DATE			

Richard Norton Smith

THOMAS E. DEWEY
AND HIS TIMES

SIMON and SCHUSTER

New York

Library of Congress Cataloging in Publication Data
Smith, Richard Norton, 1953–
    Thomas E. Dewey and his times.

    Bibliography: p.
    Includes index.
    1. Dewey, Thomas E. (Thomas Edmund), 1902–1971.
2. New York (State)—Politics and government—1865–1950.
3. United States—Politics and government—1945–1953.
4. Politicians—United States—Biography. 5. New York
(State)—Governors—Biography. I. Title.
E748.D48S65   973.91′092′4 [B]   82–370
ISBN 0-671-41741-X   AACR2

Grateful acknowledgment is made to the following for permission to reprint the materials listed:

Columbia University Oral History Project, Governor Dewey's interview in October 1970, made as part of the "Dwight D. Eisenhower Project." Reprinted by permission of the Estate of Thomas E. Dewey and Rodney Campbell.

Thomas E. Dewey, *Journey to the Far Pacific,* copyright 1952 by Thomas E. Dewey. Reprinted with permission of Doubleday & Company.

Thomas E. Dewey, Rodney Campbell, eds., *Twenty Against the Underworld.* Reprinted with permission of the Estate of Thomas E. Dewey and Rodney Campbell, copyright 1974.

William O. Douglas, *Go East, Young Man: The Early Years,* copyright © 1974 by William O. Douglas. Reprinted with permission of Random House.

Warren Moscow, the story of the conversation between Kenneth F. Simpson and Frank Altschul, *Roosevelt & Willkie,* copyright 1968.

Richard Nixon, *RN: The Memoirs of Richard Nixon,* copyright © 1978 by Richard Nixon. Reprinted with permission of Grosset & Dunlap.

Carl Sandburg, *Harvest Poems,* copyright © 1960 by Carl Sandburg. Reprinted with permission by Harcourt Brace Jovanovich.

Acknowledgments

One's outer life passes in a solitude haunted by the masks of
others. One's inner life passes in a solitude haunted by the masks
of oneself.

—EUGENE O'NEILL

A biographer incurs many debts and enlists many allies in attempting to peer behind the masks that obscure his subject. It is a pleasure
for me to acknowledge both. The best place to begin is the third
floor of the University of Rochester's Rush Rhees Library. There,
for a year, I sifted Thomas E. Dewey's public and private papers,
seeking out as much of the man and his times as could be crowded
into 1,500 boxes and 300 thick scrapbooks. The collection is vast in
scope, rich in yield. It includes hundreds of thousands of letters, including the entire correspondence between Dewey and his outspo-
ken mother from 1935 until Annie's death twenty years later. There
are staff memos and transcripts of telephone conversations, trial
proceedings and rough drafts of an autobiography, box after box of
campaign memoranda, a quarter-century of desk calendars, and extensive notes dictated on journeys to Asia and the Near East.

Major sources on Dewey's early days are notes and interviews
with his associates compiled late in the 1950s by Dr. Harlan Phillips,
a Columbia University constitutional scholar hired to do such research for a proposed two-volume memoir by the former governor.
Then, too, the collection at Rochester includes campaign films and
commercial spots, recordings of speeches and hundreds of photographs.

A mountain of official paper makes a good hiding spot, a double-
edged legacy to history that threatens to overwhelm the most in-
trepid biographer. If this did not happen to me—and only the
reader can decide that for himself—it is due largely to the guidance
and encouragement of an impressive staff of archivists in the Rare
Books, Manuscripts and Archives Section of Rush Rhees. Karl Ka-
belac, Peter Dzwonkoski, Mary Huth, Alma Creek (who was also
generous with time and assistance on photographs), Judy Gardner-
Flint, Evelyn Cilveti, and Marguerite Barrett were, in a real sense,
my partners in making Dewey's story available at this time. More
than that, they were and are warm friends, who made my stay in
Rochester personally as well as intellectually satisfying.

Inevitably, there were gaps. In the hope of filling them, I turned to the Franklin D. Roosevelt Presidential Library in Hyde Park, New York, the Dwight D. Eisenhower Presidential Library in Abilene, Kansas, the Library of Congress in Washington, D.C., the National Archives, the New York State Museum in Albany, and Columbia University's remarkable Oral History Project in New York City. I am grateful for the assistance provided by the staffs of these institutions. The same goes for archivists at the Harry S. Truman Presidential Library in Independence, Missouri, where a small part of the research I did for my senior thesis found its way into the present volume, and for historical societies in Owosso, Michigan, and Pawling, New York.

Literally hundreds of additional kindnesses were extended to me in the course of researching this work; I can only begin to mention the most significant. At Rush Rhees, I found a vast array of details. To assemble them in something akin to real life, I went off in search of men and women who knew Dewey, worked with or against him, covered him for the press, conspired at his side, fought criminals or other Republicans under his guidance. Nearly 170 individuals contributed fragments for my mosaic. Their names pepper my footnotes; a complete list can be found in the Sources section. But I could hardly let pass an opportunity of publicly expressing gratitude to three people who gave generously of uniquely personal memories and insights. Lillian Rosse was Dewey's personal secretary for thirty-seven years. Her recollections are vivid and precise. They are also, as I have had reason to check, overwhelmingly accurate.

Thomas E. Dewey, Jr., and his brother, John, recalled their parents with a candor tinged by affection, painting a picture of both Tom and Frances that was uniquely lifelike. They also made available photographs and papers not previously sent to Rochester, helped me gain access to some of the elder Dewey's otherwise tight-lipped colleagues, and made it possible for me to attend a reunion of their father's co-workers from the racket-busting days. The information imparted by both men was equaled by the freedom granted in its use. It hardly needs to be said that the interpretations and conclusions throughout these pages are mine alone.

Many other individuals enlivened my portrait or broadened my understanding. John Burton kindly allowed me to read and quote from unpublished articles on the 1948 campaign and the New York State budgeting process. Charles Breitel performed a valuable service early in my research, advising me to treat Dewey's seemingly disparate careers as gangbuster and governor with the unity they bespoke to the man's most knowing intimates. Robert Taft, Jr., permitted me to read his father's papers at the Library of Congress. Professor William Dietz of the University of Rochester graciously shared his own perceptions into the career of Edwin F. Jaeckle, and Jaeckle himself came over one day from Buffalo and spoke with sometimes startling candor of his historic, often-stormy relationship with Dewey. Earl Mazo and Nancy Chotiner offered interpretations of the events leading up to Richard Nixon's vice presidential selection in 1952. (The former president himself first agreed, then withdrew his agreement, to be interviewed.)

Joseph Stone contributed from his own extensive research into Dewey's years as George Medalie's chief assistant, and Victor Herwitz proved a historical gold mine—the biographer's dream, an eyewitness to history with near-total recall and a pungent wit not diminished for the years. Dr. Richard Elias of the Miami Heart Institute provided details of Dewey's final illness, as well as a copy of his autopsy report. Mary Wheat skillfully combed through papers at the Eisenhower Library shedding light on the elusive relationship between Dewey and the thirty-fourth president. Richard Friedman showed me through Suite 1527 of the Roosevelt Hotel. Harry O'Donnell was an equally informative guide through the thickets of New York politics in the twentieth century. Tela Cook gave liberally of her time and remembrances of Quaker Hill as it once was, and I am indebted to Lois Sutton and Mary Pickens Sumner, respectively, for the timely loan of a personal scrapbook and candid photographs of their famous neighbor.

John Francis Rothman, a scholar of modern Republicanism, gave me a number of helpful tips regarding sources. So did Steve Neal, whose research into Wendell Willkie proved an interesting counterpart. Senator Robert J. Dole was a more than tolerant employer throughout a time when politics of the 1930s and '40s diverted me from that of the '80s. To Bill Kats and other friends and colleagues in the Dole office, and to Stephen J. Chapman, Bob Rapp, Ed Cheffy, and others who have listened to far more about Lucky Luciano and Japanese codes than I have any right to expect, a special word of gratitude. Most of all, I am grateful for the friendship, support, and encouragement of Laura J. Connally. Mrs. Connally's ear is sympathetic, her patience inexhaustible.

The same kind of belief in this project from its inception has characterized my agent, Rafe Sagalyn, and my original editor, Jonathan Coleman. It is safe to say that without them I would never have dared tackle so elusive a subject, nor followed him through so many detours. And this is a better book, more steeped in the qualities of concision and style that Dewey valued, because it was edited by Alice Mayhew.

I have been asked many times over the last decade if I was writing a definitive biography. The word has always struck me as dangerous. For one thing, it suggests such a thing as ultimate truth. For another, it tends to equate a reader's exhaustion with a scholar's exhaustiveness. I prefer Willa Cather's definition. "A book is made with one's own flesh and blood of years," she wrote. "It is cremated youth."

It has taken most of my youth to know Thomas E. Dewey, even imperfectly. At the end, I'm reminded of the story told by Judge Breitel, who as Dewey's counsel was invited late in 1949 to review the proposed exchange of letters between the Governor and his departing superintendent of banks (and close personal friend) Elliott Bell. Breitel looked at the ritualistic expressions of regret and esteem, then informed Dewey they seemed all wrong. Impersonal, Breitel concluded.

Dewey listened as his counsel decried the lack of warmth in the letters. Finally, he spoke up. "I'm not going to display my emotions in public," he snapped.

In these pages, I have tried to capture in print what Dewey refused to display in public.

Richard Norton Smith
Washington, D.C.
October 15, 1981

To Richard and Marion Conant—

For the haven of their home,
And the example of their lives.

CONTENTS

CONTENTS

IV *A Postscript to Power* 1949–1971

Who has gone farthest? for I would go farther,
And who has been just? for I would be the most
    just person of the earth,
And who most cautious? for I would be more cautious,
And who has been happiest? O, I think it is
    I—I think no one was ever happier than I,
And who proudest? for I think I have reason to be
    the proudest son alive—
For I am the son of the brawny and tall-topt city,
And who has been bold and true? for I would
    be the boldest and truest being of the universe.

"Excelsior"
Walt Whitman

Prologue
The Man in Suite 1527

I will be President. It is written in the stars.
—THOMAS E. DEWEY

The Hotel Roosevelt is accustomed to the fleeting delights of fame. A coffee-colored box of brick, perched in the heart of midtown Manhattan, named for the ineffable Theodore, the Roosevelt is more than a businessmen's in-town address of ersatz splendor. Its public rooms and private suites resound to the hushed voices of the powerful, to doormen and valets in tuxedos and white gloves, and on occasion, to some of the most expensive call girls in New York. Its ornate chandeliers and marbled lobby are fit to compete with the fustian opulence of neighboring Grand Central Station. A block north of the spot where Nathan Hale surrendered his neck in 1776, the Roosevelt can comfortably brush shoulders with great events.

Even so, the mood here at the intersection of Madison Avenue and Forty-fifth Street is exuberant and anticipatory. And why not? Before this second day of November is over, 50 million Americans are expected to go to the polls and select as their thirty-fourth President the man who resides in Suite 1527. Outside, the weather is unseasonably warm, with cloudless skies adding their benediction on a contest Wall Street figures at 15 to 1. Upstairs, the candidate himself is sleeping late. By the time Tom and Frances Dewey climb out of bed at nine-thirty, the hamlet of Hart's Location, New Hampshire, has already assembled the first fragment in a vast nationwide mosaic of popular judgment. For Dewey, it casts eleven votes, for Harry Truman, one.

An auspicious start to the last day of Dewey's third presidential campaign. For thirteen years, ever since bursting upon the scene like some glamorous, improbable comet in the war against Lucky Luciano, Dutch Schultz, and a host of Runyonesque gangsters and their molls, he has been a national figure. As New York's special prosecutor, he became an idol of millions before his thirty-fifth birthday. Americans flocked to see movies cranked out by Hollywood and based upon his exploits. They read with vicarious chills about screaming black limousines and men in shiny black suits rubbed out beneath elevated tracks or encased in cement for permanent deposit in the East River. Women in Harlem felt safer return-

17

ing home at night because of Dewey—and warned recalcitrant children to be good or Mr. Dewey would get them just as he had gotten racketeers and loan sharks. A young girl argued with her father over suing the Almighty after a prolonged spell of rain. You can't sue God and win, she was told, and she took heart. "I can if Dewey is my lawyer."[1]

For many Americans in 1948, Tom Dewey remains what he was in those gray, listless days of the Great Depression: the Gangbuster. For others, he is plain Buster, a would-be president who has yet to grow up to his own ego. Is he a man on a white horse, or a man on the wedding cake? The answer lies buried deep inside a personality that attracts contempt and adulation in equal proportion. Even inside his party, which twice has awarded him the highest honor in its possession, Dewey receives only grudging admiration for the electoral and administrative miracles he has accomplished in six years as governor of New York. Something about his fastidious appearance, the swagger in his stride, even the cigarette holder clenched between his teeth in the manner of Franklin Roosevelt; something unfathomed and yet skin-deep inspires excess.

"The little man," FDR called him, or "son of a bitch." *Life* magazine once compared Sir Galahad from Owosso to "Hitler in Boy Scout clothes." Harry Truman has revived the image in the final days of a bitter campaign. Reporters used to call him the Boy, the only man who can strut while sitting down, someone you have to know well to dislike. On the other hand, George Gallup says Dewey is the ablest public figure of his lifetime, "the most misunderstood man in recent American history." The Governor's Quaker Hill neighbor Lowell Thomas thinks he is "an authentic colossus" whose appetite for excellence tends to frighten less obsessive types. The candidate's running mate, Earl Warren, professes little personal affection for Dewey, but believes him a born executive who will make a great president.[2]

Somewhere in between these extremes lie 140 million of Dewey's countrymen, who know him little better today than in the heroic summer of 1935, when Governor Herbert Lehman invited a thirty-three-year-old lawyer and former U.S. Attorney to abandon his private practice and undertake to scour the civic face of the world's greatest city. In the years since, public life has saddled financial and personal sacrifices on Tom and Frances and their two young sons. Their six-room suite at the Roosevelt, for instance: it costs thirty dollars a day (a tab picked up by the Republican State Committee) and must double as the Governor's New York City office. Then there is Dapplemere Farm, a handsome place sixty-five miles upcountry, near the village of Pawling. Purchased for $3,000 down, in 1939, it was originally furnished with pieces taken from a nearby hotel pulled down as an eyesore. The farm still carries a hefty mortgage.

Today, the front lawn of Dapplemere contains a police box, to ward off would-be assassins and intrusive tourists eager to see the home life of a potential president. Bought as a retreat from the pressures and scrutiny of New York, Dapplemere has become a tourist attraction in its own right. Frances Dewey, a deeply private woman who much prefers discussing her children to politics, finds it impossible to sunbathe out behind the old farmhouse, or garden in blue jeans and bandana. For years, she has seen the jealous mistress called Public Service claim most of her husband's time; there have been days when she resented the Holy Grail of the presidency. It didn't have to be this way: Tom could have gone ahead with his intention, back in 1937, of accepting John Foster Dulles' offer of a $150,000-a-year position with the prestigious law firm of Sullivan and Cromwell. Instead, he took the more modest sinecure of District Attorney of New York County. Salary: $20,000. (One of Dewey's maxims: No man should be in public office who can't make more money in private life.)[3]

Frances has become a public figure in spite of herself. Yet she has no intention of emulating Eleanor Roosevelt as a shaper of public opinion. She has never even made a speech. To reporters who press for an explanation, she disarms them with a mild shaft of wit.

"I am not the Speaker of the House," she says. Only a handful know how important she really is to Tom, how none of his speeches are delivered without being critiqued first for the woman's point of view that Frances brings to them, how she clips newspapers to focus his attention on local issues, and shares letters from strangers and close friends as an attractive alkali to his acid.

Today is a day not for stale recrimination but sublime hope. After breakfasting alone, the Deweys can turn to the morning papers; they make for pleasant reading. In the New York *Times* is a state-by-state survey giving the GOP nominee 345 electoral votes, 78 more than he needs to win. *Newsweek* is even more generous, forecasting 366 electors and a popular margin of 4 million. Drew Pearson, dean of Washington soothsayers and no friend of Dewey's, is in print praising the Governor for "one of the astute and skillful campaigns in recent years." The cover of *Life* shows "our next President" gazing soulfully across San Francisco Bay, Frances at his side. Alistair Cooke has filed his own post-mortem for the Manchester *Guardian*. It is entitled, "Harry S. Truman: A Study of a Failure."

Some 78 percent of the nation's newspaper readers will wake this morning to find a pro-Dewey journal on their doorsteps. Many will glance at state polls reinforcing the unmistakable message of the major national surveys, all of which point to a decisive, if not over-whelming, Republican triumph. George Gallup and Archibald Crossley each estimate Dewey's margin at 5 percentage points, while Elmo Roper, another important sampler of public opinion, hasn't bothered to interview a voter since September 9. Roper isn't merely convinced the race is over; he believes it never really started. So does Warner Brothers, whose lighthearted comedy *June Bride* has under-gone script changes to reflect today's events. Originally, in a passing reference to changing tastes in furnishings, the film contained the line "From McKinley to Truman." Today, however, New York au-diences are hearing a revised sound track, with the name of their governor replacing that of their temporary chief executive.

It's not an easy day for the nation's news gatherers. The four radio networks have alerted affiliates to expect a victory statement from the Hotel Roosevelt as early as 9 P.M. Thus reporters are scurrying about seeking ways to extend a short night. In Paris, CBS corre-spondent David Schoenbrun has received permission to interview John Foster Dulles, Dewey's representative to a United Nations con-ference in the French capital. No one has made similar arrange-ments with Secretary of State George C. Marshall, who a week ago offered in private to transfer his authority to Dulles just as soon as the votes were counted across the Atlantic.

Television can hardly hope to compete with its older established rival—ABC radio, for instance, boasts George Gallup and Walter Winchell among its election night pundits—but for those along the East Coast who have access to the round glass tube and its kinetic mix of hucksters, opera stars, magicians, baggy-pants comics, and sober-faced men reading headlines snatched from wire service copy, NBC is going all out to make the evening a visually memorable ex-perience. In conjunction with *Life* magazine, the network has in-stalled in its Rockefeller Center studios an enormous cardboard model of the White House, complete with a treadmill inside to carry miniature elephants as soon as Dewey's election is made official. No one bothers to lay in a supply of miniature donkeys.

At the Hotel Roosevelt, Dewey aides are more worried about the timing of Truman's concession than its eventuality. It seems the

President is spending the night at his home in Independence, Missouri, and may well retire early, thus delaying receipt of any congratulatory message until tomorrow morning. To the south, where members of Dewey's staff have for months now been laying the groundwork for a smooth transition next January, a large sign has been posted at Republican national headquarters, counting down the days until this one, and the final departure from power of those who have held it without interruption for sixteen years. This morning, the billboard carries a message: "1460 more days until election," it says, referring to Election Day 1952.

Meanwhile, campaign manager Herbert Brownell, a genial Nebraskan turned New Yorker, is experiencing the customary jitters that plague even the most optimistic of campaigns at the end. Publicly, Brownell predicts a virtual sweep of the nation outside the historically solid Democratic South, and even there the chairman expects to poach on the electoral votes of Florida and Virginia. In private, Brownell is less certain. Among other bits of evidence, he has seen a poll privately commissioned by a Wall Street brokerage house that suggests a rising disenchantment with Dewey's refusal to go beyond ritual paeans to unity and indulge in political promises and torchlight-parade rhetoric.

Dewey himself is a man who likes to touch all the bases. He overlooks nothing, leaves nothing to chance. Facts and figures are like mother's milk, a logical obsession that helps to explain why, as a United States Attorney at age thirty-one, he ordered agents to sift through 100,000 telephone slips to convict a Prohibition-era bootlegger; why, as District Attorney, he spent night-long vigils beside a stack of thick legal tomes in feverish search of an undiscovered fact, an unargued legal theory.

Even now, he boasts of the best political intelligence operation in the land, aided considerably by his own rule of phoning at least one of his fellow governors each day. When actress Helen Hayes came to see Dewey about her experiences as a member of the board of visitors to a state-run hospital for the handicapped, she was amazed to find a man who knew more about the facility than she did. Taxi drivers in New York City still shake their heads in amazement when the Governor recalls them on sight, asking about that son bound for college or daughter on the brink of marriage—ten years after their one and only previous meeting.

Dewey is a rationalist who is cast in an intuitive profession. He will hush everyone in a room for five minutes while he closes his eyes and mentally forages for the exact word appropriate to a speech. For the last month of the campaign, he has perceived slippage. A week ago, he ordered Brownell to conduct a private poll of the entire Republican National Committee. With a single exception, the ninety members phoned told Dewey to continue his lofty approach, with its refusal to match Truman's scalding language and scaremongering. Only Kansas' Harry Darby, worried about losing farm votes to the Democrats, advised a sharp turn away from the generalities and platitudes.[4]

Midwestern farmers this morning find their corn prices down to a dollar a bushel; two months ago they stood at $1.78. Like Darby, Senate Agriculture Chairman George Aiken scents a possible shift on the prairies. For two weeks he has been trying to penetrate the circle of close advisers who surround the candidate like a medieval moat. Chief among them are Elliott Bell, Dewey's brilliant, acerbic superintendent of banks and unofficial chief of staff on the campaign train, and Paul Lockwood, the Falstaffian executive assistant who has been with the Governor since the earliest days of gangbusting. But Aiken has had no luck. The nervous mood in the farm belt has hardly penetrated the quiet confidence traveling with the *Victory Special*. Over 16,000 miles of track, to 170 speeches and rear-platform talks, it has carried Dewey and his team, a shadow government in waiting, whose future policies remain subject to guesswork.[5]

The candidate has said kind things about crop supports in the farm belt, about Social Security and unemployment insurance in Boston, about water reclamation in the Pacific Northwest. Almost everywhere he has gone, Dewey gets applause with his promise of "the biggest unraveling, unsnarling, untangling operation" in history, cleaning out the cobwebs of Washington's good intentions as thoroughly and humanely as he has in Albany. He has refused to deal in wild accusation or programmatic detail, but has delivered thoughtful speeches on foreign policy and the need to match the Soviet Union's international propaganda campaign with a counter thrust extolling the virtues of compassionate capitalism. He has earned credit, along with Dulles, for giving birth to bipartisan foreign policy, and spent much of the campaign trying to still the lingering apprehensions of those who equate any Republican administration with Herbert Hoover's, with soup lines and hopelessness and reactionary swank. In a year when the nation seems ripe for change, Dewey has offered competence and teamwork. In a few hours, the team will know if that can offset the nation's Democratic majority and record levels of employment.

For now, amidst the small talk and nervous ritual filling Suite

1527, Tom Dewey seems calmer than anyone else. It is one more display of the brass guts that have earned him a reputation for chilly self-control. His mother, the former Miss Annie Thomas of Owosso, Michigan, is less accustomed to the tension. To kill the time, the woman Dewey calls Mater is chatting with her son's personal bodyguard, a onetime New York City cop named Frank Hnida. "How do you think it's going?" she asks in a voice that is part coax, part demand. "What do you think his chances are?"

Hnida looks up from his crossword puzzle book, smiles reassuringly, and speaks for every pundit in America. "It's a hundred to one, Mrs. Dewey. He can't lose."

Out in Kansas, Harry Darby is winding up his customary round of election day calls to key polling places across the state. What he has heard convinces him of the opposite. Darby confides his fears to Pete Wellington, editor of the Kansas City *Star,* who instructs his pressroom to get out the big type.[6]

Election days are both tedious and tense. Tom and Frances have decided to break this one a few minutes before noon, when they will climb into a big black limousine with New York #1 license plates, and be driven to a schoolhouse on East Fifty-first Street. The day is not without distractions: the candidate suffers from a cold and from bursitis reactivated a few weeks ago when he reached out to grab the hand of a lunging admirer below the rear platform of his train. Such is the price to be paid for "the new Dewey," the relaxed, even folksy, campaigner whom reporters have lately taken to describing. A decade ago, streetwise journalists, angered by Dewey's secretive ways and willingness to complain to a publisher, sometimes boycotted his press conferences in the Woolworth Building, where the special prosecution pursued racketeers in an atmosphere of absolute secrecy, requiring only sliding doors and hidden passageways to conform to Hollywood's notion of crime fighting. Photographers, informed by the District Attorney that they would not be permitted inside a courtroom where Tammany leader Jimmy Hines was being tried amidst a spectacular array of charges and countercharges, retaliated by staging a strike. Henceforth, they would snap flattering pictures of the defendant and his photogenic lawyer, Lloyd Paul Stryker, but totally ignore D.A. Dewey, or capture the publicity-conscious prosecutor only at the most embarrassing of moments.

Today, all that seems ancient history. Once, William Allen White had called Dewey "an honest cop with the mind of an honest cop." Now, Stewart and Joseph Alsop claim he has grown more than any public figure in American life. H. L. Mencken, the vituperative sage of Baltimore, asserts that he speaks the best English of anyone in public office. At meetings of the Castle Rock Society, reporters who went through a train wreck with Dewey during his 1944 presidential campaign laugh over the main business—an annual report by the treasurer of a nonexistent treasury—then settle back to relive memories of Dewey circulating among the injured lying on a track, telling each to hold out against the insurance companies for maximum damages. "I never said you weren't a crack lawyer," correspondent Esther Tufty tells him, and the Governor returns the compliment, informing the group, tongue in cheek, how Miss Tufty won a $2,000 settlement by claiming to be pregnant at the time of the wreck. A few weeks ago, a reporter on the *Victory Special* was severely chastised by Paul Lockwood for whistling at a pretty female spectator in a crowd. Didn't he know, Lockwood asked testily, that such conduct might reflect adversely on the candidate? "Be quiet," Dewey admonished Lockwood. "I felt like whistling myself."[7]

Now, as the Deweys pull up outside their voting place and are greeted by several hundred excited admirers eager to see the next president before he is swallowed up in the pomp and protection that inevitably overtakes any occupant of the Oval Office, the Governor goes out of his way to accommodate the press. Inside, he and Frances mark their ballots, then stand for half an hour as photographers snap away. "I know of two votes that we got, anyway," he cracks. His wife nervously twists her wedding band; Dewey himself seems relaxed and cheerful. One is encouraged to come closer, to examine the man apart from the headlines he has earned. "Physically," writes Dorothy Kilgallen, "he hasn't changed a lot. He doesn't look as if he had put on a pound or aged a day. But the chill is gone. When he smiles now, it is more than just a display of teeth."

Thomas E. Dewey is ruddy-faced and energetic, hardly showing his forty-six years. He is short—five feet, eight inches. Rumors of elevator shoes have no foundation, but the Governor has been known to stand on a dictionary while speaking, and unfriendly observers have suggested he begin each address with the words "My friends, I'm not standing in a hole." For years, even some of his colleagues have looked around Dewey's office and suspected him of using specially designed furniture to enhance his stature. Surely, no one present at last May's celebrated radio debate between the Governor and Harold Stassen in Portland, Oregon, will soon forget how Stassen tried to sidle up to his diminutive opponent, only to find the way blocked by the towering, ever-faithful Lockwood.

Tom Dewey's appearance, like his personality, is more emphatic than handsome. At least one journalist has looked at his face, with its high cheekbones, jutting jaw, and tight expressive features, and concluded it must have been squeezed in a vise. The Governor's hair is dark brown, almost black, cropped short over prominent ears and parted near the middle of a very high brow. His nose is sawed off—as a boy, Tom informed his mother that he would never forgive her for denying him his father's height and nose—and turned up over the trademark mustache beloved of cartoonists and bobbysoxers. The hair adorning the Dewey lip has been cut back since 1944, perhaps on the advice of his chief fund raiser, Harold Talbott, that campaign funds would be easier to collect if only the candidate more closely resembled Clark Gable.[8]

The mustache is unique in American politics, the subject of considerable debate. It has been likened to a swear word in an otherwise unexpressive sentence. But even it is overshadowed by the pair of luminous, unrelenting eyes that now bore through legislators and delegates as once they unnerved defense witnesses in a courtroom. "The only piercing brown eyes I've ever seen," Lloyd Stryker once called them. A former staffer from the D.A.'s office puts it differently: "Those eyes tell you this guy doesn't crap around." All by themselves, they can communicate eloquently. When cunning is called for, they close halfway and slither like those of some silent movie vamp plotting revenge. Horror and surprise—and "shocking" is a favorite Dewey adjective—send them into furious rotation. Opposing attorneys even accused the D.A. of popping his eyes at them, frightening witnesses and seizing for himself the attention of an errant jury.[9]

Restless and rarely looking satisfied, the eyes glow below a vast forehead, which in turn dominates a stumpy 160-pound physique covered with sober, well-tailored gabardine, double-breasted, with pockets into which Dewey stuffs his hands when speaking in public. On his head he wears a gray homburg or outsized fedora. Dewey worries about his weight; perhaps this accounts for his lifelong habit of drinking three quarts of water a day. Assistants in the rackets probe used to say, truthfully enough, that if you couldn't find the Chief in his office, he was probably in the men's room, singing an aria or show tune at the top of his voice, as he liked to do at the end of a sixteen-hour workday. It is an extraordinary voice, played like a cello, as befits a third-place finalist in the 1923 National Singing Contest of Asheville, North Carolina. It is cultured and silken, trained by hours of listening to recordings of itself in earlier radio appearances. It is capable of giving resonance and freshness to the most banal pleasantry—and holding the magical Franklin Roosevelt to a radio draw.

Its very polish denies the voice spontaneity, a failing reinforced by other factors. Keenly aware of missing front teeth lost in a high school football scrimmage, and a pronounced overbite that occasionally gives him the look of a dapper vampire, Dewey finds it difficult to smile broadly and often. "Smile, Governor," a photographer instructed him at one 1944 campaign stop. "I thought I was," came the reply. He refuses to have extensive dental work done, for the same reason he hasn't shaved off the mustache he grew as a lark on a bicycle tour of France twenty years ago. Frances likes him the way he is. Following the first presidential nomination, the Governor invited a group of friends in and lined up a string of recent photographs. The task at hand: to choose an official campaign picture. Dewey turned away from the collection, made a negative remark or two about his height and mustache, and finally left the visitors to make their own choice, with the comment, "If you can find a politically potent mug in that assortment, you're better men than I."

Around strangers, he seems uncomfortable with his own instincts. For years, he refused to be photographed with a cigarette in hand, fearful of the bad example it might set for the nation's youth. He still frowns on pictures including a wine glass, and although he is a superb dancer, will never take to a public dance floor if a cameraman might lurk behind the nearest potted palm. It has taken him years to shed his habit of standing aside from a group about to be photographed to study and rearrange the tableau more to his liking. Dewey refuses to pose in overalls on his Pawling farm, to pretend to milk cows or pitch hay. It would be phony, he tells the cameramen.

Like many men who appear gruff, Dewey is more shy than stuffy, an almost painfully private person trapped in an unremittingly public profession. Seventeen years ago, a shamefaced young district captain for Herbert Hoover wrote an apology to his superior. "I had intended to fill up a full Club but as soon as I got the signatures of a few . . . intimate friends, I found myself in a stalemate . . . it is simply impossible to ask many people for money for any cause, however good. The embarrassment is too great."[10]

He tries to let his hair down, to be one of the boys, but the effort is stiff and transparent. Earlier this year, finding himself trailing Stassen in the key primary state of Oregon, Dewey debated abandoning the contest there, only to be dissuaded by longtime backers who rea-

soned that, one way or another, Oregon would help determine the
GOP nominee. Styles Bridges and William Loeb came to the Hotel
Roosevelt from New Hampshire practically begging the Governor to
loosen up, to go out and show Oregonians some of the vinegary dynamism that private associates see every day, to slug it out with
Stassen as he had previously with Lehman in New York, with FDR
in 1944, and the hated "crawling locusts of special interests" who
threaten his concept of government by teamwork.

Always careful to pay heed to the best minds he can assemble,
Dewey reluctantly went along with the idea, barnstorming the
towns and cities of Oregon for three full weeks, often without a coat
or tie. He left his homburgs in New York, was photographed with
outdoorsmen, inspected lumber mills, and smiled benignly at small
children. To reporters along for the ride, the new Dewey was a
downright engaging figure. He was also a potent vote getter. In the
first national radio debate, the New Yorker demolished Stassen over
the issue of outlawing the domestic Communist party. (Albany advisers had urged him to go slow on advocating civil liberties in the
current mood of rising suspicion of the Soviets. Dewey thundered in
reply, "If I'm going to lose, I'm going to lose on something I believe
in.") He went on to win the primary and establish himself as the
man to beat at the convention in June.[11]

A few days after his victory, Dewey was back in New York, where
he found Bridges offering congratulations. Instead of thanks for the
winning advice, the Governor had only regret in his voice. "Styles,"
he muttered, "you know, every time I saw one of those God-awful
pictures of myself I wondered whether I was messy enough to please
Bill Loeb." But he'd won, hadn't he? Bridges retorted. And Dewey
sat back with a diffident smile on his face: "Indeed I did."

The Governor of New York is a complex man, molded from simple parts. Caution and courage entwine in his makeup. He hates to
go over forty miles an hour. In restaurants, he continues to sit with
his back to the wall, a legacy from the days when the underworld
slapped a $25,000 price tag on his head. He has been known to date
his autographs, lest a suspicious-seeming recipient try to cast a
friendship in retroactive terms when finding himself in hot water,
and to request a guest list before attending a party at Ed Murrow's
place, just down the road from Dapplemere. His own minister says
Dewey has never feared gangsters, only germs, and when the Governor goes on a tour of a state prison, he will not touch a door handle
himself, but wait for someone else to open it. If no one picks up his

message, he will remove a handkerchief from his coat pocket, discreetly cover his palm, and lightly brush the metal that prisoners hold daily.[12]

In private, he is a different man. Nine years ago, Dewey first met David Rockefeller, then a graduate student working on a Ph.D. thesis dealing with New York City government, and invited him to spend a day in the District Attorney's domain as part of his research. David and his brother Nelson found themselves being ushered into a spartan office at 137 Centre Street, where both were seated for lunch at desklike chairs, while their host, prim and paternal, polished off a sandwich and apple. When the meal was consumed, not a lengthy process, since Dewey insisted on ordering for guests whatever he ate himself, the D.A. startled David with an open book, from which the young visitor was told to read aloud. Too surprised to protest, John D. Rockefeller's grandson did as he was instructed, until he finished and Dewey fixed him with the patented eye-popping stare and said, "It's all wrong. Your voice won't do. It just won't carry for speeches. May I suggest, Mr. Rockefeller, that you obtain a copy of Dale Carnegie's book *How to Win Friends and Influence People*. It will do wonders for your speaking voice."[13]

Now as then, Dewey's enthusiasms have a way of overcoming his etiquette, especially when he beards an elegant matron at one of the Quaker Hill cocktail parties he loathes and proceeds to ramble on in graphic detail about the brave new tomorrows technology has conjured up for America, including his special fascinations—freezing and artificial insemination. In a corner of the room, Frances can only cringe. Whatever social embarrassments may trail in his wake, the Dewey of Quaker Hill is one that his advisers wish the public could see more often. They'd like voters to know the man who rises early Sunday mornings to drive a neighbor's daughter to Mass, who enjoys poker on Saturday nights and curses with gusto in the dime-a-hole matches he plays with Lowell Thomas and other celebrated members of what is jokingly referred to as the A-Pawling Set. They wish Americans could glimpse Dewey at Dapplemere Farm, wearing dirty corduroys and a smashed-down hat, driving his wife to distraction because he refuses to remove his dung-covered boots before trampling her carpets and giving the whole house a whiff of the barnyard.[14]

Here lives a man of middle-brow tastes, who laughs at the comic strips Alley Oop and Major Hoople, who delights in Edgar Wallace and P. G. Wodehouse, who sings "Oklahoma" in the bathtub and plays inadequate golf, despite years of lessons and careful study of manuals on the subject. Every Sunday, Dewey's inability to drive turns the family's excursion to nearby Christ Church into a five-mile pilgrimage with terror. To the Governor, his absent-minded failure to drive a straight line is easily overlooked. Driving a car is like making a wedge shot, something done well because he does it himself. In church, he likes his sermons doctrinally meaty. His farm manager times each to make certain it doesn't last over twenty minutes. Discovering that reporters expect him to open up after two martinis—few men are as charming on the threshold of a third—he imposes a strict limit on his alcoholic consumption. Only later will he look back and entertain doubt. "I've never been to a party," he will tell a friend shortly before his death, "where I didn't have to do something, make a speech, perform a function, and just have fun."[15]

Even to his friends, Tom Dewey is something of a mystery, irreverent and priggish, capable of great kindness or playing humanity like his beloved chess. He is a former printer's devil cordially detested for much of his career by the working press. An implacable foe from childhood of the evils of machine government à la Tammany Hall, Dewey in New York has constructed the most overwhelming party apparatus since the days of "Easy Boss" Tom Platt at the turn of the century. He has roused millions with his let's-get-this-country-moving-again optimism, despite a personality all but smothered beneath a driving ambition. He is the first candidate for president to be born in the twentieth century, and he cannot elude a Victorian preoccupation with appearances and small-town virtue. The Governor of New York is a onetime paper boy from Owosso, Michigan, symbolizing for indignant conservatives within his party their subjugation by the sophisticated, slightly sinful East. He is a reformed isolationist who speaks the language of international interdependence, a fiscal conservative who has carried on and extended New York's expensive tradition of socially progressive administration, an Albany autocrat who attacks Roosevelt and Truman for centralizing power in the presidency and ignoring the values of cabinet government.

In 1935, Thomas Dewey was a cartoon figure, legally gunning for gangsters and imparting his own brand of hope to a country ravaged by the Great Depression. Since then, he has proven himself better at governing than campaigning. To many Republicans, he is still a hero, to others a heretic. Now, as he and Frances prepare to return to the Roosevelt for the long afternoon ahead, the candidate declares himself as something more than a technocrat in the pulpit. Outside the polling place, Dewey catches sight of workers in the General

Electric Building, who have filled windows in the skyscraper with letters spelling out, "Good luck, Mr. President." He doffs his hat in acknowledgment, then suggests to Frances that they pass up the limousine and return to the hotel on foot. It is a warm, springlike afternoon in Manhattan, and in the crush of well-wishers surrounding the Deweys as they set off, no one notices Herbert Hoover slipping quietly into P.S. 18 to cast his vote.

Taxi drivers and passersby, startled to encounter the Governor as he strides vigorously down six blocks of Madison Avenue, shout out encouragement, and are rewarded with smiles and pleasantries. It is a good omen. This afternoon, in anticipation of victory, the public and private men have become one. Tom Dewey is thoroughly thawed.

Even Dewey's reckless acts give the impression of calculation. When he was district attorney, he once received an explicit letter threatening his life. Later on the same day, a man telephoned to repeat the threat; the D.A., he warned, would be shot to death on his way home from work that very night. When it came time to leave, Dewey was careful to walk out the same entrance he always used, ride in the same car, follow the same route up Fifth Avenue. Only one pugnacious variation altered the customary routine: the D.A. insisted that the lights inside his car be turned on.

In politics, he innovates to reduce risks, to narrow what he calls "that great gray imponderable area in the electorate." He is the first presidential candidate to have his own polling unit, and to one worried Republican ten days ago he exhibited anew an almost religious belief in the revolutionary science of public-opinion sampling. Paul Lockwood escorted a Rochester industrialist to a car filled with the latest poll data, including a chart where the lines for Dewey and Truman refused to intersect. There the Governor laughed off his guest's plea to talk specifics in his closing speeches. "Carl, always remember," he said in reply, "when you're leading, don't talk." In addition to the polls, Dewey has pioneered in using political advance men, is intrigued by the infant medium of television as a more intimate means of communicating with voters than radio, and came very near making this the first national campaign ever conducted by airplane instead of the traditional whistle-stop.[16]

His innovations are not limited to technique. Under Governor Dewey, New York is the first state in the nation to enact laws prohibiting racial or religious discrimination in employment and education. His administration has taken the lead in combatting tuberculosis, heart disease, and cancer; blazed new trails in curing the mentally ill; and created a women's council to insure that the Governor's law guaranteeing equal pay for equal work is more than an admirable, futile gesture. Dewey hates inefficiency, will not brook public displays of disagreement within his team, and looks to local government as a bridge between differences, a hardworking referee, a creative alternative to the deadening hand of Washington. As he is fond of telling audiences, government can be progressive and solvent at the same time, can feel with its heart what it knows in its head. He also quotes Jefferson: "The whole art of government consists in being honest."

It is, in Dewey's words, "a nervous world" beyond Forty-fifth and Madison in this fourth November of an uncertain peace. "Man has sprung in a few short years," he said in his second Albany inaugural address, "from the relative simplicity of the horse and buggy days to the terrifying realization that he is standing in darkness on a narrow ledge, holding in his hands the secret of the universe. One false step and we may lose not only the secret, but the world itself. Man has learned how to deal with nearly all nature except human nature. He has explored the universe, but he does not know himself. We are like children who have come into possession of knowledge without yet having acquired understanding."

Heroics are not in fashion this fall; disillusionment is the season's unhappy leitmotif. In war-torn Europe, the cold war proclaimed two years ago by Winston Churchill—one of the giants rejected by his own countrymen—has turned the Old World into a hornets' nest of conflicting ideologies. President Truman has responded to the threat of Soviet aggression with the Marshall Plan, and an airlift to the beleaguered city of Berlin. Both steps have met with Dewey's public approval. His own suspicion of the Russians is deep-rooted. He cannot forget the time John Foster Dulles returned from a tough negotiation with Soviet diplomats and said, "I sat there looking at them. They were the hardest-faced murderers I'd ever seen, and I knew that everyone of them had a gun in his pocket with many notches on it." Dewey himself believes the Russians have at least 300 secret agents on the island of Cuba, following up their wartime penetration of Mexico. He plans to increase defense spending, if elected, by $5 billion.[17]

A Dewey presidency will stress realism in charting America's international course. Closer ties are forecast with anti-Communist exiles like France's Charles de Gaulle. Nationalist Chinese forces under Chiang Kai-shek are openly rooting for a Republican win in the hope of salvaging their long, losing war against Mao Tse-tung's Communists. Yet, for allies as well as adversaries, his vision includes steel sheathed in velvet. The British, for example, can expect a get-tough approach if their Labour government tilts toward greater nationalization of the island's economy. A little nationalization, Dewey explains, is like pouring a little strychnine into a glass of milk. Others in Western Europe will find him a staunch supporter of American military and economic aid, but only in return for closer ties with the U.S. and for the first halting steps toward his long-held dream for the Continent, a United States of Europe.

Overseas demands make up only a fraction of the troublesome agenda awaiting the next president. Voters lining up in school-houses and factories this morning have borne a crushing load of postwar inflation, a severe housing shortage, petty scandals in Washington, and growing restiveness on the part of blacks and others who have been left out of the social mainstream. They have entertained gnawing doubts as to their own chief executive's competence. A single weak pun seems to crystallize a nation's disappointments: "To err is Truman." Dulles refers to the President acidly as "that shirt salesman from Missouri." Dewey has virtually ignored his opponent, overlooking Truman's jibes at the GOP as "gluttons of privilege . . . bloodsuckers with offices on Wall Street" and enemies of agriculture, guilty of "sticking a pitchfork in every farmer's back."

Truman's campaign has been lively and energetic. It has also been shrill and divisive.

"President Likens Dewey to Hitler as Fascist Tool," proclaimed the New York *Times* after a particularly vitriolic attack in Chicago on October 25. Dewey's muted response the next day: a mild slap at "fantastic fears" and "reckless abuse" hurled by an obviously desperate man. But Truman hasn't been running much against the Governor of New York. Instead, he has concentrated his fire on the Republican Eightieth Congress and its dominant figures, Robert Taft and Joseph Martin. Privately, the President delights in the Congress, calling its GOP leadership "Neanderthal men who will embarrass Dewey and Warren." To Truman, the Eightieth is representative of "your typical Republican reactionary . . . with a calculating machine where his heart ought to be." Like much he has said this year, that is a bit overstated. The first Republican Congress in fourteen years has raised public assistance spending, cut taxes by $4 billion, and voted funds for the Marshall Plan. It has also removed 750,000 persons, most of them self-employed, from the Social Security rolls, passed the Taft-Hartley Law making labor-management relations "a two way street" in Robert Taft's words, and offended Catholics and Jews in the urban Northeast by refusing to amend the Displaced Persons Act.

It has often appeared that the Eightieth's leaders were better at public incitement than public relations. Concerned about possible damage to his own cause, Dewey in August dispatched Herbert Brownell and Republican national chairman Hugh Scott to see Taft and plead for a compromise on the refugee bill before the end of a special session called by Truman as a political dare. "We're not going to give that fellow a thing," Taft snapped, referring not to Dewey but Truman, who promptly drove a wedge between Dewey and his supposed allies on Capitol Hill. The Governor has been forced to lay down the law to conservatives, who chafe at the thought of more Social Security, unemployment insurance, securities regulation, and farm supports. Such programs cost little, he insisted in a Boston speech, "when compared with the gain in human happiness." Like children rebelling at the best medicine, Martin and Taft can be expected grudgingly to go along with the new president after January 20, 1949. Their smiles are forced this November.

For ten years, Taft has battled Dewey for the soul of their party. At three national conventions, he has seen his ideological allies ground up in the relentless machinery of the Eastern Establishment, those Republican liberals who prefer victory to ideological purity and to achieve it are willing to accept the legitimacy of the New Deal. New York newspapers, New York banks, New York arrogance—the very city Taft's America loves to hate—all have become synonymous in Old Guard eyes with the man one Taft partisan calls "that snooty little Governor of New York." Taft himself is a blunt man; he has labeled a friendly newspaper column "the most puerile thing I have ever read" and denounced Dewey's 1944 plan for a permanent Anglo-American alliance as "a damned fool thing to do." He has tried unsuccessfully to reduce Marshall Plan funding, farm price supports, and defense spending. *Time* magazine has described him as "the Dagwood Bumstead of American politics." Walter Lippmann faults him for trying to lead his party down "blind alleys of dumb obstructionism."

Taft dislikes Dewey for paradoxical reasons. On the one hand, he considers his new New York rival too far to the left for the party of Coolidge and Hoover, too much the prisoner of New York's ethnic and business groups, too willing to purchase favor with labor and other constituents in the New Deal coalition. At the same time, he questions the sincerity of Dewey's convictions. He thinks of the Governor as a mere pragmatist of ferocious ambition, who locates his convictions by hoisting a moist finger in the breeze of public opinion. The Taft-Dewey courtship has all the instinctive warmth of the snake and mongoose. "I don't understand why he hates me so," the Ohioan said plaintively to a reporter after Dewey once all but ignored him on the same stage. For his part, introduction of Taft's name into a conversation has been known to move Dewey to break his firm rule against profanity in the presence of a woman. Not once but twice he has suggested within earshot of a female journalist from the *Christian Science Monitor* that the Senator from Ohio should have carnal relations with himself.[18]

There is more at stake here than differences of personality or political style. With Tom Dewey in the White House, Taft's chance to occupy the office his father held for a single unhappy term will go fluttering like October's dying leaves at Sky Hill, the family estate outside Cincinnati. The GOP itself will be refashioned, with internationalism and pragmatic liberalism its credos. To be sure, Dewey has long advocated returning many federal functions to states and localities. The Hoover Commission's recommendations on reorganization of the executive branch can expect to find in him an enthusiastic supporter. But to men like Taft, none of this alters the fact that Franklin Roosevelt, in his grave for over three years, still sets the accepted boundaries of political debate in America.

Dewey, of course, sees things differently. Repeatedly he tells audiences that before there was government there was man, and government arose to meet man's needs. In the modern age, those needs include as much economic security as is consistent with individual freedom. Critics call it "me-tooism," aping the New Deal in a vain attempt to outbid Roosevelt's heirs. But Dewey reaches back for his response to the Republican tradition of Abraham Lincoln and Theodore Roosevelt, Henry Stimson and Elihu Root. He reminds his detractors that it was conservative reforms like anti-trust laws and federal regulation of railroads, enacted under Republican presidents, that retained the allegiance of the people for a capitalist system combining private incentive and public conscience. Unlike Taft, Dewey is no child of the legislative process. He is used to giving orders that shape the day-to-day affairs of the nation's largest state, and to grappling with public housing and juvenile delinquency, race relations and bad prisons. If you really want to know Tom Dewey, you'd best see him in action in Albany.

Early this year, the Governor ran into Lillian Hellman, the leftish playwright friendly to Henry Wallace's independent presidential candidacy. Wallace, once Roosevelt's vice president and still a hero to unreconstructed New Dealers, had fallen out with Truman over American-Soviet relations, declared his own candidacy, and promptly found himself tangled in allegations of Communist domination. His main impact today is expected to come in diverting urban, labor, and black voters from Truman, fragmenting Roosevelt's coalition and swelling Dewey's electoral margin. Seeing Miss Hellman, the ever-optimistic Dewey asked if perchance she might vote for him. Nothing doing, the playwright told him. She regarded him as a reactionary. Isn't that odd, the Governor said; only that morning, someone had called him a Communist.

"Who was that?" Miss Hellman inquired, "Louis the Fourteenth?"

His own party's right wing, galvanized by the poison pen of Colonel Robert McCormick and his stable of editorial writers, distrusts Dewey as a liberal in sheep's clothing. "If you read the Chicago *Tribune,*" the Governor himself says, "you'd know that I am a direct lineal descendant of FDR—without the personal charm." George Medalie, Dewey's original mentor, reconciled the opposing camps. "Common sense," he replied when asked to name his protégé's most striking characteristic. "He was born with it to an uncommon degree."

The Governor has two favorite questions that he puts to advisers when a proposal is laid before him. "Is it right?" he asks. "Will it work?" He has another axiom that bears repeating. "Good government is good politics." In another mouth it would be a spineless platitude. What gives it weight with Dewey is his instinctive belief that politics, like government, is not an art but a science. That, and an evident contempt for yes-men. At staff meetings, Dewey expresses an opinion, marshals facts to give it support, then invites everyone in the room to respond. Those who agree readily are rewarded with a withering stare and a demand to know why. It's a device that prompted one insider to lament that Thomas E. Dewey never takes yes for an answer. Others, unable to cut to the heart of the issue as precisely, or to meet his informational demands, are curtly informed that he seeks a reason, not an excuse.[19]

He is, not surprisingly, a demanding taskmaster. Speechwriters have been known to despair at two in the morning, after the Governor appraises a tenth draft as "garbage" and sends the chastened ghost off to the typewriter for yet another try. Even Elliott Bell proclaims himself a charter member of the Brave Twisted Smile Club, an organization of all those who labor long hours on a Dewey speech, only to find the Governor has hacked their contribution down to a stray sentence or two. In his zeal to make his public utterances perfect, to wring out what he calls "85¢ words" and fashion a winning appeal to the vast jury of the American electorate, the old prosecutor gathers advice from outside experts, subjects data to rigorous investigation by his budget director, John Burton, and lavishes an hour of preparation on each minute of delivery. He practices carefully before an audience that may include Lockwood, Frances, or a visiting governor. "Practice," he tells one stupefied speechwriter, "is the difference between the amateur and the professional." Before the final version, rewritten in his own language, is consigned to an oversized typewriter for transcription, it has been through a dozen or more drafts; one speech earlier this year lived twenty-one lives before its public christening. Dewey's precautions do not end with what he has to say. Wherever he goes, he brings his own podium along, with a light at shoulder level and a nail on which to hang a watch, the better to time himself as he speaks. He is careful too, not to turn over each page as he reads, but instead move it silently to the left-hand side of the podium, face up. That way, sensitive radio microphones cannot pick up the distracting sound of rustling paper.[20]

On the second floor of Albany's labyrinthine State Capitol, Dewey sits behind a desk as orderly as his mind. He hates telephones—says they disturb his thought process—and hides one in a desk drawer. The desk itself carries only a brown morocco mail folder, the inevitable thermos jug of cold water, an elephant or two, and four pencils sharpened to precisely the same length. The passion for neatness extends to nature itself. When a fly disturbs his concentration, he will rise silently from his chair to creep stealthily about, fly swatter in hand. The Governor tracks his prey, striking it just hard enough to stun. That way, it won't smear the light tan wallpaper he chose for the room. When the offending insect falls to the floor, it can be disposed of more vigorously.

A lover of gadgets, Dewey presses a button underneath the desk to signal entry—he himself uses a private elevator installed by Franklin Roosevelt—and enjoys confounding visitors by manipulating a hidden dial to bring the lights up or down. It is a melodramatic effect that reinforces the sense of absolute mastery he projects, here or on the campaign trail. Old hands in Albany, seeing him shake 6,600 hands in two hours, all the while remaining as unruffled as his crisp white shirt collar, swear the man doesn't sweat. Four years ago, be-

fore going to the Chicago Coliseum to accept his party's nomination
to run against Roosevelt, Dewey kept the party waiting twenty minutes, the time it took to find a replacement for his soiled shirt.

For all this, he is a more spontaneous man now than when he first
arrived in Albany six years ago, taking up residence in the barnlike
Executive Mansion that dates from the governorship of Samuel J.
Tilden. He jokes fondly about the roof that leaks in the same spot
every January, and the grotesque oxblood-red color scheme that he
used to call an invitation to suicide. He came to Albany suspicious
and suspected. Legislators feared he might wiretap their phones.
Barbers and shopkeepers in the staunchly Democratic city didn't
know quite what to make of their first Republican governor in
twenty years. In the first few months of this term, a close friend of
the Deweys said that going to the mansion, with its depressingly
frayed appearance and subaqueous light, was like going to a funeral.
Frances has changed that now, performing the impossible transformation from red brick fortress to livable, inviting home. The change
has been reflected in the Governor himself.

When entertaining the state's top judges and lawyers, Dewey relaxes nervous guests by asking each to recount the most interesting
case from his own repertoire. Cigars are passed around with the
stories, and before the evening is over, the Governor and First Lady
may entertain their guests with selections from Rodgers and Ham-
merstein, played on the grand piano that is Frances' best therapy
against political life. Her husband seems to blossom at night; his administration has been called the first ever that works after dark.
Three shifts of stenographers are required to answer Dewey's vast
correspondence, while most of his evenings are spent with paperwork in the ground-floor study at the mansion. It is a quiet change
from a hectic daytime schedule, when callers are whisked through
his office, four shifts to the hour, and lunch is taken at his desk, the
one the Governor himself designed to have four sliding shelves so he
could conduct informal skull sessions with the professional managers
who lend his administration its slightly gray tint of excellence. He
has defined his chief administrative task as persuading $50,000-a-
year men to take $12,000-a-year jobs, then turning them loose with
far too much work for ordinary mortals to get through.[21]

The conversations here are liable to be freewheeling and contentious. They range from the latest roadblock athwart Dewey's
cherished thruway—an unprecedented high-speed four-lane highway, without stop signs or traffic lights, that will connect New York
City with Buffalo, 486 miles away—to the controversial idea of a

state university, which, following two years of painstaking study, the Governor has recently decided to embrace. Once each year, usually around Easter, aides walk in with armfuls of legislative bills for his consideration during what is known as the thirty-day period. A thousand or more, they cross Dewey's desk at the rate of three dozen a day, without the accompanying memos that Governors Roosevelt and Lehman insisted upon. With the same feel that made him the most successful prosecutor in New York's history, Dewey listens to succinct summaries of each bill, its financial efficacy and legislative history. Most days, he interrupts state business long enough to call Pawling and request a cow-by-cow report of overnight milk production in his herd of fifty-two animals.[22]

In this room, Dewey slapped down advisers urging him to go softly in criticizing Stassen's Communist registration scheme. Here also he filed a top secret letter dispatched from General George Marshall in September 1944 confirming that American code breakers had uncovered Japanese diplomatic and military secrets even before Pearl Harbor—and promised Marshall he wouldn't make his knowledge public. Here he cracks the whip ruthlessly on legislators who stray from the party fold. Assemblymen have found themselves under investigation by the State Tax Department after opposing the Governor over an insurance regulation bill. Others discover job-rich construction projects, state buildings, even highways, directed to friendlier terrain. Ever since he took his first oath of office, Dewey has insisted on having every prospective holder of a job paying $2,500 or more rigorously probed by state police. He has forced the legislature his own party dominates to reform its comfortable ways of payroll padding. Now legislative workers must certify in writing every two weeks what they have been doing to earn their salary; every senator and assemblyman must verify that he is telling the truth. All this has occasioned more than grumbling. Assemblymen have quit in protest. Others have been denied renomination by Dewey's formidable political organization. Reporters mutter among themselves about government by blackmail.[23]

But the voters are in no mood to complain about a governor so suspicious of malfeasance that he will accept no anonymous campaign contributions, has every large contributor not known personally to him investigated for motive, and once called in his staff to instruct them against buying a stock touted by friends as profitable. "It isn't that I don't want you to make a good living," he explained, "but this stock is not known to the general public, and we should not use information we gather as public officials for our own profit."

Most of all, the people of New York seem to appreciate their governor's unique pay-as-you-go liberalism.

In six years, Dewey has piled up more than $623 million in budgetary surplus, while reducing the state's tax rates by 50 percent. The surplus, made possible by wartime restraints on construction, has been salted away in the Governor's patented Postwar Reconstruction Fund, ready to fuel a vast rebuilding program and ease the economic transition to a peacetime economy. Under Dewey, state aid for education and public assistance has more than doubled. A new formula for local aid not only increases the amount the state returns to hard-pressed localities, but for the first time provides a stable climate in which to plan for future growth. The PRC is making possible 14,000 new beds in the state's mental health system, public housing for 30,000 families, slum clearance on an undreamed-of scale, reforestation of 34 million trees, water pollution control, and a model veterans' program. When Dewey took office in 1943, he found some state workers being paid $900 a year. "They love the poor so much," he says of his Democratic opponents, "that they make it their business to keep everybody poor." Since then, state workers have been given hefty raises, some as high as 150 percent. So have teachers, and workers receiving unemployment benefits.

Everything, it seems, has gone up in Dewey's budget—except the amount allocated to debt service. That has declined from $49 million a year in 1943 to $27 million this year. "I hate debt," the Governor tells anyone who will listen, and his actions give force to his words. In six years, he has reduced total indebtedness by over $100 million, partly by husbanding the wartime bounties and partly by cutting expenditures to the bone. For all the patina of generosity to Dewey's administration, there is a strong Republican tilt to it as well. When legislative leaders came to the Governor demanding a $360 bonus for every returning veteran, Dewey blanched. Such largesse wasn't in his plan to make New York a businesslike place. Recognizing the idea's popularity, however, the Governor struck a bargain: He'd embrace the bonus if the legislature and voters took the novel step of voting its financing through short-term bonds. When he first came to Albany, Dewey found some bond issues dating to the 1870's—the Bronx, he discovered, would be paying for a long-since-disused plank road called Central Avenue until the year 2147—and he resolved never to resort to what he calls "the pickpocket scheme of government." A generation that wants benefits and public works will pay for them. As a result, the $400 million veterans' bonus will be entirely paid off within ten years, and bondholders will not reap the financial whirlwind that attended the end of World War I.

When juvenile delinquency forged to the front of public concerns, Dewey was besieged with proposals to make it a state priority. He agreed, but the methods he proposed to fight it were not what conventional liberals had in mind. In place of a large bureaucracy in Albany, Dewey created a modest office of three dozen staffers administering $2 million each year. The bulk of the money goes to local communities, 700 of which have followed Dewey's suggestion and launched their own initiatives in the field, drawing upon parents, teachers, ministers, and adolescents themselves for antidotes to crime. This governor is friendlier by far than his predecessors to the private sector. Under Dewey's leadership, a Department of Commerce has been born to lure new businesses and tourists to the Empire State, ease the shift from wartime boom, and steer small businessmen, in particular, through the maze of federal regulation and restriction. A million more jobs exist for New Yorkers than in 1939. Since the end of the war, 135,000 new businesses have been started.

Dewey is an activist when it comes to revitalizing state government, and a liberal when it comes to winning for his own party adherents in neighborhoods where the very word Republican has not for twenty years been admitted to polite conversation. In 1937, harried election officials in Brooklyn posted large signs at polling places reading, "Dewey Isn't Running in This County." The secret of his success in Albany, of his hold over Republicans in the state and nation, the heart of his appeal as an admittedly unorthodox presidential candidate, lies in this demonstrated power. Two years ago, the voters of New York re-elected their governor by nearly 700,000 votes, the largest majority ever accorded a gubernatorial candidate in the Empire State. In conventional times, such a combination of political and administrative success would earn a man the White House. Yet in 1948, timing, instinct, and habit may outweigh ability, vision, and organizational prowess. Timing cast Warren Harding as president, and cast Henry Clay aside. Chance elevated Theodore Roosevelt and Harry Truman to the highest office in the land. Fate overcomes the most finely calibrated mind, and no one ever named a child after an organization.

At the Hotel Roosevelt, 150 city police have been joined by half a dozen Secret Service agents, whose director, James J. Mahoney, has voluntarily forsaken the incumbent in Independence, Missouri. By 2 P.M., Mahoney's decision takes on the glow of prescience: Houston's leading newspaper, in a survey of voters leaving the polls, has Dewey narrowly ahead of Truman, an ominous tiding for the Democrats in their Dixie stronghold. In Suite 1527, the Governor's sons, Thomas, Jr., and John, are expected at any moment from Albany, where they have spent a full day in classes. Until now, both boys have been sheltered as much as possible from the rigorous unreality of the campaign trail. John's only emotion today is a fear of leaving behind his friends and classmates.

Merriman Smith is already at the hotel, having chosen to cover Dewey instead of Truman, the assignment usually drawn by the Associated Press's senior White House correspondent. He is riding in an elevator with a colleague, eavesdropping on two youthful Dewey partisans who are chatting in the tone of mock suspense with which secure people await sure things.

"Wouldn't it be awful," one says to the other, "if something were to go wrong?"

Smith cannot resist an involuntary shudder. "Jesus," he tells his fellow reporter, "if Truman wins, you know what'll happen to me? I'll wind up as rewrite man in our Tahiti bureau."[24]

By late afternoon, New York is sinking into the premature shadows of a November dusk, and the Deweys prepare to go to dinner. The Governor is a creature of habit, and one of his favorite traditions is election night at the Ninety-third Street residence of Roger and Gladys Straus, longtime friends and generous supporters of all his campaigns. Mr. Straus, president of the American Smelting and Refining Company, and formerly chairman of the National Conference of Christians and Jews, is expected to become secretary of commerce in the new administration, a title his father held in Theodore Roosevelt's time. Ordinarily, the Deweys and Strauses spend election nights at backgammon. Tonight, they will content themselves with a dinner of roast duck and fried apples, joined by Annie Dewey, Paul Lockwood, Elliott Bell, and Alger Chapman, a close friend and manager of two Dewey campaigns in New York. During the meal, a radio feeds fragmentary returns from upper New England, as solidly Republican as the bedroom communities of Nassau and the apartment towers that line Park Avenue. The company is about to carve a cake in honor of Chapman's birthday when Dewey hears a first report out of Connecticut. "Oh-oh," he says. "We'd better get back." The cake is still there, untouched, the next morning.[25]

Not far away, Herbert Brownell is convening his own celebration in a private dining room of the Ritz-Carlton. Toasts are being drunk to members of the next cabinet when a young receptionist, gaily dressed for the evening ahead, is called to the phone. Her father is on the line wanting to know what she is wearing and the name of her favorite restaurant. Sparkling beads and the Stork Club, Louise Gore replies, before asking why.

Louise returns to the dinner table poised between fear and disbelief. Her father has suggested she get her favorite young man to take her out, "because I think you've lost yourself an election." Someone shouts for a radio. A few minutes pass, and another voice blurts, "To hell with this." Within seconds, the cream of the Dewey administration is sprinting through the lobby of the Ritz-Carlton, summoning the limousines that will return them to the Roosevelt and the security of friends.[26]

On the sixth floor of the hotel, Brownell's command post is cluttered with charts and long columns of numbers—mostly old, a few just received. Here, Allen J. "Goody" Goodrich is in charge, overseeing other accountants from the racket-busting days trained to interpret the raw tallies in more sophisticated fashion than NBC's tote boards or cardboard animals. It is a legend in the Governor's inner circle how Goody Goodrich (who is married to Dewey's personal secretary, Lillian Rosse) bested the New York *Times* on election night 1938, when the D.A. was locked in an achingly close contest with Herbert Lehman. While the *Times* was calling at midnight for a victory statement, Dewey was listening on another phone to Goody offering his condolences on a narrow loss. Tonight, it will be Goody's assessment that will justify the repast ordered from Bernstein's Delicatessen in expectation of quick victory.

By seven o'clock, New England's rock-ribbed hamlets are being overwhelmed by the Democratic bastions of New Haven and Waterbury and Stamford; and George Gallup, like Goody Goodrich, is paying special attention to the size of the vote accorded Henry Wallace. The first tallies out of Connecticut and her sister state, Massachusetts, fail to give Wallace the 8 or 9 percent of the vote Gallup and others have forecast. Instead, the race between Truman and Dewey is close, with Wallace an insignificant factor.

At eight o'clock, Gallup turns to his co-workers with the first distress signal of the day. "Boys," he says, "I think we're in trouble."[27]

Caravans of doubt are converging on the Roosevelt now, bringing Tom and Frances to Suite 1527, and Brownell and his party to the sixth floor and the main ballroom. The latter is rapidly filling with 600 partisan Republicans, many in dinner jackets or evening gowns.

Capital is having its fling tonight; the celebration has spread throughout the hotel's corridors as noisy, happy Dewey supporters toast their victory in champagne and make passage for anyone else all but impossible. That's the way Lillian Rosse finds the sixth floor a few minutes before eight. Something is wrong with Goody, who sits white-faced and silent in a room shared only with his statistics and notepads. Half frantic with worry, Lillian tries and fails to get a response from her husband. Outside, the chants of victory provide an ironic backdrop. Finally, one of Goody's colleagues appears to explain the situation to Lillian. Goody, it seems, has discovered a trend.[28]

Miss Rosse is barely back in 1527 when the Governor and his party return. Gruffly, the candidate orders Brownell to follow him into the suite's master bedroom. Later, gossip columnist Cholly Knickerbocker will report, falsely, that Dewey broke a lamp over his campaign manager's head—other versions will make it a chair. Actually, Brownell spends most of the night on the phone taking calls from key precincts around the country.[29]

Goody's message is relayed to the Governor, with no apparent effect. Instead, Dewey retreats to the bedroom, where, yellow legal pad in hand, he will spend the rest of the night virtually alone. Occasionally, Frances goes in with news of her own. So do Miss Rosse and Paul Lockwood. But the candidate leaves to others the entertaining of guests.

Pat and Marge Hogan are in 1527 tonight. Pat is Dewey's closest friend—"the brother I never had" in Tom's words; Marge and Frances are fellow veterans of the music hall circuit. The women have different outlooks on political life. One revels in the unhinged schedules of campaigning; the other hates to be routed out of bed each morning to gaze with worshipful eyes at the latest rendition of her husband's stock stump speech. "It is good to sleep in a bed that doesn't move," Frances has written, and while she would do nearly anything for the man she calls "my sweet," it is a sore trial for this retiring woman who prefers the company of a few close friends to exhibiting herself before crowds of curious strangers like one of the prize cattle at Dapplemere Farm.[30]

Tonight, the Deweys and Hogans are anticipating their New Year's Eve custom of poker in the Executive Mansion, the only change being a move to another official residence several hundred miles south of Eagle Street in Albany. Just before nine o'clock, their hopes rise with a report that the impregnable Democratic fortress of Philadelphia has been scaled and taken. Another call corrects the news, but reports a Truman margin so small there that the President cannot possibly hope to pocket the Keystone State's twenty-nine electoral votes. The news of Pennsylvania's capture is especially welcome to Hugh Scott, who represents Philadelphia's suburbs in Congress and has since June served as Dewey's handpicked chairman of the Republican National Committee. A stocky, professorial man, whose thick mustache and glasses give him the air of a scholarly penguin, Scott has seen the same Connecticut returns as Gallup and Goodrich, and is grateful for some good news to announce from the podium of Washington's Statler Hotel.[31]

"Now we come to the Republican half of the evening," he says, referring to the historic pattern of election night in America, when the Democratic urban East predominates until midnight, only to give way in the small hours of Wednesday morning to the farmers and Rotarians of the Middle West, as habitually loyal to the GOP now as when they elected William McKinley and Warren Harding. Scott's optimism is understandable at 9:15 P.M., when Harry Truman leads by 100,000 votes. The night is young, the Midwest out, and Dewey running consistently ahead of his 1944 showings throughout the Northeast. Pennsylvania is the best proof of that. Scott decides there's no reason to use the $1,500 hotline established by Brownell as a direct link between the Roosevelt and the Washington Statler.

The temper in Albany, where many of the Dewey team have gathered at the De Witt Clinton Hotel on State Street, lies somewhere between annoyance and apprehension. Many of the people there have given time to the campaign instead of their regular jobs (and been meticulously shifted from the public to the party payroll). As the hour of ten strikes without a decision, liquor begins flowing against a result delayed for several hours beyond what these loyalists have anticipated. In Rome and Syracuse, Rochester and Troy, scattered returns point to a close contest in Dewey's own bailiwick. The mood in Manhattan approaches boredom; in Times Square, the crowds that have come together to watch and hold their breath are the smallest in memory, signaling the death knell for an election night tradition that predates Abraham Lincoln. On Broadway, most theaters are packed, testament to the relatively pallid drama of an electoral runaway.[32]

Midnight nears. Russ Sprague is en route to the Roosevelt from Nassau County, where his machine has turned out a record vote for the Dewey-Warren ticket. Listening to the returns on his car radio,

Sprague wonders out loud, "Was the campaign tactic wrong?" In Suite 1527, Dewey silently jots down numbers in his bedroom, while Frances does what she can to make her guests relax in an atmosphere rapidly becoming surreal. At Sky Hill, Robert Taft is on the phone to Walter Trohan, veteran political correspondent for the Chicago *Tribune*, checking the latest tallies from the bellwether state of Illinois. He hears a mixed verdict: Dewey is running half a million votes ahead of Republican Governor Dwight Green, a lackluster executive being buried in a torrent of votes for Adlai Stevenson, an attractive first-time candidate and bearer of a distinguished name in Illinois politics. Indeed, ticket splitting is the rule tonight, as the presidential nominee runs 150,000 ahead of his party in Massachusetts, 135,000 ahead in Iowa, ahead in Indiana and Maryland and Connecticut and New Jersey.

But not enough, so it would seem, to insure victory in Illinois. At least that's the message Trohan imparts, telling Taft that the presidential candidate is outpolling the typical Republican vote in and around Chicago, but trailing among rural and farm voters downstate. Taft does not seem astonished, nor does his voice contain any hint of trauma when he confides to Trohan his belief that Dewey is licked. The Republican ship may be listing badly. Taft himself may be consigned once more to a minority position in the Senate. But there is little bitterness to his words tonight: Taft's mood is that of a partner wearily grateful to have escaped a loveless marriage.

Trohan and Taft notwithstanding, the *Trib* itself is buoyant. Tonight's lead story was outlined hours ago and now, even though Congress appears likely to return to Democratic hands and Truman himself clings to a half-million-vote lead, the night editor still credits this to an alliance of Eastern machines and rotten boroughs in the South. Confident that later returns will reverse the current trend, the *Tribune* decides to go ahead with a morning edition whose banner headline will proclaim the historic news: "Dewey Defeats Truman."

Lights are burning late in Pawling, where Mayor John Sheridan and the local business community have anticipated this night ever since Tom Dewey moved to Quaker Hill in 1938. The village expects a new railroad station to replace the shabby one shaming downtown, and a post office as good as or better than Hyde Park's. The president of the Pawling Rubber Company has made his own investment in the next administration, having purchased the old

Dutcher House, once favored by Astors and other well-heeled summer guests, for restoration and reincarnation as a summer White
House.

Seventy miles to the south, the proprietor of Dapplemere Farm is
still in his suite as Tuesday turns to Wednesday, and the nation outside is awash in doubt. The corridor leading to 1527 is lined with an
impressive phalanx of state troopers and city police, while Secret
Service agents guard entrances and plan to throw a protective net
around the president-elect as soon as victory is his. But at midnight,
with Truman holding a thin edge in New York as well as Illinois and
Indiana, Dewey's friends and neighbors notice agents casting side-
long glances at one another. Whispered words are exchanged, then,
one by one, the Secret Service men begin slipping as unobtrusively
as they can out of the suite and into the hall.[33]

On the sixth floor, a member of Goodrich's statistical team stum-
bles on an uneaten banquet of potato salad and sandwiches. Roused
from his thoughts by the sound of distant clatter, he walks over to a
window now streaked with raindrops. Down on Madison Avenue,
barricades have been set up and mounted police assigned to control
the mobs of happy Republicans expected to storm the Hotel Roosevelt. But the crowd has never materialized. Suddenly, Abe Poeretz
identifies the rat-a-tat sound that drew him to the window. It is the
clatter of horses' hooves against pavement as the patrolmen sent to
keep order melt away, disappearing into a Manhattan night as
black as onyx.[34]

In the red and gold ballroom of the Roosevelt, the early shock has
given way to cautious optimism. At one o'clock, Herb Brownell appears to lay stake to Dewey's own New York, in a narrow win made
possible largely because here Henry Wallace has done what George
Gallup and others expected him to do nationwide: strip off votes
from the old Roosevelt coalition, 500,000 in all. But the mood is
fragile. Boredom has degenerated into anguish. An elevator operator
asks if it's true that nets are being stretched beneath the windows of
1527. Russ Sprague has left Suite 2K to "go downstairs and hold
some hands," as he puts it. Somewhere in the crowd, McGeorge
Bundy is bidding good night to his evening's guest, Felix Frankfurter. For most of the campaign, Bundy, the youthful biographer of
Henry Stimson, has worked with Allen Dulles in the foreign affairs
section. Tonight, he is escorting Justice Frankfurter through the tumult of a victorious election-night headquarters, something the justice has always wanted to see. But Frankfurter's powers of analysis
are not limited to the law. Around the time Abe Poeretz glimpses

the retreating police and the votes from Long Island nail down the
Empire State for its governor, Bundy's companion utters a silent
apology and makes his way out of the ballroom and through the
blazing television lights in the Roosevelt's red-carpeted lobby.
Unrecognized, the justice walks out the door and heads for Democratic headquarters at the Biltmore, two blocks away.[35]

Other observers react in their own way to what is happening
around them. A former office boy from the rackets probe, who once
helped to house and feed a bevy of prostitutes forming the backbone
of Dewey's case against Lucky Luciano, has for months expected to
follow his old boss to Washington. Now he sits down to dash off a
telegram to his mother. "Am unpacking," it says.[36]

John Foster Dulles is wide awake on a chilly Parisian morning
when David Schoenbrun calls back to ask if Dulles is still amenable
to the previously arranged interview. Momentarily staggered by the
returns Schoenbrun passes along, the man Wall Street lampoons as
Dull, Duller, Dulles manages a self-deprecatory joke. Perhaps, he
suggests, he might be introduced as "the former future Secretary of
State."

On the fifteenth floor, the candidate himself has emerged from seclusion to wander over to Pat and Marge Hogan and softly break
the news. Composed as ever, strong of voice, he says it looks like
there won't be any New Year's Eve poker in the White House. To a
friend just outside the suite, Dewey sounds a more bitter note.
"What do you know?" he asks sardonically. "The son of a bitch
won."[37]

Dewey's press secretary, Jim Hagerty, causes a sensation on the
Hotel Roosevelt's mezzanine waving aloft a yellow Western Union
slip and shouting to the assembled press corps, "This is it. This is it."
It is 11:14 A.M. Less than five minutes ago, Democratic chairman J.
Howard McGrath had claimed victory. Truman partisans toast
their upset victory with champagne from a galvanized tub, and parody the Whiffenpoof song to devastating effect.

> "Gentleman pollsters, up in a tree,
> Doomed from here to eternity,
> God, please save us from Tom Dewey,
> Baa, baa, baa."

One of the first to congratulate McGrath is Hugh Scott, who nevertheless is furious. Already, Dewey has called to assume personal responsibility for the debacle, and he found his chairman in a fighting

mood. Scott has several scapegoats in mind, especially "those mastodons" within his own party who saddled a progressive nominee with a congressional record tailor-made to Truman's ferocious assaults. Wounded by defeat, Scott lashes out at those he considers responsible. "Now," he vows to a friend, "maybe those sons of bitches will go out and pass some social legislation."[38]

Usually, those out in the cold huddle closer for warmth. Not this morning. Already, Taft's staunch supporter Alice Roosevelt Longworth, famed for her barbed tongue—it is she who, wrongly, has gotten credit for the famous bon mot about Dewey looking like "the little man on a wedding cake"—is stamping out the last of a long parade of cigarettes in Scott's Statler suite. "Well," muses the sage of Dupont Circle, "you can't make a souffle rise twice."

In the office of the District Attorney of New York, Frank Hogan has called a staff meeting. "The best man didn't win the election," Hogan announces, "and anyone who says anything to the contrary, I will personally throw through that window." Elsewhere in New York, workers in the garment district have tossed open windows of their own, hurling bits of colored cloth to the streets in celebration of Truman's win. Switchboard operators at the New York *Times* are inundated by 25,000 calls seeking confirmation of the news from the city's newspaper of record. Hundreds of calls are similarly swamping Washington hotels as crestfallen Republicans cancel reservations made weeks ago for the January inauguration festivities. The Detroit *Free Press* contains an editorial based upon Dewey's election. The Alsop brothers are looking ahead to the new president's cabinet choices. But in the *Times,* there is a letter from the paper's own James Reston suggesting that, rather than spend their time "analyzing Governor Dewey's failure in the election," the nation's journalists examine their own.[39]

"There were certain factors in this election that were known (and discounted) by almost every political writer," Reston says. "We knew about the tradition that a defeated candidate had never been nominated and elected after his defeat. We knew that the national income was running at a rate of $210 billions a year. . . . We knew also that this prosperity applied not only to the people in the industrial areas but to the people on the farms as well. . . . We were, moreover, conscious of the fact that a whole generation had grown up under the strong influences of the Roosevelt era; that there were (and are) more poor people in this country than rich people; that personality is a force in American politics as strong as principle; and that the American people have always loved a fighter."

When he lost the 1940 nomination to Wendell Willkie, Dewey wandered down to his headquarters and found Goody Goodrich alone in a corner of the room wearing the dejection that clothes every failed candidacy and its backers. "Keep your chin up," the D.A. told him. "If you're going to be in this business, you've got to learn to roll with the punches." This morning, the lesson is repeated as the Governor appears before his staff for a short pep talk. "When I wished Mr. Truman well, I meant it," he tells them. "I think Mr. Truman is a good man. This nation will go on now, it will prosper and flourish. And so will we." He circulates through the room shaking hands and saying over and over what he has already told Hugh Scott—that the onus for what happened last night rests on his shoulders alone. Willie Schilling, a twenty-two-year-old stenographer on the Albany staff is not to be consoled. "It's awful," she sobs. "It was my first vote."[40]

At one o'clock, Dewey attends a press conference for 150 newsmen jostling for position and a piece of crow. Freshly groomed in a gray suit and tie, Dewey begins with a question of his own: "Is there anything I can tell you that you don't already know?"

He refuses to speculate in detail about the returns until he can study them more carefully. What about the pollsters? someone asks. The smile on his face flickers for a moment, then returns with irony added. "I hate to comment on anyone else's misfortune." As for the future, "I simply have no plans." Resignation is out of the question, although the Governor leaves an impression that he'd like to retire in 1950, when his present term will be up. To friends, he has confided his longing to return to the law, and a chance at last to earn financial security for his family.

"How do you feel, Governor?"

"Fine," Dewey responds, doing his best to look truthful, "and greatly relieved of the responsibilities that would have come to me otherwise."

And what about Frances? "She's been through this before. We've won and lost . . . all in good fun." A female voice rises above the din. "Do you think the American people are ready for any intellectual appeal," she wonders, "or that they still like corn?" Dewey brushes the question aside without comment. Glancing at the clock, hands in his pockets, his discomfort is plain. Clearly, he would prefer to be anywhere else. But the questions keep coming, until one-thirty when he turns to leave the room, then raises a hand to wave goodbye. "It's been grand fun, boys and girls. I've enjoyed it immensely. Good luck."

In his wake, there is a smattering of applause, a rare tribute from reporters who must scurry to their telephones and typewriters and explain within hours what went wrong and why. At four-thirty Frank Kirsie of the hotel staff knocks on the door of 1527 to offer help in escorting the Deweys to Grand Central Station and a train ride north to Albany. To Kirsie, the Governor seems dazed and remote, an interpretation soon disproved as the two men stride down the hallway. Kirsie is anxious to say something consoling, yet fearful of intruding on private grief. From previous conversations, the inquisitive Dewey has learned of Kirsie's fascination for flying machines, and now he breaks the silence by abruptly asking the bellboy for his opinion of helicopters—doesn't he think them the coming thing in aviation.[41]

Outside the Roosevelt, the weather has turned cold and wet, as if reflecting the mood of the little party crossing virtually unnoticed through the vast concourse of Grand Central to a private car attached to the Chicago-bound Water Level Limited. In an adjacent car, a few staffers and two reporters sit in silence, their strain eased by scotch. The gloom is deepened by a heavy rain drenching the Hudson Valley, collecting in deep puddles around the solid granite walls of Albany's redoubtable Union Station as the train pulls in at 8 P.M. Five hundred loyalists are on hand to greet the Governor, along with a few photographers. There are no welcoming ceremonies, no speeches, no bands; only two cars waiting to take the family up Columbia and Eagle streets, pausing en route for traffic lights, finally depositing them at the tomblike Executive Mansion. There the Governor assists his wife and mother from the car before saying good night to his guards. He waves absentmindedly, before a new thought moves him to speak.

"I'll see you on the weekend," he calls out, "if you're still with me."

An answering voice comes through distantly, disembodied in the clammy fog. "I'll be with you, Governor." It could have been a ghost speaking.

I

A BOY FROM
PIANO STREET

1902–1935

1

The Right Side of the Tracks

There was nothing interesting about my youth, except that I was
working all the time.

—THOMAS E. DEWEY

The Deweys were born to contention, raised on conviction, and nurtured by intolerance. It was an inheritance dating to the second half
of the sixteenth century, when a French Huguenot family named
Douai forsook northern France and all things Popish for the Protestant Canaan across the Channel. Yet even in England, the true faith
was a perishable commodity, and by 1630, Thomas Duee of Sandwich could no longer tolerate the relaxed standards of Anglican
Britain. That year, he left for the New World, where he put down
roots at Dorchester, Massachusetts, in the shadow of John
Winthrop's city upon a hill.

Whatever side of the Atlantic the clan called home, restlessness
remained in the Dewey genes. "The Settler," as he was known by descendants, abandoned the orthodoxy of Massachusetts Bay in 1635
and moved to the infant community of Windsor, Connecticut. Four
years later, he married a widow and started a family that eventually
included four sons and a daughter. His second boy, Josiah, drifted
north, to the overgrown drumlins and exhausted soil of Vermont.
Combative blood flowed in his progeny; Deweys fought red men in
King Philip's War and lobsterbacks in the American Revolution. In
Bennington one golden Sabbath in 1777, the Reverend Jedidiah
Dewey was preaching to his congregation when word of a Hessian
advance reached town. Closing his Bible, descending from his pulpit, the minister led the men of his flock out the door to war; then,
once victory over the invaders was assured, returned to the church to
complete his sermon.

Deweys and domestic peace mixed like the devil and holy water.
The family historian counted 200 of the brethren in Civil War uniform. Others, like George Martin Dewey, fought the battle against
slavery and Southern aristocrats with words instead of bullets.
George was the son of Granville Dewey, born in a colonial farmhouse on New Hampshire's Mount Support in 1832. As a boy and a
man, he was unable to savor the fat, prosperous peace of his time. At
sixteen, he enrolled in Harvard College. But the Yard held no allure,

and in his sophomore year George left Cambridge to join an eighteen-month astronomical expedition to the headwaters of the impossibly distant Amazon River. Returning to Massachusetts, he
found life as a Lowell schoolteacher a poor answer to youthful ambition, and before long he took to the road once again, now pointed
west toward the empty and beckoning land of Michigan.

In 1852, he found himself in a young state racked by political and
moral growing pains. It was an epoch of violence and spittoons, of
rugged individualism and immature democracy. It was also a perfect age for the opinionated, as George Dewey found when he became the neophyte editor of the Niles, Michigan, *Enquirer.* America
and her frontier were in ferment in this last tumultuous decade before South tore asunder from North. Well-intentioned reformers and
charlatans alike were talking up women's rights, Utopianism, Swe-
denborgianism, spiritualism, and phrenology. In lyceums across the
land, powerful oratory roused Americans to a frenzied pitch, and
politics seized their imagination as never before or since.

Editor Dewey's personal passions were temperance and abolition-
ism, matched after 1854 by the new cause of Republicanism.
Proudly, he took his stand with hundreds of like-minded advocates
of free soil and free labor who gathered under the oaks at Jackson,
Michigan, in July of that year to create a new and stainless party
with which to reform and cleanse America. From his modest journalistic Olympus, Dewey hurled thunderbolts of abuse at "southern
traitors and northern dogfaces" who aimed at nationalizing "the
barbarous institution of negro slavery." Yet, for all his dogmatic at-
tachment to the party, George Martin Dewey remained his own
man, prickly and prone to attack, when it came to individual Republicans.

With the war won and Lincoln martyred, George Dewey took to
the wing again, adding the Hasting *Banner* to his quiver of polemical
arrows. By 1879, he was taking credit for never having printed a line
"giving the least aid or comfort to traitors or their apologists, to the
vendors of liquid damnation" who would emasculate prohibition in
Michigan. The editor promised more of the same, "sternly opposing
every species of vice and immorality, every attempt to dishonor the
nation's fair name, and every effort to put the Government in the
hands of the chieftains of the late Rebellion."

In other words, to wave the Bloody Shirt against any Democrat,
crushing any Democratic attempt to rise from the grave that party
leaders had dug for themselves in 1861. A man so convinced of his
own rectitude was better suited to preach than seek votes in the

cider-loving precincts of rural Michigan, even if the state was a GOP fiefdom for all of Dewey's adult life. The editor served a single term in the State Senate, and he took a lively interest in party organization wherever he lived. After 1881, that meant a little rail junction on the Shiawassee River, first glimpsed by Dewey as a fresh-faced newspaperman twenty-five years before.

"We have come to Owosso to stay," he proclaimed in the *Times,* a seven-volume folio he now proposed to turn into a powerful organ of the party he'd helped found in the oak grove at Jackson. His new home was itself less than fifty years in existence, the product of a former New York schoolteacher and his friends who set out in July of 1835 in two covered wagons for the Big Rapids of the Shiawassee River, the place the Chippewas and their chief, Wasso, called Chiboc-wa-ting. It was a desolate land then, where silence ruled and the only signs of life were left by fur trappers, missionaries, and the soft scrape of the bear's paw against the forest floor.

Log cabins had been built, the river dammed, a sawmill and trading post erected in pale imitation of the economies of Saginaw and points east. A Baptist minister arrived to save souls, and settlers with more prosaic concerns discovered that rotten wood kindled after dark could shoo away the mosquitoes infesting Michigan's night. The river powered prosperity, and the earth gave its blessing to agriculture. If the northern climate made for a late corn crop, it was more than compensated for by the sweet sugar beets that thrived in Shiawassee County's rich black soil. In fields outside of town, haycocks stood like sentinels of farm wealth, while placid Holsteins in their slow gait seemed to imitate their owners' contentment.

Within a generation, the iron horse arrived. Halfway between Chicago and Detroit, twenty-seven miles from the new state capital at Lansing, Owosso found itself a major rail junction, where no fewer than four lines met. It was a promising venue for George Dewey, who by April 1882 was the proud owner of a new Taylor press "only two months behind schedule," churning out a weekly paper bristling with the editor's self-assured politics. On the side, he did as much printing work as a friendly administration could provide. The life of a country editor was not a lucrative one. Before the end of his second year in Owosso, Dewey was pointing to $500 in debts owed him, "which we very much need and respectfully wish our patrons to favor us with."

Yet his family of three boys and two girls now reaching for adulthood was hardly impoverished. The *Times's* circulation had tripled, and when its editor left his office in the evening it was to go to a comfortable home in a neighborhood labeled Piano Street by the envious, who reasoned that anyone living on what the maps called Oliver Street was prosperous enough to own a parlor piano. All his life, money counted less for George Dewey than controversy, and he was never happier than when called to the oratorical circuit of his native New England, to lambaste Democrats and spellbind audiences with three-hour harangues on arcane urgencies like the tariff and bimetalism.

By 1884, the editor was much in demand by national Republican leaders, who called upon him to scorch James G. Blaine's opposition eighty-two times. A few years later, he was invited by the chairman of New York's GOP to take up the battle against Tammany Hall. Delighted, George turned the *Times* over to his twenty-nine-year-old son Edmund—who added a furnace and clients appreciative of an editor who stayed home and minded his business—and returned to the bad hotels and irregular hours of the speechmaking trade. When William McKinley ran for governor of Ohio, he put Dewey's leather lungs to good use as a backup speaker. Later, with McKinley in the White House, his orator was offered ambassadorial posts in Turkey or Spain.

Unwell physically and financially, George turned the offers aside—a pattern to be repeated in his grandson's career. So was his personality. Something about George Dewey's unyielding certainty, his fanatical contempt for alcohol, and his austere carriage repelled potential followers. He was easier to respect than enjoy. When he died, a day before his fortieth wedding anniversary, the local chapter of the Odd Fellows invited an Illinois preacher to assess the passionate, partisan, slightly disappointing performance of George Martin Dewey, Senior.

"Mr. Dewey did not have that—call it tact, call it diplomacy, call it political instinct," according to his eulogist, "that something by which men attain to position." Summarizing the editor's life must have called for all three.

The Reverend George R. Wilson went on, in words that might have echoed across seventy-four years and a thousand miles to the St. James Episcopal Church on Madison Avenue in March of 1971.

"To such a man, the world of thought is a battlefield. . . . He does not speak to please; he does not tarry to adorn with rhetoric; he does not look for stories to enliven, far less to amuse; he does not seek to provoke laughter, but slaughter. Life is too serious in its great efforts to stop and laugh. The very voice of the man will gather to itself a quality . . . alive with the agony of intensity."[1]

The dead editor's children emulated his restless nature. Three of them never found any permanent peace in the four square miles of sunburned brick and topheavy maples of Owosso. The oldest boy, Henry, left Michigan to teach in Tacoma, Washington, ran an unsuccessful Republican campaign for Congress, and became a textbook editor for Houghton Mifflin. His sister Hannah married a biology professor from the University of California, while Grace Dewey attended Wellesley College, taught in an Ohio seminary, and conducted European tours for the raw daughters of Midwestern bankers and grain dealers. In middle age, Grace decided to become an accountant. As usual, she did what she set out to do, with a doggedness enshrined in her maxims. "There is nothing wrong with the world today that hard work won't cure" was a favorite. Matronly and intimidating, this unblinking old spinster was the first to inform her nephew that he would grow up to become a lawyer.[2]

Edmund Dewey was most unlike his father, a large phlegmatic man, hitched for life to the *Times* and the dairy cattle he liked to display for the ribbons they won every year at the state fair. "Save your money and buy yourself a farm," he told his younger brother's only child, Tom, a bit of advice that bore fruit long after Edmund's premature death by heart attack in 1918. As contemptuous of alcohol as his father was, Edmund enlivened the residence on West Oliver Street with the piano and recorded music he loved in common with his wife, May.[3]

His younger brother by nine years was also the baby of the family, a handsome six-footer with the flashing dark eyes and high forehead of all Dewey men. When he met his future bride in 1897, George Martin Dewey, Jr., was a twenty-seven-year-old with considerable disappointment under his belt. As a boy, his fondest ambition had been a career in the Army. After finishing first in a congressional examination, George had proudly taken his place at West Point, only to leave the school when a gymnasium accident broke a bone in his lower spine. He returned briefly in the fall of 1890, with an ailment diagnosed incorrectly first as epilepsy, then kidney trouble. The pain finally grew so excruciating that the cadet was forced to abandon forever his military aspirations. Yet something of the soldier remained behind, a precision about words and people, and a granitic reserve that led friends and neighbors to call him the Rock of Gibraltar.

In the early 1890s, the frustrated soldier drifted west, in the footsteps of his older brother Henry. He landed a reportorial job at fifteen dollars a week on the Tacoma *Ledger,* only to return home when Edmund invited him to lend a hand in running the *Times.* George drifted naturally into the masculine haunts of Owosso: the Elks Lodge, with its polished antlers and cathedral ceiling; the varnished floors and stale aroma of the newspaper composing room, the no-frills piety of the squat Congregational church. But something was missing. To relieve his loneliness, he was soon courting a vivacious girl seven years his junior.[4]

Annie Louise Thomas was the daughter of a local merchant, raised in her father's general store on the banks of the Shiawassee. Alfred Thomas was a gentleman of the old school, who believed advertising undignified and who extended credit to hard-pressed laborers whenever Owosso's unpredictable economy went bust. An easy democracy pervaded his brick store at Washington and Main, where factory workers from the west side of town mingled comfortably around a vast American cheese with prosperous managers like the Storers, who ran the town's leading haberdashery.

It was in the seven-room apartment over the store that his second daughter was born in July 1877. From girlhood, Annie was as mischievous as County Cork and respectable as Main Street. Raised to respect a dollar and avoid credit, she did not crowd out of a head trained for numbers a buoyant enthusiasm for life and all its wonders. She loved the outdoors, went skating on Lake Hopkins in the winter and swimming there when the weather turned warm. In between she forsook both for intense competition on Owosso's municipal golf links; bridge games filled countless evenings. Annie liked to excel at whatever she did, and barely tolerated those who played with less single-minded absorption. Bridge partners found it impossible to complete a game without her advice or criticism. Regulars at the country club began slipping away at the sight of her, confident they would not meet her exacting standards. Even today, friends recall her as "a strong character . . . with a wicked mouth . . . apt to be opinionated."[5]

She was a methodical woman who could order a friend driving her to Chicago in 1944 to see her son nominated for President to keep a close watch on the clock; noon was approaching, "and I always eat at noon." To her minister, she railed against excessive repetition in a sermon; and long-absent acquaintances were apt to find the first words of greeting a sharp inquiry about their tardiness. Thrifty to a fault, she complained when her son was governor of

New York that her grandchildren stayed too long in the shower, and used altogether too much toilet paper. On one visit to Albany, "Mater" suffered through a game of hearts with her two grandsons, agonizing as John Dewey debated his next move. As the boy's indecision lengthened, the old woman's face grew red and her impatience rose to the surface. Finally, unable to stand the suspense, she burst out, "Play your card or get out of the house."[6]

It was that insistence that the world meet her on her own terms that made Annie Dewey a character in Owosso, a trait she passed on at an early age to her son. Yet she was multidimensional, endowed with an Irish humor that softened her sharp edges and confused New York shopgirls. Ordering one of the patented hats that gave her in old age an air of self-parody, Annie looked at a questioning clerk with wide-eyed sincerity and said as fast as she could, "Oh, don't you know Owosso? It's in Shiawassee County on the Shiawassee River."

She was a woman without pretension, although dignified in public. In private, she could be coarse and profane. A contradiction in terms? Not according to her grandson. The dignity, after all, was important "only when other people were watching." At the Dewey farm on Quaker Hill, Annie thought nothing of turning over one of the ashtrays her chain smoking filled so rapidly, then wiping it clean with her slip. "It's the quickest way," she explained to the maid. Nor was it unusual for her to sit, legs apart and elbows planted on her knees, transfixed before a television set, gazing at the flickering image of her son parrying reporters' questions on *Meet the Press*.

"Attaboy, Tom," she exhorted the set, "you give 'em hell."[7]

To her son, she bequeathed a clear head, and a healthy respect for common sense and the average man or woman who possessed it. She left also a headstrong assertiveness that many took for conceit, a set of small-town values never entirely erased by exposure to the sophisticated East, and a sense of proportion that moderated triumph and eased defeat. In 1948, when Tom was virtually conceded the White House and reporters desperate for a fresh angle on a dull contest sought her out, Annie was pressed for motherly expressions of pride and a forecast of her son's performance to come.

"Well," she told one of her questioners, "I don't know anything about politics, and I don't know whether Tom will make a good President. But I'll tell you one thing: he's a lousy poker player."[8]

January 25, 1899, was a day of intermingled joy and sorrow in Alfred Thomas' home. At four o'clock that afternoon, his daughter was scheduled to become Mrs. George M. Dewey, Jr. At the last minute, the ceremony was advanced to noontime so that the bride's grandfather might look on from his sickbed. Within three days, the honeymooning couple were called home to attend George Thomas' funeral. Later, the couple, hailed by a local journalist as "among Owosso's favorites," settled in Lansing, where George worked as a clerk in the state auditor's office, and commuted every Thursday night to represent Ward 1 on Owosso's Board of Aldermen. A more permanent return was forecast in the summer of 1901, when Annie discovered she was pregnant, and her indulgent father insisted that she come back to Washington and Main streets for her lying-in. And so it was in the apartment over Alfred Thomas' general store, at seven o'clock on the evening of March 24, 1902, that Annie gave birth to a son. The "City Chat" column of the *Press-American* announced the glad tidings.

"A ten-pound Republican voter was born last evening to Mr. and Mrs. George M. Dewey. George says the young man arrived in time for registration for the April election."

American youth was awash in the brittle tales of Horatio Alger and Tom Swift, of *McGuffey's Reader* and Frank Merriwell. Alger's 119 titles set a tone for an entire generation: *Work and Win, Slow and Sure, Jed, the Poorhouse Boy, Strive and Succeed.* In Owosso, the struggle to establish a pioneer settlement had given way by 1902 to the parochial self-pride that turned America's open spaces into closets of conformity. Now, residents boasted without reservation about their splendid new sidewalks. "In municipal improvements," a local brochure trumpeted, "the city of Owosso is fully up with other cities of her class, and to a very large number of them sets an example of what may be accomplished by thrift, enterprise and plenty of spirit."

Owossoans were pleased with their three miles of finely paved streets. They talked with wonder of the electricity coursing through their homes and factories. They counted precisely the one million window screens and 180,000 snow shovels produced each year at the Estey Manufacturing Company. They cherished their three hotels and the Prolato Detachable Tire turned out by the Owosso Tire Company. They flocked to listen when the town band was enriched by four saxophones; and when the new Central High School was opened—it cost $100,000, without equipment—they were properly awed. They dispatched ambitious sons to Owosso Business College, and daughters not already consigned to snoring husbands and moist offspring to the Ladies Country Normal School.

Owosso in 1902 was a shared community of values, where people worked hard and worshipped regularly and satisfied their intellectual curiosity at Chautauqua. By the time of Annie Dewey's confinement, it had become a miniature chapel, festooned with crinoline, in the American gothic cathedral. Its most mystical rites were card parties and ice cream socials, and the icy fellowship of the dead months between November and April. In religion, the town was diverse if not broad-minded. In the ballot box, it knelt without reservation before the blood-spattered faith of Lincoln and Garfield and McKinley. Religion and politics were reflections of Owosso's comfortable certainties. "It was one of those things we took for granted," Tom Dewey would later write of the Almighty, "as it was assumed that all good people were Republicans."[9]

There was another side to America, another America really. There was a land whose children didn't read the Rover Boys stories, as George Dewey's son did in Owosso, in which young men had no backyard to do chores in. The ethic in the other America was less salvation than survival. Salvatore Lucania was Sicily-born, one of 12 million immigrants who formed the bulk of an urban country so unlike its pastoral Western complement, and who filtered through the turnstiles at New York's Ellis Island between 1890 and 1910. Together, they transformed the old Dutch haven of Manhattan into a patchwork of ethnicity, where foreign tongues and bright ambitions all too often led to crushed hopes and criminal reactions. As a boy, Lucania was reared in the fantastic ghetto of the Lower East Side, where crime bred faster than rats. The old dumbbell tenement had been outlawed in 1901, but over half New York's population continued to live in the six-story high rises for the poor, where a whole family might share one living room, and a narrow air shaft and central hallway turned a man's castle into an eerie world of shadows and dank air.

Only Bombay suffered worse slums than New York. Some 3,500 people lived in one block on Mulberry Street on the Lower East Side, where many tenements still lacked fire escapes, banisters, or a water closet for every twenty inhabitants. Yet, for all the deprivations of life in Mulberry's warrens, the neighborhood itself seemed like a vast human carnival. Open air markets sold fresh vegetables and meats. Pushcart peddlers and hurdy-gurdy players filled the air with the music of commerce. There were knife sharpeners and cloth cutters, shoeshine boys and hot-corn girls. The very streets of New York sweated humanity. When horses fell dead on the pavement, they were left to be picked up by the city. Young men and women alike picked rags or toiled in sweatshops for a dollar a day. When Christmas came around, resourceful children made a tree from a pail and mop handle.

Never before had New York, or the nation whose unofficial capital it had become, seemed so stratified. Visitors to Manhattan could stroll from the rococo palaces of Vanderbilt, Astor, and Carnegie that threw shadows across Fifth Avenue to desperate and sometimes murderous street corners where Jewish seamstresses could, with luck, earn eight cents an hour in the garment trade. The immigrant had little for consolation besides his faith, his ethnic identity, and an alliance of convenience with the city's dominant political machine. In an age when government was weak and reluctant to provide jobs or ease social integration for the newcomer, it was Tammany Hall that won over the Italian or Polish immigrant with a turkey at Christmas, a few weeks' work cleaning streets, some greased justice in a magistrate's court.

Not everyone availed themselves of Tammany's welcoming embrace. Salvatore Lucania, for one, sat mute in the back of a classroom at Public School 10, embarrassed and isolated because he knew no English. By his fourteenth birthday, he had left school behind for good and turned to petty crime, which for many residents of the Lower East Side was the only rags-to-riches story with any credibility. Lucania joined the 104th Street Gang, befriended another resentful youth named Frank Costello, and endured his six-dollar-a-week job as a runner delivering women's hats. In 1916, the boy was arrested for the first time, caught after stashing narcotics in a hatband. For his offense, he was sentenced to a year's imprisonment at Hampton Farms penitentiary, from which he emerged Charley Lucania. Soon, friends shortened the name to Lucky; and an aspiring felon, just as ambitious as a Dulles, a Truman, or a Dewey, was developing his own philosophy of success.

"I never wanted to be a crumb" he explained later. "If I had to be a crumb, I'd rather be dead."

The two Americas, street corner and cornfield, were latent antagonists in 1902. Not long before his death, President McKinley, whose imperialist policies were under attack from the left, listened to a Gridiron Dinner comparison of the newly won Philippines, Cuba, and "our other island possession—New York." As for the liberated natives now seeking union with the mainland, "they are not in touch with American sentiment. Neither is New York. They are accustomed to a monarchical form of government. So is New York. They are not yet ripe for assimilation. We have been trying for two hundred years to assimilate New York, without success."

The old America looked askance at the new, could not fathom the squalor and street crime infesting immigrant neighborhoods. Even more alien than the languages overheard in New York's overcrowded doorways and courtyards were the politics—strange hybrids of socialism and communism and trade unionism and a general leveling of the established and serene order. More than a continent separated the two Americas in 1902.

Attempting to bridge the gap was a seemingly unlikely pacifier, a blueblood by birth, a jingo by instinct, a dynamo aptly summed up by Henry Adams as "pure act." His name was Theodore Roosevelt, and to those bored with the bloodless etiquette of the Victorian administration, he seemed all thunder and lightning, blood and guts, a gift from the gods. Everywhere Americans looked in the first year of the Roosevelt presidency, there was TR breaking precedent and reaping headlines; inviting a black man, Booker T. Washington, to dine at the White House; threatening to break up the vast industrial conglomerates called trusts; announcing America's new role as international policeman, in his famous Corollary to James Monroe's Doctrine of national hegemony over the Western Hemisphere.

To muckrakers—Roosevelt coined the word as he coined the era—McKinley's successor was an invaluable ally in their shrill assault against the seamy underside of the nation's economic life. To conservative Republicans, he was an object of mounting horror, pressing reform after reform, bringing under government's watchful eye the production of meat, food and drugs, railroad shipping rates, and vast areas of the unspoiled West. He sent troops to Santo Domingo; alerted Admiral Dewey, the hero of Manila Bay and fifth cousin to the child setting out in life from his grandfather's general store in Owosso, to prepare a fleet should Great Britain and Germany try to force impoverished Venezuela to pay her debts; and agitated a revolution in Colombia that he might obtain a strategic slice of the continent on which to dig his cherished path between the seas.

Yet he mediated other nations' wars as skillfully as he risked involvement for his own, winning a Nobel Peace Prize in the process. To the average American, Roosevelt was easily the most captivating, democratic chief executive since Lincoln. Yet he was at heart a thoughtful conservative, a pragmatic product of his milieu and the elegant brownstones of Manhattan's Twenty-first Assembly District. In a moment of candor, he once summed up his political career; it was due, he mused, "to the single fact that when I came out of Harvard, I was firmly resolved to belong to the governing class, not the governed." This was the Roosevelt who balanced budgets and worried not at all about the propriety of accepting substantial campaign contributions from the very titans of industry whose stranglehold he was pledged to break, who told a close friend that as for the Negro race, "they are altogether inferior to the whites" and suspended 167 black soldiers after shooting broke out in Brownsville, Texas, on a fetid August night in 1906. No evidence was ever produced to convict the men; TR was unmoved. "I care nothing whatever for the yelling of either the politicians or the sentimentalists," he wrote his secretary of war, William Howard Taft. The soldiers were dismissed.

It was to forestall more violent changes that Roosevelt threw open the windows of a musty society on the brink of international standing. "He serves his party best," according to this father of modern Republicanism, "who most helps to make it instantly responsive to every need of the people."

Others disputed so sweeping an edict. Andrew Carnegie, for example. "We accept and welcome as conditions to which we must accommodate ourselves," the steel magnate and philanthropist wrote, "great inequalities of the environment, the consolidation of business . . . in the hands of the few, and the law of competition between these . . . essential for the progress of the race." Yale's W. Graham Sumner went even further in espousing the might-makes-right philosophy of social Darwinism, claiming flatly that "millionaires are the product of natural selection."

So it was that TR found himself presiding over two Americas, and two Republican parties. Purist versus pragmatist, financial kingpins versus iconoclastic journalists, Nelson Aldrich and J. P. Morgan versus Hiram Johnson and Gifford Pinchot. Twice during his term of office, President Roosevelt was forced to ask Morgan to do what he, a mere president of the United States, could not do—stem a gathering economic panic. By the end of his administration, TR was more popular outside his party than within. He could not even persuade the Republican platform committee to endorse a tough anti-injunction measure for labor disputes, despite the fact that William Jennings Bryan and his left-wing allies in the Democratic party had lured previously neutral labor chieftain Samuel Gompers to their standard with just such a plank.

The purist Republicans would cling to principle, even if principle were reduced to flotsam floating in the wake of a sunken ship. For them, Republicanism was less free labor than reliable profits, and the success of American business a testament to their own faith in Sumner's natural selection. They looked upon TR as a dangerous flirter with the left, whose pragmatism was a mere false front for expediency. They grudgingly accepted his dictation of William Howard Taft to succeed him in 1908, only to be pleasantly surprised when Taft turned out to be far more conservative than his old chief. Within four years, the two parties fighting for the Republican label were formally split asunder, with Roosevelt veering sharply to the left, and his enthused partisans standing at Armageddon. Taft retained the GOP machinery, and the rotten boroughs of the solidly Democratic South—enough to win a nomination, but not to extend his lease on the White House.

All over America, loyal Republicans were forced to choose which party to belong to. George M. Dewey, like his ten-year-old son, Tom, lined up with the Bull Moose. The boy's very nickname was Ted, both because of his initials and his impassioned support for Teddy Roosevelt. Who could imagine that loudly contested summer that George's boy would one day fall heir to Rooseveltian Republicanism, while Taft's son Robert would carry the conservative torch his father had held aloft so unhappily? Who could conceive of the parallels between TR and his youthful disciple from Owosso: that both achieved early fame as crime fighters, that both were governor of New York at the age of forty, that both were presidential contenders within months of assuming office? TR busted trusts; Tom Dewey busted rackets. Both men wielded authority with undisguised delight, rarely shying away from the personal pronoun. Both were heroes in an age longing for the heroic, who rose almost tragically fast, and lived out abbreviated lives in the shadow of premature acclaim and great ambitions rashly pursued.

Both were compassionate conservatives, more pragmatic than profound in their philosophy of government. Both sought to bridge the two Americas, rejecting what Dewey called "the blind obstructionism which Democrats claim is our habit and some Republicans would like to take as our role."

Owosso was a good place to be a boy in the first decade of the new century, when George Dewey moved his family back from Lansing and rented a house on West Oliver Street, close to the school where Tom was first enrolled. George's son could develop his senses in his grandfather's store, in fragrant recesses scented by fresh produce and gooseberry jam. A cellar jutted out beneath Main Street, providing a perfect hideaway for fresh eggs under glass or a fat Christmas goose. When troubled, Alfred Thomas invited his grandson into a luxuriant garden of wildflowers and berries, or onto the front seat of the sleigh driven by his deliveryman, Otto. For Tommy, it was a heady experience, riding in all weather behind a shivering horse that pranced confidently down every street in town. He committed those streets to memory, recalling them at will when selling the *Saturday Evening Post* and *Country Gentleman* a few years later.

There were diversions for an energetic youngster. Across the Shiawassee lay the old railroad trestle, where children anxious to prove their mettle could leap twelve feet into the deep, placid waters below. Boys played, as they always have, at cowboys and Indians, in tree houses and on baseball diamonds. On Halloween, they scouted out vulnerable outhouses, and inscribed terrible oaths in soap on residential and shopwindows. When the Fourth of July came around and Sousa marches filled the air, they sent lighted snakes wriggling across freshly laid sidewalks, then paused to inhale the patriotic commandments of a flag-loving age. When Tommy was seven, he celebrated one Fourth by dressing up as Uncle Sam, posing for posterity behind Margaret Ellis, a pint-sized Miss Columbia from next door.[10]

As an editor's son, he could take advantage of free tickets when the circus came to town, as he did in August 1911, rising with the dawn to look at elephants and acrobats and hear the steam calliope that signaled frivolity amidst the sober-minded purpose of Owosso. In the woods around the town, there were rabbits to hunt, and in the skies overhead kites seemed to hang suspended from the clouds. When the weather turned hot, the family retreated to a resort hotel at Glen Lake in Michigan's northern peninsula, where Tommy learned to construct a rudimentary sailing vessel from an old rowboat and bedsheet. A photo of him taken there in the dry heat of 1911 shows a little boy with a mischievous grin and pants rolled up to his knees. Behind him stands his father, stony-faced and as out of place on a vacation island as an iceberg.

George Martin Dewey, Jr., was not an incandescent figure in his son's life. Later, Tom said his father had "an extraordinary intellect" and might well have become "a famous writer" if ambition had steered him in that direction. At a more candid moment, Dewey couldn't recall his father's ever taking up "a problem of what I should or shouldn't do." Instead, he remembered the editor's absences, and the long days at the *Times* office that began before seven in the morning and lasted until supper was set out at six. Evenings found George Dewey absorbed in the paper, the small-town politics of a school board meeting, or a bridge or poker game with Annie and friends.

In later years, Thomas Dewey seemed deliberately to avoid pleasant memories of the man with whom he caught fish for the evening meal, and who lent him an office at the *Times* from which to conduct his own burgeoning newspaper and magazine distribution business. Yet George Dewey has not been entirely obscured by time, and his influence upon his son was undoubtedly greater than Tom himself realized. There was, he acknowledged, "a great sense of urgency" in whatever his father said, along with "an intolerance for anyone who could think differently." The editor had a habit of whipping out of his pocket his latest feverish denunciation of a Democratic administration, subjecting friends to vivid readings before posting the finished product on a galley at the *Times* office. His son never forgot the repeated message, "Tammany Hall represents all that is evil in government."[11]

Sometimes, Tommy sat wide-eyed for hours listening to his father talk politics with local luminaries like Congressman Joseph Fordney and Governor Chase Osborne, the Bull Mooser who epitomized Republican progressivism at its zenith. Osborne was a frequent visitor to the sun porch of the Dewey home, where he bounced young Tom on his knee and argued for Negro rights and a progressive income tax. A mature Dewey would recall Governor Osborne as the hero of his youth. He remembered, too, the front-porch rally held for the statewide ticket in 1910, and his mother liked to tell of an argument in her home between the man she called George M. and a refugee from the orthodox faith of Owosso. Hot and heavy the dispute waxed, interrupted only long enough so George could tuck his eavesdropping son into bed.

In the morning, the elder Dewey was confronted by a puzzled partisan. "I thought you said Mr. Jones was a nice man," the boy said.

"Why he is, Tom."

"But he's a Democrat!"

When Tommy was three, he was given a bicycle, with the strict admonition that it would be reclaimed if he were to fall off while riding. The child promptly mounted his new plaything, and promptly lost it to his mother's unrelenting grip for a full year. Three years later, he suffered from migraine headaches that ended in vomiting. Whistling or singing on his way to school, fidgeting in the armchair to which Annie condemned him for long periods of silence as punishment for a boyish misdeed, the boy seemed more than usually energetic. Years later, he was diagnosed as a hypothyroid, prone to tire easily, able to work long hours through willpower alone. His own doctor suspected he might have been born hyperthyroid, and burned out his excessive energy by adolescence.[12]

Dewey's aunt would later refer to "the rigid discipline of your boyhood, uniformly maintained and guided by the deepest love." Those who knew Annie Dewey agree that she was an old-fashioned parent, who was capable of indulgence. The only thing strict about the family dinner table was her edict that if Tommy didn't like what was being served, he could go to the kitchen for a bowl of cornflakes. He was encouraged to have friends over to play in the cellar, while the living room at 421 West Oliver was turned into a "workroom" for the boy. When he hooked one contraption to a light socket for power, his proud mother showed it off to visitors, oblivious to the clutter and inconvenience around her.

When Tommy was seven, he dragged a cart to a neighbor's house and asked if he might collect her old newspapers to sell. A few minutes later, the woman heard a strong, angelic soprano coming from her attic. Delighted, Annie plunged her son into a musical world for which she had no talent of her own. Every week, he walked across town to take piano lessons from an elderly German schoolteacher, and his mother saw to it that he practiced at least an hour every day, even if classmates stood outside and hollered for Tom to come out and play ball. In the evening, he seemed the first of his friends to be called in for bed, while a hated cuckoo clock in an upstairs hallway mocked his unwilling efforts at sleep.[13]

Much of his boyhood was spent around older people, at church suppers and choir practice and Sunday dinner at his Thomas grandparents'. Each week when the family gathered for dinner and conversation, Alfred Thomas vanished into the kitchen to fetch a huge shiny bread tin. Filled to the brim with hot, lavishly buttered popcorn, it made a small boy's day complete. In the evening, there were musical soirees at Uncle Edmund's house, where Tommy begged his aunt and uncle to play over and over the thick cumbersome platters on which were stored the quartet from *Rigoletto* and the sextet from *Lucia*. Then, over the hushed stillness of a rural evening, he was transported by the magic of Caruso, Melba, Chaliapin.

A picture survives of the family ranged around Ed and May's

piano, their faces wreathed in anticipation of the next popular standard. In the foreground, head on his hand, one button-shoed foot thrown over a knee, sits young Tom, his features trained on an open book. Before the party broke up, there would be peach ice cream and the onion sandwiches he inexplicably devoured. He might even pull his cousin Harriet's inviting blond pigtails or wrestle with his surrogate sister under the piano. For now, he sits oblivious to the spontaneity around him, comfortable in a private universe of inscrutable design.

Owosso's America believed in work, perseverance, and confidence in one's own mission as the surest route to its realization. No Horatio Alger hero toiled against a more prosaic backdrop than Dewey. When he was still in grade school, he set type and fed boilerplate at the *Times* for ten cents an hour. At home, there was a furnace to clean, a lawn to mow, and a long sidewalk along Oliver and Pine streets to shovel each winter. At the age of nine, he began selling magazines and newspapers, and when the local agent of the Curtis Publishing Company quit in 1913, Tom eagerly took his place. Each delivery day thereafter, he hurried to meet the four-fifteen train out of Detroit, then carted his precious cargo home for divvying up among the nine boys who worked under his supervision.

A year later, he was invited to tour the Detroit *News* plant, where he impressed an editor with the volume of questions he fired, and he gathered up a bundle of information to take home to the *Times*. In the backyard of the Dewey house, he talked a friend into helping him build chicken coops, reasoning that there was money to be had from selling eggs and birds for Sunday dinners all over Owosso. The worst part of the enterprise involved chopping off heads and plucking and cleaning bloody carcasses. Dewey never entirely forgot the crawling lice that offended his fastidiousness.[14]

Then there were a couple summers spent sweeping floors at Otto Sprague's drugstore on North Washington Street, and the Christmas vacation when he washed windows in the local sugar beet factory, until a sprained ankle sent him to the packing room. His dedication was sometimes carried to curious extremes. To Mrs. Paul Pulver, society editor of the Owosso *Argus-Press*, Tom seemed possessed when he came around selling the *Saturday Evening Post*. "I told him I didn't want the magazine," she said afterward, "but he just looked at me defiantly with those dark, piercing eyes and left it on my desk. He gave me a dozen reasons why I should buy it. I couldn't outargue him; it was easier to become his steady customer." In February 1915, his grandfather Thomas died suddenly. Tom went to the old man's funeral, but only after attending a full morning's classes at Central High.

"Much as I love my grandparents," he explained, "my job is to be at school learning what I can . . . it's all part of the preparation for the future." Alone of his fifty-eight classmates, Tom was never late or absent once in twelve years. When he was invited to testify at anti-trust hearings involving Curtis paperboys in Chicago, his class had first to designate him their "delegate" who would make a full report on the proceedings upon his return. No other stratagem could get around Annie Dewey's perfect attendance fetish.

"It is hard for many people to understand," Dewey wrote his mother in 1944, in response to her questions about reporters inquiring into his youthful attendance record, "and many will not believe it." By then a presidential candidate sensitive to his public image as something of a prig, Tom urged her to make light of the whole thing, to joke about scheduling bouts with chickenpox during the summer months, as he did. By then, of course, it was slightly embarrassing, a politician flirting with perfectionism.[15]

It was after Mr. Thomas' death that Tom and his family moved in with his grandmother in a well-scrubbed Victorian bungalow at 421 West Oliver. There, sliding doors divided a formal parlor from a less remote sitting room. A telephone occupied a place of honor in the main hall, while a sun porch behind the kitchen was usually filled with cigar smoke and talk of primaries and platforms. Outside, tall maples shielded the house from wind and rain; inside, Annie and her mother, who liked to sprinkle sugar on bread for the grandson on whom she doted, spread their protective wings.

It was a comfortable life, over and above the $1,800 a year George Dewey brought home as editor or later postmaster, a post given him in 1921 by President Harding. Annie employed a cook, whose wages were paid for by a boarder who lived in a second-floor room next to her son's. George Valentine was a welcome source of masculine companionship for Tom, always ready to help the boy mend a kite or listen to whispered confidences. One morning over breakfast, he heard revealed Tom's latest ambition—to one day own his own Packard.[16]

There were books in the house, four glass-fronted cases filled with Dickens and Thackeray and Shakespeare. While his father preferred the Congressional Record, Tom spent hours with the bard or the adventure tales of James Fenimore Cooper. It was to be his last enjoyment of creative literature, before law and government took possession of his brain, and imaginative fiction lost its hold. Near the end of his life, a friend asked half-jokingly if his reading had ever extended beyond *David Copperfield*. No, he replied ruefully, he'd been too busy with practical things to read stories for pleasure.[17]

By the time he attended the second-floor high school at Central, Tom was a promising alloy of Tom Sawyer and Sid, sass and Sunday school. When Annie asked why he didn't bring home straight A's, he replied he didn't want to be thought a freak. Preferring music to manual training, the boy did especially well with history and languages. "His mind," according to George Valentine, "was a sponge for absorbing everything." C. C. Tuck, Tom's principal at Central, agreed, with one important reservation.

"By all odds the smartest kid in school," Tuck judged, "but so egotistical we threatened to expel him because he couldn't get along with his classmates."

There are still people in Owosso who remember Dewey's feisty theatricality, and a tendency to resort to fists when shouted orders failed to have their desired effect. When Tom sold his magazine distribution agency to another boy, he went down to the train station to initiate the new owner in the routines of small-town free enterprise. One young salesman, spying an opportunity to skim some cream off the transition, picked up more than his usual allotment of magazines. Tom ordered him to stop, and fists flew as the undersized Dewey administered a more or less thorough beating to his larger adversary. Others felt the lash of Tom's verbal combativeness, as when he ordered a girl off her own tennis court because he wished to use it, or marched up to his mother and coolly informed her that henceforth it would cost her twenty-five cents to have her lawn mowed.

C. C. Tuck saw a boy whose arrogance was matched by a doggedness to succeed. At the beginning of his senior year, he called Tom into his office to warn him that he was making himself unpopular among his fellow students.

"That's awful," Dewey responded. "I like them, and I want them to like me."

Then don't act so bored in classes, Tuck told him. "Don't act as if you know so much more than the other fellows."

Surprised and hurt, Tom agreed to try. But he couldn't resist a parting shot. "Some of those fellows are just as bright as I am," he said, "and they don't even try. I think a fellow who has brains and doesn't try is worse than one who doesn't have any."

Tuck came to know a vulnerable side to George and Annie's son, especially after he started boarding with the family in George Valentine's place. Football was one of the pleasures Tom shared with his father, and one of the few areas in which Annie could be overridden. When the smallish left tackle sustained a bad shaking up, Tuck found him limping to class, arm in a sling, and suggested he take a day or two off to recover. That was impossible, Dewey responded—it would spoil his perfect attendance record. Well, Tuck persisted, at least he could get some bed rest after school.

"What," the boy inquired, "and miss football practice? I couldn't do that either. The boys might think I was a quitter."

It sounds almost too perfect, a Parson Weems invocation of youthful dedication. Yet in Owosso, it all made sense, and in George and Annie's household it was probably inevitable. A generation later, a somewhat mellowed presidential candidate returned to his hometown to publicly thank "former playmates who taught me to use my fists, former teachers who tried to get me to study, businessmen who tried to get me to work." A more accurate recollection would have revealed a boy who did all of these things without much urging.

Tom was fifteen when Woodrow Wilson took America into World War I. By inclination and geography, the citizens of Owosso were isolationists. The daily *Press-Argus* hadn't prepared them for the world beyond the Appalachians, and to most, World War I had all the earmarks of an irrelevant nightmare. Sugarless oatmeal was painless patriotism. So was the banning of German from the high school curriculum, a fine, hollow gesture to buttress the sons of farmhands and factory workers who were called on to sacrifice far more.

Too young to be vulnerable to the draft, George Dewey's son could not escape the martial mood engulfing Owosso once war was declared. The same week that Wilson issued his first call for soldiers, Tom was drilling two nights a week with forty other boys who belonged to the Cadet Corps. A year later, with no end in sight to the war, and a serious labor shortage caused by departing doughboys, he signed up for the Boys Working Reserve, a national volunteer effort that pressed young men under draft age into civilian jobs. Early in June 1918, the sixteen-year-old found himself in George Valentine's Studebaker, enroute to the Ovid, Michigan, farm of Earl Putnam.

The Putnams lived in an old farmhouse devoid of indoor plumbing and hot running water, set amid 140 acres of beans, corn, and oats ten miles from Owosso. Earl was a man who worshipped God and work with equal fervor; most days began at 5 A.M., when Tom was rousted out of bed and set to cleaning stables, milking cows, and feeding horses and hogs. Breakfast followed, an enormous meal of boiled potatoes, ham and four or five eggs, washed down by coffee and accompanied by spiritual nourishment—a different chapter from the Bible read aloud each morning.

Until now, Tom's most intimate acquaintance with the back-breaking labor that turns soil and sun into food and fiber had been his daily visits to Uncle Edmund's to pick up a pail of warm unpasteurized milk for the George Dewey household. Like the Detroit *News* editor, Earl Putnam found himself confronted by a barrage of questions. His first day on the farm, Tom learned to ride a heavy steel roller, which flattened the ground before seeds could be planted. It was hard work, but when he wrote his parents that night, his humor seemed intact, even jaunty. "Dear Folks: It's 8:00 P.M. and am thru chores . . . the woman who went to the M.D. for a corn cure after riding 300 miles in a Henry had nothing on me now. Tomorrow I do it all day. . . . Lots of eats and pretty good but not like home. . . . Bed has plenty blankets. You win on the napkins but they have tablecloth."

The day after George and Annie got this first bulletin, they received another update from "Mr. Dewey, R.F.D. No. 1."

Last night I found out how hard one bed could be. My mattress is straw and immediately on sitting on the bed we find out how hard the slats are. The springs might as well be in Hong Kong. Slept well, however, as long as they sleep out here. Rode the roller all day today, that is, all the time I was not in the air directly above it. Farm machinery sometimes has a seat which is iron. I found out today that iron is the hardest metal on earth. I am sitting down very carefully this P.M. . . . I didn't know so many rocks could collect on one plot of ground. I did 16 acres today.

In later years, few glimpsed the good-humored farmhand of 1918, whose cockiness was mingled with a slangy self-deprecation. "Wasn't much good anyway," he wrote of a watch lost in a bean patch. "I got stepped on again," he informed his parents near the end of his nine-week stint, "but it didn't hurt much. Today I hit a large rock too suddenly and the laws of gravity and two or three other things set me off, scraping my leg some but it doesn't hurt now hardly at all. Very thrilling, this farmwork."

Earl Putnam grew to admire the boy's ambitions, the way he stayed up late under a kerosene lamp memorizing words out of the

Saturday Evening Post—all preparation for college, Tom explained. He acceded to the boy's insistent request for boxing lessons to build himself up for the coming gridiron season. He enjoyed his boarder's maturing baritone (Tom was known to sing arias from *La Bohème* while milking cows), and the pride the boy showed when he escorted his visiting parents around the farm, or hitched up a team to carry a load of beans into Owosso. Tom never complained, even when Saturday night came around and he was forced to take his weekly bath in an iron tub placed in the middle of the kitchen and filled with hand-pumped water heated over a wood stove.

To Putnam, the young man at his side seemed more intense than emotional, too preoccupied to mention a girl. But when a political argument arose, he could vie with a passion. Tom noted disdainfully the way his uncle's opponent in a mayoral contest spoke to every single person on the street. Uncle Edmund, his nephew pointed out, spoke only to those he ought to.

"But Tom," Earl Putnam warned the boy, "in politics you've got to be friendly to everybody, whether you like them or not."[18]

Dewey shed his reserve in his last year at Central. He carried a bass horn in the band, accompanied his classmates on sleigh rides, and was cast in the senior class play as Bertram Lancelot, "a temperamental composer who could roar like a lion." He also performed behind Monte McFarlane's interlocutor in a minstrel show entitled *The Dudes of Blackville*. These and other productions were mounted on the modest proscenium of the Strand Theatre, where once a week Tom went to see the more sophisticated entertainment of silent movies.

He also edited the *Spic*, Central's yearbook, in which a parody called "24 Hours of School Life" is revealing: "2:00 A.M. Mrs. Dewey is surprised at the terrible language used by her son, who is undoubtedly dreaming of the splendid (?) teamwork of the Spic Board." Tom honed his feel for language by joining, then starring on, Hazel Goodrich's debating squad. Speaking without notes or prepared texts, he found it good training for an aspiring student of the law. There were unfortunate side effects, though: the stock oratorical devices taught in the rosy afterglow of Victorian poets and William Jennings Bryan. On a political platform, the exaggerated gestures and histrionic rhetoric smacked of artificiality. In Owosso, they cinched a case.

When the yearbook finally appeared, it described him as "first in the Council Hall to steer the state, and ever foremost in a tongue debate." Above the testimonial was a photograph of a confident boy in a stiff collar, with a great shock of coal-black hair swept over a high forehead. The face is rounded, like his mother's, but dominated by George's high cheekbones, jug ears, and penetrating almond eyes. It combines precocity with enigma, and a touch of smugness befitting one who has finished eighth in the class, with a ninety-two average, a full year ahead of his schoolmates.

At graduation, Owosso celebrated the virtues it considered the sources of its strength. The Reverend Ernest B. Allen addressed the Class of 1919 on "Service, the Goal of Life" and set out to illustrate three great rules by which he defined a useful life: "Know Thyself, Deny Thyself, Self-Control."

For Tom, there was the last fling before college. Before her death in January, the boy's grandmother had planned a cross-country excursion for them both. Now, Tom went alone, riding for three days in steaming, dirty parlor cars that snaked their way west to Los Angeles, stopping three times a day to permit meals to be taken in Harvey Houses along the way. Once in California, he was met by his Aunt Emily and her family, who loaded themselves into an ancient Hupmobile and set off to explore the San Bernardino Mountains. There, Tom went hunting and hiking with his cousins, took boxing lessons from a semipro, and slept beneath the stars, after first drawing trenches in the dirt to ward off rattlesnakes otherwise inclined to slither up beside a warm body.

Later, he headed south, to visit his Aunt Hannah in Riverside. He swam in the Pacific, stared in fascination at sting rays, and hauled in mackerel to be salted down against the coming winter. Then the summer turned to memory, and the time came to retrace his steps. A transition was under way, barely perceptible at first, that would educate the boy from Piano Street in the ways of a world far beyond the Shiawassee.

Tom arrived in Ann Arbor in September 1919, to a one-time agricultural college on the verge of great tomorrows. Seventy-three-year-old Harry B. Hutchens had that spring submitted his resignation, and the Board of Regents was about to settle on his dynamic successor: a former president of Smith College and the University of Minnesota named Marion LeRoy Burton. Dr. Burton was a hybrid of New England Congregationalist virtue and red-haired controversy, a builder who immediately embarked on a vast program to expand and improve Michigan's plant and faculty. The university hospital complex was completed, along with engineering and physics classrooms, a vast new fieldhouse and the William L. Clements Library. A Tudor Gothic quadrangle was built, as were dormitory and dining facilities for the law school. Administratively, Burton was just as productive. The Board of Regents was reformed, and greater authority centralized in the president's office. Weekly conferences were instituted with deans, and salaries and research opportunities were boosted substantially. Chase Osborne was persuaded to donate $5,000 to endow a fellowship in creative art; Robert Frost came to Ann Arbor for the 1921–22 term and was such a hit with students that he stayed an extra year.

Under Burton, the grading system was overhauled to reduce the number of "pipes" and what the president disdainfully called "scattering and smattering." "Fellow freshmen," he informed Tom Dewey's class, "you and the university are going to mature together."

There was an ascetic side to the forty-six-year old president, an intellectual bewilderment at the Jazz Age. "Learning has a quiet and simple beauty all her own," he told the student body. "Our jazz bands, our saxophone orchestras, our whirling giddy parties, our 'busts,' our proms, our hops, our moving pictures . . . all these and many other things gather into a noisy rushing rabble and banish learning." In truth, Ann Arbor was a riot of bobbed hair, rolled stockings, coonskin coats, sideburns, and pomade. On Friday and Saturday nights, there were jazz dances in the union, the first of a kind of recreational facility that housed under a single roof a cafeteria, barbershop, bowling alleys, billiard rooms, and reading lounges that catered to 7,500 students a day. In the evening, students gathered outside Betsey Barbour House to listen to Jemima Miller of the Class of '21 play siren songs on her ukulele. The big man on campus was Paul Eaton, for eight months a German prisoner of war and now president of the Glee Club, Psi Upsilon, the Mimes, Michiganensia, and the Comedy Club.

Tom Dewey arrived at a time of bright prospects and severe overcrowding. There were 8,500 students at Ann Arbor in the fall of 1919; by the time he left, four years later, the number had swelled to nearly 11,000. Forty percent of the student body worked part-time to pay expenses. For all the social frenzy, it was a conservative campus, caste-conscious and patriotically proud of its role in the war. In an editorial entitled "Note These Traditions," the student paper, the *Michigan Daily,* welcomed the class of '23. Don't smoke on campus, it warned—a ban local legend has Dewey trying to overthrow—and avoid the first four rows at the Majestic Theatre. Toques, green hats assigned to all freshmen, were mandatory, as was their tipping whenever the president or dean of the college appeared. To these, the chief of campus police added one more commandment: "Don't drive faster than twelve miles per hour."

For all his liberality, President Burton hated automobiles, and he pleaded with parents not to permit their sons and daughters to bring them to school. He also frowned upon campus queens, and radical dress. Most students conformed to his preferences; blue serge was popular in 1919, along with thick wool sweaters and felt hats. For Dewey, the $1,200 saved from his various boyhood jobs didn't afford him the imported English tweeds that wealthier students bought at Tucker and Company. Early on, he developed a habit of noting precisely every expenditure, no matter how minute, in a special notebook, a routine which persisted through his days as New York's racket-busting special prosecutor. To his parents, he prudently wrote asking that they not send him his entire quarterly allowance. Other students had secured theirs, only to exhaust their funds within days. Tom may have entertained doubts about his own resolve. More likely, he figured that this way he wouldn't be a soft touch for hard-up friends.

He submitted with relative grace to Hell Week's hazing, and celebrated when his class defeated the sophomores in the annual cane rush. He renewed his old tie with printer's ink as a cub reporter for the *Michigan Daily,* and in his second year was named telegraph editor, a job he held for a single term, perhaps in pique at having been passed over for the more coveted title of night editor. Or perhaps reporting was simply a victim of his growing passion for music. On one occasion, he wrote a story called "Who Will Succeed Caruso?" and fecklessly asked the popular John McCormack whether standards like "Mother Machree" and "Little Gray Home in the West" weren't debasing the public's taste.

The boy soprano may have descended the scale, but his aspirations were definitely on the rise. Under the guidance of William Wheeler, a former football hero who now headed Michigan's voice department, Tom pursued an opera career full tilt. He paid for his lessons by singing in a Methodist church quartet, and he polished his diction, intonation, and feel for language in courses over and above the hour-a-day instruction he took from Wheeler. He joined the glee club, directed its freshman contingent, and was elected president.

In his second year, Tom abandoned the boardinghouse he'd been living in on East University Avenue for the Phi Mu Alpha fraternity. Known as Sinfonia ("The manly musician and the musicianly man in America"), it was less than a bastion of scholarship. Dewey himself coasted to a B-plus average in the School of Literature, where he made initial contact with Leonardo da Vinci and Prax-iteles, Confucius and Hamlet. Late-night bull sessions took prece-dence at Sinfonia over Renaissance drawing, followed on Sunday night by belated bookishness. Politics seemed distant here amid the smoke and chatter.

The university was, like the rest of Michigan, overwhelmingly Republican; a poll taken among students in Dewey's first spring showed the GOP supported by 85 percent of the student body. By substantial margins during the 1920 campaign, Herbert Hoover, the feeder of war-torn Europe and identified domestically with progressive Republicanism, was the first choice for president of both parties on campus. Among Republican collegians, Warren Harding was a weak fifth. Nearly 90 percent of those polled in Dewey's class favored entry into the League of Nations, with or without Henry Cabot Lodge's reservations.

In many ways, Ann Arbor for Dewey was the logical next step from Owosso. Here there were old friends from Central High, and his cousin Harriet. Here, too, were the values of perseverance seen as a prelude to personal success, in itself testimony to an individual's worth. Socially, Tom seems to have abstained from sowing wild oats. While some of his classmates dated girls from Ypsilanti and bought illegal drinks from rural blind pigs, he asked for no money from home with which to escort a girl to a show or dance. He had little inclination and no time to play on the twenty-seven billiard tables gracing the student union.

Yet he displayed a capacity for friendship. One of his closest com-panions was Carl T. Hogan, Pat to his friends, a jovial engineering student from Spokane, Washington, who pledged all those around him to the fraternity of laughter. Pat became Dewey's alter ego, one of the few men who could address him as Tommy. Hogan's friend also joined the student opera company, and in his sophomore year was cast as Patrick O'Dare, evil pretender to the Irish throne, in *Top o' th' Mornin'*. He got to stop the show with "A Paradise for Micks" and to travel with the all-male company—which included husky athletes cast as the Fairy Queen and the DuCann Sisters—to Chi-cago, Detroit, and other cities along an eight-stop tour. Usually on these train trips, he could be found alone, often in the last car, un-comfortable with the camaraderie and alcohol.[19]

A student reviewer praised the "velvety texture" of his voice, and in a performance on Detroit radio station WWJ he so impressed musicians that violinists tapped their bows in appreciation. Then, in the spring of his senior year, Tom entered and won a statewide singing contest and was sent to Asheville, North Carolina, to compete in the national finals. His third-place finish was heartening, enough so that large decisions began to gestate in his head. Caution had been bred into him, and Aunt Grace's insistence that law was a more acceptable vocation than the stage was not overlooked. But he loved music, and as he admitted in later years, was enough of a ham to savor the sound of applause. He decided that he would have both by enrolling in Ann Arbor's law course while simultaneously completing his regular schedule in the School of Literature—and keeping up his musical studies on the side.

It was an ambitious agenda. Before it could be kept, however, he went home to Owosso for the summer of 1922. His father was abandoning the family business in favor of a postmastership, the natural reward for Shiawassee County's leading Republican as well as manager of the Dry Campaign Committee. Unable to run both the paper and the post office, the party regular turned the former over to his son for a few weeks' trial run. When business grew hectic, Annie came down to fold and address copies and take advertising. As for Tom, he seemed comfortable supervising other employees, all two or three times his age. Not yet twenty-one, he still exuded a kind of natural authority. But when the summer was over and the classroom beckoned once more, George Dewey's son was certain of one thing at least. He would never follow in his father's journalistic footsteps. A year later, the *Times* was sold.

He had left the town behind, as surely as he had discarded tree houses and circus parades. Yet he could not forsake the values of Owosso or shed his Midwestern birthmark and bedrock devotion to the party of his forebears. When he returned in October 1948, it was to pay extemporaneous tribute to the neighborliness and horse sense that thrived along Main Street, a community of mutual dependence "where we all go to the stores and we all work for a living. Every single person in town does something. We are all useful."

Owosso was tolerant, according to its most famous native son. People didn't ask your church, your job, your instincts in the privacy of the voting booth. If neighbors were in trouble, "we help them and we don't call on a distant government. We just do it." In Owosso, there was another common axiom—"decent respect for the value of a dollar." Doubtless, Dewey meant what he said. Yet after 1923, he consigned his birthplace to memory, to be revisited only on special occasions.

In March 1921, George and Annie Dewey were lost in the throng of jubilant Republicans who listened to Warren Harding take the oath of office and pledge normalcy for a nation weary of heroics and death. In ensuing days, he reached out to the "best minds" within the party, inviting Charles Evans Hughes and Herbert Hoover to join his cabinet, and appointing former President Taft Chief Justice. He toured the South and talked boldly about equal rights for Negroes. He convened a Naval Disarmament Conference in Washington, and did not oppose American membership on the World Court. When he died in August 1923, detractors hinted at foul play—poison was the favorite culprit, allegedly administered by Florence Harding, who preferred for her husband an early grave to sitting in a docket at impeachment proceedings. The scandal called Teapot Dome enveloped the dead man's memory in unpleasant odor. It posed initial problems for his successor, a sphinxlike Vermonter of desiccated virtue, Calvin Coolidge.[20]

Coolidge stood foursquare for the status quo. He was a pithy advocate of the tried and true, a product of the nineteenth-century museum of rural Vermont. He slept eleven hours a day, and near the end of his five and a half years in office boasted "one of the most important accomplishments of my administration was minding my own business." An unlikely father confessor to a whole decade of flappers and speakeasies mortgaging future prosperity, Coolidge was widely admired and little heeded, except by his own party, overjoyed to have survived the shock of Teapot Dome. In celebrating their historic landslides of 1920 and 1924, Republicans all but buried their past progressivism. The party of Emancipation and the Homestead Act, the transcontinental railroad and railroad regulation, of conservation and the 2 percent income tax: this party was now the property of men who blew the trumpet of laissez-faire, and promised to make war only on debt.

2

Foundations and Cathedrals

What am I doing actively at present? I am working on a new Constitution and set of By-Laws for the National Fraternity, studying the finances of the City of New York as Chairman of a committee of the New York Young Republican Club, engaged in a small amount of district political work (Republican, although wholly altruistic), apartment hunting, acting as Secretary-Treasurer of the University of Michigan Club of New York, and, between the hours of nine-thirty and six, and frequently thereafter, practicing law. Does this answer your question?

—THOMAS E. DEWEY.[1]

Dewey's study of the law of Ann Arbor was brief and less than happy. In the lecture halls of the college, an exceptional instructor or book might ignite curiosity; the tentative law student found such selectivity an unattainable privilege. Fifty years had passed since Christopher Columbus Langdell invented the case study method at Harvard, asking students to take a logical step beyond general principles and common law, and immerse themselves in actual cases. After Langdell, mere facility would not be enough to guide the aspiring lawyer past the shoals of legal instruction. For first-year students there was considerable frustration as they were forced to memorize an unending stream of facts to regurgitate in something akin to logic.

Michigan embraced the reform with enthusiasm. But no legal evangelist arose at Ann Arbor to awake from Tom Dewey and his classmates more than a grudging respect for the statutory code. Common Law Pleading, Criminal Law and Procedure, Torts, Contracts and Property, which he later characterized as "scrivener's work," remained objects on a distant intellectual shore, unbridged by the bored and suspicious instructors at Michigan. "You learn how to lay a foundation," he said afterward of law school, "but not how to build a cathedral." Nonetheless, he maintained stoutly to his death, his own experience to the contrary, that law school was the best possible training for anyone seeking any career, a sort of educational boot camp where young minds were toughened and the very dreariness of the routine prepared one for the worst after commencement.[2]

It must have come as manna from heaven when Bill Wheeler suggested to Tom that he spend the summer of 1923 in Chicago, at one of the refresher courses conducted for former pupils by a New York singing coach named Percy Rector Stephens. "Stevie," as his students called him, was a gray-haired, clarion-voiced man, renowned as the discoverer of stars like Paul Althouse and Jeanette Vreeland of the Metropolitan Opera. He might have had an operatic career of his own, had stage fright not paralyzed him, leading him to teach instead. "A dog can bark all day and not get hoarse," he told disciples in his teakwood-floored studio on Seventy-second Street. "That's how a singer should be."

George and Annie were unenthusiastic about their son's musical aspirations, but consented to the Chicago interlude when he agreed to work part-time with his cousin Leonard Reid in a downtown law office. Dewey hated the Windy City, regarding it all his life as a moral cesspool. Neither was he pleased with his worm's-eye view of the legal process—serving papers, answering court calendars, scouring the law library for fine points with which to enhance other men's arguments. Not once that summer did he set foot in a courtroom or witness a trial. He did take the elevated train to a suburban park for evening concerts, and on weekends he joined other Sinfonians to belt out standards and mutter under his breath a determination once and for all to reject the law for music. He also met a woman who changed his life.[3]

If 1920 was Warren Harding's year, it was also Sinclair Lewis'. In his corrosive novel *Main Street,* the iconoclastic author stripped away the gauzy nostalgia of Yankee enterprise to unveil hypocrisy and sloth in the archetypal Midwestern town of Gopher Prairie. Carol Kennicott was Lewis' representative heroine, a library aide from Minneapolis who rejects her leatherbound future for the conventions of home and hearth, only to find herself trapped in the airless tedium of the Thanatopsis Club, subjected to mirthless stunts performed for the thousandth time at funereal parties, and ostracized by a parvenu society made hideously fashionable in the rickety grande dame of rustic architecture, the Minniemashie House.

The 1920s were filled with Carol Kennicotts, young women newly aroused to their potential, yet forced to grapple with society's strictures against any female avoiding matrimony. Frances Eileen Hutt was one. Born in Sherman, Texas, on February 7, 1903, she was the daughter of a railroad brakeman named Orla Thomas Hutt, whose formal education had ended abruptly when he ran away from boarding school, and Audie Lee, an ambitious Southern woman who had once aspired to the glamorous life of a concert pianist, and more recently took pride in her distant relative Jefferson Davis.

As a girl, Frances listened to her grandfather Moses tell of the battle of Shiloh, in which he fought as a Confederate infantryman. She learned instinctive regional feeling for lineage and bloodlines, and later was delighted with an alleged family tree tracing her ancestry to colonial Virginia and, further back, to the Emperor Charlemagne. Preoccupation with the past was not the only Southern habit she inherited. Audie Lee ran a strict Southern Methodist home, in which groceries could not be purchased on the Lord's Day, or ice taken in from the neighborhood vendor. A self-confessed tomboy who excelled as a swimmer, high jumper, and tennis player, Frances was not permitted near the courts or the baseball diamond on the Sabbath.[4]

The family's faith had a liberal dose of stoicism. Orla and Audie had already lost an infant son and a six-year-old daughter. It made them all the fonder of their precocious, quick-tempered Frances, whose special status was beyond question, whether in the Hutt household or in the mock school she conducted in their backyard, complete with disciplinary whippings for the fractious children of Sherman. She was used to being the boss, her older brother remembers, but there was a feminine counterpart to the nine-year-old baseball coach who wrote poetry and drew pictures on the side, who cherished family recipes and never forgot Sunday afternoon hymn singing around a parlor piano not much different from Ed and May Dewey's, more than a thousand miles to the north in Owosso.[5]

When Frances was eleven, her family pulled up stakes, and headed for Sapulpa, Oklahoma, the dusty terminus of Orla's railroad line. There they lived in a modest five-room cottage. Frances dreamed of better things and displayed a streak of ambition that sent her, like her future husband, through the high school curriculum a year ahead of her classmates. She also had a fine, if untrained, mezzo-soprano singing voice and began perfecting it Sunday afternoons in the church, where she often played the organ. As an adolescent, she cut a narrow social swath, but her character and potential were evident. So was her talent, displayed at countless benefits and church socials. In 1920, she won a statewide voice contest at Norman and was offered a scholarship to the University of Oklahoma.

But Bess Hughes had other ideas. Mrs. Hughes, herself a former student of Percy Stephens, wanted her promising pupil to go north to New York, a place of decidedly un-Methodist sympathies. The Sapulpa Kiwanis gave a benefit concert, and early in 1922 Frances set out for the big city enriched by $400. After settling in at a Manhattan YWCA, she was soon getting up at the crack of dawn to sing in a Plainfield, New Jersey, church as one means of supplementing her small kitty. Percy Stephens offered another. From the first, he was under her spell, a Mona Lisa charm that complemented gracious manners and a voice of bell-like clarity.

Five feet, three inches tall, with soft brown hair parted in the middle, with a pale china complexion and a demure voice that could purr magnolias or erupt in a crisp witticism, Frances had a gift for calming whatever chaos surrounded her. It was a resource her future husband was to find invaluable, and which Stephens recognized almost immediately. He hired her as his secretary and studio manager, and in the summer of 1923, when he penciled in Chicago on his schedule, she was glad to go along. Not the least of her functions there was to serve on a panel of judges who would award a scholarship large enough to pay for a summer's study to some gifted young vocalist. The judges listened to several contestants, then voted the prize to an energetic youth of twenty-one whose ruddy complexion and protruding ears gave him the air of an adolescent prodigy, but whose rendition of Handel's "Hear Me, Ye Winds and Waves," was authentic with adult promise.

Once again, Tom Dewey had uncovered a doorway marked success. Learning just that morning of the existence of the scholarship, he auditioned impulsively, found himself victorious, and went on to impress Stephens to the point where the coach strongly urged that he continue his vocal training in New York. The suggestion could not have been more eagerly received. Tom decided to leave Ann Arbor but to continue his legal studies at Columbia. That way, he would gain additional experience in both music and law, while seeing more of Frances Hutt, a fetching young woman whose vote had already influenced his future. It was to be a triple encirclement he had in mind, a grand pincer around the law, the stage, and love.

New York in 1923 was a shimmering magnet to ambitious outlanders like Tom and Frances. Optimistic and brash, it looked forward to a future that must, in the words of a popular self-improvement method of the time, "every day, in every way, get better and better." It was a decade when New York finally overtook London as the world's leading financial center, and land values along

Park Avenue and other fashionable boulevards were skyrocketing. More cars plied the streets of New York than all the roads of Europe, and thousands of the upwardly mobile flowed each weekend through the new Holland Tunnel or over handsome suspension bridges thrown across the East River, to tour the rural pastures of Long Island, or party under the stars at Jay Gatsby's West Egg.

Fifth Avenue was called Millionaire's Row, a fitting appellation for stores like Saks and tony watering holes like the Plaza Hotel and J. P. Morgan's Metropolitan Club. At the Algonquin Hotel on Forty-fourth Street, Alexander Woollcott, Franklin P. Adams, Dorothy Parker, and a wickedly witty coterie of the literati gathered regularly around their famous Round Table. Elsewhere, camaraderie was dimmed by the Eighteenth Amendment, which made the sale of alcoholic beverages illegal and thereby loosed a flood of lawlessness.

"This measure was born in hypocrisy, and there it will die." The words came from Jimmy Walker, a dapper state senator and songwriter much admired for the cut of his clothes, the tilt of his hat, and the devil-may-care self-indulgence he brought as mayor to City Hall after 1925. Walker had a point about Prohibition. In basement dens reached through heavy wooden doors with iron grating and peepholes, New Yorkers gathered to forget their cares and defy legislated morality. On the Upper West Side of Manhattan, in the ghetto called Nigger Harlem by its own inhabitants, whites went slumming at rent parties, drank bootleg booze at the Cotton Club, and dined on "yardbird and strings"—local jargon for fried chicken and spaghetti—in Sugar Hill. Harlem was still a Republican stronghold in the 1920s, supporting Harding and Coolidge in national elections and represented on the Board of Aldermen by a member of Lincoln's party.

Downtown in Greenwich Village, artists of all kinds lived and created cheek by jowl with Irish, Jewish, and Italian workingmen. Not far from the second-floor walk-up at 89 Christopher Street that Tom Dewey moved into in 1925, Eugene O'Neill saw his first plays produced, and Edna St. Vincent Millay breathed fresh life into the sonnet. Other artists toyed with the Ashcan School, with cubism and post-impressionism. Dewey worked on his voice.

On his arrival in September, 1923, he had taken up residence with a Canadian engineering student in a single room on West 122nd Street. Much of his time was spent on the West Side subway, hurrying back and forth between morning classes at Columbia and lessons with Percy Stephens and a new coach named Charles Baker, recom-

mended by Stephens. On Sundays, he earned fifteen dollars by singing at the Episcopal Church of St. Matthew and St. Timothy on
West Eighty-fourth Street. He picked up spending money performing in a synagogue.

Bred to compete, Tom found little time for recreation, although
on occasion he and Frances would climb long stairways to cheap
seats in the second balcony of a Broadway theater or the Metropolitan Opera House. Frances herself was on stage in 1924, understudy-
ing the lead in *George White's Scandals* at the new Paramount Theater. Later, she joined the cast of a John Murray Anderson
roadshow, replacing the leading lady when she fell ill. But theater
wasn't her idea of a respectable living, and she rarely discussed these
years afterward, avoided mention of dressing rooms and hotel
rooms, impermanence and cigarette smoke. She wanted to be a concert singer, not a chorus girl, and the hours she devoted to language
and harmony and composition were not to be confused with the
agenda of a Broadway starlet.[6]

As for her suitor, the musical road was proving to be rocky. On his
twenty-second birthday, Tom was scheduled to perform in his first
solo recital in New York. Programs were printed, his parents drove
in from Owosso. Among those in the audience that pivotal night in
March 1924 was Deems Taylor, a well-known music critic come to
appraise the young performer's artistry. Unknown to him, Tom had
woken that morning with a case of incipient laryngitis, and by the
time he set foot on stage he was no longer in control of his own voice.
The program started off well enough, but then came "Der Dop-
pelgänger," a long and taxing German lied. Midway through the
number, Dewey's voice disappeared, replaced by a froggy croak and
acute embarrassment. Taylor, in his review, wrote that the young
man tended to telegraph his dramatic effects before they were due.
Stephens was equally diplomatic. His pupil sang "too intelligently,"
he decided, with more precision than feeling.[7]

Tom was appalled. A cold-blooded reckoning of the odds convinced him against resting his future on anything so unreliable as a
human voice. From that point on, the basso cantante would shun
voice training for the Socratic probing of a still-untested legal mind.
After 1924, Dewey confined his singing to snatches of *Pagliacci* in the
bathtub and duets with Frances of favorite tunes from Broadway
shows. All that remained of his singing career were an instinct for
drama, a tenor's temperament, and an inclination to take himself,
and his work, with the utmost seriousness. In league with imagina-

tion and a public outcry, such debris could transform an average law student into a powerful contender for justice.[8]

Columbia University in the Jazz Age was a fertile factory of ideas, crackling with creative tension between progressives like John Dewey and Stanley Gill and traditionalists led by President Nicholas Murray Butler. Like thunder answering lightning, Butler held out for classical learning in the face of those who would stress the relevance of knowledge. A gentleman and scholar, erudite in Roman and Greek literature, Butler by training was a political scientist. More than a few regarded him as a potential Republican Woodrow Wilson. Instead, he was fated to guide Columbia through thirty groundbreaking years, in which he stamped upon the place his own obsession with excellence.

It was from the law faculty that Butler drew the sharpest attacks, and not simply because he mourned "the wide and distressing gap between membership of the bar and a knowledge of the law." With the departure of Dean Harlan F. Stone in 1923 to become Coolidge's attorney general (and later, chief justice), Columbia's legal scholars were split badly between those espousing pure legal scholarship, and others who would study society as well. One school defined the lawyer's function narrowly, as an agent of the law alone; the other saw him guiding society's advance.

Thomas Reed Powell was a leading advocate of "sociological jurisprudence," who dared to argue that judges were motivated by social, economic, and psychological as well as legal factors. He combined a grasp of behaviorism with a belief in astrology and the browbeating manner of Simon Legree. Every Powell student was expected to devote at least ten hours to research for every hour spent in class. "I will guarantee not that you will know any constitutional law," he promised students at the start of each academic year, "but that you will absolutely know what the constitutional law is not." Powell also liked to toss coins into the air to illustrate the capriciousness of the Supreme Court, whose stupidity was such that "it's unfathomable even to me at times."[9]

Underhill Moore pounded the lectern and could not abide sloppy expression. He also baffled legal purists with questions like "What are the stimuli that motivate the human animal on the bench?" William O. Douglas, a classmate of Dewey's who later resigned a teaching position at Columbia when President Butler and his chosen agent of conservatism, Young B. Smith, gained control of the law school, was one of the young revolutionaries who rejected logic alone as insufficient to meet the challenge of a modern complex society.

"We wanted to join forces with other disciplines," Douglas wrote in his memoirs. "In finance we wanted to teach the anatomy of finance as well as the rules of law. In criminal law we wanted psychiatry as well as the criminal code. In credit transactions, we wanted to explore all the institutions of credit as well as the commercial code."

Critics of the new school clung to their casebooks in horror, yet however fuzzy such legal theorizing might seem, the sociologists were anything but casual in their pursuit of academic rigor. Underhill Moore thought nothing of humiliating in public students who failed to meet his exacting standards for the use of language. Professor Richard Powell, an acknowledged genius in property law, launched his course each fall with the words "Gentlemen, if this is not the hardest course in law school, I am not teaching it right." Herman Oliphant, whose trust classes were credited by Dewey with first exciting him to the legal poetry, imparted a similarly stringent feel for words and their proper use.[10]

With music now consigned to the background, Tom blossomed in the classroom. He earned a B-plus average and was admitted to Phi Beta Phi, a select legal fraternity that in the absence of top-notch grades or law review work indicated promise of a bright future. He organized a night seminar on economics, and a moot court with two friends. He met and befriended Elliott V. Bell, a native New Yorker and brilliant student of the dismal science, with a biting wit and a hunched back that some considered more of an emotional than physical handicap. The two men met at a Wednesday night seminar conducted by one of Columbia's more influential thinkers, Rexford G. Tugwell. Tugwell was only a few years away from becoming the nucleus of Franklin Roosevelt's New Deal Brain Trust, but his impression on Dewey was less favorable. Tom abandoned the seminar after a single semester; privately, he considered it too undemanding.

To classmates, the young man from Owosso seemed intense and unrelenting in his curiosity. "He can ask more questions in five minutes," one said, "than anyone else could think up in two hours." Bill Douglas became a close friend, another outlander who, unlike his Michigan counterpart, never became a convert to Manhattan's unique allure. Douglas had arrived from Yakima, Washington, with six cents in his pocket, and never forgot the cold indifference with which Park Avenue strollers had brushed aside his good-natured inquiry, "How do I get to Columbia?" Later, he ate pork and beans at an Automat and did settlement work on the Lower East Side. On the Columbia campus, he struck classmates as moody, ambitious, intolerant of the ideas of others, and possessed of a first-rate mind. Secretly, he nurtured an ambition to become dean of the law school. Around Morningside Heights, it was also said that he hoped to open a law office with Tom Dewey, a plan that died a natural death when neither man would agree to let the other's name precede his own.[11]

In his first days at Columbia, Tom joined none of the traditional study groups with which legal students brave the rigors of torts and contracts. Instead, he read and prepared cases alone. By the fall of his second year, 1924, he began to make up for lost time. Evenings were spent in the company of friends like Bill Douglas and Al McCormack. It was McCormack, ranked first in the class, just ahead of Douglas, and destined to win some fame as a special assistant to the secretaries of state and war, who engaged an older student named student named Arthur Schwartz in speculation as to future stars in the Class of '25. Douglas was a natural. But what about the non-A students, for whom extracurricular jobs or other impediments blocked entry into the charmed circle whose legal and financial success were assured long before commencement day?

McCormack told Schwartz that there were two such men in the second-year class. One went on to an established Wall Street firm, only to run afoul of women and money. "The other one you don't know," McCormack went on. "His name is Tom Dewey."[12]

Not long afterward, Arthur and Tom met for the first time, over an orange blossom in a dry fraternity. It was the start of a lifelong friendship. Another intimate was Marland Gale, descended from a line of Rochester abolitionists, who was outraged at the burning of a cross on the Columbia campus in 1924. The Ku Klux Klan was at the height of its nationwide revival that year, and for the six blacks in the Class of 1925 (the singer and actor Paul Robeson was one, boxing to earn his tuition), the ideal of equality did not go unchallenged, even in so urbane an environment as Columbia. Gale was manager of Furnald House, a dorm housing a group of Southern students suspected of the cross burning. After he kicked the charred symbol to the ground, he went out and organized a campus-wide committee to cleanse the university of racial antagonism.

It was about this time that Gale was approached by a friend asking if he'd like to meet a possible study partner. A meeting was arranged, the friend was called away, and Marland found himself being questioned by a young baritone from Owosso, Michigan. The talk turned to music, specifically Schubert. Both men expressed a fondness for "Der Wanderer," which led Tom Dewey to sit back stiffly in his chair, fling his right arm into the air and gulp a lungful. Suddenly, the room was filled with a lusty rendition of Schubert's marching song; the very ceiling and pictures on the wall seemed to shake, Gale remembered. A few months later, he was even more surprised when Tom encountered him in a registration line, recalled every detail of their initial meeting, and invited Marland to join him and a lady friend, Frances Eileen Hutt, for dinner that evening.

After commencement, in the fall of 1925, Tom and Marland settled in a three-room apartment on Christopher Street for a year, then moved to an old brownstone in the Chelsea section of the city. They argued for hours over politics, Tom being unable to distinguish the reformist Democratic governor Alfred E. Smith from his Tammany Hall sponsors. He was generously endowed with opinions on every subject, but especially politics and music. For the living room of their apartment, he'd bought a Steinway piano, which was in almost constant use by Miss Hutt and her fellow voice students. In the shower one afternoon, Tom heard a tenor rendering a song in less than robust fashion. Shortly, the bathroom door flew open and there in the middle of the room stood a dripping Dewey.

"For God's sake," he demanded, "put some guts into it."

Gale noted a tactical cunning in his friend, and a never-say-die persistence. The men played squash often at the Columbia Club, and more often than not Marland built up a lead as Tom seemed to have the wind go out of him. Then, after a quick pause for rest, Dewey began walloping the ball with renewed force, to roar ahead with a mysterious reserve held back until the moment of maximum psychological impact. "There was nothing that was more of a challenge to him," the loser finally concluded, "than to be behind."[13]

By the fall of 1924, any questions about Dewey's future in the law were fast disappearing. Already he had decided to stay in New York, which he liked "a thousand times better" than Owosso, and which offered great orchestras and singing companies. It was Frances Hutt's adopted home and the ark of the legal covenant. That fall he began his visits to the Wall Street firms to which aspiring law partners had made pilgrimages since long before his birth. He did so knowing his prospects for the immediate future were severely limited. Dewey never forgave the firm of White and Case, a pillar of the establishment, where he was told airily, "Of course, you will realize that we regard a young man as nothing but a pair of legs the first two years."[14]

Sensing one's unimportance was one thing; being reminded of it was quite another. Still, Dewey endured such condescension with more equanimity than Bill Douglas. To a patronizing John Foster Dulles at Sullivan and Cromwell, the hoydenish rebel from Yakima expressed gratitude for help in donning his coat by presenting the partner a quarter tip. Dewey confronted more practical indignities. Everywhere he went, the starting salary held out to him was the same: thirty-five dollars a week. Usually he found mere indifference in the face of his ambition. But in the end, three firms offered him employment, and after a month's deliberating he cast his lot with Larkin, Rathbone and Perry, a substantial office with twelve partners and twenty-eight associates. It was not the sort of place where a young man anxious to be noticed was likely to achieve his wish.

Final exams came next, admission to the bar to be announced later that summer. In the meantime, Tom set off with Marland Gale and an Owosso friend named Ward Jenks on a 25,000-ton German ship for Plymouth, England. For $140, the trio bought an old Ford touring car and began a leisurely tour of quaint fishing villages and boisterous pubs. In one of the latter, they picked up a Tasmanian architecture student from Cambridge who guided them through the venerable buildings of London and Oxford. Following a sojourn in Paris, they bicycled into the French countryside with wine, cheese, and bread. They persuaded a guard at Verdun to show them the vast underground bastion where, less than ten years earlier, thousands of mud-spattered French soldiers had surrendered their lives.

Back in London, the Ford was sold, and the travelers embarked for home. Penniless after missing his train for Detroit, Dewey managed to cash a check at the University Club, then live off a dwindling supply of sandwiches until he got back to Owosso. He was twenty-three, a Columbia graduate, world traveler, authentic New Yorker, broke. He brought home with him more than happy memories of foreign countries, or the jittery stomach of the neophyte at the dawn of self-support. While on the Continent, Dewey and Jenks entered into a bet to see who could grow a mustache first. In the process, Tom obliterated a high lip and set Frances' heart apounding. Because she liked it, the mustache stayed, to delight cartoonists and dismay political advisers for twenty years.

By August, Tom was back in New York, installed in the Christopher Street apartment he shared with Marland Gale. He returned to good news from the bar association, and mixed tidings from the legal profession itself. Fate had assigned him, with six other junior members of the firm, to a crowded bullpen at Larkin, Rathbone. One of its inhabitants, Noisy Newhall, earned his nickname while dictating at the top of his voice. Others paced back and forth in the cramped confines that were, to one as orderly as Dewey, a professional torture chamber. Over at Cravath and Swaine, Bill Douglas was sharing similarly spartan quarters with John J. McCloy. The future Supreme Court justice witnessed a graphic display of professional dedication late one night, when an older associate wrenched a ringing telephone off his desk and barked a greeting into the offending instrument. "Why the hell bother me?" the man asked before hanging up and returning to the work at hand. To Douglas, he explained: It was his wife calling. Their house was on fire.

Dewey was also capable of such single-mindedness, but the professional agenda at Larkin, Rathbone induced slumber before passion. Much of it entailed corporate leases, in which title searches were followed by written assurances to a mortgage-holding bank that it would receive payment or security when a customer disposed of property. Dewey composed these by the score, before sending them for final editing to an associate or partner. It was dull, monotonous labor, the main compensation for which was what he later called "the greatest training there is at the bar—the insistence upon perfection."[15]

Dewey wanted trial work. He was assigned only paperwork. At long lunches with a Columbia buddy named Joseph Panuch, he bemoaned his fate, only to be told he was being unrealistic. "Christ," said Panuch, "they're not going to give you any good cases. You've got to take the dogs." As for the courts themselves, "They give you the works. You've got to play the clerks, get to be buddies with them, make damn sure they get liquor around Christmas, or some cigars. It's a political deal."

To which Dewey replied, "But these guys are all Democrats." How could you possibly deal with such people? The more worldly Panuch told him to forget the lessons of Owosso, and Columbia's ivy-covered towers. If you wanted to get ahead in the world, you had to play the personality game, know who to butter up and who to ignore. In the courts as elsewhere, politics held sway—a perverse testimonial to the tenets of sociological jurisprudence. To Tom, this was sad confirmation of all he'd heard about Tammany Hall. Now, with politics as usual staring him blankly in the face, infesting his chosen career, he resolved to dip his toe in the partisan waters.[16]

A few days after joining Larkin, Rathbone, he met fellow bull-pen-dweller Sewell Tappan Tyng, a tall, broad-shouldered blueblood who was the grandson of New York's Episcopal bishop and a relative of the Vanderbilts. Tyng had earned official recognition for his hero's part in the World War, and his book on the Battle of the Marne would be considered definitive enough to win him an annual invitation to lecture at West Point. In common with other men of his station, Tyng was contemptuous of the hammerlock over New York's civic life enjoyed by Tammany Hall. But, unlike many of them, Tyng was willing to do more than express his concern. Active in the junior committee of the Republican Committee of One Hundred, Tyng had links to party bosses by virtue of his position as a district leader in the Tenth Assembly District. On the prowl for other young men who shared his aggressive idealism, Tyng spotted Dewey as a ready ally in the lonely and uphill crusade against a political machine founded more than a century earlier on the myth of an ancient Indian warrior named Saint Tammany, and which, in the intervening years, had attained mythical status and fabulous power for itself.

The United States Constitution was barely ratified when a New York furniture dealer named William Mooney founded the Society of Saint Tammany in the fall of 1789, as an anti-English, anti-aristocratic organization, precursor to the rise of formal political parties and a social division between conservative men of property and the landless masses. Members wore Indian regalia, met in a hall dubbed the Wigwam, and earned rank as hunters, sachems, and warriors. With the dawn of partisan politics, Tammany took its stand with Jeffersonian democracy—going so far as to hold a discreet celebration the night Alexander Hamilton lay dying from Aaron Burr's dueling pistol.

With the last property restrictions on voting removed by the New York legislature in 1826, Tammany began courting Irish immigrants. Two hundred of the newcomers were marched to the polls by machine braves carrying cocked pistols when Andrew Jackson ran against John Quincy Adams in 1828; they stayed to cast three votes apiece. Later, such "floaters" would have their ears marked with red circles and be dragged from ward to ward to swell Tammany's natural base of support. Immigration was like mother's milk to the bosses who gradually came to rule the city, none more brazen than William Marcy Tweed, whose handpicked judges swore in new citizens a thousand a day in the weeks before a crucial election.

It was Tweed who perfected the art of graft in municipal government, who padded every contract for stationery, carpets, furniture, printing and a thousand other services by 50, 60, or 70 percent before it was submitted to his comptroller, Slippery Dick Connolly.

The difference was returned to the Tweed Ring, as marvelous a take as any Vanderbilt or Astor might imagine in his most rapacious dreams. For thirty-five chairs and four tables for municipal armories, a Tweed crony billed the city $170,729,60. The County Courthouse wound up costing four times as much as the British Houses of Parliament. Budgeted at $250,000, it finally cost taxpayers $13 million, including a $3 million bill for plastering and enough chairs to stretch from one end of Manhattan Island to the other.

Tweed and his ring bilked New York out of perhaps $200 million. No one blew a whistle until guests at his daughter's wedding deposited $700,000 in gifts—Jay Gould contributed a set of silver nutpickers—and an unfriendly city auditor began spilling the beans to the New York *Times*. Slippery Dick offered the *Times* $5 million not to publish the information, but to no avail. An austere fish-eyed reform Democrat, Samuel J. Tilden, formed the Committee of Seventy to focus public outrage on Tweed, who was indicted on 120 counts, convicted after his second trial, and later escaped to Spain before being brought back to the Ludlow Street jail to die a pauper in 1878. Tilden, meanwhile, was elected governor of New York, and nearly reached the White House, only to see his popular victory thrown out by a Republican-dominated Congress in the final hours before Rutherford B. Hayes's inauguration.

To pick up the pieces Tweed left behind came Richard Croaker, who explained the secret of organizational success that lay behind the machine's resurgence:

I worked over the business like an artist over an etching. Discipline was brought to a pitch never known before. My district leaders were the pick of the covey, and every one, for force and talents of an executive kind, fit to lead a brigade into battle.

Under these were the captains of election precincts, and below the latter came the block captains, one for each city block and personally acquainted with every voter in the block—yes, every soul in the block.

Tammany was, to Boss Croaker, "like the wheels and springs and ratchets and regulators of a clock, sure, when wound up, to strike the hours and announce the time of day in local politics with a nicety that had no precedent."

As a boy, Croaker had led the Fourth Avenue Gang. Later, he fought in the prize ring, and won a seat on the Board of Aldermen before his twenty-sixth birthday. The boss lived well, traveled in a private railroad car, owned a half-interest in a breeding stable, and moved into a $200,000 residence on East Seventy-ninth Street. He succeeded because he knew his city, and he never forgot the base of his power. "Politics are impossible without spoils," he said candidly. "It is all very well to argue that it ought not to be so, but you have to deal with men as they are ... you must bribe the masses with spoils."

There was a bond of kinship between Tammany and the Irish newcomer, a common perception of exclusion and the plight of the downtrodden at the hands of the rich and powerful. The city they shared was often a savage place, with street gangs like the Plug Uglies or Bowery Boys contesting with pistols, chains, and bats, coming together only on Election Day to swell the margins turned in by Tammany's well-oiled machinery. As Daniel Boorstin has pointed out, machine politics was politics without ideology. Tammany acclimated the immigrant to strange surroundings, found odd jobs for the jobless, food for the hungry, medicine for the sick. Tammany warriors went to wakes and greased municipal justice.

Reformers might fume, wrote James Bryce in his classic work, *The American Commonwealth,* but "the hated political bosses were in truth, buffers between the rich and the poor; buffers who taxed the one to keep the other in good humor" and, as for the brokers' fees involved, they were small indeed "as compared to the cost of riots and revolutions."

"Well, well, well, reform has gone to hell!" chanted a writhing column of Tammany braves snake-dancing their way through New York's streets after taking back City Hall and the 60,000 jobs it controlled in 1886. Seven years later, reformers rose up once again to indignantly second the denunciation of the Hall leveled by the Reverend Charles Parkhurst, a Presbyterian preacher whose verbal blast at "a lying, perjured, rumsoaked and libidinous lot" led to a legislative investigation that turned up extensive corruption within the city's police force. Cops were taking money regularly from Italian fruit dealers and German saloonkeepers. Worse yet, they were raking in thousands from bordellos and gambling houses. Every captain, it seemed, had his own wardman, deputized to collect cash from such establishments once a month. After deducting 20 percent for his own expenses, the wardman gave the rest to the captain, who in turn paid off the inspector over him. Eventually, money found its way into the hands of the police commissioner and Tammany's district leaders.

It cost $300 to be a simple roundsman in the force, the legislature found, $14,000 to attain a captaincy. Theodore Roosevelt was brought in to clean up the department, Boss Croaker resigned after an uproar over his refusal to renominate an independent Tammany judge, and the machine, backed by the unshakable loyalty of the poor, went back to running the city. A new boss rose, a onetime Hudson Duster named Charles J. Murphy. It was Murphy who defined the essence of Tammany's appeal as he leaned against a Second Avenue lamppost in the evenings, ready and willing to dispense aid to blizzard victims, petty lawbreakers, even a struggling Episcopal mission. Later, he bought a Long Island estate with its own nine-hole golf course, and conducted secret meetings with financiers and bootleggers at Delmonico's, in what tabloid reporters dubbed the Scarlet Room of Mystery.

But Murphy never took his hand off New York's pulse. He knew that Christmas baskets and street sweeper positions wouldn't forever cement the machine to its constituency. Already, middle-class Jews were becoming susceptible to the socially liberal, fiscally conservative good government appeal of the city's Republicans. Organized labor was growing, and restive at the same time. Then, in 1911, a disastrous fire at the Triangle Shirtwaist Factory on the Lower East Side took the lives of 141 garment workers, most of them Italian and Jewish seamstresses burned to death at their sewing machines. A new kind of Democrat emerged from the Tammany cocoon, loyal to the machine yet liberal in outlook, and passionately concerned about the rights of working people and the poor. Robert F. Wagner and Al Smith were sent to the State Senate to represent what Murphy's successor would call "the new Tammany." Speaking forcefully and blessed after 1920 with a reactionary Republican opposition, Smith and Wagner kept their distance from Tammany's dirty laundry, winning national reputations for themselves and their part as advocates of social welfare legislation.

Even Jimmy Walker, otherwise celebrated as the man who legalized professional baseball on Sundays, and boxing seven days a week, was hailed by the New York *Times* for his bill to compel publication of the Ku Klux Klan's membership roll, and his stouthearted support of Al Smith's legislative program after Smith outgrew Tammany and developed into a widely admired governor. It was Smith who succeeded in electing Walker mayor in 1925, temporarily misplacing his own doubts about the man's capacity for serious work in the name of party loyalty.

Charles Murphy was dead by then; 60,000 New Yorkers lined Fifth Avenue to see his coffin taken out of St. Patrick's Cathedral. When his will was read, Boss Murphy's wealth was placed at $2 million, not bad for a man who hadn't held a salaried job since 1900. But Murphy was discreet, tight-lipped, a man who worked best behind the scenes. Jimmy Walker, the heir to Murphy's machine, was as flamboyant as the dead boss was secretive. Colorful in his morning clothes and spats, the new mayor told a joke better than any Broadway comic. His weakness for a shapely ankle was hardly frowned upon in the Fitzgerald decade of flappers and bootleg booze.

Before long, every day in New York was a party, with Walker's gardenia-sporting gladhander Grover Whalen leading ticker-tape parades from the Battery to City Hall, where, if the guest was of the pedigree of Rumania's Queen Marie, he was likely to be met by Mayor Walker, military guards, and the Sanitation Department band. Whalen welcomed Charles Lindbergh and Amelia Earhart. He roused noonday crowds to cheer the Belgian Debt Refunding Commission, French Boy Scouts, and a Ukrainian backstroke champion. The Mayor himself preferred partying in the private luxury of the Central Park Casino, reserved for his own inner circle and refurbished at a cost to the taxpayers of $350,000.

Somewhere in this careless decade, Tammany got out of hand. While the city's population rose 15 percent, its budget went up 250 percent. The municipal work force doubled, bloated with purely political appointments, from county clerks who sold official records on the side, to the son of a Walker campaign manager rewarded with a $7,500 job as secretary to the superintendent of schools. Public improvement projects were turned into lucrative indulgences for Tammany to market at rates that would have astonished even Tweed. The Independent Subway System, for instance, wound up costing twice its original price tag of $400 million. Aldermen unloaded worthless property on the city for astronomical prices, and magistrates' courts were sold for $10,000 a bench, with more cash demanded to wear the robes of a general sessions judge. Newsstand sites, traditionally allotted apolitically to the blind or crippled, were divvied up for the profits they might bring.

This was the picture greeting Tom Dewey upon his arrival in New York, a dark and brooding canvas of democracy corrupted by greed and debased by the man on the street's willingness to acquiesce in his own fleecing. In the face of Tammany's army, the city's Republicans were a fragile host, relying for support upon nabobs like Frederick Chauncey Turner, eligible for the Order of the Cincinnati and the Society of Mayflower Descendants; a garrulous and high-pitched alderman named Fiorello H. La Guardia, who made a reputation attacking his own governor, Nathan Miller, over home rule and the five-cent subway fare; and a Hungarian-born Jew, Sam Koenig, who cared little for esoteric debate—he dismissed the League of Nations as "over my head"—but excelled at grass-roots organization.

Koenig became chairman of the GOP in New York County (Manhattan) in 1911, when Henry Stimson persuaded him to take on the thankless task of rallying voters around the anti-Tammany standard. To survive, the chairman had been forced to scrounge off scraps dropped from the Democratic feast—a few minor patronage jobs, once in a while a judgeship, but little more. It was standpattism of a high order, but to less flexible men, like Tyng and his youthful recruit to the organization, it was an illegitimate response to a machine they saw as evil incarnate. It was not a healthy party in which Dewey enlisted, ringing doorbells in the Greenwich Village area in October 1925. Yet, as Marland Gale had already observed, being in a hopeless situation rarely slowed Tom's drive or dimmed his optimism. It wasn't long before Tom was making a name for himself as one who called upon voters repeatedly, wrote letters to those he couldn't track down personally, and hammered home in every face-to-face encounter the time-honored priority of at least supporting the party's local State Assembly candidate. Hundreds of New Yorkers, it seemed, might be treated to the dogged salesmanship first displayed to Owosso's society editor.

While all this went on, the new United States Attorney for the Southern District of New York—Uncle Sam's lawyer in the city— was pursuing his own effort to revive the party as an organization of young men and fresh ideas. Emory Buckner invited his staff to meet Thomas C. Desmond, a Newburgh shipyard owner enriched during the war and eager to breathe new life into the dormant New York Young Republican Club. Once proud, the club had more recently fallen victim to the torpor overtaking the senior party in the wake of the TR–Taft rivalry and Wilson's eight years of noble-sounding governance. Buckner urged his own men to join up. Two who did were Lowell Wadmond, a Wisconsin native and Harvard Law honor student, and J. Edward Lumbard, a native New Yorker who also bore the polish of Harvard Square in his bearing and speech.

Wadmond became vice president of the revitalized club, and Lumbard chairman of a policy committee that devised a Republican manifesto for the city of New York. In it, the club called for public swimming pools, baths, and gymnasiums in all sections of the city, and decent housing and strict enforcement of sanitary codes in slum as well as silk stocking districts. They insisted on cleaner streets, reduced utility rates, and abolition of costly and overlapping city offices. It was a liberal program for the 1920s; a platform TR himself could have stood upon. The Young Republicans described it as "scientific treatment of human welfare problems."[17]

Every Thursday, the bright young professionals gathered for lunch and earnest talk in the Governor's Room at the downtown Lawyers Club. By the summer of 1928, their numbers had grown to nearly 3,000, and they were able to provide significant help to the Hoover Engineers in watching the polls on Election Day in November and preventing the theft of up to 50,000 votes for the hero of Republican liberals, the Great Engineer who mingled the humane and scientific impulses that powered the Young Republican Club under Desmond. Two of the newer additions to the roster were Sewell Tyng's friend Tom Dewey and a transplanted Nebraskan by way of the Yale *Law Journal*, Herbert Brownell. Brownell's obvious flair for organization led him away from board meetings and out onto the streets, while Dewey was assigned to the City Affairs Committee, which soon called for a campaign against noise and for reduced fares to the Statue of Liberty. In 1927, he was asked to chair another committee, this one investigating the city's finances and, as assistant managing editor of the club's newsletter, to publicize "by means of pamphlets, radio addresses, and other methods" the larceny quietly being committed against the citizenry.

The result was "Drunken Sailors," a deft critique that bore the debater's stamp.

Ever since Isaac Newton discovered the law of gravitation, it has been generally accepted dogma that "what goes up must come down." So, year after year, the taxpayers of the City of New York have placidly watched the Budget of the City rise like a fire balloon, sure of its eventual descent. But the Budget of the City of New York vigorously denies the existence of all natural laws, and condemns sane finance as the idle amusement of the feeble-minded.[18]

More seriously, Dewey assailed the Jones–White Merchant Marine bill as "involving government ownership and operation of a great industry. . . . It establishes a very bad precedent which we may well see next followed in our very sick coal industry and which may be invoked in the expansion of government ownership or aid in water power, weak railroads and other national or local necessities."[19]

It was an orthodox, if forward-looking, Republican writing for the newsletter, one whose adherence to the club's "scientific" humanism was entirely in keeping with the faith of Owosso's priests and pharisees. Like Wadmond and Brownell among others of the club's leaders, Dewey was still an outsider to the city he hoped to save from itself, an emissary from the other America looking askance even as he tried to lure converts.

Dewey spent his political adolescence in a city where organization was everything. Political clubs, whether Democratic or Republican, chose party officers and convention delegates, designated preferred candidates in primaries, and reproduced themselves through captains and assembly district committees, slates and propaganda. Socially, they were black-tie versions of Tammany's streetwise clubs, ones in which ambitious young men and women met at formal balls and engaged in animated conversations, about personal and political opportunities. Most clubs had their own pianos. Masquerades, dinner dances, chop suey dances, spaghetti dances, poetry contests, fashion shows, Jimmy Hines's "June Walk" to Central Park, and countless beefsteak dinners given to honor party chieftains—in all, politics in New York combined conviviality with the killer instinct. Democrats seemed to be more blessed with the latter than Republicans—or so Dewey lamented—and thus when a pugnacious young disciple of Coolidge and Hoover appeared, one who actually worked as hard as he talked, he could expect to be noticed.

Dewey was. By May of 1927, he was being asked by Sam Koenig to join "a small group of the most active" Republicans for lunch. Then the regulars of the senior party invited the newcomer to take over a vacant district captaincy in the Fourteenth. This was the era of genteel persuasion, when headquarters served tea on Sunday afternoons to prospective voters—a gambit unlikely to be repeated at Democratic gatherings—and sought with almost painful sincerity to explain to the uninitiated how a voting machine functioned. Dewey was more direct in his appeals, wearing out considerable shoe leather in tracking down apartment-building and brownstone residents. Later, he reported twelve dollars in meticulously recorded expenses, for taxi fares and janitorial tips.[20]

By primary day 1928, Tom was handling two adjoining districts. He found himself unable to attend a captains' meeting because of schedule conflicts with two other party functions. He showed every indication of winning a foothold in the senior organization, traditionally suspicious of youthful do-gooders. Yet politics remained an interesting sidebar to his main preoccupation, the law. Moreover, for all his aggressiveness when selling the party ticket door to door, there clung to Dewey a residual reserve, and more than a little insecurity. This was the son of a Michigan postmaster who still sent his laundry home to be washed by his mother, and who looked forward to the jars of homemade meat relish wrapped up in the return package, the country boy who whispered to Lowell Wadmond after one Young Republican luncheon, "You and I have to stick together. We're both Midwesterners and we don't understand these Easterners." This was the champion debater who turned down Sam Koenig's first request to organize a speakers' committee when Fiorello La Guardia ran against Jimmy Walker in 1929. "As a speaker," Tom replied to the county chairman, "I do not believe that I will be available or effective." A minor throat operation the previous fall had forced him to curtail even normal use of his voice, but "I doubt whether I am a particularly effective speaker in any event."[21]

In the end, he relented, stumping for Frederick Coudert's candidacy for district attorney from the back of a flatbed truck. In 1930, he convinced thirty-five other men, mostly young lawyers like himself, to urge support for Republican candidates in that year's congressional and gubernatorial races. To his cadre of inexperienced speakers Dewey stressed issues that might have special appeal— water power and President Hoover's commission on unemployment among them—and he carefully reminded his flock to be positive: "People will respect our speeches more and listen more closely if we have something affirmative to say."[22]

Freshmen lawyers, like children, were supposed to be seen and not heard. The talent most valued in New York's most prominent firms, where Jews were rare and blacks nonexistent, was not independence but obedience. Each fall, the incoming group of hopefuls at Larkin, Rathbone were casually informed that half their number would not survive their first year. Instead, they were on professional probation.

Dewey failed to pass the test. Bored with the work assigned him, anxious to make his way in a hurry, he quarreled with an older partner named Stickney and, early in 1927, was informed that his services were no longer needed. "To show you how dumb we are," another member of the firm cracked after 1935, "we fired Tom Dewey."[23]

Barely had his anger cooled when Tom found another opening, with the small firm of McNamara and Seymour. It was headed by Stuart McNamara, a barrister who had once served as Theodore Roosevelt's assistant attorney general. McNamara insured himself against time off by keeping his staff deliberately small. At its peak, the firm engaged two partners and five lawyers, including Dewey. His employment was not automatic; McNamara confided fears to his partner that the self-confident applicant from Owosso might be "a little too bumptious." Yet Dewey's obvious ability and enthusiasm carried the day, and in February 1927 his name was added to the firm's payroll at $2,300 a year.[24]

Grateful at last to have escaped the anonymity of the bullpen, Dewey impressed his superiors with a willingness to devote long evenings to library research—even if the secretarial pool resented his cavalier directive that one of the girls stay late. Occasionally, his manner alienated more powerful colleagues. Raymond Seymour never forgot the day when Dewey, red-eyed and distraught, emerged from the senior partner's office to lament, "Mr. McNamara just gave me an awful bawling out." Yet personal rebukes could not diminish the luster of professional advancement. McNamara's list of clients was select. They included T. Coleman Duont, who owned the Chateau Frontenac, New Willard and Waldorf-Astoria hotels; and Joseph Baldwin, whose Empire Trust Company was also located at 120 Broadway and was a source of business that would have a profound, if accidental, impact on McNamara's ambitious junior colleague.[25]

There were other concerns in Tom's mind in 1927. At the end of May, he received a telegram from Owosso. "Your father not well," Annie reported, "wants you to come home." Tom took the six o'clock train for Detroit to go sit beside his father's sickbed. By early June, the crisis seemed past, and he was able to return to New York. Then, on June 19, George Dewey suffered a fatal heart attack, the same ailment that killed his brother Edmund at the same age.

Once again, Tom retraced his steps westward, and this time stayed with his mother for two weeks. His father's will left $27,000 in real estate and cash, a tidy tribute to the thrift and application preached as part of his political gospel. Annie, who had always been the business-minded member of the family, simply went on running and repairing the downtown block and speculating in Wall Street stock, usually with her son's advice and admiration for support. His own feelings about his father's death were obscure. To a friend who wrote expressing sympathy, and mentioning his own loss of a mother, Tom returned the condolences, and hurried on to a bantering invitation for the correspondent to come visit him in New York soon, "before we both grow beards." His silence hardened, swallowing up any personal recollections of the parent he resembled more closely than he realized.[26]

Back in New York, Tom found new problems, this time in his

courtship of Frances Hutt. Sometime later that year, the two had an argument, apparently over Frances' continuing interest in a career, and in a moment of anger, she signed a contract for a new roadshow version of *George White's Scandals*. Dewey himself hinted afterward that considerable persuasion was called for before his intended would finally relinquish her operatic ambitions, lately heightened by the offer of a place in the San Francisco Light Opera Company. Early in June 1928, Tom advised a Republican friend that he could not possibly attend an upcoming committee meeting. "I am working days, nights, and Sundays," he explained, "and expect to continue doing so for at least another week."[27]

He failed to mention that, at the end of that week, he was getting married. On June 28, he knelt with Frances in the little chapel on the Fifty-third Street side of the St. Thomas Episcopal Church on Fifth Avenue, as three friends looked on. Afterward, the bridegroom presented to Marland Gale, his best man, a fashionable duplicate of the walking stick he had brought back from Paris. Then the couple set sail for Havana and a two-week honeymoon. They returned to a two-room fourth-floor walk-up on East Eighty-third Street; its seventy-five-dollar-a-month rent was in keeping with the finances of young marrieds who hadn't been able to afford an engagement ring. Tom and Frances served their first dinner party in their new home on a bridge table shoved up against one wall. In the evenings, cheap entertainment came from word games or the company of Pat Hogan and his wife, Marge, who often came over on Saturday nights for a midnight meal of scrambled eggs and bacon.[28]

"He is as charming a fellow as you will ever meet," Tom said of Hogan, "and he has a grand wife, whom he took off the stage, to the great detriment of the stage and the great benefit of his own home." The friendship extended to Frances and Marge, fellow troupers from the theatrical circuit. Around the Hogans, Tom could relax, loosen up, laugh at himself. He seemed once more the bright, if prickly, collegian who enjoyed people as well as their problems.[29]

A classmate sent greetings in January 1929 to "Old stick in the mud."

"Hope you make half a million soon," he wrote, "and have your dignity ruined occasionally by your most excellent wife." Dewey's reply was breezy. "Why only a half million? As long as one is being ambitious, let's not limit the ambitions." As for "that inherent pomposity which frequently passes as dignity" and which saddled his own efforts at relaxation, "even that is being whittled away as the

years go along." Meanwhile, he sighed in agreement with the sentiment expressed by President Clarence Little of his old alma mater:
"Dignity is the greatest curse of mankind."[30]

The year of the Dewey's marriage was a year of disappointment.
Early in 1929, it seemed as if the stock market were bound for infin-
ity, as bullish small investors like Dewey and his friends spent feverish hours whispering hot tips and inside information. Invest in
Jewell Tea, a tax consultant at Irving Trust advised Tom. Buy Fox
Film, the knowledgeable lawyer replied. It was a good tip; within a
few weeks, the tax man was writing "to see what dope you can get on
two or three other sleepers."[31]

By summer, however, Dewey's optimism was wilting. He warned
his aunt that the market was entering "a very dangerous phase, although the leading stocks may go higher." To another correspondent he admitted that "the very best authorities" might disagree,
but to him it seemed that the market had become "thoroughly unsound." On September 3, Wall Street peaked. Softening set in, and
in the third week of October the prosperous bubble finally burst. On
the twenty-fourth, leading bankers met to try to stem the psychological panic feeding an apparent collapse of stock prices. The House of
Morgan dispatched Richard Whitney, an eminently respectable financier, to take to the exchange floor and purchase U.S. Steel and
other stocks at inflated prices. It was a bold, ultimately doomed attempt by Thomas Lamont, Charles Mitchell of the First City National Bank, and others to rescue a sinking economy by symbolic
gesture.[32]

Public relations could no longer sustain the market, and on October 29 the roof fell in. Dewey stood with silent fascination in a broker's office that disastrous afternoon staring wordlessly as $30 billion
of paper value was sucked into an economic black hole. His own
portfolio, which ran to established stocks like General Motors,
Woolworth, and New York Central Railroad, was hardly immune to
the general havoc, but he displayed no emotion on Black Friday,
only a blank stare as Owosso's virtues came under assault by forces
as yet unimaginable. He could not conceive, looking at the mounting pile of financial rubble around him, that a time would arrive
when his own career might entwine with those of Lamont, Mitchell,
and Whitney.[33]

3
The Ruby Nose of Uncle Sam

Too often, life in New York is merely a squalid succession of days.
—FIORELLO H. LA GUARDIA

There's no need to bang on a table to prove a point. Facts will
do it.
—THOMAS E. DEWEY

Four months before the crash, Tom and Frances Dewey left their
two rooms on East Eighty-third Street for a more fashionable address on East Seventy-third. That summer they took a cottage on
Long Island, in company with others who worked all week in the
scorching heat of Manhattan, and sought escape in the sea air and
unspoiled marshlands east of Queens. Even the collapse of stock
prices moved Tom only to an expensive I-told-you-so: "Perhaps the
appalling events of the last two months," he wrote his aunt at year's
end, "have served to justify my hesitancy about investing your
bonds in any common stocks." As for himself, he would risk nothing
more uncertain than Sears, Roebuck.[1]

Dewey wasn't immune from the disaster—his profits from stock
dealings fell sharply in 1930—but his rise at McNamara and Seymour was steady, and was reflected in his earnings. Within three
years of joining the firm, his salary had tripled. For a while, he
thought of indulging his old love of sailing by buying a houseboat.
That plan gave way to summers on Long Island and a small sailboat, in which he and Frances arrived at the blue arena off Newport
in September 1930 to cheer on the American yacht *Enterprise* as she
whipped the last of Sir Thomas Lipton's five *Shamrocks* and tightened a grip on the Auld Mug first won by the racing schooner
America eighty years earlier.

Back in the city, other contests beckoned. "Dodging taxis," Dewey
wrote his uncle, "continues to be the most popular sport, and the
odds are more or less against you. . . . So far, we have been lucky in
the game."[2]

It was an understatement applicable in other areas. For Dewey,
1930 was a busy year, brimming over with clients and paperwork.
Fewer and fewer of his fellow New Yorkers were so fortunate. After
October 1929, New York was a city divided against itself. Infant sky-

scrapers like the Empire State Building and Rockefeller Center were poor palliatives for men who stood in the street watching their construction, with no jobs of their own. The glittering ambiance of George Gershwin and Cole Porter, the Oak Room, and the St. Regis hardly disguised the hunger of people camped in newspaper and tin shacks, nor did it satisfy the beggars haunting Park Avenue like ragged ghosts.

New York didn't collapse overnight; it takes time for an entire nation's economy to deflate. Not until the fall of 1930, when the International Apple Sellers Association found itself with a surplus of product, did street corners in every neighborhood begin resounding to desperate hawkers vending fruit for their livelihood. Fall apartment rentals in the city were running slightly behind the previous year, but, all in all, were considered healthy. Some 2,086 banks in the country failed in 1930, and the National Council of Federated Churches, led by Mrs. John D. Rockefeller, Jr., announced that birth control was "morally justified." It was a time of flux, of old certainties dying, and new ones awaiting birth.

The one thing obvious to everyone as 1930 turned into 1931 was that the Depression was for real. In New York, saleswomen at Woolworth's were lucky to take home eight dollars a week in wages. On a March day in 1930, 35,000 New Yorkers attended the largest Communist rally ever staged in the United States. And as this unfolded, President Hoover sat in Washington, a prisoner of indecision, waging internal warfare between a humanitarian's instincts and his philosophical commitment to rugged individualism. "Economic wounds must be healed by the action of the cells of the economic body," the chief executive announced, "the producers and consumers themselves."

In 1930, Tom Dewey was one of a host of Republican campaigners who saw their best efforts at explaining the President's policies crushed by the weight of a hundred million discontents. Hoover himself cast aside his doubts, banished Andrew Mellon to the Court of St. James's, and launched his own program aimed at recovery. He spent a billion dollars, in vain, trying to raise farm income. He pressed for the creation of 3,000 voluntary brigades in a war on joblessness, refused to accept his own presidential salary, and urged other government workers to practice similar self-sacrifice. When Dewey joined the federal payroll as an assistant United States attorney at the start of 1931, he faithfully led his own campaign to turn back at least one day's wages each month for unemployment relief.

Confronted with a tough re-election campaign in 1932, Hoover started the Reconstruction Finance Corporation to spur local construction and hiring. In a radical departure from Republican orthodoxy, he sought a moratorium on international war debts. And still the spiral descended. In 1930, 26,355 businesses went under and the president of the Baltimore and Ohio Railroad told a gathering at the Wharton School of Economics, "I would steal before I would starve." Was it surprising, then, that hungry or disillusioned Americans might vicariously begin to identify with the newest Horatio Algers, the anti-establishmentarians with a fondness for shiny black in their cars and suits alike? Franklin Roosevelt might consider himself the leader of national government after March 1933. But in New York, the 1930s were overseen by a shadowy regime of insouciant rogues and gun-toting thugs, a logical denouement to the historic alliance between Tammany Hall and the gangs that now threatened even the Hall's pre-eminence.

Prohibition opened the floodgates to crime on an undreamed-of scale. In New York City alone, the U.S. Attorney prosecuted 63,000 violations of the Volstead Act; nationally, the figure topped half a million. New Yorkers bought booze wherever they could find it. In such a climate, lawbreaking became fashionable. Hoover appointed a commission to study the situation, and even it could produce only a hopelessly muddled mishmash that led one wag to conclude,

> Prohibition is an awful flop—we like it.
> It can't stop what it's meant to stop—we like it.
> It's left a trail of graft and crime, it's filled our land
>   with vice, and crime,
> It don't prohibit worth a dime—nevertheless, we're for it.

Before 1919, the underworld consisted of little more than a ragtag collection of dope peddlers, cat burglars, and highway robbers. Now, with big money to be made from bootlegging, organization began to tell, often with violent results.

"Being outlawed, the liquor business cannot be regulated by law," wrote Walter Lippmann in 1931. "It cannot call upon the law for protection. Thus, it is driven to improvise its own substitutes." It wasn't only the Prohibition law that bootleggers broke; they also discarded tariff and tax laws, bribed local police and politicians, and in settling internal disputes customarily resorted to gunfire. In New York, the last years before Prohibition saw gangs like Dopey Benny Fein's selling themselves to the highest bidder in savage labor-management wars in the city's garment district. But Benny was becoming an anomaly in his own neighborhood. The Lower East Side was home to a sleeping giant of Italian ancestry.

Building on the foundation of the Black Hand, a semi-secret criminal society founded at the turn of the century, Joe Masseria—Joe the Boss—created the Unione Sicilione, and a vast subterranean society that thrived on bootlegging profits. As the money rolled in, rivalries sprang up. Joe the Boss was challenged by Salvatore Maranzano, a native Sicilian whose adolescent aspiration to the priesthood may have accounted for his magisterial behavior.

With diversification taking place, as in any big business, the underworld found itself in need of financial backing. Arnold Rothstein entered the picture. The son of a Jewish tailor, Rothstein was a dapper bon vivant who had his office at Lindy's, the Broadway restaurant famous for its cheesecake. In truth, his domain was as unlimited as his imagination. "Rothstein," his lawyer once said, "is a man who dwells in doorways. He's a gray rat, waiting for his cheese." Best known for his alleged fix of the 1919 World Series, Rothstein had branched out into narcotics, stolen and smuggled goods, and gambling with millions on the line. He had an eye for criminal talent, and a fine disregard for the artificial barriers of religion and ethnicity that formerly had prevented the underworld from pooling its strongest resources. It was Rothstein who looked with favor upon Meyer Lansky, Vito Genovese, and a former thief turned aspiring racketeer named Louis Buchalter, better known as Lepke. It was Rothstein who took a crude and ill-educated Charley Lucania, now nicknamed Lucky, and taught him conservative dress, graceful dinner manners, and other social rules enforced in the swank saloons frequented in the 1920s by social-climbing gangsters.

Lucania, in turn, brought into the fold associates like Frank Costello, whose specialty was slot machines, and bootleggers like Dutch Schultz, previously a strong-arm riding beer trucks on the West Side, later graduated to ownership of his own speakeasy in the Bronx. By 1931, Schultz controlled at least eleven businesses creeping south into Harlem and the West Side precincts where rival bootlegger Waxey Gordon was king. By then, Rothstein himself was dead, shot in November 1928 after welshing on a $340,000 gambling debt. Underworld rumor had it that the dead man stood to pick up a cool million in bets on Herbert Hoover against Al Smith had he only lived another forty-eight hours. At City Hall, Rothstein's murder caused a panic; his connections with Tammany politicians were said to be extensive. So a local judge ordered that all the gambler's voluminous files be placed in the custody of a district leader—who later informed the court that they'd been stolen. Mayor Walker fired his police commissioner, and brought in Grover Whalen to see if the flamboyant official greeter could impart some of his public relations razzmatazz to the unsolved crime.

In the hopeless race against Walker in 1929, Fiorello La Guardia tried to make the Rothstein case a springboard for his own candidacy. Among other charges leveled at Beau James was one that Albert H. Vitale, a magistrate and mayoral friend working the Bronx for the incumbent, had accepted nearly $20,000 in loans from Rothstein. Walker won the contest, but La Guardia had set fire to a long and deadly fuse. A month after the election, Vitale attended a testimonial dinner in his honor at the Tepecano Democratic Club in the Bronx. The evening was disrupted by seven masked gunmen who robbed the magistrate and others of thousands of dollars. Afterward, the well-connected Vitale hurried to his Democratic clubhouse and, within two hours, retrieved all the stolen loot—evidence that he knew how to push the right buttons with the underworld. A subsequent investigation revealed that at least seven of Vitale's admirers at the dinner that night had police records, including a prominent racketeer named Ciro Terranova. All seven had records balanced by dismissed charges in magistrates' courts, including Vitale's own.

Now events gained a helter-skelter momentum of their own. George Z. Medalie, a respected private attorney best known for his investigation of payroll padding in the Secretary of State's office, was asked to undertake a probe of Vitale, who later resigned. Then a State Supreme Court justice named Joseph F. Crater vanished into thin air, never to be heard from again. His name became a synonym for disappearance. In the wake of his departure, he was identified as a notorious womanizer and friend of Ziegfeld, who had almost certainly paid for his court appointment. Simultaneously, other magistrates came under suspicion of financial irregularities, and thus it came as no surprise when the appellate judges of the Supreme Court invited a fifty-eight-year-old former court of appeals judge and antiTammany Democrat named Samuel Seabury to undertake a complete examination of the city's judicial system.

Judge Seabury was a pillar of virtue, aptly described by his biographer as "the twentieth-century man with eighteenth-century manners," an aristocratic product of four generations of Episcopal clergymen, born in the parish house of the Church of the Annunciation on Washington's birthday 1873. His first political involvement was on behalf of Henry George, the single-tax advocate who sought the mayoralty in the 1890s. Later, he enjoyed a spotty political career of his own, culminating in a narrow loss to Charles Whitman in the governor's race in 1916. Tepid support from Tammany Hall was widely suspected as the leading cause of the judge's defeat that year; now he was in a position to avenge the humiliation and rescue the city and party he loved in his distant, patrician way.

Seabury began by exposing corruption in the women's court, where innocent housewives and brides-to-be had been subjected to extortion and blackmail by crooked members of the vice squad. In April 1931, he raised his sights and broadened his inquiry into a general unearthing of municipal jobbery. The Sheriff of New York County, Thomas A. Farley, was asked repeatedly how he'd come into $100,000 in 1928. Farley claimed to have discovered it in "a wonderful tin box," enriching the language even as he cut his own throat. Before he was done, Farley also explained to Seabury that men ranged around a table behind the locked doors of his political clubhouse at two in the morning weren't gambling, but only packing baseball bats, ropes for skipping, and other toys to be handed out at the club's annual children's party.

The Sheriff was followed by the Registrar of Kings County, James A. McQuade, who justified deposits of $510,000 as a series of loans, needed after a string of untimely deaths in his family. Now, according to the sorrowing official, he was personally responsible for supporting no fewer than thirty-three people—and "the thirty-four starving McQuades" became a standing joke. Spectacular as all this was, emboldened reformers were pressing for more, including the scalp of Mayor Walker. But crime in New York was hardly limited to City Hall, and its investigation could never succeed so long as Tammany's sixty-nine-year-old figurehead District Attorney, Thomas C. T. Crain, was in charge. It was precisely to bypass such roadblocks in the path of justice that Seabury and his staff were poring over city records. For similar reasons, the administration in Washington was casting about for a new U.S. attorney to replace Charles H. Tuttle, who had resigned the office to crushing defeat in a gubernatorial contest with Franklin D. Roosevelt in November 1930.

The search would not be easy, especially with warring factions in the New York State GOP at loggerheads over the patronage-rich, politically potent job. Since the days of Henry Stimson, through Emory Buckner and Tuttle, the U.S. attorney's office had been identified with progressive Republicanism. President Hoover's friends in the state were promoting the candidacy of Alan Fox, his

1928 campaign manager there. Indigenous organization men like
Sam Koenig and the new state chairman, W. Kingsland Macy of
Suffolk County, preferred Keyes Winter, overseer of the silk stocking
Fifteenth District and a loyal ally of both men.

While the maneuvering was going on, and possible dark horses
were being scouted, Tom Dewey was occupied with more prosaic
matters, including his first major court case, a customer suit against
the Empire Trust. But as the case approached trial, Dewey's senior
partners advised him to bring in a seasoned trial lawyer for the defense. Thus George Medalie entered his life.[3]

Medalie was forty-seven years old at the time, a moon-faced man
of average height who looked out at the world through steel-rimmed
glasses. The son of a rabbi, raised in the teeming streets of the Lower
East Side, George had gone to work after the death of his father and
simultaneously entered Columbia on a Pulitzer scholarship. A voracious reader whose interests ranged from Talmudic to ancient
Roman and canon law, Medalie was also an authority on the grand
jury as the community's chief investigative tool. Throughout his
married life, he wrote affectionate little notes to his wife in Greek,
which she answered in the same tongue.

After graduating from Columbia Law School, Medalie had distinguished himself as an assistant to Charles Whitman, the crusading district attorney whose scouring of Tammany's graft-ridden police department catapulted him to the governorship in 1914. From
Whitman, he gained a deep respect for the tedious essence of any
investigation, which is detail. "The smallest fact," he quoted Aldous
Huxley, "is a window through which the infinite may be seen." By
1920, Medalie was in private practice, passing up large retainers for
the freedom that comes to the independent barrister, taking cases as
they roused his interest or challenged his mind. He maintained a
small staff, for whom he was an awesome figure.[4]

Ideologically, Medalie was a perfect progressive Republican: a
worrier about the growing tendency to rely too readily upon Washington for solutions to local problems and a social liberal who publicly repudiated the segregationist policies of the American Bar Association. He was also an internationalist, who warned in 1931 that
"no nation today is sufficient unto itself . . . no nation dares or cares
to live in self-sufficiency, and in disregard of its neighbors." Finally,
he was an indefatigable worker (for whom public office would result
in a pay cut of 90 percent or more), simultaneously endowed with
an old-fashioned sense of obligation that overcame purely financial
concerns.

His influence over Dewey—as he came to know the younger man he called "a legal prodigy"—was immense. Every morning, the pair made a ten-minute journey on foot from 120 Broadway where each had his office, to the state Supreme Court building in Foley Square, where the widow Annie Kaufman pressed her claim against Empire Trust. Tom carried Medalie's briefcase and listened intently as his more experienced partner mapped the day's events in his mind.[5]

The trial was in its final hours, in the first week of January 1931, when Medalie was called to the phone. On the other end of the line was President Hoover's attorney general, William Mitchell, formally tendering the office of U.S. Attorney for the Southern District of New York, the oldest and largest of the nation's ninety-four legal divisions. Among other distinctions, Medalie would be the first Jew ever named to the post. When he returned to the courtroom, he asked his assistant to consider other bright young Republicans who might serve on his staff and told Dewey, "Put your own name down, too."

For his chief assistant, Medalie sought out Lowell Wadmond, but Wadmond, having stalled a downtown law firm for two years already, had no intention of continuing in public office. Medalie persisted, promising to have Wadmond appointed U.S. attorney whenever he himself retired. The younger man still refused, agreeing only, and enthusiastically, to help Medalie recruit Tom Dewey. To be sure, Tom had little courtroom experience, but then, the chief assistant's role traditionally had been largely administrative, and Medalie was concerned about housekeeping functions, including personnel and mail. Besides, both men had already been associated in the Kaufman case, and the chemistry between the Midwestern Protestant and the East Side Jew seemed promising.[6]

The next day, Wadmond was asked to lunch by a distraught Dewey, who rattled off a long list of reasons why he shouldn't take any such job. McNamara and Seymour had promised to make him a partner within five years. Then, too, Hoover was likely to be defeated in 1932, "and I'll be swept out of office with all the other political hacks." The discussion was renewed that night at dinner and in Dewey's car, which circled Central Park endlessly as Tom, Wadmond, and Frances joined the issue with another Young Republican friend. A salary cut was involved, and in 1931 that was no mean disincentive. On the other hand, there were administrative experience and influential contacts to be had; already, Dewey was casting ahead to the day when he might run a large law firm. A few days later, he told Wadmond he'd made up his mind to take the job.[7]

Dewey's own version of the sequence of events leading to his appointment as chief assistant was considerably different. It included two previous offers before he finally accepted the highest position below the U.S. Attorney himself. Yet his memory for dates could be faulty: He had Medalie taking office on March 1, instead of the actual date of February 12. His correspondence during the period, in fact, suggests anything but blushing reticence. In mid-February, he wrote to the new U.S. Attorney offering to escort him to a meeting of the New York Young Republican Club. Less than three weeks later, he was forwarding his Columbia Law School grades, almost certainly with political clearance for a high-level job in mind.[8]

As it turned out, Sam Koenig wanted his own man for the office, a crusty veteran of the organization. Medalie wouldn't hear of it—indeed, he informed those who ultimately did make up his staff that Republican politics ended at the door—and by the middle of March was involved in apparently intense dickering with Dewey and Stuart McNamara over the young man's future. It may be that the earlier offer Wadmond remembered was either tentative or for something below the chief assistantship. In the end, Dewey said he was willing to come to work for Uncle Sam, but only as Medalie's chief assistant. It was an audacious demand, but Medalie was willing to agree. Meanwhile, Tom received a letter from his mother written from a cruise ship in the mid-Atlantic.

"Mr. Medalie must approve of the way that Brief was written. Isn't it a fine satisfaction to have been offered the position. I rather hope you will decide against it, for you might have to send someone to Sing Sing, and with Mr. M[cNamara] you don't."[9]

On April 1, the news was made public, the New York *Times* sighed with relief for all the city's good government forces that Medalie showed no inclination to be a "political prosecutor," and a college friend of the new chief assistant wrote flattering congratulations. "I know you will acquit yourself with great credit, and who knows but what some day you may be Governor, or mayhap President."[10]

At the end of March 1931, Dewey reported for work on the second floor of the old Post Office Building at 270 Lexington Avenue, a dissonant medley of Italian Renaissance and French mansard roof. A hundred and seventeen columns of Dix Island granite supported the fortresslike structure, which had taken nearly a decade to build and still carried iron bars and shutters as daunting reminders to those who might wish to re-enact the Civil War draft riots that engulfed New York in violence a few years before its construction. Inside, an old-fashioned cage elevator transported Tom to the oval office he occupied next to Medalie's. The Criminal Division, headed by Ed Lumbard, was also headquartered on the second floor, as was Samuel Coleman's Civil Division, charged with the dreary assignment of settling customs and contract disputes. Upstairs, Arthur Schwartz had the thankless task of enforcing Prohibition, with a separate division that, despite shortages of manpower, managed to suppress more than 900 speakeasies in 1931.[11]

In all, the staff numbered fifty-two lawyers, and, as chief assistant, Dewey was their nominal supervisor. He took the job seriously—too seriously for some. On most mornings, he arrived an hour ahead of the others, then prowled his gloomy old command post for similarly zealous colleagues. Anyone unwilling to put in sixteen hours a day, he informed the staff, "is putting one over on me." It wasn't an empty boast: After spotting one associate leaving the office at seven the previous night, he upbraided the same man for arriving at 9:45 A.M "Don't you know our office opens at nine-thirty?" he demanded.[12]

Dewey's actions betrayed his lack of interest in the chief assistant's traditional preoccupation with administrative detail. Barent Ten Eyck, a Columbia classmate, was brought in to read mail and greet visitors while his superior put his feet up on a desk and dictated a blizzard of precisely worded memos. All old files were to be ransacked and shifted to the chief assistant's office, where over 1,200 outstanding indictments, some dating to Benjamin Harrison's time, were uncovered. A drunken clerk was fired, and order brought to an unruly stenographic pool. Personal calls were discouraged as an impediment to efficiency. Newspapermen were asked to keep mum about impending investigations.[13]

Secrecy, Medalie made clear, was to be their most potent weapon in the war on crime. There would be no announcements before indictments were ready, and leaks from inside the Post Office Building would be plugged by the simple expedient of evicting the army of bail bondsmen who hovered there like vultures, eager to pass on the smallest scrap of news to their allies in the underworld. A host of rules forbade photographs of any assistant with any defendant, outside practice, or independent contacts with the press. Aggressiveness was to be the hallmark of Medalie's office, imagination its prerequisite for success.

"We are not sludges or political hacks," he reminded the staffers. At their command were all the forces of federal justice, from FBI agents to Post Office inspectors and the Narcotics Squad. There was no such thing as overpreparation, he preached. Neither should the men be afraid to delay action when such delay might enhance the psychological climate favoring conviction. He taught them to freeze witnesses, a legal blitzkrieg in which every conceivable witness was rounded up and presented to a grand jury, thus committing them to stories that could only be changed under risk of a perjury charge. By the time defense lawyers reached the same witness, they were long since imprisoned by their own immediate recollections.[14]

Medalie asked his men to take a view of the grand jury as broad as its powers of investigation. It should be treated as an ally in a campaign in which petty crooks would be indicted mostly for the assistance they could offer in pursuing and convicting the real criminal powers. Through contempt citations, and charges of conspiracy or obstruction of justice, the U.S. Attorney was determined to pry open the lips of drones in the underworld army, and take up a trail that would inevitably lead to the big fry. To his youthful staff—Dewey, at twenty-nine, was typical of the men around Medalie, men young enough to be ambitious yet without constraining ties—Medalie promised no lack of drama. But even that would be sifted and analyzed for its potential impact upon a jury. Heterogeneous as his staffers might be, they were united by a certain soberness of mien, a whiff of the crusader's ardor, and a tireless emulation of their boss's concern with facts.

Medalie had his own pet phrase for the single telling detail that might, properly presented and polished, excite a jury's outrage, sweeping aside in one electric moment their previous confusion or hesitancy. "How do we put a ruby nose on it?" he asked. Before long, his chief assistant, who patronized Medalie's tailor and copied the older man's habit of tossing coins in the air as he spoke, developed his own more prosaic question for investigators reporting in their findings. "What's the dirt in the situation?" he inquired. What followed was likely to be an exercise in frustration for the hardworking gumshoe.[15]

"Dewey was the perfectionist to end all perfectionists," remembered one federal agent who worked closely with him in probing the Harlem policy game. "His thoroughness is beyond description. . . . An agent, his briefcase jammed with the results of a good and thorough investigation, would meet with him. . . . The confident agent would disclose the situation, explain all the documents, and offer his opinion that the evidence was sufficient to convict."

Dewey would peruse what had been gathered, and stare off into space, lips pursed in a quizzical smile. Then, like a wild animal anticipating his dinner, he would pounce, "and methodically tear the perfectly good evidence to shreds with about a million questions, give or take ten. Wearily, the agent would leave, determined to get more."

Piling certainty upon proof, the chief assistant refused to halt the process even after a defendant indicated willingness to plead guilty. "We want to be ready if he changes his mind," he told exasperated agents.

Sometimes Dewey's obsessive pursuit of facts, like his perfectionism, bordered on the absurd. There was an office boy named Sidney who was asked a series of questions about what time he mailed some of Medalie's letters. The boy answered in general terms, but Dewey pressed for the precise moment. Finally, Sidney said he'd mailed the letters on his way to meet the 5:15 P.M train—just before the train left, in fact.

"Thank you," Dewey concluded. "That makes it five-thirteen."

Another time, Jacob Grumet, like most of Medalie's assistants a Columbia graduate, was asked in to compose a letter to the Attorney General in Washington, setting forth the facts in a case the U.S. Attorney wished to drop for lack of proof. Grumet was to draft a formal request to the Justice Department, then take it personally to Washington for official approval. Several pages long, and complex, the letter took most of a day to write. When it was finished, it was brought to Medalie and Dewey for review. The chief assistant began to edit it with his usual insistence upon the ideal, suggesting a different word here, a more erudite phrase there.

Finally, Medalie interrupted. "Look, Tom, I'm not interested in whether the letter is rhetorically perfect. I want him to get all the facts down; if we go and start changing words, it could take all day. Let's get the thing out."[16]

Some thought Dewey brusque and arrogant. At lunch with an old friend shortly after his appointment was announced, the conversation turned to historical greatness, and the dangers of an overactive ego. Self-confidence was one thing, Dewey's companion asserted, necessary so that others would believe in you. But conceit was quite another, a malignant force that could spoil the entire effect. Dewey agreed halfheartedly, but then offered his own dissent. "If you stop to think about it," he mused, "all the great men we've been talking about were conceited."[17]

Others chalked up his bulldog manner to precocity, and the natural vulnerability of one so young that he dressed in chesterfields and sober homburgs to erase the boyishness of his appearance and manner. "I am a youngster," Dewey told his own staff when he was District Attorney of New York County seven years later, "and I remember it very sharply when I am dealing with senior members of the bar. . . . I remember it every minute." But he was happy, and modest too, as he made plain in a letter written less than two weeks after taking the oath of office. "This is the most fascinating job I've ever had," he informed a well-wisher, "and I am trying hard to learn something about it."[18]

Meanwhile, as Dewey settled in at 270 Lexington Avenue, a crescendo of violence overtook criminal society, and new leaders surged forward to streamline the underworld as never before. Rothstein was dead, but he bequeathed a generation of successors who shared his organizational talent and larger than life ambition. The older gangsters—"Mustache Petes," in Lucky Luciano's derisive phrase—were sensitive to the threat, and responded with savage tactics to maintain the status quo. Lucky himself was taken for a ride one night in October 1929 to a Staten Island warehouse, where he was suspended by his thumbs and had his throat nearly slashed through, probably by Salvatore Maranzano himself.

In the aftermath of his brush with death, Lucania ("Luciano" found its way into common usage at the time of his trial in 1936) entered a convenient alliance with Joe Masseria, a pact that lasted only as long as Charley's self-interest permitted. On April 15, 1931, he climbed into Joe the Boss's steel-plated sedan, rolled up the two-inch-thick plate-glass windows that shielded Masseria from attack, and drove out to the new Coney Island restaurant of Gerardo Scarpato, a friend who was active in the Surf Democratic Club. The two men dined there—Lucky abominated Masseria's wolfish table manners—and then Lucania excused himself to go to the men's room. As he did, five gunmen materialized in the courtyard. Masseria went down, his fleshy figure pockmarked with bullet holes. In his left hand he clutched an ace of spades.

The Boss went to his grave in style, in a $15,000 casket, beneath fragrant floral clocks set to the precise hour of his death, 3:20 P.M. With his rival's body barely cold, Maranzano convened a meeting of the Unione Sicilione to proclaim himself the new boss—capo di tutti capi. But Lucania had not forgotten his nocturnal ride, nor had time banked the fires of his own ambition. Five months after Joe the Boss died, four fresh recruits dressed as plainclothes detectives strolled into Maranzano's real estate office, his Park Avenue front, and directed the student of Caesar into another room, ostensibly to frisk and question him. Bo Weinberg, a professional hit man and associate of Dutch Schultz, did the shooting, then rid himself of the murder weapon by dropping it in the jacket pocket of a homeward-bound commuter inside the frantic concourse of Grand Central Station.

Within the underworld, Lucky Luciano was easily identified as the unseen hand behind Weinberg's trigger. In the months after Maranzano's death, he moved quickly and skillfully to consolidate his position, personally visiting outposts of the Unione and hastening to explain the new democratic methods by which it would be run. Like a modern corporate executive, Lucky would cast a vote at board meetings equal to any other, but would also set the style and tone for the entire organization. Only a handful of New Yorkers might recognize his name or his record in 1931. Soon, millions of them would feel the expensive effects of Lucky's shadow government.

Having rid himself of the U.S. Attorney's office's humdrum details, Dewey now gravitated toward the courtroom. Medalie believed in entrusting assistants with as much responsibility as they could handle—letting them sink or swim, as he put it. And with the Seabury probe almost daily uncovering new cases of municipal corruption, an activist U.S. attorney was bound to prosecute his share of lawbreakers left untouched by Tammany's own district attorney.

In mid-April, Dewey secured an indictment against James J. Quinliven, a plump, ruddy-faced veteran of the Vice Squad, whose personal enforcement of the Volstead Act was presumably compromised by his ownership of a speakeasy called the Nedana Club on 125th Street. Handed the case as a baptism of fire, the chief assistant devoted most of the summer to preparing it, then, when the trial finally began in September, warned the jury that the Quinliven affair "goes down into the sewers of the city." As his chief witness, Dewey called Harry Levy, an unsavory police informer and criminal errand boy who had, for fifty dollars a week, served Quinliven as chauffeur and collector. What he collected, it turned out, was $7,500 a month in bribes paid by speakeasies and brothels to protect themselves from the cops.

The defense attorney, James D. C. Murray, assailed Levy's credibility. In Murray's hyperbolic words, "He is as slimy an individual as it will ever be your misfortune to listen to." But Dewey had the last word. To buttress Levy's testimony, he introduced the incontrovertible evidence of bank records, reviewed over many weeks with the help of Hugh McQuillian, chief of the Intelligence Unit of the IRS. Handwriting experts were called in to compare Quinliven's signature on his police check with the penmanship of one S. A. Duffey, whose account at the First National Bank exactly matched the deposits and withdrawals attributed to Levy's patron. Sure enough, the experts testified, the two handwritings were identical—and the noose tightened around Quinliven's neck.

Desperately, Murray ridiculed Dewey's case as unproved, because he hadn't produced a single speakeasy owner to swear to the payment of bribes. Besides, the court lacked jurisdiction, as the alleged crimes took place in Brooklyn. Ridiculous, Dewey snorted; did anyone ever hear of a speakeasy owner standing up to announce himself as such? The jurisdictional dispute was similarly brushed aside, and the jury retired, to return with a guilty verdict and a three-year term at the federal penitentiary in Atlanta for the miscreant patrolman. Within a week of Quinliven's conviction, forty bootleggers, including seven of his police colleagues, materialized at the federal building to pay back taxes.

It was Dewey's first victory before a jury, the Empire Trust case having been won on appeal. As important as the verdict was his justification of Medalie's faith, an evident flair for organizing facts and a talent for giving coherence to numbers beyond ordinary comprehension. Tom was learning how to give a case a ruby nose. In the process, he opened the way for assignments of greater scope and potential for professional growth.

Five days after Quinliven was indicted, Dewey was dispatched to Washington to confer with an assistant attorney general over a wave of complaints against the American Bond and Mortgage Company. American Bond was the brainchild of a former bricklayer named William J. Moore, who transformed a small Chicago-based firm into a national business with a high-powered sales force and an expensive advertising campaign which promised, "No one ever lost a cent in American." The company sold bonds, millions of dollars' worth of them, which in turn allowed it to buy up mortgages and finance hotels, office buildings, and apartment houses.

For four months, Dewey pored over American's records. Behind its once glittering facade, he discovered a scrim of fraudulent claims and worthless promises. The Hudson Towers in New York was but one example. In 1922, a doctor named Leo Buerger had approached American Bond with a proposal to build a combination hospital-hotel, where wealthy patients could make a vacation out of an illness, and enrich Buerger and his medical colleagues in the bargain. The company shared his enthusiasm, and promised help. It sent its appraisers and engineers to estimate the value of the site and the cost of the Towers, and thereafter issued a mortgage in the amount of $1,600,000. It informed its investors that Dr. Buerger and his colleagues would invest a million dollars of their own. Actually, the doctors didn't have $70,000 in all. American then subtracted a 15 percent fee, leaving far too little to even finish the building or pay off a second mortgage.

In August 1931, Dewey completed a marathon presentation of the complicated case to a Manhattan grand jury. By then, he could point to $90 million in defaulting bonds (out of $160 million outstanding), and a string of foreclosure proceedings already under way. On August 25, the grand jury returned a seventeen-count indictment, charging the Moores with mail fraud and conspiracy in thirty-four separate bond issues. Then, having done the investigative spadework, Dewey turned the entire case over to a special assistant attorney general in Washington for trial.

There was a wealth of work in Medalie's office to keep him busy. In a landmark case against the Manhattan Electrical Supply Company, Uncle Sam's lawyers convicted stock manipulators of inflating prices from twenty dollars per share to fifty-six before selling out en masse, bilking honest investors in the process of $10 million. The prosecutors also broke up the Diversified Corporation, a scam promising to make a feature film entitled *The Life of the Blessed Virgin*, but not until its officers had taken more than $5 million out of the pockets of former governor Al Smith and Roman Catholic cardinals, as well as devout altar boys and housewives.

There were front page cases aplenty, none more electrifying than the capture and conviction of Arnold Rothstein's onetime bodyguard, Legs Diamond. In the first week of August, with Medalie vacationing in Canada, Dewey was left to call the shots. Defense attorneys offered to plead guilty in return for a reduced sentence, but the chief assistant instructed Arthur Schwartz, who had overall supervision of the case, to reject the deal out of hand and proceed with his prosecution. Diamond was convicted of operating an upstate still, and before going on the docket in other pending cases, he asked to be let out on bail for a final taste of freedom. Schwartz argued strongly against it, but Legs got his wish.[19]

A few days later, lying drunk in a Catskill motel room, he proved an easy target for Bo Weinberg, the ubiquitous assassin, sent by Dutch Schultz to rub out his rival. It was the latest battle, one-sided and bloody, in a criminal War of the Roses that temporarily thinned mob ranks even while swelling the coffers of New York's tabloids.

· · ·

The politics on Dewey's mind at this time was less personal than paternalistic, the elevated desire of the Young Republican Club "to correct in our own party the tendency of all parties to make organization an end rather than a means . . . to resist and expose political corruption, to advocate merit rather than partisan service as entitling to public office." What saved such a scientific approach from tepid do-goodism was Tammany's own public excesses. A vast amount of unclean laundry was being washed in Seabury's probes, and Dewey was one of many reformers stung by what they saw and heard into demanding that the municipal rug be lifted still higher.[20]

"I am frequently nauseated by it," he wrote of the machine's overpowering embrace, "and am always disgusted by it. Yet we cannot abandon the fight." Initially, that meant joining forces with alienated New Yorkers as congenitally repugnant as Norman Thomas and the *Daily Worker,* in calling for a deeper investigation by Judge Seabury into the Walker administration and the Mayor's own increasingly reckless conduct. The Governor of New York, Franklin Roosevelt, had his eye on the 1932 Democratic presidential nomination, and thus no desire to offend either Tammany or its reigning mayor. FDR wished the issue would go away.[21]

Dewey wished the opposite. That summer, he teamed up with Herbert Brownell, who received from Republican elders the right to seek an unattainable Assembly seat, as one way of publicizing the GOP's pressure upon Governor Roosevelt to act. Brownell made support of Seabury the cornerstone of his crusade, while Dewey concentrated on reviving a weary organization populated largely by grizzled veterans prone to golden reminiscence about TR and Taft. Nostalgia was never part of Dewey's makeup. Soon he replaced the old men with aggressive young ones, each assigned a different neighborhood. He handled finances himself, scheduled the candidate, and drummed up publicity.

"He never wasted time chewing the rag," Brownell said later. "He was a busy fellow. He gave you the impression of having a goal, and getting there fast, and if you were kind of a drag on it, or didn't quite follow what he was saying . . . he sort of didn't bother with you anymore."[22]

It may have cost him some personal popularity, but in organizational terms Tom was moving mountains. In the daytime, he put in a full load with Medalie, then spent evenings and weekends mastering campaign strategy and details. Frances wasn't spared; she led two dozen women and a district captain in door-to-door appeals for Brownell and civic virtue. Her husband matched her efforts call for call—on the telephone, which he preferred to doorstep conferences with voters. When the votes were tallied in November, Brownell had been narrowly defeated. The professionals were impressed.

On Election Day, Dewey and his friends scoured the streets in search of Democratic floaters brought over via the Staten Island ferry to augment the usual Tammany vote. They found polling places swarming with gangsters, members of the Dutch Schultz mob who used physical intimidation when verbal threats didn't suffice. A few days later, Brownell's manager accepted an invitation to speak before the Harlem Republican club, in which he was also asked to put an end to conditions "which make it possible for beer-runners to flood Polling Places with gangsters, to make policemen disappear, and also to add to the Campaign Chest of the Tammany Organization."[23]

With his own eyes, the chief assistant U.S. attorney had seen enough to convince him that such an appeal did not rest upon electoral sour grapes. One of his best friends, Carl Newton, was kicked down a flight of stairs for daring to challenge fraudulent voting in one mob-ridden district. Within nine months, Mayor Walker would tender his resignation, flee to Europe, and redeem the promises made to New York by Judge Seabury. By then, Tom Dewey was immersed in his own twisting, often tantalizing pursuit of criminals and galvanized by an indistinct but ominous alliance for profit between the politicians of Tammany and the mobsters epitomized by the mousy, unglamorous figure of Arthur Flegenheimer.

After he became famous, Herman Flegenheimer's son Arthur, also known as Dutch Schultz, said he changed his name to that of a locally revered street puncher because the name he was born with would not fit into the headlines. Schultz wasn't like other mob leaders, who swaggered around New York like petit monarchs. For one thing, he hadn't grown up on the Lower East Side, but as the son of a Bronx saloonkeeper who deserted his family when Dutch was fourteen. (Later, Dutch insisted his father hadn't run out, but died.)

Dutch's mother, a devout Jew, supported her family by taking in laundry. Young Arthur was encouraged to peddle newspapers and deliver groceries. To the end of his life, he carried a membership card in the roofers' union, a pathetic souvenir of the respectability he craved. As a fledgling bootlegger, he liked to be at work by eight in the morning. He avoided society gatherings at which he was exhibited as a novelty; he called newspapermen "sir" and once upbraided the city's paper of record for suggesting in print that he was a sucker for pretty blondes. Yes, he readily acknowledged, the story was true, but that was beside the point. "That's no kind of language to go in the New York *Times*."

But Schultz was quietly lethal. When trapped in a gangland war with Vincent "Mad Dog" Coll early in 1931, Dutch took advantage of his organizational instincts—and well-greased friendship with the police—to finally eliminate the murderous upstart. Coll was as violent a figure as Schultz was cautious, no boardroom mobster but a street terrorist who came alive behind a gun. In one shootout in July 1931, Mad Dog had killed a five-year-old child and wounded four other innocents caught in the crossfire. Coll's savagery was likely to give bootlegging a bad name, so Schultz sent for the faithful Bo Weinberg; and, when Bo failed to bring down his target, he planted agents inside his enemy's own camp.

As it happened, Vinnie was in close contact with Owney Madden, another mobster, whose "Madden's Number One" was widely regarded as the best home brew in New York. One day Madden was sitting in a phone booth at the Cotton Club, a favorite hangout, when he felt a nudge in his ribs. Looking up, he found a small corps of Schultz lieutenants. "Keep him talking," they ordered. "Don't let him hang up." A friendly cop traced the call to another phone booth in a Chelsea drugstore, while other Schultz henchmen were dispatched to do their bloody work. Within minutes, Madden could hear the rattle of machine gun fire on the other end of the line. Vinnie Coll was dead, and the way cleared for Schultz to re-emerge and lay claim to a new and potentially vast enterprise that the prescient gangster, anticipating an early end to Prohibition, had already staked out for himself.

With the Depression in its third autumn, and jobs scarcer than ever, millions of New Yorkers found a cheap diversion in the daily numbers game, a poor man's sport more formally dubbed "policy." Policy was gambling on the cheap, for the masses, in which a player chose any combination of three digits, and wagered anything from a penny up. In the years just before World War I, when policy was new, the daily numbers on which winnings were figured came from the city's bank clearinghouse. Later, as the game skyrocketed in popularity, payoff totals from racetracks were used.

The game's appeal reached phenomenal levels, and by the early 1930s there were perhaps 15,000 New Yorkers working as "collectors," gathering up bets placed in tenement houses and butcher shops, candy stores and Harlem churches, for delivery to "bankers," the game's well-heeled supervisors. It was a sport preying especially hard on destitute blacks, who were already being dunned by an itinerant evangelist preacher named Father Divine. Father Divine's followers hailed him as God, and many trailed after him when he forsook Harlem to establish his kingdom on a Hudson Valley estate across from President Roosevelt's at Hyde Park, sold to him by a spiteful Republican.

But policy was a business fraught with very special perils. By the early 1930s, it was mostly the province of a few West Indian blacks, men like Henry Miro, Wilfred Brunder, and Spasm Ison. From elaborate suites, they oversaw their profitable empires, which grew to include apartment buildings and neighborhood grocery stores. They wore flashy diamonds and drove around in long limousines. Their business proved vulnerable to one law only—the law of chance. The day before Thanksgiving 1931, enshrined in policy circles as Black Wednesday, thousands of Harlem bettors consulted dream books or a hunch and simultaneously bet on the number 527.

When 527 came up at the Coney Island Racetrack in Cincinnati, the bankers were threatened with their own miniature Crash. Ison lost $18,000 that day and Alexander Pompez, another mainstay of policy, was hit for $68,000. So it was a crippled industry that Dutch Schultz, newly freed from the threat of Mad Dog Coll, moved in on in February 1932. The precise details of his takeover wouldn't come out in court for more than six years. When they did, they would rock New York and catapult Tom Dewey to the very doorstep of the White House. But even now, there were those on the street who knew that the Dutchman was taking over, dispersing scattered resistance at the point of a gun.

Henry Miro, typical of the bankers, was coolly informed that failure to pay Schultz $500 a week from his numbers income would lead to violence, perhaps terminal violence. A black woman known in the neighborhood as Madame Queen of Policy even took out newspaper ads alleging a corrupt bargain between politicians and criminals in the underworld, squeezing out the independent bankers. But threats proved a powerful incentive, even for the traditionally feisty entrepreneurs of policy. Before the year was out, Schultz had established a combination; the bankers that were gathered under his authority forked over funds with which to bribe police and politicians, and numbers players within a 200-mile radius were enriching the Dutchmen as bootleg beer had never done. Twenty million dollars a year, according to reliable sources, flowed from the pockets of the poor into the accounts of Herman Flegenheimer's star-crossed boy.

Except for the fact that it was all illegal, it was the kind of rags to riches tale that Frank Merriwell himself couldn't have resisted.

New York's District Attorney did nothing. However, the Hoover administration launched its own war on organized crime. Whatever his failures as a popular leader, Herbert Hoover encouraged innovation when it came to prosecuting underworld kingpins, almost grateful that one enemy, at least, could be made to respond and suffer for its misdeeds. The economy might remain beyond his control, but Hoover and his Treasury agents threw Al Capone behind bars. Fresh statutes broadened federal authority in the crime-fighting field, as bank stickups and the kidnapping and murder of Charles Lindbergh's son outraged the public and inspired an all-out counterattack.

The imaginative prosecutor, armed with new laws redefining federal offenses, from tax fraud to transporting stolen autos across state lines, might hope to convict the smartest criminals if he could force the silent witnesses—bank records, deposit slips, income tax forms—to speak loudly enough in court. One of Medalie's first acts as U.S. Attorney was to deputize his chief assistant to head up a secret division within the office, a team of forty IRS agents and accountants who would work full time in pursuit of major gangsters vulnerable to tax evasion charges. The first area to be investigated was policy, and especially those calling the shots in policy in New York.

Within a month, Henry Miro was indicted for evading taxes on more than a million dollars. Knowing that Joe Panuch was a friend of the U.S. Attorney's, Miro asked Panuch to work out a deal with Medalie. Medalie and Dewey agreed to let Miro write his own ticket as to a plea in exchange for only one thing.

"Look," Dewey snapped at Panuch, "we're after one guy. We're after Hines."[24]

James J. Hines, the dapper straw-hatted blacksmith's son and leader of the Eleventh District, was the most powerful single man in Tammany Hall. He was, moreover, a political ally of Governor Roosevelt's, and an offstage operator who hadn't deposited a check in his own name since 1907. Hines liked to remind aspiring politicians, "The thing to do is build yourself an army. Get an army, boy, get an army; and if you've got one already, get another one."

Warily, Panuch transmitted the offer to his client, who gasped. "Christ, my life wouldn't be worth a nickel. I'll pay you ten thousand dollars for what you've done, and goodbye. I'll go in the pen."

Panuch couldn't know that, in going after the policy bankers,

Dewey had discovered explosive evidence. A long list of expensive gifts handed out by Henry Miro was being compiled, proving among other things that the man who claimed no income between 1927 and 1930 had bought at least forty-two suits during the same period. In the course of the slow, painstaking reconstruction of Miro's spending spree, agents had come across slips showing the purchase of fifteen-dollar silk shirts, monogrammed a dozen at a time, and sent with Miro's best wishes to a Mr. J. J. Hines. Similar records showed more shirts dispatched to Tammany minions at the Owasco Club, and still others to "the Honorable Dutch Schultz."

Tantalizing as the lead was, it was followed by no hard evidence to link Hines and Schultz, and thereby confirm the suspicions of both Medalie and Dewey that the Tammany boss was cooperating in making Harlem and other neighborhoods safe for the new gang leader and his game. Moreover, Miro refused to cooperate, choosing instead to be convicted and go to jail, for Dewey had built an air-tight case.

Dewey learned to enjoy the cat and mouse game of pursuing and trapping wrongdoers. He learned that lethal testimony could be extracted from bank and telephone records, produced on order of the grand jury. He sent agents to tail suspects, relied on wiretaps and handwriting analysis, and developed graphics that might dramatize an otherwise confusing collection of paper proof. In the courtroom itself, he was discovering his depth, finding that a voice trained for the stage could be even more effective in cross-examining a hostile or forgetful witness. From Medalie he picked up an emphasis on facts instead of Victorian oratory, and a sotto voce delivery that, in his mentor's case, had once brought a judge down from his bench with the explanation, "I'd like to hear what this is all about, too." Dewey learned how to lull a witness with gentle reassurances, before verbally locking the door when contradictions arose in his testimony. In summing up a case, his voice would rise in a theatrical aria of damning proof, his eyes would burn like glowing coals, and he would appeal to and flatter the jury as the guardian of community decency.[25]

Increasingly, Dewey and his colleagues were focusing their efforts on a new kind of crime and a new kind of criminal who masqueraded behind the appearance of legality. The word "racket" was coming into the public jargon. In Chaucer's time, it had defined a game of dice. Shakespeare applied it to disorderly conduct. In nine-teenth-century Britain, it meant certain kinds of fraud. In America, a racket was taken to mean a noisy disturbance or public commotion. But to the crime fighter, rackets were far more sinister. Step-children of the Depression, they were criminal reincarnations of trusts, Teddy Roosevelt's old blood clots in the economic arteries of America that had been outlawed in theory since 1890.

George Medalie defined the innocent beginnings of a racket in tickets sold to a dance at a fixed price, or protection against street gangs sought by a small shopkeeper. In hiring a rival gang, the busi-nessman unwittingly set off a vicious circle in which capital and labor alike fell victim to an underworld Frankenstein's monster. In its classic form, the racket operated simultaneously to secure obedi-ence from unions and the business world. By using physical force where threats didn't work, racketeers first narrowed the field of competition. Phony "trade associations" were established, and prices inflated through monopoly of production or distribution. Lawyers were hired to advise the associations, which resembled le-gitimate businesses in structure and perquisites. Labor was co-opted by the same campaign of physical terror, as thugs moved into unions and took them over by stuffing ballot boxes or literally holding guns at the heads of honest leaders. Some rackets were petty, like the Pea-nut Vendors' Association, which collected five dollars a month from members after 1929. Others were outrageous, like the Physicians and Surgeons' Economic League, organized by Chicago doctors in an effort to keep prices high and bar indigents from receiving medi-cal treatment.

With Prohibition enriching the underworld's coffers, and millions of dollars crying out for reinvestment, racketeers moved in to take over ordinary industries and jack up the cost of consumer goods. The United Seafood Workers, led by Socks Lanza, imposed an extra tax on every shipment of fresh fish that passed through the Fulton Street Fish Market. The critical artery of transportation was espe-cially vulnerable to the racketeer, who, even if he had too few men to occupy every aspect of shipping, from wholesalers to retailers, could still cripple the industry by controlling the truckers who pro-vided a vital link in the whole process by which goods reached the marketplace.

In this way, even the artichoke business had become a million-dollar racket. For years artichokes had entered New York through six commission houses, which sold them at wholesale to retail gro-cers, vegetable stores, and pushcart peddlers. In 1929, retailers began to get anonymous phone calls warning them against using existing markets, and directing them to buy only from a new firm, Union Pacific Produce. Union Pacific, in turn, was attempting to corner the city's entire supply and was slapping a fifty-cent tax on every box, passing the increase on to retailers and consumers. Physical violence enforced the monopoly, including at least one incident in which a truck driver was stopped on the road and beaten, while his load of produce was dumped and his vehicle smashed.

All of this emerged in vivid imagery during the trial of Joseph Castaldo, known to friends and frightened grocers alike as the Artichoke King. Dewey unraveled the racket within the context of a tax evasion prosecution. Castaldo's lawyer was not happy. "Is this a vegetable trial," he demanded, "or an income tax trial?" He was less happy still when the chief assistant paraded forty bookkeepers to the stand, spelling out in minute detail the scope of Castaldo's illegal business and the bank deposits that followed. By the second morning of the trial, the Artichoke King had had enough and pleaded guilty. Preparation had carried the day for Dewey. Another racket had been exposed.

By this time, Judge Seabury was probing District Attorney Thomas Crain, whose own investigation of rackets was a desultory affair, consisting mostly of moves against the school yearbook trade and the posting of a sign reading "Complaint Room," over an empty corner of his offices. The judge rendered a mixed verdict on Crain, concluding that the D.A. of New York County was probably personally honest, but also woefully ineffective in doing anything about racketeering.

Some forty cases a day rolled down the legal assembly line in the old Post Office Building: so much work that additional judges had to be imported from other federal districts to handle the load. Indians came to the U.S. Attorney demanding wages from a circus. President Roosevelt's decision to take the nation off the gold standard had to be defended. Communist propaganda had to be suppressed without damage to civil liberties. In March of 1933, the president of the Macmillan publishing company called upon Dewey, bearing with him a copy of an as-yet-unpublished book detailing secrets of American military code breakers. Dewey immediately impounded the manuscript for presentation to a sitting grand jury, before acting as intermediary between its author, a disgruntled former State Department employee seeking a formal apology for his abrupt firing, and the new Secretary of State, Cordell Hull. In the end, he succeeded in getting a letter of regret from the secretary, and potentially harmful information was kept out of the public realm.[26]

With a new administration taking power in Washington in March 1933, it appeared it wouldn't be long before Dewey's prophecy

about being swept out of office would come true. But George Medalie enjoyed a friendly personal relationship with Franklin Roosevelt,
and the New Deal seemed in no hurry to discharge the U.S. Attorney in New York. Dewey himself was concentrating more and more
of his attention on rackets, about which his office had received 2,500
complaints and which seemed to be multiplying like beetles on a
leaf, with the same destructive impact upon the city's shrunken
economy.

In a confidential report to his Washington superiors in August,
the chief assistant argued against giving rackets and racketeers further publicity, lest their leverage over businesses and unions actually
be increased. As for the extent of racket control, Dewey reported
that it was virtually impossible to find a slice of the city's commercial life not crawling with extortionists and payoff men. Grapes, fish,
chicken, and milk—all were being held hostage by thugs who demanded exorbitant payments for unloading or delivering each product. Delicatessens and laundries were falling under racket control.
The unions were honeycombed with racketeers, mindless of their
members' welfare as long as they got their under-the-table take.
Schultz, moving successfully to take over the policy game, was in a
perfect position to finance still further expansion of racketeering.

Nationally, it was estimated that rackets in the United States were
draining off $11 billion from the legitimate economy. In New York
alone, they were said to raise the average cost of living by 20 percent.
Yet, evident as they were, rackets were difficult to prosecute. Threats
of violence rendered usually honest businessmen or union leaders
mute or downright supportive. Bribes neutralized the police, and
Tammany's own somnolent district attorneys didn't even bother to
look the other way.

To break apart a single racket, Dewey estimated, would take half
a dozen men six to twelve months of full-time labor. Multiply that
by every racket in the city—and Judge Seabury was being typically
conservative in estimating that number at thirty—and law enforcement officials would have time for nothing else. Dewey concluded
that the racketeers must be severed from their base of political invincibility. They must be forced into the daylight, there to wither under
the scrutiny of young, aggressive prosecutors in a D.A.'s office that
owed nothing to any political machine.[27]

He could not conceive, in August 1933, that his comprehensive
memo would be turned into a personal blueprint, or that he himself
would be called upon by a desperate city to rescue it before the criminal leeches bled it white.

4

The Baby Prosecutor

With a jury, nothing is so boring as extended reasoning, unless it's sugar-coated. You've got to give them a sort of motion picture of the evidence.

—GEORGE Z. MEDALIE

My only vices are good clothes and a beautiful home.

—WAXEY GORDON

In September 1932, the Republicans of New York offered George Medalie their nomination for United States Senator, to run against a popular incumbent, Robert F. Wagner, in a year when Hoover and his Depression were tarring nearly every candidate with an R beside his name. Inauspicious as his prospects seemed, Medalie took on the job in the interest of the party, left the public payroll for the duration of the campaign, and invited his chief assistant to manage the effort, in fact if not in title. Once again, Dewey found himself juggling hats. Each day, he worked at 270 Lexington Avenue. Most nights, he planned campaign strategy and saw to its execution until midnight. For an editor's son from Owosso, it proved a crash course in the infighting of big-city politics.

Tammany Hall, for instance, took to distributing leaflets in Jewish neighborhoods asserting that Medalie was not Jewish but Portuguese. In response, Dewey booked time for his candidate on the foreign-language radio broadcasts that made the dial in New York an international bazaar of different tongues. He also devised scenarios to make Medalie's radio advertising more credible. "This is to be by a newspaper reporter," he wrote for one commercial interrupting the *Polish Hour,* "who is welcomed into the hour and has just come from Medalie's headquarters and is so enthusiastic about him and he wants to tell the people . . ."[1]

Dewey's appreciation of ethnic sensibilities, which Medalie would heighten with the years, was little developed in 1932. In one radio text he polished the theme of voter disenchantment with sandpaper.

"You and I know what it means not to have descended from the Americans who helped to found this country," an announcer confided. "We know it because, despite all of the Americanism we hear about and read about, there are still Americans among us who call us Hunkies, Heines, Chinks, Dagos, Wops, and Polacks."[2]

When not busy writing speeches or ad copy, Dewey answered Medalie's correspondence, selected photos for newspaper use, and directed others carrying the Republican cause throughout New York City. It was a terrible year to be a Republican, worsened by the violent dispersal of the Bonus Army of destitute World War I veterans camped out in the nation's capital. Some Hoover loyalists in the Young Republican Club pressed its Board of Governors for a public defense of the President's action. Disagreeing, Dewey counseled pragmatism. The Bonus March, he wrote, "is stone dead for political purposes, and I think it should be left in its grave ... we should close this chapter as quickly and silently as possible."[3]

But no amount of judicious silence could halt the Democratic juggernaut that swept America in November 1932. Roosevelt and Wagner crushed Hoover and Medalie in New York by more than 800,000 votes. "The result is a sad one," Dewey told a friend, "but it seems to have been in the cards. You can't stand up against a whirlwind. All you can do is give it a fine fight." About the only consolation to be found in the post-election rubble was Herbert Brownell's upset victory in a State Assembly contest, snatched from the Democrats by 307 votes. It was a hopeful sign for younger, more aggressive members of the GOP.[4]

Meanwhile, in the hectic closing days of Medalie's Senate campaign, on October 2, 1932, Frances Dewey had borne a son, christened Thomas, Jr. The proud father rose each morning at six to give the child its bottle and enjoy what little time with him his political and investigative careers permitted. During one especially rushed period, when Dewey was deeply immersed in the case of Waxey Gordon, he showed up for dinner at home precisely three times in four months. Fortunately, Frances plunged enthusiastically into the rituals of motherhood.

In any decade but the 1920s, Waxey Gordon's jaundiced skin, sullen eyes, and ungrammatical English would have assured him deserved obscurity. But Prohibition extended a hand of opportunity to such a man, paid for the gray oxford suits and pearl-colored fedoras with which the bootlegger draped his doughy frame. Prohibition turned the two-bit East Side criminal into a public enemy of tragicomic proportions. Born Irving Wexler in 1886, Waxey first landed in jail as a nineteen-year-old pickpocket. From there, he drifted into Dopey Benny Fein's gang, was indicted along with other gang members in the shooting death of an elderly clerk in the crossfire between Fein and rival Chuck Trigger, beat the rap, and became a bookmaker who alternated lavish seasons with dead months in a jail cell. He learned caution the hard way when he was convicted of shipping a trunk of cocaine disguised as luggage from Chicago to New York, after his signature was found on a baggage receipt. Thereafter, Gordon never affixed his name to any document if he could avoid it.

Waxey spent two years in Sing Sing, secured financing from Arnold Rothstein to open fifty flop joints—where for three-dollars customers could smoke opium and sleep—and married the daughter of an East Side rabbi. By the early 1920s, he had a gang of his own, picking pockets and pushing dope. Gordon's men also pimped for girls in the Fourth Avenue Hotel. His top henchmen included Max Hassel, who had a taste for real estate, and Max Greenberg, a former river hijacker in his native St. Louis, who left that crime-infested city during a murderous struggle for dominance between Egan's Rats and Hynn's Jelly Rolls.

Another hotel, the Piccadilly, joined Gordon's growing portfolio, along with a fashionable nightclub and, after the Crash, three breweries across the river in northern New Jersey. In March 1930, Waxey moved into Suite 109 of Paterson's Alexander Hamilton Hotel, lately occupied by Bugs Donovan and his gang. With Prohibition promising fabulous wealth to the visionary, or the faster gun, men like Gordon were inevitably attracted. Donovan's breweries, which had operated under the friendly eyes of authorities in Union City and Hoboken, as well as Paterson, now fell into the hands of a stronger, more ruthless adversary.

With Gordon in charge, the smokestacks at the Eureka Cereal Beverage Company belched twenty-four hours a day, and cash poured in, refreshing as a tall glass of Waxey's brew. Flushed with his profits, the gangster began comporting himself like a reputable businessman, wintering at the mob mecca of Hot Springs, betting on horses at Palm Beach and Saratoga. Waxey soon owned three Pierce-Arrows and a Lincoln, sent his son Theodore to Staunton Military Academy, and became a Broadway angel.

On non-theatrical evenings, Gordon retreated to his suite at the Piccadilly, stuffed doorways with cotton and muffled windows with heavy blankets, the better to saturate the air with opium's dull euphoria. When he felt domestic, the bootlegger repaired to his ten-room apartment at 590 West End Avenue on Manhattan's West Side. There he built and stocked a handsome library with $4,200 worth of unopened books, including crushed-leather sets of Dickens,

Thackeray, Cooper, and Twain, and retained a half-dozen domestic servants.

Waxey lived as well as he did because he provided goods and services much in demand, and because he had a very bad memory whenever income tax time rolled around. In 1930 and 1931, as Dewey would demonstrate, Gordon had taken in over $4.5 million from his hotels, breweries, and nightclub. In 1930, he paid a federal tax of $10.76. A year later, suspicious of the IRS agents Dewey had tailing him, Waxey asked for and received an extension, then he filed a single-line return estimating his income for the year at $35,000.

But those who live by the sword die by it, and with Prohibition's days clearly limited—beer had been legalized in April 1933—the bootleggers were confronting a violent scramble for survival in a shrinking market. For Gordon, that meant taking on Dutch Schultz, whose Yonkers brewery was the cutting edge of an all-out assault, backed by a small army of sharpshooters eager to carry out the Dutchman's orders.

Schultz, to be sure, had his own problems. For many months, quietly, without publicity, Dewey and his task force had been combing records and talking to grand jury witnesses in an effort to trap Dutch on tax evasion charges. Bo Weinberg was called to testify, as was another strong-arm man named Rocco Delarmi; both were cited for contempt after refusing to tell what they knew. Schultz went on the lam, waiting for the day when a new U.S. attorney took office and he felt safe to return. Rumors had him globe-trotting from Paris to the Bahamas. In fact, he remained in New York, secure against local prosecution as long as he could afford to buy political protection, and with the policy racket making him $20,000 a day richer, that was unlikely to be a problem.

For now, Schultz's immediate objective was to defeat Waxey Gordon and take possession of the post-repeal liquor and beer market. On April 13, gunmen appeared in an Elizabeth, New Jersey, hotel, and shot both Hassell and Greenberg, while Gordon himself escaped death by taking refuge in bed with a fetching blonde named Nancy Presser. Before the afternoon was out, the bootlegger vanished, conceding that his decimated gang could no longer stand in Schultz's way. A few days later, more trouble appeared for Gordon, in a four-count indictment on tax evasion charges secured by Thomas Dewey. Waxey's known haunts were all searched, to no avail. Then a tip led agents to White Lake, a Catskill resort, where the underworld notable was found in a small cottage, a motorboat docked outside for a quick getaway.

If Dewey had seemed thoroughgoing in preparing earlier cases, his handling of the Gordon investigation was exhaustive. For thirty-three months, lawyers and Treasury agents under his supervision had worked two shifts a day seeking needles in an enormous paper haystack. Gordon had kept his bootleg money in more than 200 bank accounts, not one of which carried his name. Thus Dewey and his agents found themselves sifting over 200,000 deposit slips, piecing together earlier transactions, tracing wealth and its sources deeply camouflaged behind Gordon's subordinates. Five of his henchmen had been killed, one on the eve of a grand jury appearance. Yet the corpse in this instance was carrying a single deposit slip, and from this modest beginning Dewey and his men made investigative history.

Taking the transit number from the slip—a banker's code used to identify the bank on which a check is drawn—they unraveled obscure accounts and endorsements. Suspicious accounts were isolated and compared with other records. If withdrawals and deposits coincided, hunches were confirmed. It was a tedious process, offering no assurance of ultimate success. After twenty months of digging, a federal agent went to see Gordon and asked out loud: The fancy apartment, the extensive travel, fine schools, state-of-the-art automobiles—how was all this possible for one who had paid less than $100 in taxes over the previous three years?

"When you get your figures together so they prove something," Waxey said airily, "come on back and I'll be glad to talk to you."

But Dewey was probing far more than bank accounts. Subpoenas were being issued in droves, for Gordon's tailor, antique men, and interior decorators. The bootlegger's insurance agent revealed that the supposedly impoverished bookmaker carried $30,000 of protection against harm on the golf course. Over 100,000 telephone calls were being traced to and from contact points frequented by gang members. Handwriting was being analyzed, from letters, cleaning bills, rent receipts, auto loans, and sales slips. Dewey found records of brewing equipment sold to Gordon, along with repairs to electrical wiring and barrels at his brewery. In all, a thousand witnesses were interviewed; after a careful review of all the transcripts, the chief assistant chose 150 of the most damaging for presentation to the jury.

Putting together the vast mosaic of Gordon's enterprises took time—and caused problems. Bankers, desperate for accounts in

1933, willingly tipped off mobsters whenever federal agents appeared in the lobby. One bank treasurer went to jail for three months after refusing to hand over financial records sought by Dewey. Gordon's men bribed New Jersey police and politicians so that every time a Treasury agent set foot in Hoboken he was arrested and held on the pretext of carrying false credentials. In the most flagrant example of cooperation with the mob, a United States commissioner climbed out of bed in the middle of a July 1932 night secretly to post $500 bail on a Gordon bookkeeper long sought by Dewey and now forever free.[5]

Then, early in November, with Gordon at last on the verge of trial, George Medalie announced his resignation. It was timed so that no one could step in at the last moment and snatch the big case away from his chief assistant. Without delay, the nine federal judges of the Southern District, acting under a precedent first established in 1894, unanimously chose Dewey to succeed his mentor as U.S. Attorney on an interim basis. At 9:15 A.M. on November 22, Judge Frank J. Coleman swore Dewey in outside the north courtroom in the gloomy old Federal Building. At thirty-one, Thomas Dewey was the youngest man ever to hold the title. For the press, he offered characteristically little on which to chew. With the Gordon trial under way, he curtly reminded them, "I am too busy at this time to be interviewed."

Dewey opened to the jury with uncommon bravado. "Gentlemen," he informed the blue-ribbon panel of stockbrokers, bankers, architects, and artists, "there will be lots of dead men mentioned during this case. In fact, almost everyone who doesn't want to tell the truth will point to some dead man as being the one who owned this or did that." But no one should entertain doubts as to the identity of the true owner of the $6 million enterprise, he said, run openly until federal agents began to pick up Waxey Gordon's beery scent.

"Then began an infamous system of intimidation and covering up," Dewey charged. "Witnesses began to disappear, banks began to change records, and some business organizations, so-called, came to have complete new sets of books and records." As for Gordon himself, Dewey asserted, he earned more than a million dollars a year, yet could spare his government in taxes barely half the cost of a new hat.

Judge Coleman imposed herculean working conditions on the principals, seven days a week, 9:30 A.M. to 10:00 P.M. The jury was sequestered in the McAlpin Hotel—the first time such a precaution had been taken since the trial of Legs Diamond—and prevented from making or taking phone calls except in the presence of deputy marshals. Federal marshals were employed to guard against physical harm to jurors, whose minds were kept open by the warders' snipping all references to the trial from the newspapers that provided one of the few means of recreation. Gordon himself was rejailed at Dewey's request, lest witnesses be intimidated out of taking the stand against him.

At the start of the prosecution's case, the new U.S. Attorney unveiled a boldly lettered chart on an improvised easel next to the jury box. Containing the names of Gordon and twenty-three others, it was aimed at establishing and unraveling the dual identities lying at the heart of the case. More displays went up on the ensuing days: charts tracing bank accounts opened and closed under different names, charts explaining phone calls, and check payments, charts recording the purchase of beer trucks and insurance policies, charts comparing handwriting samples and mapping out Waxey's double-faced world of breweries, warehouses, and phony offices disguised as legitimate businesses. It was a battle of charts, soon reinforced by witnesses to give resonance to the details of Gordon's power. George Henege, the bootlegger's accountant, took the stand. Henege was an old acquaintance from lean Bowery days, introduced by a mutual friend no longer alive to confirm the story, Arnold Rothstein. Dewey called on Wilbur Wright, a *Journal-American* reporter who had written a series of revealing articles about the Gordon gang and for his troubles was summoned to the Alexander Hamilton Hotel and offered $200 a week to cease and desist.

The prosecution sustained a minor setback when a barrel maker who had, in private, identified Gordon as his employer, refused to repeat the allegation on the stand. Cowering with fright, the man was dismissed, to be replaced by another cooper made of sterner stuff. He cheerfully picked Waxey out of the courtroom crowd as the man responsible for his livelihood. Still another witness provided details of a deal arranged inside Suite 109 for the purchase of 3,200 beer kegs, and a former hotel clerk recalled for good measure how the defendant had run up a $2,000 bill in eight weeks' time.

On November 23, Dewey hit his stride, with a flaxen-haired waitress named Helen Denbeck who ran a short-order restaurant opposite a Gordon garage at Main and Van Winkle Streets and apparently felt no solicitude for Waxey. With Dewey leaning over the witness box, Helen began to describe trucks hurtling in and out of the garage across the street at all hours of the day and night. What kinds of trucks were they? the prosecutor asked. Surprised, Helen said they were beer trucks. But how did she know that? Dewey persisted. "I smelled the beer," the witness answered. "Lots of people smelled it." Determined to nail his point down, the U.S. Attorney wondered if she really knew what beer smelled like.

"I drink lots of beer," Helen told him. "I know how to smell it too. . . . When the boys came in my place, they were all wet with beer."

Her credibility established, the witness went on to tell of an office boy from the Gordon garage who stood in the middle of the street surveying the traffic around him before waving a handkerchief and shouting permission for trucks to roll. Then Dewey held photographs before her expressive face, which lit up in recognition of bodyguards, office workers, truck drivers, and keg rollers. Frankie the Chauffeur was named, along with Big Bill Oppenheimer and the Kaiser. Even Waxey laughed when she looked at one of Dewey's pictures and announced, "Oh sure, that's Joe—Joe the Fleabag they call him."

Most of the time, Gordon looked on sullenly, his heavy-lidded eyes wide open and nervous. When an auto backfired outside the courtroom, he jumped halfway out of his seat, and he sat bolt upright as Helen Denbeck painted a vivid word picture of Old Man Kelly, who stood all day dressed in a butcher's apron in a meatless butcher shop that actually served the gang as a lookout post.

Gordon's lawyers found themselves reduced to using ridicule. Even that backfired. "You know everybody," Frumberg suggested in a patronizing tone. "You know Bills and Petes and Eddies and Franks. Next you'll be telling us you know an Oscar."

"Sure," Helen fired back. "Oscar Brockert. He was Waxey's brewmaster."

Brockert trudged to the stand to describe a party Gordon had thrown for at least thirty mayors, police chiefs, and speakeasy owners. It cost Gordon three dollars a barrel to make his beer, he testified, which, backed by a shotgun-toting sales force, could be marketed for as much as fifty dollars a barrel in the captive gang-dominated cities of New Jersey and Pennsylvania. More telling still, Brockert explained how Waxey managed to turn out hundreds of thousands of gallons of real beer under the noses of local authorities. Small trucks would be loaded with near beer (legal), while "the real stuff," as Brockert put it, was pumped underground, through pipes attached to the Paterson sewers, to a barreling plant disguised as a garage.

The parade of witnesses passed by, connecting the defendant to subordinates, and the whole gang to the lucrative bootlegging operation. A Long Island entrepreneur named Joseph Bissell acknowledged having sold half a million dollars of malt to Waxey, all paid for with checks signed L. J. Sampson and James Henderson, familiar aliases also used to open and transfer Gordon's bank accounts.

The case was being built in the courtroom as it had been developed, gradually and with increasing effect, off stage. And, for the first time, reporters began turning away from the torrent of facts and figures, to focus on the prosecutor himself. Dewey was a slight man, they reported, looking younger than his thirty-one years, apparently without nerves. One journalist, noting a different conservative outfit each day, called the U.S. Attorney "a perfect sartorial masterpiece . . . with a Hitler-Chaplin mustache," an infectious smile that began at the eyes and consumed his face, and, in the prominent eyes, "a fighting glint." Dewey's chin seemed to jut out a half-inch under stress, while his voice remained soft, rising only to score a point or heap sarcasm on a ridiculous tale. Most of the time, he stood motionless before the jury, hands clasped behind his back. He used no notes, despite the complexities of the case, turning to papers on his table only to retrieve an exact quote or date. His cross-examination was conducted in a conversational drawl, comforting enough to lull witnesses into betraying themselves.

When it came time to sum up, defense counsel, G. F. Wahle pronounced himself lost in admiration at Dewey's skill in presenting his case. Compliments aside, Wahle depicted his client as a man caught up in desperate times. It was Prohibition, the defense lawyer cried, that was on trial, "a law nobody loved and nobody could enforce." Holding up a passport photo of the Gordons, Wahle made a mawkish appeal. "Look at this close-bound little family one tender moment. Whatever his past, whatever his lawlessness in making a living now, I ask you: Was it not his sole ambition to provide as best he could under the handicaps of his record for that little woman?"

Wahle tried to turn his client's bootlegging to advantage. "If this defendant is all the government claims he was, he provided employment for thousands of men . . . in the Mack Truck plant, the blacksmith shop, the tire factory, for the cooper and even the farmer of the Middle West . . . whatever the government charges, he was constructive." Before he was done, Wahle referred to King John and the Magna Charta, Napoleon and "the little red schoolhouse of our childhood."

Dewey was more to the point. Alluding to attacks made on his witnesses, he declared, "I cannot prosecute a case against a crime racketeer with bishops, social leaders, and Sunday-school teachers ... my witnesses were the men with whom Waxey Gordon associated. He knew only scoundrels and jailbait." Then, too, the prosecution was, of necessity, based on fragments. "The rest was destroyed by the defendant." Gordon had insisted that Greenberg and Hassell were the real masterminds behind the breweries and other investments. But what about the witness sentenced for contempt after refusing to publicly identify his own handwriting on a check, "Waxey for beer."

"Was he afraid of the government?" Dewey asked rhetorically. "Was he afraid of two dead men? No! He was afraid of what would happen to him if he did testify." Other witnesses, equally reticent, Dewey dismissed as "that poor little frightened soul" and "that lamentable shivering victim from Paterson." Yet the defense would have jurors believe that these "pale tremblers" were all tongue-tied by fear of ghosts. Hundreds of Gordon's subordinates, Dewey went on, might have been called upon to support his story, "but all we have is the rotten, perjured tale" of the defendant himself. Books had vanished, records disappeared, all for the benefit of "the laird of West End Avenue." Look at the automobiles, the suits, shirts, handmade underwear, and silk ties: "Are these the clothing of a messenger?"

The courtroom was silent now, the tense still broken only by Leah Gordon's subdued sobbing. Dewey bearded the defendant and flung out his arm in theatrical denunciation. "By his own admission, the defendant is a cheat, a fraud, a pickpocket, a liar, a professional criminal who ... cheated the government, gave it a pittance, and left its support to the honest citizens." The note was amplified in a swelling crescendo of patriotic notes against a populist backdrop. "If the revenue laws of this country are not enforced," Dewey proclaimed, "then the honest citizens of this country will break their backs carrying the load for these criminals. If the revenue laws break down, disband your Army, sink your Navy, fire your President, and have anarchy. . . . In your hands," he concluded with a flourish, "lies the decision of whether this country is to be run by gangsters, racketeers and thieves, or whether it will be a place for honest men, where justice shall triumph."

The jury was out fifty-one minutes. By 4:25 P.M. on December 1, Waxey Gordon was found guilty on all four counts. Frances clung to her husband's arm, giddy with relief, as Judge Coleman saluted his performance from the bench. "Never in this court or any other court has such fine work been done by revenue agents and the government attorneys," Coleman said. "If ever again I hear the criticism that there are no longer enthusiastic and able young men in the government service, I shall refer to the speaker in this case."

For Gordon, Coleman had harsher words. Denouncing Waxey as "a gang leader of the worst kind," he sentenced the bootlegger to ten years in jail and fined him $80,000. Outside the courtroom, the U.S. Attorney publicly expressed his gratitude to "overworked and underpaid government servants" who had devoted thousands of hours to preparing the case. As for Gordon and his allies in the underworld, Dewey had a parting shot, a pledge that if any witness for the prosecution was ever harmed, the federal government would never rest until those responsible were punished "to the fullest extent of the law." Then he and Frances went home. While Dewey savored his first sleep in four nights, Waxey Gordon ate corned beef hash and coffee in a marshal's office, posed for photographers, then was bundled off to the Tombs to await an appeal and confirmation of his guilt.

Five days later, Utah became the thirty-second state to ratify the Twenty-first Amendment, and America's long dry spell was finally broken. Some 19,000 policemen were needed to handle delirious New Yorkers jamming Times Square and other gathering places, happy yet desperate for a drink. At Bloomingdale's, elaborate preparations had been under way for days, and the store could boast at 5:32 P.M. of selling the first legal dose of rye since 1919. Dewey seemed just as pleased as the rest of the city, for entirely different reasons. "Now the bootleggers will have to go back to picking pockets," he told reporters. What about his own plans for the evening? someone asked.

"Well"—he chuckled—"I'm entertaining a few dinner guests. You can say that."

On December 16, Dewey made his first national radio address, a blast at political corruption delivered over a forty-six-station grid put together by NBC. His language was blunt. "In the decade of unequaled prosperity prior to 1930, the American people sold their birthright. The cold, clammy hand of politics descended firmly on local police departments and prosecutors' offices and ruled them to the benefit of politicians and criminals," Dewey told his listeners. "Conceived in corruption and flourishing on graft, municipal government in the United States was left to its own devices to bankrupt our cities and surrender our citizens to the rule of the underworld."

By then, Dewey had achieved a middling national celebrity. It was possible for moviegoers that December to see Thomas Dewey in a Pathé news feature that also included a rodeo in Los Angeles, a New Jersey train wreck, and a canary that sang "Yankee Doodle Dandy." But December was also Dewey's last month on the federal payroll. At last President Roosevelt had chosen a replacement for Medalie: Martin Conboy, a Roosevelt intimate who had served the then-governor as counsel in the Jimmy Walker hearings. Swearing Conboy in on the day after Christmas, as Dewey looked on, was a grandfatherly U.S. circuit court judge named Martin T. Manton, who would figure prominently in Dewey's subsequent fame. On the twenty-seventh, Dewey spent seven hours in consultation with his successor, turning down Conboy's invitation to stay on as chief assistant, choosing instead the greater professional recognition and financial security held out by private practice.

Before he left, Dewey pondered a return to McNamara and Seymour, but after talking it over with Medalie, decided to hire his own office and staff and develop for profit his natural gift for litigation. He took over his friend's old lease at 120 Broadway, along with the furniture in Medalie's quarters. And on January 2, 1934, Dewey resumed his interrupted career as a lawyer.

To a close friend, Dewey confided his largest ambitions: to become head of a great downtown law firm, and, as he put it, "to make a hell of a lot of money." His first weeks of private practice pointed him in the direction of both. Joseph Proskauer, the former judge who was almost a legendary figure among his fellow lawyers, invited Dewey to join him in a million-dollar suit against Bankers Trust. Armenian-Americans asked the former U.S. attorney to gather evidence against the Tashnag, a fanatical sect campaigning for an independent Armenia, suspected of hacking Archbishop Leon Torrian to death at a Christmas Eve High Mass. A sealing company hired him to secure damages from a rival that had stolen a secret bottle cap.[6]

The law is a paradoxical discipline, absolute and flexible, fixed and evolving. It demands respect for institutions, yet relies upon individuals to give them life. It is as conservative as tradition, and as liberal as compassion. The law is a dispassionate passion, a career for technicians with ideals. For Dewey, trained in Columbia's sociological jurisprudence, steeped in the flavorful heritage of a small town's Victorian devotion to duty, the law was exciting drudgery, an intellectual challenge, and the surest path to success as measured by the standards of Owosso. After his victory in the Gordon trial, he publicly expressed disdain for what he called "prosecution by ballyhoo." The public might wish to deify a district attorney and turn the cool, precise search for truth into a gaudy crusade. Only facts could lend flamboyance to such a man as Annie Dewey's son.

"Things have been moving very well here," he wrote in the fall of 1934 to Bill Douglas. It was a laconic statement of the facts. Now as in college, Dewey continued his methodical notation of every fifteen-cent shoeshine and eighty-five-cent dinner in a tiny pad that measured a thrifty existence. Fifty dollars might be slipped to Frances from time to time for household necessities and a child's shoes. Dewey himself, even when his annual income was approaching $50,000, got by on forty or fifty dollars a month. Yet if out-of-pocket expenditures remained penurious, the Dewey family was moving up in the world, and surroundings suggestive of luxury were a logical reward. In October of 1934, Tom moved his wife and son into an eight-room apartment at 1148 Fifth Avenue. At the same time, he took a house in the manicured suburban community of Tuxedo Park.[7]

Tuxedo Park was designed as a retreat from the spotlight, the expression of a deep-seated need for privacy in comfortable surroundings that Dewey never lost. Much later, he said his decision to pull up stakes and move to Pawling came after he found a copperhead snake slithering in the grass near his son's playpen. At the time, however, he expressed a passionate dislike for "all those goddamned cocktail parties" around which Tuxedo revolved, and to a magazine writer in 1939, he confided that his high-living neighbors in the Park were "a bunch of snobs."[8]

He was not an easy man to work for.

"I think you'll stay," Goody Goodrich told Lillian Rosse, an Alabama-reared temporary in 1934. Puzzled, Miss Rosse asked why. Goodrich replied with a reference to Dewey's praise of Miss Rosse as "the first person who's worked here who can get along with me." Goodrich himself was a mathematical whiz, able to defeat an electric adding machine in head-on competition, who became a Dewey intimate because of a brilliant performance in the investigation of a crooked municipal court judge named Harold L. Kunstler.[9]

Judges worked fewer than 200 days a year; the average workday didn't exceed four or five hours. Not surprisingly, justice in New York was suffering from severe hardening of the arteries. The tort calendar in Manhattan's central court was over two years behind schedule at the end of 1933. As bad as the quantity of judicial work was its quality: about 40 percent of all court decisions reached in the municipal courts, often called the poor man's tribunal, were reversed on error by the time they reached the appellate level.

Judge Kunstler typified the human problem behind justice's breakdown. He was appointed to the bench by Jimmy Walker in 1928, and elected to a term of his own a year later. His florid face, startled eyes, and horn-rimmed glasses made Kunstler resemble a miscast Harold Lloyd. Certainly his record on the bench had its comic overtones, nowhere more than in his relationship with a Second District power broker named Charles Leef. It was a matter of public record that "Charlie the Thief," as he was known in the neighborhood, was a Kunstler intimate, who sometimes shared the judge's bench.

"Don't try any of your district attorney stuff on me," Leef once warned Dewey from the witness stand. But Dewey had the best of the exchange.

Kunstler himself revealed bank deposits of over $166,000 during a period when his judicial salary amounted to a quarter of that. Slowly, for maximum effect, Dewey began reading off 107 individual deposit slips, recording almost daily transactions by the judge, while Kunstler stared at the ceiling, his silence broken only by monotonous repetitions of "I don't know" and "I can't remember." The damning series of "loans" piled up, $5,000 or more each month. Suddenly, Dewey halted in his presentation. July 1928: only $3,743.82 deposited in Kunstler's account.

"Court wasn't in session in July was it?" he asked the squirming witness. The judge could only nod his head in agreement. Kunstler explained his many trips to the bank as a desperate financial shuffle that journalists immediately dubbed Put 'n' Take.

On June 16, 1934 Walker's judge handed in his resignation. Within a week, he had left town, eloped, as it turned out, with a former prostitute who would herself later accuse him of stealing her jewels.

"Curiously enough," Dewey wrote a friend in the wake of his triumph, "there is no real pleasure in winning a case like the Kunstler matter, because you have such a bad taste in your mouth afterward. The best I can say about it is that it is a nasty job of which I am well rid."[10]

II

THE GANGBUSTER

1935–1940

5
The Chief

The law is bigger than money—but only if the law works hard enough.

—THOMAS E. DEWEY

It seems to me, old man, that you have the opportunity of a lifetime.

—A FRIEND, TO DEWEY, JULY 1935[1]

There was a new district attorney in New York in March 1935 when a grand jury was impaneled to investigate the policy game and bail bonding, on top of the regular round of felonies to which the D.A. gave his attention. William Copeland Dodge was a Tammany warhorse, chosen for the job by Jimmy Hines, and elected despite the Fusion victory of Fiorello La Guardia (and a stiff challenge from Ferdinand Pecora, who campaigned as a reform Democrat). Dodge seemed perfectly willing to overlook the industrial rackets proliferating in New York, adding twenty cents to the cost of trucking every barrel of flour into the city, making it twice as expensive to unload and crate a rail car of poultry as in Philadelphia, inflating the price of restaurant meals, kosher meats, vegetables, and milk. Rackets, according to some estimates, were soaking up a half-billion dollars from the city's already crippled economy. Policy diverted at least $100 million more from the pockets of the poor, establishing a vast slush fund with which to bribe police and buy off politicians.

When the March grand jury began its work, no one expected much to come of it, especially as Dodge was in charge. The D.A. assigned as his liaison with the jurors, the youngest, least experienced man on his staff, a self-styled "child detective" named Lyon Boston. Before long, Dodge lost all interest and began talking instead of the threat of Communism in New York. But the grand jury, led by Lee Thompson Smith, a real estate broker and president of the Grand Jurors Association of New York, was not interested in prosecuting the *Daily Worker,* or chasing prostitutes, another target suggested for its attention. It wanted to get at the heart of racketeering in the city, and the civic corruption that followed in its wake.

Throughout March and April, a mounting war of words took place between Dodge and more zealous reformers outside the grand jury room, while Smith and his colleagues complained of something less than full cooperation from the D.A.'s staff. Then, on May 12, a Congregational pastor and president of the Society for the Prevention of Crime, G. Drew Egbert, blasted Dodge for delaying tactics in a sermon preached from his Flushing, Long Island, pulpit. Lee Thompson Smith joined in the assault, publicly calling for the appointment of a special prosecutor, to be chosen by the grand jurors themselves. The next day, Dodge's assistants were forcibly excluded from the jury room. The bar association added its voice to the growing demand for an independent investigation, and newspapers fanned the flames.

On May 17, a list of six names compiled by past and current presidents of the city and county bar associations was submitted first to the grand jury and then to Dodge. One of the six was George Medalie. Young John Harlan, who had already made a name for himself on Wall Street, was another. At the top of the alphabetical list was Tom Dewey, fondly remembered by Smith for the Waxey Gordon trial, on which the jury foreman had sat and been impressed by the prosecutor's presentation and command of fact. Dodge regarded the list as a deliberate political provocation and he selected his own man for the job, a friend of both Max Steuer's and Nathan Miller's named Harold Corbin. Smith denounced Corbin as unacceptable, and Dodge threatened retaliation by discharging the entire grand jury.

"I am the District Attorney," he raged, "and not the foreman of some runaway grand jury. I don't intend to surrender."

Thus was born the saga—half truth and half legend—of twenty-three jurors who took justice into their own hands, a story powerfully aided by indignant journalists. "Dodge Gives Himself Away," one paper editorialized. Another spoke of "a sinister plot" to obstruct justice, and suggested that Dodge himself should resign. The sound and fury raged on, without any comment from Dewey, who was busily earning a good living in private practice. He did take time out to chide a good-government group in Chicago for considering abolition of the grand jury in that criminal paradise. Without the Lee Thompson Smiths of this world, gangsters would thrive unimpeded, "because businessmen do not dare complain, and they are the only available witnesses," he said. Only "an agent of organized crime" could advocate such a radical amputation on the body politic.[2]

On June 6, Harold Corbin declined the special prosecutor's job, and Governor Herbert Lehman was drawn in. Within four days, the runaway grand jury had suspended operations, but not without having insisted beforehand on a prosecutor "of unusual vigor and ability" to combat a criminal element both well organized and well financed. Foreman Smith sat down with Lehman and asked the Governor for two things: a special prosecutor to focus attention on the policy racket, and an extraordinary term of the city's Supreme Court, to hear evidence and vote indictments. Lehman listened to Smith, to the grand jury, and to District Attorney Dodge. He reviewed the grand jury testimony, and conferred with Mayor La Guardia, Police Commissioner Lewis Valentine, and others.

Meanwhile, the name of Thomas Dewey kept popping up as a possibility for special prosecutor. Lehman, however, was reluctant to make the appointment. On June 24, he handed Dodge a new list of names, four in all; Dewey's was conspicuous for its absence. Publicly, the Governor worried about the former U.S. attorney's relative obscurity. Privately, it would appear, he worried about just the opposite. Lehman had no desire to build up a potential Republican contender for future office. Moreover Jimmy Hines was dead set against the choice of Medalie's protégé.

On the other hand, William O. Douglas, by then chairman of the Securities and Exchange Commission, spoke for many when he described Waxey Gordon's prosecutor as ideal for an even larger, more onerous investigation into the rackets of New York. Approaching Roosevelt braintruster Tommy Corcoran in late June, Douglas emphasized the desperate state of the city, and of a government drowning in venality. He urged Corcoran to get clearance for Dewey's appointment from the White House, so that Lehman, well aware of the President's protective attitude toward his home turf, would be relieved of any doubts over Roosevelt's attitude. Corcoran agreed to try.

"You never could tell how much the President was listening," when he was being asked to make a hard choice, Corcoran recalled, but at least FDR voiced no specific objection to Dewey's appointment, and word of his endorsement of sorts was duly passed north to Albany.[3]

On June 27, all the men on Lehman's revised list declined the position, citing "professional and public obligations," and recommending Dewey in their place. Now, the newspapers took up the plea and made it their own. "Make it Dewey!" one demanded. "He is poison to crooked officials, racketeer labor leaders, and dishonest judges," another argued.

June 29 was a Saturday, and Dewey was in Boston, giving away his cousin Elizabeth in marriage. Medalie and the others on the

Governor's list were at a stormy two-hour session in Lehman's apartment at 820 Fifth Avenue. A few minutes before one that afternoon, a haggard-looking Lehman appeared before reporters to announce that "despite all my endeavors," none of his preferred candidates would take the special prosecutorial job, and that, under the circumstances, he would urge Dodge to appoint "Mr. Thomas A. Dewey." If Lehman's error about Dewey's middle initial was indicative, perhaps he had been partly right about the young man's obscurity.

Somewhat better known was the sixty-two-year-old gentleman farmer from Connecticut whom Lehman appointed to preside over the extraordinary Supreme Court term sought by Lee Thompson Smith. Phillip J. McCook was a crusty, patrician World War I hero, three decades older that Dewey, in whom, however, the young prosecutor was destined to find a staunch ally.

Dewey was still in Boston, dressing for his cousin's wedding, when Lillian Rosse called with news that Smith was now publicly demanding his appointment. The actual announcement from Lehman did not catch up with him until he returned to New York and read about it in an evening paper. Then he went home, without comment. He hadn't planned for any of this to engulf his well-ordered life; he had expected to be in Washington for a trial early in July, then vacation for a few days in Owosso and Chicago.[4]

But by Monday morning, July 1, when he spoke for the first time to reporters pressing him for his answer, it was clear he had given the job a lot of thought. The prosecution would take a year or two to complete, he said, and call for a staff of twenty lawyers, "young enough to be free of entanglements, but old enough to have acquired the requisite experience." If he did take the job, Dewey made clear, he would broaden its scope far beyond the policy game, to include all forms of racketeering, organized vice, bail bonding, and political protection in the city. Most important of all, he would demand complete independence from Dodge and the existing district attorney's office. He spent less than half an hour in conference with an apparently amiable Dodge that same afternoon, before leaving the D.A. to make a formal announcement that Medalie's favorite would indeed accept Lehman's offer.

A few days after his appointment as special prosecutor, Dewey asked a crime reporter what "they" thought of him. Who was "they?" the journalist wanted to know, to which Dewey replied, "The underworld." To be perfectly honest, the reporter replied, "they" regarded the prosecutor as a Boy Scout, hopelessly mismatched against their terrorist tactics and political connections. Leaping from his chair, crackling like a high-tension wire, Dewey spit out a prophecy: "In a few months, they won't be calling me that."

It seemed an impossibly optimistic forecast at the start of July. Dewey was like a general without troops, whose most potent weapon against the racketeers was civic outrage. He had no staff, no budget, no headquarters, no broad plan of attack, and only vague promises of cooperation from state and federal authorities. There was only Dewey himself, some crusading journalists, a mildly supportive governor, a flamboyant mayor, a hostile district attorney, a skeptical populace, and a cowed legion of businessmen and labor leaders willing to perjure themselves before telling the truth about the systematic extortion of money by racketeers. Even friends cloaked their congratulations in cheeky irony.

"This is a hell of a town," one wrote, "where the only fellow who knows anything about vice and rackets is a young squirt named Dewey." Editors foresaw a rugged contest between "courage and ability" and "an extremely potent combination of talent, money, and self-interest." One likened Dewey's task to charting the Gulf Stream, while readily admitting that accurate cartography would prove of national interest.[5]

Dewey himself realized his work would necessarily involve a multifront war. First, he would have to prove that a crime had been committed, that the "trade associations" or corrupted unions in professions from window washing and garment trucking to construction, taxicabs, baking, and boxing were actually illegal. Harder still, he would have to extract testimony from intimidated victims. To do this, Dewey would have to make himself more frightening than the racketeers. Those who knew him believed he could do it. "Dewey knows when to be lawless," said an elderly pillar of New York's legal establishment. Others were reminded of an earlier crusader carved from ice, the brilliant, bloodless enemy of insurance and utility cheats whose achievements earned him the governorship in 1908, and a shot at the White House against Woodrow Wilson. Charles Evans Hughes was on the mind of one Dewey correspondent who told him that "no other lawyer of our generation . . . has made the reputation you have in such a short time." One man offered his services at president-making, and received a lukewarm response from the new prosecutor.

"As to you being my 'Colonel House' or 'Jim Farley,' " he answered late in July, "I honestly hope that I won't have any use for such a person, since, when I get rid of this job, I want to go back to private practice and again making a living." Admirers might look forward to great tomorrows, but Dewey found himself in a dark wood of dismal reality, the odds stacked heavily against him. He wasted no time in adjusting them. On July 5, he traveled to Albany to confer with Governor Lehman. It was their first meeting, and it would be hard to imagine two men less similar in background or outlook: the youngest of eight children of a German-born cotton merchant, a partner in the multimillion-dollar Lehman Brothers banking firm who taught three nights a week at the Henry Street Settlement House, a financial mainstay of liberal Democrats, himself nominated for second place on Franklin Roosevelt's 1928 ticket because of his close ties to Al Smith; and the country editor's boy from Owosso, hard-driving and bumptious, dynamic as Lehman was colorless.[6]

When he emerged from the Governor's office, Dewey pronounced his new superior "delightful" and Lehman's public words of support "a knockout." Before long, the relationship would founder on the rocks of mutual ambition and envy, but for now the Governor was squarely in the prosecutor's corner. So, it appeared, was Mayor La Guardia, with whom Dewey had a frantic twenty-minute conference in a car speeding toward Newark Airport. The prosecutor visited Washington on July 10, when Treasury Secretary Henry Morgenthau promised to turn his department "inside out" to help, and Dewey denounced inefficient Secret Service agents and a Treasury press relations expert who bribed waitresses to eavesdrop on restaurant conversations.[7]

From meetings with Attorney General Homer S. Cummings and J. Edgar Hoover, a friend from U.S. attorney days, Dewey returned to New York. There he found his crusade threatened by city clerk Albert Marinelli, a Tammany district leader who on his own had gathered a grand jury pool, and a perennial mayoral candidate named Henry H. Klein, who as head of the Five Cent Subway Fare party had attracted 2,600 votes in 1933. In an abstrusely worded appeal to the courts, Klein and his Property Owners Protective League dismissed the Dewey probe as a smokescreen to cover District Attorney Dodge's failure to prosecute "bond and mortgage racketeers." The prosecutor himself had a single-word retort: "Rubbish!" When Klein continued his quixotic campaign, Dewey amplified upon this slightly: "More rubbish!"

Klein's obstructionism was reflected in the city's Board of Estimate, dominated by Tammany holdovers, which was suddenly moved to speak out against waste and extravagance, subjects on which it was an acknowledged expert. The board objected to Dewey's budget; he threatened to quit if it were cut. As chief assistant under Medalie, he had slashed office expenses 40 percent. The same conservative instincts were at work in planning the new investigation. No one working for Dewey was likely to get rich. The prosecutor himself was settling for the same salary as the District Attorney, $16,695 annually. (Seabury, by contrast, had been paid $100,000 for two and a half years' work.) Assistants would receive less, ranging downward from $8,000 to a dollar a year, the salary paid aggressive youngsters freshly minted by the best law schools and recruited by Dewey as a practical solution to the shortage of money and manpower. Three dollar-a-year men were hired that July, assigned to research, and front-row seats in a legal drama of surpassing interest. In the end, powerless to do anything more than nibble at public confidence in Dewey and his motives, the Board of Estimate went along with a five-month budget of $121,000.

The summer of 1935 was a time for precedents, and the new special prosecutor was busy making them. After Marinelli tried to limit his range with the grand jury pool, Dewey launched detailed investigations of each prospective juror, sniffing out political and underworld ties. He sought and obtained from Lehman permission to hire outside of regular Civil Service lists, placed an accountant in his own pay on the state tax commissioner's staff, demanded his own stenographer in order to prevent leaks from the grand jury, and held out for separate office space, away from the Criminal Courts Building, where Dodge had his quarters and clusters of Tammany acolytes imparted the flavor of a political clubhouse.[8]

New Yorkers sweltered through one of the hottest Julys on record, but the man whom friends suspected of carrying his own built-in deep freeze worked around the clock, writing letters of resignation from outside jobs, winding down a private practice, greeting delegations of civic well-wishers, honing his budget, and poring over blueprints for an investigative office that would be airtight. There were long phone calls to George Medalie and Joseph Proskauer, lunch with Lee Thompson Smith, meetings with Police Commissioner Valentine and U.S. Attorney Frank Adams. On July 23, Dewey dined with Arthur Sulzberger and the editorial staff of the New York *Times*, where he asked to be forgotten for a while, leaving behind the front pages for the prosaic obscurity of successful investigation.

To photographers, he promised cooperation and sought the same.

They were welcome to take all the pictures they wanted, but if they came away with shots of him with his mouth open, or biting into a sandwich, it could impair his dignity and encourage those who sought to ridicule the entire probe as the latest in a long, ignoble series of vice raids destined to die after a few highly publicized arrests, while guiding its erstwhile director into a comfortable law firm or political sinecure. Most of the press responded well, as did all the city's publishers, who realized that the investigation about to begin was in large part their doing. Individual journalists, impressed but also a little frightened by the short young man with fierce eyes and a bulldog manner, slipped in references to a cutting tongue and hair-trigger temper. "His love of criminal prosecution," one wrote at the end of July, "amounts almost to a mania." Cynicism persisted, even if mingled with personal admiration for the job the former U.S. attorney was tackling. At lunch with Hearst columnist Arthur Brisbane and department store mogul Bernard Gimbel, Dewey laid out his plans and sought support. As soon as he was out of the room, Brisbane turned to Gimbel and bet $100 that the special prosecutor would be out of a job in three months. Gimbel took up the challenge; he gave Dewey six months before admitting failure.[9]

Back at 120 Broadway, Dewey spent countless hours interviewing job applicants. Most days, he was at it from nine until five, only to find twenty or more hopefuls lined up outside his door at day's end. Three thousand lawyers—one sixth of the profession in New York—wanted to work for him. Many were victims of the Depression, almost desperate to fill one of the twenty slots on the new legal staff. Other positions were sought just as eagerly. Seven hundred accountants applied for ten openings. Five hundred stenographers and secretaries desired twenty jobs. Dentists wrote in and doctors, chemists, bricklayers, and 225 New Yorkers whose talents earned admission to a thick file labeled miscellaneous. Ten applicants volunteered to do anything at all, without compensation, while overcrowded private agencies proposed to give the natural tidal wave even greater force by directing their own favorites to the Equitable Building.

Instinctively, Dewey turned to familiar faces, trusted associates. Stressing "long and intensive" background in criminal investigation, he wanted a combination of imagination, youthfulness, and iron pants. Barent Ten Eyck, his old Columbia classmate and administrative assistant in Medalie's office, met the criteria. He was soon joined as a chief assistant by two other alumni of the Medalie school, William Herlands and Murray Gurfein. Both had worked in the prestigious office of the city's Corporation Counsel. Other subordinates would recall affiliations with eminent private lawyers and judges like John W. Davis, Learned Hand, and Samuel Seabury, even some of those in Roosevelt's New Deal. Seven of the twenty were Republicans, six were Democrats, the rest Fusionists or independents. Half were Jewish. Seven held Phi Beta Kappa keys, with fourteen graduated either from Harvard or Columbia Law School. The oldest man was forty, the youngest twenty-five, reflecting Dewey's desire to find men, as he put it, with their careers ahead of them.[10]

He moved with deliberation, filling only twelve of seventy-six positions by July 29, when the extraordinary grand jury was due to convene. The full complement would not be reached until October 11. But his caution was a mark of precision, not hesitation. So fine were his rushed calculations during July that there would be only one change in the original number of staffers over the investigation's two and a half years—the addition of three copyists in the stenographic bureau in 1937.

Almost as automatic as the selection of Ten Eyck, Herlands, and Gurfein was that of Goody Goodrich to be chief accountant. From past experience, Dewey had learned that investigations such as this rely upon silent witnesses for their most damning evidence, and that only trained accountants could coax cooperation out of bank records and company books. Goodrich was empowered to choose his own staff, which included an assistant to Herbert Hoover in the American Relief Administration, and two refugees from the recently dissolved National Recovery Administration. (Ironically, the artificial codes established by the NRA in an effort to limit competition and stimulate production and jobs helped to blur the illegality of the very rackets to which they bore a faint resemblance.) The rest of the staff was as diverse as New York. There was a stenographer from County Sligo and a messenger from Syria, a clerk once employed as a Wall Street broker and a process server whose amateur photographic talents were put to good use in tailing and identifying suspects. Two of Dewey's young lawyers, Frank Hogan and Charles Breitel, were destined to become, respectively, Manhattan's longstanding district attorney and chief judge of the New York Court of Appeals.

Dewey scoured the private sector for weeks before settling on a filing genius who had been responsible for creating large corporate systems for twenty years. Phone operators were requisitioned from the cream of the work force at New York Telephone. For his chief inspector, Dewey selected John A. Lyons, a tweedy veteran of the Pinkerton Agency, fondly remembered for his work on the Waxey Gordon case. Lyons was set loose to select and organize a squad of seventy-five investigators, many of them recent graduates from the police academy.

It wasn't easy luring top-grade people with second-rate salaries. One of the reasons for Dewey's visit to Morgenthau was his pursuit of a chief investigator, finally solved by reducing the stenographic crew and scraping together $10,000 to pay Wayne Merrick, an Iowa-born FBI agent held in awe by city police, who hadn't forgotten the job he did in capturing a bank robber and cop killer named Leonard Scarnici. The romance of Dewey's crusade reached as far as Texas, where a former ballplayer and oil rigger named Arthur Robinson heard what was planned for New York and promptly packed a truck, slapped on a ten-gallon hat, and shipped off for 120 Broadway. Impressed by Robinson's spunk, Dewey was more grateful still for his fluent command of Spanish, useful indeed for long stretches in a Harlem basement or coal bin interpreting the wiretapped conversations of Dutch Schultz's Spanish-speaking lieutenants.[11]

To those he took into his confidence, Dewey outlined an investigative approach both direct and tortuous. There would be no time wasted on what Dewey called "small fry." Only the major figures of the underworld interested him. But to get at them, it would be necessary to climb a long, slippery ladder, accusing lesser criminals to secure their testimony against higher-ups.[12]

To some, the prosecutor seemed cunning, to others cocky. If he was brassy, he admired brass in others. Among the hundreds waiting to be interviewed that sultry July was a young Knickerbocker Democrat recommended to Dewey by George Trosk, an influential lawyer familiar with the qualifications of young Victor Herwitz. Herwitz had spent months working with the egocentric and controversial Irving Ben Cooper probing the murky world of the bail bondsman, and now he found himself being asked more questions about Cooper than about his own record. It was a tight fix for the young job applicant, who if he told Dewey the truth, that in his opinion Cooper was "a crazy son of a bitch," would appear disloyal.

"He's a great investigator," Herwitz finally fudged. But Dewey wasn't buying. "That's not what I'm asking. I want to know what kind of a guy he is."

Herwitz fortified his stonewall, and gradually the questioning shifted to his own history. He started explaining his single year at Dartmouth, when Dewey interrupted sharply. "What happened?"

he asked. "You get thrown out?" No, Herwitz answered, the Depression had invaded his household a year early, and with his older brother already in school, he decided to leave Dartmouth and return to New York, to work days and attend evening classes at the Brooklyn School of Law.

"You know," Dewey broke in, "you're the only one I'm interviewing from a lousy law school."

Herwitz didn't retreat. "There must be a good reason for that."

"Why should I hire you?" Dewey demanded.

"Because I know more about investigating than anyone else."

"How do you know?"

"I've been doing it for four years."

Two egos crackled in the small room. When Herwitz finally left, he felt certain his job prospects were demolished. A few days later, Trosk telephoned the special prosecutor and, unable to restrain his curiosity, finally asked Dewey's opinion of the young man he'd sent over to 120 Broadway.

"I think he's a snotty little son of a bitch," Dewey informed him.

Taken aback, Trosk sputtered apologies, but Dewey cut him off in mid-sentence. "I'm not sorry," he said. "I'm going to hire him."[13]

With a crack staff taking shape, Dewey next pushed ahead with his search for a secure base of operations. Paramount in his mind was a building whose accessibility would insure anonymity for his visitors. Thurston Green was deputized to scour the city for such a building, and found it in Frank Woolworth's sixty-story Cathedral of Commerce. Close by City Hall and the Supreme Court in Foley Square, where the extraordinary grand jury would be sitting, the Woolworth Building had eight separate entrances on Park Row, Broadway, and Barclay Street, including one direct link to a subway line, permitting witnesses to slip away in the vast commuter congregation coming and going underneath Manhattan. Inside, there were six elevators to carry visitors to the fourteenth floor, where 10,500 square feet were divided into thirty-five cubicles set off from each other by frosted glass, arranged around a long hallway that bisected the whole suite.

Furniture was bought secondhand, for $16,000, and part of the savings reinvested in venetian blinds. That way, as Dewey told a visiting contingent of reporters, "no one can get up in the Transportation Building over there with a telescope and see who's in here talking with us." The blinds were put to good use. There would be no interrogating, Dewey decreed, until they were lowered and reluctant or terrified witnesses reassured of their privacy. All stenographic work was to be done in a single large room, with strict precautions against leaks. Lead disk and wire seals, the kind used to fasten box-car doors, were bought to safeguard filing cabinets and, since the building had no incinerator of its own, Dewey made arrangements to burn each day's wastepaper in a furnace. You never could be certain when a bored or sinister charwoman might riffle the contents of a cluttered desk. He ruled out any general waiting room in which witnesses could size up one another. Instead, twenty-four-year-old Michael Monz, who had undertaken similar chores for the Seabury inquiry, would be posted at the main entrance to the floor, a receptionist adept at spotting members of New York's substantial population of cranks and misfits. Staffers were instructed to escort visitors to their individual quarters within five minutes of their arrival, and if a potential ally was too cowed to come to them, they must be prepared to meet the informant any place of his choosing.

Nervous visitors who did show up on the fourteenth floor had the option of leaving via a freight elevator next to Dewey's inner sanctum. This had the added advantage of allowing the prosecutor to see people without his own staff knowing about it. An untappable phone cable was installed and Dewey, who detested the interruption of a ringing telephone, asked for and got a phone booth placed just outside his door. That way, he explained, he could make the calls he wanted, without wasting time talking to people calling in. A uniformed officer was stationed on the floor night and day, and detectives were posted at inconspicuous spots in the main lobby. Elevator operators were investigated, along with porters and cleaning women who frequented the area.[14]

Under Green's direction, the work proceeded quickly. Before the month was out, Dewey himself came by to peer into the glass-fronted boxes his assistants would occupy, the freight elevator, the entrances and exits. He scanned the neighborhood for possible enemy outposts, and when it was over, he demanded of Green why no ashtrays had been provided. Then he invited reporters over to 120 Broadway for a get-acquainted session.[15]

To his newly assembled staff, Dewey described a forbidding world, in which each member must exercise caution in choosing whom he spoke with on the street, dined out with, drank with. Nightclubs were verboten—later, it was said, not wholly in jest, that Dewey's idea of an acceptable nightclub was a Child's Restaurant—and racetracks frowned upon. Liquor could not be brought into the office, nor could any of the prosecutor's men borrow money except through Dewey himself. Personal problems were to be shared with him; secrecy was to be their watchword.[16]

More injunctions followed. Assistants would under no circumstances make public speeches, nor pass on private confidences about their work to wives or families. Caesar's wife was mentioned often, along with the sorry state of the bar in New York, where lawyers Dewey considered legal prostitutes were willing to truckle to gangsters if the price was right. The staff must not put too much faith in individuals, he warned, for on close examination most people had an angle. "Bear in mind," he told a similar meeting at the start of his district attorneyship, "that every public official is sold out by the guy he spoke to on the street corner . . . when you want to associate in public with anybody, be careful who it is . . . use your horse-sense all day and all evening and particularly after midnight. The most important thing of all is to remember that everybody is capable of being your enemy."[17]

"If you want to have a good time," he told the staff, "go to New Jersey."[18]

On July 30, in his new domain on the fourteenth floor, Dewey put finished touches on a radio speech—he said he hoped it would be his last—to be delivered that night, explaining his investigation and appealing for help from victims of racket thievery. At eight-thirty that night, New Yorkers tuned in to hear from their newest, and most unlikely hero.

The special prosecutor began his half-hour address by saying what his probe was not meant to be. It was not, he insisted, a chase after prostitutes or gamblers—regular investigative machinery could handle regular vice. Neither was it an anti-labor crusade, even though racketeers had infested many unions. Who, then, was the enemy? Dewey was unsparing. The enemy was "organized gangs of low-grade outlaws who lacked either the courage or the intelligence to earn an honest living. They succeed only so long as they can prey upon the fears and weaknesses of disorganized or timid witnesses. They fail, and run to cover, when business and the public, awakened to their own strength, stand up and fight." Hardly a household in New York didn't suffer from their depredations, didn't pay a tribute "levied by force and collected by fear." No family could sit down to dinner without first rendering "a huge, unofficial sales tax" on chicken, fish, vegetables, flour, and other staples. No businessman dealing in these or many other commodities could hope to escape mob violence.

A racket could begin innocently enough, Dewey explained, with a self-proclaimed "watchman" presenting himself for hire to a shopkeeper seeking protection. If the offer was rejected, the consequences were costly. "Truck tires are slashed in the night. Fresh vegetables and fish are soaked with gasoline or stolen. Customers are intimidated, employees are beaten up, plate-glass windows are broken, and often whole stores are completely destroyed." Tragically, some legitimate businessmen had thrown in their lot with the racketeers, hoping to force out competitors and jack up prices. Other times, racketeers themselves launched the process, using threats and violence to bring a reluctant industry to its knees.

"The result," Dewey told his audience, "is always the same. The businessmen and the public pay, and the racketeer takes the profits."

It didn't have to be this way. "You can be free from organized racketeering in this city." But he would need their help. He would also need their patience. Nothing would happen overnight, and nothing at all would happen unless victims came to the Woolworth Building and unburdened themselves.

"Every shakedown, every threat, every stink-bomb throwing, is a state crime," Dewey continued. "We will prosecute every crime which is part of an organized racket . . . every crime in the book, from conspiracy and malicious mischief to assault in the first degree, from extortion to perjury, from income tax violations all the way to murder." But that did not mean an orgy of instant headlines. Crime, Dewey reminded his listeners, "cannot be investigated under a spotlight. Publicity does not stamp out crime . . . sensational raids and arrests without months of quiet and painstaking preparation in advance result in nothing but acquittals in court."

"If you have evidence of organized crime," he concluded, "bring it to us. . . . The rest is our job. We will do our best."

At nine o'clock, the tocsin sounded, Dewey and his men could only wait anxiously for the next morning. Then they would know if their crusade was flying high or stillborn in a humiliating backfire of good intentions.

The response washed in immediately—a tide of hard fact and furtive, sometimes paranoid, whispers. In a single month, 3,000 New Yorkers jammed the fourteenth floor, a hundred a day greeted by naive young men with stacks of five-by-eight-inch cards, otherwise occupied listening to anonymous tips on the phone, reading unsigned letters, and holding hands with the lonely or lunatic. Much of the information was worthless. But the exercise itself was not. Waiters described a shadowy racket engulfing the restaurant trade. Poverty-stricken clerks told of loan sharks charging 1,000 percent interest and threatening the lives of those who couldn't pay up. By sifting and organizing the mass of data on the cards, Dewey's men by the end of the summer could follow leads into two dozen rackets. Moreover, the first major impetus to success—the support and encouragement of average New Yorkers—had been tested and found abundant.[19]

It shouldn't have surprised anyone, really, the outpouring of tall tales and mundane detail. America was a country in thrall to crime in 1935, with 120 million people fascinated by gun-toting men and their molls, by screeching black limousines and corpses draped in concrete.

It was the heyday of crime reporting, when lurid headlines electrified sullen cities, and sob sisters raced from lover's nest to city morgue before gushing over the most heinous, and therefore salable, offenses. Throughout the deadened decade that began with Wall Street's tumble, the press behaved like a shrill Greek chorus, hawked in ten editions a day by apple-cheeked newsboys with the latest atrocity on their tongues. Hearst's New York paper, the *Journal-American*, was most predictable in its theatricality, but staid journals like the *Times* and *Herald Tribune* also splashed the sights and sounds of sudden death over their front pages, and tried innocent people while New York read on in rapture.

As ever anxious to capitalize on a trend, Hollywood joined the carnage, cranking out fifty gangster movies a year, in which anti-heroes like Cagney, Bogart, and Garfield emulated the real-life illegalities of John Dillinger, who appropriately was gunned down by FBI agents oustide a Chicago movie theater in July 1934.

Dillinger's alleged killer, Melvin Purvis, proved a popular guest on radio's *Fleischmann's Yeast Hour*. Millions of middle-class children mailed in boxtops from Quaker Oats packages and earned detective badges and membership cards in a vividly imagined war on crime. But the gunfire did not cease, and 12,000 people died annually as a result. In New York, and especially in the city's marketplaces, the mythical gunslinger or avenging bank robber was a deadly force. The gangs taking over restaurants, laundries, bakeries, and movie theaters themselves—these were hardly the stuff of individualistic legend. Together, they drained off nationally ten times what America spent on defense, more than the entire cost of the New Deal's ambitious social welfare programs.

And while all this was going on, Americans were coming more than ever before under the domination of a city they professed to distrust. "It would be as iconoclastic to praise New York," wrote Sinclair Lewis in 1938, "as to damn the Y.M.C.A."

On August 7, a week after Judge McCook in his charge to the extraordinary grand jury had called for "common sense means" in finding and eradicating rackets wherever they existed, the special prosecutor found himself with an embarrassing first catch. Dominic Tossone was nineteen years old, a petty hoodlum with a single arrest and suspended sentence on his record, tabbed as a racketeer by one of the complainants who rushed the Woolworth Building in the wake of the July 30 radio appeal. Tossone, a victim of loan sharks, had slipped a note to a shopkeeper demanding thirty dollars and revealing, "This is your last chance. If you don't pay, the building won't be worth a dam cent."

At that, armed detectives emerged from hiding, took Tossone into custody, and provoked laughter among knowing New Yorkers. Their Lochinvar's debut had been less than heroic. Dewey himself tried to put a good face on a bad judgment. "I have said we will prosecute every racketeering case that comes to us, large or small, and I meant it." Tossone went to an Elmira reformatory, but not before he pointed up the iron grip enjoyed by loan sharks over people desperate for cash. Dewey filed the information for future reference.

On August 19, Dewey left the city for an undisclosed location—actually, three days with his mother in Owosso—and took along 750 pages of testimony amassed by the runaway grand jury. "I may have to pretend that I am studying evidence," he wrote a friend lightheartedly, "but if you should read that in the newspapers do not believe it. The public does not understand the necessity for vacations." He returned to find his work cut out for him. A process server named Albert Kahn already hired for the Dewey staff was found to have ties to Tammany Hall through a half-brother. Kahn's personal conduct was above reproach, his record with Judge Seabury commendable. But rumors had reached the fourteenth floor that members of a Tammany club in the Seventeenth District were boasting of "a direct wire" into the Dewey office. As far as Dewey was concerned, images were as important as reality, especially if prospective witnesses were to overcome their fears and testify. Kahn was fired.[20]

The pervasive secrecy had its drawbacks. An accountant who arrived at work early one morning walked by the bank vault where records were housed, protected by round-the-clock guards and a sensitive Holmes alarm system. Somehow, the man accidentally tripped the alarm. Within two minutes, twenty-three radio cars and a squadron of special police had thrown a cordon around the building. It was the comic price exacted for playing by the rules of a prosecutor who told his men, "Never tell anybody what you are going to do tomorrow."[21]

A more serious challenge was the reluctance of many union leaders to accept at face value the idealistic intentions of a Republican from Owosso. It was one thing for the Communist *Daily Worker* to shriek, "Hands Off the Unions" and urge workers to ignore Dewey's call for help in rooting out racketeers within their ranks. And few on the fourteenth floor were surprised when the painters' union, long a captive of racketeers Lepke and Gurrah, publicly denounced "government agents" for dangerous intervention in union affairs.

More worrisome was the attitude of the city's major labor chieftains, men like Sidney Hillman, David Dubinsky, and George Meany. Early in August, Dewey sprung raids against six members of the left-wing furriers' union. At the same time, rumors floated around of large fees accepted by the prosecutor when still in private practice from bakery officials hoping to destroy unions in that important industry. In fact, as Dewey was able to prove to the press's satisfaction, the $2,500 he'd received that spring came from a Brooklyn firm threatened with dynamiting by an illegal owners' association, the United Cake, Pastry, and Pie Bakers, which sought a monopoly for itself and nothing for bakery workers.

Other than denying the charge, Dewey stuck to his silent ways. "The testimony in court will speak for itself," he said when asked if his raids on the furriers made him, in effect, an ally of "sweatshop operators." When independent furriers took the stand and told of beatings and forced membership in a fur racket, he was proven right. Privately, he was doing much more talking, over lunch at the Bankers' Club with George Meany, over dinner in his own home with Hillman and Dubinsky. Meany's pledge of support was wholehearted. His fellow labor leaders made similar promises, while stoutly denying any knowledge of racketeering in the garment industry. Dewey went to his grave convinced otherwise.

At a statewide conference on crime called by Governor Lehman in October, Dewey publicly denied that he was engaged in labor-baiting. "My only interest in labor," he told delegates, "will be when I find evidence that a dishonest labor leader has sold out." With that assurance, the American Federation of Labor issued a ringing endorsement, and Dubinsky joined an in-house committee to police unions against racketeers.

Until 1935, no one had really tried to map out the New York underworld, and Dewey had little to guide him initially besides rumors, hearsay, his five-by-eight cards, and a few leads from his days in the U.S. attorney's office. Inevitably, there were blind alleys up ahead, and detours from the main objectives—defined as Dutch Schultz and his policy racket (including Dixie Davis, the mouthpiece lawyer for Schultz and his political patron Jimmy Hines); the monarchs of industrial racketeering, Lepke and Gurrah; other racketeers like Tootsie Herbert, who controlled the poultry trade; and a pair of trucking dictators, Johnny Dio and Jimmy Doyle.[22]

In August and September, Dewey was staking out the terrain, assigning each of his assistants to the field best suited to his talents, from artichokes to pinball. A continuing flood of complaints was sifted for useful nuggets, and detectives were put to work compiling a census of the underworld. By the time it was finished, a hundred different rackets, employing perhaps 25,000 criminals, were listed on paper. The dollar-a-year men were given Dewey's card and sent to work in the County Bar Association's library, and a former NRA lawyer named Stanley Fuld undertook his own extensive research in areas as diverse as search and seizure, subpoena jurisdiction, and whether a grand jury could legally meet any place but a county courthouse.

The group around Dewey was beginning to mesh—at staff meetings where irrelevant or wordy questions were dismissed with a cold stare and harsh words, and over long lunches and dinners where the law in all its variety dominated every conversation. There were impromptu brainstorming sessions with Dewey in the men's room or the corridor, where he grabbed two or three assistants on his way out, at midnight or later, to hash over new dilemmas in his car en route to 1148 Fifth Avenue. Frances complained that he brought his work home with him, a criticism soon ragged with repetition.

Actually, she didn't get to see that much of him. Several months into the investigation, a job applicant was surprised to receive a call from Lillian Rosse at ten o'clock one night asking if he could possibly come downtown for an interview with Mr. Dewey immediately. David Worgen hurried to the fourteenth floor to find every light ablaze and the office in full swing, with assistants and stenographers bustling about, and Dewey himself issuing orders as crisp as the autumn air outside. Soon, Worgen himself was duplicating the insane hours, and admiring his boss's grasp of every detail of every investigation, those pending and those in prospect. Peppering the men with questions about leads and witnesses garnered from his daily luncheon with the chief assistants, Dewey exhibited as well a habit of picking up a conversation or running away with a train of thought before another man could get five words out of his mouth.[23]

His vitality seemed endless. Much of it rested on his ability to leave a staff meeting or case conference where his presence wasn't required, lie down on an office couch, and instantly fall asleep, waking precisely fifteen minutes later refreshed for whatever lay ahead. He also knew how to keep a discreet distance from subordinates. At one meeting with old associates from the U.S. attorney's office, Dewey fretted over his title within the new circle. He didn't want the men calling him by his first name—"Pretty soon the office boy would be calling me Tom"—and it was Murray Gurfein who hit on the happy solution: like George Medalie, Dewey would be known simply as the Chief. To his personal friends, the boss confided that, when alone, they could still call him Tom. Only in the presence of others would he have to be addressed by the more formal title.[24]

Jack Rosenblum was such a friend, an eccentric, exhaustive investigator who seemed constitutionally incapable of toiling during daylight, who as an Orthodox Jew found dining out a never-ending trial, who was found by early arrivals to Medalie's office praying, and whose superstitious instincts didn't permit him to leave a room except as he had entered it. A Lower East Side alumnus, Rosenblum mirrored the neighborhood, inspiring comparison with an untrained boxer, full of heart, quick on his feet, yet less polished than the brilliant, retiring Stanley Fuld for example. But no one ever doubted Rosenblum's investigative skill or tenacity, traits much in evidence when he joined the staff as the fourth and final chief assistant in mid-August. It was a difficult time for Rosenblum, who had just suffered his first defeat ever as a member of the U.S. attorney's staff, a heartbreaking setback in a farcical proceeding for income tax evasion against Dutch Schultz.[25]

For Schultz, the summer of 1935 was the best and worst of times, when he could win his tax trial and forfeit his policy empire, father a son and set in motion other men of equal greed and thirst for blood, including Dutch's own. And dogging every step of his way, Schultz found his old nemesis from the U.S. attorney's office.

In the dull hours of a waning life, Herman Flegenheimer's son was worried about his soul. At his second tax trial, held in the tiny upstate farm town of Malone, Schultz reached eagerly for the proffered rosary beads of an admirer. "I'm going to need all the good luck I can get," he said. It was one of the few statements made at the trial that might pass for truth.

Having barely survived a hung jury at his first trial in Syracuse, Schultz and his counsel, Dixie Davis, decided to take advantage of the new venue, a bucolic hamlet more contemptuous of New York City than of any gangster allegedly terrorizing its sinful precincts. The notoriously cheap Schultz even opened his purse strings for a change, hiring a public relations firm to bolster his image among the good people of Malone. In the process, he became his own best advocate. Small children got pats on the head, old ladies graceful bows. Flowers and candy flooded the local hospital, bartenders discovered large tips, and the whole town was invited to dance and drink, courtesy of Mr. Flegenheimer, at the largest dance hall money could rent.

When the trial opened on July 23, Davis wove preposterous spells before credulous farmers and matrons in polka-dot dresses. Within eight days, Schultz was a free man, the cheers of townspeople ringing in his ears. Only Judge Frederick Bryant refrained from joining in the merriment. "Your verdict is one that shakes the confidence of law-abiding people," he sternly informed the jurors. "You will go home with the satisfaction—if it is a satisfaction—that you have rendered a blow against law enforcement and given aid and encouragement to the people who flout the law. In all probability, they will commend you. I cannot."

In New York, Dewey joined in Judge Bryant's expression of outrage, while Mayor La Guardia went still further. The Little Flower declared his city off limits to the Dutchman, a verbal placebo typical of the man who campaigned tirelessly against "punks and tinhorns" with mixed results—witness a highly publicized raid on local slot machines, truckloads of which were dumped in the East River as cameras whirred, while the rest were hastily shipped to the more hospitable climate of Huey Long's Louisiana.

Schultz sounded less than awed. "So there isn't room for me in New York," he said with a sneer in his voice. "Well, I'm going there. And nobody is going to put us out." As for the newly appointed special prosecutor, the bootlegger turned racketeer professed no fear. "If the feds couldn't get me, I guess this fellow Dewey can't do much." Schultz intended to return to Manhattan within a couple of weeks, "just as soon as I show these people up here a good time."

Cockier than ever, Dutch enjoyed his notoriety, the bantering with reporters, even the two cents a day it cost to read about himself in the papers. Yet, beneath the insouciance, Public Enemy Number One was rapidly losing his grip on reality. Schultz was, at heart, a bourgeois gangster, who, unable to work, was forced to seek refuge from his friend Luciano. No longer did he court danger as he once had, showing up at the opening of a Times Square nightclub a few days after Dewey first indicted him in 1933. Now, 100,000 posters with his face on them cast Schultz into a private jail just as confining as any run by the state. The men around Luciano had been anticipating the Dutchman's conviction at Malone, and the day when they might divvy up his policy and restaurant rackets among themselves. Even Bo Weinberg had given Schultz up for lost, and offered to help in the division of spoils if only Luciano would protect his own hard-earned share.

Jack Rosenblum's addition to the Dewey staff signaled a fresh assault on an old, untried charge of evading state taxes, a crime Schultz had inadvertently acknowledged during the Malone proceedings. State tax officials worked in tandem with the special prosecutor's office, and Dewey assigned Bill Herlands to launch a massive probe of the restaurant racket, in which the shadowy figure of Schultz's henchman Jules Martin kept emerging. Martin himself had been murdered a few months earlier, after Schultz, drunk and unhinged by his own problems, accused his old friend of embezzling $21,000. Coming from the source, it was as good as a death sentence. "You can insult Arthur's girl," Dixie Davis said later, "even steal her from him, spit in his face, push him around, and he'd laugh it off. But don't steal even a dollar that belongs to him. You're dead if you do."

The man who shot Jules Martin himself at pointblank range, then had his body dumped in a Troy snowdrift, was a man coming apart. He was reading biographies of Napoleon and Genghis Khan— "There was a mass murderer for you," he laughed—and talking for hours about life after death and his own desired conversion to Catholicism. As he had betrayed others, so others were now betraying him, and Schultz knew it. The tensions of his life were becoming too great to sustain. He couldn't pick up a phone without imagining Dewey listening in. More often than not he was right.

"I hope your ears fall off," he'd shout before slamming the receiver down. After a few drinks, he liked to rip the instrument apart and smash it on the floor. A bizarre verbal shorthand was developed. "Listen. He cannot see. He cannot give. Do you understand?" was the message relayed to his lawyer, Dixie Davis, one day. (Later, these transcripts would be used in Davis' disbarment.) Dutch thought he could deceive the tiny microphones that picked up every word, that he could tap a pencil loudly and talk under the sound, could ignore the mike embedded in the earpiece that continued monitoring his conversation long after he hung up that instrument.

Worse yet were the ravages that self-interest inflicted on his former sidekicks, including Bo Weinberg. By the time Schultz returned to New York in September 1935, he found fewer than twenty-five of his gang members still loyal. His sensitive nose picked up a distinctly unfriendly atmosphere that prompted him to pay a call on his supposed protector, Lucky Luciano. Most of their visit was consumed with Schultz's eager quest for information about the Catholic Church. To Lucky, he confessed that Christ alone had sustained him through his eighteen-month ordeal.

Soon after, Schultz put a tail on Weinberg, whose loyalty had included serving sixty days in jail on the old contempt charge pressed by Dewey. Like Schultz, who had recently married a hatcheck girl from a Harlem nightclub, Bo too had walked down the aisle. He had also shown signs of developing independent ambitions, to Schultz an intolerable offense. The Dutchman murdered Weinberg in a Forty-seventh Street hotel, then loaded his body on a delivery truck for burial in a Catskill forest. Bo's death only caused new problems for his killer. The dead man was a popular figure in the underworld, valued for his steadfastness and daring. Then, too, the shooting was—for Luciano and his associates, who were commonly known as the Big Six—a distasteful reminder of the bloody, unrestrained competition of Prohibition. Lucky's modus operandi was an avoidance of self-destructive street warfare. Instead, he had built a criminal board of directors, bound by their word in the best Sicilian tradition, voting by hand, not trigger finger. Now, with Schultz going his unpredictable way, there might be problems for mobsters who sought, if not respectability, at least the trappings of a prosperous peace.

On September 20, Dewey upped the ante, revealing that he might impanel a second special grand jury, so mountainous was the evidence of wrongdoing piling up from tips, wiretaps, and detective surveillance. Indeed, the grand jury then sitting was being forced to give three or four hours each day to the job of interviewing some 500 witnesses between September 4 and December 27. Meanwhile, it was leaked that the men on the fourteenth floor were preparing at least 3,000 more witnesses to talk about rackets and racketeering. With that, the first grand jury pleaded exhaustion, and the prosecutor was strongly inclined to put a second investigative body into the field.

What wasn't leaked was the progress being made against the loan shark business, known by its victims as the Shylock racket, and Schultz's restaurant racket, which held over 300 restaurants, cafeterias, and nightclubs in its extortionate grip. But the rumors served a purpose. They lured victims, especially of the loan sharks, to the Woolworth Building, and lent credibility to Dewey's crusade at a time when it commanded headlines promising achievements to come rather than accomplishments under the belt. It was precisely to satisfy an impatient public that Dewey moved quickly to round up the most odious of the estimated 2,000 loan sharks bilking New Yorkers out of at least $3 million a year.

On September 25, Schultz was arrested again, but this time in Perth Amboy, New Jersey. He was picked up by local cops, in a prearranged deal that had him out on $10,000 bail within three hours. Or would have, until an assistant U.S. attorney appeared on the scene and revealed that the Dutchman was still under scrutiny by New York's special prosecutor. One way or another, Dewey and Rosenblum were determined to drag Schultz into a courtroom where his money and influence would be impotent. Once again, the scions of organized crime gathered in Luciano's suite at the Waldorf-Astoria, this time to decide on a response to Dewey's mushrooming inquiry.

Schultz had become a distinct public relations problem. Worse, in his current frame of mind, what was there to keep the Dutchman from pointing a finger at all of them? Long ago, Dewey had established his method of capturing and prosecuting lawbreakers for the information they could give against men who broke bigger laws with greater impunity. The question didn't require lengthy debate; it had already been answered by Schultz himself, who tipped off Luciano's master enforcer Albert Anastasia that he had a plan of his own to answer Dewey's menace. As might be expected, it involved violence at close range.

On September 16, Dewey took time out to address a Jewish charities dinner and explain for the first time in public his concept of sociological jurisprudence. "The criminal law is still dominated by the ancient and outworn theory that the simple cure for crime is the punishment of the offenders," he said. This was "punitive rather than preventative," a mockery of the sociological emphasis on rooting out the true causes of crime, including poverty and society's own failure to live up to its generous promises.

At a lunch not long before, a friend had expressed the wish that all of New York's criminal population might be loaded on a skiff, taken out, and then dumped into the harbor, preferably in international waters. Dewey's response had been a long harangue on civil liberties and the need to follow established procedures. But in his speech on criminal justice, he did not limit himself to legal theorizing. Instead, he dipped his toe in political waters.

"There are stupid and distressed people in this country who today are willing to sacrifice their individual rights and espouse a dictatorship," he said heatedly. If the audience concluded that an abnormally high number of the stupid and distressed lived in Louisiana, where Huey Long had just been assassinated, that was fine with the prosecutor. But he wasn't drawing state boundary lines around his arguments about "human wreckage" and "false panaceas" held out by charlatans like Long. "A hungry and ignorant people," Dewey worried, "might sell their freedom in the delusion that they will thereby be fed." Only by caring "decently and intelligently" for the needs of susceptible citizens might the American people have their character preserved and society itself pulled back from the brink of suicide.

Then he went home to a wife less than a month away from giving birth to their second son. Frances Dewey was never much of a morning person. She liked to spend mornings in bed, storing the energy needed to match her husband's late-night hours. Each morning, Tom left her still asleep a little after eight, and, not wishing to disturb her with phone calls from the bedroom, walked around the corner to a little drugstore where he phoned his office for overnight developments, ordered breakfast and then called Frances herself as a daily wake-up service. The routine wouldn't be hard to pick up, especially if you put surveillance men on Dewey's trail. Dutch Schultz had done precisely that, and out of the details of the prosecutor's domestic schedule, the Dutchman hatched a plot to eliminate once and for all the man who had made his life miserable for three years, and now threatened much worse. The plan was simplicity itself. When Dewey entered the drugstore and seated himself in his familiar phone booth, a gunman posing as a customer would drill the booth with gunfire, then whirl around and cut down the pharmacist. By using a silencer, the assassin should have his shots lost in the noise of early morning traffic and be able to slip away into the hurried crowds of New Yorkers on their way to work.

Dewey had guards—insisted upon by John Lyons after an anonymous caller had instructed Frances to come downtown to the morgue and identify her husband's body—but he objected to their presence, and insisted they stay outside the drugstore. So the plan evolved, and a date, October 25, was set for its execution. Schultz offered the job to Albert Anastasia, who promptly reported it to Luciano. More rational than the Dutchman, Lucky saw grave problems behind the plot. For one thing, there was a certain gangland etiquette, in which you killed your own without stepping across the boundary of polite society to gun down a civilian. Dewey said as much himself when asked if he feared for his life. In addition, the cold-blooded murder of the dynamic young crime fighter might set the underworld's cause back for years, exploding the carefully wrought unity within the organization, not to mention the respectability and political influence achieved since the end of Prohibition.

For six hours, Luciano and his council debated Schultz's future. Later, it was said that the most vociferous demand for his head came from Lepke, the petty thief and garment district goon turned racketeer extraordinaire. When it came time to vote, each man cast a single ballot, of equal importance, as dictated by Luciano's rules. All but unanimously, it was decided that Schultz would have to go. Only Meyer Lansky urged the long view.

"Right now," he told Luciano, "Schultz is your cover. If Dutch is eliminated, you're gonna stand out like a naked guy who just lost his clothes."

All this time, Dewey was typically preoccupied. "My new job is going smoothly and is tremendously interesting," he told his brother-in-law on October 16. "I rather think that within the next two or three months we will begin producing substantial indictments." He forgot to mention another event of the day, the birth of a son, John Martin Dewey. Obsessed with the Schultz and loan shark investigations, on the verge of important discoveries in rackets overwhelming the restaurant and garment industries, Dewey barely reached the hospital before his wife gave birth. After a short stay by her side, he was back at his desk, avoiding any display of nerves or cigars, eager to resume the work at hand.[26]

His own showdown with Schultz had been building for weeks, ever since a Harlem policy banker's son-in-law, feuding with his wife, walked into the office and offered details of the methods used by Schultz to take over the game. The man went on to describe political protection purchased from Jimmy Hines, who as de facto leader of Tammany could instruct magistrates to go easy and have cops who insisted on doing their job transferred. All this served to reinforce wiretaps from 1933 on which Schultz and his lawyer had discussed meetings at "Jim's office" and upcoming appearances before "Jim's judges."

New taps were placed on Davis, seven lawyers and accountants were instructed to burrow into the restaurant racket, and other investigators put to work examining court records for evidence of political favoritism. Eunice Carter and Victor Herwitz were sent to Harlem to pick up the local trail leading to Schultz. In a neighborhood bar, the pair were asked their mission by a police inspector. Just up for a drink, they told him, and he promptly issued an invitation to a shipboard party marking his departure for Europe in a couple days. Back at the Woolworth Building, Dewey told his assistants to accept, and keep an eye out for suspicious characters.

There was plenty to see, including gangsters handing around drinks and presenting cases of liquor, one of which went to Carter and Herwitz. Fine, Dewey responded, keep the booze, along with the next gift from the underworld, ringside tickets for a Joe Louis fight. "Let them think you've been bought," he told them, while he and Rosenblum plowed ahead with the main case against Schultz for state tax evasion. On October 21, the two men worked long after sundown, preparing the presentation that Rosenblum was to begin for the grand jury in the morning.[27]

Schultz spent October 23, as most of his days of late, in a three-room suite at Newark's Robert Treat Hotel, taking his meals with a shrinking band of loyalists at the nearby Palace Chop House. That evening, he was accompanied in a little room off the bar by bodyguards Lulu Rosencrantz and Abe Landau. For comic relief, there was a onetime court jester to Rothstein and Diamond and the model for Damon Runyon's Regret, Abba Dabba. Named for a popular candy bar, the sidekick, who had been christened Otto Berman by his parents, was a financial genius who did quadratic equations in his head and earned every penny of the $10,000 Schultz paid him weekly to forecast and doctor the racetrack numbers on which the policy game based its payoffs.

A Chinese cook was frying a steak for the Dutchman when Schultz went into the men's room at ten-thirty. As he did, three men darkened the door leading to Park Street, the bartender jumped for cover, and bullets rained down, two dozen at least. Abba Dabba and Rosencrantz fell in the first volley, while Landau, a sharpshooter from his days as a Brooklyn fish market terrorist, stayed on his feet, banging away at his attackers. Schultz cowered inside the men's room. Later, Charlie "the Bug" Workman claimed to have shot him.

The local District Attorney found a more ironic fact. It was Abe Landau, dying on the floor of the Palace, who aimed a single bullet into his chief as he emerged from the lavatory. Whether an act of revenge, or the mistaken firing of a delirious, half-blind victim, Landau's motivation was never explained.

Within ninety minutes, another Schultz lieutenant was gunned down while having a midnight shave in a Times Square barbershop. Still another mobster was found dead in a burning car in Brooklyn's Navy Yard section, while over the next five days, ten more racketeers would die or suffer gunshot wounds. Back at the Palace Chop House, police found an adding machine; Schultz had spent the evening totting up his policy take from the last seven weeks. Income: $827,253.54. Expenses: $313,711.99. They also discovered a final bit of doggerel from the self-deprecatory pen of Abba Dabba.

> M. A. Dabba, rode out of the west,
> With soot on his shirt, and egg on his vest.
> "Oh gimme," he said, "the light of the stars,
> Instead of the tinkle of bottles on bars."

The firestorm sweeping across the underworld that night deprived Dewey of his chief target. It also altered radically the lives of everyone caught up in the Schultz ring. Dixie Davis, frantic with fear, called a red-haired rodeo rider and ingenue from Broadway's *Life Begins at 8:40* named Hope Dare, proclaimed the heat to be on, and suggested immediate escape as the better part of valor. Lucky Luciano made his way to Miami, where the sun was bright, the air tropical, and the police friendly. At his side was his own favorite chorine, Miss Gay Orlova, an emigré from revolutionary Russia and actress whose main talent seemed to be for wearing diamonds.

Everything about the Schultz affair was theatrical. The victim lingered for twenty-two hours, while photographers snapped his picture en route to surgery and reporters rushed to jot down the mystifying mutterings that filtered into each successive edition of New York's papers for October 24. "George, don't make no bull moves," the old ham quoted. "What have you done with? Oh, mama, mama, mama. Oh, stop it, oh, oh, oh. Sure, sure, mama. Now listen: Phil, fun is fun. Ah, please, papa. What happened to the sixteen? Oh, oh, he done it. Please! John, please, did you buy the hotel? You promised a million. Sure, get out. I want to know ... Oh, oh, dog biscuit and when he is happy, he doesn't get snappy. . . . Oh, cocoa, know, he thinks he is a grandpa again, he is jumping around. No hobo and pobo, I think he means the same thing."

For amateur sleuths—and that seemed to include most of New York's fourth estate—speculation was rife about the meaning of the dying man's gibberish. George was thought to be George Weinberg, Bo's brother and an important enforcer in his own right. John and the hotel were interpreted to mean Jimmy Torrio, a Luciano ally and investment partner. At one point, Schultz opened his mouth, and out came a sentence acclaimed immediately by a college professor of English as great poetry in the stream-of-consciousness school.

"A boy has never wept, nor dashed a thousand kim."

In moments of lucidity, the Dutchman was approached by detectives from Dewey's office; and he said, "The boss himself," when asked who might have been responsible for his shooting. There were other reminders of past enmities, including a telegram with the cryptic message, "Don't be yellow. As ye sow, so shall ye reap." It was signed, Madame Sinclair, Madame Queen of Policy.

With evening coming on, Schultz sank lower and doctors abandoned any hope of saving him to testify in Dewey's court. The rites of the Catholic faith, which the gangster had lately embraced, were administered, and before he fell into a coma Schultz spoke one last time to those around him. "Please help me up. Henny. Max. Come over here. French-Canadian bean soup. I want to pay. Let them leave me alone." Trivia experts gnawed that one over until Charles Foster Kane said his Rosebud four years later. At 8:30 P.M., Schultz died, a confused, romantic monster who never really belonged to the underworld his organizational skills had admitted him to, who lacked both courage and charisma. But somehow he had intrigued the world's greatest city, and he had $7 million to show for it.

His body lay unclaimed in a Newark morgue for two days, while his mother and widow launched frantic, fruitless searches for wealth as fleeting as the gold of El Dorado. On October 28, Schultz's remains were smuggled out of a Bronx funeral home before dawn, in a black hearse that circled familiar streets for six hours and twice stopped at Coffee Pots along the way before a grim line of state troopers met the tiny cortege at the Westchester county line. Five floral pieces accompanied the dead man's mother, sister, and widow to his resting place in Gate of Heaven Cemetery. A carload of detectives trailed behind. Even in death, the Dutchman was not free of Dewey's surveillance.

Time would prove Schultz's grave a restless one. For now New York was embroiled in an all-out gang war following on the heels of his assassination. The morning of his rudimentary farewell, two more mobsters were shot to death outside an apartment on West

Eighty-fourth Street. But at the Woolworth Building, Dewey and his men were too busy counting the catch in their first large-scale raid to pay more than passing attention to a dead man. His own paranoia may have robbed them of Schultz, but another target nearly as inviting was being hit to maximum effect, salvaging in the process the prosaic crusade first launched in a radio talk asking for patience as well as cooperation.

6

"An NRA of Prostitution"

I didn't give up a good law practice to chase after prostitutes.
—THOMAS E. DEWEY

Six for five. That was the heartless, intransigent formula on which loan sharks punished New York's poor for their poverty. Borrow five dollars one week, pay six back the next. Borrow $100 and find yourself owing $120 within seven days; an annual interest rate of 1040 percent, compounded by beatings and threats and jobs terminated by frightened employers. With October 29 marking the end of three months in office, Dewey and his men clearly needed something spectacular to renew their mandate from a dubious public and press. When Sewell Tyng came in with the results of an extensive investigation of loansharking undertaken for the Russell Sage Foundation, he brought with him the perfect solution to Dewey's becalmed struggle against the racketeers.

From a public relations standpoint, no more odious prey existed. For years, slum dwellers and union men had been victimized by cut-throat usurers. Furriers told Dewey how they were encouraged to play card games and then sign for loans to cover their losses. Relief workers were betrayed to the shylocks by their own bureau chiefs, blacks in Harlem were warned to pay up or have their hair combed with lead, and borrowers were met outside their place of work and escorted to the East River by men carrying weapons beneath their coats. A seventy-two-year-old beautician described a 791 percent interest rate attached to a $200 loan. A transit worker told of borrowing fifty dollars, repaying seventy-five, only to be cut up by thugs and have a lien put on his meager salary when his infant son fell ill and he could no longer meet the escalating installment on his debt. Dewey repeated the story for years.

For now, he assigned half a dozen staffers to interview over a thousand witnesses. Dewey refused to move until he had more than one solid witness against a suspect; in some cases, by the time of their arraignment, the usurers found their fate sealed by up to thirty victims. On the morning of October 29, fifteen squads of investigators set out at seven o'clock to locate and arrest two dozen of the most notorious sharks. Before leaving, Dewey warned them: Make no arrest in a private home; it might only lead families of those apprehended to tip off others. Instead, the suspects were picked up on street corners, in restaurants, and in subway trains. By nightfall, twenty-four shylocks were being led into a fourteenth-floor room of the Woolworth Building, with an entrance covered by a venetian blind through which victims could peep and safely pick out their persecutors.

Rounding up the sharks was one thing, convicting them under New York's antiquated laws quite another. Dewey decided to interpret the law imaginatively, to circumvent tradition with a radical plan that transformed the extraordinary grand jury convened in July into an impromptu magistrate's court, with Judge McCook presiding from two o'clock that afternoon until three the next morning. Instead of indictments, the prosecutor asked the court to return "informations" which, in a misdemeanor case, would have the same effect. McCook signed warrants as fast as he could. Some of the defendants were charged with assault, others with threats of violence or kidnapping. All were hit with a usury charge.

By following this novel method, Dewey could speed trials, and hold them not in the regular magistrates' courts but in the Court of Special Sessions. Here the definition of due process was loose, since Special Sessions predated the U.S. Constitution. By avoiding the magistrates, Dewey not only steered clear of those havens of crooked justice but also prevented the suspects themselves from returning to the streets to intimidate witnesses. This way, not a single victim would have to identify himself until the trial actually convened, a powerful incentive to cooperate, and one unavailable under standard procedure.[1]

As they came to realize their plight, the shylocks squealed furiously about violation of their rights. They, too, were victims of the Depression, they insisted, with families to feed like anyone else. Dewey was unmoved. "I never saw a crook yet who didn't point an accusing finger at somebody else . . . every defendant produces a sad story about sick relatives or the wife and children, after he is caught."

His plan worked flawlessly. Within thirty-five days, every shark had been tried before a panel of three judges, and for good measure Dewey added six more shylocks to the original covey. Only one was acquitted, and he escaped on a procedural error. In three months, the youthful prosecutor had achieved what five district attorneys with 150 assistants and 18,000 police at their disposal had been unable, or unwilling, to attempt. The New York *Times* was unrestrained in its praise. "Thousands of poverty-ridden clerks, taxi chauffeurs, office boys and men and women on home relief hailed the stroke with fervent joy," it reported. "Shabby, broken-spirited men approached the shylocks' ratholes with money scraped up at great sacrifice of pride and honor on the day of the raids and could not believe their ears when detectives met them and told them, 'Stick the money in your pocket; your Shylock's in jail.' Dewey," the *Times* concluded, "is a savior and hero to thousands."

The successful campaign against loansharking bought time and restored faith. Early in December, the extraordinary grand jury begged to be excused, and suggested in parting that two new panels be put to work in its place. Dewey agreed, Governor Lehman began looking for a judge to complement McCook, and for the moment an eerie silence descended over the Woolworth Building. The prosecutor and his investigation abandoned center stage and returned to the wings. Forces on both sides of the law settled in for a phony war as 1935 drew to a close.

"The public has grown to like Mr. Dewey," mused the *City Journal* at the end of December. "It likes the quiet, efficient manner in which he works, AND GETS THINGS DONE." Actually, the public had only sketchy headlines on which to form its judgment. It read of sudden raids making off with the books of the Flour Trucking Association, a million-dollar-a-year conduit between the baking industry and Lepke and Gurrah. It welcomed Dewey's declaration of interest in the year-old murder of William Snyder, a trucking union officer. Most of all, it appreciated the fine impartiality with which the special prosecutor excoriated capital as well as labor for refusing to cooperate in the campaign against racketeering. At a hospital fund-raising luncheon on December 11, Dewey rose at the head table to lambaste his hosts.

"There are few rackets which do not rest securely and luxuriously upon the throne of business," he informed a startled audience. "Not one businessman out of a hundred who has paid tribute has told the truth to my assistants." That included a man recently questioned whose books included a $2,000 payment marked off to "labor trouble," which in the garment district was a euphemism for Lepke and Gurrah, the Gorilla Boys. It seemed a mockery of social justice that it took years for a hospital to raise a couple million dollars to save lives while thousands of businessmen routinely coughed up 10 million each year to the poultry racket alone.

By now, the Woolworth Building was New York's hottest journalistic beat, even if Dewey did rule most of what he said off the record.

"I won't stand for that; I'll call your publisher" became a dreaded byword of press duty on the fourteenth floor. For most public figures, with their images and prospects at the mercy of reporters, such tactics would have been the surest guarantee of harsh treatment in the press. But in 1935, Dewey was attracting attention and support precisely because he was so obviously hard-boiled.

Headlines surrounded the prosecutor's office like an inky nimbus. They were more than enough to attract Fiorello La Guardia like a shark scenting blood. The Little Flower was a complex man, a flesh and blood cartoon cutout who raced to fires and conducted symphony orchestras and read the comics over the radio. To his beloved city, he was paternal; to those who worked for him, he was more often than not impossible. Short and rotund, the Mayor had stubby legs that barely reached the floor behind the ornate desk he maintained in his Napoleonic office at City Hall. Secretaries were kept frantic answering the six buzzers His Honor pushed constantly, and coping with an explosive temper coupled with a biting sarcasm that belittled his closest colleagues. Before a meeting with his commissioner of hospitals, one of the foremost experts in his field, the Mayor blasted the man in front of others as if he were a total incompetent. When they were alone, La Guardia said gruffly, "You know, we have to do this kind of thing for front." Another time, La Guardia was talking to his water commissioner. Already late for another appointment, he had to be reminded three times by a secretary that he was due elsewhere. After the third reminder, the Mayor fixed a beady stare on his guest and barked, "She's dumb enough to be a commissioner."[2]

La Guardia liked to present members of his administration with a bronze bone in a leather case to commemorate acts he thought especially stupid. When Tammany boss Tim Sullivan, relying upon his majorities on the Board of Estimate and Board of Aldermen for continued domination over city government, reminded La Guardia that it was the majority's business to advance a constructive program, the Mayor smiled knowingly and said, "In this administration, I am the majority." In a Stetson or fire chief's helmet, Fiorello was brusque, impetuous, unforgiving, and a shameless exhibitionist. He was also hopelessly in love with his city, passionate about giving it a clean, honest, progressive administration, and adored for his very excesses. Whether driving subordinates to tears or punching a slow bureaucracy into frazzled compliance with his wishes, La Guardia epitomized the contradictions of his metropolis as few urban leaders before or since.

The Mayor could not abide playing second fiddle in anyone's orchestra; and as Dewey skyrocketed to fame beyond New York's boundaries, his relationship with the special prosecutor took on suspicious overtones. Both men were individualists, with a white hot core of ambition and strong territorial instincts. Yet, whereas La Guardia tolerated Republicans so long as they could provide the margin of victory within the broader Fusion movement, Dewey's allegiance to the party of his ancestors was deep and instinctive. La Guardia loved publicity; Dewey preferred to work in secret and reap the headlines afterward. "Gratitude was never part of La Guardia's makeup," Dewey said later. He also remembered the Little Flower as "dreadfully ill-mannered . . . about as rude as any public official I ever knew."[3]

The first run-in between the two men was more comical than portentous. On the day after Christmas 1935, La Guardia drove up before dawn to a Bronx produce market, produced from his pocket a proclamation banning the sale of all artichokes in New York, and, having earned his daily quota of sensations, retreated to City Hall. His heavy-handed attack on the artichoke racket was retracted a few days later; in the meantime, there had been congratulatory editorials and rich dividends of publicity to savor. More serious rifts would develop in 1937, when La Guardia felt that Dewey, by then running for district attorney, was claiming entirely too much credit for that year's sweeping Fusion victory, and again a year later, when a Dewey-for-Governor boom threatened whatever lingering hopes La Guardia himself might entertain for high office in 1940.

Typical of their relationship was a trip they shared to Albany one day in 1938, when the Mayor asked Dewey, by then District Attorney, about rumors regarding possible police corruption in New York. The inference was clear: that Dewey was holding out, protecting miscreants or husbanding headlines for his own use. The D.A. insisted that nothing of the sort was true, and that he would be the first to blow the whistle if and when he ever came across hard evidence linking any cop to dishonesty or graft. La Guardia persisted, finally goading Dewey into saying that he had heard some rumors —only rumors—about a certain police inspector from the Harlem beat.

That was enough for Fiorello. Within a week, Dewey received a letter on official stationery instructing him to turn over forthwith all the "evidence" he might have collected to the Police Commissioner for immediate disciplinary proceedings. The District Attorney, who prided himself on having a close relationship with the cops, and resented anyone trying to muscle in on his domain, hit the roof. For five minutes he swore a blue streak, then calmed down sufficiently to dictate the following response to La Guardia: "Dear Mr. Mayor: You must be mistaking me for somebody else. I can recall no such conversation. Faithfully yours, Thomas E. Dewey.[4]

Eunice Carter knew the streets of New York. A black woman, hired by Dewey for her command of Harlem poolhalls as well as Albany committee rooms, Mrs. Carter knew from years of work in Women's Court all about prostitution and bail bondsmen and shyster lawyers like Abe Karp. Karp's uncanny ability to get any girl off with, at worst, a suspended sentence, struck her as curious. She listened to the hard-luck stories the women told, and quickly perceived a pattern. The "innocent girl from out of town, picked up while visiting friends" was one favored explanation. What she didn't know at the time was that Karp not only coached the girls to tell a convincing tale but slipped twenty-five dollars to a cop or magistrate with the admonition "It's O.K."

Invariably, the women were released. On the rare occasion that Karp's tactics failed, he simply told the unlucky prostitute to go on the lam for a while. Night after night, Eunice Carter looked on, seeing the same women, the same lawyers, the same burlesque justice. Together with Murray Gurfein, she went to see Dewey, who promptly poured derision on the idea of reforming New York's morals. He hadn't taken the prosecutor's job to go after prostitutes, he reminded them. His interest lay in industrial racketeers, not madams and bookers. But that was precisely the point, Gurfein argued. Prostitution, the oldest of professions, and hitherto the most individualistic, had been turned into an assembly-line operation, with justice corrupted and laws flouted.

Still unconvinced, and concerned lest too much precious manpower be diverted from the main investigations at hand, Dewey nevertheless told Carter and Gurfein to go ahead and pursue a full investigation; when and if they were convinced that there definitely was a racket lurking behind the flimsy curtain of Women's Court, they were to come back and he would follow through. Armed with a court order signed by Judge McCook, Eunice Carter had wiretaps installed on dozens of whorehouses in Manhattan and Brooklyn. Detectives took up her post along Bail Bond Row. They, too, noticed how none of the suspects arraigned there ever spent more than a few hours behind bars. Men sat for hours at a time listening and copying what they heard over tapped phones. Others, inexperienced in shadowing suspects, stalked their quarry in rainstorms, only to find the prey waiting on a street corner, umbrella held out with an offer to escort the green detective back to the Woolworth Building. One investigator spent weeks looking for a suspect, before finding him listed in the Manhattan phone book.[5]

By October 1935, Dewey himself was caught up in the hunt, dog-earing a Rockefeller Foundation study on prostitution, and promising assistants that together they would find "weaknesses in the line" which might lead to criminal big shots. Frank Hogan was added to the investigative team, along with Charles Grimes and Harry Cole. Grimes was a curly-haired Yale athlete, a disgruntled exile from Harold Ickes' Interior Department, who attracted ribbing from street-smart colleagues for never being without his squash racket. His partner Cole was equally patrician, the thirty-year-old son of a banker, graduate of the Brown swim team, with his own yacht and a fierce admiration for Alexander Hamilton. Frank Hogan combined devout Catholicism with an Irish humor and a zeal for detail resembling his boss's.[6]

Together, Eunice Carter and her male colleagues sifted through tips from disaffected bookers and madams. From loan sharks they learned of vast financial transactions within the underworld, complicated by hoodlums who hit houses of prostitution for the cash they contained. They came to know criminal justice as practiced by the criminal, and tracked down whispers about a combine that herded girls from house to house, protected them when they got into legal trouble, and purchased favors from cops and magistrates. By the end of 1935, Dewey knew what his investigators had discovered for themselves, that prostitution had become a big business, administered as one. It was a vast racket employing perhaps 2,000 prostitutes in 300 houses throughout the city, "an NRA of prostitution," as Dewey put it.

Carter and her team discovered four major bookers, who phoned client madams each Sunday night and gave the word where to send their girls the next day, in a bawdy Orpheum circuit of sin. Prices were set, even if working conditions were not. The prostitutes worked a twelve-hour day, from 2 P.M. until 2 A.M., six days a week. Even in a two-dollar joint, some women could earn up to $400 a week—until the Combine stepped in. Then the women were forced to give half their pay to a madam, plus twenty dollars a week for room and board. A booker got ten dollars, a doctor five more for performing weekly check-ups. When the racket took over, it demanded ten dollars a week from each woman as a bonding fee, as well as a healthy share of each house's income. Before long, the bookers themselves became mere employees of the Combine, and even the madams, a notoriously independent lot, were beaten by strong-arm men or robbed if they resisted the collectivization of their industry.

If it all sounded like the stuff of detective pulp novels, Dewey's investigators found evidence to the contrary. Repeatedly, they heard the same names mentioned: Ralph Liguori and Abie Wahrman, Tommy the Bull Pennochio and Little Davie Betillo. To criminal insiders, what made these men interesting was their known friendship with Charley Lucky, as Luciano was called in the underworld. One detective assigned to pose as an aspiring booker soon found himself talking shop with Jimmy Frederico, a general manager of sorts who was none too impressed when the undercover agent walked in with five whores hired, with the people's money, from an Eighth Avenue dive called the Bucket of Blood.

"If Tommy was here," said Frederico, "he'd bust you up." It seemed that cops liked nothing better than nabbing prostitutes, even those employed by the Combine. "We're paying too much now," Jimmy sighed. The agent apologized and changed the topic to the mechanics of protection once a house was opened for business. Relax, Frederico told him, "we take care of everything."

Dewey knew he was getting close to something important. It was a detour from his original route that might provide, if nothing else, another dazzling headline grabber to satisfy the public while work on industrial rackets proceeded quietly. Like the illegal trade associations, the prostitution racket was a pyramid, built on the tawdry labors of prostitutes, their madams, their bail bondsmen and bookers. At the apex stood Frederico, Pennochio, Betillo, and— who? Probably no one, the prosecutor concluded as he set about planning the most spectacular raid in a city almost inured to spectacle. Here, as throughout his budding investigation, necessity was the mother of innovation. To grab a bunch of prostitutes and force them to testify against madams would be easy, Dewey reasoned. It had been done before, to no lasting effect. To grab madams and persuade them to talk against the bookers was also a fairly simple task.

But what if Dewey's forces could stage a whole series of raids, a clean sweep that might ensnare prostitutes, madams, bookers, and bail bondsmen, along with those suspected of actually ruling over this seamy society? By holding the entire lot as material witnesses, Dewey and his men could then bargain for valuable information against the princes of New York's underworld. It was an audacious plan, requiring absolute secrecy and split-second timing. There were hundreds of details that could not be entrusted to anyone lest they should somehow slip to the enemy.

At the end of January 1936, Dewey reserved the thirteenth floor of the Woolworth Building, a barren, uncarpeted expanse shunned by the superstitious, yet now prepared to house a hundred or more guests of the city for several days. He checked on food, on toilets, on coffee, stashed $500 in the office safe, and convened a staff meeting for Friday, January 31. Something major was planned for the weekend, he informed his assistants; they would all be required to report for work the next morning at eleven. Not a word of this was to reach wives or friends, but they were unlikely to be home before Sunday. More details would be provided the next day. In the meantime, everyone should go home, get some sleep, "and keep your damn mouths shut."[7]

That night, while most of his staffers slept, the first phase of Dewey's plan was carried out. The special prosecutor was in his office taking reports from sixteen detectives who for weeks had been keeping tabs on the men identified as the racket's leadership. After midnight, police seized Jack Eller, one of the four bookers, on Riverside Drive. Betillo, Pennochio, and Benny Spiller, a strong-arm man responsible for intimidating madams, were grabbed at 4 A.M. by a squad of cops dispatched personally by the prosecutor. The night was not without comedy. One cop, searching Eller's office after the nab, was startled to hear a phone ring. He realized that if he let it ring it might arouse suspicions among Eller's regular customers. So he picked up the receiver, struck a tough-guy note, and, with the aid of a map of Eller's houses, booked women all morning and into the afternoon. When Dewey heard of it, he roared with laughter.

Saturday morning found all four bookers in custody, one of them in Philadelphia, along with the reputed masterminds. Dewey had also caught in his net a presumably honest victim, a lawyer who had tried to prevent the arrest of a bail bondsman named Jesse Jacobs, and for his pains was hauled in as well. After all, as Dewey later explained to his staff, secrecy was imperative, and if a single lawyer's constitutional rights were violated for twenty hours—the length of time Dewey kept him in jail without a warrant—then how much more important was the overall success of the raid. Besides, the man had come over to the fourteenth floor "and voluntarily, I assure you, given us a long statement . . . he thanked us for our great courtesy and consideration."[8]

The newspapers were silent about Friday night's pyrotechnics. Dewey's own men knew nothing of what had happened. Even his four chief assistants were not informed of the raids until 9 A.M. when special messengers arrived at each of their houses with the news; Dewey didn't trust telephones. For Murray Gurfein, the night ahead meant weaseling out of a party at the Fifth Avenue Hotel apartment of his old employer Judge Julian Mack, and an evening out with his wife and his good friend Felix Frankfurter. Other men were sore at having to decline tickets to a Fordham basketball game, or forsake the treasured escape from work that Saturday night represented.

All that was promptly forgotten at 11 A.M., when Dewey for the first time unveiled his plan for the evening. At nine o'clock that night, eighty houses of prostitution were to be hit simultaneously by 160 plainsclothes police who wouldn't themselves know of their mission until an hour before the raids. To reduce the chance of leaks, the prosecutor had created teams of men who hadn't worked together before, and sent them to unfamiliar neighborhoods where, at precisely five minutes before nine, they would open envelopes with detailed instructions on where to go and what to do once they arrived. Not a single member of the Vice Squad was included in the army that would seize everyone present, pick up any physical evidence, and refrain from speaking to either women or customers. That was to be the job of Dewey and his staff.

The precautions unfolded: all prisoners were to be brought to 19 Barclay Street—the freight elevator entrance to the Woolworth Building—where they would be met by assistants wearing special badges. A fleet of taxicabs, already reserved sub rosa, would transport both raiders and suspects. Dewey wanted no ponderous paddy wagons to tip off underworld sources the moment a raid was under way. Telephone communications were double-checked. At 2 P.M. there was a class for receptionists on how to greet the guests expected later.

Dewey dismissed his men to lunch at the Dutch Tavern, and went back to his preparations. Police moved into the lobby of the Woolworth, ready to keep out anyone not approved of once the massive operation began. Murray Gurfein went home and then kept his date at Judge Mack's party. Around nine o'clock, he began edging toward the door of Mack's duplex. Unobtrusively, he slipped out and was on his way to work. Frankfurter and Eva Gurfein were sitting on a step and saw him go. The Harvard law professor remarked, "It was just for a bunch of whores he left us."

What did he mean by that? Mrs. Gurfein wanted to know. Elementary, replied Frankfurter. Knowing Murray, it had to be something very, very important, something unique to Saturday night, something perishable on the calendar and too sensitive to be mentioned. "It had to be whores."[9]

Frankfurter's deductive powers were on target, as raiding parties hit forty-one houses in Manhattan and Brooklyn. That left almost half the planned total unaccounted for, a suspicious rate of failure that was never adequately explained. But the successes were many and the resistance minor. Some of the women sprained ankles trying to outrace their pursuers. One fainted on a fire escape after climbing out the window, only to confront a detective lying in wait. As Gurfein left his party, little knots of men and women were gathering already at the Greenwich Street station, from which those arrested were to be escorted to Barclay Street. Meanwhile, at the raided houses, superintendents and doormen began frantically phoning others in the business all over town, only to discover that they too, had been raided. But why?

The Woolworth Building's freight elevator was busy for hours, disgorging young women in evening gowns and nothing else, in loud silks and satins, reeking of smoke and cheap perfume. Eunice Carter tagged each, then offered coffee and the hospitality of the special prosecutor's office. By midnight, a hundred suspects jammed every cubicle, every hallway and reception area on both floors. Loudly proclaiming their innocence or ignorance were some of the biggest madams in New York, women like Polack Frances, Sadie the Chink, Six Bits and the redoubtable 200-pound terror, Jennie the Factory. Most were waiting for Abe Karp to show up and spirit them away, as he had after previous busts. At this hour, silence and a brazen front seemed enough to tide the girls over until help arrived.

They could not know that the customary angels of mercy were themselves lying helpless in jail cells or scared off for fear of their own capture. As arresting officers inventoried hundreds of opium papers and several gross of condoms, it fell to the reticent researcher Stanley Fuld to utter the best line of the night. Confronted by an uncooperative tart who insisted that she always played bridge half naked, he reached over and opened a desk drawer brimming with confiscated prophylactics.

"That's very interesting," murmured Fuld, himself a fan of the game. "What rubber were you up to?"[10]

The prosecutor himself went out of his way to be gracious to the scarlet women now clogging his office. His greetings were friendly, accompanied by a handshake (which he scoured off in a washroom the moment he was alone). A secretary boiled a fountain pen used by one of the women to sign a sworn statement. But on the night of February 1, good manners seemed to have little success in eliciting from the prostitutes anything more than weak alibis and sneering resistance. One assistant tried and failed to get the truth out of Nancy Presser, Waxey Gordon's onetime companion; then he walked out shaking his head. "She says she's a virgin," he explained to a superior. Dewey himself strode down the hallway just as Nancy stuck her head out of the doorway.

"So you're Dewey," she groused. "Run along, Boy Scout, and peddle your papers."[11]

Dewey's men had weapons against the most intractable prisoners, including detailed wiretaps allowing them to impress the women with seeming omniscience. In some cases, two assistants would tackle a single prisoner, one adopting a soft, beguiling approach, while his partner let the woman know she could rot in jail unless she cooperated with the investigation. Livingston Goddard, one of Dewey's dollar-a-year men, had success of a sort after he offered a shaking drug addict named Molly Leonard a drink. "Oh, God, yes," the madam gasped in gratitude. Soon, she was talking about the Combine, and the apparently dominant position within it held by Little Davie Betillo.[12]

The more worldly of Dewey's suspects saw what was happening and marked it down as something very different from the usual raid. No bail bondsmen had shown up to spring them. No lawyers had come to coach them on what to say to a friendly magistrate. No bookers had emerged from the night with assurances that all would be well. Maybe Dewey's men were telling the truth, some reasoned, when they said they weren't interested in prostitutes and madams, but in the information they could provide against the Combine itself. Thus prodded, old resentments gradually surfaced. "They worked us like dogs for a couple of years," ran the common complaint, "and then they hurled us out." One madam pointed to an ugly scar on her head. "Look, look there," she screamed. "That's what Frederico done to me. Frederico himself. I want none of their bond racket. Things is tough enough as it is." The madam told of the economic bind in which she found herself, as the girls had complained of spending five dollars each week to see "a croaker." After she refused to join the Combine, Frederico had visited her establishment, smashed her head with a lead pipe, and sent Ralph Liguori over to rob her of thirty-six dollars. Still others told of threats if they ever talked, of slit throats and broken homes and sexual indignities that went with the job. Thelma Jordan talked of standing nude while one patron killed a pigeon, and of earning a hundred dollars for visiting a funeral director who lay in a coffin, his lips rouged and face waxen, while organ music played in the background.[13]

At three-thirty that morning, Dewey sat down, unshaven and bleary-eyed, for a quick off-the-record session with reporters, and a public expression of gratitude to the police and detectives who had carried out the operation. Then he returned to questioning witnesses. He phoned Judge McCook, who until then had been kept in the dark about the raids, with a request that he come immediately to the Woolworth Building. Dewey wanted to hold every single suspect picked up as a material witness in the case. McCook was startled by the call, and even more so by the bail he was asked to set on each girl, not the customary $300, but enough to guarantee that none of the hundred prisoners would soon return to the streets.

By five o'clock, there was a lineup, a fantastic procession of blowsy characters confidently awaiting their freedom now that a judge had arrived to set bail. "Not guilty, Your Honor" echoed through the halls, answered invariably with "Held as a material witness in $10,000 bail." For the first time that night, shock replaced annoyance as the dominant mood on the fourteenth floor. Simultaneously, another drama was unfolding in Jack Rosenblum's office, where Dewey's chief assistant was talking with David Marcus, alias David Miller, one of the bookers picked up the previous night and a man made reflective by a heart condition and a family. Miller related how he came to New York and found a job when jobs were scarce selling dresses door to door. He'd found prostitutes his best customers, and it wasn't long before he was booking girls himself, including his wife.

Rosenblum listened closely, signaling that Miller's wife might get immunity from prosecution as long as the couple cooperated. It was a twisting trail the booker took in his conversation, as he told of threats to independent operators made at the point of a gun. Eventually, talk turned to the ring's leaders. Who, Rosenblum wanted to know, pulled the strings that made Miller and others dance?

"Davie," the prisoner told him, "and Abie, and Charley."

Who was that? Rosenblum persisted. Charley, Miller told him, Charley Lucky. After a few more minutes of questioning, Rosenblum excused himself, then hurried two doors away to Dewey's office. The special prosecutor, it turned out, had some questions of his own for Miller. As the booker told of bullets fired at his car after he refused to join the Combine, word arrived that Molly Leonard was talking, and that Mildred Harris, another madam, had seconded Miller's identification of Luciano.[14]

Dewey didn't believe any of this. It was unbelievable that Lucky Luciano, boss of all the bosses, a smooth, savvy dictator whose major interests were narcotics and gambling, would allow himself to be caught up in prostitution, the one offense the Mafia held at arm's length. "I want that story investigated down to the smallest detail," he told Rosenblum. As the sun crept over Wall Street that Sunday morning, the outlines of a pattern were beginning to take shape. The real work lay ahead. Not until late afternoon were the last of the women booked and the men arrested the night before brought in for questioning. Judge McCook held the lot in $435,000 bail, then went home around seven o'clock. Dewey alone remained.[15]

Murray Gurfein arrived home to be greeted at the door of his apartment by his wife. "Did you arrest the whores?" she asked with a poker face. Gurfein was stunned. "Who told you?" he demanded. Eva maintained her poise. "Felix Frankfurter." A few weeks later, the Gurfeins had a baby daughter. The father threatened to name her Laverne or Lola, until the mother put her foot down. The girl was christened Susan.[16]

By Monday morning, Dewey had changed his tune. Now convinced by what he had heard from Dave Miller and Mildred Harris, he wasted no time in kudos for what had already been accomplished. All that, he told the assistants, was mere prologue to a far more improbable drama, the conviction of Luciano himself. It wasn't a universally shared view, even among his inner circle. Sol Gelb, destined to play a major role in soldering together the case against Luciano, dismissed Lucky's involvement out of hand. As for Dewey? "That guy's crazy."[17]

Gelb's boss was taking steps to prove otherwise. Pete Harris, Mildred's husband and a booker in his own right, was indicted and arraigned, and Charlie Breitel was assigned to get his story. Mildred herself put up resistance, until Breitel confirmed his suspicions that a child was involved, and the mother was reassured that Dewey had no desire to hurt any infant. She also won a written pledge of immunity from Sol Gelb—something she later denied at the trial. Nancy Presser continued to hold out, even took out a writ of habeas corpus and almost convinced a judge that she was an aspiring opera singer unjustly held. Then Dewey ordered a battery of tests, and the would-be diva was revealed to have syphilis, gonorrhea, and crab lice.[18]

Most of the other women took more readily to their new life after they were transferred to the Women's House of Detention in February, although some had cause to shudder when disembodied voices from the Sixth Avenue elevated warned them to remain silent or face the consequences. Special privileges included three dollars a day, all the food you could eat, a drink when you needed one, and charming young men to take you to the movies or buy you new stockings when your old ones developed runs. Some of the girls relaxed, and told what they knew. Others took to calling the prosecutor their Uncle Dee, and befriended his young staff of assistants. Ophelia Bishop, one of the city's more notorious whoremongers, adopted a maternal attitude toward one Dewey clerk fresh out of law school. "For you," she said to a callow Oscar Cohen, "you get it for nothing." In addition to the women, others with knowledge of the ring and its operations were scouted out, including a jailed former chauffeur for Jimmy Frederico who begged Vic Herwitz not to reveal his connection with the hookers. The underworld thought he was serving time for the respectable offense of peddling narcotics. Abe Karp was arrested cowering behind a piano in his brother-in-law's apartment.[19]

Behind closed doors Dewey was rewriting the very rules of criminal procedure. Along with Stanley Fuld, he was searching for an alternative to existing laws requiring suspects to be tried on individual counts, even if charged with committing, or causing to be committed, a hundred separate acts of violence. In a state court, state law applied, and in 1936 that meant separate trials on each count. But Dewey found himself confronted with a new kind of criminal, the racketeer who never personally threatened, bribed, stuffed a ballot box, or committed a murder, but left all that to underlings, distanced by a protective wall of henchmen and political accomplices.

With the acceptance of income tax evasion as a potent tool against racketeers, prosecutors like Dewey had succeeded too well by half. Thereafter, gangsters contributed at least a token of their illegal earnings to Uncle Sam. But state prosecutors could not avail themselves of the joinder indictment, a common device in federal courts, and thus no state investigation of racketeering was ever likely to succeed. Dewey set out to change this.

Supported by Governor Lehman, and by Herb Brownell in the legislature, Dewey sent to Albany a new statute providing for the joinder indictment in New York. A few civil libertarians objected, but their cries were drowned out by public applause. The City Bar

Association endorsed the measure, as did Mayor La Guardia, and by the first week in April, the State Senate had unanimously adopted what immediately became known as the Dewey Law.

Its first and most memorable target was even then soaking up the sun in Little Rock, Arkansas, the gambling mecca established by Owney Madden and Meyer Lansky, as a forerunner of Lansky's operations in Miami and Cuba. While Dewey was arguing for a grand jury indictment of Luciano, the gangster was secure in the company of his friend Dutch Akers, the chief of the Hot Springs detective force. Gay Orlova was there as well, lending her own brand of support. Then, on April 2, while strolling Bath House Row in Hot Springs, Luciano was approached by a New York detective named Stephen Di Rosa.

"You're a hell of an Italian," Lucky snorted as Di Rosa moved in to arrest him. His anger was short-lived; within four hours, Luciano was released on $5,000 bail provided by Akers. Back in New York Dewey exploded. He sent Ed McLean of his staff to join Wayne Merrick and other detectives already in Hot Springs, and gleefully jumped on a tip that Luciano had offered Carl Bailey, the state's attorney general, $50,000 to let him go after a second arrest. Threatening to expose the Razorback State as a welcoming haven for gangsters, Dewey succeeded in stiffening the AG's backbone. Luciano would not be released

Lucky seemed genuinely astonished. "I may not be the most moral and upright man that lives," he informed the press, "but I have not at any time stooped so low as to become involved in aiding prostitution." His indignation was lost in a swirling game of musical chairs. Demands that Hot Springs' sheriff turn the celebrated prisoner over to authorities in Little Rock went unheeded, until a dozen Arkansas Rangers armed with machine guns forced their way into the jail at dawn on the fourth and took Luciano over fifty-five miles of mountain road for incarceration in the state capital. "Did you need the whole militia to get me out?" he asked.

As the Dewey Law wended its way through the New York legislature, its author was finding Luciano a wily and resourceful opponent. Lucky tried to convince a judge that he was attending his sick mother in White Plains at the time the New York conspiracy was being hatched. Dewey's men testified he was at a racetrack placing bets. His bid for habeas corpus had been denied, but Luciano's lawyers moved for thirty days in which to reproduce the record of his hearing, a plan thwarted only when Ed McLean stayed up all night at Dewey's orders and did the job himself. A few days later, Dewey's long arm reached into the suspect's Little Rock cell and snatched him away. Five minutes before a legal stay was due to expire, detectives rushed in and hustled the prisoner onto a train held up for fifteen minutes by a cooperative Carl Bailey.

"Kidnap!" Lucky shouted. "You can't do this. It ain't legal." It was undeniably effective and dramatic, this unexpected return to a city that, just a few days before, barely knew Salvatore Lucania except as a shadowy figure lurking in the last paragraphs of newspaper stories focusing on the more spectacular Dutch Schultz. At Dewey's orders, Luciano's route was kept a secret. At St. Louis, fifteen guards stood outside his locked compartment, and the dapper gangster—owner of his own Lockheed to fly him to pleasure or safety—was replaced by a shaken man of less than average height grumbling about the messy business of prostitution.

There were thirty detectives on hand to greet Lucky when he arrived at Penn Station a few minutes before nine on the morning of April 18. They were backed up by a hundred repeating rifles held by regular police, and a shouting mob of cameramen and reporters. His name was Lucania, he told anyone who would listen, not Luciano, and he was "sore as hell." Fingerprinting was a prelude to the indignities of the lineup and arraignment on a staggering $350,000 bail before the stern-visaged Judge McCook. That night, the *capo di tutti capi* was lodged in a Brooklyn jail miles from his co-defendants.

Gay Orlova, who soon appeared on the fourteenth floor in diamonds and a fur wrap said to be worth $4,000, was angry over the turn of events. "Lucky was a dear," she informed the press, "and I don't believe any charges, especially that one about compulsory something or other. It just doesn't sound nice. Not like Lucky at all." Dewey had a different reaction. His current job was, he wrote his mother, "a terrible drive . . . I have had little sleep for a week and two days without any but I think the result will justify it."[20]

For Luciano, the managerial revolution in organized crime had paid off handsomely. He lived in a sumptuous suite of the Waldorf Towers, paid for with $7,600 in cash each year. He was a regular at Polly Adler's swanky cathouse, where he was careful to tip no more than five dollars, lest he artificially raise prices; and his nightly round of protected supper clubs and cafes, like his regular jaunts to Saratoga or Miami, was a carefree exercise in conspicuous consumption worthy of Jimmy Walker's New York.

By contrast, the prosecutor out to nail Luciano on the most improbable of charges, that of overseeing a prostitution racket, was still, ten years after his arrival in the city, very much a stripling of Owosso. For Dewey, wealth consisted of the seventy-five dollars a month he insisted his mother should charge a tenant in her red brick business block. There clung to Dewey a touch of the country cousin, as when he stopped a natty dresser in the hall and asked for the name of his tailor, or summoned an assistant to his office late one afternoon to inquire if he might be able to shake some contacts at Fox Films: his mother was standing in line at the Capitol Theater, anxious to see a Charlie Chaplin movie.[21]

Then there was the afternoon a group of men working on a tortuously complex garment rackets case let lunch slip by unnoticed. Finally, about three-thirty, someone suggested they send out for pastrami sandwiches. Great, the others answered.

Dewey's baritone dissented. "What's pastrami?"

Carefully, the men explained the raptures of pastrami, as only a certain East Side deli could make it. Dewey seemed impressed. It sounds delightful, he said, and promptly suggested that a messenger boy be sent out to pick up their orders. As for himself, "Tell them I want mine on whole wheat with mayonnaise."[22]

Dewey's men admired his cock-of-the-walk attitude, striding through City Hall Park, hands in his pockets, silver cigarette holder clenched between his teeth. They learned to wear bags under the eyes from all-night work as a badge of honor. Unlike his rival at the Waldorf Towers, Dewey eschewed the social limelight. Since his appointment as special prosecutor, he hadn't set foot in a nightclub, but instead organized with friends a private dance club in which to cut a rug without strangers looking on. After working late one Saturday, he went to a party where he danced until three the next morning. He sailed a boat all Sunday afternoon, and then returned to the office to toil until five Monday morning. Assistants struggled to stay awake, until one finally nodded off in his chair.

Dewey reacted irately. "He can't take it," he harumphed. For Lucky Luciano, alias Charles Ross of the Waldorf, the trial beginning in May 1936 was to be a public test of his mettle.

The State Supreme Court Building in Foley Square was usually used for civil suits. On May 11, there were submachine guns and tear gas stashed in side corridors, snipers guarding windows, and a corporal's guard of detectives and uniformed police standing watch over the second-floor courtroom where thirteen defendants arrived in handcuffs and shackles shortly before 10 A.M. The prosecutor walked in a few minutes later, dressed in a gray suit and bowler hat that added ten years to his youthful appearance. Immediately, he dropped a bombshell.

Three of the defendants, bookers Dave Miller, Al Weiner, and Pete Harris, would plead guilty and lend the weight of their testimony to the state's case against Luciano. Consternation was followed by puzzlement a few minutes later when Dewey asked the prospective jurors whether they were acquainted with Albert Marinelli, the City Clerk and Tammany mainstay. Dewey knew him to be a close friend of Luciano's, had known ever since assigning detectives to tail the powerful Second District leader a month before the trial's start. And when a jury was empaneled, Dewey warned them: "Frankly, my witnesses are prostitutes, madams, heels, pimps, and ex-convicts. Many of them have been in jail. Others are about to go to jail. Some were told they would be prosecuted if they did not tell the truth. . . . We can't get bishops to testify in a case involving prostitution. And this combination was not run under arc lights at Madison Square Garden. We have to use the testimony of bad men to convict other bad men."

Therein lay the gamble, and the potential for a successful defense counterattack. If Dewey was to convict Luciano, he must convince the jury that his down-at-the-heels band of raffish failures were truthful, and that a man as powerful and skillful as Lucky was alleged to be would actually become involved in a prostitution ring. The first could be achieved only with time. Dewey laid a foundation for the second with a carefully worded description of the "large corporate enterprise" atop which the *capo* perched. "He was the czar," the prosecutor explained, "and his word was sufficient to put other bosses out of business. His function was to say, 'Do this,' and it was done. The others were his servants." Then on down the line: to Betillo, "the man who really ran the racket," but who never placed any women in houses, to Pennochio, whose function was to receive proceeds of the bonding combination, to Frederico, who conducted beatings "when people didn't behave," to Liguori, who held up independent houses, to bondsmen, and finally down to the bookers themselves.

Dewey talked of a hotel room that served as prostitution central, where a Luciano henchman known only as Bingie answered calls and shuffled flesh. He displayed the names and addresses of 144 girls working for the Combine who had been arrested and bailed out by Abe Karp. In rebuttal, Luciano's lawyer, George Morton Levy (the seventh man approached to take on the case and a $50,000 retainer), sounded an every-man-for-himself defense. His client, claimed Levy, didn't even know any of his co-defendants, save Davie Betillo, once a gunman in Capone's Chicago army. Instead, he said indignantly, Luciano was a victim of "the distorted imaginings of broken-down prostitutes."

Dewey now marched out his parade of tarts, forty in all, beginning with Rose Cohen, who recalled getting help and legal advice from Frederico and Karp. The latter had told her to describe herself before a magistrate as a visiting seamstress from Philadelphia, and it had worked like a charm. Then came Mary Thomas, a plump, bespectacled woman of twenty-seven years who walked the streets to support two children, and much preferred it to life under Jennie the Factory or Big Rita. As she told Dewey, "there were too many rules and regulations working in with the mob."

A madam named Dixie explained her system of computing wages: she punched a card, twice for a two-dollar job, five times for three dollars, nine times for four. Dewey handed her a specimen, and Dixie computed it instantly. The girl in question had earned forty-six dollars one Friday between two in the afternoon and ten at night. She did even better the next day. Next, Joan Martin repeated what she had told Dewey's men the night of the raids, about Frederico's lead pipe and Abie Wahrman's vow that, unless she joined the Combine, she'd never again find girls to market for herself. Defense counsel Sam Siegal angered the middle-aged native of Rumania by his suggestion that hers was a less-than-elegant establishment. To be sure, Miss Martin acknowledged, she had lowered her price to $1.50, but only because of the Depression. Hard times was hard times.

Gradually, Dewey's intentions came into focus. To portray the fallen women as victims of lust and greed, condemned by the Combine to a hellish existence that lacked dignity and even dollars with which to salve their blasted pride—this was his strategy. Helen Kelly came to the stand in a fetching summer dress to tell of her stint as a prostitute at Hungarian Hilda's at 1225 Park Avenue, her refuge of desperation after losing a six-dollar-a-week waitress's job. Even defense lawyers were moved to apologize to Helen. They, too, were caught in a bind, just as securely as the men they tried to defend against a rising wave of juror outrage.

Dewey's case contained more than sympathy for streetwalkers. Joan Martin, before leaving the stand, described a visit to the Hotel York, where she saw Bingie and Jimmy Frederico release a hidden spring in an electric light socket and retrieve records of all the houses in New York paying tribute to the Combine. Booker Al Weiner limped onto the scene to tell of a meeting on Tenth Street at which a furious Betillo accused everyone of holding out on the racket. According to Weiner, Little Davie had called Pete Harris "all kinds of names," promised Jack Eller a good beating, and warned Dave Miller that if he went to the cops he, Betillo, would return the favor.

"Liar!" Betillo shouted from the defense table. "The dirty liar."

Defense lawyers did extract from Weiner the fact that Dewey had promised him consideration in return for his testimony. But that admission backfired when elaborated. The prosecutor, Weiner went on, had given his word only that he'd recommend "a jail where I couldn't be murdered."

A more serious setback for the prosecution took place in the witness room, where Dewey was talking with Good-Time Charlie, a cooperative pimp who earlier remembered in detail a crucial meeting at which Luciano himself had denounced the bookers and said, "You guys are through. I am giving the business to Little Davie." The line was dramatic enough to earn a place in the prosecutor's opening statement. But now Charlie was recanting his story. Subsequent investigation would prove his change of heart was purchased with a $2,500 bribe. It was a major blow, removing one of the four witnesses (out of over a hundred) able to link Luciano directly to the Combine. Of the three who remained, one was a hotel thief serving fifteen years to life at Sing Sing. Joe Bendix's credibility was less than sterling.

Things looked bad. But not to Barent Ten Eyck, who had gotten a note from the House of Detention from a girl who signed herself Flo. Flo, Ten Eyck was convinced, could make Dewey himself forget about Good-Time Charlie.

Cokey Flo Brown, formerly Jimmy Frederico's mistress, thereafter a madam, and more recently arrested for common streetwalking, was being held in a tiny cell whose ten-inch slit did not admit the heroin to which she'd become addicted. From the newspapers, Flo had guessed that Frederico was about to be convicted, and since neither he nor anyone else from the Combine had given her any help, she sat down and wrote her note to Ten Eyck on the fifth day of her "fast" drug cure. A meeting was arranged with Sol Gelb, a key strategist on the case who questioned witnesses not important enough to merit Dewey's personal attention. Suspicious of a plant, Gelb rejected Flo's claim to knowing Luciano. Not to be put off, Flo wrote another note to Ten Eyck, who this time agreed to interrogate her himself, in a psychiatrist's office he often used for such purposes.

For hours, Flo talked, and as Ten Eyck jotted down page after page of hastily scrawled notes, he came to believe the woman. On the night of May 20, Dewey himself listened while Flo reminisced about running a Cleveland speakeasy at fifteen, of being shared by three men in Chicago, about morphine and heroin, about Frederico and meetings with Luciano in which the boss instructed his men what to do, whom to punish, where to organize. Dewey also regarded Flo as genuine. He decided to put her on the stand as soon as possible, lest word of her cooperation leak out to the underworld.

Late in the afternoon of May 22, Cokey Flo shuffled into court, gaunt from weight lost during her heroin cure, looking far older than her age—late twenties—in a shabby, ill-fitting blue dress. Three times during her appearance, she asked for and got, per order of Judge McCook, brandy with which to fortify herself. Her legs were weak, and her eyes still playing tricks. Yet she stayed for nine hours. Her voice was clear and strong when Dewey asked her if she knew Luciano.

"I do," she answered, then went on to tell of meetings in a Chinese restaurant at which Lucky talked of syndicating prostitution, "the same as the A and P." She told of driving Frederico to an East Side garage for late-night conferences with Luciano, Betillo, and Pennochio. She told of Lucky's own doubts about the racket, once it failed to produce revenue up to expectations, and his concern over the Dewey investigation in October 1935. They won't get us, Little Davie had said reassuringly. "They'll only pick up a couple of bondsmen." Finally, Flo remembered Lucky's most audacious reform, placing the madams themselves on salary: "It could take a little time, but we could do it."[23]

When it came the defense's turn, George Morton Levy bore down for four hours, in a savage assault on Flo's character, background, and reliability. He asked her for the details of her heroin addiction, her needles, and her sex life. She admitted having been a morphine addict before switching to heroin, which was cheaper, and of taking a large white pill the previous Sunday. She denied the pill was morphine. "Nobody's that generous," she told Levy, to appreciative laughter. Still, Luciano's counsel pressed, rhetorically wondering what it was like to be "a hophead" and insisting on a lunch-hour test to see if Flo was on drugs at the time. He resurrected old love letters to Frederico, including one addressed, "Dear cousin," and including the statement "I wish Uncle Dee would die of cancer, the louse."

Weak and at times violently trembling, deep in the throes of withdrawal from heroin, Cokey Flo passed a critical test. In doing so, she had gone beyond the sympathy previously generated for girls victimized by a heartless mob. When Flo stepped down, sympathy had evolved into contempt for one man. Dewey moved to capitalize on the change of climate, and add some respectability to his own case. After requesting the defendants to move around, he called to the stand an effusive young chambermaid from the Waldorf Towers. Molly Brown was the first reputable New Yorker introduced by the prosecutor, and she rounded out Cokey Flo's harrowing story by simply identifying "Mr. Charles Ross" of Suite 39-C, who was always the last on his floor to let his room be made up each day. Asked to be more specific, Molly pointed to Luciano, who returned the favor with a graceful little bow. Then she was escorted to the defense table and told to place her hands on the men she recognized. Promptly, she reached out to Betillo and bondsman Meyer Berkman. "You didn't see this man there, did you?" asked Frederico's attorney, hoping to put some distance between his client and the others.

"Oh, yes," the maid replied, "he was there oftener than anybody else."

The hotel manager came forward to recount the day he evicted Lucky, in the wake of Dutch Schultz's murder and an onslaught of bad publicity. A Czech waiter told of serving tea and pastry to Luciano, and more robust refreshments to many of the defendants gathered for night sessions in 39-C. Bellhops confirmed the sightings. In still another accident of cross-examination, Thelma Jordan admitted having talked with Dewey's men ten times since her original arrest. When Sam Siegal pressed her on why she hadn't opened up more readily, Thelma blurted out a devastating truth.

"I tell you, I was afraid. I know what the combination does to girls who talk. Plenty of girls who talked too much had their feet burned, and their stomachs burned with cigarette butts and their tongues cut."

That afternoon, extras proclaiming Thelma's grisly explanation appeared in the streets. Her story was soon topped by Nancy Presser, the reluctant witness who was once Ralph Liguori's sweetheart. Hooked on heroin by Liguori, abandoned in the wake of Dewey's raid, Nancy slowly came around to the prosecutor's side. On the stand, the former Genevieve Fletcher of Auburn, New York, wove a lurid tale, of disappointing sex with Luciano in his Waldorf suite, and instructions from Lucky to hide in the bathroom and keep the water running to block out conversations between him and the other defendants. There had been telephone calls from Little Davie Betillo to 39-C, and complaints about a non-cooperative madam known as Dago Jean. "Wreck the joint," Lucky ordered his subordinate, while in other late-night talks he spoke about a new setup, in which Betillo would give orders to madams and bookers alike, and prices would be raised to a three-dollar minimum.

The defense zeroed in on Dewey's conversion of the witness from hostility to support. "Did they tell you that they could send you away until you regained your health and normalcy?" one lawyer put to her. "You were afraid of exposure, weren't you . . . you're afflicted with a social disease, aren't you?"

"It's something anybody can get," Presser shot back in a throaty whisper. Did she pick it up on the streets, she was asked? How many doses of dope did she need a day? Three? Four? Describe the suite at the Waldorf, Levy coaxed, or was it the Barbizon Plaza? Were there double beds? Single ones? A radio? A piano? What color were the drapes?

"Oh, I can't," the witness murmured. "I'm sure I can't."

By seven o'clock on the evening of May 26, Nancy Presser was slumped in the witness stand, her answers all but unintelligible. Hustled out of the courtroom, she was said to be too sick to continue. The next morning, Mildred Harris was also unwell. Before she could tell of being introduced to "the boss" by Little Davie, and of her own unsuccessful attempts to persuade Luciano to let her booker husband peacefully out of the business, a harried prosecutor moaned to reporters, "They've been fainting on me."

Notebooks and other scraps of paper linking the defendants to women who had testified were introduced to round out the prosecution's case. Nine of the ten charged with aiding and abetting compulsory prostitution had clearly been implicated. Dewey had won sympathy instead of skepticism for his shady collection of accusers. But Luciano himself had been tied to the racket by thin strands of evidence, unspooled by resentful women, jilted girlfriends, and known felons hoping for a break. Over the Memorial Day weekend, the prosecutor kept up his guard, drilling the girls yet again for anything at all they might know about possible witnesses for the defense. Nothing could be left unexplored, nothing left to chance, least of all preparations for Luciano's own last stand, a dicey move by the defense once and finally to declare Lucky's independence from his co-defendants.

It is an old and honorable courtroom tradition: If you can't win a case on facts, then try it on the law, and if all else fails, make the opposing lawyer the issue. On Monday, June 1, when Luciano's defense lifted the curtain on its version of the truth, the axiom was alive and well and putting Dewey himself on the hot seat. That was evident as soon as Ralph Liguori accused the prosecutor's men Gelb and Grimes of promising him a European vacation with Nancy Presser in exchange for his help in nailing Luciano. Dewey himself had said to him, in Liguori's recollection, "Ralph, you're the peddler and I'm the buyer," followed by Frank Hogan's warning that twenty-five years in prison awaited Ralph the Pimp if he refused to help the People.

Dewey disposed of Liguori quickly, puncturing his credibility with admissions of earlier lies, told to make off with the life insurance of a girlfriend's father-in-law, and later to buy a car. Denying any knowledge of Nancy Presser's syphilis, insisting that, as far as he knew, she really was a model, dismissing Joan Martin, Pete Harris, and Thelma Jordan along with Nancy as perjurers, Liguori's testimony was further littered with memory lapses. By the time he stepped down, the defense was in need of an immediate transfusion.

On June 2, looking forward eagerly to his courtroom confrontation with the prosecutor, Luciano informed the press that "when I get through with Dewey" no other witnesses would be needed for his case. The next day he got the chance to prove his boast. For twenty gentlemanly minutes, George Morton Levy invited his client to lay out the laundry of his early life. He was born in New York, the witness said, and once spent eight months in jail on a narcotics charge. Since then, with the exception of a single gambling conviction in Miami, he'd never been arrested. He was a gambler, a bookmaker, a follower of the horses. He knew none of his co-defendants except Betillo, and he had never seen any of the women put on the stand by Mr. Dewey, except for a handful of hotel employees.

As for prostitutes, Lucky tried a weak joke. "I gave to 'em. I never took."

Then came the moment New Yorkers had been waiting for, the mortal combat between the representatives of good and evil. There was silence in the courtroom as Dewey slowly approached the stand, clutching in one hand a few papers. His face was a mask. He milked the tension for what seemed an eternity before asking in a conversational tone if it wasn't true that Lucky's "little gambling rap" in Miami had included conviction for carrying a concealed weapon. Physical evidence of the charge was held before him, and the witness muttered it was true. Then Dewey retraced his steps, and Lucky was confronting a past that included peddling dope at eighteen, followed by bootlegging in the first glorious days of Prohibition.

Stoutly, the defendant had maintained that his livelihood for the decade past came from craps and bookmaking, that he had held no regular job throughout the period. Dewey had evidence to the contrary, in Lucky's own words. For instance, there was his arrest on August 29, 1922, when he told a Patrolman Clay he was a chauffeur, and his arrest on August 25, 1924, when he informed a Patrolman Harris that he made his living as a salesman. And, by the way, he told Harris his birthplace was Italy, not New York, had he not?

He might have, Luciano conceded. To continue: Dewey wondered about his arrest in December 1924, when he told a Patrolman Hart he was a fruit dealer, and after that several subsequent arrests, each with different occupations. "I may have said it," Lucky replied to each of Dewey's time capsules. "I can't remember." He did belatedly recall owning a piece of a Broadway restaurant, but couldn't dredge up its name.

When previously had he lied under oath? the prosecutor wanted to know. "When I'm looking to get something," Luciano cheerfully replied, then, casting a worried look at his lawyers, mumbled, "I don't know . . . I was never under oath like this." Well then, Dewey went on, let's be more specific. How many times had Lucky lied under oath to obtain a pistol permit? Lucky thought once.

"If it was a little thing like a pistol permit," Dewey cooed, "you are willing to lie, is that it?"

Loud objections ensued from the defense table. "I'll withdraw the question," Dewey said. "So you would only perjure yourself about a big thing like a pistol permit?"

Now, regarding an upstate trip Lucky took in July 1926 with one Joseph Saleeze, wasn't it interesting that police afterward discovered two guns in the car, along with a shotgun and forty-five rounds of ammunition. What had they been hunting?

"Peasants," a flustered witness blurted. Shooting pheasants, Dewey corrected, in the middle of July? How had they bagged the birds—by handing the gun back and forth between them? Luciano's voice began to fade. Judge McCook offered him a recess, but bravely he went on.

"Does the date June sixth, 1923, mean anything to you?" Dewey asked. Luciano couldn't recall anything of significance transpiring on the date. "On June second, 1923," Dewey went on, "don't you remember selling a two-ounce box of dope to an agent of the Secret Service? . . . Didn't you give a statement that at 163 Mulberry Street they would find a whole trunkful of dope?"

Lucky closed his eyes and whispered assent. "You're just a stool pigeon." Dewey mocked him. "Isn't that it?"

"I told them what I knew."

"You mean you went to those men and, like a big-hearted citizen, you told them where they could find the trunk?"

"Something like that, maybe . . . what I want to know is where the hell does all this come from?"

Luciano could not know that, prior to his appearance, Dewey had obtained access to the police department's complete file on him, nor that Dewey had been augmenting it with bits and pieces of recollections contributed by underworld informers and a network of cooperative madams. He could only squirm as the prosecutor forced him to admit knowing Joe the Boss, Lepke and Gurrah, Bugsy Siegel, and other criminal nabobs. Lucky denied knowing either Ciro Terranova or Al Capone, a claim pulverized by telephone slips connecting his Waldorf suite and the unlisted numbers of both men. Lucky denied Nancy Presser's story of having met him at Dave's Blue Room, and Cokey Flo's tale about the Standard Garage as a site of late-night business meetings for the mob. Once again, telephone records showed frequent calls from the Waldorf. To this, Lucky insisted someone must have gotten into his suite and made the calls without his knowledge.

"How many times have you been taken for a ride?" Dewey's question forced an intake of breath among spectators, but for Luciano, it was expected. Once, he answered. "And you told the police officer you did not want to give any information," the prosecutor went on, "that you would take care of that in your own way?" This Lucky disputed, but Dewey was ready with a new angle: In testimony before a grand jury, Luciano had admitted having in his pockets at the time of his beating $300 in cash and a $400 watch. It seemed doubly strange that his assailants touched neither, and that a simple bookmaker could afford to carry around such accouterments. "Pretty good crap games that year, weren't they?" Dewey asked sarcastically.

Finally, almost five hours after he began, the perspiring witness was asked about his chronic failure to pay income taxes, and his rush to pay six years' worth just two weeks after the start of the rackets investigation the previous July. Then too, Luciano hadn't ever paid a dime in state taxes, "because the federal government prosecutes big gangsters," Dewey suggested, "and the state does not, isn't that so?" Slouching in his seat, Lucky answered lamely, "I don't know."

"That's all," an obviously pleased prosecutor shouted, and within minutes a headline large and accurate hit the streets of New York. "Dewey Riddles Lucky on Stand," proclaimed the *Daily News*.[24]

There were no holds barred in the defense summation. Typical of the verbal assaults on the prosecutor was the language of Ralph Liguori's lawyer. Dewey was "the greatest actor I've ever seen . . . the boy prosecutor . . . a Boy Scout . . . dressed in khaki shorts." Dewey looked on with a fixed grin as he was accused of aiding prostitution by offering protection to pimps, madams, prostitutes, and drug addicts. He had condoned perjury the defense stormed, consumed "thousands of glasses of water" during the trial, and presented his mock evidence "with the charm of a beautiful cobra."

Davie Betillo's lawyer picked up and embroidered the theme, accusing the prosecutor of buying perjured testimony in a desperate attempt to launch a gubernatorial boom. George Levy was more silken in his outrage. "I'm not accusing Tom Dewey of suborning perjury," he began, but zealous assistants, "anxious for a pat on the back," had undertaken to assemble a cast of first-rate actors and actresses which Mr. Dewey then rehearsed and presented. For three hours, Levy ridiculed the sorry band of human refuse. He also zeroed in on Dewey's own failure to follow through on his opening promise to introduce a witness capable of quoting Luciano himself saying, "You guys are through. From now on, I'm putting the business under Davie."

It was a powerful performance, one to engender doubts in the minds of reasonable men and women. Certainly Dewey thought so; an hour later, he seemed depressed in discussing his own closing argument with trial strategists. That night, he worked on the statement until two o'clock. He was up again, polishing and punching it into shape at six. He arrived at the courthouse looking pale, and it was difficult to hear his opening words, delivered sotto voce. Gradually he gained force, his voice taking on a metallic edge when sinking sarcastic barbs into his opponents, or rising with indignation in warding off the personal allegations made against him and his staff.[25]

"I have heard myself described as the greatest actor in America," he said, "and the stupidest dolt. I have heard myself described as an irresponsible child of thirty-two and as Machiavelli's lineal descendant." Yet why would he and his assistants, who hoped to practice law the rest of their lives, place their professional reputation in the hands of a hundred professional criminals? It was obvious what the defense was about. "Smear everyone and everything in trying to save the rotten, stinking hides of these men. Smear me. Smear my

office. Smear every witness that got on the stand. But not one word
of defense against the material facts in the case." As for the charge
that he was running, in their words, "a subordination of perjury factory" over at the Woolworth Building, Dewey was contemptuous.
"If we manufactured it, I tell you, it would be better than this. . . .
We would have one hundred witnesses, each one of them saying
Lucky told them to go out and break up a house, or Lucky came up
collecting money. . . . Let us be realistic."

No, immunity meant immunity, and freedom to tell the truth.
Fifty-five witnesses had done just that, though not without some
persuading.

"Have you ever dealt with sheer, stark terror?" he asked in a voice
filling the courtroom. He had, with Nancy Presser and other petri-
fied young women. For two hours, he had cajoled Nancy into talking, and had taken into his own hands responsibility for her living or
dying. "If anybody thinks it is a picnic to work for four and a half
months . . . on a case involving prostitutes, pimps, gangsters, and
bookers of women, and to examine them, and spend time with them,
and persuade them to testify, and to hold their hands . . . they are
badly mistaken."

As for the caliber of those called to testify, "I admit the witnesses
on both sides are rotten, except that I make no pretense about mine.
I tell you what they are." Facts were facts: "You cannot convict
bookers of women on the testimony of anybody but the people he
booked . . . you cannot convict a criminal bonding conspiracy except
on the testimony of those who knew about it. You cannot convict
the men at the very top of a criminal enterprise . . . except upon the
testimony of the people who were their associates, their subordinates, or their intimates."

Dewey complained about manufactured defense plants calculated
to derail the prosecution and wild charges that he had bribed his
witnesses. But more than enough solid evidence remained, in the
testimony of Cokey Flo, Marjorie Brown, Mildred Harris, and
Nancy Presser. As for Presser's inability to provide a careful reconstruction of Luciano's quarters, "If I had been in twenty-five different hotel rooms a week for the last eight years, I couldn't describe
any one . . . and neither could you."

Then the prosecutor went on the offensive himself, dismissing
Ralph Liguori as "Mr. Nancy Presser," and ridiculing defense
charges of European trips and other bribes as "pure stuff and nonsense. . . . I would like to have you look at my appropriation." And

for sheer offensiveness, he asked, could anything top the cross-examination of Thelma Jordan, "whether she had not had to submit to an
operation for the removal of part of her organs," and the subsequent
implication that she had become a lesbian. "God, what a way to try
a lawsuit. What a defense," Dewey groaned. "I hope there is somebody on this jury who . . . knows something about the facts of life."

The afternoon light was fading now, throwing weak rays on a
courtroom completely silent but for the prosecutor. "Every lawyer in
this case has practically admitted his client's guilt in an effort to save
the boss," Dewey told his audience. "Why? Because Lucky's given
orders." When all the purple prose was stripped away, "the great
complaint of the defense in this trial is that the first and only commandment of the underworld has been broken, 'Thou shalt not
squeal.' " Of course, he hadn't proven that Luciano was himself
putting women into houses of prostitution. "He graduated from
that. It was back in 1927, when he had the two guns and the shotgun
and forty-five rounds of ammunition in his car . . . before he got
conscience-stricken and began filing federal income tax returns for
six years back all at once . . . but not state." The man that jurors
had seen in his "sanctimonious, lying, perjurious act" on the witness
stand was no gambler, no mere follower of the ponies, but "stripped
stark naked, the greatest gangster in America."

"Convict him," Dewey cried, "in the name of the safety of the
people of this city."

Seven hours after he began, Dewey sat down to await Judge
McCook's charge to the jury and then, at 9:31 P.M. to wait out a
verdict. Hundreds of people had gathered in Foley Square, most of
them Italian, nearly all of them hoping and praying for an acquittal.
Women with babies in their arms shared the green space with boys
playing craps and policemen hustling away parked cars—all part of
an elaborate plan to ward off any rescue attempt of Luciano or his
co-defendants.

Inside the courthouse, relatives of the men slept on newspapers or
watched with uncertain emotions as the confident group around
Lucky played pinochle. So exuberant was Ralph Liguori that he
gave Jimmy Frederico a hot foot, setting fire to a book of matches
attached to his friend's shoe. In his chambers, McCook stockpiled
razor blades and hot coffee against a prolonged deliberation. On the
fifth floor, a drained Dewey found himself an empty room with a
cot, where he dozed off until a few minutes before five o'clock Sunday morning. Then he woke with a start (he always had the ability

to answer a mental alarm clock), knotted his tie, and walked out into a hallway just as a court attendant was coming to notify him. The jury was returning.

Downstairs, it was a surreal scene, dimly lit by a gray dawn, caressed by the sound of bells calling early worshippers to Mass. "Gentlemen of the jury," the clerk asked of foreman Edwin Aderer, "have you agreed upon a verdict?" They had. "How say you, gentlemen of the jury, do you find the defendant Luciano guilty or not guilty on count number one?"

"Guilty."

The word was repeated 558 times, for the next forty-four minutes, like the slow filling of a mass grave. A WPA language teacher on the jury sat with tears streaming down his face. Frederico and Pennochio stood with fists clenched. Betillo scowled. Luciano himself displayed no outward emotion. By 6:09 A.M., the jury was finished with its work. McCook extended congratulations on "the righteousness of your verdict," then released them to their homes and jobs, their brush with history over.

Dewey listened to the verdicts in a stolid calm, the mood leading one assistant to describe him as a cross between a man and a robot. Very human emotions were churning behind the passive facade, including a stubborn theatrical pride. Assistants, worried about the charged atmosphere outside the courtroom, urged him to leave the building by a rear entrance. He would hear nothing of the kind. Quietly, alone with whatever thoughts he could sort out in triumph, Dewey emerged from the front door, walked down the long flight of granite steps separating him from the pro-Luciano crowd across the street, and climbed into a car. Ahead was a full day's rest at 1148 Fifth Avenue, and things that ambitious men could only guess at.[26]

7

"Tonight, I Am Going to Talk about Murder"

It was the Depression, and there was a complete lack of hope. You were out of school, working for nothing, going nowhere, with war on the horizon. It was like the Messiah appeared when Thomas E. Dewey came along.

—BERT SARAFAN[1]

Over and over, during the Luciano trial . . . men and women would come up to me and say, "Oh, it's all right while you're carrying on this investigation, but when it's over, things will go back to where they were."

—THOMAS E. DEWEY

Luciano's conviction, said the Brooklyn *Eagle* on June 8, was "the most useful . . . in New York in a quarter of a century." "What's the fastest way of getting to Hot Springs?" George Jessel asked, before answering his own question. "Join a mob and have your name brought to Dewey's attention." Mayor La Guardia joined in the accolades, readily agreeing when the prosecutor asked for a special City Hall ceremony to publicly promote thirteen of "our detectives." Unwilling to relinquish center stage, the Little Flower used the occasion to drop broad hints about future indictments of corrupt public officials. If New York were Tokyo, La Guardia mused, "there would have been at least six hari-karis" in the wake of Luciano's guilty verdict.

For Dewey, the bulk of his work lay ahead. For all his success in the loan shark and Luciano prosecutions, the technique of using small fry to lasso bosses, the secrecy promised and delivered to frightened witnesses, the fact that not a single Dewey witness had ever been harmed, the grand jury that asked to be released from duty early in July was undoubtedly correct in saying that the real job of tracking down and busting rackets in the city was "barely commenced."

One survey showed at least 140 businesses had fled New York because of racket-imposed costs. Dewey himself realized that breaking the racketeers' hold over trucking, restaurants, the garment district, and public marketplaces was akin to ordering an avalanche uphill. "Sometimes I feel the entire town is against me," he confided to one interviewer in a candid moment. "You'd be surprised at the places where people like these defendants have friends. Once I have finished this investigation, nothing will ever take me away from my private practice again."

On July 7, Governor Lehman invited Judge Ferdinand Pecora, hero of a Senate investigation into corrupt practices on Wall Street, to take over a new grand jury. The reaction on the fourteenth floor was wary. Pecora, despite his role in reforming the stock exchange and membership on FDR's Securities and Exchange Commission, had been a faithful follower of Tammany at least until 1933, when he broke with the Hall to run for district attorney against William Copeland Dodge. That same year, he was quoted in the *Herald Tribune* as saying, "Rackets? Why, I don't know of a racket in New York County." Moreover, those close to Pecora knew the judge still harbored political ambitions. Lehman might give up the governorship in 1938, and the fifty-four-year old jurist and native of Sicily was already being talked of as a potential successor.

For the record, Dewey said nothing. Indeed, he said as little about anything as he could get away with. "I don't want to become a talking prosecutor," he told the press. The same attitude prevailed in his office. Around the fourteenth floor, it was said that the Chief "wouldn't even tell you if it was raining outside." But behind the walls of circumspection, things were beginning to move. Late in August, thinking ahead to his own retirement from office within a year, Dewey announced formation of a Citizens Committee on Crime, to be headed by former Ambassador to Cuba Harry F. Guggenheim. "I was pretty young then," Dewey reminisced afterwards, "and I didn't know that these things turn into public nuisances."[2]

At the time, it seemed a good idea, a public watchdog to educate businessmen to the dangers of racketeering, and to hold their shaking hands when they were called on to testify. There were more raids launched: throughout the previous fall and winter, detectives and patrolmen had swooped down on dress shops and restaurants, stripping away the veneer of respectable businesses to reveal racketeers pulling strings and counting millions. In one case typical of dozens, wiretaps were placed on the offices of the Perfection Coat Front Company, which manufactured cardboard pieces sewn into the front of every suit to keep its shape. Then Dewey sprang a lunch hour raid. Five taxicabs and a truck were filled with business records, and fourteen company officers hauled off for immediate appearances before the grand jury.

Dewey redrew his subpoenas, to read duces tecum forthwith, and had them delivered in person instead of through the mails. That way, he and his accountants could avoid the last minute burnings or frantic erasures that kept earlier evidence from reaching him. Because the subpoenas were so broad, lawyers more than once threatened to contest them in the courtroom, only to discover that Dewey's rigidly enforced policy of never telling the press whom he had subpoenaed meant that any challenge would attract precisely the attention the lawyers sought to avoid. As a result they backed down.[3]

The books were crucial to Dewey's rackets cases. They were the means of legitimizing otherwise illegal actions, a hiding place for extortion within the endless maze of company finances. To get them, Dewey would do almost anything, including staging a mock trial when a terrified bookkeeper begged to be indicted on tax evasion charges to convince the underworld that he wasn't cooperating with the prosecutor. A special sessions judge was tipped off to the plan, and a three-judge panel duly pronounced Oscar Saffer guilty after a two-day "trial" prosecuted by Murray Gurfein. The whole incident might have backfired later, when one of the judges regaled guests at a cocktail party with the story. Fortunately, the sensitive ears of the underworld did not pick up that particular account.[4]

Dewey sent detectives to Canada, Cuba, and the West Indies in pursuit of Lepke and Gurrah. Agents sat in a locked women's room under a gangster-occupied cabin on a White Star liner. Unable to enter a Montreal hotel suite used by gangsters because lookouts were always posted, Dewey's men started a fire in the hotel corridors to lure the cautious mobsters outside. While detectives dressed as bellboys and elevator operators ran through the hallways spreading the alarm and causing panic, Wayne Merrick and another man crept into the mobsters' room, found two lookouts dead drunk, planted a bug, and crawled outside in the rain to hook it up.

Over and over, the same pattern was repeated: books seized in a raid, followed by hard-nosed, frustrating attempts to get racket victims to talk. New categories of crimes were invented, not by criminals but by the prosecutor's men, determined to use every weapon possible in coercing the truth from tight-lipped restaurateurs and dressmakers. Tax evasion was threatened, and prosecuted, with suspended sentences an inducement to cooperation. Second-degree perjury was devised as an offense, along with the broadest definitions ever accepted of contempt. Such imagination only reflected the lengths to which racket victims would go to avoid telling the whole truth. One man whose ledger contained the entry $1,500 for "Prot. Assn." maintained it was a fraternal order. A garment district entrepreneur insisted during five separate grand jury appearances that he didn't know a Lepke and Gurrah bagman named Abe Friedman. He clung to his story even after Dewey produced checks signed by him and endorsed by Friedman. Another suspicious entry he described as payment of a doctor's bill for the delivery of his infant son. Dewey's men did some digging, and found that the child was born eight months after the payment was made. Other victims would talk only in taxicabs, with one eye cocked nervously over their shoulders for a glimpse of racket enforcers.

"I'll go to jail for three years," one suspect finally blurted out, "before I'll tell you what I did with that money." In another case, it took days for an assistant to get the facts straight from a lawyer for the Broadway restaurant Lindy's, and then only after successively subpoenaing the man's druggist, doctor, secretary, office staff and sixteen-year-old son. Just as common was the restaurateur who testified to the grand jury to paying money for protection from stink bombs, only to deny the story in grueling visits to the fourteenth floor.[5]

One stonewaller refused to break and walked out the door at the end of a long day "fresh as a daisy," in Dewey's recollection. Half a minute later, the witness poked his head back in the door and, with a cocky grin on his face, asked his interrogator, "Mr. Hunter, would you also like a specimen of my urine?"[6]

Then, when he was most frustrated, Dewey heard from Benny Gottesman. In one meeting with one honest man, the terror gripping New York's economy was summarized and challenged to a duel.

With his thick glasses, cauliflower ears and mousy manner, Benny Gottesman didn't look like a hero. He was a union man, head of Local 1 of the waiters' union, and unionism was an oldtime religion with Benny. Even before Dewey's radio appeal at the end of July 1935, Benny was one of his callers, a semi-familiar face from the time of his visit to the U.S. Attorney's office, when he told Bill Herlands about a violent confrontation with racketeers including Dutch Schultz's crony Jules Martin.

Now Gottesman was back again, having spoken to no avail to two Tammany district attorneys. He found Dewey more willing to listen. Benny recounted a picket line he'd ordered around the Elkwood Restaurant in January 1933, at which time Martin and others had ordered him to clear out and leave jurisdiction of the neighborhood to Local 16 of the union. Shoving him against a wall, the men produced guns and threatened to use them. Benny was given an hour in which to call a meeting of his executive committee, which ordered the picket line taken off. The next day, the Elkwood's proprietor forked over $5,000, the workers were forced to accept a Local 16 contract, and Jules Martin told Benny to "get smart . . . we're going to take over the local whether you like it or not."

Martin also promised incentives for cooperation, including new members for Local 1; "All you have to do is pay us two dollars apiece." At a meeting in Albany addressed by Paul Coulcher, head of the Metropolitan Restaurant and Cafeteria Owner's Association, Benny was urged again to join up or pay a price. "We got accountants," Coulcher told him. "We got Dixie Davis, the smartest lawyer in New York. We will show you how to fix your books so that everything will be all right. All you have to do is to take in our people and you will get rich; and if you don't—you'll be found dead." When Gottesman still refused to knuckle under, he was visited outside his home by a bevy of Schultz's strongmen. Sam Krantz, a Schultz hit man, pulled a gun out of his pocket and said, "This is for you unless you behave." His partner shook his head. "Krantz, don't do that; he is just a poor yold."[7]

Gottesman refused to yield the names of his men or his executive board. So when a strike against a Broadway restaurant was called, and the mob offered to settle it for $2,000, they tried first to buy off Gottesman with marked bills. The setup failed, and Benny and a dozen waiters went to the D.A. A trial of sorts was held, in which not a single restaurant proprietor was questioned, and after three days, the charges were dismissed and the complainants all fired. This was Benny's experience with the law before July 1935.

In Dewey, he found a willing believer, enough so as to assign Bill Herlands, three assistants, and ten investigators to work for eighteen months in unraveling the racket that had seized control of the restaurant industry. Following Jules Martin's murder, Herlands visited the dead man's office, where papers linking the gangster to the owners' association led to an even more spectacular coup: the discovery of an Elkhart, Indiana, factory owned by Martin where new automobiles were assembled out of old spare parts.

Another note found in Martin's office was saved for future reference. It said, "Call Jimmy Hines."

For months, the inquiry ground on, tracking down Martin's associates, including Paul Coulcher. Once an authentic revolutionary expelled from Czarist Russia in 1905, Coulcher in the summer of 1932 was bored with waiting on tables. It was then that he hit on a scheme to take over Local 16. Dutch Schultz supplied manpower, including holster-packing thugs to stand guard at union elections that December. Martin stuffed the ballot box, only to see Coulcher defeated. Two Schultz strongmen, outraged at this display of raw democracy, grabbed the ballot boxes and burned them in the street. Within a week, a new election was called. This time, Coulcher and his gang-backed slate of officers were voted in.

The next steps were vintage racketeering. Martin went to see Max Pincus, head of Local 302 of the cafeteria workers' union, and ordered him to join up. Pincus said nothing doing. Martin threatened to cut his ears off. Pincus called a strike on his own to show his independence. Martin went to the restaurant himself, extorted $2,000 to end the strike, then sought out Pincus in a local bar. Gun in hand, he ordered his rival to pull the picket line off, placed a card carrying the name of J. J. Hines on the table, and withdrew. The line disappeared, and Local 302 joined the racket.

In return for all this, the union member got nothing. Contracts might call for six dollars a week guaranteed; three dollars was what waiters were actually paid. Eight-hour days stretched into twelve. Contrary to the terms of their contracts, waiters were forced to polish silver, paint tables at night, and buy new uniforms when a nightclub changed its scenery. Weekly pay envelopes were handed first to the racketeers, who extracted up to 60 percent of their contents before handing over what was left to the workers.

Dewey listened and grew angry. His anger was a prelude to sudden action. A former silk salesman and croupier at a Schultz gambling casino at Saratoga was subpoenaed to appear before a grand jury with the books of the owners' association, of which he was now president. Phillip Grossel refused, only to find himself hit with fifteen days in jail for contempt. He served the sentence, walked out of the Tombs, and was presented with another subpoena, and another threat of imprisonment should he ignore it. The books were turned over, and under ultraviolet examination erased notations were reassembled to tell a story of intimidation and payoffs. Accountants went to work on the records of 350 restaurants, cafeterias, and nightclubs. Among other victims they uncovered was Jack Dempsey, the ex-champ, whose smiling photo so pleased the racketeers that in return for its use they dropped the $4,500 initiation fee they had planned to extract. Another cafeteria owner was brought before the grand jury, only to waffle over the source of $1,500 paid in what his books listed as "association dues." He, too, was handed a contempt citation. To back up his novel interpretation—until now, contempt had meant the outright refusal to answer questions on the stand, not evasion of them—Dewey dispatched assistants to the County Lawyers Association library. It was nearly midnight when two of his men stumbled simultaneously on an old case that might serve as a precedent. The cafeteria owner spent thousands in appealing the decision (only confirming the presence of big money behind him) but the charge stood up. In the end, the witness broke down, admitting he paid the $1,500 in "dues" to avoid a strike.[8]

Dewey informed the press he was prepared to prosecute "hundreds" of such cases, ranging from perjury to income tax violations, from workmen's compensation frauds to something called third-degree forgery, the failure to make an entry where one belonged, or making an improper one with an intent to deceive. Late in October 1936, he sprang a new raid, this time snaring union officials, association officers, and lawyers. The charges included embezzlement of $250,000 in union funds, followed up by an indictment eight days later against the "protective association" itself, the first time an entire racket was placed on trial.

The trial that began in January 1937 lasted ten weeks. It featured Benny Gottesman's public testimony, Dewey's first mention of Hines—he warned prospective jurors that knowing the Tammany leader might disqualify them from service on the panel—and a desperate attempt by the defense to portray the prosecutor as a union buster. "The indictment charges extortion," Dewey replied icily. "There is no union on trial here." Bill Herlands took over once a jury was chosen, while Dewey and others reviewed each day's courtroom action on three-by-five cards. When Dewey saw a chance to destroy the defense by cross-examining the wife of a defendant who claimed he had been terrorized by the mob, he shouldered Herlands aside.

Mrs. Irving Epstein told of fleeing cross-country for her life, while her husband sought a new existence and job outside New York. Smothering the woman with kindness, Dewey invited her to recall all the highlights of the trip as he held in one hand her travel diary.

Mrs. Epstein remembered the cherry blossoms of Washington, shopping in an Atlanta Pig 'n' Whistle, fishing in Galveston Bay, the "quaint buildings" of El Paso, and a hired guide to show her and her husband the sights of Mexico. As she rambled on, Dewey maintaining his fixed smile at her side, it was soon obvious that the Epsteins' journey was no escape from terror, but a leisurely skip out of town. Outside the courtroom, the poor woman's husband lunged at her, and had to be restrained lest murder be added to his other offenses.[9]

It was a complicated case, but after Dewey finished his summation, the jury took only six hours to return a guilty verdict. The prosecutor then handed Judge McCook a sealed envelope containing $3,300, given a subordinate by Paul Coulcher with instructions that it be returned immediately in case of an acquittal, or held against his release from prison if the verdict went against him. There was reason to believe, Dewey told the astonished court, that at least a dozen additional envelopes were floating around, moving McCook to shake his head and wonder what "laboring men and women . . . who have struggled for a hundred years for their rights" would say if they could be present.

Sentences were passed, Locals 16 and 302 filed suits against their former masters, and Benny Gottesman was vindicated. Within a year, membership in the cleansed unions would triple, and wage increases totaling more than $2 million would take effect. Tom Dewey celebrated quietly, reminding the press that this was the first time ever that an entire industrial racket had been presented in a single case. The verdict, he felt certain, pointed to numbered days for other illegal combinations. Then he went back to the fourteenth floor to dictate a telegram to Annie in Owosso.

"All convicted on all counts. Love, Tom."[10]

He had secured his fifty-third conviction on his thirty-fifth birthday.

By then, the young man's crusade had gained a momentum all its own. January 1937 was typical of Dewey's fight against the rackets. On the seventh, his men strolled into the Loma Dress Company and strolled out again in possession of the books of a $5-million-a-year firm suspected of being a front for Lepke and Gurrah. The same day, Dewey agents picked up a former dancehall bouncer turned poultry racketeer. Tootsie Herbert (the nickname derived from his fondness for sweet-smelling hair lotions) had joined the chicken drivers' union in 1923. With the help of sluggers and a safecracking friend named Joey Weiner, Tootsie had risen to become the union's secretary-treasurer for life and, as absolute boss of the Metropolitan Feed Company and the chicken killers' union, an economic dictator. Shochtim were ritual slaughterers whose product was a staple of the Orthodox diet. Fifty million chickens a year were blessed by them: taxed by Herbert and his corrupted union at a penny a pound, they proved a lucrative sideline.

But there was more. Tootsie had organized the Greater New York Live Poultry Chamber of Commerce, which became the only acceptable outlet for nearly all the city's merchants and dealers. With the union at his feet, he doubled membership dues to ten dollars a year, looted the death benefits fund, and ran a loanshark operation victimizing his own membership. Dewey's accountants traced his holdings from a $218 insurance refund check, and when the trial began in July 1937 (the formal charge being embezzlement of $40,000 in union funds), Tootsie was quickly subdued by the irrefutable evidence of his own financial transactions. Halfway through the proceedings, he threw in the towel, took four to ten years imprisonment as his lot, and was banished to obscurity. The Metropolitan Feed Company collapsed, the marketplace returned to normal, and New York's consumers saved $5 million in 1938 alone.

The very night of Herbert's arrest, Dewey had gone to the Claremont Inn, a city-owned restaurant near Grant's Tomb, closed for the winter and thus perfect as command post for a raid even more spectacular than the one with which he launched the Luciano prosecution. For months, Dewey and his men, headed by Jack Rosenblum, had been digging into the policy game, not to shut it down but to find evidence against those who used it to corrupt justice and extend their own political influence. The time had come for a raid that would scoop up all the major policy operators from their Harlem bases, and set in motion the by now familiar chain of accusation in which small fry pointed to their bosses.

The Claremont was chosen for its proximity to Harlem and because it sat in a traffic island, the last place anyone would suspect of hosting the most unusual social event of the season. At 6 P.M. rookie cops selected for their honesty were ordered to the Tombs, then redirected to Ulysses Grant's monument overlooking the Hudson. From there, they spread out through Harlem, picking up sixty-five of the seventy suspects Dewey wanted, serving warrants signed earlier in the day by Judge McCook. At the inn, electric heaters were in place, along with liquid and other refreshments, the special prosecutor, and a squad of inquisitive assistants. One banker was picked up with $12,000 in his wallet. But Dixie Davis, whom Dewey wanted most of all, and important bankers like Alexander Pompez and Joe "Spasm" Ison, had managed to elude his dragnet.

As far as the newspapers could report, it was just one more in a series of large-scale operations by Dewey. Consequences could only be guessed at. That same week, there were additional raids, making off with books from the cleaners' and dryers' union, Local 3 of the International Electrical Workers, and the New York Electrical Contract Association. (For over a year, Dewey had been looking into a

$10 million electrical racket.) On January 17, Judge McCook was called away from research in the public library to arraign Harold Silverman, the fifth and final of Dewey's suspects in a multimillion-dollar bakery racket. The restaurant trial opened, and inside the Woolworth Building, hidden away from the glare of publicity, assistants pursued leads in rackets ranging from used bricks to funeral coaches.

Letters began to arrive on the fourteenth floor addressed merely, The Racketbuster, New York. Warner Brothers rushed out *Marked Woman,* a Humphrey Bogart–Bette Davis vehicle based on the Luciano trial, cleansed for sensitive moviegoers (the women on celluloid were "clip-joint hostesses"). The New York *Times,* asserting that Communists and Fascists posed far less threat to America than industrial racketeers, praised Dewey for dissolving their shadow government. Other journals chimed in. A Michigan paper asked the prosecutor to vacation in Detroit so he could clean up that racket-infested city. "With a few more Deweys in the larger cities," claimed the Decatur, Illinois, *News,* "the criminals that live by extortion would be on the run." The Montgomery *Advertiser* labeled him "a man of destiny," a New York humorist suggested he be named "Rat Exterminator Number One," and talk of Dewey as a potential candidate for attorney general or governor of New York surfaced in letters to the editor and postcard polls.

"If you don't think Dewey is Public Hero No. 1," the Philadelphia *Inquirer* asserted, "listen to the applause he gets every time he is shown in a newsreel."

Unknown to the public, or to the men around him, the applause was already ringing in Dewey's ears, a seductive siren's song that had led him, sometime back in the summer of 1936, to pay a call at the Oyster Bay, Long Island, residence of Henry Root Stern, a New York lawyer and treasurer of the state's Republican party. The meeting was off the record, a friendly introductory chat between a prospective candidate and some potential kingmakers. Nineteen thirty-six was a presidential as well as gubernatorial election year. In the Empire State, Republicans, desperate to shake off memories of Herbert Hoover and his responsibility for the Depression, were in the throes of intellectual and personal realignment.

When Dewey arrived at Windrift, the Stern estate, a shortage of swimming apparel forced him to spend the afternoon lounging in a late Victorian knee-length model. Sitting there in the company of a rising young political boss named J. Russel Sprague, Dewey must have made an ironic appearance. There he was, the youthful hope of Republican resurgence, in private conference with an ambitious machine builder, dressed for the beach as Theodore Roosevelt might have been were he still alive in the yellow and red bungalow perched on a nearby hillside overlooking Long Island Sound. Roosevelt had built Sagamore Hill at a similar juncture in his career, while still a young man with mutton chop whiskers, a promising reformer and latent star in the clouded Republican sky.[11]

As chairman of the New York delegation at the Cleveland convention that had nominated Alfred M. Landon to take on Roosevelt in the 1936 campaign, J. Russel Sprague was a relative newcomer to statewide power. As manager of populous Nassau County on Long Island, he had a solid foundation on which to build a challenge to the upstate power interests and conservative Old Guard that, in the person of national committeeman Charles Hilles, had dominated New York Republicanism since the days of William Howard Taft. In 1934, the Old Guard had made a disastrous mistake in choosing Robert Moses to run for the governorship against the popular Lehman. Moses' defeat, by over 800,000 votes, was so massive that the party for the first time in memory also lost control of the legislature.

There had been a scandal after that, touched off in a letter written by an indiscreet Republican senator to a power company on whose payroll he had served, expressing the hope that his efforts had matched expectation. The Senator was forced to resign, the power interests were discredited, and young rebels like W. Kingsland Macy from Suffolk County, Edwin Jaeckle in Buffalo, and Kenneth Simpson in Manhattan emerged to pick up the pieces and fashion a more liberal alternative to the New Deal and its local arm under Lehman. Financially, Hilles and his contacts in Wall Street remained crucial to the party. Once a year, the national committeeman's friend Thomas W. Lamont of the House of Morgan convened a dinner meeting of the city's leading executives at his club, followed by a sales pitch and a personal pledge of $25,000 to the cause of good— that is, Old Guard—government. Around the table Lamont went, inquiring the size of individual contributions from Bankers Trust, Union Carbide, American Cyanimid, the Reids of *Herald Tribune* fame, and so forth.[12]

Men like Russ Sprague wanted a return to organizational strength, party government, and a regime honest within the limits of electability. Sprague's no-fingers-in-the-cookie-jar inclinations were helped mightily by the investment know-how of his friend Henry Root Stern. In his own bailiwick, Sprague forbade any candidate or

candidate's family from contributing to his campaign; the race
would be financed by the organization, which in turn relied upon
local jobholders who tithed a fraction of their income to the machine. Disloyalty was the ultimate crime, rewarded by banishment
to political Siberia. Talent was generously rewarded. Sprague believed that the best way to win elections was to provide good government once in power. He also gave birth to a string of maxims. "Always know how a meeting is coming out before you call it" was one.
"Never make a two-day wonder out of a one-day wonder" was another, good advice to a candidate facing the artificial controversies
on which politics thrives. Shrewd, graceful, and blessed with sufficient prosperity to follow his instincts, Sprague in 1936 was on the
lookout for a winning contender, a candidate who could lend popular appeal to his own and others' efforts to retake the GOP for a kind
of progressive conservatism that had been all but surrendered in the
hysteria following Democratic blitzkriegs of 1932 and 1934.[13]

The talk at Windrift that afternoon was genial and vague, cen-
tering on possibilities rather than promises. The district attorney
race coming up in 1937 was mentioned. So were the 1938 contest for
governor and the 1940 presidential nomination. The meeting adjourned without firm decisions, Dewey to return to his gangbusting,
Sprague to join in the hopeless and rather forlorn little crusade to
elect Alf Landon president. At the convention that had nominated
Landon earlier that summer, the only real enthusiasm had been accorded Herbert Hoover, who brought the listless crowd to its feet
with his proclamation "Thank God Almighty for the Constitution
and the Supreme Court." The platform pursued the theme of con-
stitutionalism abandoned by the New Deal, denounced the concept
of Social Security as "unworkable," and promised both a balanced
budget and sound currency. It was an accurate measure of the
party's antipathy to anything associated with "that man in the
White House."

Dewey stayed aloof from the Landon campaign. A group of his
friends from Young Republican days—dubbed the Mallards and
including at their monthly luncheons rising young lawyer-politi-
cians like Dave Peck, Herb Brownell, Ed Lumbard, and Jack
Welles—were active supporters of the Kansas governor, hailed as a
commonsense liberal and skilled administrator. "The old budget
balancer," Landon's admirers called him, but Kansas' entire budget
in 1936 scarcely equaled the amount of money spent by New York
City to patch its pothole-ridden streets. Landon himself was a compassionate man, who in later years would grow into a forceful advo-

cate for imaginative government, including the recognition of Red China a generation before Richard Nixon set foot on the Great Wall. But in 1936 he was the chief executive of a small state, nominated because no one else was readily available, handicapped by a reedy voice ill-suited to radio, and surrounded by hard-core conservatives like his national campaign chairman, John Hamilton. It was Hamilton who told reporters of his confidence in the final result, "because every Rolls-Royce I see has a Landon sticker," and who took to the airwaves to warn America that under Social Security, Washington would issue each man, woman, and child a federal dogtag.[14]

"I am fairly well satisfied," wrote Landon's fellow Kansan William Allen White in the Emporia Gazette, "that the attempt to liberalize the Republican Party is going to be a rather sad bit of ersatz." Landon tried. He repudiated the endorsement of the ultraconservative Liberty League and sounded a moderate note in his whistle-stops, promising to keep what was good about the New Deal but administer it better, with less tolerance of political payroll padding or deference to the corrupt big-city machines from which Roosevelt derived much of his support. Landon liked afterward to tell the story of his friend Roy Roberts, editor of the Kansas City Star, who had bet a thousand dollars that Landon would carry his home state. Driving to a fair on the Saturday before Election Day, Roberts noted extra men working all along the highway. He decided to check out his hunch by returning on a different road and, sure enough, it too was lined with WPA workers. Only two months later did Roberts learn why. Jim Farley chuckled as he told of conversations with the state's IRS collector, its Democratic chairman, and its national committeeman over how many names would have to be added to the public payroll if Kansas were to forsake its traditional Republican voting habits. Three weeks before the election, Farley was given a firm figure—25,000. He then made sure that 26,723 men were hired during the campaign's final two weeks. FDR carried Kansas.[15]

In the right hands and given the proper pitch, Landon's moderate criticisms might have taken hold. But as his campaign dragged and the Old Guard took command, the candidate himself struck a shriller note. "Little Boy Blue, come blow your horn," went one GOP ditty dedicated to the proliferation of federal farm controls. "There's a government agent counting your corn. And there's one instructing the old red sow, on the number of pigs she can have and how." In November, farmers joined with virtually every other socioeconomic group in an emphatic endorsement of the new order that centralized power in Washington, established minimum wages, paid some farmers not to plant, and stretched a net of security under the capitalist system.

Dewey was busy during election week meeting with La Guardia and his new Citizens Committee on Crime, and working to counter an appeal in the Luciano case. He managed a quick stop at Republican headquarters, where he was introduced to party officials. The next morning, his party awoke to find itself victorious in only two of forty-eight states, with less then 38 percent of the popular vote for president and all but decimated on Capitol Hill. As of January 1937, Franklin Roosevelt could look out on a Congress where Democrats controlled 333 of 435 House seats, and 76 of 96 desks in the Senate.

Meanwhile, some Republicans found themselves wondering just where Tom Dewey stood politically. Had they had access to his correspondence with the militantly progressive Chase Osborne, they would have known that the Gangbuster regarded his father's old ally as a hero. They might have drawn conclusions, too, from the company he kept with Kenneth Simpson, a Phi Beta Kappa Yale graduate who, as the new chairman of the party in Manhattan, was moving to put a liberal stamp on its candidates, even to the extent of cooperating with the left-wing American Labor Party organized by unions in response to FDR's appeal in 1936. Later, Dewey and Simpson would engage in a classic bloodletting, with Dewey dismissing the redhaired, hard-drinking Irishman as "a real neurotic." For now, his interest in politics piqued, the prosecutor seemed anxious to widen his circle.[16]

He did not forget his primary responsibility. Landon's sinking ship and his own electoral potential consumed little of Dewey's time in the crowded weeks that followed the restaurant racket trial. Luciano was gone, though not forgotten; Herbert and the restaurant racketeers were put away. But the garment and trucking industries were still held in the grip of underworld bosses, none more deadly or difficult to catch than the Gorilla Boys themselves, Lepke and Gurrah.

Louis "Lepke" Buchalter was the telltale heart of racketeering in New York, one of eleven children born in an East Side flat, who got his start at crime robbing the pushcarts that clogged the neighborhood's teeming streets. He went to jail for the first time at twenty-one, after pilfering luggage in a Hartford train station. While still a teenager, Lepke (from the name his mother gave him, Lepkeleh, or "Little Louis") befriended Jacob Shapiro, another hoodlum in the making, who earned his nickname from an inability to say "Get out of the way." Thus emerged Gurrah and Lepke, a pair of thugs at the service of minor gang leaders in the 1920s, when the garment district, a fantastic world of pushboys and pitchmen and Seventh Avenue lofts, resounded to shots and screams as rival forces sought to unionize, to politicize, and to fashion thirty square blocks into something resembling an organized industry.

It was here that a gangster named Little Augie did a thriving business renting out strikebreakers, at least until December 1927, when Augie was shot to death from a passing car. Lepke and Gurrah turned themselves in at the Clinton Street station, where a magistrate thoughtfully provided them with a guard of fifty detectives and patrolmen. The next day, he even more graciously turned them loose. From then on, their rise was meteoric. Augie had been offered $50,000 by garment manufacturers to break a strike; Lepke saw much greater potential if only he could gain control of both industry and unions. Under Sidney Hillman and David Dubinsky, the garment district might be impregnable to a direct assault. But it could still be brought to its knees if the trucking industry, the lifeline for this as for so many other trades, could be taken over by the mob.

By 1929, the truckers were cowed. Union members who persisted in asking questions were beaten, labor officials replaced with lackeys, and the company bosses who had hired Lepke and Gurrah to do their dirty work now found themselves with underworld partners. The Gorilla Boys enforced their authority with hired killers who earned up to $150 a week. Lepke became overseer of Murder, Inc., the romantically dubbed enforcement unit of paid assassins based in Brooklyn and called upon for help in warding off raids on staked-out territory. Luciano himself had relied on the service from time to time. There were 300 or more "foremen" in Lepke's empire, riding herd on everything from bakery rackets to narcotics smuggling. The basic techniques of persuasion they employed were summed up by a drone in the racket army.

"My first job was to go to a shop," he told Dewey's men, "and beat up some workmen there. The men that employed me gave me ten dollars for every man I had to use. . . . I got my men together, divided them up into squads and saw they were armed with pieces of gas pipe and clubs . . . and when the workmen came from work, the men . . . set on them and beat them up."

Lepke never hesitated to resort to more drastic methods when they were needed. In September 1934, a group of union and racket figures from the Flour Trucking Association were talking shop in a restaurant on Avenue A. Displeased with the independent attitude of their local president, Billy Snyder, who had refused to accept a pay cut ordered by the racket, the union men were negotiating to head off a threatened strike when, around 10 P.M. Snyder's vice president, William "Wolfie" Goldis, left the restaurant and was replaced by his brother, Morris. Morris Goldis preferred to make his argument with a gun. Snyder was shot three times and was taken to a hospital, where he identified his assailant. He died two days later.

Detectives from the D.A.'s office traced the getaway car and questioned a friend of the Goldises', who readily admitted renting the vehicle with cash supplied him by the two. The driver, Sam Tratner, was arraigned and was represented by New York State Assistant Attorney General Charles Schneider, a Tammany power in the Eighth District. Everyone who was in the restaurant that night claimed to have jumped under two small tables, but a pair of waiters came forward to pick Morris Goldis out of a police picture book. The detectives urged District Attorney Dodge and his Indictment Bureau chief, Harold Hastings, to freeze the witnesses and go forthwith before a grand jury. They refused to do anything of the kind. No indictment would be sought until Morris Goldis was apprehended. Only then would the case go to a grand jury, and only if a magistrate so ruled.

In due course, Goldis was captured—and represented by Charlie Schneider. Sam Tratner recanted his story, the waiters proved unable to identify Morris in daylight, the defendant was set free. The truckers' union was placed more firmly than ever in the hands of Lepke and Gurrah, who now deputized a former schoolteacher named Max Rubin to consolidate the racket. All this was known to Dewey, who had in his possession a copy of the detectives' report on Snyder's murder, a letter written to District Attorney Dodge from a relative of the dead man, and checks linking Schneider's legal fee to the bakery racket itself.[17]

Appalling as the alliance was, it remained difficult to prove. Equally frustrating was the probe of the garment racket, where thousands of pages of company records were being examined, and victims of extortion threatened with jail if they refused to tell Dewey what they knew. Lepke and Gurrah were personally linked to incidents of terrorism, extortion, bribery, and savage reprisals against those who tried to elude their closing circle. A truck owner named William Brown went to the fourteenth floor and told of being shoved against a wall by men who demanded he join another truck-ing racket controlled by a former prizefight manager named Jimmy Plumeri (alias Jimmy Doyle) and his nephew Johnny Dio. After he declined to enlist, seven men returned to beat up his brother and pour emery into his truck engines. When Brown threatened to call the police, he was laughed at. Doyle bragged of being the cause of sixty-eight such complaints, all fixed by an important district leader. Getting evidence in the face of such protection called for creativity. One trucking association leader told his story off the record to Dewey assistants Gurfein and Grumet, but wouldn't repeat it for at-tribution. The debate raged, until the man finally agreed to a bet. He'd tell what he knew if Murray Gurfein could outdrink him in an alcoholic duel. Gurfein won the contest and the witness's testi-mony.[18]

In March 1937, as Dio and Doyle were preparing to leave for a Florida vacation, the prosecutor swooped down. "What do we do," Dio asked Murray Gurfein after his capture, "that J. P. Morgan doesn't do?" After a four-day trial, in which both were shown to be on the payroll of the truckers' association—their $500-a-month take was officially categorized as "salaries to directors"—William Brown had his revenge, and the trucking racket dispersed.

The Dewey probe lit fires under federal law enforcement author-ities. Lepke and Gurrah themselves were apprehended and con-victed on a charge of violating the Sherman Anti-Trust Act in the fur industry. They filed an appeal, and Dewey, getting close to an indictment of his own against sixteen racketeers whose take from the garment industry exceeded $17 million, hurried to see federal judge Martin T. Manton. The prosecutor laid out his evidence, explaining that anything less than $50,000 bail would never hold the Gorilla Boys once they saw what he had in store for them. Manton listened sympathetically, nodded in agreement, and within twenty-four hours let both men out on $10,000 bail. Lepke promptly vanished, leaving Dewey little course but to proceed with his case, post a $25,000 reward for the king of industrial rackets in America, and quietly undertake a new investigation, this time into the prosperous lifestyle enjoyed by Judge Manton himself.[19]

"The time has come when citizens must insist upon a thorough revision of the machinery of law enforcement," Dewey wrote in *Reader's Digest* in April 1937.

You can quickly recognize the new approach when it appears. No longer will you be told of the number of petty criminals who have been marched into jails and then let out again, the worse for the experience. You will hear then that those minor criminals who have in the past been regarded as the final objective of law enforcement have become of real help to the community. You will hear that they are put on probation and given the aid of society in reward for their services, and you may also hear of their ultimate rehabilitation in society . . . you will hear of petty criminals regularly coming over to the side of the people; of the arrest and indictment of their masters, and of the use of the accumulated information by prosecuting officers to wipe out whole combines of crime.

Certainly that was the method employed by Dewey throughout the rackets investigation. Occasionally, it blew up in his face. In March 1937, Cokey Flo Brown, Mildred Harris, and Nancy Presser returned with a vengeance to the headlines as part of a new appeal filed by Luciano's lawyers. Presser was now willing to swear that during most of her time on the fourteenth floor she had been drunk. Her cohorts were equally dangerous in their attempt to explode the case they helped build. A 184-page appeal was filed early in April, much of it contesting application of the joinder indictment to crimes committed prior to its passage by the New York legislature.

Stung by the allegations, Dewey fought back with affidavits of his own, 382 in all. The real hero of the affair proved to be Judge McCook, whose own close questioning of the women at the end of the 1936 trial had convinced him that they were telling the truth, and who now put two of Lucky's lawyers on a stand while Dewey pressed them to reveal the whereabouts of Mildred and Flo. "That's none of your business," Moses Polakoff snapped, but McCook persisted, and Polakoff, all the while denouncing the proceedings as star-chamber justice, finally admitted the women were in Hartford, stashed for safekeeping with a former federal agent who was working for the Luciano defense.

"A fraud upon the court!" Dewey cried. He supported his angry words with dispassionate evidence, including the original notes taken in longhand the night he interviewed Cokey Flo, friendly letters written to the fourteenth floor after the verdict by both Flo and Mildred, who'd gone to California and opened a gas station called the Rooster, and a financial plea sent hours before a similar request went to a Luciano procurer. "I sure don't want any part of rackets anymore, if I could get by," Mildred had written. "Of course, I can't . . . I am just about ready to go off the deep end."

Dewey uncovered the fact that both women were back on drugs when they signed their recantations. He produced affidavits from both to prove it. A juror who, according to defense lawyers, wished to return an innocent verdict, swore it wasn't so; actually, Joseph Blake said that one of the lawyers had tried to force him to sign such a statement, but he had refused. A detective told of a conversation with Pete Harris, in which the booker complained about his wife's original refusal to accept $100,000 in return for keeping her mouth shut. Most devastating, Dewey took the wraps off a nine-month-old statement dictated by a badly frightened Mildred Harris, given voluntarily the same day she was approached outside a movie theater by Luciano's brother. Tony Luciano had outlined a plan to get the prosecution's key witnesses to renounce their stories. He also promised to make it lucrative for them to do so. As soon as they separated, Mildred had gone to the Woolworth Building, recounted the incident to a Dewey stenographer, and left after affixing her signature.

Holding up the defense affidavits, Dewey shrugged them off as "perjurious from beginning to end. . . . Fear screams from every page. Money screams from every page. Drugs are all over these pages." On May 8, Judge McCook agreed. Later that summer, the state's highest court seconded him. On July 16, in a twenty-word statement issued from his home in White Plains, Justice Benjamin Cardozo upheld the legality of the joinder indictment. That same week, Dewey announced indictments of a dozen policy racketeers, including Dixie Davis, Bo Weinberg's brother George, and Schultz's policy treasurer, "Big Harry" Schoenhaus. Alexander Pompez was traced to Mexico; along with the search for Davis and Weinberg, his extradition kept the prosecutor firmly ensconced on the front pages of every paper in New York. Two more grand juries pleaded exhaustion and untended business affairs and asked to be replaced. Dewey won favorable publicity after refusing to intervene in a waterfront strike. Businessmen from that no man's land had suggested he confused legitimate union organizing with mob depredations.

And on the fourteenth floor, the pace never slackened. Besides surrendering social lives and the joys of marriage, some of the men found themselves in the company of guards, assigned by their boss to prevent their murder by garment district goons. Dewey himself went home nights to an island of calm, all greens and soft grays, assembled at 1148 Fifth Avenue by Frances, who throughout their life together was to throw a cloak of domesticity over her hard-charging husband. The couple found sacrifice a way of life now, their hefty private income of 1934 shrunken until Dewey looked at his bank account on the last day of September 1935 and found in it less than $300. Henceforth, his rule was to live thriftily and try to keep two months' expenses in the bank. For Frances, public life meant relinquishing her husband to endless hours of work, and the unwelcome demands made by press and public on the wife of any celebrity.

"I got home at eleven, didn't I, dear?" Dewey once inquired within earshot of a reporter.

"Midnight!" his wife said. With Tom practically a full-time resident of the Woolworth Building, there was little time for relaxation. When the couple went windowshopping on Fifth Avenue, they were followed at a discreet twenty paces by bodyguards assigned to their protection at John Lyons' insistence. Saturday nights were reserved for poker with Pat and Marge Hogan, and Sunday afternoons for recitals at Town Hall. There were a few nights at the opera, followed by a highball at the St. Regis. At home, Tom bellowed when his wife didn't answer his first call, addressed her jocularly as Francesca, and tried to spend as much as time as possible with his infant sons. He worried about their weight, pushed them outdoors for their health, and gave them piggyback rides about the apartment. He took Tommy to see Central Park flowerbeds, and winced when Johnny mistook his father's legs for wickets in a Tuxedo croquet game.[20]

But it was Frances who ran their home life, who liked to stroll through the park with the boys, who played the piano and sang to them, who read Kipling or the Oz stories to Johnny as the asthmatic little boy sat under a heat lamp each day for twenty minutes. She never seemed happier than when performing the Mother Goose rhymes she set to music for her children, enrolling her elder son in the Hamilton School on East Ninety-sixth Street, or choosing the color schemes that might turn their home into an oasis of quiet far removed from her husband's snowballing career. She found it difficult to come to terms with his growing reputation, admitted to feeling jealousy at his absences, and suffered through a healthy number of newspaper photos showing her with eyes closed. Dewey himself recalled walking through the front door of his home and not being recognized by Johnny, aged two. For Frances, such absorption in public work to the detriment of one's own family was never easily accepted.[21]

"I don't care a whole lot myself for political discussions," she told her friends. Life in "the goldfish bowl" was not her idea of happiness. Invitations to dine with such as Alexander Kerensky and Jascha Heifetz did not compensate for having surrendered her professional ambitions, only to discover the man she loved almost submerged in his own. Inevitably, there were moments of stress, whispered suggestions to Tom at a public function that he'd spoken long enough, that he shouldn't have another drink, that he should go to a dinner party without her. "Unfortunately, she doesn't like to go out," he told intimates. "Unfortunately, I do." The first time they attended a Gridiron Dinner in Washington, he danced until six in the morning; she stayed off her feet. When the mails began to swell and Frances found herself buried in correspondence, courtesy and upbringing demanded immediate and personal replies to everyone who wrote—asking for a recipe, inviting her to pour tea for a charity, beseeching her presence at a dinner or political function. Lillian Rosse, asked to take dictation, found herself being ushered into the large living room at 1148 Fifth Avenue and seated in a chair in one corner of the room, before Frances strode across a carpet that might have covered a football field to occupy another chair, as far away from the secretary as possible. It was many years before the chairs got much closer.[22]

Frances worried about dignity. There were those who thought her concern stemmed from her own theatrical fling, now a taboo subject. In her presence, Tom too seemed to stiffen, dropping the shirtsleeves informality of the fourteenth floor to assume the manner of a very young man trying to appear a very sage prosecutor. At the last Christmas party in the Woolworth Building, in December 1937, a raucous afternoon was turning into a disheveled evening, as detectives, process servers, and secretaries alike enjoyed a final fling before moving on to new quarters at 137 Centre Street.

Shortly before six, the door opened to disclose the Deweys, unsmilingly casing the joint. Tom spoke up. "Don't you think it's about time you all went home to your wives?" The staff cleared out as if a band of their racketeering foes had suddenly opened fire.[23]

Frances' unhappiness expressed itself in a host of ailments, from hay fever to chronic colds, a poor appetite—she felt fat if she weighed over 110 pounds—and an annual bout with bronchitis. Worst of all were the allergies. "Frances thought she was allergic to everything in the book," remembers one close friend. "The only thing she was really allergic to was politics."[24]

Whether in response to his wife's pleas, or with his own eye on the 1938 political landscape, Dewey in the spring of 1937 was casting ahead, pondering how he might attain his old goals of heading the best law firm in New York and making "a hell of a lot of money." In May, at lunch with his Tuxedo neighbor John Foster Dulles, the perfect avenue to both seemed suddenly to open. The senior litigation man at Dulles' firm, Sullivan and Cromwell, was unwell and likely to leave, Dulles explained. The white-haired, craggy-faced grandson of John Watson Foster, Benjamin Harrison's secretary of state, was anxious to replace him with someone both youthful and poised, capable of top-notch research and courtoom hypnosis. Someone, in short, very much like Tom Dewey. The two men hit it off at once, and Dulles soon made a concrete offer. Come to work for us, he said over lunch at the Bankers Club, and it will be worth something like $150,000 to you. For once in his life, Dewey abandoned judicious weighing of pros and cons. He seized the moment, and shook hands on a deal. The Racket Buster was joining the Establishment.[25]

In that same spring of 1937, with a re-election contest looming, Fiorello La Guardia was fast on his way to becoming a man without a party. Always an irregular Republican, La Guardia had caused campaign managers to be all but bodily tossed out of the offices of John D. Rockefeller after he attacked family property in midtown Manhattan as underassessed. In 1936, the Mayor publicly endorsed Roosevelt's re-election, and his administration often seemed an extension of the New Deal in its more theoretically excessive moments. So liberal was the Little Flower, in fact, that the Democratic candidate for City Hall in 1937, Jeremiah Mahoney, made the cornerstone of his campaign allegations against the "red" Mayor.[26]

Not surprisingly, Old Guard Republicans like Charles Hilles and Hoover supporters like Ogden Mills and Ruth Pratt wanted nothing to do with the feisty La Guardia. Besides the cardinal sin of ingratitude, Fiorello was flirting dangerously with the new American Labor party, the 1936 Democratic offshoot that now demanded publicly owned power plants, public milk distribution, and subsidies for thousands of city-owned housing units. But Kenneth Simpson, the kinetic GOP county chairman, saw an opening for himself in the disarray, and quickly slithered through. By July, Simpson was proposing to dictate the terms of Republican support for La Guardia: the Mayor would have to accept Simpson's candidates for controller and president of the City Council, Joseph D. McGoldrick and Newbold Morris. La Guardia balked, and rumors circulated that the Republicans might actually nominate for mayor the conservative and feeble Democratic U.S. Senator from New York, Royal S. Copeland.

Elsewhere in the political jungle, Samuel Seabury and his allies in reform looked upon 1937 as a historic opportunity to rout Tammany once and for all from its familiar roosting places, especially the District Attorney's office. Together with Charles C. Burlingham, Seabury that June tried to talk Dewey into running for the job. In a crosstown cab ride, the special prosecutor found himself shouting his refusal at the partially deaf heroes of good government in New York. No Republican had won the D.A.'s job since Charles Whitman a quarter of a century earlier. Party registration figures showed 563,000 Democrats, to 122,000 members of the GOP. Medalie had urged him against running, fearful that a loss would end Dewey's promising political career before it could ever get started. For five of the past six years, Dewey went on, he'd lived on the modest wages of a public servant. He had a wife and two young sons to support. He had a right to think of them as well as his adopted city.

Left unsaid was Dulles' handsome job offer, and Dewey's own interest in seeking the governorship in 1938. To run now for a position he didn't want risked defeat at the polls. To run and win meant he would be locked into the prosecutorial role for four more years, reinforced in the public's mind as a racket buster and nothing more. What was heroic now might be taken for granted in a few years. Besides, Luciano was behind bars, and likely to stay there. For good measure, Dewey was preparing state income tax cases against the former *capo*. The rackets were crippled, if not broken. The Guggenheim Committee was in place, ready to assume a leading part in educating the public and potential victims of future racketeers.[27]

Seabury, convinced of Dewey's sincerity, turned to a reform Democrat named William C. Chanler. Simpson found his own refugee from Tammany, Irving Ben Cooper. Neither man had much chance against a united Democratic party, which finally came to its senses, dumped Dodge, and nominated in his place his Indictment Bureau chief, Harold Hastings, an eighteen-year veteran of the D.A.'s office. There the situation stood in late July, when a steady stream of petitioners started beating a path to the Woolworth Building. Supreme Court justices, Sidney Hillman and David Dubinsky, social and civic leaders, all asked Dewey to change his mind and accept a Fusion nomination. All were turned down politely but firmly.

On July 24, Simpson attended a meeting with labor's political organizers. He brought with him three different statements, including an endorsement of Royal Copeland for mayor, and one for La Guardia's re-election. Adolf Berle, the Roosevelt Brain Truster who filled an important advisory capacity in La Guardia's first administration, preserved details of the machinations of the next few days in his diary. Simpson played a shrewd hand that night at Berle's. He insisted that while he hated La Guardia personally, he was willing to go along with renominating the Little Flower in order to beat Tammany. First, of course, he would have to persuade his own party against supporting Copeland. Then too, it would help greatly if the Mayor would accept McGoldrick and Morris, and pledge "not to have anything to do with state or national affairs directly or indirectly."[28]

According to Berle, Simpson was kindly invited to jump into the East River. That interpretation notwithstanding, within a few days La Guardia was warmly embracing his fellow Fusion candidates McGoldrick and Morris. Now all that remained was to talk Dewey into running for D.A. That proved neither simple nor agreeable for the Mayor, Berle, Simpson, and Seabury. A week before the filing deadline of August 14, La Guardia and Berle took the prosecutor to the River Club to talk it over.

"Dewey's vanity," Berle recorded later, "always disagreeable, was working overtime. He had somehow gotten into cahoots with Ferdinand Pecora. He made a condition that the President and Governor Lehman should ask him to run, that Seabury should guarantee him a $300,000 campaign fund, and that he should have separate headquarters, etc. My own thought was that it was better to drop him overboard. Apparently, he also wanted to be told that he was essential to the Mayor's victory. I declined to do this."[29]

The next morning, La Guardia and Berle decided to ignore their prospective candidate. Berle expected Dewey to stick to his original wish and decline the nomination. Three days later, at a meeting convened on board the yacht of World-Telegram publisher Roy Howard, La Guardia's prospects as an independent candidate were discussed. On August 11, Dewey issued new demands: There would have to be "public clamour" for him to run. Editorials weren't good enough. Actual stories were needed, at least three days' worth. All that afternoon, he talked with Thomas Thacher, the upstanding Bar Association president and former solicitor general, until he repeated his request for a $300,000 fund to pay workers with large families to vote for him (so Berle recorded). At that, Thacher rose, said he wanted nothing more to do with the idea, and stalked out of the office. Back home, he took a call from Dewey, who said he'd thought it over and was perfectly willing to leave the matter in Thacher's capable hands. Alex Rose of the American Labor party visited the fourteenth floor that same day, while Simpson and others kept up the pressure and both Chanler and Cooper expressed a willingness to withdraw in Dewey's favor.[30]

Still the conditions came. Even Seabury hit the roof when Dewey sought control over the police department in the event of his victory. Late on the afternoon of the fourteenth, with the deadline for filing fast approaching, La Guardia let it be known that he was skipping town for the weekend. He advised Berle to do likewise. Nothing else, in the Mayor's words, would put an end to "foolish demands" from the Woolworth Building. That night, Dewey was at the home of Republican County Treasurer William Chadbourne. So was Ken Simpson, pouring drinks—later it was claimed that Dewey's final assent to run came only after his sixteenth scotch—and keeping in touch by phone with Irving Ben Cooper, who sat in his office at 2 Lafayette Street waiting to dispatch a letter formally renouncing his own candidacy. At six minutes to twelve, Simpson put in his last call of the evening. Dewey still was holding out, but his resistance was weakening, and a talk with La Guardia in the morning would, it was hoped, do the trick. Two minutes before the deadline, Cooper's declaration was received at the Board of Elections.[31]

The next day, reporters called to the fourteenth floor heard Dewey assail "an alliance of long standing between crime and certain elements of Tammany Hall" and pledge to do his utmost to preserve decent municipal government in New York. Adolf Berle had the last, sardonic word.

The horrible thing to me is whether Dewey, after this explosion of ego, will not blow up completely. As a prosecutor, he is one of the world's best. He obviously has taken his own build-up seriously and actually thinks of himself as having the entire weight of the United States in his hands. He wants to run for governor next year on a combined Republican and Labor party ticket, which I think is impossible . . . the man is really proceeding on a miscomprehension . . . of course, he may develop and the situation may change.[32]

Dewey told a different version of the events that led to his candidacy. "I didn't want to run . . . any more than I wanted a great big hole in the head," he said in later years. "The general impression was about to get around that I was a skunk because I wouldn't run for an office I didn't want. I'd been a prosecutor for five and a half years, and that was plenty. I wanted to get back to the practice of the law.

"But in the final analysis it got so bad that I had to sit down with Foster [Dulles] and we talked about it. He agreed that I had to do it. . . . I thus was launched in politics."[33]

Whatever his initial reluctance, Dewey plunged into the campaign with an abandon that impressed even the most blasé New Yorker. Privately, he considered his organizational base hopeless and, after a quick escape to Cape Cod, returned at the end of August to set about building a new one from scratch in each of the city's twenty-three election districts. Some 14,000 feet of space were taken in a midtown office building, over a thousand lawyers recruited to guard against vote fraud, and a massive courtship of the city's kaleidoscope of ethnic voters begun. Millard Ellison, a Jewish Democrat, was made campaign manager, and a romantic figure named Bernie Yarrow hired to appeal in his thick Russian accent to Czechs, Poles, Germans, Swedes, Norwegians, Syrians, and his own transplanted countrymen. It was the start of a lifelong ethnic fascination for Dewey, more typical of the average Democratic precinct captain than any Republican outside Union Square. Some in his entourage were resentful.[34]

"If you persuaded him you could swing the Carpathian Russian vote," one campaigner said of the boy from Piano Street, "you were in for life." Yarrow and his ethnic recruiters (there was a separate division to court the city's huge Jewish vote) were accorded royal treatment. Dewey's assistants, meanwhile, took to the streets addressing rallies from flatbed trucks and rising at five on election morning to man the polls before they opened. Two newspapermen, the *Herald Tribune*'s Hickman Powell and Harold Keller of the *Journal-American*, were enlisted to polish speeches and handle publicity. Typical of Dewey's attention to detail were his telephone banks, 125 phones manned around the clock by students selected for their cultured voices from the enrollment of Columbia University's Teachers College. Operating out of a boiler room in the Grand Central Office Building, women working the day shift called women, men at night called men—that way, there would be no domestic suspicions aroused. Voters were called regardless of party affiliation, and informed of the deadline for registering to vote in the municipal contests. Before signing off, each caller politely expressed a hope that the voter would support "prosecutor Dewey" in the upcoming election. Registration jumped significantly, and a surprising number of New Yorkers hurried to tell their spouses of a personal call from Mr. or Mrs. Dewey.[35]

Complementing the organization, indeed soon to surpass it, were the words that came out of the candidate's mouth. From his first appearance at a September 24 rally chaired by Seabury where he declared, "The plunderers have been driven from the city," through a series of powerful radio addresses, Dewey's 1937 race was a textbook campaign. He was hailed by cheering members of the painters' union, and endorsed by the left-wing elements of the furriers, dock workers, and paperhangers. Sidney Hillman saluted him as a true friend of the workingman at the same mass meeting of the American Labor party that gave its formal blessing to Dewey's candidacy.

For his part, the candidate reciprocated with the kind of language rarely, if ever, spoken by Republicans in the 1930s. "Any gangster who tries to get into a labor union in New York City now," he proclaimed, "will be thrown out by the members before the D.A. has time to act." He attended the signing of a new contract for the restaurant workers, paid tribute to Benny Gottesman as New York's leading hero, and was mobbed in Harlem by former victims of the Schultz ring. His campaign chest bulged with over $130,000. Its two largest contributors were the Rockefeller family and the International Ladies Garment Workers Union.

By late September, Dewey had narrowed the odds against him to 6 to 5. In the process, he was displaying an exuberance previously known only to a handful of intimates. "I think this is going to be a tremendously interesting experience," he wrote to his mother, "win, lose, or draw, and I am going to have all the fun out of it I can." The spirit was contagious. Before a mass meeting of the printers' union, Dewey tossed aside his coat, reminisced about learning "with clumsy fingers" to set type as a boy, and demonstrated his art on imaginary stamp machines and cylinder presses. He ribbed his audience of "city slickers" and asked if they knew what "a hobo printer" was. "I mean a guy that comes into your shop and he works for two weeks and he saves enough money to send his wife the allowance . . . then goes on a drunk for four days." He remembered "the Saturday drunk" who showed up for work by Monday afternoon, and the annual month-long binge of Leo, George Dewey's pressman, who loved his union card even more than his liquor.[36]

He amused his listeners with the tale of Jo-Jo Weinberg, a Luciano procurer who came to the fourteenth floor one day and said, "I'm in trouble."

"You're goddamn right you are," Frank Hogan replied, and Jo-Jo said that's not what he meant, his mother had brought him a letter at jail that morning, and, "Mr. Hogan, I don't like to get in any trouble, would you mind fixing this jury notice for me?"

"Oh we had so many people like that," Dewey went on. "We had a guy whose name is all I need to bother you with; his name was Jimmy Douchbag." The men roared, listened raptly as Dewey unfurled stories of his investigations, and cheered him to the rafters when he explained, "I thought I quit prosecuting four years ago . . . and they let me practice law for a year and a half and then they hung this job around my neck. And now they hang one for four years on my neck, and I am fighting like hell to get it." He had to go, he apologized, he was already behind schedule for his next meeting, but he had some parting words. He had just learned that the current District Attorney did not require his print work to be unionized. Dewey thought a change was in order. "You may be damn sure that the printing for the District Attorney will be done in a union shop or it won't be used, after January 1."

Then he was off, to address one of the eight or ten rallies he hit each night, plugging the entire Fusion ticket, often saying no more for himself than a few sentences of introduction. He stepped up to a microphone at Benny Gottesman's testimonial and cracked, "Somebody in the City of New York is shorter than I am." Events provided a mighty boost. The same night he launched his campaign, Dewey was forced to cut short a round of appearances at Republican district clubs; Max Silverman, Lepke and Gurrah's right-hand man, had been tracked to a palatial Hollywood estate by John O'Connell of the prosecutor's staff. Silverman was indicted three days later, the same day Broadway unveiled *Behind Red Lights*, a graphic melodrama about the prostitution racket. That weekend, an orgy of labor violence broke out, incited by the Gorilla Boys. A thousand strong, union men marched behind the blood-red casket of a local president gunned down on the steps of his apartment house, whom Dodge dismissed as the victim of a routine robbery.

Then Max Rubin, Lepke's deputy in charge of the Flour Trucking Association, was shot in the neck. His crime: returning to New York against his master's instructions. But Rubin lived, and went on to become a convincing witness against his former employers when Dewey went to trial against them. For now, the shooting provided fresh drama in a campaign already filled with it.

"Tonight," Dewey told a radio audience the night of October 3, "I am going to talk about murder—murder in the bakery racket." The shot that felled Max Rubin, Dewey said, was "the frightened act of a desperate underworld. The racketeers have flung down their challenge. Tonight I accept that challenge."

It was the first of a series of Sunday night radio talks that electrified the city as no one else had since Franklin Roosevelt invented the Fireside Chat. The next day, Dewey told the Herald Tribune Forum that he entered the race "because there is too much politics in the administration of criminal justice." There was no such thing, he claimed, as a Republican, Democratic, or Socialist way to convict the guilty, protect the innocent, and rehabilitate the youthful offender. He talked for the first time in public about the loanshark raids, the Waxey Gordon case, and the deadly rackets that had nearly strangled the garment and trucking industries. At the Henry Street Settlement House, Dewey tempered his crime busting with compassion, describing the new start in life given to a small-time policy runner named Louis, befriended by the Dewey staff and encouraged to begin again outside New York. He addressed mass meetings in Italian and Slavic neighborhoods, and won the endorsement of the transport workers' union and its peppery president, Michael Quill. Quill said that Dewey "had dared more gunmen and done more to end rackets in labor unions" than anyone in New York. Everyone, it seemed, wanted to shake his hand, get an autograph, hear his dulcet baritone rise in denunciation of mobsters and corrupt politicians. When Dewey couldn't appear in person, Judge Seabury or Mayor La Guardia himself filled in.

On October 10, in his second Sunday radio broadcast, the candidate lashed out at Dixie Davis. "Five thousand dollars is offered. Not for Jesse James. Not for Billy the Kid. Not for the hold-up of the Deadwood stage, but for a young New York lawyer who betrayed his profession and turned gangster." It was all there—the law office that cost $13,000 a year, the $165 suits and eight-dollar shirts, the fashionable addresses and cheap eloquence. Dewey saved his best for last, a tantalizing promise "some night in the future" to tell all he knew about "the most powerful district politician in New York," an intimate friend of "this sinister young man" Davis. Seabury, scenting a victory big enough to finally lay to rest all that Aaron Burr and his Tammany cohorts had dreamed of, was less cautious. He named both Hines and Al Marinelli, rivals for control of the Hall who were united in a resolve to keep Tom Dewey out of the D.A.'s office.

At forlorn gatherings called to promote the cause of Harold Hastings, the Hall's regulars worked themselves into a frenzy of contempt for the enemy one called "a creampuff with a mustache." When Dewey described sixty-four assistant district attorneys in Dodge's office as "loafers" and likened Dodge himself to Mortimer Snerd, Hastings foolishly told a meeting of the Ninth District Tammany Committee, "I know who wins elections. It isn't the newspapers or the *Saturday Evening Post* or *Time* magazine. It's the district workers under leaders like Denny Mahar." Hastings also boasted of his lifetime membership in the machine, and accused Dewey, twelve years a New Yorker, of carpetbagging.

Not many people were listening. Attention was focused instead on Dewey, on his headlines, his whirlwind rallies, and the trucks outfitted with movie equipment that cruised around Manhattan and turned street corners into impromptu theaters, showing a rousing little morality play entitled *Smashing Crime with Dewey*. It had Benny Gottesman retelling his story of terror at the hands of racketeers, an Eighth Avenue restaurateur reliving the kidnapping threats made against her children before Dewey broke up the ring, and a chilling re-enactment of the synchronized raids that laid the groundwork for Luciano's prosecution.

Most of all, New Yorkers were listening to Dewey on the radio, and discovering that criminal facts could hold their own against the most lurid inventions of network scripters. Never again would Dewey strike so responsive a chord in his audiences as when assailing Tootsie Herbert, "a slim, slick-haired fellow who cowed the noisy with a cold eye or a crippling, unexpected blow," or verbally indicting Charles Schneider for abetting "the murder of Billy Snyder on Avenue A." Technique counted as much as content. Dewey's speeches, the result of an exhaustive group effort, were staccato processions of facts and figures, crafted in short, powerful sentences that fell like hammer blows. Like another would-be president, Adlai Stevenson, Dewey would rather offend a hallful of important politicians than read a speech drafted only three or four times. Yet if Stevenson's words played like chamber music, a Dewey speech aroused fans like a college fight song on the crisp afternoon of the big game.[37]

On the evening of October 24, after a day largely taken up with libel lawyers and their meticulous proofing, Dewey rocked the city on its heels.

"Tonight, I am going to talk about the alliance between crime and politics in the County of New York," he began. "I am going to tell you about a politician, a political ally of thieves, pickpockets, thugs, dope peddlers, and big-shot racketeers. Albert Marinelli, County Clerk of New York . . . attained power by staying in the dark and keeping his mouth shut. Tonight, we turn on the spotlight."

Who was "this shadowy figure" whom Dewey charged with attending the 1932 Democratic National Convention in the company of Lucky Luciano? He was a laconic survivor of the 1933 La Guardia landslide, "Uncle Al" to his friends in the Albert Marinelli Association, whose headquarters was located in the same building as the trucking racket's, and a warm-hearted patron to racketeers like Socks Lanza and Johnny Torrio. Uncle Al lived in "a luxurious estate surrounded by an iron fence . . . way out on Long Island. From his several motor cars he chooses to drive back and forth in a Lincoln limousine, and his Japanese butler, Togo, serves him well."

Dewey gave a tongue-in-cheek accounting of the Marinelli Beefsteak dinner, "a colorful affair" held in January 1935 and supported by the likes of Little Davie Betillo, Benny Spiller, and Jesse Jacobs. All this was but prologue to the main business of the evening, the exposure of Marinelli's county committee lieutenants. "I have the official criminal records in front of me," Dewey assured those listening. "Here's the first one. He has eight arrests to his credit but the only one which stood up was in the federal court for selling dope. . . . Here is another who has a great personal interest in law enforcement . . . he began in 1924 with a sentence to Atlanta for counterfeiting. Some years later, he was picked up for extortion and carrying a gun, but it took him only two weeks to get out. Only a month later, he was again in the hands of the police, charged with homicide with a gun. But he beat that rap. Last month he was named as a member of Al Marinelli's county committee.

"Here's one who started his criminal career with an arrest in Hoboken, New Jersey, as a horse thief. . . . Here's one who qualified back in 1928 by getting himself convicted for dope peddling and in due course graduated from a term in Atlanta Penitentiary."

The list went on and on, detailing arrests for auto theft, drug peddling, impersonating an officer. That was the County Committee. What about Uncle Al's election inspectors? Dewey was ready with a powder keg.

"This faithful worker who counts your votes started out as a pickpocket in 1918. . . . But he won't serve as an election inspector this year. On June 1, he ran up against the federal government and a U.S. judge sent him to Lewisburg for a year and a half." Dewey wasn't certain about another inspector, "whose police record doesn't indicate whether he is in jail at this moment." In all, he cited thirty-two Marinelli associates with criminal pasts. Their seventy-six arrests ran the gamut "from robbery to sex crimes."

Marinelli refused to say anything when reporters swarmed around him the next morning. But Dewey was just beginning. He ventured into the boss's own district and promised changes in the local lexicon after January 1. "The word big shot is going out of the English language," the candidate told 400 excited partisans spilling out of a schoolroom. "There aren't going to be any big shots anymore. There are just going to be heels." To 5,000 people who collected at the sound of his voice during a noontime rally on Wall Street, Dewey said he was still waiting for a response from Marinelli, and suggested the district leader could make a major contribution to criminal justice in New York immediately by having his entire County Committee and Election Board submit to fingerprinting.

In the campaign's final days, the candidate hit his stride, ridiculing the opposition and pledging to restore honesty to law enforcement in the world's greatest city. "Every four years voters are offered a new false face to sit in the front office," Dewey claimed of the D.A.'s quarters, while "the boys in the back room" meted out justice Tammany-style. And what of Luciano, Schultz, and Gordon? "Not one of them was ever convicted of spitting on the streets by the District Attorney."

A Tammany rally at the Hippodrome lured 1,500 on the same night as 18,000 noisy, optimistic reformers crowded into Madison Square Garden. The crowd had to be warned against sacrificing precious radio time, or it would have shrieked for Dewey half the night. At their single joint appearance of the campaign, Dewey approached the line separating sarcasm and cruelty, saying of his opponent, "Harold doesn't mean to be that unkind. He's really a nice fellow. I have always respected his ability as an indictment clerk." As for Hastings' campaign charges, no one needed to pay much attention; "somebody else wrote them for him and told him the answers." Then the prosecutor apologized for having to leave early. "One of our fugitives apparently has been reading the election returns in advance" and turned himself in. The fugitive turned out to be Alexander Pompez, the important policy banker sought in Dewey's first Harlem raids and just now extradited from Mexico City.

"Well, it's all over," Dewey said to Fusion's final mass rally on October 30. "All we have to do is to keep them from stealing the voting machines." Behind the scenes, all was not harmonious in the Republican camp. Four days before the election, Kenneth Simpson complained to Dewey that his semi-independent campaign was drying up all the funds. Simpson warned that "the polls won't open" unless someone came up with $60,000 in "walking-around money," the time-honored gift of ten dollars to each precinct worker for ferrying voters to the polls, buying candy for vote counters, or simply to pocket for himself. Furious at his county chairman, Dewey scrounged up a few thousand over the weekend and, after a sleepless night, rose before dawn on November 2 to cast his own ballot.[38]

"Boy, am I glad I don't have to make a speech tonight," he joked to reporters at the voting place. He went for breakfast at a Childs restaurant, where he thumbed through a morning paper and laughed out loud at the prediction by Jeremiah T. Mahoney, La Guardia's mayoral opponent, that the election would result in a rout of Communism in New York. "Prejudice," he muttered before eating his meal and setting off for a handshaking—and irregularity-spotting—tour of Harlem. In one precinct, a black woman approached the Little Flower to complain. Her voting booth opened, she told him, to reveal a ballot already marked with the names of four Tammany candidates. Fiorello threatened to arrest the whole Election Board on the spot.

That night, surrounded by a happy mob of well-wishers at his headquarters, Dewey sought seclusion from the backslapping and self-congratulation that accompany a successful campaign to its finale. While men in evening clothes and top hats munched on sandwiches and drank beer, the candidate was alone in an empty fourth-floor room. Occasionally, friends like Benny Gottesman intruded. "Tommy, you're absolutely in," the hero of the restaurant racket case announced, a sentiment concurred in before nine-thirty by Harold Hastings. A few minutes later, Dewey slipped out to pay a call on the County Chairman in his office at the Hotel Roosevelt a few doors away.

"Where the hell is Simpson?" he asked. When the prickly ally was located, and photographers pressed for a smiling embrace, Dewey refused. "None of that stuff," he told them. Cordial smiles would have to suffice. Then it was back to his own command post, to talk with George Medalie and telephone his running mate. "Fiorello, the funniest thing happened . . ." a reference to Dewey's astonishing win in the home districts of both Jimmy Hines and Al Marinelli. Nearby sat Frances in a wine-colored gown, turning aside all questions from the press, allowing only that the evening was "the most gratifying experience of my life."

After the votes were in, she could escape the demands of public display for two weeks with her husband in Bermuda, where she fell off a bicycle trying to match his furious pace, said nothing when he gave Miss Rosse his vacation address, and longed for her children "terribly—particularly when I see any other child." Back in New York, the final tally showed a defeat for Tammany of staggering proportions. La Guardia had become the first Fusion mayor ever reelected, and by 450,000 votes. Dewey, running in Manhattan alone, ran ahead of Fiorello, polling 326,000 votes to Hastings' 217,000.[39]

Dewey returned early in December, to savor an invitation to attend Washington's Gridiron Dinner and to read Drew Pearson's column lauding him as a full-fledged presidential prospect. He arrived to find a party in cacophonous dispute, where Ken Simpson, hoping to replace Charles Hilles on the national committee, was lunching with Dewey's cousin Leonard Reid and discussing the new District Attorney's political prospects. Stacked on Dewey's desk were letters like the one from Leo Casey, publicity director for the Republican National Committee, who wrote a tribute to the prosecutor's future in politics, and invited himself to New York for a get-acquainted chat. On December 15, Dewey replied. He would be "delighted" to see Casey at any time convenient to him.[40]

Dewey had barely unpacked when he received another message, this one from Governor Lehman, inviting him to substantiate his campaign charges against Marinelli. Within an hour of its receipt, process servers were scurrying through the East Side subpoenaing 300 of the clerk's associates. Two grand juries worked around the clock listening to their testimony, and when it was over, Dewey wrote his own letter linking Marinelli to underworld figures Vito Genovese, Joe Adonis, and Jimmy Doyle. Lehman demanded an explanation from Uncle Al, and got instead a resignation. Henceforth, city court clerks would be appointed, not elected.

Most of Dewey's time was taken up with preparations for moving to 137 Centre Street. All through December, WPA crews worked three shifts a day knocking down walls and recreating a modern investigative laboratory out of Dodge's political retreat. Waiting rooms were built on every floor, and receptionists hired to prevent free access as of old. The outmoded filing system and old-fashioned letter press were tossed out, along with Dodge's swivel chair. "The beauty parlor," as Dodge's inner sanctum was known, was revamped. Out went a plush sofa formerly used by weary assistants. Additional floors in an adjoining building were taken for the accounting and rackets staff Dewey proposed to transfer intact from the Woolworth Building. Thirty-five process servers were dismissed, and positions exempted from Civil Service slashed from ninety-seven to eleven. A night chauffeur was added to the budget, as Dewey sheepishly explained he expected to work most nights until twelve.

Only three of Dodge's staffers were retained, one of them a former shoeshine boy named Felix Benvenga, known to Dewey since their days in Bar Association work. Amid the hurricane of activity, William Copeland Dodge sat in glum silence, interrupted only by a cryptic promise one day to reveal the names of those who had prevented him from doing his job. Crime would be wiped out, said

Dodge in his benediction, by "better parental care and more attention to God." Before the final move to Centre Street, Dewey summoned exterminators to pump a million cubic feet of lethal, sweet-smelling gas into the porous walls of the Criminal Courts Building. It was more than a symbolic act.

8
Mr. District Attorney

Things are boiling along here at the usual speed with nothing out of the ordinary, but some racket cases which may reach trial soon, a nice murder conviction by Rosenblum, and the necessity of preparing two or three speeches . . . which is quite a burden but I am about ready to tackle it.

—THOMAS E. DEWEY[1]

We note in the public prints of many cities the oft repeated cry, "What we need here is another Dewey." His name is almost a household word.

—DAMON RUNYON

Ferdinand Pecora held the new District Attorney's coat as Judge Charles C. Nott administered Dewey's oath of office on the afternoon of December 31, 1937. Frances and Annie were among the little group of onlookers at the ceremony, which was kept private at the D.A.'s express orders. The next day, while Frances represented her husband at La Guardia's second inauguration, Dewey and his men moved from the Woolworth Building to 137 Centre Street, where a small army of painters and carpenters continued their ministrations to the tired structure already slated for replacement by a new Criminal Courts Building a block away.

"Scram," Dewey told reporters camped outside the door, "I've got work to do," then good-naturedly he relented and set a press conference for ten-twenty that morning. Later he stood at the head of a receiving line for judges and other court officials, ate a hurried lunch at his desk, and counted 387 prisoners in the Tombs, nearly half of whom were awaiting grand jury action. One man had lingered over a year behind bars with no word from a jury that would either indict or set him free. Appalled, Dewey made the Tombs his top priority, and by the end of the week, 80 percent of the pending cases were resolved. The rest were disposed of within a few days.

Plans were announced at a dizzying pace for a new night homicide bureau, for new rackets and fraud bureaus ("The Racket Bureau's a fraud," went a saying at 137 Centre Street, "and Fraud's a racket"), and for reduction of felony charges to misdemeanors in cases in which juries were unlikely to return felony convictions. An assistant D.A. was assigned to magistrate's court to guard against the fix in that notorious judicial marketplace, and Dewey himself began prowling the courtrooms. In one he happened upon a young offender about to draw a twenty-year sentence for robbing a storekeeper of $2.50. Skimming through the defendant's probation report, the D.A. asked permission to address the court.[2]

"The facts of the case are these. This defendant is a second offender, because before he was twenty-one years old he stole a typewriter and pawned it for eight dollars. He pleaded guilty and was sentenced to two years' imprisonment. He has experienced a hopeless family life. He is now twenty-four years old. The report indicates that he has worked whenever he could find work." No weapon was involved in his latest offense, Dewey went on, and yet "a gross miscarriage of justice" would occur unless the youth was allowed to plead guilty to a lesser offense—say, attempted grand larceny in the second degree. The change was made, sentence reduced drastically, and Dewey announced his intention to accept lesser pleas in all youthful offender cases not saddled with previous records.[3]

He asked subordinates to develop his idea of a special court for sixteen- to eighteen-year-olds that would provide discipline short of incarceration. "You get these kids on the street when they're most dangerous," he explained. "They've never been in prison. They don't know the consequences of using a knife and gun." Perhaps therapy could turn them away from crime before it was too late.[4]

Dewey also moved to purge the Criminal Courts Building of a locust army of lawyers' runners and bail bondsmen. In May 1938, he announced a new innovation, a Voluntary Defender program to provide legal services to the poor, much as doctors ran medical clinics for men and women unable to afford conventional health care. Over half the felony defendants in New York, he said in a speech to the Legal Aid Society, lacked money for counsel.

Justice for the poor, Dewey charged, was "a tragedy and a farce." The Voluntary Defender program might be an answer. Chief Justice Charles Evans Hughes produced a warm endorsement to counter the opposition of the criminal lawyers' association, and within three weeks more than 200 attorneys willing to furnish legal help to the indigent had signed on. With that, Dewey stepped out of the picture, and the program was launched to public acclaim.

On the main business of the agenda there were the routines of interviewing and choosing a staff. Veterans of the rackets prosecution were asked en masse to come along to Centre Street; nearly all of them went. When a law was uncovered forbidding appointment of anyone who had not yet passed the bar exam, Dewey secured from the state legislature permission to create for his dollar-a-year men a new title, that of "criminal law investigator." The former chief assistants were awarded Dewey's major bureaus. A deluge of job applications was sifted. Ken Simpson was among the most voracious in his patronage demands. He was also one of the first political professionals to discover that personal pressure was the worst method one might choose in hoping to sway the new D.A.[5]

While Paul Lockwood, newly advanced to the position of executive assistant, inquired into the political allegiance of job aspirants, Dewey himself thought nothing of offending those whom he saw as essentially political candidates. Bernie Katzen was an influential member of the Jewish Republican community, field marshal of the drive that ousted Sam Koenig as county chairman in 1933, and director of Dewey's own campaign among Jewish voters in the race against Harold Hastings. Moreover, Katzen was an imaginative and vigorous lawyer with a dozen years' practice under his belt. After the election, he received a tepid offer. Come aboard as a deputy assistant D.A., Dewey asked, at $5,500 a year. As a payoff, it was disappointing. In its financial implications, it was downright insulting.[6]

Friends on the staff talked Katzen into swallowing his pride. "Listen, Bernie," Frank Hogan told him, "this guy is going places. Who knows, he might be president of the United States." When Katzen finally came around, Dewey seemed perfectly able to contain his enthusiasm. At the first staff meeting, he made clear why politicians of the ward-heeling variety were not welcome at 137 Centre Street. Dewey informed his men that district leaders who did come to visit would be thrown out. Political fixes were likewise verboten. For Ken Simpson, it loomed as the start of a political ice age.[7]

Other job aspirants got a taste of acid. The first question asked of Whitman Knapp was whether he could work a sixteen-hour day.

"No," he said matter-of-factly.

"What do you mean?" Dewey demanded.

"Well, I can come to the office for sixteen hours, but I can't work for sixteen hours." "I can," Dewey admonished, and Knapp allowed that he might be able to in an emergency, but for the most part, "it's a lot of nonsense"; it was the way New York law firms burned out their most talented prospects with unrealistic demands. Ed Walsh, later president of the ABA and an assistant attorney general in the Eisenhower administration, was another of Frank Hogan's recruits. Holding Walsh's resumé in his hand, Dewey noted that he had swum and rowed for crew in college. "What did you do that took brains?" he inquired. Walsh answered that he was a coxswain. "Well," the D.A. reflected, "maybe that took brains."[8]

Louis Pagnucco, an interpreter in the court of general sessions, was assured by Sewell Tyng that Dewey was on the lookout "for good boys of Italian origin." That was enough for Louis, who went out for a fast shave, haircut, and shoeshine before meeting the D.A. He was hired on the spot. The newcomer was assigned to an apprentice program, and proved his mettle during the investigation of Wall Street tycoon Richard Whitney. All one night, Pagnucco, under the guidance of Stanley Fuld, toiled over a brief in the supreme court library, emerging the next morning with a document that was rushed to the grand jury room. Whitney's indictment followed, and Pagnucco launched a career that would take him to the bench by 1951. He still says a daily prayer for the man who plucked him from obscurity and drummed into his head the maxim "No good lawyer works from ten to four."[9]

Half the new staff was Jewish. Frank Rivers and Jim Yeargin joined Eunice Carter as the first black assistant D.A.s to represent the People in a New York courtroom. Youth remained a watchword. One of Dewey's youngest men was William P. Rogers. Volunteering to work for nothing, Rogers explained why to a curious employer.

"Nobody knows me. I come from a small town in New York. If I work for you, then everybody will know me. I'll never have to prove I'm able or honest, because people know you only hire able and honest people." It was flattery, but not far off the mark of what the average New Yorker felt in 1938. For Rogers, it was the start of a career that made him attorney general under one president and secretary of state under another.[10]

To some of the younger men, Dewey was a godlike figure, jealous of his Olympus. When he shared it at all, it was at stilted little photo sessions for ethnic newspapers, where one's hand was seized moments before the camera clicked, then dropped like a lobster's claw mistakenly clutched in a dark night at sea. Reporters fared no better. Those who asked Dewey if he feared eclipse by another fabulously successful crime fighter, U.S. Attorney John F. Cahill, received a confident answer. "No, I don't fear that. After all, the public knows there was only one Lindbergh."[11]

Few ever saw behind the bravado. A few years later, Dewey astonished a young colleague working with him on a private case with a request that he not make suggestions about its handling except when they were alone. Why? the bewildered assistant asked. "Well, I don't want them to get the impression that you have to tell me what to do," Dewey replied. "He had a very delicate interior," the aide explained forty years later, "which he was forever trying to protect."[12]

To his subordinates, as if in place of personal warmth, the D.A. promised absolute loyalty. If someone should object to their best efforts, the offended party was to be directed to Dewey personally, "especially people who claim to be my friends. I'll put them out." This was no mere verbal pat on the back. Once, when a criticism was made of a new staffer, the new man was invited in to give his side of the story. Dewey listened, agreed with the way he'd handled a case, and wrenched a phone from the bottom drawer. "Listen, you son of a bitch," he told the complainant, "the next time you come around here with an ax to grind you'd better know what you're talking about. That is, if you ever show your face around here again."[13]

Dewey sought reporters' help, but he behaved in ways that were certain to preclude it. Charles Egan, business reporter for the *Times*, started to ask the D.A. about the effect of racketeering on private industry in New York, and Dewey cut him off. "That's a stupid question." "Is it?" Egan retorted. The story never got written. The press bridled at Dewey's high-handed methods, his habit of providing stories while insisting he not be identified as their source, his posed photos, his closing the bridge that linked his own offices with the press room at 139 Centre Street, and the new requirement that any reporter entering the building provide identification and a reason for being there. Interviews with the most respected journalists were off the record and generally limited to fifteen minutes. If he was pressed for details, Dewey would say, "If I revealed what I intended to do next, how could I lock up anyone in New York?"

Dewey's precautions against leaks, which included clearance of all stories with his press secretary, Harold Keller, were a repetition of the rules instituted by George Medalie in the U.S. Attorney's office. Yet reporters now found Dewey's cloak of secrecy too flattering a garment to be easily discarded. When the *Saturday Evening Post* published a generally laudatory four-part profile, the D.A. took vigorous exception to its mention of the fact that, while a student at Ann Arbor, he was not invited to join an exclusive campus club. He asked Henry Pringle, another profiler, to change a reference to his Saturday night poker with Pat Hogan to bridge.

Dewey was uncomfortable with public display of honest emotion, and he would make deprecatory remarks that undercut his own expression, baffling his friends and alienating potential allies. Once he gave a stirring extemporaneous speech on the rights of man before a black audience in a stuffy, hot Harlem church. Many in the hall were moved to tears. Later, in his car with Frank Rivers, Dewey turned after a few moments of silence and said, "Well, I guess we put one over on them." He complained to some others on the staff that the overcrowded, underventilated hall had smelled. "After all," he said, "they've only been free seventy-five years."[14]

When a Tammany friend died, the D.A. summoned Miss Rosse in the middle of a staff meeting, dictated a moving tribute to be sent to the family, and then circulated his draft around the room. By the time it went out, the emotion had been boiled away in favor of trite, commonplace sentiments. His candor translated best into orders. When a fire on Cherry Street killed a hundred horses late one Sunday night, and Tom Gilchrest was unable to reach anyone else, the terrified assistant finally put in a call to the D.A. himself at home. Dewey wasn't in the least bothered. His only stern words came in response to the younger man's assertion that there wasn't any available vehicle in which to bring the suspects for questioning other than a laundry truck

"I don't care if you stick 'em in an ashcan," Dewey answered. "Bring 'em in."[15]

It was often hard to identify the real Dewey. The quizzical little man with his eye-popping record and crotchety manner was already intriguing political analysts with an eye on 1940, when FDR would presumably step down and the White House would be up at last for grabs. Dewey, too, was looking ahead, boning up, and listening hard as national Republican leaders like Alf Landon urged him to seek the governorship in 1938. He joined in their frustrated cries of rage at Roosevelt and his cavalier attitude toward institutions like the Supreme Court, which in the wake of his landslide re-election he had proposed to pack by adding one extra justice—one extra New Deal vote—for every incumbent over seventy. It was a blunder that split the President's own party, only to be aggravated still further when an angry Roosevelt attempted to purge conservative Democratic senators who had stood up to him. Dewey fulminated about "crimes against the people . . . which this high-handed and idealistic administration is perpetrating."[16]

"Can we ever arouse the American people to an interest in the kind of public officials who are appointed?" he wondered in a letter to Landon in April 1938. "Certainly, in such matters lies the basic distinction between the successful democracy and the one which slithers down into corruption and collapses in a break-down of complete inefficiency. There must be somebody," he suggested hopefully, "who can dramatize the issue and educate the people on it."[17] It was a preview of Dewey's own governing style, which stressed teamwork, abhorred what he disdainfully called "palace politics," and looked upon crisis leadership as evidence of failure.

Most mornings, Dewey could be heard whistling en route to the large room on the sixth floor with bare yellow walls that he used as an office. After nine-thirty he secreted himself there, letting Lockwood gladhand the public while he reviewed reports, planned trials, and dictated an armful of letters to Miss Rosse. The spoken word was in short supply here. If Dewey's carafe of water needed refilling, a buzzer brought the secretary, and a finger was pointed at the offending pitcher. She brought him messages by writing them on a slip of paper and holding them before his eyes. Dewey's desk was just as uncompromising, its clean sweep interrupted only by a blotter, a letter opener, and a brown leather folder. Lunch was a simple affair, a sandwich, milk, and an apple brought in by Miss Rosse. It was followed by an afternoon of more reading and discussions with his bureau chiefs. Dewey reviewed evidence and leads, witnesses and judges, arguing and honing his product like a city editor surrounded by cubs and veterans alike.[18]

If he no longer prowled the streets at 2 A.M. as he once had with rackets detectives, Dewey's preoccupation with the job remained intense. He addressed each grand jury on its induction and dismissal, kept abreast of the fifteen felonies constituting a day's work for his investigators, and pressed ahead with fresh reforms in juvenile justice and legal draftsmanship. During his first month at 137 Centre Street, Dewey found himself invited to dinner parties by the likes of former attorney general William Mitchell, John W. Davis, and Justice Willis Van Devanter. "Very pleasant," he allowed to his mother, "but it kept me away from office work."[19]

Early in February 1938, a stranger appeared outside Paul Lockwood's office asking if Dewey's reward of $5,000 for the arrest of the lawyer Dixie Davis was for real. Assured it was, the man offered to write down an address where Davis could be found, just as soon as he received the reward money. An afternoon-long game of chicken and egg ensued, with Lockwood insisting the informant's anonymity would be preserved, and his visitor worrying about reprisals if he revealed his secret before receiving his thirty pieces of silver.

Finally, a deal was arranged. Davis' address would be given to Lockwood, and as soon as banks opened in the morning, the $5,000 would be handed over to the mysterious informer. While Dewey got on the phone to persuade the City Controller to gather that amount in small bills, three unmarked cars filled with detectives raced for the corner of Osage and Forty-eighth Street in Philadelphia, where they found Davis in bed with Hope Dare, with George Weinberg answering the door. After a halfhearted attempt to fight extradition (the captive lawyer likened himself to President Roosevelt, also "abused by the press"), Davis surrendered. By February 12, both he and Weinberg were back in New York, held on $300,000 bail.

Hardly had the furor subsided when the D.A. found himself leading another crusade. Richard Whitney was a descendant of Puritan stock, player of football at Groton, mainstay of Harvard's exclusive Porcellian Club, owner of a seat on the New York Stock Exchange at the age of twenty-three, adviser to two presidents, and the instrument of the House of Morgan in its ill-fated attempt to boost confidence in the stock market at the moment of its collapse. Whitney was known as the Strong Man of Wall Street for his unbending opposition to the New Deal and the regulatory reforms that came in the wake of the Pecora investigation.

Whitney didn't object strenuously to stepping down as the Exchange's president in 1935. After all, he lived the good life at his 2,000-acre Florida estate, his manor homes in North Carolina and New Jersey, his private rail car, his Long Island retreat and Manhattan town house. Besides, with all his free time, the tycoon could pursue independent investments, including a scheme to market nationally a brand of applejack popular in New Jersey, a hot dog vending firm based on Good Humor ice cream selling methods, but with trucks shaped like dogs and horns that barked instead of beeped, and the Florida Humus Company, a fertilizer venture that fared no better than any of the others.

By the spring of 1938, Richard Whitney was drowning in red ink. After answering a questionnaire circulated to all brokerage houses, he came under suspicion within the business community. In Washington, the Securities and Exchange Commission, now headed by William O. Douglas, entered the picture; while in New York, Dewey found himself competing with State Attorney General James J. Bennett for Whitney's scalp. Unknown to Bennett, his rival was secretly talking to both Whitney's wife and sister-in-law, an infraction of the rules which could be called resourceful or underhanded, depending on one's perspective. On March 9, Dewey announced an indictment of the financier for stealing over $100,000 from his wife's trust fund. Douglas broke the news to FDR over breakfast in bed.

"No. Not Dickie Whitney!" the President blurted. Shaking his head, Roosevelt could only mutter to himself, "Dick Whitney. Dick Whitney. I can't believe it." Bennett could only fume. "We won't fight over the body," he informed the press, before announcing a second indictment, on a charge involving Whitney's pledge of $109,000 in New York Yacht Club funds as collateral for a $400,000 personal loan. Times being what they were, yacht clubs drew less sympathy in the popular press than fleeced wives, however, and Dewey reaped a windfall of favorable headlines. Whitney manfully pleaded guilty to all his offenses and went off for five years to Sing Sing. The day he left New York, 5,000 people gathered to gawk and point. That same day, Whitney tendered his resignation as an overseer of Harvard's School of Education.

In the summer of 1938, Dewey was an authentic national hero. His name showed up in the Gallup poll as the choice of 3 percent of his fellow Republicans for their 1940 presidential nomination, far back of the leading contender, Arthur Vandenberg, but impressive as part of a growing phenomenon. Speaking invitations flooded 137 Centre Street. The president of 20th Century–Fox complained that "about a million" ideas for movies based on Dewey's exploits were piling up on his desk, and it wasn't unusual when two Dewey flicks—*Smashing the Rackets* and *Racket Buster*—opened simultaneously to whet audience curiosity about the man America now called the Gangbuster. Dewey was offered and rejected $150,000 to portray himself in a film, and an even larger sum to go on the radio for fifty weeks in imitation of his Sunday evening melodramas of the previous autumn. Financially appealing as it was, "it would have been . . . selling my office for my own private profit," he wrote, all the more objectionable in light of his own recent criticisms of "the money-grubbing tactics of the Roosevelt family."

He was not immune to his growing fame. After Bill Douglas arranged for Tom and Frances to spend a few days at a resort in the Blue Ridge Mountains, not far from Jefferson's Monticello, the D.A. had a complaint to register. In five days, he told Douglas, only one person had asked him for an autograph. Nor was his mind entirely occupied with illegalities on the streets of New York. "We are hoping and praying that there will not be a war in Europe," he wrote his mother in May, against rising tensions caused by Hitler's lurch for territory and dominance. "I thought the Austrian coup would probably be followed by an effort by Hitler to preserve peace for a while, so he could consolidate his gains. Others think the Democracies are getting ready to fight and do so rather soon. It begins to look as if they will have to fight fairly soon or the Dictators will dominate Europe. Anyway you look at it, it is perfectly frightful."[20]

From his jail cell, Dixie Davis brooded on his friendship with Jimmy Hines. He sent Hope Dare to see the man he called Pop, and beg for his help. The showgirl was tossed out unceremoniously. Soon thereafter, Davis sent word to the D.A. that he wanted to talk. A furtive meeting was arranged between Dixie and Sol Gelb in Central Park. "You know what I'm interested in," Dewey told Gelb before he left. Within a week, Gelb was able to report back, "We've got a case against Hines." Jimmy was having problems of his own batting down unflattering accounts of his power and its abuse. The papers were filled with stories about his friendship with milk racketeer Joey Fay, and charges from reformers that Welfare Island prisoners could purchase parole through him. New Yorkers knew of the discovery of Hines's name among those regularly called by narcotics dealers, and the dollar bills handed out to faithful voters each election day in Hines's Eleventh District like candy on Christmas morning.[21]

"I'm damned tired of all this," Jimmy finally exploded. "Hines this and Hines that—and I'm going to bring it all out in the open." On May 25, 1938, Dewey gave him his chance, with an indictment alleging Hines's participation in a conspiracy to corrupt justice and promote an illegal lottery, namely, policy. The stocky red-faced borough chief turned himself in, professed unconcern about the charges, and basked in the admiration of his friends at the Monongahela Club. Then he hired as his lawyer Lloyd Paul Stryker, a one-time Republican soured on the party after the U.S. Senate failed to confirm his appointment by President Coolidge to a federal judgeship. Stryker was a man of limitless energy and ornate courtroom rhetoric, author of a book on Andrew Johnson, a crew-cut beefy figure who exuded power and was accustomed to having his way in any confrontation. By all odds, he was Dewey's toughest opponent yet.

At pre-trial hearings, Stryker charged the D.A. with a political vendetta, and demanded that Judge Pecora compel Dewey to provide a bill of particulars, including a detailed list of all judges and other officials supposedly corrupted by Hines. To do anything less, Stryker insisted, would usher in "a reign of terror, in which every judge—every Democratic judge—is left under a cloud of suspicion." Pecora agreed, and he would have gone further, forcing Dewey to unveil the specifics of meetings, places, money, and the like, but for the prosecutor's successful plea that the decision be reargued.[22]

Dewey wanted a blue ribbon jury, from which, Stryker suggested, his opponent had dropped prospective jurors in the past for not voting guilty.[23] This brought Dewey to his feet denouncing "slimy, stinking accusations" and putting a jury pool clerk on the stand to refute the charge. There were fresh contretemps after a cameraman with a telephoto lens snapped a shot of Dixie Davis, supposedly being held under the tightest of security, reclining in his undershirt in Hope Dare's apartment. Livid, Pecora demanded an explanation from Dewey, who rather lamely informed the court that Davis left his cell to see a dentist, only going to his girlfriend's place to change clothes. By now, it was apparent that the Kid Mouthpiece was turning state's evidence. On July 30, he did so formally, and was released without bail in Dewey's personal recognizance

A few days later, Dewey unveiled his bill of particulars, highlighted by allegations of corruption against former district attorney Dodge and two magistrates, Hulon Capshaw and the late Francis Erwin. The approaching trial promised to be one of the most unusual in New York's history, its cast of characters including a D.A. being boomed for the White House, a judge known to hanker after the governorship, a defendant largely responsible for Pecora's 1933 loss to Dodge, and a defense lawyer regarded as a forensic genius, whose contempt for his rival was reciprocated. "Don't be disturbed about the press reports of conflict in the courtroom," Dewey wrote his mother as the People versus James J. Hines approached the opening arguments. "It is highly necessary to cool off my noisy opponent once in a while. . . . I don't believe I can educate him into conducting himself like a lawyer, but I do think I can teach him that some things will do him more harm than good."[24]

Privately, the tension was beginning to tell. In a visit to his doctor, Dewey held out a set of deeply ridged fingernails. "Does this mean I have cancer?" he inquired melodramatically.

Of course not, Wilbur Duryee answered. It meant that the strain under which he worked was so great that his nails had stopped growing. It wasn't cancer stunting his nails. It was Jimmy Hines.[25]

The hours were brutal now, with all-night work the rule as the Hines prosecution took shape. Few honestly expected Dewey to win the battle; many resented him for making the effort. Even Judge Seabury, who had tried and failed to get the goods on the boss from Manhattanville, the onetime blacksmith and war hero, the man who stood up to Charles F. Murphy and won, said with a smile, "Jimmy

Hines is the most likable rogue I know." Then, too, Dewey had been embarrassed over the Davis-Dare visits. He stayed publicly silent when a state senator under investigation in a liquor bribe scandal put a .32-caliber revolver to his head and shot his brains out. He offered no encouragements to various Young Republican groups and upstate county chairmen who were floating his name as a possible gubernatorial candidate. He told his uncle early in May that the governorship "is definitely no part of my plans," and he dispatched Paul Lockwood with a letter saying as much to the statewide Young Republican convention. But on June 20, U.S. Senator Royal Copeland died, and Governor Lehman, whom Dewey considered unbeatable, suddenly announced his own interest in sitting in the Senate. With that, a Dewey-for-Governor candidacy seemed more credible. Meanwhile, White House political strategists like Jim Farley, who doubled as state and national Democratic chairman, found themselves without a candidate of their own. Farley tried unsuccessfully to persuade Senator Robert Wagner to come home and take on Dewey should the D.A. finally toss his hat in the ring. "If they draft me for Governor," Dewey wrote after Copeland's death, "I don't have to run, because I can refuse the draft. Such an event, however, would be avoided by a preliminary statement." As a declaration of non-candidacy, it was less than Shermanesque.[26]

Also in June, Dewey was embroiled in a controversy linked with efforts by the state constitutional convention to forbid any use of evidence obtained through wiretapping. Dewey denounced the idea as impractical and potentially dangerous. However incriminating such evidence might be, he said in doomsday tones, if the proposed amendment were adopted, "it must be given back by the people to the criminal . . . in other words, if a policeman makes a mistake in picking up evidence, then the guilty will go free." Support for his position came from his fellow district attorneys, and Mayor La Guardia, whose economic liberalism did not conceal a preference for ends over means when it came to gangsters preying on the poor. The Little Flower once called Police Commissioner Valentine to City Hall to confront a group of angry civil libertarians.

"Lewis, these people claim you violate the Constitution."

The Commissioner thought for a moment, then replied, "So do the gangsters." The Mayor beamed. The protesters were dismissed, and La Guardia returned to the task of running his city his way.

Two days after Dewey first criticized the wiretap ban, Governor Lehman joined the fray with a strong demand for constitutional restrictions on the practice. "History teaches that tyranny and op-pression invoke the procedure of unlawful search and seizure," Lehman said, in words quickly seconded by the American Labor party. What the public didn't know was that Lehman had reason to believe that Dewey, before becoming special prosecutor in 1935, had, in common with other New York lawyers, used wiretap evidence in his private practice. For the D.A., the fight was turning into a no-win battle, threatening both his cherished dream of a fall alliance with organized labor, and the wiretap material already gathered for use in the upcoming Hines trial. Compromise was the answer—not much of a compromise, only a practically meaningless ban on "unreasonable interception of telegraph and telephone communications," which would still permit such evidence "if time or other circumstances have prevented police officers from obtaining a search warrant."[27]

It was a muddy pond in which delegates to the constitutional convention swam, where white hats were stained and old alliances weakened. Lehman himself had once proposed universal finger-printing as a weapon against crime, and lent support to a bill introduced by Herbert Brownell that would have forbidden known criminals from consorting in public or private. Dewey could count among his winning majority for the watered-down amendment such Democratic luminaries as Al Smith. "You are becoming as good a politician," Leonard Reid told him at the end of July, "as you are a prosecutor." Reid arranged a meeting between the D.A. and Landon's 1936 running mate, Frank Knox. George Medalie hired a young economic researcher named John Burton to prepare speech material if and when Dewey entered the race for governor. In one portentous month, the prospective candidate met with Landon, Hoover, national GOP Chairman John Hamilton, Walter Lippmann, and the prickly county chairman with national aspirations of his own, Ken Simpson.[28]

But after the wiretapping controversy, something seemed missing. A chink appeared in Lochinvar's golden armor. Innocence had been sacrificed to ambition. The New Yorker, tart voice of cafe society, was not alone in rethinking its hero worship. It now recalled how Dewey, to nail Luciano, had held 125 witnesses incommunicado, set impossibly high bails, traded freedom and overseas travel for testimony, and used threats of tax prosecution as a club with which to compel cooperation. "He could lock you up in a minute if he wanted to," the magazine quoted an unnamed attorney. "He's potentially more dangerous to constitutional freedom than Mayor Hague" (a reference to the undisputed power of the boss of Jersey City). Sadly The

New Yorker clucked its tongue and shook its world-weary head. The white knight from Owosso, it concluded, had turned into "just another guy we have to watch."

Reporters from Boston, Chicago, Philadelphia, and a dozen other cities joined their New York counterparts packing Room 148 of the Supreme Court Building in Foley Square on August 16, 1938, when the fight already billed as the Bulldog vs. the Tammany Tiger at last got under way. "The Battle of the Century" bannered the New York *Mirror*. The *Daily News* featured its "Courtroom Clock," with exhaustive hour-by-hour reports of the duel between Dewey and Stryker. All the major dailies ran page after page of transcripts and employed courtroom artists to evoke the atmosphere inside the stifling chamber where the air conditioning was turned off so the soft-spoken prosecutor could be heard. It was a trial of almost comic extremes, the kind of underworld pageant that a hungover Damon Runyon might have dreamed up for sale to Hollywood's moguls. There was Little Joe and Big Harry, Misfit and Spasm and badminton-playing gangsters. There was a boycott of photographs of the prosecutor after Dewey banished the photographers to the front steps of the courthouse for snapping Frances without her permission. Hanging over everything else, unknown but guessed at in the D.A.'s entourage, there was Judge Pecora's own political ambition. Just before the trial began, it was stoked in a secret courtesy call from Tommy "the Cork" Corcoran, an old friend of Pecora's from SEC days, now ambassador without portfolio from the Roosevelt White House. Pecora was given to understand, in words that any hopeful man was bound to interpret as a pledge, that his gubernatorial aspirations were looked upon with favor by the President. But of course, to have any hope of realizing them, the judge did understand that Tom Dewey must first be headed off? Pecora most certainly did.[29]

The D.A. arrived at the courthouse that morning without briefcase or papers. The case had long since been committed to memory. Near the back of the eight rows of benches set aside for spectators sat Geneva Hines, a gray-haired captain from the Eleventh District and mother to Jimmy's three stalwart sons. One row behind the Hines family sat Frances Dewey, who told reporters that her continued attendance at the trial would depend on her children. Like everyone else in the tightly guarded courtroom, she strained to hear her husband begin his case, telling of a 1932 meeting attended by Hines at which the district leader agreed to provide political and judicial protection for Schultz's policy racket in exchange for $500 a week.

Dewey verbally introduced other policy kingpins, men like Pompez, Ison, and his old adversary Henry Miro. He described the methods used by Schultz to take over the game, and defined Dixie Davis as the go-between who paid Hines his weekly salary, later augmented to include campaign funds for Hines's 1933 district attorney candidate, William Copeland Dodge (chosen, according to the boss, because "he's stupid, respectable, and my man").

When his turn came, Stryker slashed the air with his right hand and denounced the moral caliber of Dewey's witnesses. He successfully detoured the prosecutor from his customary game plan of mentally building up the racket in a jury's mind before turning to specific participants able to link its operations with a defendant on trial. Already, Pecora had overruled Dewey's request that the jury be allowed to take notes. Now he ordered the D.A. to call, not the policy bankers for an overall view of the game, but a witness who could shed light on the alleged conspiracy itself. George Weinberg, tall, conservatively dressed, persuasive on the stand, came forth to describe the meeting on Washington's Birthday 1932 at which Hines guaranteed protection throughout Harlem, including the neighborhood courts. According to Weinberg, Jimmy was a man of his word, who regularly had nosy cops transferred and raids on policy banks discouraged.

Wilfred Brunder described the game in general terms, and Spasm Ison—so named for the peculiar expression frozen on his face—told of paying $5,000 into the Democratic campaign fund in 1933, along with regular contributions to Hines's Monongahela Club. Julius Williams, a red-haired district captain in the Hines organization, blew up in Dewey's face, repudiating his own grand jury testimony and insisting that Sol Gelb and Frank Hogan had forced him to sign a statement against Jimmy. Throughout Dewey's questioning, Stryker peppered the air with objections, until slapped down by his exasperated opponent. "He's not my district captain," Dewey said. Pecora ordered the remark stricken.

The bickering went on, until it consumed more time than witnesses' testimony. One morning, open warfare broke out when Pecora left an impression that Stryker should feel free to object whenever he liked. The judge, Dewey asserted, was treating the District Attorney like "an interloper in the courtroom," and apparently didn't feel that he, Dewey, "is as good as the defense counsel." When the tantrums subsided, George Weinberg was recalled, this time to record a conversation between Hines and Magistrate Hulon Capshaw on the steps of a Democratic district club following a beefsteak dinner to raise campaign funds.

According to Weinberg, Hines told Capshaw, "Judge, I have a policy case, a very important one. Would you be able to handle it for me?" to which Capshaw answered, "I have never failed you yet. I will take care of it." Weinberg, who managed the policy banks for Schultz, also testified to delivering money to Hines at his apartment at 444 Central Park West. The last statement sent Hines to his feet, shaking his finger and shouting, "You know you lie." As Stryker later proved, Hines didn't live at the Central Park address until a few weeks after Weinberg claimed to have met him there, and Dewey was frankly worried about the effect of the mental slipup.

When the turmoil quieted, Weinberg went on, recalling the delivery of $15,000 in Schultz money for Dodge's election in 1933. His story was confirmed afterward by Dodge's own campaign manager. A graveyard of memories surfaced before Weinberg was through: Vincent Coll and Abba Dabba, and the dead Magistrate Erwin who dismissed cases within forty-eight hours of a request from Davis to Hines. Weinberg named at least half a dozen cops exiled to remote precincts after making policy raids. Even before Stryker set upon the witness, his objections to the way Dewey interviewed Weinberg led him to ask for a mistrial, and Pecora to jump in and rephrase Dewey's own questions so that they might be more acceptable.

Angry with Stryker and annoyed by Pecora, Dewey testily rebuked the bench. "May I suggest, Your Honor, that you permit me to examine the witness?" Finally, at five minutes before six, with Weinberg finished and trembling outside, Dewey casually asked permission to introduce the first of his "four-minute witnesses," a business man who could ill afford, as he put it, to spend another day away from his books. Enter Dudley Brothwell, proprietor of a Connecticut riding school where Dutch Schultz came often to admire his racehorse Sun Tan, and meet with Jimmy Hines at a time when every law enforcement official in New York was looking for the Dutchman.

Brothwell's evidence came at the end of a tough Friday, a salvaging climax to the first week's testimony. But Stryker had scored too, especially in his handling of George Weinberg, and outside in Foley Square the odds had shifted in Hines's favor.

Much of the case's fascination for the press and celebrities who flocked to see it lay in the *affaire d'honneur* between the opposing attorneys. If Pecora offended Dewey with what seemed a consistent pattern of unfavorable rulings, it was as nothing compared with the effect the D.A.'s courtroom manner had on Stryker. While the defense went through its cross-examination, the prosecutor rocked back and forth at his table, eyes half-closed, glasses dangling from one ear. When his chair stopped creaking, Dewey chose crucial moments in which to rise and stride over to the courtroom water fountain. He did this so often and at such detriment to Stryker's concentration that he finally waved him aside, filled a dixie cup, and handed it to his rival. The contrast in styles was mirrored in technique. Dewey was all smiles and good temper, courtroom observers wrote, while Stryker scowled indignantly. In landing a solid blow, the D.A. looked past the jury, to the press, flashing his great brown eyes like a high school tragedian vindicated of base allegations. To Damon Runyon, he was a "firstrate thinker and a whiplash on examination," who lured spectators to the edge of their seats with his quiet tone, and provoked Judge Pecora to red-faced anger. Once, Pecora bawled him out for failing to stand up when rendering an objection. Another time, Dewey blew himself up like a bullfrog and imitated Stryker's end-of-the-world oratory. "I don't think he said it in just that tone of voice," Pecora replied, his temper barely controlled.

While the principals clashed over procedure inside, outside the courtroom a thousand or more spectators besieged everyone leaving for fresh news. New Yorkers lined up each morning at seven o'clock to get a ringside seat. They heard Dewey interrogate former Tammany boss John P. Curry, a Hines foe who provided details of police transfers; and Stryker once more demanded a mistrial after Dewey asked Curry if such a practice was known as "being broken." They sat almost breathlessly when Dixie Davis finally came forward to talk freely about the famous runaway grand jury of 1935, and how Dodge tried to deflect it from investigating rackets once Davis lodged a complaint with Hines. It seemed that Dodge assistant Maurice G. Wahle was "digging too deeply" for comfort, according to the Kid Mouthpiece, and Hines obediently asked Dodge to lay off. When next Davis went before the grand jury, Wahle was gone, replaced by Dodge himself, who was contented with a few general questions before excusing the racket lawyer for good.

But events got out of hand, Davis recalled. Governor Lehman intervened, and demands for a special prosecutor became irresistible. It was then that Davis, contemplating the appointment of Dewey, had panicked and gone to see Hines in the company of James D. C.

Murray, another prominent criminal lawyer. "He will probably have us all indicted," Davis had warned Hines, who promised to talk to Dodge about the matter.

Davis emptied paper cup after cup as he told of thousands of policy dollars paid into Hines's account, and of a meeting with Schultz at which the gangster said of Jimmy, "Give him anything he wants," followed by a $2,000 down payment and weekly installments thereafter. He described meetings on the third floor of the Monongahela Club where Hines handed over stacks of cards with phony names and addresses, to be given in turn to mobsters who would vote repeatedly under the names they contained. Davis also remembered giving Hines large amounts of cash each election day in the club's basement. Only once did his voice seem to shake and his glib confidence grow pale—as he related, for the first time in public, the gruesome details of Jules Martin's murder.

Stryker constantly interrupted the grisly tale with objections, but when he tried to demolish the substance of Davis' story, he found the Kid Mouthpiece a wily adversary. "But you must have misunderstood me, Mr. Stryker . . ." Dixie said over and over. "What I said was . . ." When he was excused, Dewey called another four-minute witness—again it was a Friday afternoon—and this time the testifier was Davis' own sister, come to tell of delivering a $500 check endorsed by J. Hines.

U.S. Treasury agents exhumed old wiretap transcripts which had Hines calling Davis for his weekly payment. Harry Schoenhaus, Schultz's sleepy-eyed bookkeeper, swore that Hines was on his payroll for three years, and that he, too, had passed on $1,500 in policy money on Election Day 1933. A fire chief from Troy, a friend of Hines's and also a Democratic county chairman, put on the record repeated phone calls from his big-city ally in which he and the Troy police force were instructed to "stop pushing Dutch Schultz around."

On September 7, Dewey rested his case, Stryker ritualistically moved for a dismissal of charges, and Pecora, hesitating, encouraged defense counsel to press his demand. The judge thought the conspiracy angle weak. Moreover, since the policy banks had been moved to New Jersey in 1935, Pecora publicly questioned his own jurisdiction. Only a furious counterargument from the D.A., buttressed by a twenty-six-page brief prepared over the weekend, saved Dewey from the ignominy of having his biggest case summarily thrown out of court. He could not know that events would prove it only a temporary respite.

• • •

Now it fell to Stryker to cast doubt on Dewey's carefully rendered portrait of Hines as corrupt heir to the tradition of Boss Tweed. Already he had characterized Dixie Davis as "a crook lawyer," George Weinberg as "a rattlesnake," and Harry Schoenhaus as "a fat, weak, and stupid slob of a man." Now, he called Lyon Boston to the stand to refute the D.A.'s allegations against William C. Dodge. Boston twisted a Phi Beta Kappa key in one hand as he told of conducting a nine-month rackets investigation in 1934, a probe that netted one lawyer and a few policy runners. He moved on to the runaway grand jury. "Tell the entire story" of his association with that body, Stryker instructed the witness, who responded with a reiteration of Dodge's orders to conduct a fair inquiry, as well as the split between Dodge and the grand jurors over the latter's insistence on indicating Jimmy Hines.

Then Dewey took the floor and quickly established that Boston was made head of the rackets inquiry despite his status as Dodge's youngest, least experienced, least paid assistant. Was Dewey trying to prove Boston incompetent? Pecora interrupted. "I want to show that this man was assigned to the utterly impossible," the D.A. replied, "all alone, and was deliberately so assigned by his superior." Amidst a storm of objections from Stryker, Dewey extracted the precise limits of Boston's criminal investigative background prior to 1934, "as a child detective during the war." Boston also admitted knowing next to nothing about the activities of Dutch Schultz. He said that Hines's name had crept into the grand jury minutes in a reporter's testimony, but that he had not followed up the mention, considering it to be "incompetent."

Dewey asked if Boston recalled any mention of Hines by William F. Morgan, La Guardia's commissioner of markets. According to the witness, the grand jury's bias against the Tammany leader was hard to understand, because the only reference to Hines and racketeering had come in some hearsay from a reporter. But Dewey knew otherwise. He knew that Morgan, Police Commissioner Valentine, and others had linked Hines to the rackets in appearances before the grand jury. Now, in an effort to punch fresh holes in Boston's credibility, the D.A. pressed for details of Morgan's sworn statement.

"Didn't you remember any testimony about Hines and the poultry racket then by him?"

Like a sputtering rocket, Stryker shot up. "I demand a mistrial, Your Honor. I demand a mistrial!" Surprised and unnerved, Dewey fixed his eyes on the bench. "The subject was raised by the defense," he declared. Pecora would have none of it. "There was no such sub-ject opened up," the jurist said with anger evident in his voice, "and I think you should not refer to it in any way, shape, or form." The matter might have died there, with a verbal reproof, but Stryker continued to shout his demand for a mistrial, and Dewey offered to discuss the whole thing with the bench. A flustered Pecora finally slammed his gavel down with an abrupt announcement that he would consider the entire matter over the weekend.

It was two-twenty on a Saturday afternoon. Within twenty-four hours, Stanley Fuld and Felix Benvenga were ushered into Pecora's study carrying a twenty-page brief upholding Dewey's position. Both were assured by the judge that no mistrial was likely to be granted. On Monday morning, Dewey and Stryker debated again in chambers, and then, a few minutes before three, Pecora ordered the doors to Room 148 locked, and guards posted to prohibit any news-paper copy from going outside until he was finished. He began to read a two-hour polished opinion ("Pecora," Dewey said afterward, "was one of the longest-winded creatures God ever made") while the D.A. sat motionless, his only betrayal of emotion the crimson color-ing slowly rising above his shirt collar.[30]

"It is one thing to say that a fourteen-word question could not, by any standard of imagination, prejudice a defendant in the course of a trial after 4,600 typewritten pages of testimony had been taken. A sounder analogy would be that one drop of poison taken into the human system might kill the individual."

With that, Pecora declared a mistrial, and inaugurated a scalding debate among legal scholars, editorial writers, and political odds-makers. Asked by the court clerk if he wished to concur in the deci-sion, Dewey snapped, "I certainly do not. I am of the opinion that the question as asked was correct and proper ... unfortunately, however, the People of the State of New York have no appeal from this or any other of the decisions in this case."

Outside the courtroom, where on earlier days lawyers gossiped and office boys took issue with Western Union deliverymen, Hines was greeted by a ten-gun salute of flashbulbs and the cheers of a large, happy crowd. For the first time in his career, Dewey heard the ugly cacophony of boos and catcalls as he hurried to a car that would return him to Centre Street. For a few minutes, he closeted himself inside his office, then emerged demanding to know why ev-eryone else was so gloomy. "Let's get to work," he ordered jauntily. "There'll be another trial. And we'll win it." The same message was conveyed to the press late that night, after a meeting with Medalie and others concerned over the political fallout of the case. "Make no mistake," Dewey promised New York, "Hines will be brought to justice. I will move for a new trial at the earliest possible date." The defendant meanwhile complained of suffering "a bad break" in Pecora's decision, since Dewey so obviously had no real evidence against him. Then, jovial as ever, Hines asked reporters if Hitler had done anything yet to take his own name off the front page.[31]

The New York *Times* led the chorus of those who felt Dewey had been cheated of victory because of a legal technicality. It was a point of view shared by most editors and relatively few trial lawyers. Drew Pearson claimed that the debacle finally exposed the D.A. as a "slipshod" and arrogant courtroom practitioner. But in Detroit, Luise Rainer opened in yet another film based on the Gangbuster's heroics, and from Kansas, Alf Landon rejoined that Pecora's decision had boomeranged.

"The public psychology is that politics entered too much into the court's decision," the 1936 Republican standard bearer wrote. "You proved your case as far as the bulk of the public is concerned and therefore you have a measure of sympathy . . . which does not ordinarily go to the prosecutor." Landon had been approached by prairie politicians in his own state seeking his opinion about 1940. When they heard the name of Dewey, they likened the New York District Attorney to Theodore Roosevelt. "There you are," Landon concluded. "I hear that everywhere."[32]

Columnist Raymond Clapper spoke for Americans of many ideologies who looked on Dewey as "a live figure in a party of snoozing stuffed shirts." Within a week of the mistrial, his chances to be governor actually seemed greater than ever. For the record, he continued noncommittal, but Dewey's interest was made clear when George Medalie showed up in Albany to review every jot of the Republican party's proposed platform before it was submitted to the state convention on September 29 at Saratoga Springs. Medalie argued successfully for a liberalized program designed to suit his protégé from 270 Lexington Avenue.

Not every Republican liked what was happening; the Borough President of Queens, for instance, threatening to run as a conservative independent, charged that Dewey was nothing more than a puppet for Medalie, who would, if elected, turn the state over "to the Communists"—his euphemism for the CIO and AFL.

While an old friend looked after Dewey's interests in Albany, a new one swung the weight of science behind a formidable decision on running. Earlier in the year, Dewey had befriended a promising young expert in the then-new field of political polling. He and George Gallup became close, and it was Gallup's numbers, as much as anything else, that finally convinced Dewey to make the gubernatorial race. To his mother, Dewey wrote on September 28 of "an authoritative poll" implying a November victory, and expressed his conviction that now was the time to run. "I can do so much more for all of the things I believe in and have fought for if I am Governor than if I am merely the District Attorney of one of the sixty-two counties of New York."[33]

The next day, the Republican convention agreed. In one of the wildest demonstrations ever witnessed in New York's raffish political history, a thousand otherwise sane men and women, by day staid stockbrokers and farmers' agents, preachers of the Holy Word and judges of the law, all abandoned their dignity to do a contagious St. Vitus' dance in the streets of Saratoga. Flags waved and female orchestras played "There'll Be a Hot Time in the Old Town Tonight." Cowbells clanged and seconding speeches were lost in the din, until a rising vote of aye shook the building, and a renewed frenzy, like a carnival trapped in a cathedral, overtook the joyous Republicans of New York. The Promised Land was coming into view.

That night, the hall was bathed in floodlights and speckled with flashbulbs as the new leader of their cause took charge, declaring his own New Deal and providing decent burial for the Old Guard. He began by hailing social and labor progress of recent years, then stung the upstate power cartel that had for so long dictated the party's credo by insisting on the "inevitable and perpetual" ownership by the people of all natural resources. He confronted the delicate issue of Governor Lehman, at that very hour subject to mounting pressure from his own party assembled in convention at Rochester to forgo the Senate and take on the foe named Dewey.

"Without meaning to be so, any Democratic governor is, perforce, the good-will advertising, the front man, the window dressing for what is, in part at least, a thoroughly corrupt machine." This reference to the powerful organizations of Ed Flynn in the Bronx and Albany's O'Connell family seemed to presage a statewide edition of the previous year's detective story thrills. But Dewey had something more in mind than denouncing what he called "politics for profit." He had blunt words for his own party, shrunken in power and prestige since "the great progressive days of Theodore Roosevelt and Charles Evans Hughes." He had in mind a doctrine that more dogmatic men would later brand "me-too" Republicanism.

"It is the job of a majority party," Dewey insisted, "to build, not to tear down; to go forward, not to obstruct. It is not the function of a political party to die fighting for obsolete slogans. . . . In a generation torn by strife between extremists and fanatics, let us have the balance . . . to prove that democracy can maintain itself as master of its own destiny, feed its hungry, house its homeless, and provide work for its idle . . . without reliance on political racketeers."

The radio broadcast of Dewey's speech was interrupted at midpoint for a report of a peace agreement signed that day by Germany and Czechoslovakia at Munich. No matter; Herbert Lehman had heard enough. Jim Farley's tireless efforts, endorsed by the White House, to persuade the Governor to run again and thus keep the Empire State safe for Roosevelt, were only boosted by Dewey's blistering attack lumping the honest, if colorless, chief executive with the pack of vote stealers and minor criminals that represented his party in some urban precincts. On September 30, the word went out: Lehman would run again. On the heels of his running battle with Hines, Dewey found himself waging a two-front war, on the one hand seeking to translate his own popularity into votes for the state's highest office, on the other trying to rebuild an anemic party and make New Yorkers extend their memories back to a time when Republicans had worn the badge of liberals, and earned their dominance by anticipating, not resisting, the momentum of reform.[34]

As New York's governor at the close of the nineteenth century, Theodore Roosevelt teamed up with tenement house reformers to investigate what in common they called "filth-soaked, dark, unventilated buildings" in which children were condemned to early deaths. He pushed successfully for a new building code and the addition of fireproof fire escapes. He favored taxation of street railway, gas, electric light, and telephone franchises, previously untaxed, and waged noisy war on tenement, sweatshop, and Civil Service abuses. Charles Evans Hughes was TR's ideological successor, raised to prominence after he uncovered in legislative investigation widespread corruption in the insurance and utility industries. Following his election as governor in 1906, Hughes achieved insurance and banking reforms over the opposition of his own party. A Public Service Commission was created and the first workmen's compensation bill enacted. The GOP justifiably presented itself as an enlightened bulwark of good government.

In a letter to Theodore Roosevelt, by then in the White House, his fellow New Yorker Henry Stimson defined the essence of liberal Republicanism, a creed not dissimilar from that of the British Tory.

"To me it seems vitally important," Stimson wrote, "that the Republican party, which contains, generally speaking, the richer and more intelligent citizens of the country, should take the lead in reform and not drift into a reactionary position." Were the party to be captured, as the Democrats under William Jennings Bryan had been, by "foreign elements and the classes which will immediately benefit by the reform," and other Republicans wander off in disgust into mere obstructionism, then, Stimson concluded with a shudder, "I fear the necessary changes could hardly be accomplished without much excitement and possible violence."

Under men like TR and Hughes, the GOP in New York had been precisely that kind of conservative shock absorber, an evolutionary force offering adjustment as well as advance. When the Old Guard seized control of the party after 1912, Democratic liberals like Al Smith, Robert Wagner, Franklin Roosevelt, and Herbert Lehman were handed a historic opportunity to create and consolidate a new majority. Smith and Wagner took the lead in labor reform and social welfare legislation, performing a nimble leapfrog over TR's original tentative steps forward. As governor, Smith singlehandedly overhauled a woefully haphazard administrative structure. Agencies were consolidated or abolished, an executive budget compiled for the first time, aid to education increased, and the governorship itself raised a level of prestige previously unknown.

Smith's successors, Roosevelt and Lehman, expanded the role of state government in providing relief or employment for the jobless, social security for those over seventy, and prison reform. Much of this was accomplished over the strident objections of Old Guard Republicans in the legislature, headed by Assembly Speaker Joe McGinnies. In 1936, two years after the Old Guard's disastrous defeat under Robert Moses' banner, a youthful assemblyman named Oswald Heck replaced McGinnies in the speaker's chair. Irving Ives, another Young Turk, became majority leader, while officeholders and organization men like Dewey, Ken Simpson, Joe Hanley, Kingsland Macy, and Russ Sprague swept away the cobwebs of the Hilles era, and helped to lay the foundation for a Republican resurgence built on the tradition of the first Roosevelt, Hughes, and Stimson. The new men grasped the new realities.

To win the endorsement of 13 million New Yorkers, a Republican candidate must join the broad consensus for activist government, yet remain within the party's heritage of local and individual responsibility. He must promote security without abolishing risk. In the words of Joe Hanley, a state senator from Perry who later served as

Dewey's lieutenant governor, the GOP had "to get out of the Pullman cars and into the day coaches." From the start of his 1938 campaign, this was Dewey's objective. To run his campaign in New York City, he chose his friend Roger W. Straus, co-chairman of the National Conference of Christians and Jews, and onetime leader of Princeton University's Bull Moose Club. Oswald Heck was named upstate manager.

At first, there was little organization to manage. So rusty had party machinery become under the ineffectual chairmanship of Edward S. Murray, a Utica chemist, that George Medalie, Ed Jaeckle, and Dewey himself had been forced to jerry-build a statewide ticket in a room of Saratoga's Grand Central Hotel the night of Dewey's nomination for governor. While Jaeckle phoned a prospective candidate for state comptroller to get the correct spelling of his name and address, Medalie called TVA lawyer John Lord O'Brien in Knoxville to ask him to run for Copeland's seat in the Senate. Or so he claimed. O'Brien himself maintained he learned of his nomination the next morning in a Knoxville newspaper.[35]

While his manager attended to building an organization, Dewey himself decided questions of strategy. The traditional motor caravan of rural counties would be dropped in 1938 in favor of weekly radio speeches, a wiser use of precious time and the candidate's own gifts. Touchy issues like milk price supports would be avoided in favor of a frontal assault on the competence of the state government and the power exercised within Democratic circles by bosses like Ed Flynn and the O'Connells. The campaign was to be lively, assertive, and as rational as the candidate could make it.

"In the old days," Dewey said of his decision to emphasize radio over pressing the flesh, "the candidate would fly through the streets and after making fourteen speeches at fourteen hitching posts . . . end up totally exhausted and then get up and read in a hoarse voice some slightly inaccurate and undeliverable material prepared by some newspaper reporter who had been hired for the occasion."[36]

Instead of this unhappy tradition, Dewey and his managers sought to stress his command of issues beyond crime control, to flood thousands of homes with apparently personal appeals from the nominee himself, and capitalize on his celebrity and youthfulness. In his radio speeches, as on the stump, Dewey associated the virtues of private compassion and public competence. Or, as Straus put it in paraphrasing his Bull Moose hero, "It is all very well to mean well, but not to mean well weakly. You must mean well strongly, and you will get something done. Mr. Dewey means well strongly."

In his first statewide broadcast, Dewey lit into Lehman for the mess in unemployment insurance, citing example after example to personalize his case. He named a cabinetmaker who had been told his claim was lost in Albany, a Herkimer woman who waited nine months after losing her machinist's job to collect any benefits, and another unfortunate beneficiary forced to trade in his life insurance after bureaucratic inertia kept him from collecting his due. "Half the duty of a state administration," Dewey insisted, "is to see the needs of the people and meet them by passing adequate laws. The other half is to administer and enforce the laws so that there shall be performance and not mere promise."

He took the same approach to the housing crisis in the state, describing the plight of a couple in a tiny fourth-floor walk-up near Harlem who paid twenty-five dollars a month "for the privilege of breathing their neighbor's cooking instead of fresh air." He had at his fingertips numbers to bolster his argument for a constitutional amendment funneling $300 million into loans and subsidies with which to construct and maintain low-cost housing. Tuberculosis ran 129 percent above the national average in the New York tenements, he claimed. Spinal meningitis was 119 percent higher. Instead of the state sending $170 million to Washington and getting back less than a third of that in housing assistance, why shouldn't New York keep the original sum and do the job itself? The theorists who would entrust all such responsibility to a benevolent federal government, he told a Harlem audience, "ought to come up and go through one of the houses that have been burned," as he had as D.A., "wade through water to the tops of their shoes, and on the top floor find a baby smothered to death." Dewey also endorsed reapportionment of the state legislature—a position unpopular with upstate Republicans—because "you haven't got a colored man in the Senate, and we propose to get one."

He attacked Lehman's handling of Civil Service and electric rates. Before the largest Republican audiences in Rome and other upstate cities since TR's days, Dewey dismissed the incumbent as "a branch manager in a chain store system of national politics." Without ever specifically assailing the New Deal—indeed, he took to calling himself a "New Deal Republican"—he took advantage of the recession that had sent unemployment rolls skyrocketing for the second time since 1929, and made oblique swipes at the shift of authority from state to federal government that had even the New York *Times* complaining about a national debt doubled in six years to $37 billion.

The Dewey train, riding north along the Hudson, drew large and enthusiastic crowds: 1,500 in Poughkeepsie, 1,000 in Hudson, 600 at Beacon, all come to catch a glimpse of the Gangbuster as he passed through, if only to remove his hat and say, "Hello, folks, glad to see you." On board, the atmosphere was radically different from most political excursions. Gone were the liquor and cigar smoke with which politicians fortified themselves, gone too the heavy geniality and local gossip. Instead, the candidate disappeared into a private compartment in between stops, to hone his remarks for the next station or, as he did once, chat with two young girls from a high school paper while important, or self-important, organization types cooled their heels outside his door.

He went to Utica and Troy, to Mineola in Russ Sprague's Nassau, to White Plains and Syracuse and Binghamton. Two old people, a farm couple from Albany County, rose at two-thirty on the morning of a Dewey appearance, hitched up their horse and buggy for the fifteen-mile drive into town, and were sitting outside the hall fully twelve hours before the candidate was scheduled to arrive. They wanted to be sure of getting a seat, they explained. A thousand supporters greeted him at one in the morning in a Buffalo train station. In Albany, he arranged for bail to be posted in case the O'Connells had him arrested, and then went on to question how a city with 79,000 adults listed in its latest directory could have 82,000 registered voters. When it came to vote fraud, "the Tammany Braves are pikers compared to the O'Connells," he said, and someone in the audience shouted, "Pour it on, Tom."

He denounced the politics of the Flynn machine in the Bronx, reminded voters that among the delegates pressing Lehman to accept renomination were Al Marinelli and Jimmy Hines, and castigated the Governor for not "promptly and fearlessly" repudiating such support. He ventured into the Bronx as a dramatic gesture, and won cheers from a crowd with his sledgehammer assault on Flynn, "that strong, silent, sylphlike figure that no one can find on the job he's supposed to get $10,000 or $12,000 a year to fill," a reference to Flynn's sinecure as New York's secretary of state.

To Alf Landon, he promised "the most thrilling fight they ever had" and pronounced himself "soberly optimistic." With polls tightening, and the odds on Lehman down from a prohibitive 4 to 1 to 8 to 5 by mid-October, Dewey had reason to hope for an upset. Campaign rhetoric escalated as Lehman talked of "hypocrisy" and "smears" and accused his opponent of "wisecracking" his way through the campaign. Dewey lashed back with talk of bosses and purges. "Mere bookkeeping is not my line," he told several audiences, a remark guaranteed to offend the sensitive Lehman. The Governor retaliated, accusing the D.A. of inexperience and well-concealed reactionary beliefs. Lehman scored a coup by invoking the power of Roosevelt to persuade La Guardia not to endorse Dewey. When a member of the New York City Council died late in October, the Little Flower even made the highly publicized gesture of riding to the funeral in an open car alongside Lehman.[37]

For all the excitement he was stirring up, Dewey still confronted a conundrum: how to oust an immensely popular governor whose personal integrity was legendary, without resorting to farfetched and ultimately self-destructive guilt by association. Several times in the campaign, he veered close, only to re-establish a higher level in his Monday night radio broadcasts. These dealt with issues beyond vote stealing, and served to keep his name in good stead among independents and nominal liberals. Besides, bossism was a heavily traveled two-lane highway in New York. The GOP was not without its tinhorn dictators. There was Sprague on Long Island, a host of local baronies in Rochester and Syracuse, Ulster and Orange counties, Manhattan and Brooklyn, and the Southern Tier that hugged the Pennsylvania line.

And in Buffalo, there was Edwin F. Jaeckle, with whom Dewey entered into a partnership that sent out ripples, disturbing first the placid pond of Old Guard New York, and then the deep waters of national politics. Dewey was too self-possessed, too suspicious, and too confident to let anyone become his Louis Howe. But Ed Jaeckle became his Jim Farley.

Jaeckle was spectacularly unphotogenic, a hawk-nosed, jowly figure, gruff of voice and manner, blunt, ambitious, not yet forty-five but a grizzled veteran of Republican wars in Buffalo. Seven years older than Dewey, whom he met for the first time on the stage of the Saratoga convention hall, Jaeckle had a well-established reputation for independence. He had bucked the Erie County organization almost as soon as he first won a place in it, as a supervisor from the Eleventh Ward. In 1926, he ran his own candidate for county treasurer against the regulars. Jaeckle won that race, and with it appointment as collector of the county's back taxes, so that by 1933, when he voluntarily retired to head a law firm that was prosperous in its own right, he had banked over $150,000 and could pursue his cause without worry over financial pressures.

Turning full-time attention to Republican politics, Jaeckle was elected county chairman in September 1935, and he set about organizing Buffalo and its environs as no one had ever done before. At his own expense, the new chairman treated 1,100 of the faithful to a chicken dinner in the city's Municipal Auditorium. He moved party headquarters from a dingy loft to a handsome suite, and staffed them with eight year-round professionals. He began a system of files on a block-by-block basis, and made himself accessible at open houses convened regularly. Fifty new ward and town clubs were founded; within two years, they counted 15,000 party workers on their rolls. Each club, though autonomous, was chartered by an executive committee, which also drew up by-laws and constitutions. Jaeckle proposed to outdo the Democrats at their own game. He and his allies handed out Christmas baskets each year to 1,400 needy families. He organized a Republican bowling league, softball and football squads. Each year, his central committee staged a get-together for Republican families, with a half-mile-long parade, games of chance, and clowns performing pratfalls. Thirty thousand people came and enjoyed themselves, and went away confirmed in their faith, or considering conversion.

When Jaeckle took over, Buffalo was a Democratic stronghold. Republicans were an impotent minority on the City Council. The mayor, district attorney, and county clerk all were Democrats. But before he'd been in his new job six months, Jaeckle's flair for organization helped double the number of GOP assemblymen from the county. By 1938, it was a Republican citadel.

Jaeckle wasn't content to limit his renaissance to a single city. In 1936, at the Cleveland convention, he supported Landon as the most liberal candidate and declared war on the venerable Charles Hilles. He rejected out of hand Hilles's casual orders about a new clerk for the State Assembly, insisting that any jobholder to come out of Erie County must bear the stamp of organization approval. He even stalked out of a New York City meeting at which Hilles and a handful of his cronies divvied up such spoils, oblivious to Jaeckle and other rising figures in the party who wished to taste democracy as well as victory at the polls. Later, Jaeckle instructed Erie's six assemblymen to stay away from the party caucus in Albany unless the principle of local selection were agreed to. Since Republicans could muster only 75 of 150 Assembly seats without his delegation, Jaeckle

was in a strong position to carry his point. After a nightlong series of
bluffs and blandishments, the Buffalo Mahatma, as he came to be
known, had his way. Ansley Borkofski was the new Assembly clerk,
who stayed for twenty-seven years.[38]

Jaeckle won other concessions, including the party's first executive
committee, representing each of New York's fifteen judicial districts.
And, with Dewey's rise, he had at last a candidate capable of trans-
lating personal appeal into party regeneration. A deal was worked
out with Ed Murray, under which the State Chairman would retain
his title, and his $12,000 a year salary, while Jaeckle took the reins of
actual authority. That done, Jaeckle signed a personal note to cover
the $40,000 debt run up under Murray's regime. He surprised Re-
publican legislative leaders by insisting on weekly meetings to hammer out a positive alternative to Lehman's program, and to provide
continuous liaison with Dewey and his campaign. Jaeckle also laid
down the law to Hilles's crowd: henceforth, they would be appreciated for their fund-raising abilities but would also understand that
responsibility for allocating party finances rested with the chairman
and his executive committee.[39]

Jaeckle's relationship with Dewey was complex, less friendship
than mutual use. Dewey appreciated Jaeckle's crisp efficiency, admired his accomplishments in Buffalo, and found compatibility in
the homely, direct boss, who chomped on cigars and was so secretive
he preferred to use telephones whenever transmitting sensitive information, and if forced to send a package through the mails, never
put a return address on it. Jaeckle was completely honest, would not
tolerate sticky fingers of any political persuasion, and resented any
attempt at co-optation.[40]

"I don't want anything," Jaeckle would inform the Governor-
elect in November 1942. "I want to be free." Taken aback, Dewey
wondered if his friend might not like to be secretary of state. "The
job will pay you $12,000. You get a car and a chauffeur and the ex-
penses to go with it." Again, Jaeckle demurred.

"You don't quite understand my values and philosophy," he told
Dewey. "I want to be a leader of the party and cooperate with you,
but I don't want to have any commitments. . . . You and I are going
to have a lot of conferences and talks. And, I'm sure that if I'm not
on your payroll you're going to give more consideration to what I've
got to say. . . . If we don't get along, we can meet and otherwise be
free and nobody is obligated to anybody else."[41]

For now, and for two years after Dewey's first election, he and

Jaeckle worked together in harmony, as opposites attracted and fundamental equals. Only when Dewey began to chafe in the role of partner did their marriage of convenience hit the rocks.

"It will seem queer indeed," Arthur Sulzberger wrote Dewey at the end of September, "not to be on your bandwagon." The New York *Times* decided to endorse Lehman. So did the American Labor party, most unions, and the state's Communists, usually good for 75,000 to 100,000 votes. But polls everywhere continued to show the race too close to call, and from the White House, President Roosevelt dispensed some helpful advice of his own to a Democrat wondering how to counter Dewey's growing appeal. "The best line that can be circulated in upstate New York," FDR wrote on October 11, "especially among Republican or Independent voters, is 'I propose to vote for Dewey—to continue as District Attorney for the balance of his term.' " It was a powerful argument, as was its extension, that Dewey was biting the hand that had fed his nascent reputation in 1935.[42]

Less defensible was another tack taken by Roosevelt, for whom a Lehman defeat would represent a stinging rebuke in his own backyard. En route to Hyde Park, where he was scheduled to make a radio broadcast on behalf of the Governor's cause, FDR told reporters that an anti-Semitic whispering campaign was underway in upstate counties, and that he, Roosevelt, had been invited to throw his personal weight against it. In fact, the "whispering campaign" was the modern equivalent of the post–Civil War bloody shirt, a useful shibboleth to be hauled out on the last weekend of any close contest and flogged in front of New York's 2.5 million Jewish voters. In this instance, it assumed credibility because of the foolish display by Dewey's running mate, Dutchess County State Senator Fred Bontecou, of posters instructing New Yorkers to "Vote the American Way," which Lehman seized upon as physical evidence that FDR was right.[43]

Even more important in the Dewey-Lehman contest than the injection of religion was the injection of Roosevelt. On November 4, the President took to the airwaves to endorse his former lieutenant governor and criticize Dewey as one "yet to win his spurs." Roosevelt also took the opportunity to compare "old-time Republicans" with both Fascists and Communists as potential threats to American democracy. In a hard-hitting speech laced with personal animosity, he sought to portray Dewey as a captive of the Old Guard. He even lifted a Biblical quote to prove his case. "By their promoters ye shall know them," the President reminded voters. Dewey took up the gauntlet at his own closing rally the next evening, in Brooklyn.

"I stand before you accused of one crime—I was born in the twentieth century. To that I plead guilty. I am of the twentieth century. We look forward, not backward." As for his promoters, he flung the charge back in Roosevelt's face, holding up before a delighted audience a sheriff's commission once given to Dutch Schultz by Ed Flynn himself, who was not only not hurled from Democratic councils, but actually promoted "to become chamberlain of the city of New York under the old regime," secretary of state and Democratic national committeeman. Dewey closed the campaign with a reassertion of the rights of labor, the farmer, the elderly, the blind, and infirm "to shelter from the winds of chance," and proclaimed a final anathema upon the Lehman administration as "weak, sloppy, and lazy . . . supported by corrupt political machines."

Earlier that day, Ken Simpson climbed into the back seat of Dewey's car and made a request that sounded like a command. Simpson wanted Dewey to promise that if he won out in the gubernatorial contest, he would name the county chairman to take over as district attorney. Dewey had no intention of making such a commitment, which he brushed aside with the observation that it would be illegal to pledge anything prior to election day.[44]

On Tuesday, November 8, 1938, 4.5 million New Yorkers rendered their verdict. The count was close and Dewey's nerves on edge as he closeted himself in a Barclay Hotel command post with George Medalie and the Hogans. He rejected requests to have his picture taken with Senate running mate Edward Corsi, or holding a telephone receiver in his hand. "We don't get reports by phone," he explained. There would be "no dishonest pictures."

At midnight, with Lehman clinging to a 70,000-vote lead and only a handful of districts still out, the candidate was more gracious. Frances seemed downright happy, a radiant smile lighting up her face as reporters asked for a comment. "You know I never say anything," she told the press, but when someone in the crowd shouted to her husband, "You're a sure bet for 1940!" her expression of concern was eloquent. It was not a totally farfetched prediction. When the sun ascended the New York skyline on Wednesday morning, the dimensions of Dewey's achievement shone far brighter than any thin rays that November might be able to summon. He had slashed Lehman's margin to 64,000, just over one percentage point, and in doing so had swept every county but one outside New York City. Upstate, his plurality of 620,000 shattered even Herbert Hoover's landslide record of 1928. He carried Erie County by 35,000 and came within 6,000 votes of taking the borough of Queens. Telegrams of congratulation were piling up at 137 Centre Street as if he had won. Included was an invitation to represent his party at the Gridiron Dinner in Washington at the end of the year.

Dewey made arrangements to assume a role as his party's titular leader, to discuss the coming year's agenda with Republican legislative leaders, and to applaud Jaeckle's elevation to the chairmanship. For its part, the organization, half stunned by its own showing, readily deferred to his whims. Jobs were found with the legislative leadership for John Burton and other Dewey hands, the weekly meetings with Jaeckle were institutionalized, and new financial angels were scouted out in the persons of George Reid of Marine Trust and the Chase Bank's Winthrop Aldrich.

Dewey had lost an election but won a national audience. William Allen White compared his showing to Lincoln's defeat by Stephen A. Douglas in 1858. The simile was strengthened by publication of a Gallup poll taken a few days after the 1938 elections. Gallup had the District Attorney of New York County the first choice for president of 33 percent of Republicans surveyed, far in front of a field that included Arthur Vandenberg, Herbert Hoover, Alf Landon, and two freshmen senators named Robert Taft and Henry Cabot Lodge. Roosevelt himself took notice of the situation. Learning of Dewey's Gridiron invitation, the President tried to force its retraction. When that failed, he indicated his own refusal to speak at the dinner, although he was obliged to attend.

Dewey had no such reluctance. In a graceful, humorous talk, he poked fun at himself and pointed the way for his party. "I have gained a lot of experience in the last few months. First, I asked a question. Instead of getting an answer, I got thrown out of court. Then I was nominated for governor. For a few hours, they let me think that I was going to run against a fellow named Elmer. . . . You gentlemen down here in Washington may never know what a fine Senator Herbert Lehman would have made. Even I thought he would make a fine Senator.

"Now, the President doesn't take part in local elections, so they brought up the titular head of the Democratic Party. . . . I never felt so much like a Democrat in my life as I did the Friday before the election, when the distinguished guest of honor this evening came to New York and made a speech against me. . . . The underlying theme in support of my opponent was 'Once a Governor, always a Governor.' But I am still not clear as to whether it also meant, 'Once a

President, always a President.' " Dewey turned to FDR and hailed him for his social leadership, a salute in which he felt certain the whole nation could join. "The elections of last month did not create a pause in the progress of liberal government in this country. Nor, in this election, did the people turn their backs upon the sound social progress which had been made ... a resurgent Republican Party comes to Washington to encourage federal leadership but to resist government domination. It comes with instructions from the people to make every effort to achieve their dreams, but to do so with a little less sleepwalking."

It was not a pleasant evening for FDR. Not only was he forced to sit through the oratorical triumph of a young and already despised rival, but he also had to pretend to enjoy himself as two farmers in a skit debated New Deal agricultural policy. The only thing the hayseeds could agree on was that it had cost Roosevelt $30 billion to give them a meager standard of living, "and Hoover gave us fifty-cent wheat for nothing." Finally, the President had to endure a chorus line of Santas kicking up their heels in a tuneful forecast of political rebellion.

> We're hunting for our reindeer, the GOP is back.
> They took our Christmas gifts and toys and there's
>   nothing in our pack.
> Oh, you better watch out, Franklin D.
> Find a brand new Christmas tree.
> Santa Claus has been voted down.

For Dewey, all this was sweet music, reverberating along with the sound of warm applause for his state-of-the-party declaration. As 1938 slipped through the hourglass, all things, including Roosevelt's job itself, seemed possible. At a New Year's Eve party hosted by Roger Straus, Dewey listened carefully as Medalie and Straus discussed the next presidential campaign, and Straus pledged financial backing should Dewey decide to make the race. Only Hickman Powell of the inner circle urged caution. He reminded Dewey that Jimmy Hines had yet to be convicted.[45]

9

The Charge of the Electric Light Brigade

I agree with you that Dewey is the best bet for the Republicans.
He is a curious type. . . . To me he talks like a genuine liberal. But
I am aware all the time that he is a prosecutor, that he is arrang-
ing facts for the jury and not for the truth . . . truth as truth has
not yet come into his interest so much as the arrangement of facts
to prove a case.

—WILLIAM ALLEN WHITE[1]

You are getting as much publicity as Hitler.
—A FRIEND, TO DEWEY, JANUARY 1940[2]

Republicans rubbed sleep from their eyes on the morning of November 9, 1938, and discovered that their house, so recently condemned
as a crumbling bastion of reaction, was suddenly crowded with
well-wishers and prospective presidents. Overnight, the party had
added eighty-one seats to its once pitiful corporal's guard in the
House of Representatives. There were six new Republican senators,
and eleven new governors. Among the latter were such promising
newcomers as John Bricker of Ohio, Leverett Saltonstall of Massachusetts, Raymond Baldwin of Connecticut, Arthur James of Pennsylvania, and, in the old Democratic–Farmer Labor stronghold of
Minnesota, a thirty-three-year-old wunderkind named Harold Stassen. In vital industrial states from New York westward to Illinois,
the party's gains over its dismal 1936 showing ran from 8 to 10 percentage points. Outside the Solid South, it actually won a majority
of the votes cast, while New York Republicans took special pride in
having dislodged the Democrats from their coveted first spot on the
state ballot. Lehman's re-election, narrow as it was, came about only
with the help of 400,000 American Labor party votes and the support of 100,000 or more Communists. And New York State, as any
experienced nose counter could plainly see, was the most alluring
possible capstone in any triumphal arch to be built in 1940.

With the Republicans' newfound potential, however, came new
problems, or, more precisely, new antagonists thrust forward to in-
vigorate old arguments. Tensions flared afresh over how much of the
New Deal to accept and how vigorously to criticize the rest. A strong
sense of déjà vu invaded the veterans of earlier fights between the

276

internationalist leanings of Wall Street, and the party's Midwestern heartland, where hatred of Roosevelt competed in ferocity with distrust of Europe. Missouri's Dewey Short was typical of the GOP's congressional wing. He told reporters he feared no foreign nation as much as "the concentration of power in the hands of a single individual." Of course, if the concentrated power were utilized in the cause of American intervention abroad, then no constitution could preserve George Washington's venerated doctrine of non-involvement. Some of the Midwestern Republicans added myopia to their xenophobic outlook. North Dakota's Gerald Nye boasted in 1938 that the threat of war in Europe was less than at any time since the Treaty of Versailles, "thanks to America's refusal to encourage the warmongers in the British and French governments."

Short and Nye epitomized for most Americans the attitude of their party in the 1930s toward a world for which it had little affection and almost no understanding. But here, as in other realms, the ghost of Theodore Roosevelt issued a silent rebuke. It was TR who had campaigned for preparedness and helped to bully a reluctant nation into the Spanish-American War, who authored the Treaty of Portsmouth, which ended the Russo-Japanese War, who built the Panama Canal, who sent the Great White Fleet around the globe in contemptuous defiance of congressional wishes, who established constitutional governments in Cuba and the Philippines, and gave rise to an entire generation of like-minded followers, from William Howard Taft and Charles Evans Hughes to Elihu Root and Henry Stimson. By contrast, it had been congressional Republicans, blinded by the personal hatred felt by Senator Henry Cabot Lodge for President Wilson, who denied Wilson membership in the League of Nations. More recently, it had been ideological (if not intellectual) first cousins of Lodge, men like Nye, Short, and the fiercely isolationist New Yorker Hamilton Fish, who loudly continued to insist that Americans regard the Atlantic and Pacific as walls not worth scaling, divinely erected to safeguard the New World from the Old's polluting influence.

And then there was Herbert Hoover, who, not satisfied to assail the New Deal as inept and wasteful, insisted that what Roosevelt was doing was "a negation of Christianity." With plain Quaker fervor, Hoover likened European power politics to a corrupt "game" at which no upstanding American ought to sit. Recalling the horrors of World War I, the former president predicted for the losers of the game the forfeiture of millions of lives, decades more of national impoverishment, "perhaps even the sinking of intellectual and spiritual liberty for a century." It was Europe's nature, he claimed, that "has made a general war inevitable every hundred years since the Romans kept the peace." As for preserving European democracy, that, he asserted, was a question of their national will, not ours.

Hoover offered one bright ray on his otherwise gloomy horizon. If Europe's democratic nations should fall to continental tyrants, "the exhaustion of the dictators will be such that these countries will leave us alone for a quarter of a century at least."

Herbert Hoover was too recent a memory to command any chance at electoral vindication in 1940. But his heirs were in place. There was Michigan's owlish parody of the Senate at its most fog-hornish, Arthur Vandenberg, the former newspaper editor from Grand Rapids, author of two shallow and idolatrous lives of Alexander Hamilton. Vandenberg's appearance was Edwardian but his rhetoric had the thick, waxy otiosity of a high church rector in Victorian England. Once he had editorialized that he was better able to sleep at night because Warren Harding was in the White House. Now he professed unconcern over the European caldron as it heated to a boil. "This so-called war," he expounded after Hitler invaded Poland on September 1, 1939, "is nothing but about twenty-five men and propaganda. They want our money and our men." Vandenberg was determined that they should have neither. He didn't seem overly eager to have his party's presidential nomination. As he put it in an uncharacteristically direct observation, "Why should I kill myself to carry Vermont?"

More intriguing as a prospective nominee was Vandenberg's freshman colleague from Ohio, Robert A. Taft. It didn't take long for Washington to be impressed by Taft's intellect, his integrity, and his undeviating loyalty to the principles of an earlier time. Harding or Coolidge would not have felt uncomfortable at his side. Both could have subscribed with conviction to Taft's unfettered individualism and nationalist outlook. (The Ohioan never developed any empathy for the Europeans whom he had helped feed as an aide to Hoover in the First World War.) About the only thing Taft shared with Dewey was a Midwestern birthplace. Taft's father had been president, Dewey's a rural editor of dubious allegiance. Taft finished first in his class at Yale, repeated the feat at Harvard Law School, and remained disdainful all his life of those who would substitute argument for facts. He was, moreover, a shy man, ascetic in bearing and speech, whose voice took on a prideful tremor when telling of "the laboring people" who had defied their "bosses" to vote for him. Alice Roosevelt Longworth, who admired Taft as wholeheartedly as she detested Dewey, said that having the Senator replace FDR in the White House would be like a glass of milk after a slug of Benzedrine.

Dewey was better at polemics than profundity, comfortable after years of exposure to the dizzying array of religious and ethnic groups that composed polyglot New York. The Ohioan went to his grave with moral and political qualms over an America overextended in the world. His rival had long since assumed a dominant role in articulating a modern version of TR's ambition to stride the world stage. The two men did have in common a barely disguised contempt for slower minds. Around Capitol Hill, it was said that Taft's was the finest mind in town, as least until he made it up.

For fifteen years, beginning in 1938, these two combatants waged political warfare in the tradition of Lincoln and Douglas, Hamilton and Jefferson, TR and William Howard Taft. Their dispute pitted East against Midwest, city against countryside, internationalist against isolationist, pragmatic liberals against principled conservatives. Each man thought himself the genuine spokesman of the future; each denounced the other as a political heretic.

Initially, Dewey's attitude toward Ohio's junior senator was merely patronizing. He looked on as Taft stumbled through a humorless, partisan text at a Gridiron Dinner in April of 1939, then afterward accepted congratulations from Washington *Post* publisher Eugene Meyer.

"It is a shame that Sen. Taft is so maladroit in some of his speeches," Dewey informed his mother, "and unwilling to take advice . . . he is a very able and conscientious man and it is regrettable that he is not more skillful as a politician."[3]

Meanwhile, Dewey's own political skills were employed in building a New York organization both loyal and seaworthy. From Suffolk County, Kingsland Macy beseeched him to move decisively against "Old Guard hoggishness." Ward Jenks, Dewey's onetime traveling companion through Europe, wrote from Owosso to urge "Old dear" to "keep the silk hats off the Republicans." On January 5, 1939, Dewey gave his response at an Albany dinner for 300 county chairmen and their organizational cohorts. His purpose was twofold: to produce a physical demonstration of unity behind Jaeckle, and to bask in the homage of a grateful band. In league with Jaeckle, Dewey was determined to take the reins of power. He sought as well to establish with help from the legislative leadership a shadow government, and a record on which victory might be achieved in 1942. Before the evening ended, he poked fun at his own perfectionism on the campaign trail (recalling how both Jaeckle and Paul Lockwood stood with arms crossed to prevent him from leaving the rear platform to work on a speech before his train actually pulled out of the station), and listened as Ozzie Heck pledged support for a 1940 presidential campaign.[4]

It was a time of seething optimism for a party that had known little since 1929. It was also a time when the Republican center of gravity was shifting rapidly. A Gallup poll in October 1938 had shown that 56 percent of the rank and file preferred a liberal candidate and platform in 1940, as against 15 percent who said they favored a conservative. Simultaneously, party chiefs tried to fashion a response. The Republican Program Committee, under the guidance of former University of Wisconsin chancellor Glenn Frank, was working behind the scenes to distill a winning platform for 1940. Avoiding moralistic attacks on the New Deal, Frank and his colleagues offered instead well-documented criticism of Roosevelt's domestic failures. After six years of pump priming and deficits, of war with business and administrative chaos, Frank's committee found 10 million Americans out of work in April 1939 and the nation's productive plant seriously eroded. It condemned as "profoundly reactionary" the methods used to finance Social Security and relief, without breathing a word of criticism against the programs themselves. Frank took special pains to fault what he called "a separate relief economy" for black Americans. By fixing prices and wages in federal codes, the National Recovery Administration had thrown thousands of black workers off their jobs, he alleged. The National Labor Relations Board, established after the NRA's demise, negotiated with fifty-two unions that barred blacks from their membership rolls. The Agricultural Adjustment Administration counted no blacks among its 115,000 field agents.

The Frank report, like the returns of the previous November, argued for a party unencumbered by the Hoovers, the Landons, and the Fishes. The horse and buggy would be retired as a Republican conveyance, in favor of a prudent driver who knew when to halt for a red light. In a profession of cautious men, the architects of future Republican glory were scrambling to get as close as events would allow to the middle of the road. They found Dewey already there.

Herbert Hoover was addressing a convert in October 1939, when he passed on some advice to the youthful District Attorney he called "the best bet in sight" for the coming presidential nomination. "The man who talks least now will be in the best position then," Hoover argued. "I don't suggest that he shouldn't appear in public, with discretion, but that he talk about local issues and especially about his own job. There he has one of the most popular of all topics. It's sure fire. Everybody's against crime."[5]

The former president presumed that "local issues" would continue to predominate in the public mind. Indeed, as late as January 1940, Hoover could dismiss as irrelevant and farfetched a question put to him at a meeting of New York City Young Republicans about the proper American response to a Nazi invasion of France.[6]

Other Old Guarders were less willing to advise Dewey. Joe Pew of Philadelphia was one of the entrenched power brokers who took umbrage at the aggressive young man who seemed eager to snatch the nomination from the hands of elders like himself. Discreetly, Pew let it be known that he could support anyone other than Dewey. The D.A. was, for his taste, entirely too irregular. "Unsafe" was the way the oil tycoon and financial angel of Pennsylvania's GOP put it.

Ignoring his critics, Dewey busied himself earning fresh headlines. He indicted New York's Commissioner of Motor Vehicles on a charge of taking bribes from cab companies, and he unveiled the chairman of the state legislature's Transportation Regulation Committee as a crook enriching himself with boodle from the same businesses. In the first month of 1939, the D.A. arraigned a dozen state agents and maintenance men who had bilked the Independent subway system out of 25 million nickel fares. Dewey was also ready to move against Judge Manton, whom he had been investigating for more than two years, ever since coming across in the garment racket probe a curious "loan" of $25,000 to the judge from a virtual stranger. The lender insisted it had nothing to do with the pursuit of Lepke and Gurrah, and the matter had been filed away for possible future reference.[7]

In the third week of January, Dewey learned that Burton Heath of the New York *World-Telegram* was nearing deadline on a series of articles exposing Manton, a former ambulance chaser widely suspected by those familiar with his courtroom of merchandising justice and serving for a price some of the city's most unsavory elements. Heath was ushered into Dewey's office, and an arrangement of mutual convenience worked out. In return for retention of his exclusive, the reporter and his paper would offer unlimited access to their sources and findings. On January 27, the first article hit the streets. By then, the D.A. had plenty of evidence that Manton had, in his zeal to influence President Hoover to appoint him to a vacant seat on the Supreme Court in 1932, awarded the lucrative receivership of a New York subway to a prominent Catholic layman who was willing in return to bend the presidential ear. It had done no good; Hoover had taken an instant dislike to the pushy Manton, and named Benjamin Cardozo instead.

Dewey was also able to link the old "loan" of $25,000 to Lepke and Gurrah, the price of their release on ridiculously low bail, and compile a lengthy list of cases in which Manton had sold his judgments, reaping more than $400,000 in the process. Within twenty-four hours of Heath's disclosures, Attorney General Frank Murphy, whom FDR was predicting would soon outclass Dewey as a gang-buster, announced his own investigation. As with Richard Whitney, Dewey found himself racing against an envious law enforcement rival, while Manton dropped hints of his willingness to leave the bench forthwith if assured of immunity from prosecution.[8]

It was an eventful period for the District Attorney and his men. On January 26, 1939, Dewey was back in the courtroom, handling jury selection for Jimmy Hines's retrial. Two nights later, as was his Saturday custom, he stayed up until three in the morning playing poker with Pat and Marge Hogan, then went into work on Sunday morning to confer with Goody Goodrich and others on Manton's financial skullduggery. While he was there, word came of the jurist's impending resignation. "If this is true," Dewey told his mother, "he will be the sixth public official I have driven out of office in the last four and a half years . . . a sad list but in the interest of the community, nowhere near long enough."[9]

Dewey had no intention of permitting Manton to take a dive, with or without Washington's connivance. He marshaled the evidence at hand, and was dictating a long letter setting forth the allegations for Hatton Sumners, Chairman of the House Judiciary Committee—under whose jurisdiction any federal action against the nation's ranking federal court judge would fall—when investigator Bill Grafenecker burst into the room.

"Weinberg's killed himself."

First silence, then consternation greeted the news that Dewey's star witness against Hines had blown his brains out in the White Plains mansion where the D.A. had secreted him, along with Dixie Davis and eight plainclothesmen. Having suffered through Stryker's bruising cross-examination at the first trial, dubious of his chances for survival in a jail cell, Dutch Schultz's bank manager had slipped into a bathroom and shattered the calm of a Sunday morning in Westchester with a single shot in the head.

"That son of a bitch," Dewey muttered, half to himself. His anger was directed not at Weinberg but Pecora. There was no time for re-crimination, though; a way had to be found to salvage the Hines case. Why not simply read Weinberg's testimony from the first trial's transcript, suggested Goodrich. Of course, the D.A. agreed. It was perfectly legal, "and it had to come from someone who isn't a law-yer."[10]

The next morning, the New York *Times* carried news of Manton's resignation, and the full text of Dewey's letter to Representative Sumners. At 137 Centre Street, all that was ancient history. Some-how, news of Weinberg's suicide had to be broken to the jury, and a dead man summoned to the witness stand.

Inevitably, the second Hines trial lacked the drama of its prede-cessor. Permeating the testimony in a half-empty courtroom was the feeling of warmed-over sensationalism, legal used goods. The jury learned of Weinberg's death in a tactful, restrained account from Judge Charles C. Nott. Two Dewey assistants re-enacted Weinberg's original appearance, followed by Stryker, whose emotional rendition failed to stir the jury from its boredom. Jurors' faces creased with cu-riosity only when Mrs. Dutch Schultz took the stand as a prosecu-tion witness, to recall meeting Hines with her husband in a popular night spot and being instructed by "Arthur" to immediately forget the encounter. Harry Schoenhaus remembered forking over $2,300 so that Hines could buy Thanksgiving baskets for the poor of his district in 1932. Dixie Davis relived his warning to Pop on the links at the time Dewey was being boomed for special prosecutor.

Hulton Capshaw took the stand to deny having been influenced by Hines or Schultz in his courtroom, but Dewey sensed an opening, and quickly breached the magistrate's defenses. Capshaw admitted ordering the arrest of a policy informer at a time when Schultz was known to be on the lookout for squealers. "Did you want the under-world informant murdered?" Dewey asked, prompting a mistrial demand (the sixth) from Stryker.

Dewey had prepared a similarly grueling reception for former district attorney Dodge. Might his relationship with Hines, the D.A. wondered, be likened to that of a mother and her son? "I've never been a mother. I can't say," Dodge cracked, to appreciative chuckles from courtroom spectators. Dewey had the last laugh. He produced a thick volume of grand jury testimony and quoted Dodge using precisely that homely metaphor on July 22, 1938. Next, he held up a roll of names, contributors all to Dodge's 1933 campaign. One was a

WPA worker down for $250. Others were minor courthouse employ-
ees said to have given $500 apiece. Still other gifts were attributed to
people who didn't exist, or who, when questioned by the D.A.'s men,
denied having made any such donation. A sneer at "gangster contributors" prompted yet another mistrial request from the defense,
and wrangling so heated that Judge Nott threatened to fine both
men.

On February 22, with Hines apparently prepared to take the
stand in his own defense, Dewey resorted to a psychological stratagem. That morning, he had wheeled into the courtroom a large file
cabinet, its contents correctly diagnosed by Stryker as material for a
withering cross-examination. Outside, hidden under the watchful
eye of assistant D.A.s, was Dewey's ace in the hole—none other than
Hines's mistress, kept under wraps but ready to blast apart what remained of Jimmy's reputation as a God-fearing family man. It was a
measure of Dewey's anxiety over the result. Ordinarily, he warned
his men against making a big deal out of mistresses. After all, he explained, no prosecutor could ever be certain that no juror had one of
his own.[11]

Jimmy Hines didn't testify that day. Instead, Stryker summed up
his case by roaming far afield in a search for historical and spiritual
allusions. He reminded his listeners that Jesus himself had sat with
"publicans and sinners" and in an impassioned parody of Patrick
Henry, implored the jury, "If you can't give him liberty, give him
the electric chair . . . take twelve iron bars and beat his head in."

Dewey could not resist a verbal sideswipe at his opponent's excess,
wondering out loud if Stryker had swallowed the dictionary, and
vowing to make no emotional detours to Gettysburg, Williamsburg,
Germany, or Soviet Russia. The facts spoke for themselves, he declared, even Capshaw's lies. Stryker had attacked Schoenhaus' credibility, an idea Dewey found contemptible. Schoenhaus, he maintained, "is too stupid to lie . . . if he could lie, I am a wooden Indian
with tin ears." Look at the facts, at the cops transferred, the campaign contributions, the cooperative magistrates, and the flourishing
policy game. Think on the many identifications of Hines together
with Schultz. Ponder the inside stories of Dixie Davis and the late
George Weinberg.

Dewey professed indifference to Hines's sentence. "The important
thing is that you declare to the people of New York, the police of
New York, that they are free, that they won't be betrayed any longer
by a corrupt alliance between crime and politics." On February 24,
1939, with two dozen seats in the dingy general sessions courtroom

vacant, the jurors did just that. Stryker wept. Hines said he felt as if he'd just been kicked in the belly. Dewey slipped into a quiet room to dash off a statement thanking by name each member of his staff involved in the case. He declared the verdict "a victory for decency," a feeling most of America seemed to share.

In Chicago, Colonel Robert McCormick's fervently anti–New Deal *Tribune* splashed a banner headline across the front page hailing Dewey's triumph over "Roosevelt job giver . . . Boss Hines." Columnist Ernest Lindley proclaimed the D.A. the most talked about, most admired young man since Charles Lindbergh flew the Atlantic alone. Caldwell, New Jersey, renamed a street in Dewey's honor. Republic Films announced plans to make a movie based on the Hines case, and in 14,000 theaters across the country, 55 million moviegoers saw pictures of the Gangbuster in Movietone, Pathé, and other newsreels. A woman in Brooklyn called Fred Allen's radio broadcast to predict a pennant for the Dodgers; Allen quipped that if the team won two more games that season, Dewey would investigate them. *Good Housekeeping* wanted to profile the D.A. So did *The New Yorker, True Detective,* and the *Jewish Morning Journal.* At the Inner Circle, Gotham's facsimile of Gridiron, "Diogenes Dewey" was portrayed looking for an honest man, while a chorus sang, to the tune of a popular song . . .

> Who has served faithfully?
> Guiltless of bribery?
>   Juries wearing ribbons of blue
> Check up on whatever you do.
> Who isn't being sought?
> Who hasn't someone bought?
> Who'll be the next one caught? Who? Who?
> Maybe it's YOU![12]

The Hines trial completed Dewey's metamorphosis from local figure to national hero. It also sent his presidential stock soaring. In the Gallup poll, he went from 27 percent among those Republicans with a preference for their party's 1940 nomination to 50 percent, far outdistancing his nearest rivals, Vandenberg and Taft. In May, Gallup weighed in with a survey testing the D.A. against Roosevelt, a mythical match-up, given the two-term tradition, and showed Dewey in the lead, 58 percent to 42 percent.

Democrats took note; six of seventeen articles in the next edition of the national committee's newsletter were anti-Dewey, and the President himself confessed concern over facing the Gangbuster to

Jim Farley when the two men met at Hyde Park in July. Similarly, FDR's former law partner, Basil O'Connor, took his own informal poll among customers in Southwestern hotels, theaters, and restaurants and reported himself "flabbergasted" by the trend toward Dewey, which O'Connor called "overwhelming."[13]

It was a situation without precedent in American history. A thirty-seven-year-old prosecutor for president? Dewey himself maintained afterward that he had a sense of "unreality" about seeking the White House from the office of the District Attorney of New York County. Prior to his victory in the Hines trial, he urged at least some old friends to disregard the optimistic polls. Public opinion was, after all, a fickle creature. Yet, behind the facade of disinterest, an overheated engine of ambition was stoked with flattering reports from around the country. "To my great surprise," Dewey discovered New Jersey's Arthur T. Vanderbilt, deliverer of that state's delegation for Landon in 1936, to be in his corner now. He lunched with Old Guard stalwarts like Iowa's Harrison Spangler and Charles Hilles, kept up a courtship of convenience with Ken Simpson, dined privately in Washington with Vandenberg and House Minority Leader Joe Martin. He savored Taft's "colossal failure" at the Gridiron Dinner, complained of living on a fifteen-minute schedule and having to brake premature partisans—like a former classmate in Owosso who launched a Dewey-for-President Club in April. He calculated his chances, his platform, and his financial wherewithal at a series of conferences with Medalie, Dulles, and Roger Straus.[14]

He invited Elliott Bell, his Columbia classmate and more recently assistant financial editor of the New York *Times,* to lend an expert hand at speech production, economic policy, and overall campaign management. It was a bad time for Bell, suffering from stress and nerves "in an uproar of apprehension." Perhaps, as Dewey suggested, the presidential fling would be a tonic. Thus began a professional and personal relationship that would have profound impact on the course of American politics. The men had long been close friends—Bell, in fact, was godfather to both Dewey boys—but 1939 marked the start of the Dewey-Bell team as a political venture. Even now, survivors of the period regard Bell and his role as a subject of white-hot disagreement. That he was brilliant, capable in state office, and absolutely trustworthy as the man closest to Dewey in his official family no one disputes. Bell had a razor-sharp mind, something Dewey found appealing, and an ability to look at a problem with clinical detachment. He had as well a facility for puns and verbal swordplay sufficient to elicit a smile from the lips of John

Foster Dulles. But there was another side of Bell, an acerbic disdain for such popular innovations of mass culture as "the idiot box," the academic's preference for an ivory tower, and the closest thing to mastery over Dewey that the suspicious, self-willed candidate ever permitted.[15]

Other men had Dewey's ear in 1939, including George Gallup, who introduced Dewey to Gerard Lambert, head of the pharmaceutical company bearing his name (and that had made Listerine a household word) and a public-relations whiz fascinated by the young science of opinion sampling. Dewey asked Lambert to supervise speechwriting and political research as well as polling, and Lambert gave generously to the campaign. With Bell and John Burton for partners, Lambert secured free of charge an entire floor of the Carlton House, then went to work creating from scratch separate polling and research operations. For Dewey the empiricist, there was no such thing as having too much information at one's command. By the end of June 1939, Burton and his men had analyzed and indexed every speech made by Roosevelt since his first inauguration, probed Woodrow Wilson's 1912 campaign, compared the relative strengths and weaknesses of the American and British economies, and compiled the best information available about housing, labor, and relief conditions.[16]

When Lambert cut back his personal involvement to spend more time on the polling work, Bell became final arbiter of speech production. It was no easy task, given Dewey's insistence on personalizing each sentence in a draft. For those who tried to add their own two cents' worth of advice, Lambert had a stock admonition. In one corner of a room at the Carlton, he hung on the wall the words FRESH FISH FOR SALE HERE TODAY, and went on to relate the tale of a Bronx fishmonger who, hoping to reap the benefits of advertising, raised such a sign over his place of business and sat back in anticipation of a commercial flood. Instead, he was deluged with questions about the slogan: did TODAY mean he wasn't open other days, did FRESH suggest a stale product ordinarily, was HERE really necessary—after all, he didn't sell fish at Grand Central Station? As for the words FOR SALE, since when had he given away anything? Finally, all that remained was the lonely identification FISH, when a small boy happened by the shop and demanded an explanation. Since when was it necessary to proclaim in print what any passer-by could unavoidably smell?

As Lambert told his story, he turned each word to the wall, "You know," he remarked at the end, "that was probably a pretty good

sign after all, but it got edited to death." From then on, "fresh fishing" was a notorious byword in the Dewey organization. Only the
candidate seemed immune to its implications. At the start of December, days away from his first major address as a presidential contender, Dewey convened a series of general discussions with an advisory group dominated by Bell and Burton. A draft emerged, was
checked for accuracy, then torn apart and rewritten. The writing
began at noon on a Thursday, continued through the night, until
dawn Friday, when another collection of advisers, this time broadened to include recognized experts in different fields (such as Dulles
on foreign policy), performed surgery of their own. That evening,
yet another draft was banged out, ready for five more hours of polishing on Saturday. Critics charged Dewey with delivering speeches
bleached white, but no one present in the Municipal Auditorium
in Minneapolis on December 6, 1939, part of an overflow crowd
of 14,000 come to see Harold Stassen introduce the scourge of the
underworld, could deny the galvanizing effect of speaker and subject.[17]

"America Is Not Finished" was Dewey's theme, and to bolster his
case against the New Deal, he used specific examples—6,500 men
standing in a New York line to apply for fifty-eight jobs as auto mechanics, and a bank in Boonesville, Iowa, shut down although entirely solvent. Why? Because in the still-constricted economy of
1939, the bank could find nothing in which to venture capital. After
seven long years "of lending and spending, seven years of priming
the pump, seven years of pushing the accelerator to the floor . . .
after seven years what does the New Deal repair crew tell us? It
admits defeat. It says, 'The American economic machine is stalled
on dead center.'" Especially among the young, Dewey worried,
there seemed to be taking hold an expectation of permanent depression. It wasn't enough to sing "Happy Days Are Here Again." It
wasn't enough to recognize society's "permanent, deep-rooted" obligation to the aged, the sick, the blind, the jobless. It was "a cruel illusion" to pass laws promising relief without long-range measures to
reduce the need for relief.

The New Deal, according to Dewey, "has thought it well enough
to make the promise, leaving the performance to come from the savings of the last generation . . . and mortgaging the earnings of the
next generation." There was, in truth, "only one source of real
money in any free country," the enterprise of its citizens. The "one
unforgiveable crime" was to despair of the free enterprise system, to
discount its continued efficacy and accept economic defeatism.

"There is no limit to America," Dewey shouted. "There is a force in America that has been held in check which, once released, can give us the employment that we need. It has nothing to do with slick monetary schemes. It has nothing to do with slick economic panaceas. This force is the energy of American enterprise, great and small. . . . Is it true that America is matured and completed and overbuilt and incapable of further expansion and new achievements? Is it true that all we can do from now on is to administer the achievements we already have? I do not say no temperately. I say no with resentment and anger."

As for himself, the D.A. claimed his objective was to "help make the courage of youth flow once more in the veins of my party and my country." Reaction was predictable, mostly along party lines. *Life* praised with faint damns "New York's Number One Glamour Boy." Many faulted Dewey for a lack of specifics. Harold Ickes, FDR's terrible-tempered interior secretary, and a man labeled "pure psychoneurotic" by Adolf Berle for bugging his department and hiding tapes in a secret room adjoining his office, issued a comment worthy as usual of a headline in the next day's papers. "Tom Dewey's thrown his diaper in the ring," Ickes sneered. More worrisome to the D.A. was Hickman Powell's disappointment with the speech's lofty tone and gilt-edged rhetoric. "This wasn't Dewey," Powell wrote a few days later. "Dewey is a hard-bitten, brass-tacks guy who lays it on the line, with names, dates and places . . . every time he opens fire another bad man bites the dust."[18]

Powell's critique kicked off a decade-long debate within Dewey's privy council. On the one hand were advisers like Bell and Dulles, cerebral men who argued for an educational approach to campaigning, treating the electorate as an intelligent, rational body capable of filtering fact from falsehood. On the other hand were the Powells. They wanted Dewey to run for president as the toughest cop on the beat.

Ruth Simms was sixty years old, the daughter of William McKinley's manager, Mark Hanna, the sister-in-law of Colonel McCormick of the Chicago *Tribune,* the widow of an Illinois congressman. Following Medill McCormick's death, she had run for and won his House seat, located next to that of Albert Simms, a Republican representative from New Mexico. After Ruth's defeat in a senatorial primary she and Simms were wed, and went off to live at Trinchera Ranch, not far from Albuquerque. Wherever she was, politics remained her passionate hobby. As a girl, she had been her father's Washington secretary, listening and learning as Marcus Alonzo Hanna planned two landslide victories for McKinley over William Jennings Bryan and the forces of agrarian radicalism. Ruth got a distressing taste of poverty and disenchantment herself, as a volunteer working in Chicago's grimy settlement houses. From there, she joined the McCormick brood, where pioneering views were nothing new. Besides the Colonel, Ruth was related to Anita McCormick Blaine, daughter-in-law of James G. Blaine and a multimillionairess who spent lavishly promoting the cause of world government—and later, that of Henry Wallace in 1948.

Ruth herself became a fixture of the Republican National Committee where she accumulated a vast storehouse of friends and favors. In the spring of 1939, bedridden with a broken hip, dependent on newspapers to provide her with political reconnaissance, she discovered Tom Dewey. The more she read, the more excited Mrs. Simms became, until she put in a call to Joseph Patterson, publisher of the New York *Daily News* and another of her relations by marriage. "This is the kind of man we need for president," she told Patterson. "Young, vigorous—someone who isn't afraid to take on the corrupt forces in society." The publisher agreed, and when Ruth expressed a desire to go to work promoting the Dewey cause, the prospective candidate said nothing to discourage her. It didn't take long for the beer-drinking, cattle-roping, delegate-corraling heir to Hanna's tradition, "the ablest woman I have ever known" in Dewey's words, to conclude that at last she had found her own McKinley.[19]

Far more equivocal in his enthusiasm was Ken Simpson. Admirers compared him to Jim Farley, pointing for proof to the coalition with the American Labor party engineered by the shrewd red-headed Irishman that assured his own Republican party a majority at the state constitutional convention in 1938, not to mention the coup that placed three Republicans on La Guardia's winning ticket the year before. Simpson struck them as a genuine liberal—despite his Hooveresque high collars—and they cheered when he bluntly warned in public against any return to Hoover, the Liberty League, "and some of the reactionary influences of the past." Simpson's friends chuckled at his pungent one-liners, and readily forgave temporary lapses of judgment, such as his refusal, early in 1939, to shake Hoover's hand at a Washington cocktail party.

To his detractors, Simpson was a budding tyrant with a talent for self-promotion, who looked down his well-bred nose at the clubhouse crowd, who treated assemblyman and precinct worker alike as

ABOVE—Three-year-old Tom Dewey with the bicycle given him by his mother on condition he not fall off it—and withdrawn for a year after he fell. It was not the last display of Annie Dewey's influence over her son. BELOW—The Dewey clan relaxes at a summer outing. Tom dangles his legs in front of his father, a country editor of fierce partisanship and mixed success. Annie smiles from her perch above the left wheel—a rare break from her usual pursuit of perfection.

"Where did you get that thing?" Dewey demanded when a friend showed a copy of his high school yearbook picture twenty years after it was taken in 1919. By 1925, he would grow the trademark mustache that pleased a prospective wife and dismayed political advisers; they urged him to trim it back, in the manner of Clark Gable. BELOW—Dewey's original ambition was to be an opera star. Critics said he had a tenor's temperament, but lacked spontaneity. Here is the University of Michigan junior (second from right) cast as Patrick O'Dare, pretender to the Irish throne, in a student operetta.

Discarding his musical plans, Dewey found himself drawn to the law, and Republican politics, in a New York City held hostage by the Tammany Hall of Boss Tweed (ABOVE, RIGHT) and dapper James J. Walker (LEFT). Aided by his original mentor, George Z. Medalie (BELOW, at left), Dewey became United States Attorney for southern New York in 1931, the youngest man ever to hold the title. It proved an unexpected springboard to elective politics for one who claimed his real goal was to run a great law firm and "make a hell of a lot of money."

Dewey's entry into public life nearly coincided with Franklin Roosevelt's election to the presidency; by 1944, the two men would be bitter rivals in a campaign marked by private maneuverings over Pearl Harbor and FDR's alleged foreknowledge of the Japanese attack. Fiorello H. La Guardia (BELOW, LEFT) was an irregular Republican and an uneasy ally in Dewey's war on New York's rackets. Herbert Lehman (BELOW, RIGHT) was responsible for Dewey's appointment in 1935 to lead the special prosecution of racketeering. Within three years, Lehman found himself hotly challenged for the governorship by the young prosecutor. Dewey lost, but his admirers across the nation took heart from a contest they likened to the Lincoln-Douglas campaign.

"The Gangbuster" at home, with Frances and his two sons, Tom, Junior, and John. Ever conscious of his public image, Dewey refused to unbend in public, allow photographs in shirt sleeves or with a wineglass in hand, or demonstrate the vinegary exuberance known to intimates. It cost him dearly as a presidential candidate. BELOW, LEFT—Dutch Schultz, a target of the rackets probe who was killed by underworld assassins before he could put into play his own plan to murder Dewey; RIGHT—Irving Wexler, alias Waxey Gordon, a bootlegging kingpin, "the laird of West End Avenue," whom Dewey convicted of tax evasion in 1933.

UPI

UPI

Lucky Luciano (LEFT), Boss of all the Bosses, was a ruthless if suave gangster whose prosecution on racketeering charges—the evidence was tenuous—stunned New York and made Dewey an object of popular acclaim. The conviction came largely on the testimony of Cokey Flo Brown (ABOVE, RIGHT), a streetwalker whose eyewitness account of Lucky's role in supervising "an NRA of prostitution" was all the more dramatic for coming in the midst of drug withdrawal. BELOW—Hollywood cranked out movie after movie based on Dewey's exploits; radio followed with *Gangbusters*. Here, Bette Davis and Humphrey Bogart portray the Brown and Luciano characters, in a script doctored to avoid offending public sensibilities. The girls were no longer hookers—just clip-joint hostesses.

Even Judge Seabury called Jimmy Hines (at left, with his flamboyant lawyer, Lloyd Paul Stryker) "the most likable rogue I know." Dewey disagreed, convicting the Tammany chieftain of protecting the policy racket after a dramatic mistrial. The courtroom victory catapulted the 37-year-old D.A. to the gates of the White House. BELOW— Ed Jaeckle (center) and Ken Simpson (right) were two of Dewey's earliest political advisers. Both would clash with him before long— Jaeckle falling out during the 1944 presidential campaign, and Simpson ostracized for his support of Wendell Willkie in 1940. Jaeckle survived to marshal delegates for Dewey in 1948. Simpson was crushed, and died an embittered alcoholic in January 1941.

Alf Landon (ABOVE, LEFT), encouraged Dewey to run for president after his own disastrous defeat by Roosevelt in 1936. Robert Taft (RIGHT) fought Dewey for fifteen years to control the party he wished to keep within the conservative tradition of his father. Dewey beat Taft in 1944 and 1948, and used Dwight Eisenhower in 1952

to polish off the Ohioan once and for all. LEFT—An impassioned candidate denounces the New Deal before an audience in Boise, Idaho, in 1940. Dewey's partisans were both noisy and numerous at the Philadelphia convention that followed (BELOW), but they could not prevail against the Willkie blitz—or the Nazi blitzkrieg in Europe.

Wendell Willkie (LEFT), "our fat friend" to Dewey, proved better at winning a nomination than capturing the White House. A different kind of opponent was Louis "Lepke" Buchalter (RIGHT) whom Dewey pursued as D.A. and sent to the electric chair as governor. BELOW—1948 running mates Dewey and Earl Warren meet at Dapplemere Farm, Dewey's Pawling retreat. The amiability was bogus; Dewey and his associates came to regard Warren's selection as a mistake. Dewey himself referred to the Chief Justice in later years as "that big dumb Swede."

In 1942, Dewey was chosen as New York's first Republican governor in twenty years. From his position in Albany's fortresslike Executive Mansion (LEFT), he proceeded to give the state an administration combining social progressivism and fiscal conservatism, including tax cuts, balanced budgets, and the nation's pioneer civil rights laws. CENTER—Dewey and his inner circle: from left to right, Lillian Rosse, Dewey, Jim Hagerty, Paul Lockwood, Lawrence Walsh, Hamilton Gaddis, and Charles Breitel. BELOW—Elliott Bell (left) and Herbert Brownell.

ABOVE—Dewey accepts his party's 1944 presidential nomination, with a blast at the "tired old men" of Roosevelt's administration and a warning against repetition of peace-keeping blunders at the end of the First World War. BELOW—The Governor and his family outside Dapplemere, their country house 65 miles north of New York City, where Dewey liked to don overalls and tramp through his milk barns. His neighbors included broadcasters Lowell Thomas and Edward R. Murrow, as well as Norman Vincent Peale and other celebrated men. Twice, Dapplemere contended for the honor of being the nation's summer White House; it remained instead what it was when Dewey moved there in 1938—a 486-acre working farm.

WIDE WORLD

UPI

ABOVE—J. Russel Sprague (left), Nassau County Republican boss and a premier Dewey strategist; (right) Harold Stassen, in 1948 a serious contender for the GOP nomination, defeated by Dewey in Oregon after a seminal national radio debate over a move to outlaw the Communist Party. Stassen took the affirmative, supported by his debate second, Joseph McCarthy, while Dewey argued vigorously and effectively that "You can't shoot an idea." He won the debate, and the nomination. BELOW—The candidate wages his own whistle-stop campaign.

UPI

The Morning After ... Harry Truman (BELOW) holds aloft the famous mistaken front page of Colonel McCormick's *Chicago Tribune,* while the loser (LEFT) leaves an afternoon press conference, doing his best to exude sportsmanship and put the disaster behind him. "It's been grand fun, boys and girls," he told reporters. "I've enjoyed it immensely." Few guessed it then, but Dewey's greatest service to his party still lay ahead of him.

RIGHT—Robert Taft's forces, desperate to prevent Eisenhower's nomination at Chicago, resorted to a last-minute attack on his most prominent—and politically savvy—backer. It did no good; Ike won on the first ballot, thanks in large part to Dewey's maneuverings and arm-twistings; BELOW—The Governor enters hearings into corruption along New York's waterfront in 1953, ignoring angry demonstrators outside.

SINK DEWEY!!
END DEWEY'S CONTROL OF OUR PARTY
EIGHT YEARS OF <u>DEWEYISM AND DEFEAT</u>

By now every delegate knows that it is Tom Dewey who is calling the shots in this convention. He is not the candidate this time but he is the man who pulls the strings. *He is the candidate in everything but name.*

Every delegate knows what Dewey and his *ruthless* team have been doing. They stop at nothing. They have no qualms and no scruples. They go to any lengths to *pressure* delegates. Where promises are enough, they promise the moon. Where threats can do a job, they use threats. They dangle juicy offers before the eyes of some. They use every bit of political pressure they can bring to bear where that is the most effective method.

Tom Dewey is the most cold-blooded, ruthless, selfish political boss in the United States today. He stops at nothing to enforce his will. His promises are worthless. He is the greatest menace that the Republican Party has. Twice he led us down the road to defeat and now he is trying the same trick again hidden behind the front of another man.

Behind Tom Dewey is the same old gang of Eastern internationalists and Republican New Dealers who ganged up to sell the Republican Party down the river in 1940, in 1944 and in 1948. They are trying it again this year.

The whole Dewey crowd has made it plain that they will play only under their own rules. They are willing to wreck the Republican Party if they can't have their way. Fair play is only a two word phrase to the Dewey boys. They hide behind a screen of sweetness and light the better to slander, villify and connive. They practice politics to the hilt—gutter politics.

Tom Dewey, his machine and his cold-blooded, self-seeking ruthlessness have meant only sorrow and defeat to the Republican Party. Until and unless Dewey and Deweyism are crushed our party can never win and America can never be made safe from the insidious efforts of the New Dealers, whatever their party label, to take us down the road to socialism and dictatorship.

Issued by TAFT COMMITTEE
DAVIS S. INGALLS, National Chairman
CONVENTION HEADQUARTERS
CONRAD HILTON HOTEL — CHICAGO

UPI

ABOVE—Dewey, now out of office, speaks for the Republican ticket in 1956; BELOW—He greets Richard Nixon in May 1968. Nixon owed much to Dewey, including his original vice-presidential nomination and his survival in the Fund Crisis that followed. In return, he offered the former governor the chief justiceship or State Department. Dewey's support waned as the Nixon presidency evolved. In the last weeks of his life, members of Nixon's cabinet sought to enlist him in a campaign to purge presidential aides H. R. Haldeman and John Ehrlichman—before it was too late.

ABOVE—Dewey is greeted by supporters on the floor of the New York Republican convention in the summer of 1970, as he endorses Nelson Rockefeller, a man he had once said could not be elected dogcatcher. BELOW—A final wave to his last national party convention, in August 1968. Three years later, Dewey was dead at the age of 68, to the end of his life a man who might have been.

UPI

instruments of his personal will. They attacked him for playing loose with facts. His diatribe linking Hoover and the Liberty League, for example, failed to take into account the former president's blistering assault on the League in the September 1938 *Atlantic Monthly*. Having married into money, Simpson had plenty of time in which to cultivate gubernatorial ambitions, to pursue intrigue and alcohol in roughly equal measure. A difficult ally, he was a formidable opponent, and his relationship with Dewey was, at its warmest, a case of mutual use. To anyone who would listen, Simpson quoted the D.A. after his victory in the second Hines trial as saying he had no intention of ever entering a courtroom to personally conduct a prosecution again; the potential dangers of trying and failing to top his own record were simply too great. For his part, Dewey disliked Simpson's manner, obsequious in times of need, distant or downright hostile the rest of the time.[20]

Still, they were practical men, adept at the pretense and horse trading that passes for friendship in politics. Each had a stake in keeping the other happy, never more so than late in November 1938, when separate meetings of the party's state and national executive committees convened. Dewey wanted Jaeckle designated chairman of the New York executive committee, permitting Bill Murray to retain his title and $12,000 annual salary while transferring real power to the Buffalo Mahatma. Simpson wanted to take Charles Hilles' old place on the national party's board of directors, from which to fight for a liberal candidate and platform in 1940, and advance his own interests back home.

A deal was struck. At a stormy session of New York's leaders, Murray at first refused to walk the plank. Tom Broderick and Rolly Marvin backed him up, and nearly succeeded in adjourning the meeting without a vote. Then Simpson and Jaeckle went to work in earnest, Murray was importuned into a lukewarm endorsement, and the change went through on a vote of 16 to 4. Simpson was less fortunate in his aspirations. Dewey instructed both Jaeckle and Sprague to work for his election to the national executive committee, but he reckoned without a still angry Herbert Hoover. The former president apparently feared that Simpson might become national chairman in the event of a Dewey takeover. He was confirmed in his distaste by the abrasive Manhattan leader, who in his short time as national committeeman had managed to roundly offend most of his colleagues, either personally or politically. In the end, the committee settled on Delaware's Daniel Hastings, a reactionary known for his business connections and voting record as DuPont Dan.[21]

A year earlier, Simpson told Dewey's campaign manager in the district attorney fight that he had received from the winning candidate "nothing but the finest degree of cooperation." Now his opinion shifted abruptly. At a meeting with Dewey and Russ Sprague not long after his executive committee defeat, Simpson invited the D.A. to prove his organizational strength by running for district leader in the Fifteenth. Impetuously, Dewey accepted the challenge, only to be warned out of it by the more seasoned Sprague. The professional from Nassau pointed out that Simpson was baiting a trap. As the county chairman, whose friends extended throughout Manhattan, Simpson could concentrate all his resources in the fifteenth to defeat Dewey and thus, in one crushing setback, blast away any chance the D.A. might have for 1940.[22]

On March 13, Dewey dined at his apartment with Herbert and Lou Hoover. (He never forgot how, when a plugged chimney filled the room with acrid smoke, the resourceful Mrs. Hoover—not for nothing a past national chairman of the Girl Scouts—got down on her hands and knees and repaired the offending flue.) More serious than a smoke-filled dining room was the impression given that Dewey was shifting to the right in hopes of attracting Old Guard support for the White House. The image was reinforced a few days later when the D.A. spoke to the annual legislative correspondents' dinner in Albany. Off the record and often ribald, the dinner gave politicians a chance to say in private what could not be said on a public platform. Charles Evans Hughes had once used it to denounce conservatives within his own party who were ganging up to block his utility reforms. But even Hughes never caused the ruckus now created by Dewey.[23]

Dewey began with a few potshots at "Butch" La Guardia, then moved on to Simpson, whose public tirades against Hoover and fellow conservatives were proving obnoxious to many within the regular organization. "He is really a very nice fellow," Dewey claimed, "in between his speeches." In truth, the D.A. had been defending Simpson for more than a year now. "Ever since 1937, Jim Farley has been trying to get me to indict Ken for kidnapping Jim's child—the American Labor party." The only trouble with Simpson "is that he doesn't suffer from laryngitis at the right time." As for his own recent meeting with Hoover, he continued, its real purpose was to negotiate a deal whereby the former president would give all his old collars to Simpson. "We both hope they don't choke him."[24]

The speech seemed to have caused "a number of repercussions," Dewey informed Hoover a few days later. It was a rare understatement. Party pros interpreted his remarks as an open declaration of war. Simpson himself seemed temporarily stunned. "Can't you get a hold of your friend Tom Dewey," he asked Lowell Wadmond, "and tell him to lay off. . . . Why's he picking on me?" By now, Simpson was under fire on his own turf. Late in May 1940, a dissident group mailed out 15,000 circulars attacking his courtship of the ALP and his failure to produce for Dewey in the Fifteenth District what William Bleakley had polled as the GOP candidate for governor in 1936. A poll of the district showed 60 percent convinced that Simpson had outlived his usefulness. "There is no room in this country for two radical parties," asserted Louis D. Hopkins, a Simpson critic from the Twelfth District, "and I believe the Republican party should be the conservative one."[25]

Dewey found himself walking a tightrope. Both Jaeckle and Sprague, concerned about the possible damage Simpson might do among delegates to the 1940 convention, urged compromise. They had reason to worry, for their foe displayed a real gift for jungle warfare. Already, Dewey had been burned when an upstate Republican congressman, egged on by Simpson, rose on the House floor to denounce the D.A. as an Old Guard captive, seeking to "purge" the liberal New York county chairman. Early in July, a new deal was worked out. Dewey would back Simpson in the Fifteenth, where victory would insure Simpson's re-election as county chairman. In return, Simpson signed a pledge promising to assist Dewey's presidential campaign for as long as the D.A. was "a serious candidate." Simpson went on to win his contest, and promptly disregarded his promise to Dewey, whom he was soon dismissing among friends as "a favorite son" and nothing more. He had begun an active search for someone to support against Dewey in Philadelphia, when he was approached in September of 1939 by Frank Altschul, Herbert Lehman's brother-in-law, who was also an influential banker and Republican fund raiser.

Altschul was a close friend of Russell Davenport, editor of Henry Luce's *Fortune* magazine and himself a dedicated GOP liberal. At a recent meeting of the Fortune Round Table in Stockbridge, Massachusetts, Davenport had met and been captivated by a rumpled, spontaneous, charismatic man whom Altschul now proposed as the answer to Simpson's presidential dilemna. The county chairman was understandably dubious.

"So I am supposed to go back to the clubhouse," he said to Altschul, "and tell the boys that we will all have to pull together now to get the nomination for Wendell Willkie. They'll ask me, 'Willkie, who's Willkie?' And I'll tell them he's president of the Commonwealth and Southern. The next question will be, 'Where does that railroad go?' And I will explain that it isn't a railroad, it's a public utility holding company. Then they will look at me sadly and say, 'Ken, we always have thought you were a little erratic, but now we know that you are just plain crazy!'

"And that would be without my ever getting to mention that he's a Democrat!"

Wendell Lewis Willkie was forty-seven years old, a child of Booth Tarkington Hoosiers, reared by two lawyers in Rushville, Indiana, and treated to a picaresque adolescence that included stints as a short order cook, vegetable picker, and barker for a South Dakota tent hotel. Along with an exuberant and sunny personality went a tendency to rash decisions and cheerful contradiction. In high school, Wendell joined a social club. In college, he joined an anti-fraternity chapter called the King of Beasts. He took his religious stand with Methodism, until a fetching damsel converted him to the Episcopal Church. At Indiana University he wore red turtlenecks and questioned the literal truth of Scripture. He pledged to the Jackson Club and wrote an admiring essay on the New Freedom of his political hero, Woodrow Wilson.

With a grin and a shrug of his massive shoulders, Willkie explained away his confusing loyalties. "Any man who is not something of a Socialist before he is forty has no heart," he said, "any man who is still a Socialist after he is forty has no head." Willkie was no Socialist in February 1919, when he arrived in Akron, Ohio, to fill a legal department opening with the Firestone Rubber Corporation. Harvey Firestone himself took a shine to the gregarious, tousled youth, although convinced that his politics posed an impediment to future success. After all, said the tire magnate, Willkie was a Democrat, "and no Democrat ever amounts to much."

In the next few years, Willkie proved Firestone wrong. He remained a Democrat—who supported the League of Nations and denounced the Ku Klux Klan as a delegate to his party's 1924 national convention—but he amounted to a great deal within legal and business circles. Two weeks before Wall Street's nosedive, Willkie found himself in New York handling legal affairs for the Commonwealth and Southern, a large holding company responsible for most of the electric power generated in the Tennessee Valley. Within four years, he moved up to the president's chair, at $75,000 a year, and when the New Deal proposed first to wipe out holding companies and then to expand the TVA's functions to include generating power of its own, Willkie found his calling. In countless speeches and articles over the rest of the decade, the genial Hoosier proved himself one of big business' few articulate or sympathetic critics of the Roosevelt revolution.

Wall Street applauded when he called TVA "the most useless and unnecessary of all the alphabetical joyrides." Walter Lippmann hailed him in print as a public-minded entrepreneur, whose differences with Washington came over federal competition with the private sector rather than the regulatory concept itself. Roosevelt had cause of his own to take notice, especially after the utilities executive demolished his personal favorite to succeed Lehman in Albany, Assistant Attorney General Robert Jackson, in a *Town Hall of the Air* broadcast. In a powerful defense of the work ethic, Willkie set the stage for his declaration that would ring throughout 1940: "Only the strong can be free, and only the productive can be strong."

It wasn't long before stories by or about Willkie showed up in journals like *Time* and *Life, Reader's Digest, Barron's* and the *Literary Digest. Fortune* described him, with a certain license, as "the Mississippi Yankee, the clever bumpkin, the homespun, railsplitting, cracker-barrel simplifier of national issues." *Fortune* did not explain if Willkie split his rails in his luxurious apartment at 1010 Fifth Avenue, or if he was looked upon as homespun by his circle of friends, which included Thomas Lamont, Sloan Colt, Roy Howard, John and Gardner Cowles, and Russ Davenport. As for being a bumpkin, that was a ruse, along with the suits better fitted to a Fort Wayne shopkeeper than a Wall Street executive. Willkie read four books a week, and he never learned to drive, because his restless mind refused to concentrate on the road ahead. He abandoned golf as impossibly dull, and purposefully dressed in rumpled, shiny garb that cast him as "an Indiana farmer" (his own words) among city swells.

Until 1935, Willkie was a member in good standing of Tammany's Thirty-seventh Election District Committee. He told Jim Farley of his personal admiration for the President over a lunch in December 1938, mentioning as well a vote cast for Herbert Lehman in his re-election dogfight with Dewey. Six months later, Davenport sounded him out about running for the presidency himself. The unorthodox suggestion was seconded by Charlton MacVeigh, a New York publisher who had assisted John Hamilton in Landon's doomed crusade three years earlier. For Willkie, bubbling over with self-confidence, ever eager to tilt at windmills, it was a welcome diversion, at first hardly to be taken seriously.

After all, everything about the man cried maverick. He had never held public office, never run for one. How was he to go before the American people, as a latter day Moses from Indiana, proclaiming, "Let my utilities go"? Arthur Krock was not alone that fall in calling attention to the president of Commonwealth and Southern as "the darkest horse" in the 1940 field. At the same time, hidden like the shrewdness and drive his small-town lawyer's wardrobe concealed, was a chameleon whose very spontaneity argued against organizational appeal. "I can still see Willkie," says a contemporary, "late for a speech, running through the library, raincoat over his shoulder, half done up, like his mind."[26]

In stark contrast to Willkie's carefree buoyancy, his chief rival remained in public what he was in the courtroom, a stalking panther in pursuit of facts. "I don't remember him doing anything that wasn't deliberate," Russ Sprague recalled. "He had to be sure in his own mind, and when he was, he moved and moved quickly." Contrary to a growing reputation for smugness, Dewey asked for the unblinking criticism of his friends. Chase Osborne warned against letting his picture be taken with cigarette holder in hand—too Rooseveltian, too Eastern, he implied. Lowell Thomas advised he do something about "the grand canyon" between his lower set of teeth, and volunteered to work on the D.A.'s speaking voice. Together, the two men made recordings of Dewey talking, then played them back countless times to produce in the end a more resonant timbre. "No monkey business," wrote another friend, who needn't have worried; Dewey had no intention of allowing himself to be trapped in foolish poses like the one recently struck by a reluctant Robert Taft, standing in a field in business suit and starched collar, all the while holding up a dead fish in feeble imitation of a relaxed, self-satisfied angler.[27]

The headlines were characteristically generous that summer of 1939 and fall, what with an honorary degree from Dartmouth, the Kuhn indictment, and Lepke's decision to turn himself in to Walter Winchell and J. Edgar Hoover rather than face New York's district attorney. Most warming of all were the opinion polls, which at the start of December showed an astonishing 60 percent of all Republicans in Dewey's corner. Popular acclaim notwithstanding, Dewey persevered with a caution born of the very tenacity and will to win that had raised him to such lofty heights.

Dewey described as "perfectly swell" the advice of Barak Mattingly, a supporter and veteran national committeeman from Missouri, that he not speak out on major issues prematurely. It called to mind Hoover's reason for dismissing Taft as a candidate—that as a member of the Senate the Ohioan would find himself compelled constantly to stake out positions on all manner of public controversies. Mattingly also summed up dispassionately the candidate's assets and liabilities. Dewey's strongest support, he wrote, lay with "the younger and more progressive element of the party, particularly those Republicans who want a candidate that can win." As for his greatest weakness, Mattingly had no trouble in reaching a diagnosis. It was, as he put it, "your age and lack of executive experience."[28]

Like another young candidate who promised twenty years later to get America moving again, Dewey recognized that his one chance for the nomination lay with his party's primary voters. While Taft confined his efforts to Republican professionals and Southern rotten boroughs, and Vandenberg waltzed around a formal declaration of candidacy, Dewey set out to demonstrate overwhelming popular support, enough to deflect Old Guard opposition with the sweet smell of success. In January 1940, he traveled through New England, gained the endorsement of former Massachusetts Governor Alvin T. Fuller, and delivered an upbeat address to 12,000 supporters in Boston's Mechanics Hall. There were two kinds of politicians, he said, "one who comes into office by pretending to soak the rich and be the friend of the poor; the other who tries to tell the truth." The truth as he saw it was an indictment of New Deal extravagance. "Government spending can't create jobs," he insisted. "All it can create is stopgaps." This for a nation "in the morning of its destiny" was not nearly good enough.

In February, Dewey took a 7,500-mile swing through thirteen states in the West. In Portland he charged a $7 billion erosion of capital since 1933, and when a bystander in one prairie village shouted as his train was pulling out, "What have you got against President Roosevelt," Dewey cupped his hands and shot back, "Nine million people out of jobs." The crowds turning out to greet him were a campaign manager's dream, halting the Dewey train repeatedly and forcing the candidate to step out for rear platform appearances. It was zero at Olivia, Minnesota, but a hundred residents were waiting at the local depot to see the Gangbuster. Five hundred more gathered at Miles City, Montana, at one in the morning. Webster, South Dakota, closed its schools so that local children might glimpse the hero.

"When an astronomer makes a miscalculation in terms of billions of light-years," Dewey told a cheering crowd at the Oregon cross-roads of The Dalles, "it may mean nothing more than that Halley's Comet will be along Tuesday instead of Thursday. But when the federal government repeatedly miscalculates its finances in terms of billions of dollars, it is a symbol of a deeper, even more widespread incompetence." Such bungling was measured ultimately, according to Dewey, "in misery, lack of jobs, heavier taxes, and the eventual undermining of the nation itself." Then he returned to the rails, and a schedule of appearances that prompted a bantering complaint to Ruth Simms. Dewey was contemplating receipt of a ten-gallon hat at 12:45 A.M. somewhere in South Dakota, when he wired Simms, "Yielding to local pressures worse than New Deal . . . patient doing nicely but treatment guaranteed to kill or cure."[29]

"Go 'long with you," he told reporters back in New York who asked him to wear one of the hats garnered on the trip. "I'll hold it but I won't put it on." He never got over his prickly distaste for the stunts required of would-be presidents. He gave the impression that the campaign trail was an extension of the district attorney's office, subject to rational conduct and personal dictation. Sometimes it got him in trouble, as in Portland, Oregon, where he lost his temper with a persistent photographer. "How am I supposed to relax," he demanded, "with you snapping away in my face?" Dewey ordered a candidate for the Senate from Nebraska to stop waving at crowds from the windows of his train. "Let us handle things our way," he notified the man, "and we'll get along better." Accustomed to calling the shots, he had his organization give precise instruction to local party officials two weeks in advance of a visit.

David Simpson, his Portland contact, received a typical set of marching orders. Dewey men would choose a local reception committee, program chairman, and committee on arrangements, this county chairman was alerted. Breakfast would be followed by a 30-minute press conference. "Morning and afternoon conferences," the memo went on, "will have to be divided among the following groups: politicians, businessmen, women, farm, labor, Young Republicans—press included. Luncheon: to be arranged to meet businessmen, about 35 persons, with distinct understanding Mr. Dewey will make no speech. He prefers roundtable gossip. Press may be included." In the afternoon, there were to be additional conferences, arranged by Simpson.

Rest period for Mr. Dewey from 4:45 P.M. until 9:08 P.M. Leave hotel at 9:08 P.M. for the Auditorium. Doors of the Auditorium will open at 8 o'clock

P.M., and at 8:30 P.M. the regular Lincoln Memorial Day program will start. It will be interrupted at 9:15 P.M. for Mr. Dewey's entrance. This will allow Mr. Dewey 15 minutes on platform before his scheduled speech. . . . Mr. Simpson is to control applause. Gov. Charles A. Sprague's introductory message is to be timed to 30 seconds. Mr. Dewey's speech is timed to 24 minutes.[30]

A prisoner of his own perfectionism, Dewey in 1940 was unable to climb down from his racket buster's pedestal. Running for president, at best, is an artificial experience, in which strangers must be treated like old friends, and fools not only suffered but embraced.

Dewey was temperamentally better suited in 1940 to prosecuting his opponents than generating a personal bond between the electoral jury and himself. He found it "absolute torture," in the words of one who was active in the campaign, to plunge into a crowd of strangers and shake their hands. He rejected without debate the idea that Frances' theatrical background might be exploited for human interest, and did so in a way that suggested shame on his part, or at least fear that his wife's days on the stage would damage his own prospects. "You never wanted to waste his time," Ruth Simms's assistant in the campaign says of the man she called T.E.D. "Everyone around him was very sensitive to that. . . . He was brilliant, thoroughly honest, and his staff were willing slaves. But he was cold—cold as a February icicle."[31]

When he stuck to what he did best, crowds went wild. Reviewing the New Deal's "report card"—national income down $8 billion, dividends down $5 billion, exports down $12 billion, average take-home pay for industrial workers down 11 percent since 1933— Dewey could not escape a conclusion that "the New Deal will soon be called to the woodshed." Comparing the U.S. with other industrial nations, Dewey found eighteen of twenty countries had better recovery rates; sixteen had surpassed their 1929 industrial levels. "The New Deal not only doesn't get a passing grade," he concluded, "it is at the foot of the class."

In Lincoln, Nebraska, he urged farmers gathered as part of the largest crowd in the history of Founders Day, to "foreclose on the New Deal." In Milwaukee, he did a little figuring and told his audience that under Roosevelt the country was going deeper into debt at the rate of $8,000 a minute. In Denver, he claimed for the New Deal authorship of a new beatitude: "Blessed are the young, for they shall inherit the National Debt." There were 16,000 on hand in Chicago Stadium the third week of March, to hear Dewey tick off instance after instance of waste and political favoritism within the WPA. The candidate mentioned 450 workers hired three weeks before the Illinois primary, and dismissed the day after, at a cost to the taxpayer and the needy of $23,268. He told of a dozen Arkansas WPA workers shaken down for $500 in campaign contributions, of Pennsylvania seamstresses forced to buy tickets to a Democratic fund raiser, and Republicans who refused to change their registration, only to find themselves reassigned to new jobs forty miles from home.

"What kind of people are those who will pick the pockets of road workers, mail carriers, and servants in a soldiers' home?" Dewey demanded. "What kind of people are these who hide behind the smiling mask of the New Deal? . . . For an ordinary person, extortion is a felony. In the New Deal, it is known as 'remembering the forgotten man.'" This was Dewey at the docket, the small-town boy who had cleaned up New York and now proposed to clean out Washington, running a campaign invigorated with contempt for the status quo, and setting off vehement responses from the opposition. Senator Scott Lucas of Illinois denounced Dewey as "the number one rabble-rouser of the nation"; and Ken Simpson, carrying his still-undeclared war against the D.A. into Ohio, wryly reminded one audience that the object of the campaign was not to put the President in jail but out of the White House.

Concentrating his fire on the weak links in Roosevelt's administration—the bloated budget, the city machines, the use of relief as a political tool, and the cool relations between Washington and the business sector—Dewey grossly oversimplified his opponent's performance. He failed to credit the New Deal with 8 million jobs created since 1933; and to casual followers of the campaign, it might seem as if he was pronouncing an anathema on all that had been undertaken since Herbert Hoover left the White House.

Unlike Hoover, however, Dewey wasn't warning of doomsday but of defeatism. Everywhere he went, he faulted the administration for resigning itself to permanent contraction of the nation's economy. His own polls showed a heartening response. Wherever he spoke, they revealed a quick leap in his favorability rating, sometimes twenty points or more. Twenty thousand Hoosiers attended a barbecue in Washington, Indiana, hoping to see him. One woman in the huge crowd spoke for the rest, murmuring, "He's got it," over and over as Dewey plugged for private enterprise as the only realistic solution to the nation's ills. A Sioux City, Iowa, reporter, presumably more skeptical, found himself wondering aloud just what it was that gave the D.A. such a hold over his followers. Finally, he concluded, it was "nothing less than a phenomenon."

Dewey's first major test at the polls was slated for Wisconsin, on April 2, where the powerful La Follette organization was backing Vandenberg, and where Gerald Nye came into the state in the closing days to support his Senate colleague and preach their shared gospel of American isolationism. Dewey campaigned tirelessly, delivering twenty-two speeches in fourteen counties in two days. Ruth Simms and Theodore Roosevelt, Jr., supported his efforts with tours of their own. The polls looked startlingly good. So good, in fact, that Jerry Lambert cooked up a poor-mouthing scheme guaranteed to make his candidate look good no matter what the final results. He showed Dewey his final poll, conducted among 4,000 carefully selected voters and putting Dewey in front with 62 percent of the vote. On the day before the primary, the candidate fretted to local and traveling reporters, complained of nervousness over the outcome and even offered to split the delegation with Vandenberg fifty-fifty.

It worked like a charm. When the votes were counted, Dewey emerged victorious with 61.8 percent. He carried all but four of the state's counties, captured 75 percent of the farm vote, won as easily in working-class neighborhoods as in white-collar suburbs, and swept all twenty-four of Wisconsin's national convention delegates. Party pros were impressed, and worried. "Not only has he upset the apple cart," a Wheeling, West Virginia, editor wrote of Dewey's landslide, "but he's taking most of the fruit."

Hurriedly, the Old Guard concentrated its forces behind Vandenberg in Nebraska, scene of the next primary contest. Senator Charles McNary, the Senate Minority Leader, dropped in on the state to call his friend from Michigan "safe" on farm issues. Arthur Capper of Kansas and Gerald Nye developed their own variations of the pro-Vandenberg theme. According to the New York *Journal-American*, organization Republicans feared that Dewey "is going to set their prairies afire."

On April 9, he did exactly that, beating Vandenberg 109,000 votes to 71,000, all but eliminating the reluctant Senator from contention, and forcing Robert Taft to beat a hasty retreat from primaries in Maryland and New Jersey. Dewey's campaign chest bulged now with contributions from such pillars of American business as John D. Rockefeller, Walter Chrysler, Lamont DuPont, Edgar Queeney, Alfred Sloan, and Henry Luce. To be sure, some liberal journals began stepping up their attacks. The *New Republic* ran a scathing piece entitled "Pollyanna for President." Harold Ickes in *Life* professed to see evil implications in Ruth Simms's prominence, and the *American Mercury* compared the D.A.'s publicity with techniques employed by Goebbels in Nazi Germany.

All this might be dismissed as so much panic on the left, a backhanded compliment from Roosevelt's most devoted followers. What could not be ignored as the spring unfolded were the desperate events overtaking Europe. Americans who had been hard of hearing for a decade could not fail to listen to the sounds of a goose-stepping Wehrmacht as it knifed through one European democracy after another. The sound grew deafening in May 1940, drowning out the noisy acclaim for gangbusting, rendering all prior commitments as impermanent as the waves crashing against the shores at Dunkirk.

Later, it was said, only half in jest, that Tom Dewey was the first American casualty of the Second World War. More precisely, Dewey paid the price for mirroring the national mood of uncertainty. Other Republicans were anything but vague in their conviction—the old one, enshrined since Washington's Farewell Address, that rejected involvement in a world impossibly impure for a chosen people. Ten weeks before Hitler invaded Poland, House Republicans voted against an increase in the Army Air Corps, 122 to 5. When Roosevelt moved to repeal the arms embargo provisions of the 1935 Neutrality Act, 58 percent of the American people told George Gallup they approved. House Republicans, by a 7-to-1 margin, did not.

On the other end of the political spectrum, pacifists acknowledged the clear and present danger to Europe, but urged inactivity on purely pragmatic grounds. Self-styled liberals agreed. "The hard fact," according to the *New Republic* after the German invasion of Norway and Denmark, "is that if Hitler were on the verge of winning, and we were to declare war tomorrow, we could hardly contribute an extra ounce to the present capacity of the Allies to defeat him. If they cannot get at him, still less can we. It is not merely our preference, but the unimpeached fact, that they must win the war for us if it is to be won." Deeply ingrained were the memories of petty bickering that followed the Treaty of Versailles; as late as April 1937, Gallup had found 71 percent believing U.S. entry in the First World War had been a mistake. Three years later, when the Democratic chairman of the Senate Foreign Relations Committee, Key Pittman of Nevada, advised Churchill's government to calmly withdraw to Canada in the face of Hitler's relentless advance, the idea generated applause within both parties.

It was a confused time providing the backdrop for Dewey's first presidential campaign, and he did little to counter the confusion.

His own foreign policy views were strongly shaped by John Foster Dulles, whom Eisenhower would compare to an Old Testament prophet and whose affiliation with the church militant could be felt in attacks on Bolshevism as "a product of the Devil." In countless dinner conferences and speech writing sessions, Dulles expounded his opposition to American intervention in what he publicly called "the cyclical struggle between the dynamic and the static forces of the world." His younger brother Allen, staunchly pro-Allies, bluntly asked Foster how he could consider himself a Christian and overlook what was happening inside Germany. But that was precisely the kind of appeal guaranteed to have no effect on the senior partner of Sullivan and Cromwell, a ponderous, immovable man who expressed to Charles Lindbergh the fear that the United States, "under the influence of emotion," might yet be dragged into the conflict.

Dewey, a novice at international politics, drank deeply from the Dulles cup. He listened to both brothers, but heeded Foster more often. "He felt that the Germans were the strong, aggressive force in Europe," Dewey later summarized his chief adviser's attitude of the time, "that Hitler was a passing phenomenon who would disappear and was reflecting a basic economic problem." America's proper role in 1939 was "to stand aside and hopefully wait until a stalemate would occur and then exercise our weight to bring about a peace." Dewey thus began his campaign wedged somewhere between Vandenberg's ironclad isolationism and Roosevelt's cautious, brilliantly crafted efforts to edge the nation closer toward outright support for the Allies. It was an erratic path Dewey pursued. In an early speech in Boston, he ignored Europe to criticize Roosevelt's 1933 decision to recognize the Soviet Union, "a perversion of a government, abhorrent to mankind." A few days later, echoing Walter Lippmann, he called for establishment of a two-ocean navy, something the White House contemptuously dismissed as "plain dumb" (and embraced within two months).[32]

Dewey kept his ear to the ground, his hand on the popular pulse. Consistency was not his hobgoblin. In Wisconsin, a hotbed of isolationism, he sounded like Vandenberg, contending that America could not remain true to herself "unless we resist every entanglement in the affairs of Europe." On May 10, Hitler invaded the Low Countries. That night, Ed Jaeckle told a meeting of Dewey's chief backers that the game was up; the radical turn in European affairs now guaranteed that the Republicans would nominate someone other than "a 38-year-old kid," whose foreign experience was limited to a bicycle tour of France fifteen years before. But Jaeckle also urged the candidate to go on. With his usual grasp of the long haul, the Buffalo politician looked on 1940 as an opportunity to solidify Dewey's grasp over the fractious New York party, and position himself for a gubernatorial win in 1942.[33]

Pat Hogan had a different reaction for his best friend. "Two months ago," Hogan wrote, "an isolationist was a sound fellow who minded his own business." Now, in the gray dawn of a Europe threatened by Nazi hordes, the word had taken on a new and chilling connotation: "one who believes we have no interest in the European mess and is willing to sit back and watch Nazi aggression conquer the world by terror."[34]

Hogan was pleased when Dewey that same day endorsed Roosevelt's call for a billion dollars in defensive armaments, coupled with a request of his own for a civilian defense board "not subject to the whims of a temperamental administration." Others disagreed, in tone and temper. With British forces trapped on the beaches of northern France, Robert Taft journeyed to Topeka and told his fellow Midwesterners, "This is no time for the people to be wholly absorbed in foreign battles." Two days later, in St. Louis, Taft went further still, saying that a German victory would be preferable to American participation in the war. Dewey meanwhile fell back on prosecuting the administration for unpreparedness. It was Roosevelt, he charged, who in 1933 had sabotaged the London Economic Conference, "the final effort" of civilized nations to fashion an economic order that might have stayed the Nazi menace. And it was Roosevelt's seven-year war on domestic producers and defense budgets that had all but disarmed the country.

At the spring's Gridiron Dinner, two figures representing Taft and Vandenberg were arguing the necessity for isolation when they were interrupted by a short, bustling man with a mustache striding out of the wings. A reporter asked the stage Dewey for his solution to the dangers posed by Mussolini and Hitler. Without a moment's hesitation, the young man replied, "Indict them!" Gridiron's satirists presented Dewey in another skit, dressed as Little Lord Fauntleroy, crowing over his lead in the polls.

> N'yah, n'yah, n'yah, I'm the wonder boy.
> N'yah, n'yah, n'yah, you can't catch me.
> N'yah, n'yah, n'yah, I'm the glamour boy—infant prodigy
> On each fine speech I work for weeks,
> Casting a blinding spell.
> I want a chance to wear long pants,
> And give the New Deal hell!

President Roosevelt asserted on May 17 that the nation was well on its way to rearmament, pointing for proof to thousands of planes and other weapons "on hand and order." Dewey, using first-hand information supplied him by Jimmy Doolittle and federal aviation officials, painted a far different picture in Dallas ten days later. The Army's own leaders estimated 240,000 rifles as the acceptable minimum; 38,000 were on hand. Less than 1,000 functioning aircraft were in military hangars or on military runways, roughly one week's toll in the ferocious dogfights decimating European air forces. "We cannot produce airplanes the way the New Deal produces a billion dollars," Dewey said, "by printing government bonds. A blueprint is no protection against a bomb." To achieve the 50,000-plane goal set by the White House, the nation would need to quadruple its military plant, at a cost of over $3 billion. It would cost even more to organize a pilot force capable of flying and maintaining such a fleet of aircraft. Ahead lay "a staggering job," manufacturing and manning tanks, artillery, rifles, bombs, and battleships, the entire arsenal of modern warfare. Could the New Deal be entrusted to work harmoniously with the private sector in getting the job done? For Dewey, it was a rhetorical question.[35]

His own speeches edged closer toward accepting the inevitability of America's participation in the spreading war. He forecast "a world greatly different from the world we have known in the past," filled with "revolutionary fires" and new powers arising in Asia and Africa as well as Europe. He tried to recapture the first bloom of his candidacy, now wilting under merciless exposure to world disorder. It had become "a gangster world," he told Vermont Republicans on June 17. "I know something about gangsters. I know that soft-minded men and guns 'on order' are no help against them." Finally, he returned to his bill of indictment against the New Deal.

Yet nothing said by Dewey could compete with the drama kicked off by the German invasion launched on May 10. What followed thereafter can only be described as an explosion of support for a fresher face on the political scene, the commonsense liberal who flatly declared Britain and France to be America's first line of defense.

"We don't want a New Deal," Wendell Willkie proclaimed in a special edition of *Fortune* called "We the People." "We want a New World." Oren Root, a Wall Street lawyer and political neophyte, inspired by Willkie's sweeping idealism, met the messianic candidate and set in motion an independent petition drive that was to collect 4.5 million signatures urging Willkie on a reluctant GOP. It was the spectacular christening of what Hearst columnist George Sokolsky labeled "an advertising man's holiday," in which all the resources of business and public relations were happily and profitably wed. One adman staged an Indiana box supper to emphasize the candidate's rural origins. Others worked on chain letters, Willkie clubs, and articles by and about Willkie for national publications. Henry Luce came aboard, along with the Cowles brothers, Roy Howard, and Ogden and Helen Reid, whose New York *Herald Tribune* was plastered with a three-column front-page editorial hailing the utilities president as "heaven's gift to the nation in its time of crisis." Other journals were only slightly less hyperbolic in their claims.

"It should never be forgotten," said Fred Smith, one of those who masterminded the brief, spine-tingling campaign leading to Philadelphia, "that the 'Willkie boom' was one of the best-engineered jobs in history." As early as May 18, Dewey was told of pro-Willkie letters being sent to supporters in Kentucky and Indiana by banks and businessmen. Ironically, this was only a week after Dewey himself had filled the 10,000-seat Municipal Auditorium in Louisville, prompting his state campaign manager to proclaim him the most popular Republican in Kentucky since Theodore Roosevelt in his prime. But in the fluid, unpredictable, ominous atmosphere of May 1940, crowds were a poor harbinger of delegate strength. Besides, no circle of Eastern industrialists or editors could have invented Willkie's unorthodox charm.[36]

Visiting Topeka in Taft's wake, Willkie delighted a crowd by announcing, "I'm the cockiest fellow you ever saw. If you want to vote for me, fine. If you don't, go jump in the lake and I'm still for you." He electrified a hall full of Minnesota Republicans, tossing a dull text into the air and proclaiming, "Some damn fool told me I had to read a speech to you. Now let me tell you what I really think." He proceeded to demonstrate a gift for stirring oratory ("a bit of hypnotism," in Dewey's words), and by the time he was through that night, the crowd was on its feet shouting for more.

The war in Europe didn't create the Willkie candidacy, but without it, the renegade Democrat with grass-roots support, according to Alice Roosevelt Longworth, "in every country club in America," would doubtlessly have been laughed off the national stage. With the war, Willkie's cause acquired a sense of urgency to clothe personal ambition. It was a time for rule breaking, as the globe-trotting newspaperwoman Dorothy Thompson recognized in proposing that both parties cancel their summer conventions and unite on a Roosevelt-Willkie ticket. The Willkie crusade gathered momentum in almost direct proportion to the success Hitler's forces were having in overrunning France. On May 16, Dewey led the Republican field with 62 percent; Willkie trailed far back at 5 percent. Two weeks later, the margin had slipped, to 52 percent to 17 percent. On June 20, as delegates arrived in Philadelphia to begin their deliberations, it was down to 47 percent to 29 percent, and Willkie actually took the lead sometime during convention week. The man and the moment had met, in perfect if startling unison.

It was against this rising threat that Dewey forces moved in mid-April to consolidate their home base. Jaeckle assumed the title of state chairman, in keeping with the eighteen-month-old agreement with Murray; and Ken Simpson immediately announced that he would no longer feel bound by any prior pledge of support to Dewey's candidacy. This was specious in view of the county chairman's tireless and well-known search for an alternative to the D.A. A lawyer with friends in both warring camps ran into Simpson late that spring in an elevator at the Ritz. At his side were Wendell and Edith Willkie. "Oh Ken," he asked impishly, "what are you doing here? Finding yourself a candidate?"[37]

The rift within New York Republican ranks was front-page news by June 12, when delegates to the national convention were scheduled to elect a national committeeman. Simpson, fighting hard to prevent his ouster from the post, accused Jaeckle and, by implication, Dewey of "Hitleresque" purges. The state chairman fired back. Simpson, he declared, was a wolf in sheep's clothing. Fiorello La Guardia leapt into the fray, declaring that city workers who sided with Dewey could expect to find themselves unemployed. Frank Gannett, a right-wing publisher from Rochester who was conducting his own quixotic, costly campaign for the nomination, lined up with Simpson, as did the Southern Tier leader Billy Hill, long a voice of the Hoover faction within the party. It was a crazy-quilt coalition joining hands to block Simpson's defeat, but when the vote came in an Albany caucus, Simpson was out and Russ Sprague in.

Smarting and resourceful, Simpson vowed public revenge. Forty-one New York delegates, he claimed, would vote against the state's presumed favorite son at Philadelphia. Personally, he issued a call for a challenger who would "salvage, not destroy" the New Deal, and pursue a "realistic, not an isolationist" foreign policy. One required little in the way of political sophistication to guess the identity of Simpson's mystery man.

Two days before the convention got under way on June 24, Dewey and Jerry Lambert motored down to Philadelphia from

Princeton. Frances remained behind on the family's Pawling farm. At a strategy session in the Walton Hotel—also known around the Dewey high command as the Rat Trap—Lambert expressed surprise at the decision to "shoot the works," cashing in every delegate chip in hopes of amassing 400 first-ballot votes. Then and later, the game plan was criticized; but confronted with a host of delegates won in the primaries and of dubious loyalty, not to mention Trojan horses planted in several delegations by Taft and Vandenberg, Dewey had little choice.

Twenty-four hours later, a similar meeting hatched a very different stratagem. Willkie's inner circle—including Indiana congressman Charles Halleck, Russ Davenport, Sam Pryor of Connecticut, and Ken Simpson—met in a room of the Bellevue-Stratford Hotel. Unknown to the public, most of the convention leadership, privately or openly, had swung by this time behind the dark horse from Indiana by way of Wall Street. Pryor, for instance, as chairman of the vital arrangements committee controlled access to thousands of gallery tickets and, in tandem with permanent chairman Joe Martin, the right to limit or exclude visitors on the convention's floor. Unlike Dewey, Willkie and his managers calculated for psychological momentum. Starting small, with a modest beachhead of fifty or sixty first-ballot votes, they planned to build steadily, until they swept away the regulars and their doubts by sheer immutable force. Ray Baldwin, Connecticut's governor and a Pryor ally, offered his state's sixteen delegates intact, and in return was all but promised the vice presidency. Still another important piece of convention machinery was in attendance at the Bellevue-Stratford that Sunday night: Harold Stassen, earlier designated keynote speaker after promising Dewey that he would remain neutral between opposing camps.[38]

Arriving delegates found a fresh Dewey poll in their hotel mailboxes. It showed that the D.A. was preferred to Willkie by 7 to 1 among the half of America's population earning $1,200 a year or less. Affluent voters were much more evenly divided, but since they were outnumbered four to one, the Dewey managers argued, didn't it make sense to choose a candidate who could poach on the Democrats' strongest preserve? The poll was easily overlooked in a deluge of telegrams and phone calls demanding Willkie's nomination. William Bleakley, chairman of the New York delegation and a strong Dewey man, counted 7,500 telegrams at his hotel, with 20,000 more piling up in his White Plains home. Thousands more—perhaps a million by week's end—flooded delegates by the hour. They came

from everywhere, many genuine, many spurious, and many somewhere in between, the work of utility companies whose network of
contacts with banks and other important men in hundreds of communities provided a ready lever. Alf Landon was just one of the delegates who tried to answer the blizzard of paper addressed to him
once he returned home. Eighteen sacks full of the answers he wrote
to pro-Willkie messages came back to him marked "addressee unknown."

While Willkie was strolling the streets of Philadelphia, reporters
in tow, and operating an apparently amateurish campaign out of his
private two-room suite at the Benjamin Franklin, Dewey visited
with delegates around the clock, greeting knots of the uncommitted
on a fifteen-minute schedule at the Walton Hotel before moving
next door to another suite full of more potential supporters, and another round of personal salesmanship. It quickly became apparent
that the original strategy was the only one with a chance of success—demonstrate overwhelming strength early, or run the risk of
being stampeded by Taft or Willkie. In lobbies and caucus rooms,
talk bubbled up of a Dewey-Taft coalition, able to command a majority of delegates and halt Willkie's bandwagon in its tracks, if only
one of the two men would agree to be the other's running mate.

Inside Convention Hall, loyalties were melting down in the hun-
dred-plus-degree heat. Young men learned ruthlessness; old men
surrendered their dignity. It was a grand surreal pageant unfolding,
as illogical and aromatic as Frank Gannett's elephants defecating on
Broad Street. The girls, with their buttons and badges promoting
one cause or another, were pretty rather than beautiful. Numbers
replaced names as passwords admitting one to temporary prominence. Clare Boothe Luce sat in the gallery wearing pearl earrings
and shouting herself hoarse for Willkie. Herbert Hoover was reported slipping into Taft headquarters disguised in a long red beard.
A Buffalo drum and bugle corps, the Uncle Sams, serenaded Dewey
supporters in the hall, interspersing their brassy welcome with tedious speechmaking from the podium. And everywhere there were
rumors: Dewey running for vice president with Taft. Taft taking the
second spot on Dewey's ticket. Vandenberg taking second billing to
anyone. Hoover preparing to announce his candidacy. Willkie going
over the top with Joe Pew's help. Willkie being undercut by a congressional revolt of Old Guarders behind Joe Martin.

It was all grossly unreal, the very antithesis of calm or reasoned
deliberation, and thoroughly American. On Monday night, young

Willkie partisans packed the galleries, admitted with the help of forged tickets provided them by Sam Pryor and Ken Simpson. Their unending chorus, which no one who was there will ever entirely forget, was both simple and frenzied. "We want Willkie! We want Willkie!" Over and over again, like waves crashing on a beach before a building storm, the chant was repeated, annoying many of the delegates and sending Renfro B. Creager, Taft's Texas chairman, rushing to the podium to tell Martin that he was going public with his complaint about forged passes. Creager was talked out of it by the presiding officer, who persuaded him that such publicity would only hurt the party. Not far away, Ed Jaeckle had grievances of his own, stemming from his exclusion from the floor and the fact that Ken Simpson, still a member of the national committee until the last day of the convention, held all fifty-two of New York's floor passes.

Tuesday, June 25, was reserved for the orators. Stassen gave his speech, then went to the Walton Hotel to apologize and inform Dewey that he would serve as Willkie's floor manager. No sooner had he departed than Herbert Hoover rose to address a packed, expectant audience at the hall. Hoover hoped to make his own move at the right time to gain revenge on the President he hated with a passion uncharacteristic for an Iowa Quaker. At nine-thirty that night, he strode dramatically down the central aisle of the auditorium, transformed for the occasion into a floodlit cathedral. He stood for a moment at the rostrum, bathed in applause and sentiment. He began the liturgy of rugged individualism. "Almost everywhere in the Old World the light of liberty for which men have struggled and died has gone into a long night," Hoover said. "Men and nations have lost their moral and spiritual moorings . . . the whole world is in confusion."[39]

It was a powerful speech, flawed only in its logic, which assailed Europe's "totalitarian liberals" and promised that America's ocean and her navy could together buy plenty of time for "sober preparation." Away from view, in rooms off the main hall and under the stands, Hoover placards awaited the right moment for their unveiling. Others were just as determined that that moment would never come. The next day, many delegates complained of being unable to hear the former president's speech, and to the end of his life, Dewey believed that a convention official, hoping to spike any Hoover boom, had deliberately tampered with the microphones. Tuesday night, the D.A. had problems of his own keeping a bandwagon in motion. He continued to meet with delegates, and he professed optimism about the final result. But the Willkie blitz grew still more intense, the telegrams still piled up, and sensitive ears picked up stories of money talking in the most seductive convention oratory of all.[40]

Later, a Georgia delegate told of receiving an insistent call from his hometown banker on Willkie's behalf, a banker who happened to hold the mortgage on his acres. A Rocky Mountain car dealer got telegrams urging him to vote for Willkie from practically every Packard customer he'd ever seen. South Carolina's chairman was offered $19,000 in "expenses" in exchange for second-ballot support, and an Arizona delegate invited reporters to eavesdrop on an extension while a Willkie backer called him from the Bellevue-Stratford and said, "You name your price, because we have a roomful of money." Intrigue bred faster than flies in a garbage pile. Vandenberg offered to flip a coin with Dewey, the loser to take the vice presidency. Dewey rejected this as "an uneven exchange." On the eleventh floor of the convention's headquarters hotel, Hoover kept up a steady barrage of appeals to more active candidates. His message to all was the same: Stand fast against the Willkie juggernaut. Ruth Simms, fatigued and ashen with doubt, confided to Dewey on Tuesday night, "Tom, we're facing the Fascist movement of America."[41]

In the galleries, Mrs. Theodore Roosevelt, Jr., shouted, "We want Dewey," and found herself rebuked by hissing friends. Dewey dispatched Simms and Sprague, his co-managers, to meet with Taft's cousin David Ingalls, in the hope that some deal might be arranged. Taft did, in fact, maintain an observer in Dewey headquarters throughout the balloting, and subsequent events followed a pattern suggesting that some kind of arrangement was indeed in place.[42]

On Wednesday, the convention heard candidates being put in nomination, and delegates performed the snake dances with which politicians proclaim delight in a winner and sympathy for a forlorn cause. John Lord O'Brien, the defeated U.S. Senate candidate from New York and a forceful advocate of aid to the Allies, spoke for Dewey. He emphasized his candidate's status as "a lifelong Republican" and earned a twenty-eight-minute demonstration for his efforts. The editor of the Toledo *Blade* nominated Taft, whom he called "common as an old shoe," and then it fell to Charles Halleck to present Willkie's case. There were scattered boos ricocheting through the hall as Halleck approached the microphone, from delegates who could not know how close Halleck's Indiana colleagues had come to forbidding him from designating Willkie as the state's favorite son. Only John Hamilton's threat to nominate Willkie from his seat in the Kansas delegation overcame the Hoosiers' reluctance.

"Is the Republican party a closed corporation?" Halleck inquired before asking delegates to respond to extraordinary times with extraordinary actions. When he finished, a scuffle broke out for possession of the New York standard, which was finally wrenched away from the Dewey forces by burly Rolly Marvin, who hurried off to hold it high in a bobbing sea of place names. Creager of Texas could only sneer at what he called "the station wagon set" out to take over his party. Indiana's former senator, Jim Watson, snorted contempt of his own when Willkie inquired if the Old Guarder didn't believe in conversion. To the contrary, Watson replied. He believed that even the town whore could be converted—but that didn't mean he expected to see her leading the choir the next Sunday morning.

On Thursday afternoon, the presidential balloting at last got under way. Dewey sat alone in his hotel suite, with a scorecard spread out in front of him and a radio spitting out numbers. Mrs. Simms was at Convention Hall, along with Russ Sprague, Jaeckle, Lockwood, and Foster Dulles. Like the rest of the vast crowd, they were buffeted by Willkie's screaming, dancing, delirious admirers in the galleries, who seemed totally oblivious to Dewey's 360 first-ballot votes, as to Taft's 189. What amazed everyone was Willkie's unexpectedly strong showing of 105 delegates. To reporters at the Walton, the D.A. called his own tally "great" and forecast a healthy gain on the second call of the states. His managers counted on additional support from Landon's Kansas—which on the first roll call cast a complimentary vote for Senator Arthur Capper—as well as Iowa, Oregon, and West Virginia. Instead, Dewey dropped 22 votes, to 338, while Taft and Willkie both registered substantial gains.

The convention adjourned for dinner. Jaeckle reached agreement with Taft's manager to open negotiations, only to have the deal shot down by Taft and Dewey themselves. When Joe Martin signaled a third ballot, Kansas finally broke open, swinging 11 fresh votes Dewey's way. But as New York was reached, and Bleakley announced Willkie's total as 13, Ken Simpson had his revenge. Walter Mack, one of Simpson's co-conspirators, rose to his feet and demanded a poll of the huge delegation. Boos filled the hall, out of anger at a delay in the proceedings just as Willkie seemed ready to take off. The crowd soon changed its mind, however, when New York's revised numbers were read aloud: for Dewey 53, for Willkie 27. For two ballots, against all logic, Simpson had held out for Frank Gannett, biding time until the moment of maximum psychological impact. Then he shoved all his delegates into the Willkie column. The result was everything he hoped for.[43]

Arthur Vandenberg got on the line to Dewey, warning him against raiding the Michigan bloc lest the entire anti-Willkie front suddenly crumble. On the fourth ballot, Willkie surged in front, with Taft second and Dewey fading fast. From the floor, Sprague practically begged his candidate to see the handwriting on the wall and give his campaign a decent burial. On the fifth ballot, when Iowa failed to restart his momentum, Dewey surrendered. He called the Wisconsin delegates and urged them to support Taft, a message also conveyed to the New Yorkers, with some strange results. Theodore Roosevelt, Jr., cast his vote for the son of his father's old foe, as did Kingsland Macy. Encouraged, Taft's supporters tried to adjourn the convention overnight at the end of the fifth ballot, hoping to solder together new coalitions of convenience and still prevent Willkie from laying claim to the nomination.[44]

Ken Simpson, learning of this, raced to the podium, where he conferred with John Hamilton, Chairman Martin, and Harold Stassen. Martin ruled out any adjournment, and Manhattan's county leader smiled broadly, his lips curled around a dead cigar placed there instead of the habitual pipe. Now Michigan was ready to join the Willkie parade. Mrs. Vandenberg had passed on written instructions from her husband, in the event his own nomination became impossible, to get behind Taft. But Frank McKay, the state's national committeeman, owed a favor to John Hamilton, and the national chairman was now anxious to collect. McKay said his delegates were concerned over Willkie's attitude toward federal judgeships. Would he in the White House heed the advice of his amateur backers or would he listen to the organization?

A direct line to Willkie's suite had been installed on the podium for just such emergencies, and now Sam Pryor used it to put the question to his candidate. "To hell with the judges," Willkie rasped, "get the delegates." With that, Michigan cast 35 votes for the unlikeliest presidential nominee ever to emerge from a major party convention. Dewey telephoned his congratulations, and he concealed his own disappointment well in a 1:30 A.M. session with reporters. He was, he confessed, "relieved" by the result, and Frances was even more so. "I led on three ballots," he explained when asked for the reasons behind his loss, "but they were the wrong three."

Willkie's nomination proved the crest of his wave, almost immediately dissipated through inexperience and a stubborn disregard for the judgment of other men. On Friday morning, Raymond Baldwin was summoned to meet the nominee, who apologetically told his first important public supporter that "the oldsters" inside the party wanted him to balance the ticket with a Westerner. Manfully, Baldwin stepped aside in favor of Senate Minority Leader Charles L. McNary, an Oregonian who opposed Willkie on public versus private power and aid to the Allies, and who at first refused to run with him. Finally, McNary gave his consent and met Willkie for the first time in his life, sitting in the bathtub in his hotel suite.[45]

Even more bitterly disappointed than Baldwin was John Hamilton, once he learned that Willkie wanted Joe Martin to replace him as national chairman, on the assumption (mistaken, as events proved) that Martin could do a better job of welding together Willkie's grass-roots amateurs and party regulars. Such moves stamped Willkie at the start of his crusade against Roosevelt as a man whose commitments were subject to whim, a kind of corn-fed Ken Simpson. Dewey himself immediately endorsed the new standard-bearer, turned over to Oren Root some 300 Dewey clubs, and won plaudits for his poise from Landon and Hoover, who agreed on little else. "If we can't take it," Dewey told Landon, "we shouldn't be in politics, and I hope by now, I have learned to take it."[46]

Herbert Hoover wrote a different kind of congratulatory letter to the defeated candidate. "It is," he said, "a time of effervescent public moods, of short duration thoughts instead of long duration deliberation, of rapid shifts to meet emergencies of the moment rather than the deeper currents of national life. A great responsibility is going to fall on the young leaders of the party, of which you are the outstanding person . . . you have the fundamental sense of the long view rather than the transitory."[47]

Eager to put behind him the sounds of band music and promises, to escape the artificial life of politics for brook trout, a nine iron, and some rural solitude, Dewey left Philadelphia, Bob Taft in tow, and retreated 200 miles to the north, to play one o' cat with his boys and grill hamburgers on a hilly ridge overlooking the Harlem Valley. There, at a place called Dapplemere Farm, he could temporarily forsake the mixed pleasures of fame. There, as nowhere else in the world, he might even enjoy a trial separation from ambition.[48]

III

A FIRE
IN THE BELLY

1941–1948

10
The View from Purgatory Hill

If Tom had a grocery store, it would be the first one to open in the morning, and the last one to close at night.
—FRANCES DEWEY[1]

Lowell Thomas was a collector. Experiences, anecdotes, foreign places, and, above all, people stuck to Thomas as if to flypaper. His interest in the human species was implanted early, as the son of a curious doctor-geologist who lived in the gold-rush community of Cripple Creek, Colorado. Young Lowell left town about the time the gold was exhausted, then, after receiving an M.A. from the University of Denver, he drifted into the newspaper business, to find himself working in the Chicago *Journal* newsroom, where at one time or another Charles MacArthur, Ben Hecht, Carl Sandburg, and Ring Lardner would also work. When the First World War broke out, Thomas hopped the Atlantic to report from the battlefields of France. He pursued Lord Allenby to the Near East and, in a stroke of luck that changed his life, was introduced to a blue-eyed Oxford graduate who dressed like a prince of Mecca. Lowell Thomas became America's eyes, peering through desert sandstorms and maddening mirages, tracking T. E. Lawrence on his triumphal campaigns at Aqaba and Damascus.

Having achieved it, Lawrence renounced fame and thereafter courted death and release. Thomas basked in his own notoriety, wrote a hugely successful book called *With Lawrence in Arabia,* and took to the lecture circuit, where he packed Madison Square Garden for eight solid weeks with his movies of Arabian camels and buccaneers. From his friend Dale Carnegie, he learned how to exude confidence in public. But it was his own innate gift for the dramatic that filled out a visual experience that, for many Americans in an age when movies were still silent and the world still impossibly large to comprehend, was nothing less than revolutionary. "Come with me to lands of history, mystery, and romance," Thomas invited at the start of his illustrated travelogue. "What you are about to see is an untold story, part of it as old as time, and part history in the making."

Overnight, he became an international celebrity. King George V desired a command performance of the show. Among the thrill seek-

317

ers of London who drank in the heroic exploits of Allenby and Lawrence were Lloyd George and Winston Churchill. Later, the peripatetic newsman navigated the globe by air, went barnstorming in Europe, dropped in on revolutionary Germany, and cranked out book after book on air travel and the Khyber Pass and whatever else crossed his restless, boyishly excitable mind. By the mid-1920s, he was looking for a place to settle down. He had in mind a private refuge from the public acclaim, as well as a watering hole for the growing circle of the famous who were flattered by his admiration and appreciative of his lavish hospitality.

Thomas discovered his Shangri-la in 1926, on Quaker Hill, a verdant twelve-mile-long ridge straddling the borders of New York and Connecticut, set in a natural bowl scooped out of the Catskills to the west, and the Berkshires to the north and east. Two miles from the village of Pawling, the Hill in colonial days had lain at the heart of the Oblong, a two-mile-wide buffer zone between the English of New England and the Hudson Valley Dutch population. Even earlier, it had been home to Mohawk Indians, giving way early in the eighteenth century to a community of Quakers, from which the area took its name. In the old Quaker meetinghouse on the Hill, the first anti-slavery protest meeting in North America convened, and during the American Revolution the Society of Friends remained loyal to King George, even while General Washington's troops were bivouacked on adjoining Purgatory Hill ("halfway between Quaker Hill and everywhere else," so went the local legend).

Washington and Lafayette came here to attend the military negligence trial of General Philip Schuyler. A century later, the Hill was crowned by the Mizzentop Hotel, while fashionable summer visitors favored the sprawling old Dutcher House downtown. J. P. Morgan's daughter, who lived in an estate at Mount Kisco, in Westchester County, persuaded her father to install steamboat whistles on the trains pulling into town so as not to offend sensitive ears. In 1903, a Wall Street tycoon named Albert J. Akin died at the age of ninety-nine, leaving most of his estate to the Akin Hall Association. The group held its meetings in a rococo stone library on the Hill, built by an architect who used the same blueprint in constructing an Indiana jail. Money and its frequent consort, eccentricity, did not long outlive old Mr. Akin. By the time Lowell Thomas first set eyes upon the neighborhood, Pawling's reputation as a resort was in decline. The area around the Dutcher House was a sore sight to greet the two dozen New York Central trains that pulled into the depot each day.

But the Hill—the Hill itself remained unspoiled, even by the grandiose estate of New York real estate developer Fred French. French went bankrupt before the Depression, and his palatial country house stood empty in 1926. Besides such man-made wonders, Thomas found a maze of roads snaking through woods ablaze with azaleas and apple blossoms. Everywhere in this enchanted region the traveler was rewarded with spectacular views and a pervasive peace broken only by the lowing of cows on the dozen or so farms situated on the Hill, the dull thwack of an ax going into wood, and the rustle of the hilltop wind as it brushed over two states at their frontiers. Thomas fell in love with the place, and promptly purchased 350 acres, later enlarged to 2,000 and including the deep glacial cistern he renamed Quaker Lake. Home was Clover Brook Farm, thirty-two rooms stocked always with interesting people and the potential for new books to take their place in the prolific collection bearing his name. Around the Hill, there were quite a few who thought Thomas got considerable help on his literary assembly line from Prosper Buranelli, a gnomish little man, whose collected crossword puzzles had laid the foundation in 1924 for a new publishing house called Simon and Schuster.

Buranelli could play five chess partners at one time, engage in scintillating conversation, eye a pretty woman, and still remain Herbert Hoover's favorite fishing companion. Hoover was a frequent visitor to Clover Brook Farm in the 1920s, along with everyone from Franklin Roosevelt and Prince William of Sweden, to Count Felix von Luckner, the Sea Devil of World War I. In 1930, Thomas took to the air, as the voice of the *Literary Digest* on CBS, and a decade after that he made the first televised newscast, an innovation temporarily stalled by the war. Meanwhile, the books continued to pour out, with royalties invested in a world of his design on Quaker Hill.

Thomas liked to ski, and so ski tows were built on the Hill. He enjoyed golfing, and talked Gene Sarazen and Robert Treat Jones into creating a magnificent eighteen-hole course on the brow of North Quaker Hill. He liked sometimes to swim or fish, so he stocked Quaker Lake with smallmouth bass and perch, and limited its use to sixty families, the better to preserve a rustic character. Saturday night socializing, de rigueur on the Hill, centered on the Barn, a community center produced and directed by the Squire of Quaker Hill. In its fireplace, Thomas installed stones from the Great Pyramid of Cheops, the Parthenon, St. Peter's, China's Great Wall, and Mount Vernon. He disliked the view from Akin Hall, so one winter when most of his neighbors were away he had it moved and remodeled into a nondenominational place of worship in Christopher Wren style. He carted off trees and hills that were similarly offensive, outlawed liquor and smoking in the Barn, prohibited power-boats on Quaker Lake.

The Hill became a thriving community of the rich and/or successful, to whom old houses or freshly carved building lots were sold by agents under Thomas' scrutinizing eye. About a hundred families settled there. At one time there were twenty-one lawyers, as well as Casey Hogate, publisher of the *Wall Street Journal;* George H. Sibley, vice president of Squibb and Sons; Norman Vincent Peale; and Edward R. Murrow. It was all a reflection of one man, as much as Windsor Castle reflected the British Royal Family or the Vatican mirrored a procession of Roman pontiffs.

In exchange for admission to this scenically unsurpassed, socially rarefied atmosphere, Thomas' golfing cronies looked the other way when he put down inflated scores, played on his famous Nine Old Men ball teams (a typical roster included Westbrook Pegler, Gil Hodges, Dale Carnegie, Will Hays, Casey Hogate, and Dewey himself), and flocked to the Fourth of July celebration at Hammersley Hill, the estate to which Thomas moved in 1953. Each year, the evening's final illumination was of a sparkling, hissing American flag, the stars in the upper left-hand corner replaced by the Squire's face.[2]

In April of 1938, Thomas caught sight of an item in the *Herald Tribune* saying that District Attorney Dewey and his family were planning on spending the summer in Connecticut. Ever vigilant for what he called "desirable parties," Thomas called Dewey, whom he had never met, and asked pointedly if he thought Connecticut would play an important part in his political future. "Have you ever seen Quaker Hill?" he probed, and Dewey replied, "We'll be right up." Before the month was out, the D.A. came over from New Milford, Connecticut, where he was on the verge of renting a summer place, and the Thomases escorted their guests across a pastoral landscape, freshly renewed with the annual outburst of spring in Dutchess County. They saw some of the 200 miles of bridle paths crisscrossing the Hill—Thomas liked to ride—and called on publisher Hogate, whose eighty beef cattle as well as his milk cows, pigs, and ducks struck a responsive chord in the native of Owosso.

Something about Dewey always seemed to be in New York City but never of it. The city, he maintained, was not a melting pot. "It's a boiling pot." He advised his brother-in-law against moving to any large city and spoke wistfully of lawyer friends who had abandoned the urban canyons for rural retreats—and saved a bundle in taxes to boot. This was the Dewey who asked a reporter, "Who's Stravinsky?" who adhered to the maxims of Owosso that held all blond men to be weak and all bearded men to be hiding something, who loved aisle seats at Broadway musicals, and had more fun than his six-year-old son when he took Tommy to see a four-hour circus performance at the height of the Hines investigation.[3]

In May, Tom and Frances returned to the Hill. This time, their host took them off on a dirt road leading northeast from Pawling, out a mile or so, where the countryside turns into cornfields, and over Purgatory Hill. The road dipped, then climbed sharply, and in a few minutes, the visitors from Manhattan found themselves standing outside a white frame house flanked by twin pillared porches, and shaded around a generous expanse of lawn by towering oak, horse chestnut, and tulip trees. It was the residence of Evelyn Haskins, a widow looking to sell but willing, at Thomas' request, to rent it out for a summer if the District Attorney preferred such an arrangement. Encumbered by his limited means and officeholder's salary, Dewey couldn't hope to buy any property in 1938, nor again the next summer, when Mrs. Haskins once more agreed to rent to his family. It didn't take long for the Deweys to become enamored of the place. The breadwinner himself found it the best therapy possible for overcrowded schedules and political gladhanding. "I work like a horse five days and five nights a week," he wrote in October 1939, "for the privilege of getting to the country for the weekend."[4]

By then, Dapplemere Farm was his personal property. Two months earlier, Thomas had prodded Mrs. Haskins into accepting Dewey's price: $30,000, with $3,000 down and the balance on mortgage. Jubilant, the D.A. borrowed the down payment from his cousin Leonard Reid, and took in some furniture from the recently demolished Mizzentop Hotel to supplement what little he and Frances could afford to buy.[5]

Money was to be a problem in their lives for the next fifteen years. "Too many years in public life," Dewey wrote six months after assuming the governorship, "have left me with nothing but a farm with a nice big mortgage on it. Maybe the fun makes up for it. Sometimes I am not sure." It wasn't unusual for Dewey to ask Lillian Rosse to find out if he had sufficient funds in his bank account to add another Holstein to his flock. First, however, he reminded her, "Don't tell Goody about this." As late as 1950, when considering a school for young Tom, Dewey's choice between Princeton and Amherst was heavily influenced by the fact that the Massachusetts college cost $500 a year less than its older, more prestigious rival. In the end, Tom attended Princeton, but only after fervent pitches on its behalf by both George Gallup and Jerry Lambert.[6]

All was not perfect harmony at the Hill: Dewey wrote to Thomas of a "rather ugly rumor," alleging that Jews calling for information about housing there were asked to supply both their name and religion, and that an ad for the development seeking "old American stock" had appeared in a New York paper. Thomas replied that his agent was "not diplomatic" and had been fired. Beyond that, he maintained, "nothing was said about demanding a pedigree of prospective purchasers." In his zeal to befriend another famous man, Thomas offered every amenity in his well-stocked arsenal of comforts. Join him on a sailboat, he asked, ride my horses, join me trap-shooting, skating, skiing (which Dewey tried once, to everyone's merriment but his own). Come to the Help Finland Mass Meeting and study the speakers' techniques. Play golf on my private course. Attend this dinner. Address that function.[7]

"All speeches," Thomas tartly reminded his new neighbor, "should be boiled down and then cut in half." Of course, Dewey's advisers might not know this, "because, after all, there are only a few top-flight speakers in this whole dizzy world." The broadcaster could be smothering in his embrace.

He never changed. A few weeks after his father's death in 1971, Tom Junior heard from the broadcaster of a planned service on the Hill, presided over by Thomas himself and featuring his parents' interment in a new burial ground started at one of the Squire's favorite overlooks. Patiently, Tom explained that his parents would be buried in the mausoleum they had planned together before their deaths, not far from their closest friends, Pat and Marge Hogan (whom Thomas thoughtfully proposed to move as well, from consecrated ground in Pawling's Catholic cemetery). A service would be held in June, on what would have been their forty-third wedding anniversary, and Thomas would be receiving his invitation shortly.

"But you can't do this to me," sputtered the dean of network newsmen. "I've already got both Javits and Nelson coming."[8]

The main house at Dapplemere Farm had weathered 140 winters on its crest overlooking the Harlem Valley, a stately sentinel of twelve rooms and four baths. On three sides, the land sloped away gently toward open fields and spreading trees. Ranged around the residence were four barns, greenhouses, stables, and a house for the farm manager and his wife. A white picket fence set off grounds from the unpaved road bisecting them. It looked like what it was, a working farm, producing hay and corn. When the Sheffield Dairy opened a few miles away, Dapplemere's new proprietor tapped a fresh source of revenue by selling a ton of milk each day for shipment to the masses of New York City.

Here, just sixty-four miles from Grand Central Station, he could shed the city, and forget about reporters and criminal suspects. His Pawling wardrobe didn't include a black tie. Double-breasted suits gave way to work boots and heavy overalls, deposited in a special room off the back stairs maintained by Frances, who had no intention of inviting the barnyard into her immaculate sanctuary. In her first weeks at Dapplemere, she was described by her husband as "very lonely." It was a difficult passage for the self-confessed introvert, who showed a serene face to the world if only to mask her disappointments.[9]

Two years earlier, an emergency operation, performed in the wake of John's birth, had ruled out any more children, including the daughters she always wanted and spoke of wistfully as the years passed. It was hard work to care for two growing boys and twelve rooms simultaneously, and servant problems seemed a way of life at Dapplemere. But when she finally latched on to Fred and Helen Stohl as helpmates who might lend order to her establishment, Frances began to enjoy the country, to remember things as they had been many years before on her uncle's farm near Lake Texarkana. She took to the informality of country life, enjoyed gardening and dabbling with an easel. She mended her own clothes and picked up most of her wardrobe—which leaned heavily to blacks and whites, easily washed and ready-made—at a little shop in the heart of the village. She tried her hand in the kitchen, cooking up Creole dishes and okra, drove the boys to school, read them stories, and relished Agatha Christie and E. C. Bentley for herself. In the afternoons she spent hours at the piano relaxing with Bach or Mozart, and on weekends she frequently played golf with her husband and never missed an evening of poker and camaraderie with the Eightsome, an all-but-inseparable group of Hill neighbors that included, besides the Deweys and Hogans, New York Supreme Court Judge Charles Murphy and his wife, Elizabeth, and advertising executive Lyn Sumner, who was married to America's leading authority on sewing.[10]

Pat Hogan—"Monsignor" to his buddies—remained Dewey's

dearest friend. G. Lynn Sumner was equally appreciated for his wry wit and stylish wife. "Sit down and tell me a story," the D.A. commanded Sumner at the start of a marathon poker session. "I haven't laughed all day." Charlie Murphy was more irreverent, a Brooklyn Democrat and onetime New York corporation counsel who slyly introduced himself as "famous newspaperman, brilliant advertising executive, noted barrister, renowned jurist, heroic army officer, profound critic and philosopher, celebrated raconteur, gallant horseman, Olympic champion, the toast of drawing rooms in the capitals of the world ... unaffected by the acclaim universally showered upon him."[11]

"We shall have a gay time," Murphy promised in inviting his golfing buddies for a drink. "I shall read some of my opinions aloud." If not asked to spend New Year's Eve with the Deweys, Murphy warned that he and Shorty, his four-foot, ten-inch wife, would probably be condemned "to a Salvation Army hut in the Bowery." To Dewey, the Irish Catholic lawyer and player par excellence of liar's dice was "an angel," the only man capable of shaming him with one glance into apologizing for blowing up at a hapless waiter.[12]

Around such intimates, seemingly his polar opposites in temperament, Dewey relaxed, laughed, and talked freely of anything but politics. That alone was a forbidden topic; those who ventured to introduce it were crisply informed that Dewey had come to the Hill for relaxation, not business. His candor did not evaporate around friends. If anything, it grew sharper, less guarded. He once debated with his mother over a dress being worn by Mary Sumner, their hostess, who stood less than five feet away. In the end, mother and son publicly agreed that the outfit was unbecoming—it didn't show Mary's legs to advantage.[13]

According to the farm manager who helped Dapplemere turn a profit, Dewey's critical standards extended even to recreation. "His greatest fun was finding out someone else had made a mistake," Arnulf Mueller recalled, and verbal retribution could be swift and sometimes brutal. Discourtesy was as objectionable as sloppiness. When a state farm agent arrived two hours late for a Sunday appointment, then apologized by explaining he expected to see "only" the farm overseer, Dewey's eyes blazed and his tongue cut loose. "Mr. Mueller is just as important as I am," he upbraided his visitor. "His time is just as valuable." Besides, how could anyone be so rude as not to call when he realized he would be late for an appointment?

Sheepishly, the agent apologized. He had been detained elsewhere in Dutchess County, at the farm owned by Franklin Roosevelt, Jr.[14]

Dewey loved Dapplemere as no other place. He could tell a fair-going audience in 1947 with a straight face that "farming has been the principal interest in my life for the last ten years." At the Barn or on the lawn outside Thomas' church, around a poker table or at one of the cocktail parties he dreaded, the D.A. talked farming like a small boy talks baseball, reverently yet joyfully. He told of his $1,600 milking machine, his revolutionary pen stabling of milk cows, and his 150-foot trench silo, which cost a fraction of what the conventional silo did, and could be filled easily as long as you wore thick boots—otherwise, the sulfur dioxide used in sealing it shut would freeze your toes. He was proud of his experiments that cut costs, enjoyed buying his own feed from Town Supervisor Emery Cole, joined the Grange, and bored his wife with endless hours spent in comparing milk production charts.[15]

His routine on the farm varied little. Most days, he was up early, stalking through the kitchen dressed for work, whistling or singing a favorite tune like "Oh, What a Beautiful Morning." Then he rode horseback alongside Lowell Thomas, or checked his fences in an old four-wheel-drive vehicle that bounced and veered as its erratic driver pondered in his head a speech draft or overnight crisis. Dewey had 300 acres to call his own. A fraction was given over during the war to his sons' victory gardens, where berries and beans were grown and marketed back to the household at OPA prices. Young Tom was soon established as the best pitcher on the local team, coached by the Reverend Ralph Lankler. (His father was not often asked back by Thomas' Nine Old Men; it seemed his pitching style was a little too ferocious for friends merely playing a game among themselves.) John, still an infant when the family first took up residence on the Hill, grew into a round-faced boy, usually carrying a book or two under one arm.[16]

Frances' domain was the house, a well-ordered and dusted antique that received loving attention. On the ground floor, her husband installed folding doors to a library which he could also enter from the outside. A formal dining room was located between the kitchen and library. Across the hall was a living room, thirty by eighteen feet in dimension, and dominated by the grand piano around which Tom, Frances, and their closest friends often sang until two or three in the morning. In back of the dining room was an enclosed sun porch, where the family took most of their meals. The sun's rays filtered through the house much of each day; in the evening, the proprietors liked to sit in silence on the west porch, gazing off at amethyst hills and a buttermilk sky on the brink of dusk. Sometimes, on the spur of the moment, they invited Arnulf Mueller and his wife to join them there, for the nightly spectacle that moved Dewey to remark, "No man could live here and not believe in God."[17]

Upstairs, the house contained five bedrooms. The Governor often met visitors at the door himself, then showed them to their quarters. When able to escape from the city for a few days, he often slept nine or ten hours a night. His doctor had given him warnings, prescribing a less hectic pace after diagnosing a thyroid condition in 1936. His father and uncle had both died at fifty-seven, Dewey reminded his family. Perhaps the small, clear voice of his own mortality led him to Norman Vincent Peale's house one night, a week or so after the two men had disagreed at a community meeting. Peale had to catch a plane that same evening, and didn't return from a speaking engagement for several days. Subsequently, at eleven o'clock at night, his phone rang. It was Tom Dewey, insisting he had to see Peale immediately and would be over in a few minutes. When he arrived, Dewey found Peale standing in his doorway in a robe, a quizzical smile fixed on his features. "How come the Governor has to see a preacher at midnight?" he asked.

"Norman, I had a notion that I may have hurt your feelings by my clumsy humor a week ago at the meeting. You went off in a big hurry. It's been bothering me ever since." At the door on his way out, Dewey put an arm around the minister's shoulders and looked him squarely in the eye. "Whenever you feel you have hurt a friend of a lifetime, heal that hurt at once. I love you." With that, he slipped into the night, his emotions briefly bared like the Hill itself under a quick flash of summer lightning.[18]

On July 8, 1940, two weeks after the Philadelphia convention, Dewey and Willkie met at the latter's office on Pine Street. Afterward, Dewey reported that their hour and a quarter conversation, interrupted often by the telephone, was "very pleasant." Willkie himself confided a different version. To one intimate he described a torrent of suggestions, people to see, places to go, approaches to the issues to stress or avoid. Finally, according to the Republican candidate, he interrupted his visitor. "Tom?"

"Yes, Wendell."

"Since when did the party make you its nominee?"[19]

Such a response was in keeping with the self-confidence of one who complained of "free advice ... worth just what it costs." Dewey's own attitude was different. To Ruth Simms he wrote, asking her to serve on Willkie's advisory committee, and reminding her that their own campaign had not been simply to replace a president, but to "eliminate what we regarded as dangerously unsound government." He volunteered to collect "high grade legal talent" to assist Willkie, and persuaded Jerry Lambert to stay on as pollster, a decision that seemed to please the nominee greatly. Dewey turned over the cream of his own preconvention staff: John Burton did research for Willkie; Elliott Bell tried to bring order to a chaotic speechwriting effort; and when Willkie turned out not to have a press secretary, Dewey assigned him his own, Lem Jones.[20]

Mrs. Simms agreed to serve as well, and in her own assessment of the candidate struck a perceptive note. "Mr. Willkie is fundamentally indifferent to Party labels and he believes that more Democrats will openly support his candidacy than I think likely." She discounted an appeal to Southern Jeffersonian Democrats—Herbert Hoover was to urge the same course upon candidate Dewey four years later—as symptomatic of the unreality of much of the Willkie campaign. On July 26, the nominee met with Russ Sprague, a very realistic Republican, and pronounced Dewey's cooperative attitude "magnificent." Willkie sought ways to capitalize on his own burst of popularity, which had brought him neck and neck with a president whose coy plans regarding renomination led to some embarrassing moments at the Democratic convention in mid-July. At one point, Chicago's Mayor Kelly found it necessary to station his superintendent of sewers at a subterranean microphone, where the man attempted for an hour to rouse lethargic and confused delegates with booming, disembodied chants of "Illinois wants Roosevelt. New York wants Roosevelt. The World wants Roosevelt!"[21]

Late in September, delegates to the New York Republican convention listened and cheered as Dewey delivered a keynote address linking FDR with corrupt machines in Chicago, Newark, and elsewhere, and attacking the contention that the President was indispensable to the nation's welfare. "Only ideals and principles survive, and these through the leadership of many men," he said. "Where one man would destroy all others who might uphold those ideals and carry on those principles, he believes in no ideals. He believes in no principles. He believes only in his own personal aggrandizement."

The next day, Dewey introduced Willkie to a roaring crowd of

50,000 at a Yonkers racetrack, where the candidate, in a spontaneous coda to his formal text, solemnly proclaimed, "If we do not prevail this fall, this way of life will pass." It was a characteristic action for Willkie to take, but to thoughtful observers such rhetoric smacked of previous "crusades" against the New Deal. The New York *Times* called Willkie "the biggest smash since Mickey Mouse." Gloria Swanson and Mary Pickford were just two of the passionate supporters who donned some of the 30 million buttons with Willkie's name on them. But Wendell Willkie was discovering daily that winning a presidential nomination is not the same thing as winning the presidency.

Quite simply, Willkie didn't like professional politicians. He still believed his nomination to have been solely the product of his own labors, and he continued to place his faith in the amateurs who idolized him and to ignore the organization. (Charles Hilles, still influential although no longer a member of the national committee, had wired his congratulations and an offer to help. He received in return a form letter urging him to join his local Willkie Club.) Willkie insisted on seeing the press whenever the mood struck him, and talking to everyone, everywhere, who might be converted to his cause. "My God," exclaimed a throat specialist called in to treat the candidate when Willkie's voice gave out in mid-August, "I can't make him stop! He goes on night and day."

Sometimes, overcome with the importance of his cause, Willkie talked rashly. At Joliet, Illinois, Lem Jones had to step in and clarify the nominee's statement accusing Roosevelt of contacting Hitler and Mussolini at Munich and instructing them "to sell Czechoslovakia down the river." Just as bad was the utter disorganization around Willkie, which George Gallup forty years later termed "a farce from day one." The car occupied by Willkie's speechwriters was dubbed the Squirrel Cage. To a sputtering New England professional angry because no one on the train stepped forward to be briefed before a scheduled stop in Boston, one of Willkie's writers captured the essence of what made his campaign so exciting, unpredictable, intensely emotional, and an organizational disaster: "This place is like a whorehouse on a Saturday night," he explained, "when the madam is out and all the girls are running around dropping nickels in juke boxes."

It wasn't long before Willkie's vanquished foes entertained thoughts of "I told you so." By the middle of September, Taft was complaining to Dewey. If nothing else, the Senator wrote, the botched-up crusade should teach the party never again to nominate a political novice. As for Willkie's tendency to trade quips with the press, the starchy Ohioan commented, "It may be that wisecracking which keeps the nominee on the front page every day really gets results, but I rather doubt it." Dewey responded with similar sentiments, adding that two-thirds of his own time since the convention had been spent "straightening out messes."[22]

As September wore on, the tide began to turn—not to Franklin Roosevelt, but to a world insistent on dragging a reluctant America into its war. FDR himself displayed increasing boldness in preparing for a conflict he probably regarded as inevitable. In upstate New York, the President briefed Canadian Prime Minister Mackenzie King on a secret plan to trade fifty over-age American destroyers to the British in exchange for ninety-nine-year leases on British bases in the Western Hemisphere. It was an audacious step for a professed neutral, and no one could guess how the public would accept the idea. To find out, Roosevelt asked George Gallup to undertake a poll, which showed surprising support for such a plan.[23]

Dewey heard of the proposed swap from Allen Dulles, who was then in the early stages of forming his own aid-the-Allies committee and concerned lest Willkie allow partisan pressures to keep him from adding his own stamp of approval to the destroyer deal. After hearing Dulles out, Dewey got on the phone to Colorado Springs, where Willkie was resting, and offered to make a public declaration of his own in favor of the trade if Willkie thought it might ease the way for him to do the same. Curtly, Willkie informed his former rival that he had events well in hand, and would soon be in a position to come out for the deal. Until then, he preferred silence on the issue. When he later did endorse the swap, Willkie's support was double-edged, coupled with a blast at Roosevelt's circumvention of Congress as "the most dictatorial and arbitrary act" ever perpetrated by an occupant of the White House.[24]

The 1940 campaign was one of lights and shadows, in which real issues were submerged in conflicting personalities and an unspoken pact ruling out the truth when it came to U.S. participation in Europe's war. The Battle of Britain was raging, Americans were tuning in nightly to hear Edward R. Murrow's galvanizing reports from London, German and Italian diplomats were negotiating a Tripartite Pact with Japan (formally made public on September 27), and the first peacetime draft in American history was churning through Congress; yet Willkie and Roosevelt found themselves engaged in bitter long-distance media debates over who could provide the most ironclad guarantees of American isolation from the fighting.

In Los Angeles and Chicago and Louisville, Willkie promised that a vote for him was a vote for peace. In Baltimore, he flatly predicted that Roosevelt's re-election would have American boys loaded onto troop carriers by April 1941, a statement he later retracted smilingly as "a bit of campaign oratory." Charles Lindbergh, now the foremost spokesman for isolationism, all but endorsed Willkie in a nationwide radio broadcast on October 14. Some former supporters began to drop away, disgusted. Walter Lippmann wrote to Henry Luce, "I hoped and believed he would be the man this country needed, but I think he set his campaign on a fundamentally wrong line back in July and has lost ground since." Dorothy Thompson switched to FDR. So did Dewey's "boyhood hero" Chase Osborne.

Roosevelt himself had two major advantages in the contest, the tendency of Americans to rally to their president in times of crisis, and Willkie's own exploitable errors. But he, too, was kept busy pledging solemnly that there were no secret agreements with any foreign power to come to their aid; and in Boston, weary of responding to Willkie, Dewey, and other Republican critics who dismissed his promises as worthless—Remember the 1932 vow to balance the budget? Dewey asked—Roosevelt made a mistake of his own. It was close to the finish line of an intense, often virulent campaign (the New York *Times* featured a regular scorecard of the eggs, tomatoes, potatoes, and other objects tossed at Willkie) when the President gave his word "again and again and again" that "your boys and girls are not going to be sent into any foreign war."

Dewey was occupied with his own speechmaking tour. Having promised the nominee to give a few addresses on his behalf, the D.A. found himself traveling as far afield as Caldwell, Idaho, to preach the Willkie gospel. At the tail-end of his tour, Willkie wired a request to add St. Louis to the itinerary; Missouri was close and Dewey might be able to swing it with a hard-hitting speech. Dewey agreed to do his best. His own mood was pessimistic. On October 21, he worried out loud to Alf Landon that "Mr. Big" appeared headed toward another term. Landon advised Dewey in his own speeches for the ticket to stress economic and social issues as well as graft and good government. He also urged Dewey to inject some warmth into his texts, advice Dewey said he should be reminded of every day.[25]

Meanwhile, the D.A. pulled no punches in assailing the administration. At Kingston, New York, on October 10, he spoke of "a sudden mysterious entanglement in the Far East" which could mean "the lives of men in this very hall. Yet we are allowed to have no in-

formation as to what is going on. We are asked only to have faith in
the supposed wisdom of the same men who have sadly mishandled
our domestic problems.... Having weakened our domestic economy," Dewey asserted, "having left us woefully unprepared in a
world crisis, is the New Deal administration now leading us to war?"
A week later, at Pittsburgh, he was more specific, asserting that
rearmament plans had been stalled by the Budget Bureau with the
President's knowledge and support. "If this be the indispensable
foresight of the indefensible man," he thundered at Peoria, Illinois,
in the campaign's closing days, "then let us have just the common
sense of the competent man." Dewey indicted, tried, and convicted
the New Deal of fomenting internal strife, fostering unemployment,
repudiating its own pledges of a balanced budget and sound currency, attempting to subvert both Congress and the courts to its will,
and creating a "regimented party" marked by "political execution
of critics and rivals."

If government should perpetuate itself by such methods, Dewey
told an audience in Saginaw, Michigan, then the freedom of the
American people was all but ended. He lambasted the Democrats'
Chicago convention, the voice in the sewer and a nomination "conceived in secrecy, nourished on cynicism and reared in arrogance to
its ugly maturity by the most corrupt elements of American political
life." The language was blunt, even extreme, but, then, Americans
had grown conditioned to such talk since 1932. Something about
FDR, his charm, his guile, his talent for flouting rules by which
other politicians were judged, his stance as a man of the people who
happened to live on a Hudson Valley estate; something about the
man's magic, the way he taunted his opponents, riddled them with
sarcasm, reached into their ranks and recruited cabinet members
like Henry Stimson and Frank Knox (appointments brilliantly
staged on the second day of the Republican convention at Philadelphia)—all this and more made reasonable men unreasonable, and
cautious men arrogant with anger.

Grounds for criticism surely existed, especially on the sensitive
topic of military preparedness. The Army relied for firepower on a
twelve-ton tank with no periscope. It still had a horse cavalry division, and was proposing to add another. Military posts were distrib-
uted to fight Indian wars. Political procurement contracts were the
rule. A serious race problem hobbled the force, hardly mitigated
when Roosevelt, in an obvious political move, elevated Benjamin O.
Davis, a black, to brigadier general status eight months before

Davis' scheduled retirement, and a good deal closer than that to Election Day. Roosevelt himself trailed in his wake a lengthy string of isolationist statements for public consumption.

Yet the President displayed courage in overruling Harold Ickes and going ahead with the first military draft drawing ten days before the election. If the nation's defenses seemed weak, her commander in chief's remained all but impregnable.

In the event, Willkie went down to defeat by a little over 5 million votes (and in doing so polled the highest Republican tally in history).

Ken Simpson did better that day than his political protector. He claimed for himself the silk stocking House seat that had been vacated by Bruce Barton to wage a hopeless Senate campaign. But Simpson found himself in the gray light of dawn dangerously exposed. No longer could Willkie guarantee safe cover from Dewey supporters out to complete their takeover of the state party machinery. Simpson's new office afforded little more than a platform from which to wage a kind of oratorical scorched-earth campaign. None of this prevented the county leader from a bold toss of the dice. Early in December, he moved to replace an able and popular elections commissioner named David Costuma with a man of his own. Dewey assistants Bernie Katzen and Aaron Benenson went to work, hoping to re-elect Costuma and thus deal Simpson a telling blow. Tom Curran, another district leader and Dewey ally since their days as fellow doorbell ringers in the Fifteenth Assembly District, spearheaded the Costuma campaign.

Chase Osborne and others urged Dewey to end his feud with Simpson. "I can't make friends with a man whose word is no good," he told Osborne, "at least I can't do so and be consistent with my conscience." In the end, it was Simpson's own brashness that forced a showdown. By a vote of 2 to 1, the foot soldiers of Republicanism in Manhattan rejected his candidate for elections commissioner. Four days later, on December 20, the Congressman-elect tendered his resignation as county chairman. Dewey was hosting a party that night at a favorite restaurant in the financial district. Ostensibly, it was to thank workers from his own campaign, but when news arrived that his bitterest foe was finally and decisively defeated, the celebration took on a giddy exuberance. By midnight, Paul Lockwood and Sewell Tyng were leading a conga line to the music of a slightly inebriated Syrian band. The D.A. took more restrained delight in his victory.[26]

"It is now eleven o'clock," he wrote to a friend, "and for four hours

New York County has reached the blessed state of freedom from its local Republican dictator." To Jerry Lambert, he was philosophical. "The mills of the gods grind slowly, but they grind exceeding small."[27]

Embittered and politically broken, Simpson returned to the bottle. Five weeks later he was dead. He was forty-five years old. The papers called it a heart attack. Simpson's death opened the way to a virtually unimpeded nomination for Dewey for governor in 1942. Already, he was determined not to run again for district attorney. Instead, Dewey planned on entering private practice for a year, making some money, and investing his spare time and energies in a county-by-county courtship of the party leaders who now looked to him for guidance. He did not hesitate to state his plans, nor to claim credit for his achievements. "I made Ed Jaeckle chairman of the state committee," he reminded Kingsland Macy. "I made Tom Curran county leader in New York, and I propose to create the strongest Republican organization New York has ever had."[28]

In January, 1941, President Roosevelt introduced the Lend-Lease Act, formally House Bill 1776, to provide Britain and her allies $7 billion worth of armaments and ammunition with which to carry on the fight against Hitler. Early in the month, Dewey issued his own call for "every possible aid to Great Britain short of war." At the same time, he faulted Lend-Lease as originally drawn for granting the President unlimited authority to decide what would be given to which ally and when the gift would be made. Such surrender of congressional initiative, he insisted, posed a grave threat to free government. Even so staunch a friend of Britain as Allen Dulles concurred, while Willkie asked only that the life of the legislation be limited to two years. At the opposite end of the spectrum, Robert Taft opposed the whole concept of Lend-Lease, while Herbert Hoover, whom Dewey thanked for taking "a fatherly interest" in his career, sought to persuade the younger man to stump the country for its defeat. Arthur Sulzberger probably came closest to an accurate description of H.R. 1776. He termed it "an affirmative act on our part, and a warlike act."[29]

Under the circumstances, it was hardly a time for either sober reflection or long-range philosophical development. "The world hangs in a state of suspense," Dewey told his mother late in February, "and the war of nerves clamors across a vacuum." For him, the beginning of 1941 was, as always, a time of too many demands and too few hours in the day. He complained to Oswald Heck of "a ruinous schedule" of speeches. He devoted several hours each day to his work as district attorney, began traveling around the state and befriending Republican chieftains in advance of the race for governor, and maintained a vast correspondence with new friends gathered in the 1940 campaign.[30]

For the first time, Dewey began to associate foreign failures with domestic ones. He spoke out for a Republicanism more in the mold of TR than Taft. "We have only put patches on the wounds of the last decade," he told a Lincoln Day audience in Washington in February (the same dinner where he called for "all-out aid" to "the heroic people of Britain" and endorsed a congressionally revised Lend-Lease). "We have bought and paid for them with government deficits. Social gains have been made, but they rest upon the insecure foundation of a mounting debt. Economic opportunity has actually declined. Real social and economic security have yet to be achieved."

He spoke of a need for medical insurance for the poor within a private enterprise framework, greater opportunity for millions left outside the social mainstream, and economic decentralization that might one day render industrial slums a bleak memory. It was a thoughtful, if abstruse, plan. Few of his countrymen listened. For most Americans, whatever their political faith, 1941 was a steep, slippery incline toward war.

On May 27, Roosevelt took note of recent German military successes by declaring an unlimited state of emergency. Two weeks later, he froze German and Italian assets in the U.S. and shut down German consulates. In July, Japanese assets were similarly quarantined, and an embargo declared on all shipments of scrap iron and gasoline to the warlords in Tokyo. In August, the President and Winston Churchill met on a warship off Newfoundland to devise the Atlantic Charter, and a 900,000-man ceiling on the peacetime army was declared invalid. Within six weeks, German submarines were retaliating by sinking American vessels, and formal entry into the war seemed only a question of time.

Robert Taft watched the gathering storm from his Senate seat, and steadfastly opposed what he considered to be warlike steps on the part of the Roosevelt administration. Taft disapproved of Lend-Lease, seizure of Axis shipping, the occupation of Iceland. He denounced the draft extension and repeal of the Neutrality Act. Ten weeks before Pearl Harbor, Taft told an audience that "if isolationism means isolation from foreign wars, I am an isolationist." He was hardly alone in that sentiment; 135 of 164 House Republicans echoed his stand against Lend-Lease, and when the draft finally was extended, it was by a single-vote margin. Meanwhile, the America First Committee, backed by such luminaries as Lindbergh, Henry Ford, Joseph P. Kennedy, and Alice Roosevelt Longworth, raised the banner of isolation for millions to flock to. At one America First rally in Chicago, fiefdom of Colonel Robert McCormick and his fiercely anti-British *Tribune,* a huge crowd lustily booed Churchill's name.[31]

Dewey advised a Wisconsin supporter against joining a local chapter of the organization, arguing that in the East its supporters were widely viewed as "appeasers." His own feelings about the war were beginning to crystallize into a sort of gloomy acquiescence in the unavoidable. He fretted to Alf Landon at the start of March 1941 about the long-range effects of a five-to-ten-year war of attrition on the domestic economy and political structure. He found discouraging omens on battlefronts from the Balkans to Gibraltar, but owned up to a Hobson's choice. "If we stay out, the prospect of being ruled by an atavistic set of conquerors with international ambitions is equally bleak," he wrote, and concluded with a sympathy never shown in public: "Franklin Roosevelt is faced with the most difficult situation and set of choices of any man in our history."[32]

Landon's reply was a plea to avoid discussing foreign policy. "Your job is to do nothing that will keep you from being elected Governor of New York." The Kansan's antipathy to FDR was close to paranoia, and to his New York protégé he confided stories of Roosevelt at the start of the New Deal informing friendly reporters of his intention to call in Chief Justice Hughes to consult over economic and social legislation in the hope of preventing the Supreme Court from declaring his program unconstitutional. Landon quoted Roosevelt in 1936, the day after his NRA was dismissed by the Court on just such grounds, as likening himself to Victoria, who, told by Gladstone that she could do nothing to help his legislative program—which was up to the House of Lords—replied that she could choose a new House of Lords.[33]

Roosevelt and Lend-Lease produced much bitterness throughout Republican ranks. When Dewey arrived in Washington to deliver the Lincoln Day speech in February, he was met at Union Station by an elderly GOP congressman. In the cab ride that followed, the legislator tried to smoke out the D.A. on the subject of Lend-Lease, then in the throes of amendment. Informed that Dewey's text did indeed mention the bill, and favorably, the congressman halted the cab, climbed out in disgust, and declared that he would ride no further with such a heretic. The middle ground found few takers in the furious debates of 1941. Some Republicans resented what they took to be Willkie's hectoring over the issue. Callers at Pine Street found Willkie voluble as ever, eager to express doubt over the stand— which he perceived to be isolationist—taken by every Republican from Hoover and Landon to the Indiana delegation in Congress and Dewey as the hidden power in New York Republican politics. Darkly, the titular leader hinted that all those who opposed Roosevelt on the foreign question, especially over extension of the draft, would pay a heavy price for their obstinacy at the polls. In the process, he left the impression that he would willingly join in a purge of such elements from the party.[34]

   That spring, Dewey found himself once more called to organize rather than theorize. Arthur Sulzberger paid a visit to Centre Street and stayed to ask the D.A. if he would undertake fund-raising responsibilities for a still embryonic amalgam of religious and fraternal groups called the United Service Organization. It was the USO's plan to operate recreational facilities for the 1.5 million men already suctioned into the armed forces by the draft law. The federal government would put up the money to build the centers, 250 or so, but the USO would need $10 million in its own coffers if the idea of volunteerism in their operation was to move beyond a good intention. Sulzberger personally expressed doubt that the entire amount could be raised. Instead, he pitched the job to Dewey as a useful educational experience for the country. It would have beneficial side effects for an aspiring governor as well. The D.A. thought it over, agreed, and after checking out the orange crates and telephone that were USO headquarters in the Empire State Building, flew to Washington to meet with top military brass and accept General George C. Marshall's offer of his personal DC-3 to transport Dewey and his party on a series of cross-country inspection and speaking tours.[35]

   On May 8, Dewey was in the air again, this time bound for Hampton Roads, Virginia. There, at the confluence of army and naval facilities housing 200,000 men, he found severe morale problems and a force almost ludicrously inadequate to the task before it. A third of Langley Air Force Base's 12,000 population slept in a converted hangar; some soldiers spent their nights sprawled uncomfortably in old rowboats. Recreation was all but nonexistent. Half the force at nearby Fort Monroe was regularly "out on the front porch" for three or four nights a week, subject only to reveille at six in the morning. It was hard to know what they did. The only town serving the area was Phoebus, a dusty little crossroads of 3,000 with entertainment facilities consisting of a 450-seat movie theater, segregated, and a drugstore dispensing chocolate sodas.

Dewey spoke to groups of the enlisted men, seeking their opinions about the USO and what it should become. Some told him they longed for swimming pools and skating rinks, others wanted help in combating a syphilis epidemic—morality lectures to the contrary. One boy expressed a desire to see more of "those Southern bellies." Everyone, it seemed, had complaints about the attitude of the locals to men in uniform, from a swimming pool sign proclaiming "Dogs and Soldiers Not Allowed" to higher prices on such simple pleasures as bowling and beer, and laundry bills that consumed a third of their twenty-one-dollar monthly basic pay. A morale officer insisted that the most pressing need was for "a place to go to pee." Dewey replied wryly that this might make a less than stirring battle cry. Besides, he said, he couldn't use the word toilet on the radio.

For six weeks, he immersed himself in the gripes of barracks life. He examined a Garand rifle and rode a tank, ate in commissaries and shared rustic showers with crewcut men from Syracuse and Mobile. His pace was breathtaking in those days of lumbering flight. One morning, Dewey ate breakfast in New York, lunch in Atlanta, and dinner in New Orleans. It was, he admitted, "all new to me and . . . really lots of fun." Taking to the airwaves, he dramatized the plight of boys stationed in Florida who walked nine miles to the nearest movie theater, hailed the Military Maids of Shreveport, Louisiana, for agreeing to set aside at least one night a week for dating locally stationed soldiers, and pressed his argument that the USO was a quintessentially American response to the problem at hand. The government might build service clubs, he said, but it ought not to run them, ought not be entrusted with "the private lives of American boys when they have a night off . . . their only chance to be free from discipline . . . to be ordinary American boys."[36]

Within five weeks, Dewey had his $10 million pledged. By the time the drive ended, he was able to turn over $6 million more to the fledgling organization, to staff and administer recreation centers equipped with movies, games, books, writing materials, and comfort stations, which could sponsor dances, parties, and checker and chess tournaments. Dewey had done his part. The private sector had responded generously.

Now it was time for Washington to step in and do the building. "I am willing to wager a month's salary," the D.A. angrily wrote a friend, "that no soldier or sailor will cross the threshold of a government-built USO building this year." The Federal Security Administration, headed by Paul McNutt, was ill-equipped to handle a crash program. Adhering vigorously to a long list of regulations, two sets of field office inspections, architectural reviews, and personal presidential approval, the FSA had permitted fewer than 10 percent of the proposed centers to pass its gauntlet of paper by the end of summer.[37]

In September, Dewey flew south "with an olive branch in one hand and a shillelagh in the other," in hopes of unsnarling the red tape and raising "some particular hell." He talked with the brass and fired off a blistering memo to Secretary of War Henry Stimson, who finally agreed to take the program away from the FSA and give it to the Army. General Brehon B. Somervell, whose toughness as New York City's WPA administrator had impressed Dewey, was handed the task of dismissing loafers, booting out chiselers, and slicing through the bureaucratic Gordian knot. Within a month, Dewey could inform his USO colleagues that a hundred or more recreation centers would be open for business by Christmas. As the last golden hours of peace ticked away, his dolorous brush with the New Deal only reinforced his pervasive gloom.[38]

"The whole system seems to be under . . . systematic attack from the highest places," he wrote in mid-September. ". . . it is being said that capitalism is dead and that the social revolution is in full swing. This may well be true. The problem is which direction it will take. . . . If we can keep the reward system in our economy, this will survive as a free country. It is true, we will have controls and priorities and price fixing. But we will also still have our freedoms." For Republicans who regarded the 1930s as a decade-long grudge match against "that man in the White House," and whose hatred of FDR was profound enough to include betting the family farm on a single roll of Willkie's dice, Dewey's message that conservatives must adapt or perish was not likely to rouse enthusiasm. It had little to compare with the delicious irresponsibility of unbridled contempt.[39]

In May of 1941, as Dewey prepared to fly south on a USO inspection tour, Louis "Lepke" Buchalter was arraigned on a five-year-old murder charge. The arraignment came not in Manhattan but in Brooklyn, where District Attorney William O'Dwyer's mayoral aspirations were being fed by Deweyesque headlines about an assault on Murder, Inc., and the notorious garment racketeer already serving a fourteen-year term at Leavenworth on narcotics charges. With eight months left in his term, Dewey remained hopeful of pressing his own long list of criminal charges against Lepke, who instead sought to make a deal. Through his own lawyer and through Victor Herwitz, the racketeer conveyed word to Dewey at the Empire State Building that he could provide testimony against Sidney Hillman of the Amalgamated Clothing Workers and the CIO. The offer was rejected, and Lepke started down the road that finally led to execution.[40]

While Dewey pursued gubernatorial backing at such political esoterica as a Greek War Relief rally and the Empire State Potato Club, he also found himself fending off efforts to extend his tenure as district attorney. Early in July, Tammany itself offered to endorse his re-election if the city's Republicans would run their own candidate for mayor against La Guardia—a tribute to Dewey's controlling stature in the party since Simpson's eclipse. Alf Landon was one of many urging that he oppose the Little Flower's bid for a third term, as one means of accomplishing a larger goal, namely bringing down La Guardia's friend in the White House, who had been able to count on his strong support in both 1936 and 1940. Dewey disagreed. To be sure, he told Landon, La Guardia had enough faults "to fill a large volume." Moreover, few men were as intimately acquainted as he with mayoral treachery. But the interests of the party and what he called "the present decent moral atmosphere" in New York outweighed personal considerations. "I would rather have one SOB in City Hall and know where he is than to have a whole lot of them scattered all over the city, with the enormous patronage of the Mayor, his Commissioners and the New York Police." By mid-September 1941, with O'Dwyer's mayoral victory a distinct possibility, Dewey wrote out a statement of his support for the embattled La Guardia, at a midnight snack of milk and cookies in the kitchen of Frank Gannett's staunchly teetotaling home.[41]

At the same time, he had some fun with Tammany, whose Businessmen's Committee for O'Dwyer had somehow placed his name on a mailing list.

"I am in receipt of two delightfully unexpected letters from you, one addressed to the old Racket Investigation Office in the Woolworth Building, and the other to the recently vacated building of the District Attorney of New York County. The first letter I thought was just a mistake which could have been corrected by any one of a number of Democratic Leaders who have unhappy reason to remember that Woolworth Building Office." Dewey thought it ironic that he, as a D.A., had been criticized in 1938 for seeking higher office, while O'Dwyer was merely answering the public's demand. Moreover, wasn't it a little ungrateful of a party which managed to retain the governorship largely because the Communists had run no candidate of their own against Lehman now to turn around and disclaim such support within the city limits?

"Blow, blow thou winter wind," Dewey quoted the Bard. "Thou art not so wicked/As man's ungratitude."

"When he is defeated," he continued, "Bill O'Dwyer will only be the mellower and the sweeter for it." He signed his letter, "Sorrowfully, but with good will," and promptly released the entire correspondence to the press.[42]

His own political dilemma was resolved with relative ease. At the end of July, Dewey once more asserted his intention to retire from office at year's end. Private practice was a must if he was to "feed the babies—and incidentally, to try to pay off the second mortgage on the farm." A deal was arranged with Tammany in which Dewey identified four of his own assistants as worthy successors, and the Hall agreed to back one, thereby avoiding a partisan fight over an office that should, he argued, be above partisan politics. Frank Hogan's name was immediately seized upon by Tammany's diminutive boss, Christy Sullivan, and Dewey was asked if he could deliver the GOP nomination. Some Republicans preferred Paul Lockwood, but Dewey was interested in winning, not sentiment. On July 24, he met with his own county leader, Tom Curran, who surely owed him this favor. A week later, Tammany made its choice official, and a pleased Dewey hailed his assistant from the Hines and Luciano cases as "the finest fellow in the world." With the succession assured, he could now retire to the sidelines and marvel at the ensuing donnybrook between La Guardia and O'Dwyer. Neither was exactly a shrinking violet when it came to invective.[43]

"This campaign is certainly a beaut," Dewey wrote his mother. "Everybody is calling everybody else names, including liar, thief, doublecrosser, cad and faker. The Democrats are fighting among themselves and La Guardia is fighting with everybody. I'm glad I'm not in the middle of it." His pleasure was reinforced by La Guardia's narrow re-election, coupled with the victory of his own "pet candidate" for Manhattan borough president, Edgar Nathan. A month later, coming off the Quaker Hill golf course at five o'clock on a wintry Sunday afternoon, Dewey was told of the Japanese attack on Pearl Harbor. "Well, it is a different world now," he sighed. Frances, fearful for the children's safety in the city, wanted to move the household immediately to Quaker Hill for the duration of fighting. Dewey was more concerned with the political dangers. Since the news from Hawaii was so "devastatingly bad," he predicted the government would never release a truthful account of the attack until after the war.[44]

For Dewey, the end of America's phony peace was also his last month in office, a time to say goodbye to men and women with whom he had worked for half a dozen years, growing up together in a crusade about to be entrusted to the workmanlike Hogan.

New offices for Dewey's private practice on the forty-fourth floor at 20 Exchange Place were rented, and Charles Breitel was invited to accompany Dewey into the new firm for a fresh crack at prosperity. It was a time for summing up. There had been disappointments, the most recent coming in a frustrated investigation of racketeering along the city's docks. With customary attention to detail, Dewey and Gurfein had hired ten city buses and placed them so as to block off the entire waterfront on the Lower East Side. Detectives were brought in from Queens. Movies were taken of kickbacks and salary extortions conducted by Frank and Carl Salvio, and showed in hopes of refreshing the memories of 200 longshoremen who had been picked up in a single swoop. The men were herded into the largest room in the Criminal Courts Building, the films projected and there followed—absolute silence. "Who the hell wants to be a dead hero, mister?" asked one relatively voluble dockworker.

But the failures were overwhelmingly outnumbered by the successes, the 94 percent conviction rate of those brought to trial, the spectacular victories over Whitney and Hines, colorful small fry like a Princeton Club treasurer caught on embezzlement charges, cop killers and ambulance chasers. More important than statistics of prosecution were the methods of modern crime fighting installed at Centre Street, the principle that a district attorney should be aggressive in pursuing lawbreakers, and imaginative in applying mercy to those, especially the young, who could and ought to be rehabilitated. There were the new bureaus—Fraud and Rackets—a new division of juvenile justice under Eunice Carter, the accountants, and a Bail Bureau that collected ten times as much money for the city as ever before, because Dewey insisted it clamp down on forfeitures. There were the "Dewey Indictments," more than a hundred in all, drawn up by the D.A. and Stanley Fuld, that replaced the old legal purple prose with simple, planed-down language comprehended by the layman and adopted almost at once throughout the state. There was a Homicide Bureau directed to undertake the

first prosecutions ever of tenement-house firetraps; by the time
Dewey finished with manslaughter cases against owners of buildings
in which New Yorkers had died, the city's law against those jerry-
built torches had teeth. In a single year, their number was cut from
13,000 to 3,500.

Before Dewey left the D.A.'s office, it had been professionalized,
at less cost than Dodge's politics as usual, in faithful adherence to
the sociological jurisprudence of Columbia, Class of '25, and with a
tip of the hat to orthodox Republicanism. "No nation was ever
made good by laws alone," Dewey said near the end of his term.
"The pretended strength of government is never a substitute for the
real strength of the individual." As for the lessons of gangbusting,
"the people have learned they need no longer tolerate the furtive alliance between the upper and underworld. In high places it has been
learned that clean government can also be good politics." In
Hogan's election, Dewey bequeathed a district attorney's operation
beyond the tentacles of machine politics. "I don't like Republican
thieves any more than Democratic ones," he repeated, and when
Wendell Willkie, then in private practice, brushed past a young deputy D.A., insistent on seeing the head man to voice a complaint
about his client's treatment, Dewey passed on instructions to look
again at the facts of the case, and only the facts. Willkie, like La
Guardia before him, discovered that the law was for Dewey his holy
of holies. His client got no relief.[45]

On December 31, 1941, the D.A. convened a final staff conference. He called each man and woman to his desk for a handshake
and inquiries about the future. With one he spent forty-five minutes
in a vain attempt to assure great things down the road if only he
changed his registration to Republican. Dewey took care of his own,
a mark of friendship and of astute politics. For these veterans of his
toughest campaigns, there would flow countless letters of introduction and recommendation, business or jobs, appointments to the
bench or a taste of public service in Albany or Washington. Now as
later, Dewey preferred the company of the Gurfeins and Gelbs to
that of legislators and state chairmen who always wanted something
from him: his time, his O.K. on a pet project, his immediate intimacy in the way vote seekers barter privacy for popular esteem. Before he dismissed the staff, the normally unsentimental chief surprised each one with a wooden reproduction of the huge bronze
doorknobs that had graced the 1893 County Courthouse, now demolished to make way for the new Criminal Courts Building. Years
later, the group would recharter itself as the Dewey Associates and

stage annual reunions where Dewey amazed the young men, no longer young, who had thought of him in godlike terms, by singing around the piano and, aided by a couple doses of Scotch, reminiscing and roaring with laughter. It was at such a nostalgic evening he told the story of three assistants—Frank Hogan, Herman Stitchman, and Manny Robbins—known for their investigative skills, who were assigned to come up with some good Irish Catholics for a heavily Jewish office.[46]

"Hogan brought me Ed Walsh, an excellent lawyer, who just happens to be a Methodist," he explained. "Robbins went out and found Jim O'Malley, the son of a judge, holder of an impressive record, and I hired him on the spot. But he happens to be a Presbyterian. Then in walks Stitchman with a fine lawyer named Herman McCarthy—and he's a Jew. And these guys are my investigators."[47]

There was never any doubt in Dewey's mind that he would seek the governorship in 1942. It was something he began working toward the morning after his loss to Lehman. To achieve it, he must navigate the shoals of his own party's left and right wings, as personified by Wendell Willkie and his own fiery isolationist congressman in Dutchess County, a six-foot three Harvard All-American football star who had recently been denounced for permitting his office to serve as headquarters for isolationist propaganda that bordered on pro-German. Hamilton Fish had been voted "the least useful member of the House" in a poll of Capitol Hill correspondents. His opposition to Roosevelt in 1940 (the President won storms of applause with ritual denunciations of Old Guarders "Martin, Barton, and Fish") made him a liability in the wake of Pearl Harbor. Still, he was entrenched at home.

Meanwhile, Willkie was trying to smoke Dewey out on the question of postwar planning and American membership in an international peacekeeping organization. Early in the year, Willkie served notice that he would support no Republican candidate out of line with Roosevelt's foreign policy. In calling for outright repeal of the Neutrality Act, he was bolder than FDR himself. Arthur Krock described him as "the follower who got ahead of his leader." In March Willkie attended the legislative correspondents' dinner in Albany, where he begged off Warren Moscow's request to speak. "Goddamn," he told Moscow, "if I do get up and make a speech, I'll have to make the speech I don't want to make."

Which speech was that? Moscow wondered.

"The one about why Dewey shouldn't be governor."[48]

When it came his turn, Willkie reeled off a list of ten names including that of Dewey's close friend Roger Straus, a virtual stranger—as eminently acceptable gubernatorial fodder. The former district attorney, sitting barely a dozen feet away, was conspicuous by his absence from Willkie's roster. "Our friend Wendell is out to do me dirt," he complained to his mother a few days later. "I am not as worried as I ought to be, probably." And why should he be, considering the overwhelming support from rank-and-file Republicans as well as the organization Jaeckle had fashioned since 1938? Straw polls in 1942 reported the same overwhelming trend throughout the state: 20 to 1 for Dewey in St. Lawrence County, 2 to 1 for Willkie's rival over the combined total of three others in the Bronx, 104 to 1 in the New York Young Republican Club.[49]

Willkie responded with a barrage of hints that he might be available himself. He advised restraint lest Republicans commit themselves too early to any one contender. He all but endorsed Representative James Wadsworth, and voiced puzzlement over Dewey's lukewarm endorsement of a resolution condemning isolationist policies that had been pushed through the Republican National Committee at its April meeting in Chicago. Avoiding a strong stand in public, Dewey had wired Russ Sprague, his personal representative on the scene, to promote passage of Willkie's resolution and to oppose the Hoosier's attempt to oust Joe Martin from the national chairmanship. Slowly, deliberately, Dewey was staking out his position. "It will be impossible to put back into their bottle," he told a Republican women's group on May 9, "the genii which have been released. National and racial aspirations, long subdued, have been awakened. The hopes of hundreds of millions of people all over the world are on the march. The victory at arms will be only the beginning."

To the New York Bond Club, no liberal hotbed, he warned against the consequences of trying to turn the clock back. Should conservatives refuse to meet "well and fully" the problems of society through the methods of free enterprise, "the stock of collectivist planners will surely be here to take over the job." Dewey anticipated the Marshall Plan by five years when he advocated the U.S. lease, lend, and give away—mostly give away—"both to our allies and our defeated enemies," food, medical aid, machinery, and other equipment "to rehabilitate their destitute peoples and rebuild their bomb-torn lands."

Not fast enough for Willkie, far too rapidly for Fish, Dewey was becoming an internationalist. His commitment remained intellectual, however, rooted in political and military reality. On May 22, Fish, facing a stiff primary challenge from within his party, phoned Dewey to warn against any intrusion into the fight, and threaten to run for governor himself should Dewey persist in attacking him and his record. Dewey replied that he could no longer support Fish. "Your office was used by our enemies," he said. To stay in the race would be "a terrible disservice" to the party. Fish protested his innocence, maintaining that his greatest usefulness was as a watchdog of Communism, a claim Dewey dismissed with a contemptuous snort. Angered, Fish told Dewey that a man of his age ought to be in the armed forces. Dewey shot back that Fish was confronting him with "about as complete a case of blackmail as I have heard." Not at all, the Congressman demurred. All he was doing, Fish repeated, was issuing a warning "not to butt into my district."[50]

The next day, Dewey publicly announced himself "unalterably opposed" to Fish's re-election. Two weeks later, he ventured into the Congressman's lair for a speaking engagement before the Republican women of Mahopac. "For the first time in my forty years and three months," he said, he found himself in disagreement with a "substantial majority" of a GOP audience. "I have never responded well to threats," Dewey continued, explaining that his opposition to Fish was more than a matter of conflicting views. "I am against him, not for his views only, but because of the misuse of his office and the associates he has had." The next day, Jim Hagerty of the New York *Times* printed a story in which he quoted Dewey without the word "only," a small but important distinction. Guests at a prespeech reception remembered hearing Dewey use the word in ruling out any compromise with Fish, but the disputed text renewed the doubts felt by Willkie and his followers over the sincerity of Dewey's internationalism.[51]

Ken Simpson's widow attacked Dewey in a series of newspaper ads. Along with Russ Davenport and a host of political, literary, and theatrical supporters, she announced the formation of a committee to draft Willkie for governor. Jaeckle responded by shifting the 1942 state convention from Buffalo's commodious 13,000-seat arena, susceptible perhaps to a repeat of the miracle of Philadelphia, to the little hall at Saratoga Springs where Dewey had been nominated in 1938. It was a step taken, according to Brooklyn boss Johnny Crews, in the name of "wartime conditions." Briefly, Willkie toyed with the idea of running. To friends, he confided his belief that the American Labor party, perhaps Roosevelt himself, would support him as the Republican nominee against the colorless Democratic State Attorney General, John J. Bennett. But the draft campaign was doomed from the start, an amateurish exercise in fingerwagging from those outside the party councils. By mid-June, Dewey could count on at least 1,000 of the 1,680 delegates who would do the nominating, and on July 1, Willkie formally disavowed any thought of running himself. Soon afterward, he sought and perceived presidential sanction to undertake a global journey, visiting and reassuring America's allies in the face of Hitler's latest advances. "We have had no trouble from my fat friend for some time," Dewey wrote Annie on July 29. "I hear he is going to Russia before the Republican Convention, so he will be where he belongs, and I hope he stays there until Christmas."[52]

Four weeks later, in an optimistic mood engendered by the split between liberal and conservative Democrats, New York Republicans watched a ten-minute movie recalling the Gangbuster's exploits. When it ended and the screen rolled back to reveal a larger-than-life portrait of the candidate, Saratoga's convention hall rocked with applause. A thousand people had to be turned away from Dewey's acceptance speech—in which he vowed to devote the next four years "exclusively" to the service of New Yorkers—after the local fire marshal declared the hall unsafe for further occupants. The four-year promise was inserted in Dewey's text only after strenuous debate between Jaeckle, who argued it was necessary to deprive the Democrats of a potential issue in the gubernatorial race, and Sprague, who considered it a boomerang that might come back to haunt them before 1944. Dewey also pledged total support to the war effort, and he dusted off his gift for sarcasm with a reference to Ed Flynn—the Bronx boss recently implicated in a petty scandal involving paving blocks for his driveway—as "that delicate flower of machine politics, that great friend of the people . . . better known for his discriminating taste in antique building blocks."[53]

Republicans had even greater cause for optimism when Jim Farley prevailed over the White House and rammed through Bennett's nomination over Buffalo Representative James Mead, a faithful follower of the New Deal. Rebellious liberals bolted the party and put up a New York City reformer and Columbia classmate of Dewey's named Dean Alfange. Alfange expected, wrongly as it turned out, "a good hunk of moral support" from the Roosevelt White House. Meanwhile, his presence in the race could only serve to divide an already fractious coalition of do-gooders and city bosses, New Deal visionaries and Tammany wardmen. Dewey tempered his great expectations with a note of caution. "Of course we cannot stay ahead," he wrote at the end of September, "without keeping in character, which means I have to wage a strong campaign."[54]

The Dewey-vs-Bennett race produced the first appearance of Herbert Brownell as Dewey's political helmsman. It also witnessed the consolidation of the candidate's authority over a once-autonomous Republican organization. The two events were not coincidental. In 1940, Brownell's participation in the Dewey-for-President cause was limited to volunteer work with delegates from his native Nebraska. A year later, he was asked by his old friend and former campaign strategist to run Edgar Nathan's race for the Manhattan borough presidency. When Nathan won out despite the odds, Dewey moved quickly to entrust his gubernatorial prospects to Brownell's organizational wizardry. Working with Jaeckle, Brownell devised a strategy to force insurgents to surrender over $300,000 left over from 1940. Henceforth, it was ruled, all funds would be collected in a single pot, to be divided on a county-by-county basis by the state chairman. This had the effect not only of consolidating the executive committee behind Dewey and Jaeckle but of instilling gratitude or fear in local bosses dependent on the central organization's largesse.[55]

The same trend toward centralization was revealed in Dewey's edict that all candidates on the GOP ticket would answer to a single manager, Brownell. Headquarters would be consolidated at the Hotel Roosevelt. There would be no repeat of Fred Bontecou's "Vote American" fiasco of 1938, not only because Dewey would not tolerate it, but because Brownell's own five terms as a state legislator from an ethnically diverse Manhattan district had made him sensitive to the need for Republicans to reach out to untraditional sources for support and success. The transplanted Cornhusker was a skilled, talented manager, someone able to keep the big picture in view while attending to myriad details. Brownell made certain that Dewey's radio broadcasts followed popular shows like *Amos 'n' Andy*. He organized hundreds of dish suppers and knitting bees on October 5—Dewey Day. Blessed with the candidate's confidence, Brownell in turn perceived and grappled with Dewey's obstreperous ways, what one reporter defined as "the untamed aggressiveness of a wounded she-bear."

"He was a tough man to herd," Brownell recalled. Dewey insisted on widespread consultation with every imaginable expert, especially pollsters, whom he had come to regard with near reverence.

After his Wisconsin primary victory in 1940, the question had arisen whether or not Dewey should enter a contest in West Virginia. Theodore Roosevelt, Jr., canvassed the state, and returned to New York with an upbeat report on the D.A.'s chances there. Dewey shook his head. "Jerry says not," a reference to Gallup's friend Lambert. Young TR continued to argue, and Dewey cut him off. "No," he reiterated, "Jerry has a poll just in, and it shows Taft running very close to me. If there is an error, he could win, but even if not, it will be the first time he has come anywhere close. We won't do it." Such decisiveness was always preceded by careful—and time consuming—calculation of the odds. Decisions were delayed, and details minutely examined. Dewey debated whether he should leave one engagement at six and be in the next town at seven, or whether his schedule should be reversed.

Even worse, from Brownell's point of view, for a politician Dewey could be astonishingly impolitic. "He'd see a local political leader who wasn't doing a very good job and he'd tell him so. Well, he should have left that to his managers to do . . . he could tell another person what to do brilliantly, but he wouldn't do it himself. He'd give me the perfect formula for handling a person, but then he'd get annoyed with something the guy said, or because he couldn't keep up with him intellectually."

Dewey's greatest obsession was his speeches. In September of 1944, Brownell would persuade former Nebraska governor Sam McKelvey at considerable expense to arrange a rodeo at Valentine, to which Republicans from all over the prairie states would come to meet and, presumably, be charmed by Franklin Roosevelt's opponent for the presidency. Dewey arrived wearing a favorite homburg, and while potential supporters dined on Western grub and yahooed themselves hoarse, the candidate stayed in a hotel suite polishing his speech. "He thought he was doing the right thing," Brownell reflected. "He was working on that speech to make it perfect, and he overlooked all the handshaking. That was for the other fellow to do." Perfectionism had its price, and Dewey paid it. Without the polishing, the speech might not have read quite as well in the next morning's paper, but, as Brownell put it, "who would have cared?"

"He didn't really like handshaking," according to Brownell. "He wasn't good at it . . . he'd climbed up the ladder the hard way. He worked harder, studied longer than anyone else. He could take a problem, break it down into component parts, assign it to talented people. He organized people. He was a real fighter. As president, he would have been boss . . . a Fala speech, that part of politics, he just could not do."

Did he enjoy life? Was he happy in politics?

Brownell mulled over the question, then answered with the candor that drew to his side many Republicans whose loyalty to his candidate was less instinctive. "I don't think he was ever happy. He got joy out of attainment. He was satisfied with many of his accomplishments. But as for happiness, in the usual sense of the word . . ." A pause, and a pronouncement: "He wasn't really geared to our political system."[56]

"I am having the delightful experience of finding a campaign headquarters which really functions," Dewey wrote his mother on September 9, 1942. The polls were universally favorable, and the split in opposition ranks showed no signs of healing. Indeed, not until October 5 did Roosevelt issue a perfunctory endorsement of Bennett, whose campaign proved lackluster in comparison with that of the smoothly functioning Republican organization, with the star quality of its nominee. The creaky Republican machinery was oiled and humming, especially upstate, where Bennett's strong support among the American Legion was thought to pose a threat. On the other hand, money was in short supply. Brownell rustled up $35,000 for radio appeals, but Dewey was forced to borrow $5,000 on his own from George Medalie.[57]

He took nothing for granted, despite the polls. He spoke twenty times in two days, fell sick and was forced to cancel a motorcade through Staten Island. He abandoned the rail progression of 1938 for the traditional upstate motor trips and handshaking tours; sometimes Frances went along. He reaped more than his share of headlines, even in competition with Guadalcanal and North Africa. In Albany, he renewed his assault on the O'Connell machine. He proposed "humanizing" the state's tax system, with new deductions for unusual medical expenses—a legacy of his own near-bankruptcy at the time of Tommy's birth—and pledged a fair reapportionment of the legislature over the opposition of rural Republicans who feared it would mean sacrificing power to regions south of Westchester County.

He went into Harlem and denounced the hypocrisy of fighting a world war against racism while tolerating it at home. He flung back Bennett's charge of inexperience, arguing that the time for change was overdue, and decrying what he called "the deep ruts of comfortable routine." The Democratic candidate accused him of being a prohibitionist, and a reporter sent out to ascertain the facts was assured by Dewey that he was dry "only behind the ears. And you can quote me on that." At other times he tapped into the frustration of voters just beginning to feel the deprivations of war, of gas shortages and rubber shortages, of OPA regulations and the threat of too little food on the table. He invited New Yorkers to take shelter from theory beneath the protective roof of common sense.

"Good government is not an abstraction," Dewey insisted over statewide radio. "It is not a disembodied spirit fluttering vaguely around the gables of the Capitol at Albany. It is made up of a team of live, active, vigorous men and women doing vital tasks with energy and intelligence."

For the most part, the campaign attracted little interest from a public worried about war casualties and the fate of the Allied cause. When Franklin Roosevelt entered a voting booth in Hyde Park a few minutes before noon on November 3, 1942, only 175 of the town's 803 voters had cast a ballot. Some were overseas, involved in the fighting. Others had moved, their lives disrupted by an economy regenerating itself through production of bombs and bullets. Still others were simply uninterested, or convinced that the final polls showing Dewey an easy winner were not worth contradicting. There were dissenters, of course. Wendell Willkie confidently forecast in private that his rival would lose the election by 500,000 votes.[58]

Willkie was spectacularly mistaken. Dewey crushed Bennett by 647,000 votes, forcing a concession from the Attorney General before eleven o'clock. Jubilant Republicans sang and strutted "We'll Heil! Heil! Right in der Führer's Face" as the numbers were posted showing a sweep of historic dimensions. Tammany Hall never even opened that night. Dewey had carried the entire GOP slate along with him. He came within 12,000 votes of taking Manhattan, where Alfange cut deeply into traditional Democratic strength, and actually did win in Staten Island and Queens. Increased Republican majorities in both houses of the legislature provided the icing on the cake.

"We are not here to share a party victory," the winner told 3,000 partisans in the Roosevelt Hotel's ballroom. After all, November 3 was a Meatless Tuesday. News of the election would share tomorrow's front page with the withdrawal of Field Marshal Erwin Rommel's forces from El Alamein. "We are all of us interested in only one victory—total, uncompromising, crushing victory over our country's enemies. . . . We all belong to one great opposition party—the party of uncompromising opposition to Hitler, his allies, and all the hateful things they stand for." The crowd cheered and chanted "Dewey for President."

Between his election and inauguration, Dewey would receive 20,000 letters, many urging him to seek the White House in 1944. On the last day of the year, he left New York for Albany, met his wife and sons at Pawling, and proceeded to a private low-key oath-taking in a ballroom bedecked with Christmas holly and poinsettias. He hadn't wanted to live in the Executive Mansion but had hoped to stay at Pawling and keep a suite of rooms at the DeWitt Clinton Hotel in Albany for use during the legislative season. He couldn't afford to live in the state's official residence, he confided to Ed Jaeckle, who promptly dismissed the idea of his governing New York from Dapplemere as impossible. As for maintaining a New York City address, Dewey said that that, too, was out of the question for financial reasons, prompting Jaeckle to suggest a compromise: the state chairman would contact the management of the Roosevelt Hotel, where wartime business was down and several floors closed, and sell the idea of the Governor of New York maintaining a suite there. Prestige and publicity would accrue to the hotel—and Dewey could still run for office as a city resident.[59]

Dewey still had Albany to contend with. There, in a hideous house in a ramshackle neighborhood of a political backwater, he stood behind the desk once used by TR and took the oath of office administered by Phillip McCook. Like his boyhood hero, Dewey was forty-two years old, widely assumed to be a president in the making. His formal inauguration, stripped down because of wartime necessities, would come a day later, before an Assembly chamber packed with happy, expectant, and open-handed Republicans. For now, the Deweys staged their own quiet celebration, before setting off to marvel at the perfect ugliness of their new address.

11
The Governor

It is our solemn duty . . . to show that government can have both a
head and a heart, that it can be both progressive and solvent, that
it can serve the people without becoming their master.
—THOMAS E. DEWEY

Have you been investigated yet?
—A POPULAR REFRAIN AROUND ALBANY, 1943

Albany in 1943 was a drowsy city of 130,000; its grimy face looking
eastward over the brackish river named for Henry Hudson, whose
Half Moon had dropped anchor there in 1609. As a capital, Albany
was both provincial and proud, a city in pentimento, whose distinguished past was varnished over with block after block of drab
brownstones and a more recent tradition of genteel thievery. A
Dutch flavor still clung to Albany, as it had since Walloons settled in
what they called Fort Orange fifteen years after Hudson's explor-
atory feint. Later, the Six Nations and their palefaced counterparts
gathered in the Stadt Huys to make peace for the Mohawk Valley.
Another assemblage, this time of American colonists, listened to
Benjamin Franklin's 1754 "Plan of Union" rejected by both colonies
and the Crown as too moderate to be practical.

Beneath the floor of St. Peter's Episcopal Church, where the new
governor was a vestryman (who in addition to his regular duties
taught the rector backgammon), lay the remains of Lord Viscount
Howe, killed by a stray bullet while trying to wrest Fort Ticon-
deroga from the French in 1758. At the Albany Academy, where
Tommy and Johnny Dewey were now enrolled, Joseph Henry had
discovered the electric dynamo, and Henry James the elder lost a leg
in an accident involving a flaming ball of tow used to heat student
balloons. The DeWitt Clinton Hotel, filled to the rafters with pat-
ronage-hungry Republicans, occupied a full city block near the site
of Fort Frederick, Burgoyne's chief objective in his 1777 campaign
to divide New England from her sister colonies in rebellion. Aaron
Burr studied for the law here. Washington Irving relaxed in a residence on North Pearl Street. Martin Van Buren dictated to the Albany Regency, and Thurlow Weed for thirty-five years edited the

influential Albany *Evening Journal.* Millard Fillmore was once greeted by flag-waving citizens at the Old Capitol, where John Quincy Adams a few years earlier defended the right of petition, and Abraham Lincoln a generation later lay in state on a black catafalque.[1]

In the last years of the nineteenth century, Irish and German settlers mixed their blood with the Dutch. The Barge Canal opened, and Albany, 145 miles north of New York City, was reconfirmed as a leading inland port. Politics became the town's main occupation, especially as America turned its way in looking for presidents. Old-timers in 1943 could still recall Grover Cleveland, 300 pounds heavy, complaining without conviction how a colored steward had forced him to devour the leftovers of a reception at the Executive Mansion. Theodore Roosevelt arrived there at the age of twenty-three, a citified dandy with glasses on a silk cord who rapidly earned the nickname Oscar Wilde and soon rose to become Minority Leader of the Assembly. There he delighted in attacking Jay Gould as the "arch thief of Wall Street" and the Gould-controlled New York *World* as "a local stock-jobbing sheet of limited circulation and versatile mendacity." TR struck many as effete and lordly. He made no secret of his disdain for Albany's twenty breweries. Yet Governor Cleveland liked the young man, whom he thought a bit "cocksure." Teddy's fifth cousin Franklin was a newly elected state senator from Dutchess County when, with his wife Eleanor, he took a three-story residence on the treacherous slope of State Street in 1911 and from the first displayed a Rooseveltian knack for gaining headlines. The fife and drum corps brought along from Hyde Park to celebrate his swearing-in all but drowned out the inaugural prayer of an elderly bishop. A few years later, Al Smith was a governor who cracked jokes with servants and vetoed bills over Irish whiskey. Smith kept in the back yard of the Executive Mansion a menagerie of tigers and bears, goats, elk, dogs, and raccoons sent him by admirers. He may well have regarded them as tamer than the Republican-dominated legislatures he was forced to deal with.

The 5,000 men and women who worked for state government gave Albany in 1943 a deceptive appearance. Away from State Street, the city remained pugnaciously blue-collar, boastful of its factories, which turned out billiard balls, checkers, carbolic acid gas, and toilet paper. It did not blush at the cultural wasteland that greeted legislators and out-of-town correspondents, for whom the capital of New York was considered hardship duty. Albany had no

opera—Frances Dewey had to content herself with listening to Tex-
aco radio broadcasts on Saturday afternoon—no legitimate theater,
an indifferent symphony orchestra, and thirteen movie houses.

Dewey was indulging in understatement when he told Ruth
Simms that his new home was "not the sprightliest of cities." It
could have been a political rather than esthetic critique. For Albany
lay under the iron rule of "Uncle Dan" O'Connell, a powerful boss
whose early experience as a tax assessor well equipped him to reward
the faithful and punish the independent. Before the O'Connells, Albany had been the private property of Republican overlord William
Barnes, whose popularity was never greater than when he was under
attack from TR or a grand jury investigation. Eventually, however,
Barnes gave way to a new master and a new party, which in 1943
controlled every seat on the City Council, and thirty-two of thirty-
nine county supervisors. Slot machines co-existed with church stee-
ples in Dan O'Connell's Albany. Bookmaking vied with political
gossip as a popular pastime. Saloons open all night sold Hedrick's
Beer, manufactured by the O'Connell family. Taxes were held down
by the simple expedient of paying current operating expenses out of
capital borrowings. Assessments were measurements of loyalty to the
dominant power, and election frauds were commonplace. Nothing
was done to change any of this, because Albany was content in its
petty corruption, because old patroon families made a handsome
living in partnership with the machine, and because the O'Connells
controlled the local district attorney, and the grand and petit juries.[2]

Dominating the city architecturally was the massive State Capitol,
set atop what nineteenth-century Albany residents called Pinkster
Hill, for the orgies of gingerbread, cider, and apple toddy staged annually by free Negroes. The building was commissioned in 1868, at a
cost of $4 million. Part French château, part Gothic cathedral, part
Pharaonic tomb, the enormous structure took thirty years to complete, and wound up costing nearly six times the original estimate.
Along the way, falling bricks caused one assemblyman to introduce
a resolution that New York State take out $25,000 life insurance pol-
icies for its legislators. A planned 320-foot central tower was
scrapped when it proved too heavy to rest on the main edifice. Instead, the roof was left a giddy riot of dormers and gables, turrets
and red tile. When finally finished in 1899, the Capitol looked like
something Commodore Vanderbilt might have constructed in his
dotage. At the State Street entrance, facing the river, was an extraordinary, seventy-seven-step staircase; another stairway inside
cost a million dollars. Throughout, rich marble and lacy arabesques

framed the vision of different architects. Tattered regiment flags
from the Civil War gave silent testimony to dim heroics. So did an
equestrian statue of Philip Sheridan, Grant's great cavalry commander and an Albany native, who stared off into eternity from the
State Street lawn.

New York's Assembly and Senate met beneath allegorical art on
the third floor, while the executive branch of government was located in the southeast corner of the building, one floor below, beside
a vast ceremonial chamber known as the Red Room, adorned with
portraits of governors gone on to the White House. The executive's
personal office was a rococo nightmare, encased in dark stained
paneling and a high gilded ceiling. Dewey took one look at all this
and blanched. One of his first projects was to make the place over
into a seat of modern government. The ceilings were lowered to
fourteen feet, air conditioning and carpeting were installed, modern
lighting was hooked up. The paneling came down. "I have just finished clearing the lumberyard off the walls," he informed Al Smith,
before having a paperweight made for the Happy Warrior "as a
continuing reminder that 13 million people have not forgotten your
loyalty to them, and that they will love and respect you as long as we
revere great qualities in other men."[3]

It was not mere pleasantry, Dewey's newfound veneration for the
great Democrat whom twenty years earlier he had been unable to
distinguish from Tammany. Dewey told reporters that Smith was
the best governor of the century, and, in the evening of his life, the
old man and his youthful successor established a warm friendship.
Dewey appointed Smith's daughter Emily to the state university
board of trustees, and invited Smith himself to visit the office he had
filled for eight illustrious years. When the old hero of the East Side,
more recently in the thrall of rich men and their politics, emerged
from Dewey's office, reporters clustered around for a reaction.

"There's only one thing wrong with that fellow in there," Smith
observed. "He's a Republican."[4]

If Dewey found the State Capitol old-fashioned, he regarded his
new residence as downright Byzantine. The Executive Mansion,
home to New York's governors since 1877, was, he decided, "the oldest and worst" house of its kind in America. The Lehmans never did
tally all its rooms (twenty-four, not counting baths, hallways, or the
basement), embellished in a red and gold scheme during the Smith
years by a decorator from Bloomingdale's. Five blocks from the Capitol, in the heart of Hermie Hoogkamp's Fifteenth Ward—an

O'Connell stronghold—the mansion had reminded Franklin Roosevelt's children of a Hollywood haunted house. Others thought of 138 Eagle Street as a mutant out of Wuthering Heights, a brick fortress with shadowy corridors as impersonal as railway terminals and a central staircase as cold as a keep. The first floor included morning, music, and breakfast rooms, the latter preferred by the Deweys to the intimidating formal dining room, which was big enough for thirty-two and was serviced with china left over from the New York pavilion of the 1915 San Francisco Exposition. There was also a frightful ladies room, mauve-colored, with walls speckled like a tollhouse cookie. The sharp-tongued Gladys Straus—already appreciated in the Dewey circle for her characterization of Roosevelt's Treasury Secretary Henry Morgenthau as "the only Jew in the world who doesn't know a thing about money"—promptly dubbed the powder room El Morocco.[5]

Running throughout the house, and overwhelming visitors to its reception hall and second-floor family quarters, were walls painted a depressing oxblood red. Paul Lockwood called them an invitation to suicide. Marge Hogan said they made a visit to the Executive Mansion like going to a funeral. There were also brocade draperies that appeared not to have been dusted since Tilden's day, a garish stained-glass window blighting the grand stairway, and a heating system so erratic that one winter the first family found themselves taking their meals in the kitchen. The house came complete with an eighteen-member staff, supervised by a tall, unflappable major domo named Whitehead. Among his functions, Whitehead told stories of other occupants and their trials, including the time Governor Charles Whitman's young son refused to speak up while making the first transatlantic phone call. A hatpin stuck into the boy's posterior finally loosened his tongue.

On the second floor, Frances found nine bedrooms, including one named for William McKinley, who had slept there before going on to Buffalo and assassination. Here, too, the prevailing theme was Victorian: McKinley's room included a black-bordered picture of the martyred president over the bed, a musty shrine to a forgotten era. None of this was likely to get much better soon. With a war raging, and no money available for refurbishing the old house, Frances found her ingenuity taxed to its limit. First, she had partitions installed at one end of the second floor, creating a comfortable three-room suite for her family, and allowing her to continue the practice of listening for nighttime sounds from her sons' open rooms. She borrowed paintings from the Albany Institute of Art to replace

mooseheads and similar trophies on the walls since TR's time. She
used chintz wallpaper and lampshades to give warmth to chilly
rooms, did over McKinley's memorial in pink and blue, rummaged
in the attic for colorful screens, and devised ways to obscure thread-
bare furnishings with slipcovers.[6]

She filled the house with flowers and music. One weekend alone,
she planted a hundred tulip bulbs in the greenhouse next to Franklin Roosevelt's swimming pool. She moved furniture constantly (a
friend found her stilling her nerves on D-Day 1944 by rearranging
sofas and rugs), and one night she and Tom worked late to mix precisely the right shade of garden green with which finally to obliter-
ate the red terror all around them. Late hours were the rule at the
mansion. Often Frances sat in silence at her husband's side until
midnight or later, knitting or sewing, planning the next day's menu,
or acknowledging personally every letter that crossed her desk, as he
worked over papers in his study. She still disliked mornings, remaining in her room on many days until three or four in the afternoon.
Even her mother, a frequent visitor, complained of Frances' inacces-
sibility. When she did come downstairs, it was to play the piano, review final arrangements for a dinner or reception, or read to her
sons. She filled hours with newspapers and magazines, scanning half
a dozen each morning and clipping whatever she thought useful to
Tom. Because of the war, entertaining was kept to a minimum, and
the Deweys didn't suffer the weekly "at-homes" that had plagued
other official families. Dutch patroons griped that the Governor and
his lady were standoffish, and that the Republican restoration was
less than socially glittering.[7]

In truth, Dewey felt a stranger in his new home. He welcomed the
company of old friends like his counsel Charles Breitel, Lillian
Rosse, Goody Goodrich, the Pat Hogans, Roger Strauses, and others
in the A-Pawling Set. For Frances, Albany was worse. For many
years, she confessed to friends, she had worried about living up to
her husband's rapidly growing celebrity. Only a conscious effort of
willpower let her come to terms with the artificialities of politics, to
memorize names and interests, to be charming when she wanted to
be someplace else. Her nervousness was most evident before a major
reception or dinner, anxiously comparing the guest list and *Who's
Who;* but by evening's end, it was universally agreed that the shy
woman from Sapulpa had succeeded in making even her most intimidated guests feel at home in the rambling splendor of Tilden's
Folly.

Still, Albany remained a trial. Frances' children were wrapped in a protective cocoon spun by state troopers and their own mother's fears of assassination or kidnapping. In the mornings, they were awakened by Marcella Pollock, a personal maid who became virtually a surrogate parent. Troopers drove the boys to and from their classes, played basketball with them in a third-floor court, and chaperoned on dates. When other Albany children were playing trick or treat, the Dewey offspring did not venture out. Neither did they go to public theaters. Instead, films were shown in the mansion, to which schoolfriends were invited. In twelve years, John Dewey did not leave the mansion grounds unaccompanied. His grandfather and uncle were kept under surveillance on their own visits, driven about by chauffeurs, and escorted to the head of a line at Radio City. Isolation was not the only price of fame. On $25,000 a year, and with two sons enrolled in a private school, the Governor suffered through his share of liver for dinner, a dish he disliked but manfully swallowed. Indeed, about the only thing he couldn't eat was muckluck, pickled seal blubber served at one of the more exotic political dinners to which presidential candidates must subject themselves. Tommy and Johnny helped out as best they could. To one guest, they thoughtfully offered a bottle of catsup, explaining that almost anything at the mansion could be eaten if you had enough catsup.[8]

Always adaptable, Dewey soon became acclimated to his surroundings. Frances did her best. Inevitably, there were scenes. John Dewey found that his asthma attacked only in the middle of the night, as he listened to raised voices in his parents' room next door. When Mater came to call, the tension could be palpable, with Frances forbidding Miss Rosse, for example, to befriend the gregarious Annie. Servants came and went; troopers complained of being verbally abused by the First Lady. The socially minded of Albany whispered their disappointment when she joined nothing more elegant than the Gray Ladies of the Red Cross. Frances refused to play the Duchess of Eagle Street. Her clothes, still simple, were not likely to start any trends. A fox collar was as dashing a thing as she allowed herself to wear. Her hair, now showing streaks of gray, was deliberately left natural, and her household seemed as comfortable as the vanilla ice cream with chocolate sauce that was her favorite dessert.[9]

She adored her husband, but discouraged hero worship in others. Sitting on the mansion's wraparound porch one afternoon, she smiled sweetly as an admirer waxed rhapsodic about the "man of destiny" to whom she was married. Tom Dewey, her visitor continued, was nothing less than "a superman," at which point the Gover-

nor emerged from inside, only to be tripped up and sent headlong
into the grass by Canute, the family's enormous Great Dane.
Frances' expression barely changed as she noted, "There goes your
superman." Another time, gazing wistfully out a window at a tableau of swirling flakes, her face wearing the gaunt optimism of a
Tennessee Williams heroine, the First Lady murmured, "How I love
it here when it snows." Surprised to hear any observation from one
who had remained all but silent during his visit, a guest pounced on
the conversational opening. Why did she love it so? he asked.

"Because it covers up Albany."[10]

The Governor of New York strides a national stage, crowded with
precedent and superlatives. Like a gigantic box-toed shoe, indented
at Lake Erie and trailing Long Island as a loose spur, New York is
the largest state east of the Mississippi, save Georgia. Within its
49,000 square miles in 1943 lived 10 percent of the American people,
responsible for one fifth of the nation's economic output. New York
was a nation-state, an international crossroads where Italians grew
potatoes and worked in the steel mills of Syracuse, Poles manned
Buffalo foundries, Czechs listened to a weekly Slavic-language radio
broadcast in Binghamton, and Swedish cabinetmakers contributed
to the wealth of Jamestown. In New York City, there were more Italians than in Rome, more Irish than in Dublin, more Jews than anywhere else in the world.

The Empire State was much more than Tin Pan Alley and the
Statue of Liberty. The new governor was reminded of this in choosing a commissioner of conservation. He took eight months and rejected dozens of applicants for the job, which, according to Lowell
Thomas, would make its holder the real power in the state north of
the New York Central Railroad. Dewey himself was one of thousands of dairy farmers who sold their milk to the Sheffield and other
cooperatives. Far from the smokestacks and slums of the world's
greatest city, upstate farmers made New York the leading producer
of ducks, cabbage, fluid milk, and onions. A third of the nation's
buckwheat was New York–grown, Long Island was the home of a
thriving poultry trade, Cattaraugus County exported much of its
maple sugar crop to neighboring Vermont. Grapes and cherries, potatoes and apples, beets and hay, all helped to feed the nation and
enrich the people of New York.

Thomas E. Dewey was the fifty-first governor of the home of
Washington Irving and Walt Whitman, of Lewis Mumford and
Abner Doubleday, of ghettos inhabited by Stephen Crane's "crea-

tures that were once men," and the manicured neighborhood units of Forest Hills. New York was the birthplace of Susan B. Anthony and the Mormon Church, of Finger Lakes said to be the imprint of an Indian Great Spirit pronouncing a benediction on his tribes, of Broadway and Frank Lloyd Wright and Richard Hunt's Ecole des Beaux Arts. It was a tapestry of rural beauty and urban squalor, of whitewashed hamlets and decaying slums, a place where Communists gathered in Union Square and luxurious apartment buildings lined Park Avenue for three miles. It gave rise to Kodak and General Electric, West Point and John D. Rockefeller; and it served to incubate most of the nation's political and social reforms. Franklin Roosevelt may have been reared on a Hyde Park estate and Al Smith in an East Side walk-up, but the two men shared a common dedication to making government strong enough to guarantee security to millions previously ignored by laissez-faire capitalism.

Workmen's compensation, a six-day week, old age pensions, agricultural and individual relief: the programs rolled up and the responsibility of government and the private sector to attend to the needs of citizens and workers reached historic highs. Some 1,167 social agencies catered to every imaginable need among New York's people. A million acres of forest and field were bought for state guardianship, by a government that bred 400 million fish to populate its rivers and streams. New York was a hothouse of dreams translated into law, of good intentions as the credo of sound administration. But there had been no change of party in twenty years, and Albany found itself putting the social welfare cart before the financial horse. Dewey took office in a state whose economic pre-eminence was under challenge, most clearly in its share of war contracts and an unemployment sickness affecting 400,000 in New York City alone.

In his first address to the legislature, the new governor pledged to step up New York's contribution to the war effort, and to revitalize the whole concept of state government in an age when federalism itself seemed a possible war casualty. "We seek security from the economic hazards of large-scale industrialization," Dewey reminded his audience. "But we cannot rely solely upon government for that security. . . . Only in a society which gives scope and opportunity to individual initiative can we expect to continue the economic progress that has made our country unique. Only in a society which provides economic freedoms can we preserve our other freedoms."

In a wide-ranging message to the lawmakers delivered a few days later, Dewey outlined an ambitious program to "humanize" the tax system, change the state's fiscal year from July 1 to April 1, investigate what he called "dry rot" in various welfare agencies, and reapportion the state legislature for the first time since 1917. The last was a particularly bitter pill for upstate Republicans, who enjoyed the benefits of a gerrymandered formula allocating one assemblyman to as few as 12,000 rural farmers, while another represented as many as 300,000 tightly wedged apartment dwellers in Queens or the Bronx. Dewey took on another GOP shibboleth, the power companies, in demanding that the state be reimbursed for water diverted for generating purposes by Niagara Mohawk. Democrats for years had been beating their opponents over the head with both reapportionment and the power issue. Dewey proposed in ninety days to rid himself of both monkeys.

It was shrewd politics, a kind of pragmatic idealism that offended orthodox Republicans and invited bewilderment from orthodox Democrats. Dewey explained it in historical context, by examining the conflict between economic security and individual freedom in the machine age. "People have looked for a new way to make the old and beloved words fit the new time," he said of slogans like "self-reliance" and "liberty." There were advocates of "all-powerful government," who saw the modern era as one in which to redefine the catchwords for sinister ends. "According to the neo-liberals, freedom in its classic sense meant only freedom to starve. They say the real meaning is freedom to receive from government all the comforts and security of life. In exchange, the individual is expected to do the bidding of government.... Not only in America, but all over the world, we see men use the world 'liberalism' to promote the very policies of government which liberals rose up to destroy."

Those who would warp the concept of traditional liberalism had a powerful word at their command. Welfare. "The centralized government people have taken it over as a latter-day Ark of the Covenant," Dewey complained. Even worse, "some very clumsy Republicans" had joined in attacking what they foolishly labeled "the welfare state," and only succeeded in strengthening the Democratic hold over popular loyalties. This was nonsensical as well as self-defeating, he maintained. "Of course they are running a welfare state," Dewey said. "There has never been a responsible government which did not have the welfare of its people at heart ... anybody who thinks that an attack on the fundamental idea of security and welfare is appealing to people generally is living in the Middle Ages." The issue, then, lay in how to achieve agreed objectives without sacrificing personal freedom. Means could be as important as ends. "Mussolini made the trains run on time and cleared the streets of beggars. But at what cost?" Powerful government at the federal level, Dewey warned, might move faster too, but only at the expense of a stifling bureaucracy and high taxes. If the national government should ever succeed in acquiring "total power in exchange for promises of total security" it would either collapse from within or be overthrown by "hardier, hairier men who are still prepared to work and achieve."

To make government an encourager of individual incentive as well as an insurer of social security, to do so within the Republican tradition of diffuse authority and fiscal restraint, to recapture the very word "liberal" for the party of Lincoln and TR—this was the challenge posed to New York's first Republican governor since Nathan Miller. It made Albany an exciting place to be in 1943, an outpost of political and intellectual ferment. The sleepy old town was suddenly transformed into midwife for a new idea struggling to be born.

One of Dewey's first actions was a sweeping review of the state government's form and function, with the object of eliminating duplication and reducing the budget by $20 million. What followed must have confirmed his worst suspicions. One office door was found to have been locked for two years, while its erstwhile occupant went on collecting a healthy stipend from the state. Another man complained loudly when his job, which occupied fully five minutes of his time per month, was abolished. After all, he said, the money he earned from public employment paid the office rent on his more lucrative sideline profession. Dewey discovered that it took twenty-nine public employees to order seventy cents' worth of glue; Form 76-A was promptly abolished. So, too, over the loud squawks of farmers, was the Milk Publicity Board, a $300,000-a-year nest of patronage jobs. The New York Transit Commission was axed, and an investigation was launched into the Labor Department's worker compensation system. Other probes looked for possible violations of state anti-monopoly laws by big oil distributors, and reviewed the economy of New York City with an eye toward postwar development.

Then, early in March 1943, a Queens Republican named Seymour Halpern, disguised as a visitor to the violent ward, slipped inside Creedmore, a 4,500-patient mental hospital located in his district and long the subject of rumors regarding living conditions and inadequate care. What Halpern found horrified him, enough to take

his story to the Governor's office. Dewey in turn invited a New York
lawyer of impeccable credentials, Archie O. Dawson, to investigate
Creedmore for himself. Within seventy-two hours, Dawson was
feeding back to Albany reports of an epidemic of amoebic dysentery
at the hospital, of nine deaths over the last three years, of open milk
cans in an employees' lavatory and mice nesting in a room beside
the kitchen. In a telegram to the Governor on March 14, Dawson
said that such offenses "should not be allowed to continue even for
another day"; and that night, Dewey instructed his commissioner of
health, Edward S. Godfrey, to go to Creedmore and take immediate
steps to improve conditions. The Commissioner of Mental Hygiene,
meanwhile, was granted immediate retirement. The superintendent
was relieved, the state-appointed Board of Visitors faulted for abandoning its duties of oversight, and the Mental Hygiene Department
criticized for running eighteen mental hospitals, six schools, and two
institutes like custodial cages. Dewey called Creedmore a "bastille of
despair" and appointed a panel of experts in the field to devise a
better approach. On June 3, he announced selection of a new mental hygiene commissioner, Dr. Frederick McCurdy, director of the
Vanderbilt Clinic and professor of hospital administration at Columbia University. McCurdy promptly went to work, removing elderly patients consigned to state hospitals merely because of their
age, cleaning up a prisonlike epilepsy hospital, and instituting a new
emphasis on curative treatment instead of warehousing.

"My job," Dewey once said, "is to get $50,000-a-year men to take
$12,00-a-year salaries." Most of those around the new governor tes-
tified to his persuasive powers. Dr. McCurdy was one. For his public
works commissioner, Dewey traced Charles H. Sells to Iran and finally nabbed him at a Miami airport en route to South America.
Sells said flatly he wouldn't take the job if it involved politics, and
Dewey, who considered public works the most important job in his
administration, assented readily. Surprised at his own success,
Dewey asked what had changed Sells's mind. "You did," the engineer answered. "You finally convinced me that this job is more important than yours!" The new commissioner of health was an assistant U.S. surgeon general. Agriculture was awarded to the president
of the State Farm Bureau. Dewey moved slowly in assembling his
cabinet. It took him almost a year to fill all the slots, and even then
he retained two Democrats from the Lehman administration. He
was having "the devil's own time," he complained to a friendly editor four months into his term, finding an insurance commissioner. "I
want a lawyer of outstanding ability, with a liberal, open mind

who does *not* know much about the insurance business," he explained. "If he knows much about insurance he has acquired that knowledge in the service of the insurance companies which he is called upon to regulate."[11]

The *Wall Street Journal* picked up on his favorite image, that of a pragmatic Team "that must run fast, hit hard, pass accurately—and never quarrel in public," and for whom the Governor was both captain and quarterback. Dewey had no patience with subordinates who disdained assignments outside departmental jurisdiction. "Who do you work for?" he would say with a sharp look; further complaints were effectively stifled. He used his elephantine memory to check waste, as when the Mental Hygiene Department decided to hire forestry experts to appraise timber on its property, only to receive a curt reminder from Dewey's second-floor office that the Conservation Department had more than enough personnel already available at no extra cost. Dewey's power of recall caused problems for Charles Breitel, who guarded against any of his fresh-faced assistants meeting the Governor for at least several weeks after their hiring. Otherwise, Breitel knew from unhappy experience, they ran the risk of saying something stupid or inaccurate, which Dewey would file away and never forget.[12]

Although impressive in the aggregate, to some Republicans the Team seemed a curiously ungrateful way of rewarding their party's long years in exile. Every state job paying $2,500 a year or more, Dewey decreed, would be filled only after a complete investigation of the applicant by state police. (Later, a Criminal Investigation Bureau, headed by William Herlands, was created for this and other purposes.) Would-be assistant attorneys general discovered that it was not enough to have contributed generously to the campaign war chest. They must also supply written answers to a wealth of questions about their religion, income, courtroom records, and local bar association endorsement. Even Dewey's own lieutenant governor was not immune to investigation—or gubernatorial ribbing. "What's the matter, Joe?" he asked Joe Hanley. "Afraid to go to jail?" Around Capitol Hill, it was said you needed a Dun and Bradstreet rating to get a job, but Dewey's caution served him well. In the course of personnel checks, he was spared a boss-recommended doctor who turned out to be a veterinarian, and a potential assistant D.A. who was conversant mostly with the laws of Sullivan County brothels. Dewey had no intention of fighting rearguard actions on behalf of dubious appointments. He had enough on his hands.[13]

His inner circle included the devoted Paul Lockwood, jack of all trades, political ambassador, confessor, and alter ego; the cabinet members, with whom he worked closely for a while before setting them loose to meet his elevated expectations; and outside advisers like George Medalie (appointed in 1945 to the State Court of Appeals), Herbert Brownell, John Foster Dulles, and Roger Straus. Ham Gaddis, a Dewey advance man from 1940 and an integral piece in the Nassau County party apparatus, became chief patronage dispenser, working alongside Jaeckle, Sprague, and the county leaders, who consolidated organization support through a generous helping of gravy.

Closest of all were the Three B's—Breitel, Burton, and Bell. Charles Breitel was virtually an assistant governor. Thirty-four years old, he was Dewey's liaison with state agencies that were used to bringing their bickering to the second floor for a decision. Breitel was also a careful critic of every important legislative proposal filed on the floor of the Assembly and Senate.

John Burton was a year older than Breitel, an Ohio native, professional researcher, and co-author of the book *Valuation of Vacant Land in Suburban Areas*. Burton combined with his skills at burrowing for facts the crisp instincts of a budget maker and the finesse of a born politician. It was his job to reform the way New York collected and spent its revenues and to devise the first functional organizational chart of state government. When Burton came to Albany, he informed Dewey that there were virtually no Civil Service employees in the budget division. By the time he left, that was corrected. In line with Dewey's desire to professionalize the financial heart of government, no Democratic holdovers were fired. But other changes were made aplenty. A research unit was created to improve income forecasting and give the Governor greater leverage over spending. The budget division took out membership on numerous committees and commissions. Management specialists were hired for the first time, and the fiscal year was advanced to save the state hundreds of thousands in anticipatory borrowing and allow for quarterly payment of individual income taxes. Tax forms were simplified, and new deductions granted for emergency medical expenses such as childbirth, for life insurance premiums, and for college-age children. In 1944, a 25 percent business tax cut was announced, along with individual reductions on a similar scale.

All this happened because the war made it impossible for the state to undertake major capital expenditures. Soon a surplus began accumulating. Local legislators cried out for further tax reductions or, even better, for allocating the windfall to a variety of pet projects.

Dewey refused. Instead, he moved to lock up the surplus—which eventually reached $623 million—in a Postwar Reconstruction Fund, naming Burton to chair a committee that devised its own agenda of 3,000 road, public building, sewer, and water projects. The state offered to pay half the cost of any local community's postwar planning, and looked for ways to stimulate the peacetime economy. Its favorite device was tax cutting. Indeed, when Dewey left office in 1955, New York State tax rates were 10 percent lower than in 1942, although inflation had vastly increased the revenue collections.

The most important of the three B's was Elliott Bell, forty years old in 1943, Dewey's best friend in Albany, who also owned a place of his own not far from Dapplemere Farm. Bell was one of the bright young men lured from private industry—in his case, the editorial board of the New York *Times*. On paper, his assignment was to supervise 1,308 banking institutions. There were muffled roars of outrage when the new superintendent insisted on bringing state savings banks into the FDIC system, but Dewey backed Bell, and the change was made. Bell, in return, became the closest thing to a Harry Hopkins in this administration of Teamwork. His influence ranged across the landscape of state government and spilled over into national politics.

It was Bell who shaped Dewey's economic thinking, even more than Dulles influenced his attitude on foreign affairs. An Adam Smith disciple, Bell argued against such innovations as "incentive taxation," and preached successfully the combination of budget and tax cuts to stimulate investment and spur the state's lagging economy. Bell's premier status was unmistakable in the advisory group that came to be known as the swimming hole cabinet for their frequent meetings around the pool, where Dewey liked to relax with his sons.

It was at such conferences that Dewey prodded, poked, and sometimes bullied the men around him, thoroughly ventilating every issue and tearing to shreds speech drafts already rewritten half a dozen times. Critics were invited to try their own hand with troublesome passages or excoriated mercilessly if they lacked facts with which to support their criticism. At the same time, the swimming-hole set didn't hesitate to fault a speech they thought imperfect. After Dewey read back to them a passage that had been especially troublesome, he asked for their counsel. A brief silence ensued, broken by a unanimous chorus: "It's lousy."

The Governor sank a little lower in his chair and growled, "At least I'm not surrounded by yes-men."

The year 1943 was the year of Stalingrad and a new alliance with Soviet Russia, of Patton's invasion of Sicily and a bloody campaign to liberate Rome. It was the year when Admiral Doenitz's U-boats were finally mastered in the Battle of the Atlantic, when Roosevelt, Churchill, and Stalin decided at Teheran on a policy of unconditional surrender, and the people of the United States lived by the ration book. For Dewey, the war limited new initiatives but encouraged him to test his theory of strong state government as a balance to Washington. His inaugural itself had reflected wartime austerity: no ball, no parade, no nineteen-gun salute. Almost immediately, he was plunged into questions of military production and civilian privation. In his first week in office, he signed an emergency amendment allowing a Texas refinery turning out daily 336,000 gallons of aviation fuel to draw on the repair facilities of a state-owned machine shop in Syracuse.

Another immediate problem was food and grain, reaching critical levels in parts because of a cumbersome federal system that allocated responsibility for growing and distribution to a half-dozen feuding agencies. The War Production Board, for example, had seen fit to allot exactly one manure spreader to the 2,100 farms of Albany County. Everywhere it was the same. Bostonians mobbed stores for fresh vegetables. Meat was scarcely to be found in Baltimore or Birmingham. Memphis was out of poultry, and a black market in potatoes had sent the price of that hoarded commodity far beyond its official ceiling price in Pittsburgh. The Office of Price Administration tried to combat the spreading panic with a point system—half a pound of butter equaled half a pound of sirloin steak—but the shortages persisted. (Leon Henderson, OPA administrator, did not.) Even worse, northeastern dairy farmers found themselves husbanding feed and grain supplies that at one point diminished to four days' worth.

Against this backdrop, Dewey announced formation of the Emergency Food Council, to be chaired by H. E. Babcock, the state's leading farm expert and head of Cornell's School of Agriculture. Each council member was assigned a different facet of the problem—such as labor, transportation, machinery—and handed responsibility to act for the State of New York. A scout found 10,000 tons of oyster shells in Norfolk, Virginia, to be ground up and fed to egg-laying hens as protection against too-soft shells. The state went into the Canadian market for 26 million bushels of barley, then taught chickens to eat the unfamiliar feed. Five tons of twine were begged from Washington to bind the Long Island vegetable crop. Some 1,300 sawmills were canvassed to find those not manufacturing ammunition containers, and they were then asked to make apple boxes instead. A law was passed permitting classes for schoolchildren on Saturdays, freeing up to 30,000 schoolboys to work as farmer cadets and in the victory gardens that blossomed across the state. The Dewey boys were two who sold their vegetables at OPA prices to their mother. Frances herself introduced a soybean luncheon at the Executive Mansion, and after learning of a nursing shortage in an Albany hospital, she volunteered to work for several months without fanfare.

The Emergency Food Council designed a monitoring system to rush tractors and trucks wherever they were most needed, and state colleges offered short training courses in farming. On his own, Dewey used the 1943 Lincoln Day Republican Dinner as an occasion to appeal to the patriotic instincts of New Yorkers in the campaign to grow more food. Within twenty-four hours, Chinatown alone tendered 3,000 volunteers in answer to his call. Five hundred factory workers in Broome County harvested hay on weekends. College girls picked apples. State workers were encouraged to work extra hours, and in return Dewey raised the wages of the lowest-paid among them by a third. Labor unions agreed to forgo some of their privileges in exchange for overtime. New York established the best record in the nation of time lost to strikes, in part because the Governor doubled mediation funds, established a State School of Labor and Industrial Relations at Cornell University, added 400,000 workers to the ranks of those covered by minimum wage laws, and pushed ahead with his highly publicized investigation of corrupt doctors and lawyers who bilked the workmen's compensation system out of millions.

In all, New York State enrolled 111,000 volunteers in its food production efforts during the summer of 1943. Even more worked the fields and orchards the next year. Other problems included gasoline shortages—the Deweys set an example of conservation by discarding the ancient Albany tradition of sending a chauffeur to acknowledge calling cards left at the mansion—and human roadblocks athwart the war production effort. A house-to-house survey was made of working mothers, before the state designed a $15 million program of child care, to be funded in equal parts by the state, localities, and the mothers. An oil shortage was eased somewhat by dredging the old Barge Canal. A new Department of Commerce was created, to aggressively assist businesses in bolstering their share of war contracts from twenty-eighth among the forty-eight states to second place. Clinics were held throughout New York for small businessmen on the fine points of applying for contracts. A census of every shop and every forge from the St. Lawrence River to Staten Island was undertaken. For the first time, a state opened its own office in Washington, what Dewey called his "ligation," to lobby for federal largesse and guide New York entrepreneurs through the maze of wartime regulation that stood between them and prosperity. When the war ended, New York had a leg up on the other states; its postwar planning was so far advanced that all but ten of its 113 federally built war plants simply converted to peacetime uses.

While he coped with the emergency, Dewey saw his legislative program move smoothly through the Republican Assembly and Senate. He had called for a new budget year, new tax deductions, quarterly payments, spending cuts, and elimination of departmental fifth wheels. Within three weeks, he had them all. He headed off a Democratic attempt to put the state in the power business, by declaring the right of the people to hold in perpetuity their natural resources, and by compelling Niagara Mohawk to pay for the 15,000 cubic feet of water it siphoned off each second to turn its dynamos and pad its profits. Here a complication arose and, with it, a reply that went to the heart of Dewey's first year in office. During the campaign, the Republican candidate had promised to exact a fair price for the water, leaving the impression that he might well move to amend the state constitution to achieve his end.

Now, however, before his first month in office was over, Charles Breitel informed Dewey that the statute in question, an old legislative grant that read like a legal deed, could be amended only at the risk of violating the U.S. Constitution's due process clause. When Dewey seemed unconcerned, Breitel reminded him of his campaign promise. To settle now for a new statute instead of a constitutional amendment would look bad politically, perhaps confirm every lurking suspicion about the party's old allegiance to Niagara Mohawk and the new governor's willingness to sever the special relationship.

"What would a lawyer do?" Dewey asked his counsel. Breitel replied that a lawyer would pass a statute. "Well then," Dewey told him, "that's what we do." The counsel again protested; the Team was likely to be severely criticized. This time, Dewey cut him off. "We do what a lawyer would do."[14]

• • •

When Dewey spoke his mind, the result could be refreshing. At a meeting of state governors in Columbus, Ohio, in June 1943, New York's chief executive came down hard on the food crisis in his state, going so far as to suggest that Midwestern farmers should reduce their pig population in order that Northeastern dairymen might use the corn saved for their herds. The only alternative, he added, would be to turn to Canada for imports. Governor Shriker of Indiana jokingly asked if Dewey really proposed slaughtering pigs so that New York cows could eat their corn. That's exactly what he was proposing, Dewey told Shriker, but if it was any consolation, at least he wasn't following the way of the New Deal and demanding that the pigs be "plowed under."

Pig farmers rose up in righteous anger. "I represent thirteen and a half million people who are getting hungry," Dewey told one letter writer, people whose hunger would grow much worse "if we do not get grain into this state soon." As for the rumors circulating in the wake of his remarks, Dewey sought to reassure the anxious. "Honestly, I am not pressuring anybody to eat hay. I don't eat hay myself, and I can't ask anyone else to eat it." He also assuaged an angry WCTU: "My concern and worry was to get milk for New York's children, not liquor."[15]

I. F. Stone came to Albany to profile the potential president and pronounced himself bored. Dewey was not, Stone concluded, "a regular guy." His speaking style was "too perfect to be pleasant." In his habits, as in his politics, Dewey was economical. He ate the same lunch every day—a chicken sandwich, an apple, and milk. His phobia about germs was unrelenting. When a chauffeur sought escape from gubernatorial duty, the man hit upon the simple, foolproof idea of coughing miserably, unceasingly, until Dewey asked Paul Lockwood if the man had tuberculosis and ordered him transferred. The same driver was instructed in the Dewey system for newspaper reading. Whenever the Governor climbed out of his car, there remained behind three precise little piles of newsprint. The one on the right of the seat was already read but was to be saved for future reference. The one on the left was unread and also to be preserved. On the floor, a third pile of paper represented news given the once-over and chucked.[16]

On a typical Christmas Day, it took the Deweys several hours to complete what John called "the stately progress" of unwrapping their presents. This was because the master of the household, with characteristic deliberation, insisted that each gift be opened individ-

ually, displayed to the assembled kin, sampled or put through its
paces, analyzed and commented upon before the next ribbon could
be torn off the next package. Here, in the bosom of his family,
Dewey was not staging a performance, merely being himself. Others
were at a loss to understand his methodical ways. Reporters accustomed to drinking gin from open bottles at Lehman's annual reception now found themselves being served off silver platters. Former
associates from the D.A.'s office, called to Albany for clemency
hearings, were astonished at the little parade that brought Dewey,
Charles Breitel, and assistant counsel Lawrence Walsh into the Red
Room, where the Governor, without the slightest sign of personal
recognition, stared down at the papers on his desk and conducted
the hearing in a brisk, businesslike way. When it was over, Dewey
rose and, looking neither to his right nor left, exited the chamber as
he had entered, trailed once more by the silent, obedient retinue.
They reminded one attorney of tin soldiers all in a row.[17]

Much of this could be put down to a newcomer's insecurity.
Dewey was, after all, for the first time learning to grapple with other
powerful men instead of merely giving orders to hero-worshipping
young lawyers. He had few friends and almost no intimates in Albany, and relished most of all the days he could escape to Quaker
Hill, where good management involved his dairy herd instead of legislative committees.

Dewey elevated his lack of public heartiness to the level of principle. A friend discovered him at his desk, in suspenders and shirt
sleeves, glasses perched low on his nose as visitors bustled in and out,
and gingerly suggested that perhaps the Governor would do well to
appear the same way outside his office.

"There's a dignity that comes with this job," Dewey admonished
the counselor. "If you lose that, then the office isn't worth having."[18]

Dewey had come charging into Albany sniffing corruption among
the cobwebs. The state's pioneering effort in safeguarding the rights
of the worker was in tatters as fee-gouging lawyers ganged up with
unscrupulous medical men to split kickbacks and deprive injured
employees of their just due. The Department of Labor, organized
medicine, the bar, even Tammany Hall, which held sway over some
of the commissioners charged with enforcing the law—all were exposed in a series of public hearings filled with exchanges like the following, between a Dewey-appointed investigator and a state claims
referee whose job it was to determine the validity of individual
claims.

Q: How long have you been hard of hearing?
A: How long have I been what?
Q: (shouted into witness's ear): How long have you been hard of hearing?
A: What?
Q: How long have you been hard of hearing?
A: How long have I been what? I don't hear.

The director of the Division of Workmen's Compensation, called to explain the presence of a deaf referee on the payroll, advanced a novel theory. "I am not sure," he said, "but what a physical handicap of that sort keeps his record from becoming too cluttered with nonessentials." The panel went on to uncover patterns of influence buying, almost total inaction by the State Industrial Council, and mandated physical examinations being conducted variously in venereal disease clinics, police department fingerprinting rooms, a jailhouse bathroom, and the Wellesville City Engineer's office. At least $5 million a year, it concluded, was being withheld from the pockets of injured workingmen. Dewey quickly accepted recommendations that benefits be raised and a new, less political workmen's compensation board be created. Long delays in locating files would become a thing of the past. Other administrative reforms would eliminate the "antiquated and inadequate" methods Dewey found clotting the unemployment insurance system.

"If more than one agency handles a problem," the new governor said to Elliott Bell, "that is an injury to the solution of the problem, as well as a waste of public funds." In the crucible of administration, Dewey refined his pragmatism into a system of logical values. "Every government degenerates when trusted to the rulers of the people alone," Dewey told a 1944 Lincoln Day Dinner crowd. The Great Emancipator had faced the crisis of secession from Washington; modern Republicans confronted the urge to abdicate to federal authority. Government must plan, not only the things it would do, but equally important, what it would refrain from doing. Most of all, Dewey decried those who would look for "magic formulas" to solve America's problems.[19]

Washington would retain its appeal for Americans as their only reliable protector against the economic insecurity branded on the national psyche by the Depression. This Dewey understood, and never ceased to regret. It was, he noted, an appeal based on fear. "Life is more than unemployment, sickness, and old age. Life is alive and vital, to be lived and enjoyed. A morbid government that insists only on acquiring power to spend more and more money from more and more taxes for the negative aspects of life, will end up as all history shows, with no money, no taxes, and no security for its people. Government," he went on, "has nothing it does not take away from the people. It is an illusion that it alone can deliver security and leisure," which could only result from "a vigorous and productive economic system" charged, in turn, with promoting equal opportunity and "a sharing of the good things of life." Here was the heart of the liberal Republican dogma, what Murray Kempton has called "the religion of property holders."[20]

If the Republican ship of state was to sail serene waters, Dewey realized it must first be shorn of the barnacles clinging to its hull from the long years of political isolation. In New York this meant passing his water power bill, which the Senate did unanimously on February 15. It would entail reapportionment of a Republican legislature as required by the state constitution every ten years but neglected for twenty-five. By the first week of March, with adjournment fast approaching and nothing as yet done, Dewey stepped up the pressure. Legislative whips were called to the Executive Mansion for a frank discussion. Ed Jaeckle, who lived at the Ten Eyck Hotel throughout the legislative session and who was a familiar gubernatorial emissary on the floor of the Assembly and Senate, informed county leaders that reapportionment was must legislation. Assemblyman William Stuart of Steuben County rose in response to denounce the plan as "party suicide" and call for a rump caucus to challenge the Governor. One of Stuart's colleagues claimed that unnamed men around Dewey had asked him if his county had already received all the appointments it desired. Important jobs were left unfilled pending the crucial vote, as a cherished Republican icon— legislative supremacy over the executive—fell by the wayside of personal ego and political necessity.

On March 16, Dewey issued an emergency message, which by law took precedence over any other business. In it, he attempted to cast the issue in stark moral terms. Failure to pass his plan, he now argued, would violate each legislator's oath to uphold the state constitution. Far worse, it would be a travesty on young men "fighting and dying in every part of the world for free representative government." Within a week, the combination of an aroused public and a determined executive carried the day, although twenty-four of the Assembly's eighty-eight Republicans stood up against their presumed leader. As for Dewey, he considered the vote "a great political triumph for the people. . . . Of course it created a good deal of ill-feeling but I hope it will evaporate."[21]

It did not evaporate. Given the Governor's methods and personality, it could not. By training and instinct, Dewey was an administrator, accustomed to finding the best possible men and exacting absolute loyalty in return for considerable latitude in the performance of official duties. That was how the Team functioned. The legislature, however, was not a team, not a stellar gathering of keen minds and disinterested opinion, but a slightly shabby peerage of job-hungry provincials, given to gabbling and squabbles, respectful of no authority but local political machines. The Governor acted like Oliver Cromwell wearily dismissing the Long Parliament. When his first legislature went home, leaving behind more than a thousand bills to sign or veto during the constitutionally prescribed thirty-day period that followed, Dewey bemoaned having to read and judge far too many poorly drawn or worthless ones, "but I guess that is part of the job and I cannot expect the legislature to accept responsibility either for draftsmanship or for failing to kill off some of these extremely bad, but sometimes popular, proposals.[22]

Dewey figured his veto rate at 1 for every 3.6 bills passed. Among the legislation he rejected were bills to license bingo games (in violation of the state constitution) and a "hopelessly confusing" statute forbidding the consumption of horse meat. As a result of his ordeal, he came up with a new approach. Henceforth, he would kill legislative vermin before they had a chance to swarm over his desk. Beginning in the fall, months before the new legislative session was to begin, Breitel was told to anticipate the most pressing problems likely to confront the state and its localities in the immediate and long-range future. A master list was compiled for review by Elliott Bell and others acquainted with financial realities. Then the legislative leaders themselves were called in for consultation. Every Sunday evening, once the session was actually under way, Dewey, key members of the Team, and the five ranking Republicans in the legislature gathered at the mansion for dinner and drinks. Afterward, the Governor led the little group into his study, where he plumped down in an easy chair, lit a cigarette in a short holder, and spread a pile of three-by-five-inch cards on his lap. All week he had kept careful notes whenever a new problem arose. Now he turned to the men around him, and for the balance of the evening New York's government was a true partnership.

"Well," he began, "what do you want to talk about tonight?"[23]

In the verbal free-for-all that ensued, the Governor's men shot off an enfilade of questions, friendly or critical. "No man was ever overruled more often by his own advisers," Dewey rued, in tribute to the collegial spirit of his Sunday night war councils. Nothing came out of these meetings unless agreed upon unanimously, and nothing so agreed upon failed of eventual enactment. In large part, this was due to the power granted legislative leaders to bottle up or promote controversial bills inside an omnipotent rules committee (whose presiding officer was also Speaker of the Assembly). Before 1943, with opposing parties splitting the executive and legislative functions, the system led to compromise and negotiation on a grand scale. Now it narrowed the legislative process to a handful of men and made the Governor himself the real power in passing or killing bills. Feeling his oats, Dewey even invented the so-called "pre-veto." Another child of the Sunday night bull sessions, it ordered in advance that proposals not to his liking be sidetracked without so much as a public hearing, let alone the indignity of a vote on the floor. Only later, after being assured of his control over both houses, did Dewey relent and permit bills he was certain would be defeated come up for open debate.

Inevitably, there were displays of rebellion from the proud, suffocated legislature. In March of 1944, Dewey would embrace a proposal to strip authority over New York's school system from a nine-member supervisors' board—subject to domination by the teachers' lobby that in private he likened to Hitler's stormtroopers—and place it instead in a single professional superintendent. The bill was bitterly opposed by education lobbyists, already smarting from the Governor's refusal to restore cuts in state aid to education imposed as part of the general wartime economies. Buttonholing legislators and reminding them of their power at the polls, the teachers were confident of victory. Then Dewey counterattacked. March 20 was the last day of that year's session, a mindless marathon in which 183 bills were adopted in the Assembly during a twenty-hour stretch, and Speaker Heck broke two gavels in trying to secure order. All day, Dewey summoned legislators to his office to exert his persuasive powers on behalf of his own proposal. Ed Jaeckle played mailed fist to Dewey's velvet glove, threatening to go to the local leaders if obedience was not prompt. Still, the teachers expected to win as the clock ground on, past midnight and into the predawn hours. If nothing else, cowardly assemblymen could always desert the chamber when the critical roll was called, thus aiding the teachers' cause without actually voting against the Governor.

Dewey would have none of it. A few minutes before five o'clock, his ally in the Speaker's chair, Oswald Heck, ordered the sergeant at arms to round up any missing legislators. Then the doors were closed and the vote taken. One assemblyman from Buffalo was discovered hiding beneath his desk. When his turn came, the man crawled to his feet, held two fingers over his nose, and let out a high-pitched aye. Dewey won, 77 to 61. Over in the Senate, Democratic leader John J. Dunnigan lost his temper, jabbing at the majority as "mannikins" leashed firmly to the Governor's standard. "Who runs this legislature anyway," Dunnigan shouted as he stalked about the roiling mass of angry, exhausted lawmakers, "us or the Governor?" It surprised no one when Dewey was heard soon afterward to refer to Dunnigan's colleagues in both houses as "my legislature."

Almost as contentious as Dewey's relationship with the legislators was his courtship of the fourth estate. The leftish daily *P.M.* habitually referred to him as "the Little Brain at Albany." This could be charged to political differences. But it was on the personal level that the new executive had the most to learn about journalists, who tend toward slang and irreverence, seizing on a personal foible the moment its entertainment possibilities are uncovered. Dewey, for instance, was extremely sensitive about his height.

It was a reporter who took one look at the Governor's Great Dane Canute and asked if he rode it to work. "Someday I am going to catch the guy who said I wore elevator shoes in a dark alley," he warned friendly columnist Westbrook Pegler, "and I am going to give him a personal demonstration of my opinion of willful falsehoods." Even allies in the press found themselves upbraided for suggesting overattention to politics. To Pegler, Dewey complained of "being loused up" after following the "ancient, honorable, and not unpleasant practice" of reviewing New York City's ethnic celebrations on St. Patrick's Day, Pulaski Day, and Columbus Day. He enjoyed himself at these festivals of Old World diversity, he told Pegler. Why should anyone fault him for that?[24]

Before he had taken the oath of office, Dewey was angered by reports that he was planning a vacation at Sea Island, Georgia. Reporters were called in, directed to a stack of impressive-looking volumes, and assured that the Governor-elect would devour the entire pile "on my so-called vacation." One newspaperman looked closer, only to discover that half the budget supposedly going to Georgia was missing. The rest of the totem was equally suspect. To forestall future such embarrassments, Dewey reached into the heart of the enemy camp, inviting the respected, soft-spoken political writer of the New York *Times,* James Hagerty, to become his press secretary. Hagerty, more amazed by the offer than anyone else, told Dewey he expected to continue his friendships with men not necessarily friendly to his employer. Dewey made no objection, and on January 15, 1943, after two weeks of deliberation, Hagerty took the job.[25]

Almost immediately, a thaw came to the second floor. Reporters found speeches and press releases available hours in advance of a scheduled event. Dewey himself proved accessible, holding press conferences twice a day during the early stages of his administration, and appearing in the Legislative Correspondents Association room while his own quarters underwent renovation, the first governor in memory to do so. He struck up warm friendships with several journalists, including Leo Egan of the *Times,* the AP's Kurtland King, and Leo O'Brien of UP. Background information flowed freely, as long as it remained, in Dewey's phrase, "within the room."

On July 17, 1943, Dewey's lieutenant governor, Thomas W. Wallace, died after less than six months in office, and after prolonged wrangling in the courts it was decided that a new election would be required to fill the vacancy. For Dewey, it was an important test, not only as a referendum on his first year in office, but also of his relative freedom to maneuver outside the state as a prospective presidential candidate. Privately as well as in public, he played a reluctant tune throughout the spring and summer of 1943. He canceled a planned national broadcast of his Lincoln Day food speech, so he wrote his mother, because such an appearance might cause "inferences which were not warranted." In July, he asked John Foster Dulles not to go ahead with a reprint of the 1940 speeches that formed *The Case Against the New Deal.* While expressing pleasure that others had come around to his viewpoint since, Dewey warned his foreign affairs adviser that "nothing in the world would explain to the cynics that I was doing it only in the interest of the country."[26]

Still, the Governor was a man who liked to hedge his bets. Lieutenant Governor Wallace had won the previous year by only 30,000 votes. Should the upstate vote fail to match that of heavily Democratic New York City in turnout, even that margin would be impossible to repeat. To surrender second spot on the Team to an outsider or, worse, a Democrat, posed incalculable dangers to Dewey's entire concept of governing. Once again, Ed Jaeckle stepped in to help. On August 24, he secured a unanimous endorsement by the GOP state committee of Joe Hanley, the sixty-seven-year-old State Senate president. Hanley was Iowa-born, a 32nd-degree Mason, commander in chief of the National Spanish-American War Veterans, for thirteen years a regular on the Chautauqua circuit. Unlikely to be confused with Winston Churchill as a statesman, he was nevertheless an appealing choice upstate, popular within party circles, and a reliable ally in persuading his friends in the legislature to Dewey's support. Hanley might not be exciting—neither was his Democratic rival, General William Haskell—but he was no prima donna.

Dewey worried about winning the special election. When he worried, extraordinary precautions had a way of following. On registration day, every Republican state worker who could possibly be spared was sent into the field. In rural areas, where Democrats had wisely all but abandoned local races to discourage voting, Dewey's organization designated the most important farmer as Republican captain, charged with responsibility for getting out the maximum vote. His incentive—friendly relations with the Department of Agriculture—was as evident as his personal influence in the semi-feudal atmosphere of upstate New York. In an appeal to minority voters, Dewey appointed Frank Rivers, his black assistant district attorney from the Centre Street days, as a New York City judge. At $17,500, Rivers became the highest-paid black officeholder in the nation. Even the left-wing American Labor party was forced to go along with the choice, endorsing Rivers for a full term in November lest it be accused of racial bias.

In other appointments throughout the state, Dewey was capitalizing his party for a generation of dominance. It may have been true that only nonpolitical professionals of the highest caliber were considered for Dewey's cabinet. It was also true that more traditional standards were applied to build up a Republican organization where one was weak or nonexistent. A new state judicial district was created in populous Nassau County, giving Russ Sprague two supreme court judgeships and $100,000 worth of patronage jobs to dangle before the faithful. Tom Curran, successor to Ken Simpson as party boss in Manhattan, became secretary of state. The chairmen of Wyoming and Montgomery counties became his deputies. The head of St. Lawrence County's organization was named director of the state fair division of the Agriculture Department. The weak Albany machinery was liberally greased, with jobs for its chairman, vice chairman, secretary, and ward leaders. The GOP boss of Utica County became commissioner of motor vehicles, and Rochester's Tom Broderick, once hostile but now amenable to Dewey's control, was appointed a municipal finance commissioner.

Rolly Marvin, more adamant in his opposition, was less fortunate. In the spring of 1944, with Dewey's presidential availability rising daily, and Marvin still pledging loyalty to Willkie, Jaeckle began scheming to replace him on the executive committee with a friendlier Republican. Publicly, Dewey kept hands off the quarrel. Privately, he allowed the impression to surface in Syracuse that the city might suffer as a result of Marvin's obstinacy. Practical-minded organization men began pressuring Marvin to quit; Dewey's insurance commissioner, Robert Dineen, was the new power to deal with in Syracuse, they argued. To those who wrote protesting such moves, Paul Lockwood sent an indignant reply. "For your information," it read, "the Governor never interferes in a local matter, either in the selection of a chairman or vice-chairman. The Governor believes in the free electoral process." Insinuations to the contrary, Lockwood continued, were both "shocking" and "astounding."

On April 4, 1944, Dewey upset Willkie in the Wisconsin primary. Two weeks later, the anti-Marvin forces went public. Insisting the feud was entirely local in origin, the group did not conceal their fear that Marvin's mulish attitude toward the first Republican governor in twenty years might prolong a "starvation diet" of state jobs. Marvin publicly recanted his support for Willkie, promised to toe the line and carry out Dewey's wishes in Onondaga County. For a while, he stayed on as county chairman. But his days as a real power were ended. The professional politician had been upended by the citizen crusader. In having Dewey for an enemy, he was by no means alone.

One day after Joe Hanley's selection to run for lieutenant governor, Dewey sent off a more resounding charge. Through his state tax commissioner, Rollin Browne, he revealed the first move in a long-awaited investigation of Albany County and the O'Connell machine. Browne was assigned to look into assessing practices in the capital, a feint leading up to the main assault, the appointment early in October of J. Edward Lumbard to examine election frauds surrounding voter registration. Ostensibly, the probe was to be statewide in scope, but no one politically astute could miss its immediate target, especially when Lumbard came back to the Governor within a week with preliminary findings pointing to "widespread and flagrant" abuses throughout the city. These included enrollment booths hidden behind fire trucks, supervisors instructing voters how—and in which party—to register, and a host of registrars who peered over shoulders as the voters pondered their choice. In Albany, this was chicken feed, as much a part of daily life as winter snow and the nocturnal pleasures in the Gut, the city's bawdy red-light district.

Dewey released Lumbard's findings on October 13, 1943. That same day, the O'Connells brought up heavy artillery of their own.

District Attorney John T. Delaney served subpoenas on, among others, the state comptroller, seeking legislative expense accounts to verify long-rumored payroll padding by Republicans for whom the legislature remained, until 1943, the only game in town. Then too, there were stories drifting around Capitol Hill of all sorts of perks—known officially as "in lieu of" expenses and popularly by the name given them in a moment of genius by Al Smith, lu-lus—that substantially raised the annual legislative emolument of $2,500. Suddenly, it was Republicans who were put on the defensive. But Delaney hadn't reckoned on his opponent's tactical gifts. On October 19, Dewey's attorney general, Nathaniel Goldstein, successfully argued for a show-cause order against Delaney's subpoenas. The O'Connells took out full-page newspaper ads alleging "terrorism" in the city, but their claims rang hollow when the A.G. pointed out the composition of Delaney's grand jury. Twelve of its members were found to be district political leaders, committeemen, or precinct workers. Three others were contractors doing business with the city.

The mayor of Albany, Erastus Corning, was called to testify on the matter of $1,600,000 of public funds said to be missing. Corning labeled this a "temporary diversion" and loudly objected to use of the word "shortage" to describe the use of bond-issue monies for regular operating expenses. Before the shock waves of his testimony could die down, Dewey staged a raid on the city's election bureau, seizing records for a broader inquiry into graft and corruption throughout the county. He moved a step further, forcing his own legislative leaders to invite him to launch still a third probe, this time into the alleged payroll and other abuses by legislators themselves. By now, Dewey had investigations under way into the Labor Department, the state's mental health care system, the state police, and the municipal government in the capital city. The elderly, esteemed New York lawyer Hiram C. Todd assumed leadership of the legislative probe, while a former assistant district attorney named George Monaghan took on the fast-expanding inquiry into Albany County. Delaney was forced to resign, discredited, and Monaghan ultimately secured fifty indictments, mostly for minor offenses. Todd won still less: two indictments, both of them leading to acquittals. But while they continued, Dewey's latest efforts at ferreting out crooks from the public payroll produced a sensation. One state worker even charged that investigators had dangled him head-first from the twenty-ninth floor of the State Office Building. "There ought to be a truce so prisoners can be exchanged," a wag observed.

All of this came on the heels of the Aurelio affair, with its strong reminder that, as Dewey himself put it, "the Tiger does not change its stripes." Frank Costello was the new, undisputed boss of the underworld in New York, and Frank J. Kennedy was his mouthpiece within the allegedly reformed corridors of Tammany. Manhattan magistrate Thomas Aurelio's taped expression of gratitude for Costello's aid in getting him on the supreme court, first made public by Frank Hogan in late summer, could not have come at a better time for Dewey and his hand-picked nominee for lieutenant governor. In Brooklyn on October 23, the Governor harkened back to Costello's relations with Jimmy Hines, "whose present address is Sing Sing, New York," and how, when Luciano was arrested in Hot Springs back in 1936, the only piece of paper found on him contained Costello's unlisted phone number. "The faces change, but the system remains the same," he declared. "One hundred and fifty years of Tammany history, from Aaron Burr to Frank Costello, proves one simple thing: no one can vote the Democratic ticket in New York City without knowing that gangsters have participated in the selection of that ticket." He cautioned against being taken in by protestations of "a new Tammany ... with a brand new suit, its hair brushed and its face and ears glistened with soap."

The campaign wasn't all accusation. After expanding minimum wage coverage and promising equal pay for equal work by women, Dewey won an unprecedented endorsement for Hanley by the state chapter of the American Federation of Labor. Speaking before the organization's convention late in August 1943, he drew a line connecting a postwar economy buoyant with new jobs in the private sector, and labor's own aspirations for economic justice. He divided mankind into two classes, "the kind that have things happen to them and the kind who makes things happen." The former were victims of totalitarian systems, where they had no right to conduct their own business, join a trade union, or live lives according to their own wishes. A democracy, Dewey continued, relies for its sustenance upon those "cut from quite another bolt of cloth. A democracy must have an increasing number of people who do things for themselves and for others—people with starch in them, with initiative, imagination, and vision." This, he implied, set his own administration apart from the one in Washington.

In November, Joe Hanley was swept into office by 350,000 votes. For Dewey, it was a ringing mandate, greeted nowhere more warmly than in Republican circles hostile to Wendell Willkie. Dewey remained cautious. "Your stock is at a new high," wrote his Missouri comrade Barak Mattingly. "Shall we start selling?"

"The answer to your wire is no," Dewey replied three days after the election. Kingsland Macy publicly stated what was privately obvious—that the vote had greatly increased pressure on Dewey to come down from his mountaintop of non-candidacy and make plain his intentions. Alf Landon joined the rising chorus, comparing the New Yorker's disclaimers with those of Theodore Roosevelt in 1900, and Charles Evans Hughes sixteen years later. Both men insisted to the last that they wanted no nomination; both accepted it when it came without the slightest sign of reluctance.[27]

The stage was set for a showdown, between the visionary Willkie and the pragmatist Dewey, between an internationalist in the Wilsonian mold and a gradualist who decried "fuzzy-minded theorists" and whose greatest ambition was to develop a postwar position that might unite his badly divided party. One man found all party discipline too confining for his political and intellectual free spirit; the other was devoting himself in New York to building a formidable political machine. One man was drawn inexorably to uplifting generalities; the other preferred to dwell in the valley of practical administration. One worried about a world gone haywire; the other fretted over a constitution trampled by Washington. Each man shared a common contempt for the other; both spoke for intense bands of admirers. The first volleys in what promised to be a war without quarter were fired in the pages of a book.

In April 1943, recently returned from a trip around the globe, Willkie published *One World,* an account of his fifty days on board the converted C-87 bomber *Gulliver.* Throughout his trip, the once and prospective Republican candidate for president had spoken with typical candor, angering the White House by endorsing in Moscow Stalin's demand for an immediate second front in the European war, and forcing both Churchill and opposition leader Clement Attlee to take issue with his call for an end to empires once the fighting was over. Willkie's response was characteristic: "When I speak for myself," he told reporters seeking his reaction to the ruckus his opinions caused, "I'm Wendell Willkie and I say what I damned please." In *One World,* he followed the same course. What emerged was a powerful warning against an imperialistic pipe dream that might set in motion the forces of an even greater conflagration.

"Men and women all over the world are on the march," he wrote "physically, intellectually and spiritually. After centuries of ignorant and dull compliance, hundreds of millions of people in Eastern Europe and Asia have opened the books. Old fears no longer frighten them. They are beginning to know that man's welfare throughout the world is interdependent. They are resolved, as we must be, that there is no more place for imperialism within their own society than in the society of nations. The big house on the hill surrounded by mud flats has lost its awesome charm."

In Willkie's new world, there was no room for nationalistic empire building or trade barriers. Anticipating what would later be christened the Third World, he pleaded for "a new society of independent nations, free alike of the economic injustices of the West and the political malpractices of the East." Willkie also wrote admiringly of the Russia he had seen, "a dynamic country, a vital new society, a force that cannot be bypassed in any future wars." He described Stalin's "robust" sense of humor, and depicted the Russian dictator as a man of simple tastes who dressed in pastel tunics and directed a fully working and therefore valid society. In the idealistic atmosphere of 1943, when the Soviet Union was leading a heroic resistance and Americans devoutly sought reassurance that the death and mud of European and Pacific battlefields could be given a sense of nobility, response to *One World* was overwhelming. Within weeks, Willkie's book sold a million copies, only the third work of nonfiction to achieve that lofty plateau since 1900.

More and more, the Hoosier who had idolized Woodrow Wilson was sounding like a latter-day version of his doomed hero. The parallels were not precise; Wilson destroyed himself and the chance of American participation in international peacekeeping with his unyielding insistence on every detail of a League of Nations as he envisioned it. Compromise for his stern Calvinist soul was a sign of weakness. Valiant defeat was preferable to success with Lodge's reservations. But Wilson could at least rely upon his party's machinery and the White House itself as his personal pulpit. Willkie, by contrast, was rapidly forfeiting whatever influence he once possessed in his adopted party. He was not married to the GOP, he liked to say, he was still courting it. It was a clumsy courtship.

It was bad enough that Willkie went off on his trip rather than staying to campaign as the titular head of the party in the fall of 1942. Equally bothersome was Willkie's hectoring tone, expressed in print in *American* magazine, where he took other Republicans to task for what he called their "psychopathic hatred of the President" and warned, in ominous tones, that "the party that pussyfoots . . . during a national emergency, writes its own death warrant." Incredibly, Willkie had gone to see Jim Farley to suggest the idea of joint backing for any congressional candidate, regardless of party label, who agreed to support Roosevelt's foreign policy. He told a closed-door session of Republican congressmen in Washington that he could go over their heads and win the 1944 nomination by appealing directly to the people. He alienated Harold Stassen, a key 1940 supporter, who now entertained his own hopes of running. At a reception attended by business leaders in St. Louis, angered by insinuations from his onetime backer Edgar Queeney, Willkie lost his temper and blurted out, "I don't know whether you're going to support me or not and I don't give a damn. You're a bunch of political liabilities who don't know what's going on anyway."

A steady stream of reports filtered into Albany, where Dewey continued to insist he was not a candidate, even while the men around him prepared for that eventuality. "Willkie not only ignored . . . all of the people who helped him," the Governor commented in August. "He has ignored their brains, their advice, and the party which gave him his opportunity. It is not merely a case of being an ingrate. It is a total failure to understand the working of the American system of government and a total absence of any capacity to work in association with others." To Alf Landon, he went further still, criticizing "self-seeking individuals who would like to create about themselves the aura of a Messiah who alone can save the Republican Party from itself."[28]

Ever since Pearl Harbor, the GOP had been struggling to find a common ground on the divisive issue of postwar cooperation with other nations in preserving the peace. Willkie focused attention on the issue, and liberals friendly to his cause joined in creation of the Republican Postwar Policy Association. At the other end of the spectrum, Herbert Hoover and former U.S. ambassador to Germany Hugh Gibson wrote a series of articles that summer decrying as "damaging nonsense" the Willkie approach of immediate and detailed planning. Hoover wanted a transition period after the war, during which the victors might provide relief and reconstruction, while gradually designing a workable world organization to bequeath to a grateful planet. Still further to the right, Gerald Nye opposed any league whatsoever, and found an appreciative audience in the Republican Nationalist Revival Committee, which noisily proclaimed at its Chicago (where else?) convention, "WE DON'T WANT WILLKIE." Against this confused background, national chairman Harrison Spangler, himself a compromise choice between the party's left and right wings, announced at the end of May formation of the Post-War Advisory Council. It was designed to bring together forty-nine leading Republicans to ponder postwar challenges at home and abroad. A conference was called for mid-September, on Mackinac Island, between Lake Michigan and Lake Huron.

Arthur Vandenberg accepted the job of writing a compromise foreign policy plank that might unite the party's disparate elements without sounding entirely bleached of meaning. Several times, he and Dewey reviewed the statement, once at a secret meeting in the Governor's suite at the Hotel Roosevelt. Just before he left for Michigan, Dewey received a letter from Hoover imploring him not to say anything that might accidentally wed him to any New Deal for the whole world. "Roosevelt has no peace plans or peace policies," wrote the former president to the man widely assumed a likely Republican candidate in 1944. "He has only war policies and peace 'aims.' He cannot produce a real peace plan and policy without creating disunities with other nations during the war." Instead, Hoover continued, FDR was likely to unveil something unacceptable to Republicans "the minute firing ceases." Stay away from the trap, he concluded; "it is buying a cat blind."[29]

Personally, Dewey favored a middle course, "something concrete, though not specific," as he told Landon. He favored the Six Pillars of Peace, a broad but forward-looking program put together by John Foster Dulles and the Federal Council of Churches of Christ in America. The Pillars would commit Americans to international cooperation, economic and financial controls, establishment of a world body to adapt a global peace treaty to changed conditions, autonomy for subject peoples, control of armaments, and both religious and individual liberty.

Dewey arrived at Mackinac on September 5, a candidate despite his continued protestations to the contrary. A poll in his hands taken privately among delegates to the 1940 convention showed him to be the first choice of 36 percent, with Ohio's photogenic but unexceptional Governor John Bricker (whom William Allen White called "an honest Harding") the favorite of 21 percent. Willkie and General Douglas MacArthur trailed the leaders. MacArthur was already being lionized as the war's greatest hero for his gallant defensive tactics in the Pacific, a battle zone that Republicans believed was being neglected in favor of the European theater of operations. Unfortunately for his prospects, as a friend eagerly informed Dewey, the General suffered from an overriding vanity that made it impossible for him to pass a mirror without stopping to adjust his hat or signature corncob pipe. This led the first Mrs. MacArthur to reply, when asked to assess her former husband as a dark horse for 1944, "It depends which end you look at."[30]

Invited to choose the man they thought of as the weakest candidate their party could nominate, the 1940 delegates picked Willkie over Hoover by a five-to-one margin. Then came Bricker, Landon, Taft, and Vandenberg. No one, so it seemed, thought of Dewey as a potential liability. A poll of House Republicans turned up similar results, except that Willkie enjoyed even less support among these largely conservative party regulars. The public, too, was shifting to Dewey. George Gallup found the New York governor, despite his avowal of non-candidacy, moving ahead of Willkie in December 1943, 55 percent to 35 percent. Yet a large tactical problem remained. Dewey had promised repeatedly not to leave the governorship before his term was over. The pledge tied him to Albany and discouraged delegates from boarding a bandwagon early. At the same time, it freed him from the demands made upon other announced or likely candidates like Willkie and Bricker. "The best way to campaign," Dewey once told Vandenberg, "is by the performance of public service that the people know about." Certainly, with the national press beating a path to the second floor to write favorable stories about his successful blend of fiscal conservatism and social concern in the nation's largest state, Americans were beginning to rediscover Dewey as something more than a gangbuster. Set in a context of domestic shortages and administrative overlaps, of growing dissatisfaction with what many perceived as the arrogance of old men too long in power in Washington, the youthful, efficient problem solver in Albany was fast becoming an attractive alternative.[31]

Dewey's prospects were enhanced at Mackinac when, in an offhand response to a newspaperman's report of agreements between Roosevelt and Churchill—the latter was in the United States to make a speech at Harvard—he came out for a permanent postwar alliance with Great Britain. After all, he reasoned, ever since the War of 1812, America and Britain had enjoyed "a de facto military alliance." In two great wars since, the U.S. had gone to the aid of her mother country. Formalizing such ties "would be very likely and . . . in our interest." In addition, Dewey "hoped" that China and Russia might join a postwar partnership. As for those who feared a sacrifice of national sovereignty, he claimed that nothing was surrendered except international tensions when a group of nations determined to build a peace made treaties among themselves.

Hardly had he finished speaking when other Republicans reacted noisily to his proposal, which overshadowed the "Declaration of Mackinac" itself—a call for international disarmament and "cooperative organization" that Vandenberg himself could not define precisely. Robert Taft denounced the Anglo-American idea as "a fool thing to do." The Chicago *Tribune* headlined its reports from Mackinac, "Gov. Dewey Goes Anti-American." Colonel McCormick's editorial writers summoned all their considerable bile to lambaste Dewey as "a tragic example of a man who was not quite big enough to rise above his immediate environment. In his anxiety to hold New York City he has lost the nation . . . now he has finished the pilgrimage to Downing Street by way of Wall Street. He has bought and been bought by the prospect of millions for his campaign fund from New York bankers, but he has lost the millions of votes of New York Republicans just as surely as he has lost the support of voters in the more American states." For his part, Dewey told his mother that the *Tribune*'s harsh words were "quite satisfactory . . . the support of that paper may be useful in Illinois. . . . It is a terrific liability in other states."[32]

Alf Landon, a more sophisticated observer, also found flaws in the Anglo-American idea, prompting Dewey to defend it as "a core, a beginning" for what would undoubtedly prove an arduous process. Besides, he went on, his proposal was far better than the "sweet dreams" of Willkie and the Democrats. Peace, he reminded his Kansas friend, was not likely to be built upon their shifting foundation. At Harvard, there was another kind of response as Churchill, hearing of the Dewey suggestion, rewrote his scheduled address to speak of Americans and the British as "one family." Cynics noted the publication within three days of a Gallup poll showing 61 percent supporting such an alliance, a finding that might easily have been leaked to Dewey before he set off for Mackinac. Meanwhile, President Roosevelt had on his desk a confidential report by political agents sent to observe the Republican conference, including an account of someone's practical joke, consisting of a bogus paging of Willkie (who was not invited to Mackinac) over the loudspeaker of the headquarters at the Grand Hotel, while assorted Old Guard politicians huddled in fear.[33]

The President's political intelligence men reported that Dewey was definitely running for the nomination, that the men around him believed the prize to be his, and that they were going to great lengths to avoid friction in laying claim to it. Their strategy reportedly was to say complimentary things about MacArthur, counter Willkie's appeal with the postwar alliance plan, hold out the prospect of a position for Willkie after the 1940 nominee's defeat, and in general "make no enemies among the other candidates, so that the

Republicans will have a united front behind Dewey against Roosevelt."[34]

The report was not without foundation. It is impossible to say precisely when Dewey decided to run for the presidency. He maintained until he flew to Chicago in June 1944 to accept the nomination that he was not a candidate. But almost a year earlier he agreed with Ruth Simms that it would be disastrous if Colonel McCormick were to seek delegates in Illinois, as some were urging him to do in an effort to stop Willkie. Such an extremist opponent, Dewey predicted, could give Willkie "exactly what he is looking for." He certainly didn't discourage prospective backers like Karl Mundt of South Dakota, who wrote in early September, "Now is your chance to be President. Another opportunity may never arise." Dewey replied with something less than blushing reticence that he was "anxious to hear all of the things you couldn't write."[35]

In October, Ruth Simms worried that the strategy for a national campaign "is not being considered as I think it should be" and urged a private meeting of Dewey's advisers at which the Governor would not be present. From this gathering would emerge another, larger one in Chicago early in 1944, which in turn would appoint a committee to approach Dewey and ask him to reconsider his stated refusal to run. Actually, Straus, Medalie, Dulles, and Brownell had already convened, and on November 19 Dewey all but ended any doubt that he would, indeed, become a candidate when the time was right. He sent Mrs. Simms a confidential delegate count compiled by five leading men in the party, showing Willkie with fewer than 150 first-ballot votes. He passed along Willkie's latest gaucheries, including his refusal at the Herald Tribune Forum to shake hands with Vice President Henry Wallace, and his standing on a table, knocking over a pitcher of water, and throwing kisses to a group of New Jersey Republican women. Willkie had antagonized downtown bankers, according to Elliott Bell, offended every Republican in Washington, and, so reported both Republican and Democratic sources in Wisconsin, stubbed his toe badly on his first campaign swing through that critical state.

"This thing is going well, I believe," Dewey apprised Simms. "Willkie is being hysterical and the most conspicuous characteristic of his peregrinations to date is that they have not been successful." There was more: Governor Earl Warren's agreement to hold on in California as a favorite son—an assignment for Brownell; Hoover arguing, wrongly Dewey thought, for a short, late-starting fall campaign; and "a long, confidential session" with Alf Landon at Roger

Straus's home in New York City, after which Landon publicly forecast Dewey's nomination no later than the second ballot—while Dewey himself refused comment. "Remember," he concluded his report to Simms, "at this time four years ago there was not even an announced candidate in the field. Today, there are three and other favorite sons. You and I know better than most people that this is just plain too early."[36]

By the end of 1943, Dewey's draft was blowing at gale force. Barak Mattingly reported that the New York governor was a virtually unanimous choice of Midwestern party chairmen. John Hamilton made a nationwide swing in Willkie's wake in which he all but endorsed Dewey as the only practical alternative to the man whose 1940 nomination he had helped make possible. In mid-December, Dewey feared that his rival might be fading too rapidly. He once more fretted over the possibility of McCormick's running in Illinois: "Our fat friend would get a brand new lease on life." Two weeks later, Ruth Simms was able to say categorically that the publisher had no such intention. The New York delegation, Dewey wrote Landon, would be solid. At a meeting of the national committee in Chicago, Brownell, Jaeckle, and Sprague, although operating without any formal green light from the Governor—Jaeckle later said, "He never gave a nod and he never gave me a no"—quietly passed along word that a draft would not be refused.[37]

It was at this national committee session that Jaeckle told a leading Dewey supporter in Wisconsin that his candidate might win 65 percent of the vote against the field, and, as if to second that judgment, a Gallup poll published on June 26 showed Dewey out in front of Willkie in that state 2 to 1. Yet in Albany, caution prevailed, and Dewey made strenuous efforts to have would-be delegates pledged to him withdrawn from the Wisconsin primary ballot. Mrs. Simms disagreed. Hoping to test and defeat Willkie early, she was encouraged by a groundswell of support for her reluctant champion, evidenced in thousands of petition signatures collected by volunteers within the first few days of the year. Vandenberg joined the fray, acting as a go-between with Dewey's insistent Wisconsin backers, now that his own first choice, MacArthur, seemed out of the running. Fifteen Dewey delegates refused to abandon the fight, even after the Governor dispatched his cousin Leonard Reid to argue for such a course. North Carolina Republicans issued their own invitation to Dewey to declare his candidacy. On February 16, Tom Curran announced a ninety-three member New York delegation, all but one member of which enthusiastically supported their governor.

New Gallup polls showed Dewey leading Willkie nationally, 42 percent to 23 percent, and by greater margins still in such pivotal states as Pennsylvania, Kansas, Michigan, and Willkie's own Indiana.[38]

Willkie responded with a verbal assault on his phantom opponent, crisscrossing Wisconsin to warn that "in times of crisis . . . trimmers and dodgers lead their party to destruction." Gallup had indicated that, if the war were over by Election Day, Dewey would defeat Roosevelt, 58 percent to 42 percent, while FDR would win handily if the fighting continued in November. It was the best evidence yet that the contest might be won for the GOP, if only the nation's attention were focused on the homefront, a thesis Willkie hastened to dispute.

"There are some persons in the United States," he told the voters of Racine, "who believe that the issues in the campaign . . . are the gasoline shortage, food rationing, the fact that they have to work hard and the sending of their sons abroad." He attacked Dewey's Anglo-American alliance as too narrowly militaristic and implored the citizens of Superior not to buy "a pig in a poke." Meanwhile, Dewey remained in New York, brushing aside all talk of politics, concentrating instead on his second legislative session. By the middle of April 1944, having polished off 1,079 bills with three days to spare, the governor was able to boast of an additional $148 million in surplus funds secured in his Postwar Reconstruction Fund, against the many "pleasant and useful" suggestions by legislators for bridge repairs and salary increases. When the war ended, Dewey was determined, New York would respond not with blueprints and bond issues but with "cold cash" put aside in trust for the men who would be coming home. Already, his Postwar Planning Committee was buying up land and commissioning designs for new housing projects, additions to overcrowded hospitals, and a vast network of arterial highways. The Department of Commerce was devising plans for peacetime conversion that might ward off mass unemployment. Taxes had not only been reduced but simplified: the average New Yorker now found himself filling out a single-page form.

Both the Health and Social Welfare departments were being reorganized to eliminate technicalities blocking assistance to the blind, aged, and to dependent children. For the first time, modern methods of treatment were being employed in the state's hopsitals, some of them eighty years old and unsafe for human habitation— "left to me," Dewey said scornfully, "by those who claimed to be liberals." Major structural changes would have to wait until peace; manpower and materials both were scarce. But that was the whole idea behind the Postwar Reconstruction Fund. In the interim, Dewey shook his head over the Batavia School for the Blind, where 152 children were taught in a flimsy wooden structure whose electrical wiring hadn't been touched in fifty years, a century-old mental hospital in Utica, a half-finished tuberculosis hospital at Islip. He did raise salaries for hospital workers, add dietitians to the staffs, and give his mental hygiene commissioner, Dr. McCurdy, a free hand in stressing occupational therapy, child guidance clinics, and the teaming of psychiatry and social work "to cut off at the source" part of the flow of patients, 18,000 a year, that filled the firetraps and violent wards to overflow.

Finally, the legislature had agreed to Dewey's demand that a system of unemployment insurance for returning veterans be set up now, so that there would be no delay in benefits when peace broke out. Washington, by contrast, had done nothing.

Orthodox Republicans admired Dewey's signature on the Coudert-Mitchell Bill, drastically reducing the number of so-called nuisance suits filed by minority stockholders against large corporations. Voters in general seemed satisfied with a soldiers' ballot proposal which met New York's constitutional demands while extending suffrage to more men and women in uniform than most of her sister states. All this was known in Wisconsin, where on April 4, 1944, a quarter million Republicans trooped to the polls. Willkie was in Nebraska that day, site of an upcoming primary contest. His archrival stayed home, posing for pictures in his suite at the Roosevelt Hotel with the head of the American Legion Auxiliary Poppy Drive and signing and vetoing legislation as part of his thirty-day period chores. In the evening, Dewey returned to Albany, where Jim Hagerty informed him after midnight of an overwhelming victory in Wisconsin. Seventeen of the state's twenty-four delegates were in the Dewey column. Stassen had won four, MacArthur three. Shut out in the voting, Willkie realized his plight and the next day withdrew from any further campaigning. To friends in the press, he confided that his ultimate support would depend upon Dewey's postwar policies.

"I supposed you noticed the Wisconsin primary," Herbert Hoover dryly wrote on the morning after. Dewey's leading Wisconsin backer, Carl Rix, was more openly enthusiastic. "He not only talked himself out as you said he would," wrote Rix in reference to the vanquished Willkie, "but he was utterly unconvincing. In some sections of the state, it seems as though the entire voting strength had decided, as if by agreement, to vote against him." Dewey issued no public statement on the primary that practically sewed up his early nomination at the convention in Chicago. He continued to slice away at the pile of bills on his desk, hurried south to christen the baseball season, and made it back to Albany in time to see Tommy play the Modern Major General in a school production of *The Pirates of Penzance*. Beyond that, he remained an enigma on his Albany hill. To his mother, he complained of "too many callers and a welter of optimism which I suspect is somewhat overdone." To Ruth Simms, he couldn't suppress his déjà vu. "Everything seems to be going altogether too well for comfort," he told her on April 12, "and I am beginning to feel a little bit like I felt four years ago at this moment."[39]

Three days later, Dewey made his second annual report to the people of New York. In it, he listed the achievements of the year past, the fresh winds blowing through and invigorating state government, and the plans in readiness to ease the coming transition to a peacetime economy. He could not resist a swipe at "that type of personal government which talks fine phrases of liberalism while seeking to impose its will and whims upon the people through centralized bureaucracies issuing directives from a distance." If it wasn't a formal declaration of candidacy, it came as close as anyone was likely to get.

12

Taking on the Champ

You ought to hear him. He plays the part of the heroic racketbuster . . . he talks to the people as if they were the jury and I were
the villain on trial for his life.
                                        —Franklin D. Roosevelt

If any man is indispensable, then none of us is free.
                                        —Thomas E. Dewey

Dewey was scheduled to address the American Newspaper Publishers Association on April 27, 1944. But first, he had to deal with his
own supporters. Hoover, John Hamilton, and others were urging
Dewey to avoid any pronouncement on postwar policy, recalling
Calvin Coolidge's advice to a prospective candidate: "Talk about
patriotism; everybody seems to be for it." Ruth Simms was reporting solid delegations for Dewey in the Far West; Dewey had polled
156,000 write-in votes in Pennsylvania's primary; Alf Landon was
telling the Governor to concentrate on the platform; Willkie was
unhorsed: and Bricker was stalled in the starting gate. There seemed
good reasons for Dewey to talk about patriotism. He didn't want to.[1]

Dewey wanted to recover his naturally combative stance, throw
off the suffocating cloak of silence, and put to rest questions about
his command of international affairs. He wanted to build a bridge
that the Willkie and Stassen men could cross to his own campaign,
to upstage John Bricker, and nail down State Street and Walnut
Street, as well as Wall Street. Elliott Bell agreed, and the two men
retreated to Dewey's first-floor study at Dapplemere to compose an
address that would dispel the lingering traces of isolationism that
Willkie and his more fervent partisans were attempting to capitalize on.

While Foster Dulles went off to his island in Lake Ontario to
check on winter damage, Dewey and Bell drafted words of praise for
Cordell Hull, who, in a recent speech, had held out an olive branch
to congressional Republicans, inviting them to join a consultative
process on postwar policy. Dewey wished to draw the outlines of a
program that didn't depend on the whims of "tired war leaders" for
success.

Much had been learned since 1919, he subsequently told the publishers. "Then, as now, there was much wishful thinking. Men

THOMAS E. DEWEY AND HIS TIMES

everywhere wanted to feel that a treaty which proclaimed peace would suffice to assure it . . . The war leaders wanted to feel that by signing their names to a treaty, they had brought their task to an end. The very idea that fine words made a peace bore within it the seeds of its own failure." America had grown up since then, had come to understand that "unprovoked aggression" anywhere in the world constituted an attack on the peace of the whole world. The current danger lay in a possible repetition of the mistakes of 1919, when the nation had signed a treaty and, "resting on our oars," had handed over the peace to men who could muster neither the physical nor mental strength to make it genuine.

When the fighting stopped this time, Dewey said, global alliances would have to be formed. That meant with Soviet Russia, as well as with Britain. If, on the other hand, "we lapse into the old suspicions, the future is dark indeed." Chaos and confusion would rule the postwar world; Americans would have to take the lead in making such dislocation as brief as possible. All nations would be needed in a system of "general international cooperation," around a global round table hinted at in his own party's Mackinac Charter, the Declaration of Moscow, and recent congressional resolutions bearing the names of Tom Connally and J. William Fulbright. None of this would happen overnight. Peace, like war, must be waged with "infinite patience, preparation and training."

Dewey linked an American presence overseas with a solid economic base at home. Uncle Sam would deal with others, not as "a benevolent but slightly senile gentleman, who seeks to purchase the good will of his poor relations by distributing among them the dwindling remains of his youthful earnings," but out of "practical idealism . . . and because it is good hard common sense." For the party faithful, he tried to sweeten an assertion that the U.S. had an obligation to lead that was "utterly inescapable." Goodwill could not be bought with gold; it flowed to him "who successfully manages his own affairs, who is self-reliant and independent, yet who is considerate always of the rights and needs of others."

The London *Times* praised the speech in a front-page dispatch. John Cowles, Willkie's devoted Minneapolis supporter, called it "simply superb," and after lunching with the Governor the next day rethought his own assessment of Dewey. "I had always realized," Cowles wrote Elliott Bell, "he had an excellent brain. . . . I got the added impression that he had matured and mellowed considerably since 1940, and . . . done a hell of a lot of studying and thinking about the specific problems that will be confronting the next Presi-

dent." Walter Lippmann had a compliment coupled with a warning. Lippmann told Dulles that the speech said more things con-
cretely about the future of American foreign policy than anything
from Roosevelt or Willkie. "The next great hurdle," according to
the *Herald Tribune*'s Delphic Oracle, would be to convince the electorate that a Republican victory in 1944 would not launch "a period
of rampant reaction." The way to make this clear, Lippmann urged,
was simply to point to Dewey's Albany record.[2]

Within days of the speech, which also won kind words from the
New York *Times* and contempt from Colonel McCormick, Douglas
MacArthur renounced formally any effort toward the presidential
nomination, and Ralph Cake, previously Willkie's national campaign manager, predicted Dewey's unanimous nomination in Chicago on the first ballot. There were dissenters. Gerald L. K. Smith,
once Huey Long's right-hand man and now a fiery apostle of the
America First party, denounced Dewey for "slipping into the Willkie bed. . . . Let me say it so any fool can understand," Smith told
reporters in Cleveland on May 15. "We want a candidate who's
against Roosevelt's foreign policy, against Roosevelt's domestic policy, against Roosevelt's Washington policies." He criticized "the
blundering young governor of New York . . . who slopped over too
much into the international side." In response Dewey muttered
about "that rabble-rouser" who, with his followers of the extreme
right, was guilty of "polluting" American politics with anti-Semitism and various appeals to bigotry. He described Smith as "a ro-
dent."[3]

More serious than America First were the Midwestern, conservative Republicans who were liable to flock to John Bricker if they
surmised that Dewey was surrendering to Wall Street. Keeping
them in line was the Triumvirate, as it came to be known—Jaeckle,
Brownell, and Sprague—that crisscrossed the land, Gallup polls in
hand, arguing that Dewey, and only Dewey had a chance to beat
Roosevelt. Within the party's rank and file, support for the New
Yorker ran far ahead of Willkie's or Landon's on the eve of the previous conventions that had nominated them. The final survey before
Chicago had Dewey leading Bricker, 65 percent to 9 percent. Regulars might have preferred one of their own, but they could hardly
ignore such evidence.

If the delegates' hearts were not in it, neither, at times, was
Dewey's. He confessed to George Gallup that he had no "burning
desire to take over." But now to reject a genuine draft might foreclose any prospect of nomination in 1948, when Republican chances

would be much more favorable. His sons had had the mumps, he reported to Ruth Simms in mid-May, but both were on the mend and looking forward to the warmer months. His children, at least, would enjoy a pleasant summer, "while their father works at a task from which he would much prefer to be excused."[4]

Meanwhile, a presidential campaign was in preparation. Bell and Burton started research for the fall. Dewey wanted a complete inventory of Roosevelt-created agencies supplanting previously existing ones that might have done the job better. He pondered themes: "four years of chaos," a postwar climate in which Washington would necessarily have to abandon some of its newly acquired domination, and a question sure to embitter what already promised to be a divisive contest: "Why are the Communists so strongly for Roosevelt?" It was a query to which he brought a prosecutorial flourish. Dewey traveled to Hershey, Pennsylvania, for a governors' conference ("a dreary performance," he wrote his mother, "with a lot of show and very little conferring"). He earned the resentment of several of his colleagues when he suggested that they spent too much time on public relations and chamber of commerce ritual. But in public, Dewey was cheered wherever he went. Thousands shouted his name when he placed a wreath on a monument to the Gettysburg battlefield, and a crowd of several hundred gathered outside the State Capitol at Harrisburg for a glimpse.[5]

In his formal remarks to the conference, Dewey pointed to his successes in New York—the surplus being stockpiled, and burgeoning plans for postwar business and veterans' benefits—and argued that what was involved wasn't states' rights. It was merely a governor's determination not to pass the buck—and the bucks—to Washington. Photographs of Dewey and Bricker started tongues wagging about the eventual makeup of the 1944 ticket. The gossip was premature. Actually, Dewey wanted Earl Warren of California to be his running mate. He twice telephoned him to urge acceptance and was twice refused. Warren was a man of modest means and could hardly afford a $5,000 a year pay cut, or supporting his young and growing family in a faded Washington hotel. And Warren shared the widespread doubt that any Republican could put FDR out of the White House at the height of the war. It would be difficult even for the phenomenally popular Governor Warren to carry California in 1944.

Earl Warren knew better than most Republicans the potent weapon being fashioned in war plants and living rooms of union families by Sidney Hillman and his Political Action Committee of the CIO. Stung by GOP gains in the 1942 congressional elections, and fearful that a Republican might snatch away the White House on a wave of domestic frustration, Hillman and his Amalgamated Clothing Workers Union had already contributed $100,000 to start the PAC, which had ambitious plans to proselytize among millions of sympathetic but unregistered working men and women. To Republican congressmen who fumed that the PAC was illegal under the Hatch Act, Hillman insisted that his entire campaign was "educational" in nature. Besides, there were no plans to engage in any overtly political activities until July 19, the day the Democratic National Convention selected Franklin Roosevelt to run for an unprecedented fourth term.

When Lowell Limpus of the New York *Daily News* had asked Dewey back in 1940 to gauge the consequences on his own career of Roosevelt's seeking a third term, the brash District Attorney had made no effort to conceal his exasperation. "Lowell, you make me sick. You're like all the rest of them. Don't you realize that Franklin Roosevelt is the easiest man in the world for me to beat?" Germany's invasion of the Low Countries and France had prevented a test then, and now, four years later, the war continued to overshadow domestic politics. Dewey's pugnacious self-confidence, though tempered by time and maturity, was evident in a letter he wrote to Alf Landon on June 6.

"We shall have a tough row to hoe," he admitted, while reminding Landon that a recent Gallup poll gave him a nearly even chance to carry the big industrial states that would spell the difference. "On the other hand, every day of successful war brings us close to the time when our people will be thinking of the domestic future.... Certainly, if they can give their full attention to domestic problems, they will vote Roosevelt out unanimously. He has been able to bury his blunders in foreign affairs under the march of mighty events. He has not been able to bury his domestic blunders."[6]

As Dewey was committing his optimism to paper, Roosevelt committed 600 warships, ferrying 176,000 men and backed by 11,000 Allied aircraft, to the invasion of Normandy. In Washington, a sleepless President took heart from encouraging messages signed by Churchill and Eisenhower. He prayed for the safety and success of the invading force on a nationwide radio hookup. "Our sons, pride of our nation. Lead them straight and true. Give strength to their arms, stoutness to their hearts, steadfastness to their faith."

It was a touching moment. One man, speaking a simple prayer, bringing a nation together. It was a classic example of Roosevelt, the leader destined to tame enormous events, soothe contentious adversaries, and instill passion in a government that had seemed passionless and remote before he came to take hold of it. In an age thirsty for guidance, even Republicans who derided him as "the Great White Father" did Roosevelt a service. By 1944, the man and the office had fused into one. On top of everything else, FDR was a political virtuoso. "Wendell Willkie talks too much," he told intimates during the Wisconsin primary campaign. "You have to know how to strike a chord." The President lifted his hands high, then brought them down again as if performing on a piano at Carnegie Hall. "Then you wait. Then you strike the chord again." Mingled in with his sense of timing was the temperamental artist's need to dominate.

Members of his own staff liked to tell a story: The boss had died and gone to heaven. Greeted cordially by St. Peter, Roosevelt requested a grand heavenly choir to mark the occasion. "I want 10,000 sopranos," he announced. Peter went along gladly. "I want 10,000 tenors." His host agreed. "I want 10,000 contraltos." Peter promised his best efforts. Peter then wanted to know how many basses. "Oh, that's all right," Roosevelt replied with a smile, "I'm planning to sing that part myself."

In June 1944, in spite of steady advances by Allied soldiers in France and Italy, the customary charge of Roosevelt's White House was running low. The President was a tired man. He sometimes fell asleep at his desk, papers clutched in one hand, and he began to present personal mementos to the staff, including presidential cigarette holders and a cup and saucer once owned by his mother. He had lost weight. As he struggled with the war, FDR was also being pressed—"badgered mercilessly," in the opinion of one of his secretaries—by his wife to make good on the New Deal's promises of a more egalitarian society. Ed Flynn came to the Oval Office, looked at his old friend, and advised him not to seek another four years in such a "man-killing" job. Tommy "The Cork" Corcoran, once a presidential intimate, now an outsider, expected FDR to leave the presidency sometime during his fourth term, to take the helm of an embryonic United Nations. The Democratic party had atrophied, no obvious successor had been groomed, or permitted, and, considering the affront of the detested Dewey, who already was comparing him to the broken Woodrow Wilson, Roosevelt's expressed wishes to go back to Hyde Park at the end of his third term had a hollow ring.[7]

No greater contrast had faced American voters in a century. Roosevelt was the patrician, Dewey the pretender to the throne. FDR was born with the self-confidence that came with social position and honed by his bout with polio and subsequent political triumphs. His fondness for the human race was open and spontaneous. He flattered the press corps and reaped rich dividends; at a press conference twelve days before his party's national convention in Chicago, Roosevelt laughingly dismissed as "unfriendly" a question about the continued presence of Henry Wallace on the ticket. He insisted that he hadn't given "the faintest thought" to politics or platforms.[8]

Dewey had no intimates in the press. By his fastidiousness, his intensity, and his drive, the *Wall Street Journal* was moved to compare his brain to a photoelectron cell. "Put Dewey in a dark room with two bottles of ink," observed another wag, "and he would instinctively come out with the black one. Put Roosevelt in the room and he would come out with the black and red bottles of ink and make you think that they were both vintage champagne." The differences extended beyond personality and manner. Dewey practiced cabinet government; he would not tolerate public dissension by members of his team. Roosevelt's warmest admirers didn't pretend that administration was his strong suit. "The boss appoints four men to do the job of one," Ed Flynn cracked, "or one man to do the job of four."

In its early days, the New Deal's proliferation of alphabet agencies had been hailed by a desperate people looking to Washington for help. Now, they only seemed expensive. The war alone had spawned 156 competing bureaus, many duplicative and some useless. Worse than that was the backbiting that had Henry Wallace fighting Cordell Hull over foreign economic policies, and Hull at odds with Treasury Secretary Morgenthau over the latter's draconian plan to reduce postwar Germany to an agricultural cipher. The President himself seemed to enjoy the spectacle of his feuding subordinates.

All this could only horrify a man like Dewey, for whom life was meant to be orderly, and government the agent of orderly progress. Roosevelt set the heart to pound, the blood to boil. Dewey was the sort who told a man with a hangover, I told you so. "Washington will have the start of its life," Raymond Moley forecast, in the event of a Dewey presidency. "Things will move. Incompetents will vanish. Crooks will go to jail. The snap and efficiency of youth will prevail." For Ruth Simms, worried about her candidate's tendency of late to pull his punches, snap and efficiency were exactly what were missing. Surrounded by "a small group of very intelligent New York men," Dewey was ill equipped to gaze into the mind and mentality of Americans beyond the Eastern Seaboard. In 1940 he had ignited the nation by being himself, a scrappy, dynamic, assertive candidate, a prosecutor of evil and ineptitude. Now Mrs. Simms sensed a change. Partly the new subdued Dewey was a creature of his own insistence that he was not a candidate. "To hold this position," she agreed, "you have been compelled to exert extreme caution. It has been dignified and well done." But to pursue such a course to November would be disastrous. "You are tightening up," she warned. "The man, the human being, is disappearing." His speeches were too carefully prepared, too concerned with surface rather than content. (In fact, Dewey had gone to the Hershey conference with two texts, one to be used in the event of an Allied invasion of Europe, the other the speech he actually delivered.)

"People are like children and dogs," Mark Hanna's daughter cautioned Dewey. "They know the man by instinct who likes them by the way he talks to them." Look at FDR, who made "My friends" his signature, and often began a paragraph with the phrase "You and I know . . ." Simms wasn't suggesting that Dewey try to emulate Roosevelt, only that he be himself. "You are not like the sort of speeches you are delivering now," she concluded.[9]

The Republicans assembling in Chicago the last week of June 1944 were almost to a man distrustful. Robert Taft, named to chair the party's platform committee, worried that Dewey suffered from "too much of the New York viewpoint. . . . He sees the group opinions there as a lot more important than they are." Personally, Taft found himself unable to warm to the Governor; the best he could do was concede that Dewey was "a very able fellow, even if difficult to get along with." Taft's Midwest set the philosophical tone for the party, as a poll conducted by the Republican National Committee proved. Some 44 percent of all Republicans said they thought labor unions responsible for more harm than good. Hefty majorities opposed any federal involvement in slum clearance or generating electric power. This was the party whose heart belonged to a man its head rejected, John Bricker.

Bricker was a photogenic fifty, born in a log house twenty miles southwest of Columbus, Ohio, when William McKinley sat in the State Capitol and Mark Hanna was making quiet, hugely successful raids for delegates in the rotten boroughs of the solid South. As a boy, Bricker walked four miles to and from school, and earned fifty cents a week pulling milkweed from his father's cornfield. He paid his way through Ohio State by taking jobs as a janitor and schoolteacher. Entering politics, "Honest John" was elected attorney general of the state in 1932. Six years later, he moved up to the governorship, where he attracted praise for budget trimming and won friends at countless party barbecues and chicken dinners. A warmhearted man of considerable charm, Bricker was handicapped by a reputation for something less than radiant intelligence. Even Taft described him as less able than Dewey, and I. F. Stone said that his oratory, which leaned heavily to themes of "Americanism," was "of the John T. Wintergreen variety."

From Albany, Dewey ordered three new suits from the Duke of Windsor's tailor in New York City. He played golf with Pat Hogan, supervised his spring plantings at Dapplemere, and busied himself writing an acceptance speech. In Chicago, the two Republican parties, his and Taft's, struggled toward an uneasy truce. The city was suffering through its hottest June in thirty years, as temperatures soared past 100 degrees, buckling streetcar tracks and taking the life of an elderly Kansas delegate. Inside Chicago Stadium, bored Republicans struggled through the proceedings in rivulets of perspiration. Many stayed away. Deliberately bare of banners and the usual folderol out of a desire to maintain wartime sobriety, the convention hall was both oven and morgue. Louella Parsons found the chairman of Colorado's delegation less interested in discussing Dewey's strength there than in asking whether Gary Cooper was as laconic off screen as on. Taft almost fell asleep reading the 5,000-word platform, which sought like all platforms to straddle divisive issues, point with pride, and view with alarm.

"Four more years of New Deal policy," it asserted, "would centralize all power in the President, and would daily subject every act of every citizen to regulation by his henchmen; and this country could remain a Republic only in name. No problem exists which cannot be solved by American methods. We have no need of either the communistic or the fascist technique."

That was for the Tafts, Brickers, McCormicks, and Martins of the GOP. For those who wished to go to the electorate with a more affirmative position, there was a mildly internationalist plank, favoring a world court while rejecting any concept of "a world state." There was also the strongest civil rights plank yet to appear in a major party platform, including among its provisions the national Fair Employment Practices Commission, a constitutional amendment banning the poll tax, an anti-lynching law, and an investigation into racial discrimination within the armed forces.

Delegates listened manfully to the metallic tones of Robert Taft as he plowed his way through the platform. When he finished, not a single minority report was offered, testimony either to his skill at placating all shades of opinion or the lethargy engendered by temperatures inside the hall as high as 105 degrees. On Tuesday night, the convention heard Herbert Hoover hand the torch to "a new generation" of young men, headed by the Governor of New York. Later that night, Hoover acted as go-between for the Dewey and Bricker forces. Earl Warren had finally made public his refusal to accept the vice presidency. In the process, he embittered Bricker by reneging on a promise at least to sit down and talk about the Ohioan's presidential ambitions. Instead, the big Californian released his delegates to vote for Dewey. Combined with large blocs from Illinois and Pennsylvania, they put an end to whatever flickering hopes Bricker entertained. So on Tuesday night, when Herbert Brownell passed along news of Dewey's interest in having him for a running mate, Bricker's managers were interested. Hoover urged Bricker to accept. A strong party man, his selection would mollify conservatives and give the Midwest representation on the ticket— something that had not been denied it since the first Republican convention nominated Charles Fremont of California and William L. Dayton of Ohio, in 1856.[10]

By early Wednesday, Bricker was a presidential candidate only in name. That morning, the convention listened as Nebraska's youthful governor, Dwight Griswold, put Dewey's name in nomination. Griswold proclaimed his colleague from New York to be "the spokesman for the future." With Dewey in the White House, Americans would enjoy "youth instead of decadence, vigor instead of cynicism, integrity instead of doubledealing . . . faith instead of defeatism." For his efforts, Griswold was rewarded with a short, sweaty display of applause that included nearly every state standard, and a brass band pounding out "Anchors Aweigh" and "What Do We Do on a Dew, Dew, Dewy Day?" Alf Landon could be seen in the crowd doing a little dance of joy. Delegates held in their hands placards brought all the way from New York, professionally lettered. "Dewey Will Win," they promised. "Dewey, the people's choice." In a box overlooking the organized turmoil sat the candidate's mother. "I don't want to talk," Annie told reporters, wiping tears from her face, "I want to listen." In Owosso that morning, farmers milked their cows early, and party lines buzzed with the news from Chicago. The atmosphere of hometown pride was spoiled only by a dozen war plant workers who carried signs pledging loyalty to FDR and the CIO.

Seven minutes after it started, the demonstration faded away, to be replaced by an even more raucous outbreak of emotion. Cowbells clanged and a band played "Beautiful Ohio" as Bricker made his way to the podium to withdraw his name in a graceful talk interrupted by shouts of "No, no." The names of Harold Stassen and Everett Dirksen were also withdrawn, and the roll call that followed proved a mere formality. Only once was there a deviation from the script. "I am a man, not a jellyfish," protested Grant Ritter, a fifty-four-year-old dairy farmer from Beloit, Wisconsin. "I vote for MacArthur." By 2:25 P.M., it was over. In Albany, Tom and Frances switched off a radio on the second floor of the mansion, descended the huge central staircase, and climbed into a car for the short trip to the Albany airport. There, a plane was waiting to transport them and a party of thirteen to Chicago. Twelve years earlier, another plane, carrying another governor of New York, had left Albany for a convention in the Windy City, there to anoint the leader of a new era in American politics.

Dewey's arrival coincided with a break in the heat wave; a late afternoon thunder shower dropped the temperature on State Street by nineteen degrees. Even so, the 25,000 partisans jammed into a hall built for 21,000 seemed distracted, fanning themselves, gulping soft drinks, and refusing to join in when the Chicago Light Opera Company struck up the party anthem, "The Battle Hymn of the Republic." Then, a few minutes after nine o'clock, klieg lights embraced the main stage. Out of nowhere, dapper, calm, apparently careless, the candidate appeared. Cheers rose in every section of the auditorium as he bowed stiffly and crooked an arm in salute, first to one corner of the vast audience, then to another. He brought forth his running mate, who at six feet, two inches, towered over him by half a foot. He introduced his wife, who wore orchids and a silent, fixed smile. He began to speak.

"I come to this great task a free man." No pledges had been made, no promises given. Only to the people of America would he make such commitments, and to them he now promised "an end to one-man government" and a cabinet of the ablest men and women to be found, "experienced in the task to be done and young enough to do it." He declared the war to be outside the realm of partisan politics and then complimented both General Marshall and Admiral King for their part in it, but warned that how victory was achieved would ultimately be as important as when. "We won the last war," Dewey declared, "but it did not stay won." The task of winning the peace would confront the next administration, something to be entrusted to realists. "No organization for peace will last if it is slipped through by stealth or trickery or the momentary hypnotism of high-sounding phrases." Only a handful, he said, still believed that America could avoid her responsibilities on the world stage; only a misguided few advocated membership in an international super-state. Republicans could justifiably lay claim to considerable credit for having defined "a large, growing area of agreement" in between such extremes.

At home, the campaign to come would be a crusade against those in Washington who were "notoriously weak in certain branches of arithmetic but who specialized in division." After twelve years in power, the New Deal had grown "old and tired and quarrelsome." "Wrangling, bungling and confusion" were the accepted order. Indeed, little about the New Deal's economic policies ever had worked. After seven years of unprecedented spending and expansion of federal authority, America in 1940 still had found itself with 10 million jobless men and women as a costly legacy. The coming of war had replaced one human tragedy with another. Dewey looked out at his audience, slammed his fist down on the podium, and demanded in his best prosecutorial style, "Do we have to have a war in order to get jobs?"

The crowd, catching the cadence, shouted back its lusty approval.

"What are we offered now?" he asked. "Only the dreary prospect of a continued war economy after the war, with interference piled on interference and petty tyrannies rivaling the very regimentation against which we are now at war." This was strong stuff, and the Republicans loved it. "The present administration has never solved this fundamental problem of jobs and opportunity," Dewey continued. "It never can . . . it has never even understood what makes a job. It has never been for full production. It has lived in chattering fear of abundance. It has specialized in curtailment and restriction . . . it is the New Deal which tells us that America has lost its capacity to grow. . . . Is America old and worn out? Look to the beaches of Normandy for the answer. Look to the reaches of the wide Pacific— to the corners of the world where American men are fighting. Look to the miracles of production in the war plants in your own towns. I say to you: Our country is just fighting its way through to new horizons. The future of America has no limit."

Without lingering to savor the delirium his closing words produced, Dewey returned to the Stevens Hotel, to shake hands with 5,000 admirers. The next morning, he sat on a table, legs dangling, and parried questions from more than a hundred reporters. He took issue with the platform over reciprocal trade agreements (which he supported), flatly ruled out a world state, and paused amidst questions, cigarette holder clenched between his teeth, to ruminate on cabinet choices and the role of Wendell Willkie in the fall. Dewey promised to consult the 1940 nominee, "along with others" in the party. "One does not shake hands across a breakfast table," he reproached newsmen who tried to get him to strike such a pose with his running mate. Then he hurried off to private meetings with forty-five state delegations, and nearly the entire membership of the national committee. He conferred with state party chairmen and vice chairmen, turned aside Taft's attempt to keep Spangler in the national chairmanship by offering the Iowan a job as party counsel, and selected Herbert Brownell in his stead. In doing so, he bruised the feelings of Ed Jaeckle, a mistake that was to have large ramifications. Dewey also moved to consolidate the party behind him by choosing four vice chairmen, including Colonel McCormick's favorite Republican, Illinois' Warner Schroder.

Then, with the various factions temporarily reconciled, Dewey left for Albany. In three days of strenuous personal effort, wrote *Newsweek*, he had snapped his party out of a twelve-year coma. Marquis Childs agreed, but looked ahead to the race against a commander in chief in the penultimate months of a victorious war, and concluded that Dewey had just four months in which to accomplish a miracle.

Back in Albany, Dewey embarked on a whirlwind series of meetings with Republican congressmen. Charles Halleck of the GOP Congressional Campaign Committee came to call. So did Arthur Vandenberg and Clare Boothe Luce. Vermont's Warren Austin, an internationalist in the Willkie mold, went away satisfied with Dewey's interpretation of the platform's all-things-to-all-men approach to the UN. Sam Pryor, also a Willkie man, pronounced himself "overwhelmed" by the candidate's command of facts. Others found themselves astonished at his private dynamism. "Why didn't you tell me he was like that?" asked Charles Breitel's brother-in-law, hitherto an implacable critic. "He's such a warm personality!" Gubernatorial aides, before escorting visitors into the inner sanctum, took to asking how long it had been since the caller last sat down with Dewey, then remarked enthusiastically that they would find the Governor a changed man.[11]

Change had its limitations, however. Dewey first met the Pennsylvania congressional delegation in a Philadelphia ballroom, in an atmosphere of nervous tension. When Representative Hugh Scott moved to the center of the room and, in an effort to break the ice, jovially asked if Dewey would invite them all back to the White House after the election, the candidate muffed it. "Well," he stuttered, "you can all come to the White House but you'll have to make an appointment first." What a shame, Scott recalled thirty-six years later. "He never knew how to be at ease."[12]

One thing Dewey hadn't lost was his appetite for information. "Telling me about this," he informed a Western Republican concerned about federal ownership of public lands, "will do me exactly no good. Writing about this will do me an enormous amount of good. Will you do it?" Neither had he abandoned his preoccupation with the nuances of what others might think. A friendly editor wrote him soon after the convention that radio broadcasts indicating the Governor was "resting" at his Pawling farm might give the public a wrong impression, and in any event, given the concern over Roosevelt's health, it was bad politics. Jim Hagerty was given new instructions: Henceforth, he was to tell the press that Dewey was planning on nothing but work when at Dapplemere on weekends.[13]

Wherever he might be, he could not escape the torrent of advice. "Organize, Organize, Organize," urged *Look* magazne, while also prescribing "a dash of humanity" to leaven the "precision-tool impression." Herbert Hoover had a scheme to corral dissatisfied Southern Democrats. Convene a meeting of conservative Democratic senators, governors, ambassadors, and former cabinet members, Hoover advised, and from it issue a manifesto calling for a coalition government for the duration of the war. What's more, Dewey should set aside thirty cabinet and war agency positions to be filled equally by Democrats and Republicans. The candidate replied on July 20 that the idea contained "fascinating possibilities" but was probably ruled out since Henry Wallace's ouster from the Democratic slate in favor of a Missourian more acceptable to the South, Harry S. Truman.[14]

Meanwhile, there was an organization to build, nearly from scratch. Bell and Burton found the national committee's research facilities nil. Brownell discovered that most of the party's second-level leadership consisted of men from the Coolidge-Hoover era. Younger Republicans were likely to be in uniform, and so the decision was made to rely heavily on the nation's twenty-six Republican governors, many of them comparatively youthful, and nearly all more sympathetic to internationalism and social programs than the entrenched conservatives in Congress. On the national level, Brownell and Dewey hoped to repeat their accomplishment in New York, eliminating the GOP's reputation for terminal nostalgia while developing fresh talent that would be personally loyal to the nominee and his views. A conference of all the governors was set for the first week of August in St. Louis. There, the chief executives were asked who might be able to develop support among veterans, labor, young people, and ethnic groups. They also got a taste of Dewey the taskmaster. Determined to hammer out specific recommendations for a host of domestic problems left vague by the platform, the New Yorker kept his fellow governors in session until two-thirty one morning. Having slogged their way to harmony on everything from tax reduction to water power, the governors finally rebelled when Dewey looked around the room brightly and asked, "What about insurance?"[15]

By the time they finished their work, the Republican chief executives had reached unanimous agreement on plans to consolidate federal welfare programs, thus avoiding warfare among competing agencies. They also went on record in favor of simplifying and reducing taxes, systematic coordination of federal and state efforts, and reducing wherever possible Washington's dictation to the states. No one had ever placed such emphasis on the governors as a possible counterweight to the party's dominant congressional wing. Once aroused to a sense of their own potential, Dewey's associates in state government were unlikely to surrender it.

While Dewey conferred over future policies, Brownell molded the campaign that it was hoped would make the governors' conference a harbinger of things to come. National headquarters were moved from Chicago to the Roosevelt Hotel in New York; only a regional office was left behind to placate Midwesterners already suspicious of the Eastern Establishment. Brownell negotiated a truce with Colonel McCormick, whose paper, in an effort to capitalize on a whispering campaign over Roosevelt's health, began carefully choosing photographs of the candidates for maximum effect. Shots of FDR at two-year intervals since 1932 appeared, and the cumulative effect was precisely what the colonel wished: the President looked like a very old man. The publisher apologized for a picture of Dewey on the golf course. It might not be flattering, he acknowledged, but then, "it gives such distinct evidence of vigor." And vigor, at a time when the Gallup poll found 34 percent of the American people believing that Roosevelt's health would not permit him to carry out his duties in a new term, was a major selling point.[16]

In New York, Brownell prepared a publicity blitz. One hundred thousand color posters bearing the image of his candidate were in the works, along with rayon banners for rallies, campaign biographies, 2 million brochures on the Dewey farm record, and 5 million buttons. Key states like Pennsylvania were singled out for special effort. Radio time was purchased and ad copy composed. Money was tight—the national committee reported expenditures after the campaign of $2.8 million, a figure swelled by state and independent committees. Imagination supplemented the meager budget. When Dewey found a picture of himself with some black leaders being circulated by Democrats in the South, he told Brownell to reproduce it, slap on the caption "Dewey Attends Negro Cocktail Party," and flood Harlem with copies.[17]

Unfortunately, Dewey rejected the imaginative ideas of others. Almost immediately after his nomination, he had been urged by Jaeckle to go abroad to visit European battlefronts and confer with both Stalin and Churchill as a counter to Roosevelt's strategy of concentrating on the war. "God, that's a marvelous idea," he replied, then told Jaeckle not to mention it to a soul. When the candidate returned to Albany a few days later, Jaeckle returned to his idea of a European tour, only to have Dewey dismiss it out of hand. "We're not going to do it," Dewey snapped, and then moved on to other matters. Sensing that he had been sandbagged, Jaeckle all but resigned. "You can run your own campaign," he said angrily. Jaeckle believed that Dewey was reluctant to do anything that might refocus attention on his non-military record, but, whatever the cause, the exchange virtually removed Jaeckle and his blunt candor from the inner circle. Thereafter, Dewey was on his own.[18]

Fresh distractions appeared. Bricker caused one by telling reporters on July 26 that he welcomed the support of any American, including Gerald L. K. Smith. "A vote is a vote," he said to his running mate in private, "and I'm doing everything in my power to get all that I can." A few days later, when Smith's America First party nominated Bricker as its vice presidential candidate, the Ohioan raced Dewey to reject the nomination. Dewey had another problem on his hands when Hamilton Fish, with whom he had observed an uneasy truce for two years, told an interviewer that he looked forward to carrying all the communities in his congressional district in the September 1 primary, except for the town of Fallsburg. The latter, he explained, was about 90 percent "a certain people," and, after all, "the Jews are more or less for the New Deal." Dewey denounced Fish's comment as "disgraceful" and un-American. He endorsed Fish's opponent, who lost nonetheless.[19]

"What're you going to do," Dewey griped after the election, "about a man who's kissed three generations of babies?"

On July 25, Harold Keller spotted a column in the New York *Times* by the paper's Washington columnist, Arthur Krock. In it, Krock quoted President Roosevelt at a private meeting with party leaders, including Chicago's Mayor Kelly and national chairman Robert Hannegan, called to discuss the wisdom of dropping Henry Wallace from the ticket and replacing him with someone else, either William Douglas or Harry Truman. Sounding less than vitally concerned ("Roosevelt," in his opponent's words, "was convinced he'd live forever"), the President instructed Hannegan to "clear everything with Sidney." Thus was touched off one of the more bizarre side issues of American political history, and a door opened to those who suspected a Communist in every Washington cupboard.

Sidney Hillman was a Lithuanian-born Jew, dispatched to the United States as a boy, later employed as an eight-dollar-a-week pants cutter in the garment district of New York. In 1910, at the age of twenty-three, he led 41,000 of his fellow workers out on strike, then displayed a tactical gift by agreeing to modify his demands in exchange for permanent arbitration within the industry. Soon afterward, the Amalgamated Clothing Workers of America was born, with Hillman its guiding spirit. He met and married a spellbinding union organizer, broke with the AFL in 1936 to join Phillip Murray's more militant CIO, and was elevated to vice president of the organization. As a young man, he had shared the political convictions of others in his trade, joining the Socialist party in New York. He had met and been captivated by Leon Trotsky. As leader of his own powerful union, Hillman wrote a book with kind words in it for the goals of Russian revolutionaries. He gave union funds to Russian relief projects and, in common with other CIO figures, spoke warmly of the heroic resistance of the Russian people to Hitler's aggression.

In July 1943, at a CIO board meeting, the Political Action Committee was born. PAC was the first attempt ever in the U.S. to organize labor for political purposes on a national scale. Hillman pledged $1.5 million to the defeat of Republicans in 1944. More important than the money at his disposal was the manpower: 20,000 in New York City on Election Day alone. There were 20,000 more in Ohio and Michigan, plus untold thousands canvassing war plants and shipyards throughout the land, working at phone banks, building car pools, writing weekly bulletins for distribution to 1,500 labor newspapers and 255 Negro ones. Hillman's very prominence became an issue in the campaign. Westbrook Pegler, with typical disregard for subtlety, lashed out at a presumed CIO-Communist alliance, built upon "naturalized but unassimilated European parasites." No regular Republican would go nearly so far in public, but soon the Dewey high command was echoing derisively the slogan "Clear it with Sidney," and running radio spots declaring that Dewey would clear everything only with the Congress and the American people.

Getting as much publicity as Hillman was Earl Browder, the Kansas-born chairman of the Communist Political Association, a successor to the party dissolved as a measure of wartime unity. Four years earlier, Browder, echoing the party line at the time, stood on a stage in Madison Square Garden and denounced Roosevelt for scheming to lead the nation into "imperialist war." Now, at the end of August, Browder did an about-face, hailing FDR, along with Stalin and Churchill, as "one of the three great architects of the new world a-coming" (an observation that doubtless would have surprised Churchill) and warning against the election of Dewey as sending unfriendly signals to the Soviet Union.

A conscientious objector during the First World War, Browder later was arrested and jailed for using a fraudulent passport. Roosevelt had commuted the sentence in May 1942. For most Americans, this was hardly evidence of a Roosevelt-Browder alliance. As long as Stalin was a valuable ally, Browder was a tolerable pest. But as the campaign heated up, Hillman and Browder were bumped together as prominent "Forth-termites." Labor unions themselves were fractured. The New York branch of the AFL responded on August 23 with a routine endorsement of the President, while pointedly declaring Dewey to be "no enemy" of the working man. A new left-wing party, the Liberals, came into being in New York, led by David Dubinsky and Alex Rose, and formed in protest against Communist penetration of the American Labor party ranks. When voters in Maine on September 11 re-elected their Republican governor by 75 percent, the vote was interpreted as a sharp rebuke to Hillman and his PAC. Encouraged, Brownell hammered away at Hillman's "stranglehold" over the White House, a theme picked up and embroidered upon by Dewey's handpicked nominee for the U.S. Senate, Tom Curran. Curran, chosen for his appeal among ethnic and Catholic voters, hit hard in Irish, Italian, and Polish wards against what he called "the Hillman-Browder axis."

The stage was set for a very nasty campaign.

. . .

Franklin Roosevelt did not wish, he told reporters, to campaign in "the usual" way, barnstorming the country to enemy-vilify and moon-promise. In a letter of July 11, in which the President made known his willingness to run again, he used the phrase commander in chief three times. When renomination came, it found FDR in a San Diego railyard. Democratic delegates were told that their nominee was delivering his acceptance speech from "a Pacific Coast naval base." From there, Roosevelt planned a tour of military facilities in the Pacific Northwest, and a journey to Hawaii, where he would sit in judgment as General MacArthur and Admiral Nimitz debated the best means of shortening the war with Japan. In September, Winston Churchill would greet his American friend in Quebec, where the arguments would deal with postwar empires and Stalin's dogmatic insistence on having his own way when it came to voting procedures in the new world organization by which Roosevelt set so much store.

"How can you challenge a will of the wisp?" Dewey asked Colonel McCormick on July 18. The publisher wanted the Republican candidate to debate FDR in public, an unrealistic proposition. "Roosevelt won't debate anything with anybody," Dewey wrote, "and will laugh at the proposal from his positions at Pearl Harbor, Guadalcanal, or the White Cliffs of Dover."[20]

At the White House, Roosevelt was prone to fits of depression. "I shall not weep bitter tears if Dewey wins through a small vote coming out," he wrote on August 18 to a New Yorker also serving in a defense capacity. "Neither you nor I have any real right to take on any more responsibilities." Others around the President detected a less disinterested stance whenever Dewey's name entered the conversation. FDR hadn't disliked Landon, according to one of the inner circle, had mischievously referred to the Kansan as the White Mouse who wants to live in the White House. He had genuine respect for Willkie. "But he really hates that Tom Dewey."[21]

In June, presidential speechwriter Sam Rosenman met Willkie secretly at New York's St. Regis Hotel. The object: to discuss Roosevelt's cherished goal of realigning American parties, bringing together all liberals under the Democratic banner and consigning Southern conservatives to the GOP. The meeting undoubtedly had another purpose, to neutralize Willkie in the current campaign or perhaps even win his endorsement of the President. Already, the 1940 nominee had confided to Raymond Baldwin that, although he was withholding judgment on Dewey, he would never come out for

Roosevelt. Much the same thing had been told to a correspondent for *Newsweek*. Now, intrigued by the sweep of Roosevelt's thinking, Willkie wavered. On August 10, he tipped off Lord Beaverbrook, who promptly carried the news to Harry Hopkins, that he would announce his support for FDR in October. A day later, the President wrote another letter to Willkie, this time inviting him to come to the White House, ostensibly to discuss the international scene. This time, word of the approach leaked out. Roosevelt first denied, then confirmed having written Willkie, and in the ensuing controversy lost his chance at a Willkie endorsement.[22]

Now it was Dewey's turn to hold out blandishments to his defeated rival. On August 16, in an Albany press conference, he raised the specter of the forthcoming Dumbarton Oaks Conference, which had been called to implement a plan of action for the United Nations, "subjecting the nations of the world, great and small, permanently to the coercive power of the four nations holding the conference." Military might alone, he continued, "does not give us the right to organize the world so that we four will always be free to do what we please." It was quite a departure from the Anglo-American alliance of Mackinac, but Dewey's stand was sound politics, sure to attract Polish and other ethnic votes from second-generation Americans worried about the fate of their ancestral homes under possible Soviet rule. It was also an olive branch extended to Willkie, whose One World was built on the idea of self-determination.

Within twenty-four hours, Secretary of State Hull issued his own statement, reassuring Dewey that his fears were groundless, and asking him to come to Washington "in a nonpartisan spirit" for personal conferences that might quell any lingering apprehensions. Hull was in a cabinet meeting at the White House on the morning of the eighteenth, when he was handed a telegram from Dewey accepting the invitation, pledging his wholehearted support for "every effort to organize, both temporarily and permanently," an international peace, and designating John Foster Dulles as his personal representative to meet with the Secretary in an attempt to remove the issue of the world organization from the discord of a campaign. Roosevelt, looking on, voiced no objection, only skepticism. For his part, Dewey told reporters that he was taking this unprecedented step in hopes of avoiding "the abyss of power politics." He sent Dulles south in a state car, a minor concession to the severe phlebitis that later landed Foster in a hospital, and he directed his foreign policy adviser to consult with Taft, Vandenberg, and other leading

Republicans in the capital at the same time he negotiated with Hull.

He also made a fresh attempt to open the clogged channels of communication to Willkie. On the night of the nineteenth, Elliott Bell put in a call to Willkie's New York City apartment, where a butler informed him that Mr. Willkie had retired for the night. Dewey fired off a telegram requesting Willkie to call him in the morning. When no call had come by ten-fifty, Dewey picked up the receiver and dialed New York himself. Willkie said he had just gotten up, and would have an answer to the telegram "before long." Dewey pressed: he hoped that they might have a "good talk" prior to Dulles' meeting with Hull. Willkie demurred, saying he was just finishing breakfast and would send a reply "in a little while." Dewey refused to let go. "Couldn't we arrange it on the telephone?" he asked, only to be put off a third time.[23]

When a telegram did arrive, it was frosty with implication. "I wish I had known of your desire for my views prior to your original statement," it said. "For several years I have been deeply concerned about the ill fate of the small nations inherent in military alliances"—a fresh slap at Mackinac. A few days before, Willkie went on, he had sought and received from the State Department "strong affirmative assurances" on just this point. However, since the forthcoming meeting with Hull was to be nonpartisan in character, "I shall be glad to give your representative freely of my views."

That done, Willkie called newspaper friends in Albany for a transcript of the release announcing the meeting. "I don't trust the little bastards," he explained. Asked in return to divulge the site of his conference with Dulles, Willkie replied, "I ain't saying. The whole purpose of this thing is to take some pictures. They just want to show me off like some prize bull." The two men eventually got together at Dulles' home on East Ninety-first Street, where they agreed to disagree on the thorny issue of deploying American forces as part of an international peacekeeping force. A carefully worded communiqué described the session as "a full exchange of views, not animated by partisan considerations." Two days later, as Dulles sat down with Hull in Washington, Willkie let it be known that the GOP must embrace his position on the troop deployment question, awarding to the world body Congress's traditional prerogative to dispatch troops and declare wars.[24]

Meanwhile, Dulles reviewed a draft agreement for the organization provided him by the Secretary of State, and a memo on the status of small nations within it. Much of their conversation revolved around semantics: Should they use the phrase "nonpartisan," as Hull wished, in describing their approach to the UN, or Dulles' "bipartisan," the latter at least implying shared credit. For three days, the two men talked, surveying the world scene generally and tightening up ratification procedures for the new organization's charter. Dulles telephoned his patron in Albany to review the text of a joint statement he proposed to issue with Hull, and reported only a single word correction. Dewey wanted the word "full" inserted before the phrase "public nonpartisan discussion." As Dewey interpreted the agreement, it ruled out of campaign discussion the world body's mandate to use force. Hull himself said as much a few days later in seeking support from a bipartisan group of senators. To the Secretary, Dewey expressed his hope that the meetings might represent a new beginning in American foreign policy. "Heretofore, war has been the only matter which has been lifted above partisanship during a presidential campaign ... if we are to have lasting peace, we must wage peace as well as we wage war." Hull replied with his own gratitude for "a heartening manifestation of national unity."[25]

For the most part, the agreement struck between Dulles and Hull held. When Dewey sent the Secretary some suggestions of his own regarding the UN charter, Hull readily forwarded them to Edward Stettinius, his deputy at Dumbarton Oaks, who had them incorporated in the document after no objections were raised by British or Soviet delegates. Hull passed on a five-page report on the conference on September 11, and Dulles, pleased with its work to date, promised to do his best to persuade Republicans in Congress against forcing the volatile issue of a world army. Hull, in his memoirs, praised Dewey for having "wholeheartedly" followed his end of the bargain made in August. Indeed, when the deployment issue entered the campaign in its closing days, it was a Willkie Republican, Minnesota Senator Joseph Ball, who raised it. Despite his voting for Dewey in Chicago, Ball now required convincing evidence that his party's candidate was sincere in his internationalism. Specifically, Dewey, like Roosevelt, was challenged to provide a guarantee that an American delegate to the United Nations would have authority without recourse to Congress to commit American forces to battle.

In a memo to speechwriter Stanley High on September 5, Dewey stressed that a global peace could only be achieved over a fifty-year period. "Acquaintances between passing rulers," he wrote, "may make personal decisions which will make more difficult building up

. . . the basis for real peace." Two weeks before Election Day, Roosevelt undercut him by endorsing Ball's demand. The President, Dewey said twenty years later, "broke his commitment, and said in a very deft way that the town hall didn't have any power unless it had a policeman, thereby satisfying a great many people who felt that there should be a United Nations army, about which I had a good many reservations. I have been proved right, and he won the election."[26]

The best Dewey could do was express confidence that a new president who cared about working with Congress would be able to "grant adequate power for swift action." Beyond that, he refused to go. "Those who would attempt to ride roughshod over the Congress and to dictate the course it should follow before it has even been acquainted with the facts," he asserted in Ball's hometown of Minneapolis on October 24, "are trifling with the hope of the world." Ball threw his support to Roosevelt. Willkie's followers could not hope for guidance from their leader; on October 8, a few weeks after meeting privately with Brownell at Henry Luce's Waldorf Towers suite and agreeing to make a broadcast for Dewey over the Indianapolis radio station owned by Eugene Pulliam, Willkie had died of a heart attack at Lenox Hill Hospital. He died without illusions. To Brownell, he predicted a Roosevelt victory on November 7, and then declared his own intention to seek the GOP nomination once again in 1948. He even asked Brownell to be his manager in the future campaign. None of this ever reached the public, soon caught up in a fruitless debate over which 1944 candidate the dead man might finally have supported. So intense was the speculation that Edith Willkie issued a statement that her husband hadn't made up his mind at the time of his death, nor could anyone living purport to speak with authority for him. More than a quarter century later, she still held to the belief. She also said that between her husband and Tom Dewey there existed "no real quarrel."[27]

Dewey attended the funeral, issued the usual bromides of praise, then returned to the campaign trial. Privately, he might be forgiven for thinking that Willkie had enjoyed the last laugh in their stormy, ambition-plagued relationship. The death of America's original One Worlder did not end the debate over Roosevelt's UN. Ironically, when the proposed charter was criticized as insufficiently rigorous, the charges came from Dewey's camp. Those doubts, couched in the language of diplomacy, did not reach public ears. Instead, on October 8, Dulles worried in a private memo that the charter unnecessarily limited the definition of threats to world peace, ruling out as strictly internal matters such provocations as minority persecution, military buildups, and economic sanctions against a neighbor.[28]

Most of Washington cared little for domestic politics; the global variety seemed new and infinitely portentous. But some partisans still rose on the floors of Congress to prick the nation's apathy. Harold Knutson, a Michigan Republican, fumed over attacks on the honor of his colleague in the House, Clare Boothe Luce. In Knutson's mind, Mrs. Luce hadn't gone nearly far enough in assailing the administration in her series of guest columns in place of the vacationing Walter Winchell. For example, he wondered how much the American people knew about a recent presidential excursion to Alaska. According to Knutson, a naval destroyer had been sent north to pick up Roosevelt's Scottie dog, Fala, mistakenly left behind in the confusion of departure.

On August 29, the President had once more let it be known that he was too busy with the war to make any "swing around the country." No political speeches were on his calendar before September 23, when he was set to address a Washington dinner of the teamsters' union. But Roosevelt wasn't abandoning all thoughts of politicking. When Frances Perkins, his secretary of labor and herself a frequent target of Republican criticism, brought him some notes for inclusion in his text, the President waved them away. No, he told Mrs. Perkins, he was going to have some fun with the teamsters.

On September 6, Dewey left Albany for his first campaign swing. With him went seventy-five reporters, photographers, radio men, an entourage of speechwriters and researchers, Paul Lockwood, Lillian Rosse, Elliott Bell, and Frances. The train on which they traveled was a marvel of streamlined efficiency, with individual cars set aside for the speechwriters under Bell, for press conferences once a day, for the different media and for local bigwigs who joined the caravan for a few hours or a day as it whipped through their territory. Journalists found plenty of coffee and roast beef sandwiches, and a car decked out with long tables and typewriters on which to pound out their dispatches. What's more, the train was wired for sound, so one didn't have to leap into the crowd at each stop, jostle the locals to hear what Dewey had to say, and then race to catch the departing train as it headed for the next stop. Instead, one could jot down the candidate's remarks while seated in the comfort of the dining car.

For the first few days, even this proved unnecessary. Dewey told reporters that he would not be delivering whistle-stop speeches from the rear platform of the train; such conventions of American campaigning were, he explained, "unseemly" in wartime. He had his preferred methods of getting the job done. "He is working tremendously hard with the boys who run the state machines," one newsman wrote to Steve Early in the White House, "and demanding that they produce. Lockwood is giving them privately some of the most forthright talk they probably have ever heard."

Wherever he went, Dewey spent his time shuffling between groups of farmers, blacks, labor men, young Republicans, and senior party officials. Unlike Willkie, who had spent much of his time in 1940 trying to convert hostile voters, Dewey was doing his best to solidify support among ordinarily Republican groups, before he reached out in October for independents and disenchanted Democrats. His tactics seemed logical in the face of an electorate preoccupied with the war and less than thrilled with the choice put before it. "Hold your nose and vote for Roosevelt" went one halfhearted slogan, "or close your eyes and vote for Dewey." When the Republican candidate reached Philadelphia on the seventh, 70 percent of his audience was female. His motorcade was greeted with cries from the sidewalks, "Where'd you get the gas?"[29]

In his memo to Stanley High setting forth the main themes of the campaign, Dewey gave first importance to the likelihood that the next administration would be a peacetime one. "This should be said over and over again." In Philadelphia, he tried out the idea. The end of the war was "in sight," he told 12,000 supporters. The economic security of Americans after the war was an "overshadowing" issue. Was the New Deal prepared to realize the nation's potential? According to Selective Service Director Lewis Hershey, Dewey said, it was cheaper for the government to keep soldiers in uniform after the war, rather than muster them out to their homes. He went after the War Production Board, the federal agency charged with planning for reconversion, and said it was racked by "quarreling, disunity and public recriminations."

Deploring the shambles of bureaucratic agencies, the Republican outlined a staggering potential for economic growth once the fighting ended. At least 6 million cars would be needed to replace those on the road in 1941, along with 23 million radios, 7 million clocks, 5 million refrigerators. Six hundred items using iron or steel hadn't been manufactured at all since Pearl Harbor. The transportation industry—rail, auto, and air—was anxious for a signal to get going again. If government treated the private sector as a partner and not an enemy, granting reductions in taxes and cutting back on excessive regulation, then 60 million jobs were indeed possible. "I think Mr. Roosevelt is going to get very tired of you before the campaign is over," Alf Landon wired after hearing the speech.[30]

A friendly editor in Buffalo had a very different reaction. A. H. Kirchofer told Dewey that the Philadelphia speech was "way over the heads of most Americans." Landon himself urged more informal talks, including rear platform appearances of the sort that usually lead to presentations of Indian war bonnets and small children waiting to be kissed. But Dewey had his own plan of attack. "It would be nice to run for President," he replied to Landon, "and not have to write speeches, wouldn't it?" When his train reached Owosso on September 10, he asked the local welcoming committee not to stage an elaborate greeting. His mother dismissed as "asinine" reporters' inquiries about her menu for Sunday dinner. At nearby Jackson, the candidate refused to appear on the rear platform of his train. Not until the twelfth, when he arrived in Valentine, Nebraska, to be met by fifty Sioux Indians from the nearby Rosebud reservation, and a crowd of 2,000 ranch hands and cowpokes, did his icy demeanor begin to thaw. "How do, how do," he said over and over to the well-wishers lined up in greeting. The next day, he dined on fried steak under a tent at the county fairgrounds, shouted, "Ride 'em, cowboy," at a rodeo staged in his honor, and shared a box of popcorn with a four-year-old admirer.[31]

He impressed the Cornhuskers with his promise of "a first class fight," but stumbled with reporters when he asserted, with no evidence to back up the charge, that General MacArthur had been shortchanged in the Pacific theater because he posed a political threat to Roosevelt. The statement was in direct violation of his earlier assertion that the conduct of the war was not a partisan issue, and it sent him scurrying back to his charges of chaos in Washington (what E. B. White satirized in *The New Yorker* as "bun-gling and con-few-zion") and the theme, repeated twenty-eight times in twenty speeches, "It's time for a change."

"Everybody looks so swell and healthy," he told 500 people at Gordon, Nebraska, "that I don't believe there is a New Dealer in the crowd." The ban on rear platform talks was forgotten now. At places like Livingston, Montana, and Coeur d'Alene, Idaho, Dewey looked forward to developing the western half of America's continent. He accepted a ten-gallon hat at Sheridan, Wyoming, rode in a torchlight parade at Billings, Montana, and laughed at the memory of himself speaking to a full house in a blizzard four years previously, when a sudden gust blew open a door and he shouted in exasperation, "Where the hell is that wind coming from?" To wool producers, he said that Frances hadn't been able to buy sweaters for the boys in over a year, and she wasn't alone in wondering what had happened to the federally ordered wool stockpile.

At Seattle, the candidate addressed the issue of organized labor, decrying "one-man policies" in the workplaces of America. He described a recent plant election, the result of which was in dispute by both workers and management. The two sides took their argument to Washington, where they found themselves called before ten separate agencies, attended four formal hearings, and filed seven complete briefs. After 370 days of this, the union was finally certified, only to be told by the federal rulemakers that a new petition had been granted to hold a new election, thus launching the whole incredible process once more.

Dewey did his best to win over blue-collar voters. He reminded them that a Republican president, William Howard Taft, had signed the bill first establishing the Labor Department. He pointed to his own efforts in New York to ensure an economy strong enough to absorb one and a half million veterans after the war. He endorsed the principles of the Wagner Act, and insisted that Americans didn't need to resort to "gunfire and gas bombs" in settling labor disputes, but neither, he said, should they accept leaf raking and bread lines in time of depression.

Two days later, at San Francisco, Dewey assayed "two dangerous alternatives" confronting the nation. "Under one, we may slip by gradual stages into complete government regulation of every aspect of our lives. Under the other, we may become so intolerant of the restraints and interferences in our lives as to take refuge in complete reaction." Government could endanger as well as provide. "For too long we have been a nation divided and government has been the great divider. Now under the stress of war we have drawn closer together. We have come to appreciate a little better the part that each of us must play. Labor, industry and agriculture . . . are equals and are equally important. No one can disregard the interest of others save to his own cost. No one can be master over the other two. No one is entitled to a voice in the affairs of government at the sacrifice of the others."

It was undeniably true. It was also dull. On September 15, some 93,000 rabid partisans awaited the candidate in the Los Angeles Coliseum, where Cecil B. De Mille had arranged entertainment by Monty Montana, elephants doing handstands, and a parade of Hollywood stars, from Cary Grant to Ginger Rogers. When Dewey's turn came, he stood under a fifty-two-foot American flag and delivered a speech about Social Security and unemployment insurance. "My God, what was the matter with him?" Rupert Hughes overheard in the crowd. "They wanted a slam-bang rally type of speech," Herb Brownell recalled afterward, "and they didn't get it. . . . The local people felt that that hurt their local campaign unnecessarily. But of course, the Governor—that wasn't his job. The biggest part of his job was to get a constructive approach to the Social Security problem in the minds of the people all over the country who were listening on the radio."[32]

Part of the fault lay with the speechwriting team, forced to apply a grand strategy hammered out in Albany to the rapidly changing realities of a national tour. Part lay with the candidate, resolute in his desire to take the high road in the campaign, avoiding the wild swinging and missed punches of 1940. Paradoxically, he seemed to be making progress with the voters even as Brownell reported a virtual strike against the campaign by big contributors. A *Fortune* magazine poll in the third week of September showed Roosevelt's lead slashed from 9 to 5 points. David Lawrence hailed the San Francisco speech as "a milestone in the evolution of the Republican party," the most progressive since the days of TR. The candidate himself was more relaxed; after his train slammed into another at Castle Rock, Washington, on September 13, he phoned reporter Esther Tufty, sent to the hospital by the wreck, and said jokingly how the accident proved she wasn't indispensable, an epithet much hurled at Roosevelt by his critics.[33]

Having recovered from the MacArthur gaffe at Valentine, Dewey won good notices with his West Coast speeches calling for "a people's peace," one not dependent for its success upon deals struck by cynical and temporary leaders of nations. "Clear it with Sidney," Alf Landon wrote, was a "devastating" slogan, and if only Dewey would place more emphasis on big city bosses and left-wing elements within the New Deal coalition, victory might yet be his. But for all the favorable straws in the wind, there was concern on the Dewey train as it headed for Needles, California, on the twenty-third. From a Hooper rating of 20.3 for his first speech in Philadelphia, the candidate's radio audience had dipped to 14.5 in Seattle. The campaign treasury was nearly bare. There wouldn't be enough money, Dewey calculated, to bring the train back to Albany from Oklahoma City, site of his next scheduled address. Finally, there was the opposition. Roosevelt was due to deliver his long-awaited teamsters speech that evening, and no one on board the train wanted to miss a minute of it. It was 6:30 P.M. on the Pacific Coast as reporters and aides of the candidate huddled together around tinny, crackling radio sets, straining to hear FDR.[34]

A visitor to the personal quarters of the White House in the third week of September found the President attempting for the first time in three years to walk with the help of his brace. "The little man makes me pretty mad," Roosevelt explained with deceptive cheerfulness. Outside, rumors gathered force about his health. He was in a Miami sanitarium, one claimed, or a Chicago hospital. Dewey himself believed FDR to have suffered a stroke while visiting Bernard Baruch's South Carolina plantation. Walter Trohan of the Chicago *Tribune* passed along word that the President was about to have surgery, with his chances of survival only 40 percent. "One of us has to stay alive," Roosevelt remarked to his running mate, after issuing firm orders against Truman's traveling by air.[35]

But on September 23, it was the Roosevelt of old who went before the teamsters, in a speech justifiably celebrated for its hilarious dismissal of Knutson's charge that Fala had been rescued from the Aleutians "at a cost to the taxpayers of two or three or eight or twenty million dollars." As for himself, Roosevelt went on, he was used to "that old worm-eaten chestnut" that he claimed to be indispensable. "But I think I have a right to resent, to object to libelous statements about my dog." Fala was Scotch, after all, and talk of such extravagance had unnerved him. "He hasn't been the same dog since."

"They liked that, didn't they?" the President said to CIO chief William Green during a pause for audience reaction. Indeed they did. One member of the audience beat a silver bread tray with a soup ladle. Another smashed glasses with wine bottles, taking a full swing to mark each punch line in the President's text. He was kept busy, as FDR, without referring to Dewey by name, sarcastically dismissed Republican attempts to pin on him blame for the Depression ("Never speak of rope in the house of a man who has been hanged," he advised the opposition) and to drive a wedge between Old Guarders and the party's "liberal, enlightened elements." More seriously, Roosevelt lashed back at those criticizing his record of war preparedness, citing numbers in key industries to prove his case and assailing Republican "propaganda techniques" lifted intact from the pages of *Mein Kampf.*

A continent away, hecklers inspired by the speech slapped red, white and blue Roosevelt stickers on the windows of Dewey's train.

Reporters competed among themselves in praise of the President's political coup. Dewey himself read the full text of the teamsters speech in the Sunday papers, described it as "snide," and, in a series of long-distance conversations with Brownell in New York, made preparations for a reply that might once again place FDR on the defensive. There was no money in the campaign treasury, so the candidate, his friends, and associates signed notes to raise the $27,496.46 it took to expand his network from 164 to 288 stations. Then Dewey and Bell secluded themselves, working straight through the afternoon and evening of the twenty-fourth. Among the ammunition stockpiled against such a crisis were earlier criticisms of American preparedness developed by high-ranking Republicans in the House and developed at length by, among others, Wendell Willkie.[36]

Alerted to expect fireworks, Oklahoma City Republicans had packed the Municipal Auditorium to overflowing; 15,000 Dewey partisans greeted their candidate with rebel yells and foot stomping. Cries of "Tom, Tom" and "Hi, Frances" pierced the din, until Dewey held up his arms and began to speak. For two and a half weeks, he said, he had been traveling the nation, offering in six major speeches a detailed blueprint for the kind of program that should be adopted "if we are to win here at home the things for which our American men are fighting abroad." Deeply aware of the difficult circumstances under which the campaign was being waged, Dewey asserted his conviction that conduct "on our side" had contributed to wartime unity. He quoted Roosevelt's July declaration against business as usual "in these tragic days of sorrow," and compared it to the teamsters appeal, "a speech of mudslinging, ridicule and wisecracks. It plumbed the depths of demagoguery by dragging into this campaign the names of Hitler and Goebbels; it descended to quoting from *Mein Kampf* and to reckless charges of 'fraud and falsehood.' " As a result, Dewey went on, he would be compelled this evening to detour from the high road just long enough "to keep the record straight." The crowd let out a burst of applause, raised to frenzy when Dewey told them, "He has made the charges. He has asked for it. Here it is."

First came a quote from Lewis Hershey in the August 23, 1944, edition of *Stars and Stripes:* "We can keep people in the Army about as cheaply as we could create an agency for them when they are out." Did Roosevelt deny the statement? Did he "laugh off" the prospect of postwar unemployment? Maybe so. "But he cannot laugh off the record. In March 1940, Mr. Roosevelt had been in office seven years. Yet the depression was still with us. We still had ten million Americans unemployed. Those are not my figures," Dewey told the crowd. "Those are the figures of the American Federation of Labor. Is that fraud or falsehood?" Dewey professed to see desperation in opposition tactics. Because the New Deal could only thrive by "waging relentless warfare against our jobmaking machinery," it must now resort to "wisecracks and vilification" to obscure the facts.

"Now I had not intended in this campaign to rake over my opponent's sad record of failing to prepare the defenses of this country for war. It's all in the past—a very tragic past. It has cost countless American lives; it has caused untold misery. . . . In 1940, the year after the war began in Europe, the United States was in such a tragic condition that it couldn't put into the field as a mobile force 75,000 men. The Army was only about 25 percent ready. Now, Mr. Roosevelt, did those statements come from Goebbels? Was that fraud or falsification? Those are the words of General George C. Marshall, Chief of Staff of the United States Army, under oath."

Dewey quoted Hap Arnold, Commanding General of the Air Force, who, in an official report filed the previous January, wrote that when the Japanese swooped down on Pearl Harbor, the U.S. was equipped "with plans but not with planes." Did Roosevelt still claim we were prepared? Dewey turned to a Senate debate four months before the attack that dragged the nation into the fighting, in which Arthur Vandenberg and Harry Truman alike agreed that responsibility for inadequate defenses lay with the White House. He quoted Truman in May 1943: "After Pearl Harbor we found ourselves woefully unprepared for war."

"Was that Dr. Goebbels on the floor of the Senate?" Dewey demanded.

Roosevelt's own record of verbal reassurance was combed, for the 1940 dismissal of Dewey's two-ocean navy as "just plain dumb," and, "when Hitler's armies were at the gates of Paris . . . the jolly comment: 'There is no need for the country to be discomboomerated.' " The simple truth, Dewey continued, was that Roosevelt's record was "desperately bad," unworthy of support by the American people. Shouts of "Pour it on" could be heard, as the issue of "indispensability" was addressed. Dewey quoted Chicago's Mayor Kelly, "who organized that false third-term draft in 1940, remember?" (" 'The salvation of this nation rests in one man.' ") He dredged up Harry Truman's warning that "the future of the peace and prosperity of the world depends upon his re-election in November." Dewey hadn't yet heard Truman repudiated by the White House, but then, Roosevelt "usually waits to shed his vice presidents until they have served at least one term." This time, Dewey joined in the laughter his acid humor provoked.

"Let's get this straight," he said. "The man who wants to be President of the United States for sixteen years is, indeed, indispensable. He is indispensable to Harry Hopkins, to Madame Perkins, to Harold Ickes ... to America's leading enemy of civil liberties—the Mayor of Jersey City. He's indispensable to those infamous machines in Chicago, in the Bronx, and all the others. He's indispensable to Sidney Hillman and the Political Action Committee, he's indispensable to Earl Browder, the ex-convict and pardoned Communist leader.

"Shall we, the American people, perpetuate one man in office for sixteen years? Shall we do that to accommodate this motley crew?" Shouts of "No, no" punctuated the applause; thirty-eight times the crowd broke into Dewey's text to register approval. The next morning, Americans woke to realize, for the first time, that a real live presidential contest was on. From California, Rupert Hughes wired Dewey that his speech was not mere oratory, "it was an earthquake." Indiana Senator Raymond Willis exulted, "The Champ has met his match." The New York *World-Telegram* headlined its approval: "FDR Asked for It." In his quarters at the Roosevelt Hotel, Brownell found his phones ringing off the hook with pledges of support from previously somnolent Republicans. The candidate as well seemed invigorated by the large enthusiastic crowds clogging his route back to Albany. There were 20,000 at the depot in Tulsa, to whom he promised a clean sweep of bureaucrats "who have fattened themselves on your pocketbook and mine for twelve years. I should like to get rid of the wasters. I should like to get rid of that crew to whom my opponent is so indispensable ... that elegant collection of loafers contributed to the government by the Kelly machine in Chicago and your neighboring Pendergast machine in Kansas City."[37]

Dewey found 5,000 people waiting to greet him at midnight in Springfield, Missouri, to boo references to Hillman and Browder; cheer his attack on "long-haired braintrusters ... who sit in ivory towers in Washington and think they know how the American people want to live"; and laugh with approval when he promised to write laws "so that men will not be afraid to move in fear you may be violating section 3, of subdivision 2, of paragraph 8, line 5 of a Washington directive." By the time he returned to Albany on September 27, Dewey had reason to engage in horseplay with reporters

who held out war drums for him to beat. A poll of forty-eight journalists on board his train revealed that thirty-seven—by no means
Dewey partisans themselves—thought the Republican cause had
been advanced by the trip. Twenty-three assessed Dewey as the
winner in the bitter exchange with Roosevelt, Fala to the contrary.
Walter Trohan sent word via Pat Hogan that the President's press
secretary, Steve Early, was sufficiently concerned about the election
to be making discreet inquiries about post-January employment.
Jim Farley was predicting a Dewey victory in New York State; his
own wife, he confided to John Nance Garner, was "red hot" for the
Governor.[38]

The campaign escalated in intensity. People began calling it a
contest between Roosevelt's dog and Dewey's goat. Others said it
was a test between a big man with a little dog, and a little man with
a big one. His success notwithstanding, Dewey confronted a painful
choice. Still hopeful of returning to the high road he had charted
from the beginning, he told Brownell that the Oklahoma City
speech was "the worst damned speech I ever made." Moreover, before he could fully assess the results of his continental swing the
campaign took a new and startling turn, with a plea from the nation's military establishment that Dewey rule off-limits the American response to—and anticipation of—the day of infamy at Pearl
Harbor.[39]

George Marshall was a worried man. For two and a half years, he
had guided the American comeback from Pearl Harbor, had overseen creation of a vast cross-Channel invasion, and had made sensitive decisions of where and when to attack in both the military and
political wars. Throughout, like an undetonated shell, the issue of
the Japanese attack and the administration's handling of diplomacy
and military preparation in the days just before it threatened to explode a fragile unity. Originally, Washington had blamed the top
military men in the Hawaiian Department, Admiral Husband E.
Kimmel and Major General Walter C. Short, for the disaster. An inquiry headed by Supreme Court Justice Owen Roberts concluded as
much a few weeks after the raid. Others were less sure. Even as
Dewey and Roosevelt engaged in long-distance sniping, two service
boards of inquiry were working toward conclusions of their own.
Walter Trohan, reflecting his paper's vehement dislike of the President, was conducting a one-man probe of his own, and learning
from Pentagon sources that code breakers knew prior to December 7
that the Japanese fleet was on the move. Washington cocktail par-

ties were enlivened with talk of Japanese codes broken. In their frustration at being denied the issue of the actual conduct of the war, congressional Republicans were soon nipping at the administration's heels.

On September 11, Representative Hugh Scott asked some penetrating questions. Why, the Pennsylvania Republican wanted to know, was the American fleet stationed in Oahu in the first place? Why hadn't Admiral Kimmel received from Washington requested supplies vital to a defense? Why hadn't the President personally met with the Japanese prime minister in a last-ditch attempt to stave off war? And why had the Roberts inquiry been conducted like a kangaroo court, focusing blame exclusively on the field commanders and ignoring possible culpability on the part of higher-ups in the defense establishment? John Bricker was more explicit still. On the campaign trail, he accused the White House of covering up details of the "disgraceful Pearl Harbor episode." Styles Bridges rose on the floor of the Senate to say that Dewey himself was "gathering facts" that might sustain allegations of a whitewash.

Bridges was correct. For weeks, John and Dorothy Burton had been collecting data for possible use in Dewey's speeches, building a case that the government had powerful reason to expect a Japanese attack somewhere in the Pacific, and was grossly negligent in failing to prepare adequately to counter it. With the Oklahoma City speech, Marshall's fears that Pearl Harbor might become a campaign issue were revived and so it was, on his own and without checking with the White House, that the Chief of Staff dispatched Colonel Carter C. Clarke to Tulsa on the afternoon of the twenty-sixth. Clarke, head of the War Department's cryptographic intelligence unit, carried a three-page letter marked Top Secret. "What I have to tell you," it began, "is of such a highly secret nature, that I feel compelled to ask you either to accept it on the basis of your not communicating its contents to any other person and returning this letter or not reading any further and returning the letter to its bearer." Dewey halted, gave the letter back to Clarke, and explained that as a candidate for the presidency, he was in no position to make "blind commitments."[40]

Before dismissing Clarke, Dewey sparred with the colonel over the letter's implications. He demanded Clarke's word of honor that he had, in fact, been sent by Marshall. He vented his frustration at the man in the White House. "Marshall does not do things like that," Dewey told Clarke. "I am confident that Franklin Roosevelt is behind this whole thing." More explicit still, he told Clarke that he already knew that American authorities were decoding "certain Jap codes before Pearl Harbor and that at least two of them are still in current use." But if Dewey hoped for confirmation, he had underestimated Clarke's reserve. Before sending the colonel away, Dewey insisted again that he knew about such codebreaking, "and Franklin Roosevelt knows about it too. He knew what was happening before Pearl Harbor, and instead of being re-elected he ought to be impeached."[41]

Dewey wasn't through with what he called "the whole Pearl Harbor mess." He informed Clarke that he would be willing to see Marshall himself, or a designee from the General's staff, once he returned to Albany. Two days later, Clarke was ushered into the reception room of the executive mansion, where he found the Governor and Elliott Bell. Fresh arguments ensued: over Dewey's demand that he be allowed to keep the letter for his most personal files, and that Bell stay in the room as it was read. Clarke hesitated to call Washington, a necessary prelude to obtaining such permission. Bemused, Dewey assured him that the room was not bugged—"unless O'Connell has just put one on me"—and went on to claim that he hadn't bugged his District Attorney's office either (while acknowledging, "I had one in my witness room, of course"). Finally, Dewey said he would call Marshall himself. Both conditions were met.[42]

Dewey turned to Clarke and expressed his continuing astonishment at the premise that any codebreakings were actually secret. He could name "at least twelve Senators . . . that know all there is to be known about Pearl Harbor." Bell confirmed this, describing a Washington dinner party at which a naval commander regaled guests with tales of derring-do involving the deciphered codes and Japanese naval maneuvers headed off as a result. "Why in hell haven't they changed this," Dewey wanted to know, "especially after what happened at Midway and the Coral Sea?" Clarke explained the variety of codes and ciphers involved, and the various Japanese agencies tangled up in a bureaucratic web. By now, at last, Dewey was reading Marshall's letter, which, except for a new opening paragraph relaxing Marshall's original ironclad insistence against mentioning any of its contents, was virtually identical to his first missive. Now the Chief of Staff sought from Dewey only a promise that the candidate would discuss nothing learned for the first time as a result of the letter. He took pains as well to reassure Dewey that Roosevelt knew nothing of the entire operation. He was persisting, wrote Marshall, "because the military hazards involved are so serious that I feel some action is necessary to protect the interests of our armed forces."[43]

A machine capable of deciphering Japanese diplomatic and other codes had been built before December 7, 1941. Unfortunately, Marshall said, no message singling out Hawaii as the point of attack had reached the War Department until too late. Later it was learned that messages decoded in Washington on the morning of the seventh had been relayed to San Francisco, the Panama Canal Zone, and the Philippines. Radio interference had forced the message for Pearl Harbor to be sent via Western Union, whose civilian messenger was approaching the base on either a bicycle or motorcycle when the Japanese bombs fell on the U.S.S. *Arizona*.

"Now the point of the present dilemma," Marshall continued, "is that we have gone ahead with this business of deciphering their codes until we possess other codes, German as well as Japanese, but our main basis of information regarding Hitler's intentions in Europe is obtained from Baron Oshima's messages from Berlin reporting his interviews with Hitler and other officials to the Japanese Government. These are still in the code involved in the Pearl Harbor events."

Marshall credited American success in the Coral Sea and at Midway to such advance information. He linked European and Pacific operations, admitted that the Roberts report was incomplete because passages dealing with the broken codes had to be withheld, and pointed to an independently authorized OSS raid on the Japanese embassy in Lisbon, which resulted in the enemy changing its military attaché code, as an instance of the dangers the present situation posed. "You will understand from the foregoing the utter tragic consequences if the present political debates regarding Pearl Harbor disclose to the enemy, German or Jap, any suspicion of the vital sources of information we now possess." Marshall wanted still more, asking Dewey at least by inference to forestall pressure in Congress to complete ongoing investigations of the attack before Election Day.

In fact, when the Army's own board of inquiry reported its findings to Secretary Stimson on October 20, it found fault with the War Department as well as General Short. It criticized Marshall himself for failing to keep Short apprised of the tensions growing all around him, and for not sending proper instructions when he finally did conclude that Pearl Harbor was inadequately defended. Unlike earlier probes, the Army board could point for evidence to precisely the decoded messages—code-named "Magic" —which Marshall was so anxious to keep from the enemy. The group's most audacious finding was that information available in Washington as early as the fourth or fifth of December was clear-cut in forecasting a Japanese attack within two or three days, and that the War Department was derelict in not alerting Hawaii to the danger immediately.

For Dewey, who was being asked to forgo a double dose of election year dynamite, the Army board and its findings could be, at best, a subject for speculation. When the report was completed, it was suppressed by Stimson at the President's express command. Had it been released prior to November 7, the public reaction might have been explosive. But it was not released. Neither were any of Dewey's own findings.

"Well, I'll be damned if I believe the Japs are still using these two codes," he told Clarke. The colonel assured him that such was the case, that 10,000 cryptographic specialists were working around the clock making use of the codes. Winston Churchill regarded Magic as his secret weapon, Clarke went on, almost by itself responsible for having saved Britain in her darkest hours. Still, Dewey was unsatisfied. Except for the two codes and the OSS affair, there was little he hadn't already known—an admission that his earlier performance at Tulsa was part bluff. Moreover, he now demanded, "What in hell do Jap codes have to do with Eisenhower?" Again, Clarke responded with detailed descriptions of differing German codes, and the importance of the messages picked up from the Japanese embassy in Berlin. The Governor and Bell stepped out of the room, and when they emerged twenty-two minutes later, Dewey said he had no further questions, nor did he wish to discuss the codes any further. Clarke promised to provide his name, serial number, office location, and home and office phone numbers, then asked Dewey if he had anything he wished to convey to General Marshall.[44]

"No," he replied in a low voice. "No message." There was a pause before Clarke prepared to return to Washington and report to his superiors. Dewey turned to his visitor. "Well," he said in parting, "I hope we meet again under more auspicious circumstances." To those around him, he was less conciliatory. "He looked like a ghost," Lillian Rosse recalls.[45]

Shaken and angry, Dewey fumed that Roosevelt was "a traitor" who had willingly or accidentally condemned more than a thousand American men, and most of the Pacific fleet, to a watery grave. But what could he do? He talked it over with Bell and Brownell, who agreed that to release the contents of the letter would be to risk a devastating counterpunch from the administration—perhaps, in Brownell's words, "a speech by Secretary Hull pointing out that this gave information to the enemy." In the end, he chose to remain silent, muting his party's attacks and trusting Marshall's word that the Japanese had not changed their diplomatic codes between December 1941 and September 1944. He instructed John Burton to collect everything dug up to date, "put it away securely and forget it."[46]

Roosevelt himself didn't learn of the affair until late in October, when Harry Hopkins repeated a conversation he had had with Marshall. The President seemed surprised. He said Dewey "must be pretty desperate" if he was even thinking of using information that might boomerang so badly. Not for another year, when a congressional investigation of Pearl Harbor was launched, did Dewey reveal the existence of the Marshall letters.[47]

When Congress finally got around to examining the attack, Dewey invited a New York attorney to review the evidence for him. The attorney reported some intriguing discoveries, chief among them a series of twelve diplomatic messages decoded between September 22 and December 7, 1941. Sent from Tokyo to the consul in Honolulu, the cables divided Pearl Harbor into five military zones, and requested specific details regarding berthing of American ships stationed there. Later, it was surmised from maps found in aircraft downed on the day of the attack that these messages were the basis for the deadly accuracy with which Japanese bombers picked off the fleet. In addition, a journalist friend of Dewey's confided that General Bonner Fellers, a top assistant to MacArthur during the war, had expressed certainty that Japanese codes were frequently changed. It was proved that the J-19 code, used in the messages on ship deployment, was abandoned long before 1944.[48]

Dewey went to his grave believing that Roosevelt shared in the culpability of a high command that displayed a fine gift for confusion and self-inflicted disaster in the very hours when it should have been taking steps to ward off the worst military defeat in the nation's history. There is nothing to suggest that he ever retracted his private assessment of the President made in the first moments of blind rage he felt while reading the letter from Marshall.

"The closing rounds of the contest," Rupert Hughes told Dewey on October 2, "demand the body punches and head-rocking that nobody can put over better than you." That same week, Clare

Boothe Luce said in Philadelphia that the United States had been "lied instead of led" into the war. The Republican National Committee deluged friendly households with examples of New Deal indulgence: a diaper shortage caused by Lend-Lease's shipment of millions to North Africa, where Arabs liked to wear them as turbans; a million pounds of meat turned into fertilizer because of inadequate storage by the War Food Administration, Mayris Chaney's program, administered under the First Lady's supervision, to teach America to dance, a crusade transferred after complaints from the Office of Civil Defense to the Federal Security Agency.[49]

Dewey himself seemed to regard the campaign as a crusade, for government that avoided crises as well as it managed them. In his memo to Stanley High, Dewey called his race with Roosevelt a contest of "competence against incompetent bungling." In his own administration, he claimed, all races, creeds, colors, and shades of political opinion thrived. "They work without quarreling and in harmony. When there are differences they get together and thrash them out instead of running to the newspapers and carrying their battles to the point of destruction of the government's business and great injury to the people's interest."[50]

At St. Louis in the third week of October, Dewey put forward three simple criteria by which to judge a government. Was it honest? Were the people who ran it competent to do their jobs? Did it have faith in the nation itself, "and a wholehearted determination to make our system work?" By such standards, he went on, the New Deal was a dismal failure, "the most spectacular collection of incompetent people who ever held office." He described squabbles over NRA, fights between Ickes and Hopkins over PWA and WPA, a struggle between Ickes and Leon Henderson over who was named "gasoline czar," contention within the OPA, attacks by Ickes upon the War Labor Board and by Henry Wallace on Secretary of Commerce Jesse Jones. "What kind of government is this," he demanded, "that even a war cannot make it sober down and go to work?" The New Deal, he concluded, had degenerated into "little men rattling around in big jobs," capable of nothing beyond "planned, noisy chaos and bungling."

In his first speech since Oklahoma City, one containing a detailed proposal for postwar tax reduction and an overhaul of the "confused and complicated" tax laws, Dewey confined his direct assault on Roosevelt to a quote from Harry Hopkins, captured for posterity by Arthur Krock, to the effect that the administration would "tax and tax, spend and spend, elect and elect." He also faulted the New Deal for changing the tax laws fifteen times in twelve years, thereby undermining the stability necessary for economic growth. But that wasn't the sort of thing partisan Republicans wanted to hear from their candidate. Dewey found himself cornered. He knew, for instance, that Eisenhower had predicted the war might be over before the end of 1944, knew also that many military men and diplomats agreed that the Morgenthau plan had only stiffened German resistance to the onrushing Allied armies. In the closing days of the campaign, Dewey hit at the administration on the plan and its potential to delay peace. But, with polls showing the American people in favor of a hard peace for Germany and Japan, there were few votes to be garnered by attacking Morgenthau.

Money continued to be short; Dewey told a friend on October 4 (inaccurately, as it turned out) that the opposition had "twice as much." American fighting men stood on German soil at the end of September, and on October 20, MacArthur's invasion of Leyte quieted the fears of his supporters that he was being held on a leash by a hostile Roosevelt. Arthur Sulzberger informed the candidate that, despite his personal distaste for the President, the New York *Times* could hardly oppose the chief executive unless Dewey were willing to publicly repudiate the Chicago *Tribune* and other isolationist supporters of the GOP cause. Sulzberger did oblige the candidate on one item, by booting *Times* reporter Warren Moscow off the Dewey train after an annoyed Dewey sent Winthrop Aldrich to complain of Moscow's attitude. Aware of an impending endorsement of Roosevelt by his paper, Sulzberger figured he had little to lose by giving in on this demand, and Moscow was reassigned.[51]

In his anxiety to strike sparks, Dewey tried, and failed, to make an issue of the Thousand Club, a Democratic fund-raising organization suggested by Roosevelt himself, in which wealthy party officials, businessmen, and officeholders donated $1,000 apiece, in return for prestige and a loosely defined entree to the White House and official Washington. After a reporter at the Quebec Conference told Dewey he was convinced that Roosevelt was a dying man, and that the Republican contender had "an absolute duty" to reveal the true state of the President's health, Dewey and his advisers sweated blood over the issue. "There wasn't a single night went by," Herbert Brownell recalled of the campaign's final three weeks, "we didn't argue that one out. . . . Some people wanted to go all out, stating that he was on his death bed, and getting all the evidence that we could." In the end, this too was dropped, as unseemly and politically certain to backfire.[52]

Confronted with such a dearth of winning issues, Dewey fell back in the homestretch on the bogey of Communism. In a speech in Charleston, West Virginia, on October 7, he said that Washington now owned or operated a fifth of the nation's industrial plant, and accused Roosevelt of developing "little by little . . . our own corporate state." He reminded his audience that Earl Browder, just one week before, had endorsed the President before 15,000 cheering partisans in Madison Square Garden. Sidney Hillman became more than ever a lightning rod for criticism, even within the Democratic party. John L. Lewis, whose United Mine Workers were friendly to Dewey, called Hillman "a Russian pants worker." Democratic national chairman Bob Hannegan bridled when Hillman stood in for Roosevelt at the New York Herald-Tribune Forum on October 18. And Hillman himself took nothing lying down. He said Dewey's election would be "a catastrophe for the country" and accused his Republican rivals of resorting to "red-baiting and Jew-baiting."

Those closest to Dewey debated how far to go in making Hillman and Browder a major theme of the campaign's closing days. In the last week, Dewey was scheduled to speak in Boston. Before he went, he invited Charles Breitel to look over the text, and Breitel said frankly he thought it was bad. Why? Dewey wanted to know. "Because you've got that Hillman piece in there," Breitel replied. "You're speaking in Boston and everybody will know you're trying to get the Irish Catholic vote. It's going to look like a cheap play at a time when the Jews in this country are terribly sensitive, when they feel terribly threatened, they don't even know if they'll survive this war . . . and to a group they believe is largely unsympathetic, if not anti-Semitic, you've got this stuff."

Dewey countered that the speech contained praise for David Dubinsky, then feuding with Hillman over Communist penetration of the American Labor party, but Breitel dismissed this as "an obvious cover." Then Elliott Bell jumped in, telling the counsel he was only "carrying the torch for the typical Communist line." At this point, Frances Dewey stuck her head in the room, tentatively but with a decided opinion to offer. As usual, she had read the speech. What did she think? everyone asked.

"Bricker could have written it."[53]

When the speech was finally delivered, it was harsh and accusatory. It painted a picture of Hillman "stalking the country squeezing dollars for the Fourth Term Campaign" from individual union members, quoted Dubinsky on the Communist influence within the ALP, and bluntly charged Roosevelt with pardoning Browder in time to organize support for the President's re-election. Pundits and partisans roiled in controversy. Arthur Krock took to his paper's editorial page to denounce as "unwarranted and unfair" the treatment of the line he had originally reported. Harry Truman departed from his text at Akron, Ohio, long enough to label the Republican ticket "a couple of fakirs who just want to get into power." Ickes, putting his gift for vitriol to good use, said Dewey was "an adolescent playing with fire." The New York *Post* went after "the Pawling Set," which it broadened to include Herbert Hoover, John Foster Dulles, and others it called "native fascists."*P.M.* announced a contest with a $500 prize for the best "dewi" of the campaign, meaning an unsubstantiated allegation, preferably quoted out of context.

Roosevelt himself fumed that this was the meanest campaign he'd ever been in, and promised retribution for some of the below-the-belt punches after Election Day. He especially resented the whispers about his health, which he ascribed to Republican editorial writers. He couldn't know that his own Pacific commander Douglas MacArthur reported to a friend who visited New Guinea that the President was "a broken old man . . . the people can have no realization of his true condition or he could not have been nominated." In response to the rumors, FDR scheduled a grueling fifty-mile motorcade through the streets of New York. For eight hours he rode in pouring rain, while 3 million New Yorkers lined the avenues and cheered themselves hoarse for the man who spoke not of administrative efficiency and peace through teamwork but of Hoovervilles and his dog, and who offered a fitting coda on the enormous events he and his country had shared for a dozen historic years.[54]

Subsequent cavalcades wound through the chilly streets of Philadelphia and Chicago, doing much to negate the health issue and regaining for Roosevelt the nation's attention. At the end, FDR refused to use Dewey's name in public, "because I try to think I'm a Christian." Ickes openly accused the Republican of anti-Semitism, and CIO leader Phil Murray told a PAC luncheon that not in forty years had the American people seen such a scurrilous campaign. "On November 8, when you go looking for the men who have been wearing the hoods during this campaign," he went on, "you'll find a hood somewhere along the highway. Pick it up and under it you'll find a little man named Tom Dewey." In his own closing appeal, Dewey tried once more to return to the heights he'd been forced to abandon after Oklahoma City. He asked a national audience on election eve to consider how to shorten the war, secure lasting peace, and achieve jobs and opportunity in the years to come. He read a letter from a mother: "I am giving you my support and I hope it will help you win. You cannot bring back my son, lost in the South Pacific, but you can and will, I think, bring back the kind of America he would have wanted to come home to."

"We stand today on one of the strange promontories of human history," Dewey said, "with the shadows of a dismal, stormy night behind us and the first gray streaks of dawn in the sky beyond us. For thirty years since 1914—nearly half the span of a human life— we have seen a series of wars, revolutions, depressions—communism, fascism, nazism, cruelty, and suffering, and finally another conflagration that has engulfed the world. At home we have had twelve unhappy years of turmoil and dissension, of group conflicts and class strife, of divisions and hatreds and antagonism. Half a generation has grown up knowing no other atmosphere. . . . After we're through with the war and get our boys back home, then we must have a period of peace and calm within our country. . . . Let us resolve to put aside these years of cynicism and of conflict . . . to throw off the nightmare of past years and breathe once more the atmosphere of courage and good will. Our people then can have a chance once more to build, to create and get ahead."

At Hyde Park, Roosevelt refused to release the text of his own closing statement, an eloquent, above-the-fray appeal for a large vote and a ringing endorsement of all those who, like himself, were determined "to outlaw and to prevent war." He had learned, the President told Harry Hopkins, that his opponent had actually prepared two different speeches, one purely political to answer anything that Roosevelt might say along similar lines. "The President said he knew that Dewey would never have time to rewrite his speeches unless he could get hold of a copy of the President's speech several hours in advance," Hopkins noted, "so the President decided not to let him have it. The result was that at the last minute Dewey had to throw together both speeches and made a hash of the whole business."[55]

The final Gallup poll showed Roosevelt ahead, 51 percent to 49 percent, a margin likely to be swelled by 3.5 million voters in uniform. The President's own forecast of his electoral college victory was 335 to 196; others in his party were far more optimistic. In Albany, Dewey seemed relaxed on the morning of the seventh; then he and Frances motored south to Manhattan to vote at the Automobile Club of America's quarters on East Forty-eighth Street. Outside, a crowd pressed against a large window, eager to see the candidate, and applauded warmly when he turned and smiled. "Hi there, Texas," someone called out to Frances. She, too, swung around and grinned.

Early that evening, Dewey appeared at the Roosevelt Hotel to order everyone out of his private command post, only to regret the ban when the switchboard operators who were receiving returns took him at his word. The first tallies were inconclusive but promising, with Dewey ahead in New England, Missouri, and Ohio. Roosevelt's margin in Philadelphia was reduced from 177,000 in 1940 to 130,000. Michigan looked good. But around nine o'clock, the trend began to reverse itself. Roosevelt pulled ahead by healthy margins in Maryland and Kentucky, piled up a massive lead in Kelly's Chicago, and showed surprising strength in upstate New York. By midnight, only the pleas of his advisers that victory was still mathematically possible prevented Dewey from conceding then and there. Soon afterward, Illinois and Wisconsin both slipped away, and Roosevelt carried Syracuse, Buffalo, and Rome, New York. It was by now apparent that Hillman's PAC had done its job magnificently. Instead of a turnout below 45 million, voters had gone to the polls in near record numbers, 48 million in all.[56]

By three in the morning, Roosevelt led in electoral votes 391 to 140. A few minutes later, Dewey appeared in the half-empty ballroom of his hotel, to concede defeat and ask all Americans to join him in "the devout hope that in the difficult years ahead Divine Providence will guide and protect the President of the United States." From Hyde Park, Roosevelt wired thanks for the statement, "which I heard over the air a few minutes ago." The President was miffed that his rival hadn't sent the traditional telegram of congratulations. Nor was that all that preyed on his mind in his hour of triumph. On his way to bed, FDR encountered presidential aide Bill Hassett, who asked if there was anything he might do before turning in. Roosevelt said no, then wheeled his chair toward the converted dumbwaiter that would take him to the second floor. He paused for a parting comment: "I still think he is a son of a bitch."

Three days later, before leaving Albany for a vacation at Sea Island, Georgia, Dewey sat down and wrote out a message of "hearty congratulations . . . during all the trying period ahead, I wish you the very best of good health and success in your every effort for the good of our country." At the White House, FDR joked about his younger rival's weak constitution and his own ability to keep on working without a break. Then he replied with terse appreciation. "My dear Governor: I have just received your greatly appreciated message of congratulations. Thank you so much. Very sincerely yours." To a friend worried about the precedent he had established, Roosevelt wrote reassuringly, "I hate this fourth term as much as you do—and the third term as well—but I do not worry about it so much as a matter of principle. It would be a mistake, of course, to establish it as a tradition but I think I can well plead extenuating circumstances."[57]

13

The Science of Politics

A good many people have the idea that politics is a sordid business, to be left to those who cannot make a living by anything else. Others have the idea that it is a simple business, in which anyone can become qualified as a sage overnight or with a brief space of speech-making or handshaking. The fact is that politics is the science of government. So far it has defeated all the best minds in the history of the world. At least I have not yet heard of the perfect government.

—THOMAS E. DEWEY

Franklin D. Roosevelt won a fourth term with 25,602,646 votes to 22,017,592 for his rival. The President carried 36 out of the 48 states, and defeated Dewey decisively in the Electoral College, 432 to 99. Republican statisticians took heart from the closest presidential contest since 1916, from significant gains among farmers and non-union labor, and from 200 counties that were taken for the first time since the advent of the New Deal in 1932. A shift of fewer than 300,000 votes in the right states would have sent the Republican to the White House; it was cold comfort for the loser. Dewey noted wryly that he had triumphed in both Hyde Park and Independence, Missouri, "but I rather think it did not particularly embarrass my opponents. They are very hard to embarrass." To a friend, he chalked up his loss to the fact that "you can't lick a total war."[1]

John Hamilton agreed. "I do not believe that ... people were afraid of Dewey per se," commented the former national chairman and card-carrying spokesman for the GOP right. "His pronouncements on international affairs, and particularly on our postwar cooperation with the rest of the world, were clear and, I think, generally satisfactory, but there was a distrust of the Republican members of the Congress based upon their voting records of the past six years." Hamilton recognized Roosevelt's greatest advantage, the Republican party's prewar isolationism. Unreconstructed isolationists had gone down to defeat wholesale. Gerald Nye and Hamilton Fish lost their seats in Congress, while Robert Taft and Clare Boothe Luce retained theirs by the narrowest of margins.[2]

The New York returns added up to paradox, as Dewey lost the state by 316,000 and his party reached its highest level of legislative strength since the Harding landslide of 1920. The reapportionment plan had paid off in new Republican seats from Long Island, Queens, and Westchester. Upstate, Rolly Marvin was finally eliminated as an irritant when he lost a State Senate contest in a major upset. Eight days later, Ed Jaeckle stunned Albany by resigning as chairman of the party, a decision he had been contemplating over the summer as the Buffalo Mahatma found himself taking a back seat to both Brownell and Sprague, and Dewey himself had left the clear impression that he no longer felt indebted to Jaeckle or bound by his advice. Publicly, the chairman remained silent, refusing to engage in any criticism of the Governor, his decision to anoint Tom Curran as the GOP Senate nominee to run against Robert Wagner, or the way the campaign against Roosevelt had been waged. Jaeckle went so far as to laud Dewey's new chairman, State Tax Commissioner Glen Bedenkapp, whose job would be eased considerably by a $212,000 surplus bequeathed by the retiring boss.

After losing to Lehman in 1938, Dewey had moved to put his stamp on New York Republicans by convening a series of meetings with legislative and county leaders, hammering out an alternative to the Democratic program and consolidating his personal position simultaneously. Now he tried to do the same thing nationwide, asking Brownell to stay on as chairman, against his wishes, and revitalize the party structure with such modern tools as full-time researchers, support staff acting as a liaison with Republican congressmen and state officeholders, and a fund-raising system aimed at diffusing contributions geographically and across the income scale.

"The PAC woke us up," Brownell said of his intention to emphasize urban proselytizing.[3]

Reconfirmed, the national chairman publicly criticized the Republican–Southern Democratic coalition in power, and put forward instead the concept of an independently formulated GOP program. If it failed to win passage, Brownell argued, then the opposition could be assailed for obstructionism. Let the shoe be on the other foot for a change. Joe Martin sympathized, but couldn't resist a gentle rebuke. "We've been out of office so long," he said of his conservative colleagues in the House, "that [they] like to take a sock at the President any time they get a chance"

Dewey had an even more radical idea up his sleeve, a twelve-point charter for the party, which he proposed to discuss with congressional Republicans in a conference that Senator Taft helped to arrange for December 21. The Ohioan was frankly dubious about the wisdom of committing the GOP in advance to Dewey's agenda, which included continuation of a bipartisan foreign policy, increased international trade, an end to secret diplomacy, and extensive rehabilitative assistance to liberated nations. At home, Dewey wanted formal pledges of Republican backing for the Fair Employment Practices Commission, anti-poll-tax legislation, an equal rights constitutional amendment, extension of Social Security benefits to 20 million uncovered workers, individual and corporate tax reductions, a two-term restriction on future presidents, abolition of overlapping federal bureaus, and the administration of unemployment insurance by the states.[4]

When the congressional delegation gathered in Dewey's suite at the Roosevelt Hotel, their host had a poignant answer to suspicions he still harbored presidential aspirations. "I honestly did not want the nomination in 1944," Arthur Vandenberg quoted Dewey in his diary, "and I honestly did everything within my power to avoid it. When it came I did the best job I knew how. . . . As long ago as Philadelphia, in 1940, I deliberately decided that I was not going to be one of those unhappy men who yearned for the presidency and whose failure to get it scarred their lives." For examples, he pointed to Wendell Willkie and Al Smith, two men all but crushed by their defeats, both now dead. Dewey would be "totally content" as a private citizen, he maintained, and should Herb Brownell in his role as party chairman seek to promote a 1948 campaign, it "would violate not only my orders but also my wishes." To another friend, Dewey said he was "certain" that Republicans would not abandon their historic refusal to renominate a defeated candidate. The war might well produce new heroes. So might the off-year elections of 1946. What Dewey did hope for was to be taken seriously as titular leader, in a position to commit the party to a program not dissimilar to what had been embraced in New York.[5]

Nothing came of his meeting with Taft and the other congressional leaders. Brownell, for one, calculated the failure to adopt a positive program that could be sold to the public as a major cause of later tensions that led to the fiasco of the Eightieth Congress and Truman's successful attempt in 1948 to portray Dewey as either its captive or an ineffective dissident from congressional orthodoxy.[6]

The congressional leadership saw no reason to defer to Dewey. They were willing to keep Brownell on in the chairmanship—a decision reached over the objections of a few conservatives at the national committee's meeting in Indianapolis on January 22, 1945—but they had no intention of surrendering on basic principle. Still, Taft and others were more flexible than the Chicago *Tribune,* which boldly proclaimed five weeks after the election, "Gov. Dewey is through. The fact is plain . . . it is useless to try and evade it." The *Trib* dismissed as "pretentious nonsense" the idea that a losing candidate might speak with authority for the entire party.

Behind the surface unity at Indianapolis lurked a broad and widening fissure over postwar internationalism. Arthur Vandenberg seized the opportunity, on the eve of Roosevelt's departure for a Big Three conference at the Russian resort city of Yalta, to discard forever his own isolationist shroud, and he appealed in a dramatic Senate speech for world organization based on "justice." Balance-of-power politics was not just, the Senator from Michigan told his colleagues. Moreover, he suggested that the military action needed to pacify Germany and Japan after victory need not require prior congressional approval. In this way, he hoped to defuse Soviet apprehensions, and thereby reduce Stalin's appetite for a series of buffer states in Eastern Europe.

It was an original contribution to the debate over the rights and responsibilities of small countries in the new order, and it so pleased the President that he took fifty copies of the address to Yalta as evidence of American unity behind his plan for a United Nations. Dewey's re-emergence came four weeks later, when he strongly endorsed Vandenberg's proposal before a Washington audience sprinkled with congressional conservatives. It wasn't an easy speech to write, he confessed to Henry Luce. One full night of "soulsearching" had been followed by three days and nights of phrasing and argument, "during which I decided that public life just wasn't worth it." The finished product was a skillful mixture of internationalism and domestic conservatism.[7]

"We have nailed to our masthead one principle . . . we will and must take a full, responsible part in the establishment of collective security among nations." Small nations would require protection against "war-breeding totalitarianism"; and to have validity, the process must be a joint effort of both national parties. Republicans, he vowed, would accept "neither isolation nor abdication." He balanced his call for internationalism with a thoughtful critique of well-intentioned federal planners who might unwittingly turn modern man into "a soulless automaton who takes his orders from the State." He defined as "the central question of our time" the need to poise economic security and individual liberty. "It is the hard core of every political decision we make."

His listeners divided among predictable lines. Vandenberg and Vermont's Warren Austin—soon to serve as American representative to the infant world body—were enthusiastic about Dewey's demand for Republican inclusion in the approaching San Francisco conference that would write the UN's permanent charter. Nebraska's stalwart Old Guard Senator Kenneth Wherry preferred the speech's domestic criticism. Charles Tobey of New Hampshire dismissed the whole thing as "too highbrow."

On February 12, 1945, Roosevelt, Stalin, and Churchill concluded their business at Yalta, and optimistic press reports reached the U.S. that the President had gotten most of his objectives from the stubborn Soviet leader and the wily Prime Minister. Soviet concessions on UN voting procedures were stressed, along with a role for France in the occupation of a prostrate Germany, and agreement to hold "free and unfettered" elections in Poland. Roosevelt aide William Hassett was less pleased, noting in his diary that after Yalta, the Soviets would dominate Europe "from the Vistula to the Adriatic." Robert Taft had a reaction of his own. "I don't think much of the Yalta results," he told Dewey on February 26, "but I am inclined to go along with any international organization that is set up, after presenting the objections for the record."[8]

Taft did much more when it came to the Bretton Woods international monetary agreement. "I don't want to hear a thing about it," he remonstrated to Dulles, who had played a major role in drawing up the finance and currency treaty. "You might change my mind." Later, Taft also cast a vote against lending Britain $1.75 billion when America's war-drained ally confronted economic collapse in the harsh winter of 1946–47. In the process, he reinforced his image, as depicted by *Fortune* magazine, as "one of that vast group of Americans to whom other countries seem merely odd places, full of uncertain plumbing, funny-colored money, and people talking languages one can't understand."[9]

In contrast to Taft, Dewey was wading deeper into internationalist waters. He urged Dulles to accompany Vandenberg to San Francisco, and he opened a photographic chamber of horrors showing Nazi brutality to Polish and other Jews. The world should not be interpreted through such aberrant cruelty, he told the Jewish Labor Committee. Mankind had taken long strides toward abolishing famine and pestilence. War, too, might be outlawed, if men could conquer ignorance, suspicion, and abuse of power. He praised the work done in San Francisco, especially the proposed world court, and argued again for a world order in which size and might did not determine the rights of nations. Those rights could not forever depend on natural resources of oil and steel, or the ability to build navies and robot bombs. "All statements of high principles or mechanics of debate and procedure will be worthless unless mankind comes one day to recognize that all peoples great or small, have rights—Costa Rica as well as the United States, Panama as well as Russia, Belgium as well as Great Britain. The hope of the world today," said Dewey, "is to get on a staircase which leads to a higher level of international morality."

On January 3, 1945, Dewey had gone before the state legislature to solicit support for a package pulling the rug from under Democrats demanding hefty loans for returning veterans, cancellation of all taxes for the year, and distribution of the Postwar Reconstruction Fund for immediate good works. The Governor instead asked that another year's surplus be salted away—anything else, he said, would be inflationary—and that outstanding bond issues be folded into his own postwar agenda. He proposed setting up a veterans division of state government, emphasizing localism and job counseling instead of the expensive bonus and loan package favored by legislators of both parties. He endorsed merit rating in the unemployment system, wherein employers might receive tax reductions in exchange for maintaining stable job rolls. Dewey also set forth a rent control plan, which earned the enmity of real estate interests, and he called for state development of the International Rapids in the St. Lawrence River should Washington not honor its long-standing commitment to build the proposed seaway with the province of Ontario. New York City was not likely to react warmly to such a massive new power project so far to the north. But some economists were predicting that the seaway and rapids could generate up to a million new jobs for the state, as well as cheaper electricity. In promoting the project as his own, Dewey also put at a disadvantage his most likely opponent for 1946, Democratic Sentor James Mead of Buffalo, who had cast a vote against the St. Lawrence plan as recently as the previous December.

Most controversial of all the Governor's bills was an anti-discrimination measure, then in the final stages of preparation by a joint legislative committee headed by Assembly Minority Leader Irving Ives. "I cannot urge too strongly," Dewey told the legislators, "that . . . action should be taken to place our state in the forefront of the nation in the handling of this vital issue." His attitude had crystallized since a storm of criticism in the wake of an anti-discrimination package introduced the previous March. That package, put together by a commission chaired by Dr. Alvin Johnson, president of the New School for Social Research, had come under fire from the counsel's office for its shoddy draftsmanship. Dewey himself had faulted the Johnson proposal for its lack of any appeal mechanism involving the courts. With the whole idea of government as an enforcer of civil rights still considered radical by many, and with only two weeks left in the legislative session, Dewey's men hadn't wished to push a bill they considered imperfect and politically impractical.[10]

Dewey had been attacked, by the NAACP and others, for not promoting Johnson's bill. His motive had been ascribed to presidential ambition on the eve of the Republican convention, and the need to placate Southerners already unnerved by the militant talk coming from Eleanor Roosevelt and others about an end to the cherished tradition of segregation. Dewey's response was to appoint Bertha J. Diggs, a black woman from Buffalo, to be his secretary of labor, and to choose a new committee, this time rooted in the legislature itself and chaired by Ives, to redraw the bill and walk a tightrope between coercion and persuasion. Eight members of the old committee quit in protest, but Johnson stayed on. He listened to Dewey, who said that he would do everything in his power to see anti-discrimination legislation enacted—but that he could not substitute his will for that of the public. An educational campaign was called for, and to that end, the Ives Committee conducted public hearings and private consultations, in the search for just the right mix of moral and legal force. Johnson came to admire the Governor, whom he called "a liberal without blinkers," and apologized for "plunking down" the original sweeping bill "on the false theory that the Governor is a dictator" who could "jam the bill through." Dewey reciprocated, hailing Johnson as a practical idealist, "willing to wait until Monday morning if the millennium can be sure of arriving and be a little better when it comes."[11]

While Ives and others laid out their plan of attack, the legislature continued working under the black cloud of suspicion puffed up by Dewey's investigations. Todd's grand jury in two interim reports had called for total overhaul of payroll procedures and abolition of "cinch jobs" and lu-lus. Todd himself was closely scrutinizing the affairs of Minority Leader Irwin Steingut, while George Monaghan reaped headlines with almost daily exposure of petty corruption in Albany County, ranging from vote fraud to embezzlement of Democratic party campaign funds. Tempers finally exploded when a third investigating body, this one set up as an in-house watchdog by the legislature itself (but counseled by Dewey intimate Arthur

Schwartz), sent around a twelve-page form containing scores of questions regarding private activities as well as personal finances. It was one thing to have to eliminate the time-honored custom of perdiem jobs on Capitol Hill. It was permissible, if humiliating, to vouch for employees' honesty on work sheets required every two weeks. But to submit to twelve pages of intimate financial and personal probing—this was too much. Republican legislators at a stormy caucus nearly had their leaders' heads. Finally, the hated questionnaire was withdrawn.

The Governor was less accommodating on the issue of rent control. On January 23, legislators rejected on a party line vote a Democratic proposal setting a rent ceiling 15 percent above that in effect in 1943, and including all commercial properties. Republicans preferred a different formula, more generous to landlords and big business alike: they would approve a 25 percent ceiling hike, and exclude from its control all office buildings and retail stores. Dewey seemed sympathetic to the GOP plan, until real estate lobbying tactics angered him, and he grew sensitive to the potential political fallout from any significant rent increases in the middle of a war. Late on the twenty-third, word was passed from his office to the Republican legislators: Accept the 15 percent limit.

"We don't mind going along with whatever the Governor wants," one GOP senator said, "but he doesn't have to make us look like fools." A Republican from Queens went further, sputtering that this was the last time he would be guilty "of such mental gyrations," to please Dewey. Two dozen other Republicans agreed, serving notice that their future pliability was in doubt. At the end of the month, Ives unveiled his anti-discrimination package, sponsored as a measure of bipartisan support with Democratic Senate leader Elmer F. Quinn and largely the handiwork of Charles Tuttle, the former U.S. attorney buried under Franklin Roosevelt's 1930 landslide and a pillar of New York City's liberal Republicans.

The Ives-Quinn Bill would create a five-member commission, its members to be appointed to full-time service by the Governor and charged with responsibilities of education and negotiation. Local extensions of this board would be set up in cities throughout New York to serve as its eyes and ears, collecting, sifting, and passing judgment on claims of discrimination in hiring and promotion on the basis of race or religion. To this point, the bill differed little from Robert Taft's plan for a voluntary fair employment practices commission at the national level, with legal authority to compel testimony when complaints could not be settled by friendly suasion. But

Dewey recognized a need to go further. Ives-Quinn treated discrimination in the workplace as a misdemeanor, subject to a fine of $500 or a jail term of up to a year. The bill's teeth were prominent enough to invite a brawl from opponents who insisted that, however morally desirable the objective of equal opportunity might be, dictation by government was not the way to bring it about.

Assemblyman William Stuart, already having parted company with the Governor on reapportionment, rose to demand a party caucus before any vote on Ives-Quinn. "The right of discrimination is older than any law or any constitution," Stuart told his colleagues. Westbrook Pegler characteristically used harsher language to say the same thing. He called the bill "a pernicious heresy against the ancient privilege of human beings to hate collectively or selectively." Robert Moses feared "quotas" would result from the government's stepping in to enforce equality in the factory and office. The State Association of Real Estate Boards likened Ives-Quinn to Prohibition. The State Chamber of Commerce professed to see race riots following in its wake, and hinted darkly at "undesirable elements" flooding New York to take advantage of its protection. In their more extreme attacks, the bill's critics said it would force Jewish families to hire Nazi butlers, and producers to cast a black in the title role of *Gentlemen Prefer Blondes.*

Ives-Quinn divided New Yorkers down the middle. Fred Bontecou, Dewey's 1938 running mate, withheld his support pending a popular referendum. Organized labor disliked provisions that it considered barriers to the dismissal of spies or troublemakers planted by capital. Business objected to state protection of lazy or inept workers. Many felt that any bill should be held back until Washington led the way. The lobbying, pro and con, was intense. The CIO mobilized its entire membership to fight for Ives-Quinn. The Brotherhood of Locomotive Firemen and Engineers appealed for a no vote from every GOP county leader in the state. In the first week of February, with some not so gentle nudges from the Governor's office, the Assembly's Ways and Means Committee reported the bill favorably to the floor. On the fifteenth, Dewey closeted himself for two and a half hours with leaders of the Associated Industries of New York, in what later was characterized as a "very frank" session. The next day, he greeted his own anti-discrimination committee, then released a statement hailing Ives-Quinn as "one of the great social advances of our time."

Even *P.M.* temporarily forsook its habitual disregard, running an editorial entitled "Hats Off!" to salute the Governor's "forthright declaration." When opponents of the bill got a public hearing in order to air their grievances, administration forces packed both the witness list and the Assembly galleries. For eleven hours, 200 New Yorkers trooped before a joint legislative committee; overwhelmingly, they were there to give reasons for their support of Ives-Quinn. Joseph Proskauer spoke out. So did Thurgood Marshall of the NAACP, the Catholic Welfare Commission, the American Jewish Congress and the Federal Council of Churches. The air crackled with a sense of incipient history on the night of March 1, as final debate wound down and the Assembly prepared to take a vote. Oswald Heck waddled down from the Speaker's rostrum to raise his voice in partisan debate for the first time in nine years. A black Democrat from New York City echoed Heck's support of the bill, turning to reluctant Republicans and admonishing them "to stand soberly with your forward-looking Governor." When the roll call was completed, it was found that 32 assemblymen—all upstate Republicans—had voted in the negative; 109 voted aye. Five days later, after rejecting Bontecou's call for a referendum, the Senate followed suit and passed the bill. Delighted, Dewey announced a public signing ceremony in the Red Room. In Boston, Archbishop Richard J. Cushing went before the Massachusetts legislature to endorse similar legislation pending in the Bay State. Representative Adam Clayton Powell of Harlem called Ives-Quinn the most important advance for black Americans since the Fourteenth and Fifteenth amendments were added to the Constitution. The Pittsburgh *Courier* said Dewey's actions should spur civil rights legislation at the federal level.

On March 12, Dewey used twenty-two pens to sign the bill before 200 onlookers squeezed into the Red Room. He said that Ives-Quinn would give "living reality to the great principles of our culture. It expresses the rule that must be fundamental in any society—that no man shall be deprived of the chance to earn his bread by reason of the circumstances of his birth." Soon, his commission established conciliation councils in the state's larger cities, struck discriminatory clauses from application forms and want ads, and in its first year on the job investigated almost 500 allegations of wrongdoing. Rail companies abolished "colored only" sections on passenger trains, New York Telephone hired the first black switchboard operators, at least fourteen separate union clauses limiting membership to Caucasians were eliminated, and within two years of the bill's passage the percentage of black women employees in clerical and sales jobs quadrupled. All this occurred without legal wrangling; indeed, not a single complaint reached the courtroom in the first five years of the bill's life. Dewey himself told friends that the responsibility for abolishing discrimination lay primarily with middle-class whites like himself. He remained proud of the bill all his life, at one point even claiming residual credit for getting Jackie Robinson accepted into major league baseball in New York.[12]

Three years later, in 1948, New York outlawed discrimination in education; and two years after that, a similar law was passed banning the practice in public assistance housing and accommodations. Dewey's civil rights program stressed education over headlines, and reconciliation over the sound and fury of postwar America, whose minorities had been awakened to assert their rightful claim to a place in the economic mainstream. It was, like so much of what Republicans in other states derided as a pale replica of the New Deal, the "scientific humanism" expounded by Tom Dewey and his fellow Young Republicans in the 1920s, an almost Fabian preoccupation with systems and rationality as the keys that would unlock a better world.

Unlike the professional reformer, whose heart beats more strongly for the good of society than of individuals, Dewey occasionally dropped the veil of reason, allowing a glimpse of fire within. He stood before the State Colored Baptist Convention in the fall of 1945 and denounced the banning of a young Negro singer from the stage of Constitution Hall in Washington. He departed from his text, in itself a rare gesture, to compliment the soulful choir he'd just heard. He said he would like to take them on a national tour. "Most of all I would like to take them to D.A.R. halls," Dewey explained. "A great many people might discover that the American Revolution was fought for the democratic principle that all men are created equal."

April 12, 1945, fell in the middle of the Governor's thirty-day period of signing and vetoing bills. Dewey spent it whittling down the legacy of paper bequeathed to him by the legislature. He approved minor insurance reforms and okayed a note to accompany pay raises for all state workers—a step interpreted by Capitol Hill observers as a virtual announcement of his candidacy for a second term. He was still in his office a few minutes before six o'clock that evening when the United Press ticker in Jim Hagerty's office clacked to life with a bulletin from Warm Springs, Georgia, announcing the death of the President. The first shocking report was soon amplified as network radio interrupted *Front Page Farrell* and *Captain Midnight* to carry details of the event, and plunge the nation into a convulsive grief that would not be matched until John Kennedy was shot down in Dallas eighteen years later. Even the formal tributes, those strait-jacketed sentiments that come from the lips of the mighty at such times, were unguarded. Robert Taft meant every word when he described FDR as "the greatest figure of our time." The New York *Times* spoke for millions of Americans when it predicted, "Men will thank God on their knees, a hundred years from now, that Franklin D. Roosevelt was in the White House."

Dewey could not go that far. He did wire condolences to the widow, and wrote out a note of sympathetic support to the new chief executive. He pledged his loyalty and help "in every action you may take in the interest of the winning of the war and the establishment of a sound and permanent peace." Truman replied warmly, admitting that his new job was "a terrific responsibility" and transmitting through his appointments secretary assurances that the presidential latchstring would always be out. Truman expressed a desire to become better acquainted, and Dewey replied that he would be "happy indeed" to see the President and discuss anything "affecting the welfare of our society." He signed his letter "with expressions of high esteem and kindest personal regards."[13]

On April 14, Dewey sat in the East Room of the White House, near Anthony Eden, Chief Justice Hughes, and Mrs. Woodrow Wilson, while the dead President was eulogized in a simple Episcopal service.

Dewey's thoughts were less reflective than anticipatory. From Chicago, his cousin Leonard Reid wrote of meeting Vice President Truman at a St. Patrick's Day celebration there, and being impressed by the modest, straightforward man from Missouri, whom some Republicans were already likening to Calvin Coolidge. Some 87 percent of the American people approved of their new leader, according to George Gallup. Jim Farley was one. "Truman has his feet on the ground," the old pro wrote five days after the succession, "and I feel sure he will be all right. Of course, he has some terrific problems facing him."[14] "While it may be bad news for the Republican party," Dewey said of Truman's apparent success, "it will be wonderful for the country, and that is what we are all interested in."

Farley underestimated the extent of the difficulties that peace would bring. Only the most gifted of seers could have foreseen the start of the Cold War between the U.S. and Soviet Russia, as the Soviets broke most of their pledges made at Yalta, airily dismissed the idea of free elections in their new satellites, and went about the business of fomenting unrest and political instability inside the democratic nations of France, Italy, and Czechoslovakia. Moreover, the threat from abroad seemed mirrored at home, where domestic Communists saw Earl Browder recalled to Moscow in May 1946 and replaced by William Z. Foster, who, among other things, compared Dewey to Hitler, Mussolini, and Franco, and accused Truman of selling out to "Wall Street imperialism."

In July, three months after assuming office, Truman traveled to Potsdam to meet "Uncle Joe" and Churchill for the first time. "I can deal with Stalin," he wrote in his diary. "He is honest—but smart as hell." For the moment, he tried desperately to keep afloat his predecessor's United Nations and adhere to Roosevelt's version of the Yalta agreements. But before the end of the year, Truman was deeply disillusioned. In an unsent letter to Secretary of State James F. Byrnes dated January 5, 1946, he stated his belief that the Russians were intent on taking over both Iran and Turkey, to add to their "two police states" of Rumania and Bulgaria. None of the assurances given on Poland had been lived up to. Defeated Germany was a meeting ground of East-West tensions. "I'm tired of babying the Soviets," Truman fumed. They only understood one language: "How many divisions have you?"

Nor were the Russians the President's only adversaries. The American public didn't know what it liked in 1945, only what it disliked. Everyone criticized price controls, but when it was suggested that the OPA should be abolished, even Taft was inundated by 10,000 letters pleading an opposite course. As wartime censorship was lifted, virulent partisanship reclaimed its place. Truman himself carried on a spirited campaign against newspapers and columnists whom he had viewed since his days in Missouri politics as spokesman for an entrenched order. Joseph and Stewart Alsop were "the Sop Sisters," and Washington's Scripps-Howard paper became "the snotty little News." He had even harsher words for Colonel McCormick and "old man Hearst."

The first year of Truman's administration was a giddy rollercoaster ride, from the national high that followed Japan's surrender in August after Hiroshima and Nagasaki had been leveled by atomic bombs, to the bewildering spectacle the next May of a Democratic President threatening to draft striking railroad workers into the Army as enemies of the fragile industrial peace. Indeed, only frantic calming efforts by the White House staff prevented Truman from publicly calling for hanging "a few traitors" in the union leadership. The wartime labor peace was over. Confronted by slackened demand, management decided to cut back on overtime rather than the hourly wage. As a result, union men found weekly paychecks shrinking. The United Auto Workers demanded a 30 percent pay hike from General Motors. Some 400,000 coal workers were led out on strike by the redoubtable John L. Lewis. Then came the railroad fiasco. Even more pervasive than the labor unrest was an inflation set off by $136 billion in savings and bonds accumulated during the war, and now rushing pellmell to overheat an economy that had been kept under artificial restraint by patriotism—and by 73,000 full-time employees in the Office of Price Administration.

Truman's misfortune was to be standing underneath the roof when it fell in. Overnight, American consumers discovered ways to circumvent price controls in a thriving black market. Women who wanted lamé skirts, families wanting appliances, newlyweds seeking apartments—all racked their brains and pitted their considerable ingenuity against the bureaucrats. Nylon stockings were worth their weight in gold. Iowa farmers traded an automobile for a boxcar of corn to feed their cattle. Butter and cheese, building blocks and beer, all took on second labels and vastly increased price tags. "Bonuses" found their way into the pockets of landlords and butchers. A Detroit auto mechanic got around controls on labor charges by figuring 167 hours of work in a single week. And while prices shot up, shortages made even wartime deprivations seem mild. The Trumans were unable to find beef in Washington markets; sympathetic friends from Missouri sent them hams and turkeys instead.

The President was assailed. Cynical Washington ridiculed his habit of asking advisers what Roosevelt would have done. This became known as Invoking the Ghost. Harold Ickes resigned office in the spring of 1946 after telling a congressional panel that Truman had told him to perjure himself if asked to comment on the appointment of Edwin Pauley, once treasurer of the Democratic National Committee, to be undersecretary of the navy. Pauley was intimately linked with oil interests in his native Texas, and Ickes was his usual undiplomatic self in allowing inferences to be drawn that Pauley's appointment might have repercussions akin to Teapot Dome. When Truman appointed Kentuckian Fred Vinson to succeed Chief Justice Harlan F. Stone in April 1946, it seemed to confirm the suspicions of those who looked upon his presidency as a meeting of small minds, more concerned with politics than with statesmanship or history.

Before long the President was himself the target of jokes. "I'm Just Mild about Harry," people sang. "To err is Truman," they jibed. It

was said that the President would be late for a press conference because he'd woken up with a stiffness in his joints and consequently
had difficulty in removing his foot from his mouth. The common
man in the White House, so it seemed, had become merely common.
From 87 percent in the early days of his administration, Truman's
ratings had skidded to 32 percent by the fall of 1946.

Already, many were thinking of Truman's presidency as a historical non sequitur. But, for all his small failings, FDR's successor displayed a sure capacity for making big decisions. The atomic bombs,
the twenty-one-point Fair Deal domestic program outlined to Congress in September 1945, the Truman Doctrine of foreign policy—
these were not the decisions of a Pendergast hack. In truth, the new
President was both statesman and ward politician. He was faced
with challenges no less daunting than those Andrew Johnson had
confronted eighty years earlier, when he had succeeded another
towering leader at the end of another savage war.

The national stresses cut across party lines. Democrats in the Senate, fighting to pass Truman's ambitious full employment bill,
countered criticism of the plan from Robert Taft by quoting
Thomas Dewey's 1944 pledges that government should become a
last-resort employer if necessary. Taft was unmoved. "I see no reason
for a larger percentage at work in 1950 than in 1900," he said.
"There is no magic in more jobs, or more people working. We ought
to be able to do the work with less workers in each family." To some,
this was conviction of a rare purity. Others dismissed it as blind reaction compounded by personal mulishness. Taft himself remarked,
"It isn't honest to be tactful." In Albany, the titular head of the
GOP could not understand such a priori reasoning. In private,
Dewey sarcastically called Taft the only man in his acquaintance
who knew all the answers to all the problems.

At the press corps' first postwar Gridiron Dinner, held in December 1945, Dewey pronounced himself an elder statesman. "The se-
renity of this position," he went on, "is copper-riveted by the fact
that in selecting nominees for president, my party has an unbroken
tradition of never having made the same mistake twice in a row."
He couldn't resist a shot at a national administration that "wobbles
each day from left to right," and attempted to put Mr. Truman's
problems within the Democratic party in perspective. Each morning
en route to work, he claimed, the President tossed one rose apiece to
the left and the right. "The left received its favors as a matter of obligation. The right was profoundly grateful because they hadn't any

roses in twelve long years. But paradise in politics lasts such a short time. The left finds only the thorns in the roses it receives. The right finds its roses were, in truth, intended to be not bouquets but funeral wreaths."

Dewey also contrasted the federal G.I. Bill of Rights with his own veterans program. There was, he maintained, an important difference between the two. "We have in New York a surplus of something over $400 million. For the information of the Democrats present, a surplus is an excess of receipts over expenditures." Publicly, he was content to tweak noses. In private, Dewey despaired. "The tragedy," he told one friend a year into the new administration, "is that we are saddled with Truman for another two and a half years, and I am afraid he is going to get no better."[15]

At home, Dewey presided over a state immune neither to postwar social disruption nor the costly solutions advocated to meet it from the left. Determined to husband his budget surplus, the Governor set out to divide his opposition by converting or at least neutralizing interest groups pressing for immediate relief. He framed the issue in humanistic terms in his annual legislative message delivered on January 8, 1947. It was not a question of "mere bookkeeping entries" or "the academic niceties of capital budgeting," Dewey insisted. "It is the problem of feeble-minded children sleeping on mattresses spread on the floors of dayrooms; of blind children going to school in firetraps; of prisons where the inmates sleep with bars between them and a bathroom; of highways that take a weekly toll of sudden death. . . . I wish every person who would like to raid the postwar savings of this state for some pet project of his own could be compelled to view the conditions which now exist and which these savings are dedicated to correct."

Paul Fitzpatrick, state Democratic chairman, retorted that the surplus was "unnatural." His legislative allies, though outnumbered, raised a hue and cry for mandatory state health insurance, a state university, and half a billion dollars in veteran loans. Democrats also insisted that the Governor abandon his plans for a thruway costing $202 million—what Jim Mead called "a postponable luxury boulevard"—and invest the money instead in housing, education, and health care. Dewey's response was to occupy the middle of the road. He handed the question of a veterans' bonus to a bipartisan legislative investigating committee.

When his investigators reported back that state health insurance would cost $400 million a year, Dewey shuddered, then quickly proposed a $14 million public health campaign, including a statewide crusade to wipe out tuberculosis by 1966. When the State Education Department pegged the cost of a state university at half a billion dollars, the Governor asked General Electric chairman (and Democrat) Owen D. Young to chair a panel of experts evaluating the proposal. Meanwhile, he summoned eighty-six college and university presidents to Albany for a two-day conference, at which they discussed ways of providing for the educational needs of returning veterans within the existing institutions.

Dewey allotted funds to convert three military bases into colleges for newly discharged soldiers, and tripled the number of veterans' scholarships worth $1,400 a year. Instead of establishing a new agency to deal with a mushrooming housing shortage, he designated three men, including his public works commissioner, to scout out abandoned hospitals, schools, apartment buildings, barracks—even a Presbyterian seminary in Auburn—for rapid conversion to temporary housing. Before the beginning of 1946, Dewey had committed, on his own, some $35 million to emergency housing, less than Democratic critics deemed essential, but sufficient, when combined with fast results, to satisfy most New Yorkers. There were other visible tokens of gratitude for the state's veterans, including a first-of-its-kind rest camp on Mount MacGregor, a 600-bed facility set amid 1,600 acres of forest and including a lake, athletic fields and a dairy farm where fresh milk was collected for t.b. victims. Almost 600,000 men and women were counseled by Dewey's veterans affairs division; 77,000 got assistance in starting businesses. Ignoring demands for an immediate bonus, the Governor persuaded legislators to tie any such program to short-term bonds—thus saving over $140 million in interest payments—which would be paid off through increases in gasoline, utility, and sales taxes.

New York suffered less through peacetime conversion than most other states. Six months after V-J Day, fewer than half the one million predicted to be out of work were actually looking for jobs. Dewey's Reconversion Service Agency helped turn war arsenals into peacetime engines of prosperity. About 100,000 new small businesses were launched in the state in the two years following Japan's surrender. When federal rent controls lapsed for three weeks in June 1946, and the administration in Washington looked more than ever to be in over its head, New York was the only state in the union to have a control plan of its own to implement, because its governor, the previous January, had sought and obtained standby authority from the legislature. And, lest this prove insufficient to win votes in urban neighborhoods ordinarily hostile to any Republican, Dewey also proposed to the 1946 legislative session a 50 percent tax cut for individuals, plus healthy reductions for business and industry. Finally, the Governor pointed to his proposed thruway as a source of additional jobs, 30,000 in construction alone, and untold opportunities once the road was completed, bringing 85 percent of New York's population within twenty miles of its four lanes with no grade more than 5 percent and forward visibility at every point of at least a thousand feet. As Dewey enthusiastically explained, the thruway would cut nine hours from the driving time between New York City and Buffalo, and open up vast areas of the state hitherto too remote for commercial development. Legislative Democrats were not impressed. They dismissed the thruway as "Dewey's Folly," and cried out instead for hospital beds, not roadbeds.

The legislature ultimately, if sometimes reluctantly, gave Dewey almost everything he wanted. The biggest achievement of 1946 was adoption of the Moore Formula, a new package of state aid to localities devised by Comptroller Frank J. Moore in partnership with Bell, Burton, and other members of the Team that stressed stability but also increased monetary aid to New York's cities and towns. Under Moore's plan, the state doubled its 40 percent share of local welfare costs. It also institutionalized the return to localities of $100 million raised annually from utilities and other taxes. Dewey agreed to add $18 million in education assistance to the amount otherwise going to local school districts under the state's Friedsam Formula, adopted in 1927 and now coming under heavy attack from teachers. Ignoring the fact that the formula hadn't been touched by Lehman or Roosevelt, the educators pressed Dewey to allocate part of his Postwar Reconstruction Fund, nearly half a billion dollars and still growing, to provide for teacher salary raises and new school buildings. The Governor refused, appointing instead one of his now-patented panels of experts in the field to address the problem deliberately and without the glare of attention focused by the angry teachers.[16]

Dewey also compared favorably with the President in dealing with the explosive postwar labor situation. "My theory has been that I either handle a strike completely," he told his mother in February 1946, "or I keep out of it, so far as the public is concerned." A few months earlier, 15,000 building service employees, including elevator operators, had walked off their jobs, paralyzing the financial district and other sectors of New York City's high-rise economy. Dewey let the strike go on for five days before he intervened, then wired both management and the union directing that services be restored and arbitration accepted. If the dispute was not settled within ten days, he said, he would arbitrate it himself. "I expect your answer by noon tomorrow," he concluded. Critics protested that he had no legal authority, but their protest was drowned out by praise. Within fifteen hours of sending his ultimatum, Dewey had a positive response. The strike ended, the elevators moved again, and the Governor's swift intervention caught the country's attention at a time when 420,000 workers were picketing coal mines in Pennsylvania, auto factories in Michigan, and electrical appliance plants in California. New York, it seemed, still had cause to believe in itself.[17]

"It cannot be said," the Alsop brothers wrote of Dewey in December, 1946, "that he has become precisely genial. But Elks-bar good fellowship is a political asset which may well be somewhat at a discount after the Truman Administration."

Dewey still found it easier to relax among a handful of close friends than in public. But the Governor of New York did display a warmer face, especially to reporters, whom he learned to take into his confidence and regard as social equals. "I hated his guts when he first came to Albany," Leo O'Brien, recalled, "and I loved him by the time he left. It was almost tragic—how he put on a pose that alienated people. Behind a pretty thin veneer was a wonderful guy." O'Brien once told Dewey that, having worked around several so-called humanitarian governors, he was convinced that none ever did half as much to take care of the people who had helped him along the way as the present occupant of the second-floor office. Dewey quickly changed the subject. O'Brien and others noticed that the Governor talked less and listened more than in the past. He told callers that his mistakes in 1944 had made a man out of him, and when asked at the second annual reunion of the Castle Rock Survivors Association whether he, too, had been a victim of the campaign train wreck, replied dryly, "Why confine it to Castle Rock?"[18]

His aloofness from Albany itself was melting. When Senate Minority Leader Elmer Quinn died, Dewey pondered breaking his rule against attending political funerals, those tribal rituals of men with whom he had little in common. He invited Harry O'Donnell, then his press secretary, to come with him to the Catholic cathedral where Quinn's service was scheduled. "I'll watch you," he said to O'Donnell, "and whenever you stand up, I'll stand up." O'Donnell's sciatica was not improved that day; each time he shifted in pain, the Governor started to rise from his seat. Afterward, astonished pols crowded around Dewey shaking his hand and exchanging small talk. "You know," he said to O'Donnell on the way back to the Capitol, "maybe there is something to these funeral services."[19]

Back in August 1945, Dewey had set out to repair breaches in party unity, to pave the way for a re-election campaign over a year away, and in the process garner support for his anti-discrimination and veterans programs. He made thirty speeches in one five-day swing, visited fish hatcheries, state hospitals, and GOP county organizations, beamed as a small boy at the Palmyra fair took him by the hand and escorted him to see his prizewinning pigeons, and munched popcorn as he toured sideshows. Aides despaired whenever they saw Dewey disappear into a cattle barn, knowing that schedules had a way of taking a back seat to the gubernatorial interest in milk cows and mastitis. Even Democrats smiled to themselves when Dewey drove by the West Ghent farm of Herbert Engel and launched into a lengthy discourse on the numerous virtues of the Brown Swiss. Before he could finish, New York #1 blew a tire. The Governor left Frances and the boys in the car, and the chauffeur to tend to repairs, while he hoisted a thumb in midair, hitched a ride with a Brooklyn motorist, and rode back down Route 9-H to get a closer look at Engel's herd. His eye caught twin heifers about to freshen, a bargain was struck, and by the time Dewey returned to his car the herd at Dapplemere had been increased by four.[20]

Meanwhile, Dewey found more time for his family, taking the boys to the 1947 Subway Series between the Yankees and Dodgers, even letting them skip two days of classes. When Tommy, "still sprouting like a weed," went to Pawling with his mother to recuperate from appendicitis, Dewey spent a pleasant week with Johnny rambling about the mansion and playing golf. Johnny collected bugs and leaves, excelled on the tennis court, and almost never appeared anywhere on time. "With the help of God," his father once said, "and three policemen," the boy would show up at a party only fashionably late.[21]

For Frances, Johnny was a concern, less sturdy and self-assured than his older brother. She tried to protect him from the pressures inevitably exerted on a child of Thomas E. Dewey. Her own dissatisfaction with public life was concealed within the walls of the ugly old house that she almost singlehandedly made airy and livable. "Frances has her stiff neck again," her husband wrote his mother, or "Frances has the bug," or Frances "is tired but standing up." In the last week of 1946, the Governor turned down a friend's invitation to dine out after confiding the "sad fact" that, in the four years he had been in Albany, he and his wife had gone out to dinner only once.

Frances didn't like to leave the boys alone, and when she did go to New York City, she did so only to attend obligatory public functions. On one occasion, the New York *Times* mistakenly identified New York's First Lady as a skiing star named Betty Woolsey. Frances refused to pose for pictures she thought might be construed as advertising.[22]

The Governor's new attitude toward job and life may have been influenced by the untimely death of George Medalie on March 5, 1946. Six months earlier, Medalie had been appointed to the state's highest court by his political and personal protégé. Working himself into a state of exhaustion, the sixty-two-year-old judge contracted pneumonia, slowly recovered, then suffered a relapse after returning to his duties too soon. Dewey summoned the best doctor in Albany, and monitored his friend's condition around the clock, until a blood clot reached Medalie's heart, and the onetime U.S. attorney died in his suite of rooms at the DeWitt Clinton Hotel. The Governor ordered state flags to fly at half mast, calling Medalie's death an irreparable loss to New York. "There was nobody quite like George Medalie," he mused in private. "He preferred to live to the fullest, even if it meant a shorter life." Medalie's death may have stirred memories of his own father's premature end. It may have awakened a sense of personal mortality. Whatever it did, after Medalie died, Dewey seemed to shed some of the cautious reserve that he had brought to Albany from the District Attorney's office.[23]

A week after Medalie's death, Dewey rose from a sickbed to greet Winston Churchill, a man for whom he had unbounded admiration and who had been turned out of office in the same leftist tide that seemed to be lapping at America's shores. His house guest turned out "every bit as engaging and compelling a personality as I had assumed him to be," Dewey wrote a relative, "brilliant as ever and still a very great force to be reckoned with in the world." Two nights later, the governor was in New York City paying public tribute to Churchill and displaying his own growing gift for oratory. "I readily admit the difficulty of judging true greatness in one's contemporaries," he began. "It was the Greek dramatist Sophocles who cynically said that no man should be called fortunate until he had died. And it might, perhaps, be said that no man should be called great until he has been long dead."[24]

Churchill, however, was a glorious exception. "When the Nazi might prevailed from Warsaw to the Channel Isles and from Egypt to the Arctic Ocean," he alone had dared to believe in courage and righteousness. "At a time when the whole cause of human liberty stood trembling and imperiled, you breathed defiance to tyranny and with ringing words you personified the cause of freedom." The struggle was by no means over, Dewey continued, nor was it limited to distant lands. He invited his audience to look to Britain, where government was first put in its proper place "as the servant and not the master of its people." It was Churchill's leadership that had preserved the great principle of free government in the moment of greatest peril. For that, Dewey said, he would earn profound gratitude, "which will ring down through all the centuries to come," wherever men cherished freedom.

Dewey had become something of a thinker as well as a doer. "Somehow the conservative forces must relearn how to establish close relationships ... among all the classes of people," he wrote Churchill in November 1946. He had tried to do just that "with very limited success" in New York, Dewey continued. More would have to be done "if we are going to keep trade union leaders from pushing us steadily into socialism and its inevitable ... loss of personal liberty."[25]

When Republican conservatives raised objections to reciprocal trade agreements, Dewey made known his own strong personal support for freer world trade. At the conference on Mackinac Island back in July 1945, he had overridden those in the party calling for delays in ratification of the UN Charter. He outbid Truman for Jewish support, demanding that 700,000 Jews be permitted to migrate into the British protectorate in Palestine. Dewey advised Arthur Vandenberg to pass up re-election campaigning in 1946 to attend a UN conference in Paris. He promised discreetly to help quell Republican congressional support for transferral of the wartime OSS to the State Department. He repeatedly had kinder words for Truman's overseas policies than for the President's domestic efforts. Like Vandenberg, Dewey believed that partisanship stopped at the water's edge.[26]

The Democratic nominee for the governor of New York in 1946 was a sixty-one-year-old veteran of New York politics, a winner of seventeen straight elections who was once hailed by Franklin Roosevelt as one of the best vote getters in Empire State history. In the Senate, Jim Mead proved himself a loyal New Dealer. He was also a colorless and unimaginative campaigner, whose routine prescription for more of the same was seriously out of step with the postwar demand for less spending, less regimentation, less pie in the sky. Hard pressed to find an issue with which to break Dewey's hold, Mead variously accused the incumbent of "betraying" veterans, of "scandals" in housing, and of "phony reforms" in mental hospitals (whose patients, he claimed, were being forced to subsist on a twenty-six-cent-a-day diet). Mead's campaign manager, sensitive to rising distrust of left-wing influence within Democratic circles, lashed out at the GOP as a rallying point for "pro-Hitlers, the Roosevelt-haters, the anti-Semites, and the super-nationalists." The New York *Post* said Dewey's only accomplishment in four years had been the development of his radio voice. *P.M.* described the Governor as "157 pounds of bombast," while Mead contented himself with calling his opponent a latter day Rip Van Winkle, the obvious heir to Hooverism.

Dewey wasn't worried. He expected to win "handsomely," he informed his mother on September 18, "if we do not make any too serious mistakes."[27] Uppermost on his mind was the task of electing Irving Ives—the pipe-smoking Phi Beta Kappa dean of Cornell's School of Industrial Relations, known best for his work on the anti-discrimination bill—to the Senate over the revered ex-governor Herbert Lehman. America faced three crucial challenges in 1946, Ives told anyone who would listen: "international relations, race relations, and labor relations, in that order." He was clearly a Republican with special appeal to labor, minority, and other Democratic voter blocs; but in Lehman, fresh from his task as director of the United Nations Relief Administration, Ives confronted a formidable foe. The race was watched nationally as a test of Dewey's coattails.

Dewey's own contest with Mead was a case of political shadow boxing. In an attempt to strike sparks, Mead and others began attacking Dewey's half-billion-dollar surplus as "a slush fund," and the thruway as the natural enemy of housing and education. It was a weak argument, as the Massena *Observer* noted. Contrasting the combination of $443 million in tax cuts and a deficit slashed by $136 million with the profligacies of the New Deal, the paper asked plaintively, "What's so wrong about having money in the bank?" Dewey struck back at his accusers, saying that under his administration New York State had built more emergency housing than the other forty-seven states put together, doubled college facilities for returning veterans, and compiled the surplus for a vast carefully planned renovation of social services.

"Saving blind children from a firetrap and giving them a new, modern fireproof building—is that misappropriation?" he demanded. "Saving to speed the cure of tuberculosis patients; to give clean, decent wards to the mentally ill; to tear down crumbling rookeries and to put up modern hospitals—is that a slush fund?" Those who criticized the thruway, he said, overlooked the fact that great cities and upstate farms alike depended on trucking for their economic survival, and that nothing had been done to repair the state's disintegrating highways for a generation. "These incredible people ... didn't even know that in grading a road you don't use plumbers and carpenters or wallboards or flooring or bathtubs. ... They didn't know that every department of this state has been operating for months under a strict injunction not to undertake anything that will interfere with the building of homes."

The opposition, he jibed, couldn't even get its own accusations straight. "To one audience, your state government is presented as a miser, fingering one by one the gold pieces it has wrung, as pennies, out of the hearts of the people. Before another audience, the cold, clammy hand of the state is pictured as taking the money by fair means or foul, to spend it in calculating, sinister ways. Before still another audience, your state administration is a glad-hand spender, a wastrel, overflowing with misappropriations, pork barrels and slush funds, as free and easy, as profligate and open-handed as a New Dealer on a big night at the Stork Club. ... At one moment, they would have you believe that saving money is practically a crime ... that the Reconstruction Fund represents the crushing heel of the tax collector. At another moment, the Fund is a luscious melon, just waiting, and they call out for everyone to come and get it. With that Fund, they are going to build homes for everybody, right away, tomorrow, just by dishing out the money, and never mind where you get the furnace or the bathtub. With that surplus, they're going to increase relief for the indigent, raise everybody's pay. They've already promised that Fund three times over and it's still two weeks to election."

When Mead tried to blame the rise in food prices and the shortage of apartments on Dewey's administration, Dewey turned the charge on its head. "They say state government is responsible because a Democratic U.S. Congress failed to pass a Republican senator's housing bill. They say we are responsible because a Democratic Congress didn't agree with a Democratic president on what to do about OPA. They seem to think that your state government ... has been running the country this year. What is this anyway—a campaign of flattery?"

Wherever he went, Dewey contrasted what he called Teamwork Government in Albany with chaos in Washington, a capital in which men fearful of freedom itself had led the nation into "famine in the midst of plenty, weakness at the peak of our strength, and a peace that is not a peace." In Harlem, he boasted that his administration had outlawed the Ku Klux Klan in New York, and bettered the opposition's promises. On September 22, he won a pledge of neutrality from the 800,000-member AFL; only the desire of labor officials to avoid the kind of splintering going on in other unions had prevented twenty-two members of the endorsement board from overruling the two who held out for Mead. The campaign was a rough passage for organized labor, suspected by many Americans of being the real culprit behind inflation and shortages, its image soiled by Communists, who were particularly active in some CIO unions.

The year 1946 was a time for scapegoats, for suspicion and disillusionment. Stalin's callous disregard for freedom in Eastern Europe and his cavalier treatment of the United Nations encouraged a shift to the right in American politics following the nation's flirtation with heroics and One World. A confidential poll taken for the Psychological Corporation in April showed that nearly 60 percent of the voters would be less likely to support a congressional candidate if the candidate was endorsed by the CIO. Some 73 percent said they regarded the threat of Communism at home as "a very important issue"; 45 percent expected a new war with Russia. When asked to rank economic institutions, people gave a 65 percent favorable rating to the Chamber of Commerce; the CIO was approved by only 26 percent. Labor and its friends on the left were reaping a bitter harvest from the endless strikes, the economic chaos, the seeming invincibility of Soviet Russia.[28]

"The leftwingers have promised to put in two million dollars against us," Dewey told a friend early in June. His own managers, he was afraid, wouldn't be able to "come within a mile" of matching such a war chest. As late as October 10, he confided to Frank Gannett that he and his fund raisers were "breaking our necks" to get enough radio money to put on a decent campaign. He expected to be outspent 4 to 1 on the airwaves, he told the Rochester publisher. But if money was scarce, fervor was abundant, along with that most vital political ingredient, luck. Left-wing activism was an entrenched tradition in the Empire State, where Communists throughout the 1930s and early '40s could count on mustering roughly 100,000 votes in a statewide contest. In 1946, the left was even more prominent. The *Daily Worker* unveiled a list of fifty-seven distinguished New Yorkers, including Paul Robeson, novelist

Howard Fast, Dashiell Hammett, philanthropist Frederick Vanderbilt Fields, and leaders in the maritime and furriers' unions who publicly announced their intention to support Communist candidates in the impending elections. Dewey's machine had already denied renomination to Congressman Joseph Baldwin, a left-wing Republican from Manhattan's silk stocking district (once represented by Bruce Barton and Ken Simpson) and had taken back the party's designation given in previous years to Vito Marcantonio, a fiery orator and open Communist sympathizer from La Guardia's old congressional district who told a Democratic rally that the only issue of the campaign was "collaboration of this nation with the Soviet Union for peace and defeat of domestic fascism."[29]

Dewey retaliated by labeling Marcantonio and the ALP "servants of the party line of a foreign power." The very furtiveness of Communism heightened the paranoia that came to surround it. A Communist, unlike a Southern black, couldn't be identified by his color. His accent might reflect a Warsaw ghetto or a Princeton eating club. His collar was white or blue, his standing in the community impeccable or in disrepute. Eleanor Dulles, Foster's sister and a foreign policy expert herself, belonged to a group of young economists that met informally every two or three weeks. "We were seeking a better world," she recalls. "We felt the world had gone off the track with the Depression and Hitler, and the war. We wanted to put it back." Unknown to her, half the group were either party members or Communist sympathizers. She told the mother of one economist, a young man she saw ten or twenty hours a week, that she would put her hand in a fire, so convinced was she that he was not a Communist. A month later, her friend told her otherwise.[30]

The Dewey–Mead race, like all the off-year elections, took place on a stage crowded with foreign headlines and domestic alarums. An ex-editor of the *Daily Worker* quit the party, blasting it as nothing more than a conspiracy directed from Moscow. Fourteen Canadians were uncovered as participants in a Soviet spy ring operating out of the Russian embassy in Ottawa and dedicated to learning the secrets of America's atomic weaponry. Winston Churchill traveled to Fulton, Missouri, and warned of "an Iron Curtain" descending across Europe. On September 10, Secretary of State James F. Byrnes won headlines with a speech at Stuttgart that formally terminated harsh American policies toward the defeated Germans and in effect made an ally out of the defeated enemy, thus marking a turning point in U.S.-Soviet relations.

One week later, Henry Wallace, the man who had been pushed

aside to make way for Truman at the 1944 Democratic convention, and for the last few months had served as Truman's secretary of commerce, went to New York to address a Madison Square Garden rally sponsored by the CIO's Political Action Committee. In his text, Wallace singled out Dewey for criticism, especially the Governor's old idea of an Anglo-American alliance. "We must not let British balance of power manipulators determine whither and when the United States gets into war," Wallace told the pro-Soviet crowd. Adding that "the danger of war is much less from Communism than it is from imperialism," Wallace urged the U.S. to share its atomic secrets with all mankind, argued that the Soviets had a right to their own sphere of influence in Eastern Europe, and by implication impugned President Truman's efforts to contain Stalin's westward advance. At the end of his remarks, the former vice president said that Truman had read them in advance and approved every word.

Byrnes and Truman challenged that remark. The Secretary of State threatened to resign if Wallace's remarks were not repudiated, and after a three-day delay, during which Wallace leaked his post-speech conversation with the President all over Washington, Truman dismissed "the most peculiar fellow I ever came in contact with." The whole thing had been badly handled, and it pointed up anew the administration's reputation for confusion and too many cooks. Dewey warned that Wallace threatened to undermine the whole concept of bipartisan foreign policy. Vandenberg agreed. Irving Ives, no red-baiter, accused Lehman of waffling on the issue. Radio Moscow endorsed the state Democratic ticket, and New York Communists declared Dewey Public Enemy Number One—which, of course, could not have made the Republicans happier. The Governor himself delighted in attacking his opposition—"three different platforms . . . five different parties . . . a confused medley of voices"—which now formally included the Communists, who withdrew their own slate and backed Mead and Lehman.

On October 19, with all the polls favoring Dewey and Ives, an event occurred which cinched their victories at the polls two weeks later. Three thousand veterans and teachers, organized by the CIO to participate in a demonstration at the Capitol in Albany, marched around carrying signs reading "Homes, Not Slums" and "Foxholes to Ratholes, Is That Our Thanks, Gov. Dewey?" Shortly before three that afternoon, a group of about seventy-five marchers rushed an elderly guard and made their way inside to the Senate chamber, where they promptly declared themselves a veterans senate and drew up a list of demands. These included a 100 percent increase in state aid to education, a $600 bonus for all state workers, and an immediate raise of $1,000 for New York City teachers. The demonstrators also insisted on $400 million for housing, and an immediate vote on a $400 million bond issue with which to fund their ambitious program. Outside, other marchers picketed the Executive Mansion, where Dewey was said to be nursing a cold, while still others went to pay a friendly call on Mayor Erastus Corning, Democratic candidate for lieutenant governor.

In New York City and in Albany, Dewey's advisers convened and produced a near unanimous decision: find the biggest state troopers around and have them eject the demonstrators from the Capitol. Elliott Bell demurred. He alone urged caution, reminding Dewey of the disaster that ensued when Hoover ordered the Bonus Marchers broken up. Bell prevailed, as he often did. The Governor ordered no move against the protesters, but shut down the Capitol restaurants and prevented a group sent out to round up a supply of groceries from returning to the Senate chamber. That night the veterans lounged around in their stocking feet, slept in the senators' wine-colored chairs, and cheered feebly when one of their number mounted the rostrum to reiterate the justness of their cause. Shortly after ten the next morning, Charles Breitel appeared in the room. He announced that Dewey would soon be leaving for New York City, and if they wished to meet with the Governor, they had better hurry.[31]

A hundred state troopers stood in ranks three deep around Dewey's desk in the Red Room; more lined the hallway outside as the demonstrators strode in. One veteran immediately demanded that Dewey declare a housing emergency. "I don't have to," the Governor replied. "We already have one." As for their specific complaints, he was afraid they had come to Albany "about twelve months too late." They should be in Washington instead—that's where bureaucratic logjams had slowed to a trickle the flow of building materials and tied up his own construction program. He reminded the men of New York's enviable housing record compared with that of other states, defended his highway plans as the catalyst of postwar prosperity, and dismissed them all with the news that he was late for a train. Sheepishly, the demonstrators returned to the Capitol, where they proclaimed victory in having forced Dewey to meet with them, endorsed Mead for governor, and adjourned to eat ham sandwiches on the Capitol's south lawn. Twenty-two hours after it began, the siege of Albany was over. Elliott Bell had proved right, and Dewey had firmly established himself as the middle-of-the-road alternative to street mobs and raiders of the treasury.

That night, Dewey told a Manhattan women's college audience that of all the services they might render to society in the years to come, the greatest would be "an end to government by catchwords and slogans." In fact, the Governor offered up a slogan of his own: "Down with slogans; let's learn the truth." A few days later, he dedicated Sampson College, one of three hastily built with state funds to serve returning veterans, and he warned the 3,500 men enrolled there against "the contemptible noisy minority who represent the totalitarian mind in our country." Their nostrums might look attractive, he said, but in fact were nothing more than "sugar-coated invitations to suicide." Repeatedly in the campaign's closing days, Dewey returned to the theme of Teamwork Government, decrying "pseudo-liberalism . . . adopted as a masquerade by the enemies of freedom . . . so busy waving banners they have fallen behind the parade of progress." From Wallace's Madison Square Garden address to Moscow's support and Mead's something-for-everyone divvying of the surplus "at least three times over," Dewey taunted his opposition's campaign on October 31 as a cynical game of *Can You Top This?* He added up opposition promises and figured out they would lead to a budget and state taxes that would be doubled—even as Mead was going around New York calling for abolition of the state income tax.

"We of your state government do not claim any miracles," he told voters in his closing appeal. "There haven't been any. We do claim that by hard work and common sense and all pulling together, we have swept out the cobwebs of twenty years and carried this state forward in ways never dreamed of in the generation past."

On November 5, Dewey was re-elected with 58.6 percent of the vote—the largest majority ever accorded a candidate for governor of New York. His popular margin over Mead was 687,000, and some observers thought it might have hit a million had Herbert Lehman not pulled some reluctant Democrats back within the fold. As it was, Lehman went down under the GOP avalanche, losing to Ives by a quarter of a million votes. The rest of the Republican ticket did even better. The party picked up six House seats in New York City alone, where Dewey carried Queens by a 2-to-1 margin and came within 185,000 votes of taking the entire city. His margins in such white-collar suburbs as Nassau and Westchester were of record proportions: Sprague delivered a 4 to 1 victory in Nassau. Suffolk County, Kingsland Macy's bailiwick, voted for the Republican candidate 64,000 to 17,000. Dewey lost Albany County by only 8,000 votes.

In the legislature, he found his party more powerful than ever before. The Senate would be Republican 42 to 13; the Assembly 110 to 40. The scope of his victory immediately established Dewey as what Walter Lippmann deemed "far and away" the likeliest opponent for Truman in 1948. The President's own unpopularity had become so great that Democratic campaign officials desperate to counter the GOP battle cry "Had Enough?" virtually ruled Truman off the campaign trail, resorting instead to radio recordings of Franklin Roosevelt to solder together the now-shattered New Deal coalition.

Dewey's own reaction to his triumph was cautious. He thanked a friend for his good wishes on "renewal of the Albany lease" but begged off any real estate hunting in Washington. "While the climate here is not by any means perfect," he wrote coyly, "some southerly climes, particularly those which are damp and situated on rivers, would not agree with Frances' sinuses." For his mother, he had another reaction. The contest had been "exceedingly rugged," he wrote Annie when it was over. But it had taught him a lesson. "I have concluded that it is harder to wage a constructive campaign, when you are sure to win, than it is to wage a slugging, aggressive campaign when you are trying to fight your way up."[32]

14

A Second Chance

We have found the means to blow our world, physically, apart.
Spiritually, we have yet to find the means to put together the
world's broken pieces, to bind up its wounds, to make a good society, a community of men of good will that fits our dreams. We
have devised noble plans for a new world. Without a new spirit,
our noblest plans will come to naught.

—Thomas E. Dewey

The political tidal wave that washed over the American continent in
November 1946 left in its wake a vastly altered landscape. Dissolved
was the Democratic majority on Capitol Hill; in its place a tri-
umphant Republican party struggled to believe its own good for-
tune. Polling over 3 million voters more than the opposition, the
GOP picked up fifty-four House seats and twelve in the Senate.
Henry Cabot Lodge replaced David Walsh from Massachusetts.
Frank Lausche went down to defeat in Ohio. Kentucky elected John
Sherman Cooper, its first Republican senator in twenty-two years.
Even Harry Truman's old seat in the upper body would be occupied, come January 1947, by a conservative Republican. The GOP
surge was most powerful in the nation's cities, those elusive targets
that were made a top priority by Herbert Brownell before he resigned as national chairman in March. His replacement, a drawling
Tennessee banker and Taft supporter named B. Carroll Reece, carried on Brownell's program, with handsome results.

Across the country, organized labor lost many of its staunchest
backers. Forty-two of seventy-eight representatives that had been
designated 100 percent favorable by the CIO were defeated. Republicans picked up six House seats in Philadelphia, four in Chicago, and at least one each in St. Louis, Seattle, Los Angeles, and
Kansas City. Riding Dewey's coattails in New York was a congressman-elect named Jacob Javits. Even Vito Marcantonio came
within a few hundred votes of losing to a combined Democratic-Re-
publican-Liberal challenge. Among the winners who would take
their seats in the Eightieth Congress were sixty-nine veterans of
World War II, among them two future presidents, Richard M.
Nixon and John F. Kennedy, the latter a rare exception to the Republican rule.

The election struck many as a referendum on Truman's stewardship, and perhaps a belated rejection of a New Deal without Roosevelt. Whatever, it prompted painful reappraisals in the nation's capital, reappraisals tinged with panic. Senator J. William Fulbright suggested that Truman appoint a Republican secretary of state, then resign, thus delivering the government to the party the electorate so obviously preferred. *U.S. News & World Report* pegged the President's chances of winning renomination at less than fifty-fifty. It likened Dewey's New York landslide to the one in 1930 that catapulted Franklin Roosevelt to national prominence, and predicted that Dewey would be occupying the White House himself in two years. Similar talk filled the corridors of a Washington hotel in December, when the Republican National Committee met to savor its success and ponder future triumphs.

"It's just human nature to want to be with a winner," explained one committee member who was promoting Dewey. As if to confirm the New Yorker's pre-eminent status, a wintry blast issued from Chicago, where Colonel McCormick warned against a return to "the most ineffectual leadership to be found anywhere in this country." The colonel was not a happy man as he surveyed the crop of Republican contenders for 1948. On the left was Harold Stassen, self-proclaimed heir to the Willkie tradition and "a zoot suit internationalist" in the *Tribune*'s words. Stassen did nothing to enhance his standing with the tycoon who sat atop the Tribune Tower when he flew off to Moscow for talks with Stalin after announcing his candidacy in January 1947.

Arthur Vandenberg was even worse in the Colonel's view. For it was Vandenberg who had been an active collaborator with Truman in providing massive assistance to postwar Europe, and who personally shepherded through the Congress such unpalatable foreign aid measures as the loan to Britain. And it was Vandenberg who had advised the President that in order to secure $400 million to help Greece and Turkey ward off Communist aggression, he would have to scare Congress into ponying up the cash.

On March 12, 1947, Truman had done precisely that, saying, "I believe it must be the policy of the United States to support free peoples who are resisting attempted subjugation by armed minorities or by outside pressures." And one of the first voices raised in his support was Dewey's. The Governor also endorsed George Marshall's plan, which was disclosed in a speech at Harvard that June, to provide $17 billion in economic assistance so that Europe might be rebuilt along pro-Western lines.

"In my judgment we have no choice," Dewey told a group of business leaders a few months later. "It is unthinkable that after a successful war at staggering cost in blood and resources, we should stop now and surrender the fruits of victory." He did criticize those running the program as insufficiently grounded in businesslike realism—"social planners who do not know a loom from a cornhusker"—but for the European Recovery Program itself Dewey had only compliments.

Indeed, Dewey's only problem with the Truman Doctrine was that it didn't go far enough. "The free world is now in the desperate position of a man who has gangrene in both legs," he said later that month, "in Western Europe and Asia. As a doctor, our government is telling the world we have a very good cure for gangrene but we will apply it to one leg only." Dewey thought the uneven treatment of Europe and Asia preposterous. "The fact is that these governments have taken their stand on the side of human freedom, which we are struggling to preserve in the face of remorseless, spreading totalitarianism. . . . We chose our side a century and a half ago." Dewey faulted the administration for going back on a pledge first made at Cairo in 1943 to help the Chinese protect their territorial integrity. He attacked Truman's failure to give Chiang Kai-shek airplane parts when they were most needed, for permitting a half-billion-dollar credit from the Export-Import Bank to lapse, for finally providing the Nationalist forces with "grossly inadequate" supplies of arms and ammunition.

"The situation in Korea is a good example of what might well happen in China," Dewey continued. "At this moment, Soviet occupation forces hold the northern half of Korea and American occupation forces hold the southern half. The Communists have completely regimented the northern half, installed a totalitarian government, and built up a well-trained, well-armed fighting arm of 250,000 men under puppet leadership. In the American half there is no civilian government, no native military force—nothing but a political void." A plebiscite to determine Korea's future had been planned, he said, only to be boycotted by the Soviets, "because they anticipate that immediately upon the withdrawal of American and Soviet occupation troops, the armed forces of the North will engulf all of Korea. This will completely outflank northern China and will result in the delivery of the 23 million Korean people from Japanese tyranny to Soviet tyranny."

Dewey was in touch with his times; in other ways he was ahead of them. He strongly favored universal military training, in sharp contrast to Taft, who argued just as strongly against a peacetime draft.

"If we are strong enough," Dewey wrote his mother, "we will have no war. If we are weak we might well have war and then we should be so unprepared we would lose it and then everything would be lost." The universal military training debate raged against a sobering backdrop, not only of international tensions, but of America's haste to disarm. Dewey placed the military question within a diplomatic context. Standing up to the Soviets, he was convinced, was not something that Truman's people were doing with sufficient conviction.[1]

By the spring of 1947, dissatisfaction was no longer confined to Republican circles. Truman himself was dissatisfied. Both at home and abroad, the President seemed almost liberated by his party's setback of the previous November, freed at last of Roosevelt's hovering ghost, set loose to pursue his own scrappy instincts. Two weeks after the elections, John L. Lewis marched 200,000 coal miners out on strike, defying a court order forbidding the stoppage, and Truman directed the Justice Department to obtain a contempt citation. The union was fined $3.5 million, and Lewis was humbled. "He couldn't take the guff," wrote the President to his mother and sister in Missouri. "No bully can. Now I have the auto workers, steel workers and RR men to look forward to. They'll get the same treatment if they act the same way."

So, it soon became apparent, would the Russians. In March, Secretary of State George C. Marshall drew attention publicly to "certain inalienable rights . . . which may not be given or taken away" and which the United States presumably would stand up to defend. (Marshall's appointment itself had won acclaim and unanimous confirmation from the Senate the day it was announced. Dewey had forbidden Kingsland Macy, representing the First Suffolk District in Congress, to mail a letter to an editor which was critical of Marshall, his China policy, and his role in the 1944 campaign.) That same month, Truman delivered his scarifying address on the Communist threat to Greece and Turkey. The Central Intelligence Agency was created early in 1947, replacing the old OSS. The Marshall Plan was unveiled in June. Suddenly the man who had seemed, only six months before, a political dead duck, was spreading his wings and flying high.[2]

The polls told of a remarkable comeback by the President, who in January had trailed Dewey 50 to 28 and had drawn even by April. Dewey professed unconcern. "I have no doubt that Harry Truman will be a formidable candidate," he wrote on April 5. Truman had going for him a powerful strategic advantage in a fractured Congress of the other party, the same device exploited successfully for twenty years by Smith, Lehman, and Roosevelt in New York. Only a "catastrophic depression," which he did not expect, Dewey concluded, would render the President anything less than "a very powerful candidate."[3]

Dewey read election returns as well as anyone, and his 1947 legislative program was a broad reflection of the conservative mood overtaking Americans, with two important exceptions. He rejected Fred Bontecou's request for support of a bill outlawing the closed union shop in New York. But he allowed himself to be persuaded that a state university was a modern necessity of far greater long-range importance. Only one other state in the union lacked a central higher education facility. New York's was an old and distinguished tradition of providing indirect aid to rich private plants, including Columbia, Cornell, and New York University. Albany already was sending $20 million a year to twenty-nine schools, including the emergency colleges thrown together in 1946 for returning soldiers. Dewey's Temporary Commission on the Necessity for a State University was sorely divided among those who wished merely to continue or increase state aid to private schools, and others who advocated creation of an entirely new public system, inevitably in competition with the private schools. Adding to the intensity of the debate were geographical and ethnic differences. Upstaters resented the free schooling available at the four municipal colleges, while residents of the city voiced resentment at perceived discrimination within existing professional schools.

Dewey himself was wary of launching the state in the higher education business. A majority of his commission's fifteen members, influenced by the State Board of Regents, felt the same way. Upgrade the caliber of existing teachers colleges, they had argued, and undertake expansion of private facilities. Cornell's School of Agriculture, for instance, for years had functioned as an all-but-official state school. But the majority could not convince the Governor's men George Shapiro, Charles Breitel, and Arthur Schwartz. On his own, Shapiro composed a ten-page dissent, emphasizing the rank discrimination practiced against blacks and Jews, particularly in private medical and dental schools. This converted Dewey, who would in February 1948 accept a final commission report in harmony with those pressing for a network of specialized state colleges.[4]

He asked from the legislature a bill outlawing discrimination in the classroom. Higher education was "a quest for the truth," he asserted. "Baseless distinctions have no place in that quest. Education controls the opportunity for professional careers; careers should depend only upon ability to serve. Education flourishes in the controversy of divergent groups, in conflicting ideas and ideals; intellectual inbreeding has always proved disastrous."

Dewey's state university was not designed to resemble the Midwestern behemoths. Instead, it was planned from the start to be decentralized, administered and supported as much as possible by the local community. Existing schools teaching everything from medicine to ceramics would be brought together under a board of trustees appointed by the Governor. Two-year community colleges would be built as the backbone of the university's new facilities. Half the cost of construction would be assumed by the state, the rest falling on the locality hosting the school. The expenses of administering the system of two-year community colleges, would be allocated in equal portions among the state, the local community, and tuition payments from students. It was a state university with a minimum of state control. Only later, especially under Nelson Rockefeller, did the State University of New York mushroom into an operation whose annual budget exceeded that of the entire state during the last years of the Dewey era.[5]

Education dominated other headlines in 1947. At the end of February, Buffalo teachers went out on strike, demanding pay raises supposedly promised them by legislative leaders. As it happened, Dewey's commission studying educational costs and the state formula under which they were funded was due to file its report within ten days; and when it did, the recommendations included a new pay scale for both upstate and New York City teachers. New instructors would be hired at $2,000 a year in Buffalo, under Dewey's plan, and work on probation for their first three years. They would receive automatic salary hikes for each of their first five years on the job. Thereafter, while holders of a master's degree would be entitled to an annual $200 boost automatically, the rest of the schoolroom force would receive raises only on evidence of "superior merit." The latter clause enraged teachers' unions. So did Dewey's method of financing his program. The Governor proposed that the state pick up most of the $30 million price tag the first year the new aid package went into effect. At the same time, he would empower local communities to levy additional taxes of their own, including a 2 percent sales tax. To those who complained, Dewey preached the gospel of local autonomy—and responsibility.

Some cities and towns were well governed, he explained, others wastefully so. It made no sense to penalize some of New York's tax-payers to support "the inadequacies of the others." He griped in public at those who accused his administration of paying "tobacco-state wages." Educational aid per capita in his New York ran 30 percent higher than anywhere else, he pointed out. Under the new schedule of teacher salaries, New York City instructors might earn up to $5,125, while upstaters would do nearly as well. He was un-questionably correct in asserting that his administration had more than doubled state spending for education, and had revised the twenty-year-old Friedsam Formula left untouched by three Demo-cratic predecessors. At the same time, Dewey neglected to mention that, as a percentage of the state budget, money allotted to the schools declined from the Lehman years.

Angered by the Buffalo walkout, the Governor threw all his weight behind the Condon-Wadlin Bill, which made subject to im-mediate dismissal any state employee who took part in any strike ac-tion. The bill suspended for at least three years the chance of a raise for workers rehired, and withheld tenure from striking teachers for five years. Despite grumbling by some of his party, who thought Dewey's support of the bill might gain him a presidential nomina-tion at the expense of Republican strength in New York, the Gover-nor had his way. "It has always been clear," he said in a statewide broadcast explaining Condon-Wadlin on April 19, "and now it is clearer, that none of us who enter public service—and we all do it voluntarily, of our own free will—has any right to interrupt the public service. Our government is not an end in itself. It exists to serve all the people. It belongs to all of us. We cannot strike against ourselves."

Dewey reminded his radio audience that state workers had won pay raises averaging 44 percent since he took office in 1943. He di-gressed with a reference to Communists, who, he said, regarded the strike as a political tool, one that first halted government in its tracks and later rendered it vulnerable to takeover by "their small, well-or-ganized minority." Such talk was in keeping with the temper of 1947, an anxious year, when Truman issued Executive Order 9835 requiring investigation of the loyalty of every person employed by the federal government, and directing agency heads to rid them-selves of employees suspected of anything less. Dewey's theme played well at executive board meetings of the Chrysler Corpora-tion, where a Dewey supporter carrying copies of the New York papers found a warm spirit of approval of the Governor's leadership on Condon-Wadlin.[6]

Politically, it was a time of retrenchment. State aid to child care centers was discontinued after Dewey characterized it as a wartime measure, no longer needed now that most of New York's mothers had returned to the home. Rebates to employers who maintained stable work forces went up, to $140 million. Dewey salted away $58 million in reserve funds, what he called his rainy-day accounts. He signed a bill enabling the State Attorney General to restrict the public activities of any oath-taking organization (unions, fraternities, and sororities excepted) that refused to file a membership roster with the Secretary of State's office. He agreed with Frank Gannett that Hyde Park would be a bad choice for the UN's permanent headquarters, because "I don't want it to become a shrine for Roosevelt."[7]

Other actions checked the spirit of conformity settling over postwar America. On April 5, Dewey vetoed a bill making drug addiction a crime. So simplistic a formula, he wrote, overlooked the responsibility of criminal traffickers in drugs, not to mention "the contributions of modern medicine and modern psychology in evaluating the deep-seated personal maladjustments of those unfortunates who succumb to drug addiction." He also refused to sign a bill declaring illegal the writing of obscene literature. "A writing never revealed does no one any harm," Dewey explained, and even if the obscenity were to be made public, the bill in question would tread "that very narrow line between proper suppression and freedom of the printed word."

"I have been through so much in the last ninety days," an exhausted Dewey wrote near the end of the legislative session, "that I sometimes am not sure of my own name." Only a day before, he had twice called Speaker Heck to give him the same instructions on a priority bill. A vacation was in order, and early in April it was announced that the Deweys would set off in July on a 6,200-mile odyssey through the Far West, coinciding with the annual governors' conference at Salt Lake City and permitting New York's chief executive to show Yellowstone Park to his two boys. Reporters noted that Dewey's itinerary would carry him into states with over 300 of the 547 delegates required to win the 1948 Republican presidential nomination. The Governor brushed aside all such talk. The trip, he insisted, would to be strictly nonpolitical, a chance for him and Frances to show their sons the splendors of America's West.[8]

"I can hardly open my mouth without having reporters write that 'the Republicans' have decided so and so," complained Robert Taft, who was not exaggerating his influence on Capitol Hill. The *New*

Republic wrote in March 1947 that the Eightieth Congress consisted of the House, Senate, and Taft. Wallace White of Maine enjoyed the title of majority leader, but it was Taft who wielded the power, making committee assignments, setting legislative priorities, and generally riding herd on a bumptious collection of Republicans unaccustomed to the heady taste of power. Reporters cracked that White should install a rearview mirror on his desk, the better to see Taft's expressive face and judge his marching orders. Taft amazed colleagues as he mastered columns of figures faster, according to *Fortune*, "than some Congressmen can understand the dialogue in the comic strips." Taft knew the details of every domestic bill before the Senate. He wrote amendments on the spur of the moment when the majority wanted them, authored whole new bills when none that met his demanding standards existed. Few men, before or since, have held so commanding a position in the Senate.

Taft's power did not rest on affection generated in the cloakroom. One poll of senatorial preferences for president in 1948 found Vandenberg preferred over the Ohioan 2 to 1, and even those who did name Taft, as their first choice felt compelled to point out that they did so despite his personality. Only reluctantly did his colleagues suffer the snappish Taft to interrupt their discussions with the exclamation "Why, that's nonsense!" He dismissed a program placed before the Senate Labor Committee by Harold Stassen as "trivial," and a friendly newspaper column that had been guilty of the cardinal sin of getting a few facts incorrect as "the most puerile thing I have ever read." For all his intellectual powers, there was something inescapably pedantic about Mr. Republican. As a member of Yale's board of trustees, Taft voiced strong objections to building an anthropological museum on campus, because the dinosaurs to be displayed inside would have to be dusted, and that would cost money. Neither did he see any good reason for the university to own a Titian.

Facts, diamond-hard and incontrovertible, interested Taft, and little else. Facts could overcome even ideology. He proved it in the Eightieth Congress by introducing a federal education assistance program that even John Bricker could not bring himself to vote for, and a federal housing program that moved one real estate lobbyist to label Mr. Republican "a fellow traveler." Taft disagreed with Dewey over the Nuremberg Trials, which Dewey thought just and his rival said smacked of ex post facto. Nuremberg, Taft warned, was "a blot on the American record that we shall long regret."

Facts led Taft to oppose any national version of Dewey's Condon-

Wadlin Bill. Taft, in fact, had his own labor legislation in mind, designed to equalize the labor-management imbalance established under the Wagner Act. He would outlaw the closed shop, define "unfair practices" for labor as well as business, allow for an eighty-day injunction to forestall strikes in any industry related to the national health or security, and provide for a sixty-day "cooling-off" period before any strike could take place in interstate commerce. Irving Ives, looked to as Dewey's voice in the Senate, fought a delaying action on the Labor Committee, and managed a victory over those who would weaken industrywide collective bargaining. But "having made his fight," as Brownell told Dewey in mid-April, Ives threw in with the majority.[9]

Reaction to the Taft-Hartley Act in union halls across America was apoplectic. The AFL denounced it as "slave labor" legislation. Some 17,000 coal miners walked out in protest. Eleanor Roosevelt, Harold Ickes, and other prominent New Dealers took to the airwaves in indignation. Mayor William O'Dwyer declared "Veto Day" in New York City, hoping to swell the chorus of angry voices urging Truman to reject the bill. The President took their advice, only to find his veto overridden by Taft's colleagues on Capitol Hill. It was one of many battles engulfing Pennsylvania Avenue in 1947, and shaping political attitudes for the election year to come.

Taft pushed through a $4 billion tax cut weighted toward upper-income Americans. Truman refused to sign what he called "the wrong tax cut at the wrong time." The Eightieth Congress raised Social Security benefits, then removed 750,000 recipients from the rolls. It passed no civil rights legislation, and did nothing to increase the minimum wage. It did ease anti-trust restrictions on the nation's railroads. In a time of quickening inflation, when the price of eggs in Chicago went up eight cents in two months, when millions of renters were hit with a 15 percent increase approved by the Congress as part of its effort to decontrol the economy, and when, as *Time* noted, even the cost of filing for bankruptcy had risen by 50 percent, the laissez-faire attitudes of many congressional Republicans gave pause to their more liberal brethren outside Washington.

Walter S. Mack was an Eastern Establishment Republican, if any existed, chairman of the board of Pepsi-Cola, a New Yorker with kind words for La Guardia, Willkie, and Dewey. To Dewey, he expressed his fear that Truman might be setting "a booby trap" on the inflation issue, yet after meeting with a number of congressional Republicans, Mack was convinced that either they didn't understand or didn't care about the mood of the country. He went to the party's national headquarters with an offer to raise $20,000 to hire professional public relations men to burnish the GOP image; Chairman Reece replied frostily that the national committee had all the help it needed. Joe Martin and Charles Halleck, speaking for House Republicans, agreed with Mack that a problem existed, but both doubted whether other congressional leaders, Taft in particular, would ever agree to coordinate their own statements with anyone brought in from the outside. Mack spent what he called "a very disagreeable hour and a half" with Taft himself, during which Mr. Republican pounded his fist on the table and informed Mack crisply that he was "too liberal" in his approach to selling Taft-Hartley, that he, Taft, knew what he was doing and would continue giving out statements any way he wished. Besides, Taft added, the only real problem was that the press was against him.

Dewey listened to all this, told Mack he was "everlastingly right" about the image problem, and recommended a trusted young ad man to help carry out the scheme, which, for lack of clearance from Washington, died aborning.[10]

At the end of 1947, a Roper poll showed only 22 percent rated the Eightieth Congress's performance as excellent or good; 52 percent rated inflation as their major concern, far ahead of those fearful of Communism or anxious about the housing shortage. A careful reading of Roper's numbers led to the inescapable conclusion that Taft and his conservative supporters were far less attuned to the public mood than they believed. The same month that the Republicans recaptured Capitol Hill, Roper had asked voters if they thought government should provide for those who had no other means of obtaining a living. Seventy-two percent said yes. A year earlier, 77 percent agreed that it would be "a good idea" to extend Social Security coverage to everyone who had a job. More people favored than opposed direct housing construction by federal builders. Some 62 percent supported a world congress, so long as the other nations of the world agreed to make it a binding arbitrator of their disputes. Finally, a consistent majority proclaimed they would vote for "a Democrat" for President in 1948, whatever the ups and downs of Harry Truman's personal popularity.

When Taft finally got away from Capitol Hill for a national tour of his own in September, he displayed in public the biting candor that in private alienated would-be supporters. Asked what housewives might do to combat the high cost of meat, Taft said forthrightly enough that they should reduce their consumption, an answer garbled by the press into the damning headline: "Taft Says:

Eat Less." In Omaha, the Senator expressed the hope that farmers' price supports might be reduced below 90 percent of parity. In Santa Cruz and Los Angeles, he crossed picket lines; and in Seattle, angry demonstrators pelted his car with vegetables and all but physically assaulted the main author of Taft-Hartley. Back in Washington, as Taft and Truman did battle, the nation that each of them sought to speak for passed unheralded an economic milestone. In July 1947, for the first time ever, 60 million Americans held jobs. Unemployment was under 2 million. The annual rate of production growth was 7 percent and corporate profits were a healthy one-third higher than the previous year. Only inflation nibbled away at the consumer's purchasing power, and Harry Truman thought he had an answer for that

In January 1948, in a State of the Union address that might also have served as an announcement of his candidacy for re-election, the President would put forth a ten-point program to combat high prices, including standby authority to reimpose price controls and ration scarce commodities. Truman also wanted a flat forty-dollar tax reduction for every American, the cost to be paid for through higher corporate taxes. He called for a system of national health insurance, continued support for farm co-operatives and rural electrification, and a boost in the minimum wage from forty to seventy-five cents an hour.

The next day, Senator Taft responded for the opposition over ABC radio. Once again, he concluded with remorse in his voice, Washington was masquerading as Santa Claus. The Truman program would add nothing less than $5 billion to the annual budget. "Where is the money coming from?" he demanded to know.

But 1947 was a campaign year in embryo, with Taft chained to the rock of Senate leadership, Stassen crisscrossing the nation hoping to ignite a grass fire that would impress Republican power brokers, and Douglas MacArthur issuing oracular pronouncements from Tokyo, where his standing as a modern-day shogun did not in the least dull an appetite for similar power at home. MacArthur let it be known that he considered Wisconsin, site of the first big popularity test of 1948, his home state. Others touted the virtues of Vandenberg and Earl Warren, both men more admired outside Republican circles than in. In Albany, the frantic posturings seemed a world away as Dewey tended his gubernatorial chores, sifting 1,500 letters a day, smiling for the tourists who came his way.[11]

Publicly, he was a candidate for nothing. He said as much on

June 7, when Russel Sprague introduced him at a Nassau party rally as the next president. In private, the engine of ambition worked away feverishly. By mid-August, Herb Brownell was set up in a New York office, capably assisted by Tom Stephens, the state committee's secretary and perhaps the best all-around advance man and troubleshooter in the business; and Bill Pfeiffer, once an aide to Jaeckle and later an upstate congressman and state party chairman. Jaeckle himself was brought back into the fold, to handle relations with party pros and seek out delegates not already harvested by Brownell or Sprague. Their earlier relationship was never to be recaptured, but Jaeckle's loyalty to the man he believed eminently qualified for the White House outweighed his resentment of 1944 and the shabby treatment he had received from Dewey, who now told him that his very decision on whether to run in 1948 rested largely in Jaeckle's hands.[12]

On his own, Dewey worked with friends in Illinois to tone down the vitriol in Colonel McCormick. "I have received the benefit of silence of late," he wrote in January 1947. "That's wonderful progress." Perhaps, he told the publisher, they might even have a long talk together the next time McCormick was in town. A friend passed on word that Taft workers were saying their candidate would poll more first-ballot votes than Dewey, and wondered if it was really safe to bet to the contrary. Dewey replied that nothing could be safer; indeed, "the picture looks so bright that I hesitate even to make any estimates." He was not surprised when polls forecast that Henry Wallace, running on a third-party ticket, might win a million votes in New York alone. "Don't let anybody tell you that this is going to be an easy presidential election," he concluded. "We need all the voting appeal we have," presumably his strongest single argument against Taft.[13]

While Dewey carried on his own shadow campaign for the nomination, his operatives fanned out to tap financial and human resources. Tom Stephens met with garment industry members who promised to "talk Dewey up," raise funds, and compile a mailing list. The chairman of American Express could be counted on for a substantial contribution, if properly approached. Ralph Becker, national Young Republican chairman, was enlisted to carry the Dewey message to his network of youthful campaigners. Ed Jaeckle plunged into the South on a similar errand. By the first week in August, drawing upon contacts made during his days as Brownell's deputy at the national committee, Stephens was able to report a network of 376 reliable informants in 26 states. Their assignment: to learn the identities, occupations, inclinations, and personal histories of every potential delegate to the 1948 convention.[14]

Dewey perceived a threat to his chances for the nomination from Dwight Eisenhower. Elliott Bell disagreed. To Bell, the General was like the ski instructor his daughter was in love with each winter, only to lose interest once the snow melted and the instructor shed his parka.

Think again, Dewey told his old friend and trusted adviser. Only a few nights before, he had seen Eisenhower at a public function and been asked by him what he could possibly say that might be appropriate. Dewey had replied with a series of suggestions, all accepted by Eisenhower, who got up and proceeded to overwhelm his audience with a pithy spontaneous address. "He gave the best speech I ever heard," Dewey said. Bell remained unconvinced. At one point, Dewey even went to see Eisenhower with a lawyerlike assessment of all the good reasons why the General should not permit his name to be dragged through the mud of partisan politics. Eisenhower was more amused than annoyed by the whole performance. He had no intention of running for President, he said, and told the editor of one military journal that he would not allow himself to be used by political bosses hoping to block anyone who did, presumably a reference to Dewey.[15]

Spurred on by the Eisenhower boom, and memories of his own defeat in Philadelphia in 1940, Dewey set out on his ostensibly nonpolitical trip in July 1947. He visited the Hutts in Sapulpa, where he marveled at a neighbor's automatic hay baler and spent most of his time in private huddles with Republican leaders from Texas, Oklahoma, and Arkansas. To reporters who pressed for details, Dewey said he was simply relaxing and quoted Will Rogers: "All I know is what I read in the newspapers." By the time he reached Kansas City, where his schedule included breakfast with 150 local Republicans and a reception for 1,500 more, the pretense was wearing thin. It was all but abandoned in Denver, where a squad of motorcycle cops, their sirens squealing at full blast, escorted the Governor down Seventeenth Street to his suite at the Brown Palace Hotel. At the governors' conference in Salt Lake City, Dewey was the undisputed center of attention. In a private session, he proposed the radical solution of turning over to Washington the states' income taxing powers, in exchange for complete control of revenues garnered from gasoline, cigarette, and excise taxes. It was about the last unequivocal stand he took on his Western tour.

He said he was delighted to see his audience at an early morning political breakfast in a small Nevada community, then looked at his watch and observed, "That shows the depths of hypocrisy to which political life will send a man." He told an off-the-record session with Wyoming Republicans that he could find "nothing detrimental" about the Taft-Hartley Act, but expected nonetheless to see something better passed within a year or so. In a Montana speech, he offered to deposit 50,000 "hardworking and serious New Yorkers" to correct a labor shortage in the state's underpopulated ranges—his own state's hard-core Communists. Beyond such generalities he would not go. Why should he? He had won the 1944 nomination without lifting a finger to get it. His current opposition was fractured and lacking the clout developed by the Brownells, Jaeckles, and Spragues. "I wiped an awful lot of dishes," Brownell recalled of the interregnum between Dewey's first and second presidential nominations, in hundreds of kitchens of would-be delegates who were later stored for easy reference in the GOP's largest file of personal and political acquaintances.[16]

Meanwhile, Dewey continued his "nonpolitical travels," stopping off in Lebanon, New Hampshire, to visit the graves of his ancestors ("Old cemeteries fascinate me") and disdaining to reply in kind when Stassen derided his refusal to deal in specifics and sought to link Dewey with Taft and congressional Republicans, somewhat incongruously, as "riders of regal reaction." Late in August, Dewey broke his silence on foreign policy, winning plaudits from the American Legion with a plea for universal military training, a program at first advocated by Truman, then abandoned in the face of a national clamor for disarmament. Later in the fall, Dewey attacked the administration's handling of the Communist offensive in China and elsewhere. To him, the Politburo was little different from the circle around Hitler, except that it was run "by smarter men." To survive in the modern world, he concluded, Americans must awake to the realities of 1947. "We must be as hard and as cunning as they."

His own tactics reflected that view. With talk of an Eisenhower draft as strong as ever at year's end, Dewey's publicity men put together a blitz. "Every sound and cogent reason" against nominating a military man for president should be advanced, in *Town Hall of the Air* debates, magazine articles, and editorials sold by a national syndicate to rural weeklies. The whole operation, its creator estimated, could be done for $5,000, surely a minor investment compared to the danger of Eisenhower's becoming the Wendell Willkie of 1948.[17]

On January 23, 1948, the problem resolved itself when Eisenhower wrote to Leonard Finder, publisher of the Manchester, New Hampshire, *Union-Leader,* to quash any suggestion he was running for president in that state's primary or any other. Thereafter supporters of the General, men like Roy Roberts and Alf Landon, expressed willingness to fall in line behind Dewey as their second choice. "We had better batten down the hatches," Dewey had written only a few weeks earlier, in anticipation of an Eisenhower draft and savage primary fights in Wisconsin, Nebraska, and Oregon. Now visitors to the Roosevelt Hotel found him at ease, leaning back in his chair, a cigarette in one hand, discoursing at length about his nine hours of talks with Winston Churchill and a recent visit from Italian Premier Alcide de Gasperi. The implication was obvious— foreign leaders were trooping to Albany to seek out the counsel and to pool collective wisdom with America's president-to-be.[18]

Dewey would say nothing as petitions were filed to put his name on primary ballots in Nebraska and Wisconsin. He almost didn't enter the Wisconsin contest at all, and only proceeded at the last moment over the objections of Jaeckle, who warned that MacArthur and Stassen were likely to poll the lion's share of the vote there. In 1948, he did not set foot in New Hampshire before its voters went to the polls on March 8, entrusting his fortunes in the state to the organizational forces arrayed behind Governor Charles Dale. Only in the second week of January, when Mrs. Frank Schlegel of Portland walked into the office of Oregon's secretary of state and deposited a thousand names on Dewey petitions, did Mrs. Schlegel's candidate dispatch Jim Hagerty to the third-floor press room with a seventy-four-word statement of thanks to his West Coast supporters. While his legislative responsibilities precluded any active, formal campaign for the nomination, Dewey expressed a willingness to accept it should his party see fit to choose him a second time. It seemed "an appropriate way," the Governor told his mother, to get "an inevitable statement behind us."[19]

Fate had devised a hand for Harold Stassen in 1948 much like that Dewey unsuccessfully played eight years earlier. Stassen's was the fresh face, with all the potential for public acclaim and all the dubiety for party professionals. At six feet three and 220 pounds, the forty-one-year-old former governor of Minnesota certainly looked like a worthy heir to the dynamic Willkie. Unburdened by any association with the negative Eightieth Congress, and possessed of vaguely liberal ideas, Stassen could also boast of a distinguished war record, a creditable performance on the U.S. delegation to the San

Francisco conference that established the United Nations in 1945, and a broadly favorable response to his allegations before the Senate investigating committee in January 1948 that eleven Washington insiders, including Truman's personal physician and a special assistant to the Secretary of the Army, had dealt profitably and unfairly in grain commodities.

The incident boosted Stassen's stock on the eve of crucial primary tests in New Hampshire and Wisconsin. It also revealed a less flattering side to the husky moon-faced man whose youthful vigor struck a responsive chord among many younger Republicans. Stassen named only three of the alleged profiteers, and on closer examination none turned out to be guilty of anything worse than bad judgment or ineptitude—qualities it didn't take Stassen to uncover in the Truman White House. Yet the affair did contribute to another nosedive in presidential popularity. Almost simultaneously, Truman found himself the target of a Southern revolt over the administration's civil rights policies, of Jewish anger at a U.S. flipflop on the partition of Palestine, and conservative resentment in the wake of the Soviet Union's seizure in February of Czechoslovakia. Moreover, the President confronted a growing threat from Henry Wallace, now formally a candidate on the Progressive party ticket and flushed by victory in a special congressional contest in the Bronx in which a Wallace-backed American Labor nominee had easily defeated the regular Democratic candidate.

In a curious symbiotic relationship, Truman's bad fortune was also Dewey's, for with national polls predicting a Wallace vote of up to 10 million in November, some Republicans began speculating that even Taft could win back the White House for the GOP. The Ohioan himself made a humorous reference to this mood at the annual Gridiron Dinner in April. "We alone today earnestly and unanimously desire to see you renominated, Mr. President," he said to Truman. Some pundits were talking of a Taft-Stassen ticket for the fall, but Stassen, who had already abruptly dismissed any idea of playing second fiddle to Dewey, was clearly no more inclined to do so to Taft. Furthermore, polls showed him running better against Truman than any Republican except Dewey—and the tantalizing Eisenhower, if indeed he was a Republican. Stassen set out to build on his reputation as party liberal. He published a book, *Where I Stand*, which raised as many doubts as converts to his cause. It wasn't hard to see why.

As Minnesota's boy governor in the late 1930s, Stassen had incurred the enmity of organized labor by supporting a forerunner of

Taft-Hartley. In his book, he opposed the concept of federal aid to housing, urged a flat 50 percent lid on federal income taxes, and opposed Marshall Plan assistance to Britain so long as the Labour government there continued its nationalization efforts. Whatever his place in the political spectrum, no one doubted Stassen's ability to stir up enthusiasm, raise money, and organize volunteers to offset the regular party machinery. His "Paul Revere Riders" were typical, a caravan of young drivers who leafleted hundreds of doorways and parking lots for their hero, before moving on to repeat the process in the next town. In one week prior to the Wisconsin primary, 340 carloads of youthful Stassen supporters blanketed 1,000 towns and villages with the message that the age of their hero was at hand.

Working against Stassen's chances were bad memories attached to his self-seeking performance at the 1940 convention, and his bull-in-a-china-shop tactics, which included entering the primary in Taft's own Ohio in defiance of every rule of political etiquette and at the risk of making the powerful senator a permanent enemy. (For a while, Stassen considered challenging Dewey in New York, only to be talked out of it by newspapermen who knew far better than he the extent of the Governor's control over the GOP apparatus in the state.) Yet Stassen's gamble in Ohio was limited, evidently opportunistic: he entered candidates in districts with only twenty-three of the state's fifty-three delegates. His chief rival for the nomination, meanwhile, stayed entirely out of favorite-son territory, cultivating goodwill and eventual support from hopefuls like Earl Warren. If Stassen were to be nominated, he would secure the nomination in the primaries. That much was certain. If the Republicans were to turn to a smoke-filled room for their nominee, his name was likely to be Arthur Vandenberg, who was also Stassen's second choice.[20]

While rivals jockeyed for position at the presidential starting gate, Dewey was in Albany doing battle with teachers and legislators over his proposed increases in state aid to education. Fifty-seven Republican assemblymen signed a petition to Speaker Heck protesting the program as insufficient and calling instead for an additional $73 million in educational assistance. If three-fifths of the unhappy Republicans proved willing to vote with the Democratic minority, they might yet achieve the unthinkable, forcing a bill disapproved by the Governor and his legislative leaders out of committee and onto the floor.

Galvanized by the danger, Dewey swung into action. Breitel was deputized to carry his message to a closed-door session of GOP senators, while Heck went to work whittling away at the rump faction within the Assembly. In a public hearing on February 11, more than 300 witnesses portrayed a dire future should the additional money not be voted. Dewey was unmoved, complaining publicly that if all the recommendations made at the hearing were approved, his 1948–49 budget would wind up $200 million in the red. It was, he wrote to Annie, "a terrific fight, and we have had to exert all the pressure at our command." But when the Republicans caucused later that month, only twenty-five of the rebels remained outside the fold (their names were duly noted and passed along to the Governor's office on the second floor); they agreed to make it unanimous after being outvoted. Teachers howled in protest at "dictator Dewey," and vowed to wage an aggressive campaign against the Governor if his party nominated him in June.[21]

It seemed a good prospect when the Dewey command convened a war council of top Republicans from around the country at the Roosevelt Hotel in mid-February. Jaeckle and Sprague were on hand, pledging ninety-seven New York delegates of unimpeachable loyalty. Tom Stephens had the latest news from New Hampshire and Wisconsin, and there were encouraging reports from the South and Midwest. Michigan looked good, if and when Vandenberg finally ruled himself out of contention. One note of caution was sounded by Kentucky's Jouett Todd, who feared the effects of a too-rapid campaign to "humanize" the candidate. In times of such peril, Todd warned, the American people wanted a president who upheld the dignity of his office. Dewey offered no dissent. He let it be known that he intended to rely in New Hampshire on Governor Dale and other friends, rather than conduct a personal campaign prior to the March 8 primary, and his partisans there made only a modest effort, costing less than $9,000.

The result was inconclusive, although hardly discouraging. Dewey captured six of the state's eight delegates, with two going to Stassen. The top vote getter among those pledged to the New Yorker polled 28,000 votes, to 21,000 for Stassen's best finisher. Dewey called the result "deeply gratifying." Stassen looked upon the first skirmish of the primary season as no worse than a draw.[22]

Stassen had reason to look forward to the next contest, in Wisconsin, where a large Scandinavian population and the support of the state's junior senator, Joseph McCarthy, meant that the roles of favorite and underdog might be reversed for the first time. Complicating the scene was the wildcard presence of Douglas MacArthur, who enjoyed backing of his own from the La Follettes, the Hearst-owned Milwaukee *Sentinel,* and many of those active in Dewey's 1944 campaign in the state. "There is never any sense in walking in front of a truck," Dewey had written his cousin the previous November, and his decision to enter Wisconsin was last-minute and halfhearted.[23]

Not only money was lacking. Dewey was trapped by his pledge against campaigning as long as the legislature stayed in session, which it did. Meanwhile, the opposition was cutting him up in Wisconsin. Typical of the attack was a Chicago *Tribune* article by Hamilton Fish, entitled "The General and the Chocolate Soldier." One needed little grounding in the Dewey-Fish feud to know which was which in the former congressman's mind. Stassen, too, was making headway. Joe McCarthy signed a "Dear Folks" letter calling attention to MacArthur's divorce and remarriage, for distribution to the state's large Catholic population. The Paul Revere Riders galloped across the state, from Green Bay to Sheboygan, from the heavily Protestant farm communities nearest the Minnesota line to the Polish Catholic wards of Milwaukee. Stassen himself played both sides against the middle, luring young voters with his internationalist views, and conservatives and Republican ethnics by urging that the Communist party in the U.S. be outlawed. In an obvious jab at Dewey, he promised to pay special attention to the Communists of New York State, where he said 40 percent of the nation's subversives lived and plotted.

Not until five days before the primary did Dewey finally set foot in the state, and then only for forty-eight hours. He spent less than five minutes addressing a crowd in Kenosha, and his own campaign officials were conspicuous by their absence. In a statewide broadcast on April 1, Dewey ridiculed Stassen's party-banning scheme. Clear the dust from your eyes, he told those who listened in, and the confusion from your brains. "You can't shoot an idea with a gun," he insisted.

The next night, on the campus of Appleton College, Dewey returned to his theme. He found fault with Democratic foreign policy from Yalta to China, but endorsed the basic concept behind the Marshall Plan. He likened the sixteen nations of Europe to the American states, called for "a federal union" speeded by American aid, and argued that the Communists' best weapons were hunger, confusion, and fear. Six nights later, at Lincoln, Nebraska, he filled in the details of his plan for a United States of Europe, a third force countering the two superpowers arrayed to the east and west. For the U.S. merely to extend relief to the war-torn continent would be a tragic misunderstanding of dynamic forces awaiting release, he told the Nebraskans. Relief alone would do little more than restore Europe to its prewar tensions and rivalries. But the economic and political potential of the Ruhr's coal mines, France's foundries, Sweden's forests, and Italy's fertile valleys might yet be realized for the free world. Only a commitment of American wealth was needed. Whatever the ultimate direction of American foreign policy, Dewey asserted in Senator Kenneth Wherry's backyard, one thing was unavoidable. "In an age of robot bombs, airplanes that travel with the speed of sound, and atomic weapons, there is no such thing as isolation."

On April 2, resigned to finishing third in Wisconsin, Dewey returned to New York. Privately, he forecast a sweep for MacArthur, with no more than two delegates as reward for his own efforts. But when the votes were counted, Stassen emerged triumphant, winning nineteen delegates to MacArthur's eight. Dewey was shut out. In Albany, the loser took solace in a promise of ten first-ballot votes from Oklahoma. "A swallow does not make a spring," he reckoned, but the faces of those around him plainly showed their concern.[24]

The next week in Nebraska, Dewey came in second to Stassen again, but his showing was much stronger than in Wisconsin (the spread between the two men was 43 percent to 35 percent) and far in front of Taft, who had put on a strenuous campaign. Dewey had even managed to pick up two delegates. But survival was, for the moment at least, overshadowed by the Stassen juggernaut. For the first time, Dewey fell behind his rival in the Gallup poll. Money was running low, and with Stassen now regarded a 5 to 3 favorite in Oregon on May 21, the press was inclined to write Dewey off. The New York *Herald Tribune*, flagship of Eastern Republicanism, seemed perfectly content with Stassen's victories. The *Nation*, speaking for New Deal liberalism, couldn't resist a patronizing note.

"Although he is not a popular figure," the magazine commented, "there is an element of tragedy in his collapse as a leading contender. He has a good mind and considerable administrative talent. But he has pursued such a cautious course and been so clearly motivated by ambition that he stands for nothing and has no real friends."

Joseph Alsop adopted the cold, simple logic of political momentum. "The rat leaving the sinking ship," he wrote at the start of May, "is a loyal old slowpoke compared to the delegates fleeing from the weakening candidate."

Dewey knew the score. To advisers circling his wagons, he proclaimed Oregon a do-or-die situation. A loss there would end his po-

litical career. Yet he had no intention of turning Albany into a
dower house, or surrendering the field to Taft and Stassen. He
would stake his campaign on a single roll of the dice, in Oregon. On
April 20, explaining that he was bound for the West Coast "to win
or else," Paul Lockwood left Albany for Portland, to paste together
an organization and prevent his boss from turning into America's
youngest elder statesman.[25]

The Dewey battle plan for Oregon had its genesis in a July 1947
conversation between Brownell and Ralph Moores, a veteran of
thirteen campaigns in the state and owner of a card file containing
25,000 political contacts. For $1,000 a month, Moores had agreed to
organize the 300,000 Republicans scattered across 96,898 square
miles of fir forests and inland desert. Yet the plan had gone awry,
and by late March 1948 Moores was warning New York headquarters that Dewey's campaign in the state had been "drifting" for
weeks, and that it would be "desperately hard" to regain the impetus lost when Stassen had made a successful visit earlier that
month. When Lockwood arrived, he found Dewey headquarters
tucked away on the third floor of a Portland office building, all but
invisible to passers-by. So was Moores's organization. All that existed were the card file and some ambitious, as-yet unfinanced plans
to blanket Oregon with billboards and radio commercials.[26]

On April 21, New York wired a thousand dollars to Lockwood,
enabling him to set up shop in a three-room suite in Portland's
Multnomah Hotel. Three thousand more followed on May 6, and
another five thousand on the eighteenth. By May 12, Dewey forces
in the state had spent $71,000; their final investment ran to about
$150,000, three times Oregon's previous record. Most of the money
was raised by Harold Talbott of the Chrysler Corporation, possessor
of a personal fortune derived from airplane sales during World War
I. Talbott's fund paid for at least 126 billboards, hundreds of sixty-
second radio spots on every station in the state, and half-hour
broadcasts each noon on such topics as "Dewey and Women's
Rights," "A Young Voter Looks at Dewey," and "How Dewey
Would Wage Peace." Oregon newspapers harvested their share of
New York dollars. The daily Portland *Oregonian*, for example, carried five Dewey advertisements a day.[27]

Lockwood overlooked no debt that might be called in. Alger
Chapman organized a doctors' committee in New York, and every
physician in Oregon received a telegram the day before the primary
from a former Stassen supporter soured on his candidate over the
issue of socialized medicine. Winthrop Aldrich leaned on bankers in

the state. The Brooklyn Real Estate Board contacted realtors there. The New York AFL lobbied Oregon's workingmen; so did the Railroad Brotherhood. Detroit Edison, the Michigan Alumni Association, and even the Minnesota Rose Society were enlisted to sell Dewey to their various constituencies. The mailing list of the state Grange was mined for possible supporters, and Oregon's 12,000 black voters were swamped with literature paying tribute to Dewey's pioneering anti-discrimination law, as well as his habit of appointing qualified blacks to significant jobs in state government. Brokers got word from Wall Street to join in. Dewey men even threw cash into betting establishments, reversing the pro-Stassen odds and altering the psychological climate of the campaign. Dewey's conservation commissioner flew into the state to assure fishery owners of his concern for their cause. Sportsmen for Dewey, Dentists for Dewey, Lawyers for Dewey, Osteopaths for Dewey, and Teachers for Dewey all carried his message to the voters. Farmers for Dewey promised to pay a call on every farmer in the state.[28]

Lockwood was ruthless in assessing the skills of those who would organize every precinct in Oregon. "Old fart," he wrote beside the name of one aspiring district coordinator, "lead in his ass." By the time Dewey himself arrived on the scene on May 1, not knowing whether his visit would last one or three weeks, Lockwood, Stephens, and Crews had assembled a formidable piece of electoral machinery. "I am going to go out and have some fun," the Governor wrote his mother three days before he left, "even though the papers report that Stassen is now ahead. . . . As you know, I am not too happy to have the nomination anyway but am going to do a bang-up job to the limit of my capacity." Although his letter sounded like preparation for the worst, Dewey publicly exuded optimism. He told reporters on the tarmac of Portland's airport at quarter to seven in the morning that he had come west for "some good old campaigning, which I love."[29]

Frances had urged him not to go. His bursitis was kicking up, and he had a bad cold. But neither was in evidence in Dewey's first week in Oregon, where he saw and was seen by 35,000 people. He visited Sweet Home and Klamath Falls, watched loggers on the Umpqua River and spearfishers on an Indian reservation. He chatted with Chief Sunset on the Mountain and donned a headdress worn by Queen Marie of Rumania on a visit a quarter-century earlier. He toured cheese factories and salmon canneries, dairy farms and lumberyards, peppering his hosts with questions about everything and quickly shedding his image as an aloof, monarchical Easterner.[30]

No stunt was too corny for the Governor of New York to participate in. At Coos Bay, he allowed the local Pirates Club to prick his
arm and draw blood with which he might sign their guestbook. At
Grants Pass, Dewey gnawed on a bone handed him by a cavorting
group of half-naked "cavemen." He rode a 1901 Locomobile down
the main street of McMinnville, and managed a look of delight
when someone handed him a bushel of dripping razor clams. At
Salem, his bus ran over a dog and the candidate immediately wired
"my profound regrets" to its owners, who, within twenty-four hours
were presented a new cocker spaniel, promptly named Dewey.
When a crowd kept out of an overflowing auditorium knocked him
accidentally in its frenzy into the mud, Dewey never lost his smile,
but climbed back on his feet and set out to greet each admirer personally.

Dewey hated all the hoopla, but he kept at it gamely, knowing
that he was closing Stassen's lead with every day he remained in the
state, not only with stunts but with hard questions and relentless
stumping. In 200 speeches, he set forth a ten-point program for developing Western resources, and he implored his countrymen to behave like "hardheaded Americans instead of softheaded saps" in
confronting Russian aggression in Europe. "You bet," he replied
when asked if he could think of a prospective secretary of state who
could say no to Stalin, then named Dulles and Vandenberg. He endorsed the use of food as a weapon of national policy, while attacking Stassen's proposal to export to Europe a flat 10 percent of
America's food and industrial production over the next ten years as
a $110 million boondoggle that would "bust the country." He took
issue with his opponent's recent characterization of Stalin's mind as
"open" and scored Stassen supporter Joe McCarthy for being in
Oregon instead of Washington, D. C., where New York State's Irving Ives was working around the clock to pass a $40 million appro-
priation for Oregon's badly needed McNary Dam. Over and over,
Dewey lashed out at Stassen's "demagogic appeals" and "glib slogans," especially where the issue of domestic Communism was concerned.[31]

Joseph Alsop, so recently pronouncing benedictions on Dewey's
political career, now hailed the Governor's "remarkable fight . . . in
these years of the locust and J. Parnell Thomas" against those who
would punish ideas.[32] "Prosecute a man for any crime he commits,"
Alsop quoted Dewey in Oregon, "but never for what he believes."
The *Herald Tribune* pricked up its ears long enough to catch wind of
"the Dewey we used to know." Stassen, exhausted from his rigorous,

inconclusive Ohio campaign, found himself forced to return to Oregon earlier than planned, where he was on the defensive over his evasions of Taft-Hartley, universal military training, and reciprocal tariffs. Like Dewey in 1940, Stassen's ambition was overshadowing any compelling ideas or qualifications he brought to the race. The fresh face was becoming a victim of voters' fickleness.

In the final days of the campaign, Stassen centered his attacks on the Communist issue, linking Dewey to Truman and Wallace and "a soft, coddling policy," and reminding Oregonians that New York City was the center of Communist activities in the U.S. Dewey snatched the bait and accepted Stassen's invitation to debate. Both sides agreed to ground rules for a debate to be broadcast nationally over 900 stations from the studios of Portland's KEX on Friday night, May 17. Stassen had conceded on every rule set forth by Dewey's team. There would be no studio audience to erupt in noisy partisanship. Instead, the debate would be held in a quiet studio, attended by no more than fifty technicians and campaign aides. Dewey also had his way on format, closing statement, and topic. He and Stassen would lock horns on a single, explosive issue: "Shall the Communist party be outlawed in the United States?"

While Stassen prepared for the duel with his second, Joe McCarthy, Dewey made no secret of the approach he would take. In off-the-cuff talks through Oregon, he had been greeted with warm applause for his ripsnorting characterization of the Communists in his own state as "the noisiest, nastiest, most disloyal, most dishonorable, untrustworthy, subversive, seditious group of worms. But they are worms," he continued when the tumult died, "and they thrive underground. I want to keep them aboveground, where we can see them and lick them as we have in New York."

It was 6:30 P.M., Portland time, and all over America, one of the largest radio audiences in history—industry experts imprecisely estimated it at anywhere from 40 to 80 million—forsook the *Carnation Contented Hour* and Fred Waring to hear Dewey and Stassen. Before the evening was out, they had listened to a startling role reversal. The audience heard Stassen, the presumed amateur, reading slowly, confidently from a well-crafted text, ascribing to his own wartime service and subsequent world travels the conviction that an international Communist network directed from Moscow and aided by "quisling cliques" within the U.S. demanded immediate, punitive response. There was no law, Stassen held, permitting effective control over domestic Communist activities. Fortunately, however, there was a bill pending before Congress, co-authored by Senator Karl Mundt and Representative Richard Nixon, that would outlaw the party definitively. Why did Dewey—not to mention Henry Wallace—oppose such a ban? Stassen wanted to know. "We must not coddle Communism with legality," he warned.

When Dewey's turn came, he fumbled for dates, misplaced a congressional report that belied Stassen's contention that the Mundt-Nixon bill would outlaw the party, and discarded a formal text in favor of short, powerful jabs reminiscent of his earlier courtroom performances. The effect was all the more persuasive for its artlessness. Dewey praised the "fine, solid, good American job," being done by the House Un-American Activities Committee, but quoted Mundt himself to portray Stassen as being in "grievous error" in his sweeping claims for Mundt-Nixon. He cited the unhappy experience of Canada, another nation frightened into outlawing Communism, only to find itself unwitting host to an international espionage ring operating out of the Russian embassy in Ottawa

"This outlawing idea is nothing new," Dewey asserted. "It is as old as government. For thousands of years, despots have tortured, imprisoned, killed, and exiled their opponents; and their governments have always fallen into the dust." He pointed for proof to Czarist Russia, Mussolini's Italy, and Vichy France. Dewey was "grateful," he said, for Stassen's bringing up "the beautiful example" of Czechoslovakia, and asked if the American people really wished to adopt totalitarian methods to defeat totalitarianism abroad. "There's no such thing as a constitutional right to destroy all constitutional rights," he insisted. Then, in words long remembered by listeners who forgot other debating points, Dewey growled out his position.

"I am unalterably, wholeheartedly, and unswervingly against any scheme to write laws outlawing people because of their religion, political, social, or economic ideas. I am against it because it is a violation of the Constitution of the United States and of the Bill of Rights, and clearly so. I am against it because it is immoral and nothing but totalitarianism itself. I am against it because I know from a great many years experience in the enforcement of the law that the proposal wouldn't work, and instead it would rapidly advance the cause of Communism in the United States and all over the world. . . . Stripped to its naked essentials, this is nothing but the method of Hitler and Stalin. It is thought control, borrowed from the Japanese war leadership. It is an attempt to beat down ideas with a club. It is a surrender of everything we believe in."[33]

Dewey's own manager had forecast, before that evening at Station KEX, a primary victory by 7,500 votes. Ralph Moores raised his prediction after the debate to 12,000. Dewey's actual victory on primary day was by a shade under 10,000 votes. What the debate did was to halt Stassen's bandwagon cold, and to re-establish Dewey as the man to beat at the national convention in Philadelphia. It boosted Dewey's reputation as a liberal, while tarnishing Stassen's. It also set in motion an unlikely series of maneuvers in which Taft let Stassen know that, Ohio notwithstanding, he was not unfriendly; and Alf Landon was enlisted to negotiate a deal between Taft and Stassen before Dewey swept the field.[34]

A few days after Oregon, Stassen flew to Topeka, where Landon told him that he could not possibly win the nomination for himself, but could choose the man who would—if he acted promptly. Yet neither Stassen nor Taft was willing to commit himself, and on the eve of the convention, when Michigan's Governor Kim Sigler tossed Vandenberg's hat back in the ring, it only heightened Stassen's hope of a deadlock, out of which he might yet emerge the victor. After all, Dewey was stalled, despite Oregon, with only about 300 of the 548 delegates needed to win.

Brownell, however, was leaving nothing to chance. A full seven weeks before the convention's opening gavel on June 21, he had fired off a host of questions. A ballroom headquarters, switchboards linking Philadelphia with Suite 1527 at the Roosevelt Hotel, street parades and souvenir matchbooks—all came under his domain. Who would provide furniture in working areas? Where would the Texas delegation stay in the event it became necessary to challenge the host of Taft Republicans sent from the Lone Star State? Who would handle a buffet for the New York contingent? When delegates finally arrived in Philadelphia, their whereabouts were no mystery to the Dewey forces, especially the Triumvirate working out of Suite 816 of the Bellevue-Stratford, who had a carefully cross-indexed file of the convention's entire working population.[35]

"The CIA were amateurs compared to the Dewey people," recalled Ray Bliss, later a national chairman of the party but in 1948 one of Taft's badly outgunned field marshals. "They knew where your bank loans were, who you did business with, who you slept with." Brownell put it less melodramatically. To him, this was a logical payoff of four years of personal cultivation, of memorizing children's names and taking visiting Republicans to Yankee ballgames and Broadway plays. Symmetrical as a Greek temple, Dewey's machine had Brownell as chief strategist, Sprague as public contact, and Jaeckle in charge of those actually working the convention floor. Below the Triumvirate were Leonard Hall, who as chairman of the national committee's congressional division was sure to engage the attention of House Republicans; and Irving Ives, appointed to perform a similar function with GOP senators. Every state delegation had at least one official Dewey liaison, including the legislative leadership from Albany. Elliott Bell, John Burton, and Frank Moore, among others, worked the floor while Charles Breitel was left home to run the State of New York via long-distance phone with his chief.[36]

Frank Rivers was one of the army of Dewey loyalists buttonholing delegates. One of his assignments was to convert Chester Gillespie, a black delegate from Cleveland who was pledged to support Stassen on the first ballot. Every morning, Rivers had breakfast with his friend, stressing Dewey's civil rights record and laying the groundwork for a midnight conference between Gillespie and the candidate himself. Thereafter, Rivers' task was to make certain that Gillespie didn't reconsider his new pledge of support for Dewey on the second ballot.

Meanwhile, in a hotel ballroom rented for $1,000 a day, Marge Hogan and the Women's Committee for Dewey plied visitors with perfume, cosmetics, silk lingerie, and special door prizes to every hundredth caller. The president of Pepsi-Cola had been approached and persuaded to donate an unlimited supply of soft drinks. Five thousand packages of Life Savers were on hand, along with thousands of matchbooks and shopping bags carrying Dewey's picture, the latter certain to be used if enough free paraphernalia were handed out to fill them. Taft partisans ordered 10,000 copies of *This Week in Philadelphia*, only to find its cover given over to the smiling face of Thomas E. Dewey.[37]

It was all part of a vast psychological blitz designed to make Dewey's victory a self-fulfilling prophecy and to panic wavering delegates into leaping onto his bandwagon before it left the station. This explained why the Dewey forces announced a running tally of visitors to the ballroom (over 50,000 by week's end), why Brownell held twice-a-day press conferences to announce new support and drop broad hints about second-ballot conversions, why favorite sons were flattered and cajoled into throwing their weight behind an inevitability that, on Monday morning at least, was not inevitable at all.

The most important delegation holding out was Pennsylvania's,

racked by ideological and personal dissension between the forces of
liberal Governor James Duff and conservatives arrayed behind Joseph Grundy, an eighty-six-year-old woolen goods maker and mainstay of the National Association of Manufacturers, who only two
days before the convention's start had labeled Taft a socialist for his
housing and education proposals. Duff loathed Dewey and, wielding
a potent club over reluctant delegates in the form of 40,000 state
jobs, posed a formidable threat. But Grundy and his voice on the
national committee, Mason Owlett, hated Duff; and they could
bring direct pressure to bear on the Governor by cutting off his
campaign funds.

At a Sunday night caucus, Duff maneuvered for time, agreeing to
the expedient of a favorite son candidacy for the state's junior Senator, Edward Martin. It was a curious move. Martin and Dewey were
old friends from their days as fellow governors; indeed, Martin had
called his friendship with Dewey "one of the very finest things in my
public life." Also abetting Dewey's cause in Pennsylvania was Hugh
Scott, a congressman from the Chestnut Hill section of Philadelphia
who for over a year had been cultivating Martin, Grundy, and Owlett, and advising Dewey on how finally to nail down their support.
On Tuesday morning, the twenty-second, Martin took a private elevator to the eighth floor of the Bellevue-Stratford. Downstairs,
Brownell alerted reporters to be on the lookout for "a big surprise"
later in the day. Martin, it was revealed, would withdraw his own
candidacy, nominate Dewey on Wednesday night, and bring at least
thirty-five fresh recruits to the New Yorker's camp. In return, Pennsylvania's Hugh Scott would be named national chairman, which
turned out to be a largely empty reward.[38]

Belatedly, the opposition awoke to the danger if not to the means
of halting what Stassen angrily denounced as "the Dewey blitz."
The only pattern to the opposition was self-interest; that, and a
crazy-quilt mix of loyalties that defied even the illogic of convention
week. Duff came out for Taft. Clare Boothe Luce, tears in her eyes,
pleaded unsuccessfully with Vandenberg to take the field actively
against "this little chap who looks like the bridegroom on a wedding
cake." Taft would not accept Vandenberg. Moreover, the Ohioan's
delegate operation, headed up by a sweating, overtaxed, under-
trained congressman named Clarence Brown, was so amateurish
and his communications so weak that he had to get Stassen's phone
number from a reporter—to whom he also urged delay in talking
with his managers, just arrived from the last hours of the Eightieth
Congress in Washington. "The poor fellows are sleeping," Taft ex-

plained. "After all, they were up very late and then had to come here."[39]

On Tuesday night, as the convention listened to Mrs. Luce describe Truman as "a gone goose" and Henry Wallace as Stalin's Mortimer Snerd, the anti-Dewey forces found a foxhole in which to hide from the blitz at John Hamilton's apartment at 2301 Locust Street. Taft, Stassen, Duff, and Kim Sigler pooled their collective indignation. Even Earl Warren, usually the most mild-mannered of men, took a swipe at Dewey's "unwholesome activities." On Wednesday morning, those activities yielded more recruits from the ranks of the uncommitted. Governor Driscoll of New Jersey brought at least twenty-three of his state's delegates with him. Senator James Kem of Missouri, pushed along by Barak Mattingly, marched at the head of seventeen or more Dewey supporters from his state. Governor Robert Bradford of Massachusetts let it be known that he would vote for Dewey on the second ballot. Ed Jaeckle talked two black members of the credentials committee into repudiating Taft and voting to seat a Dewey delegation from Georgia. Later it was rumored that one of the men received $1,500 in expense money.

One deal that was made, only to be abrogated at considerable cost, involved Russ Sprague and Charlie Halleck, House Majority Leader and an open aspirant for the vice presidency. Sprague clearly left the impression that Halleck could have second spot on the ticket, but only if he in turn could deliver all twenty-nine of Indiana's delegates on the first ballot. Halleck promised to do his best, and he made good on his promise, talking the one-third of his delegation that favored Taft into voting for Dewey as a small price to pay for the vice presidency. Jaeckle was appalled. He told Sprague and Brownell that it was a mistake to dangle the job before Halleck, since it was agreed all along that Earl Warren would be Dewey's running mate, if he was willing. Halleck, in Brownell's words, "should have been grown up enough to realize he didn't have a promise." But he conceded that Sprague's words could easily have left such an impression on a hopeful man. Others in the high command were even more forceful in their opinion that Halleck was given a commitment not from Dewey himself but from those naturally assumed to speak for the candidate with authority.[40]

With Indiana swinging Dewey's way, and West Virginia about to break open, one impressed observer stood in the ballroom and summed up the feelings of an entire city. "Say, that crowd is good!" he exclaimed of the Triumvirate. "Why, they could put over practically anybody. They could put over Taft." On Wednesday night, it was Taft who received the loudest display of delegate affection, aided by an ear-splitting collection of cowbells, rattles, and megaphones. When Ed Martin rose to nominate Dewey, there were boos to greet him, mostly from the galleries, where young admirers of Stassen sensed their defeat but weren't about to accept it without protest. Martin didn't let the noise deter him from hailing "America's greatest administrator," or trying to turn to advantage the weakness of familiarity.

"We have known him a long time," he said of Dewey. "Through all that time he has grown in the confidence of the party and the people. Today we have reason to be thankful that he started so young on the national scene, and that he has already led us in a great national campaign. He emerges today in a robust majority, ripened by years of high responsibility—still a young man in the prime of vitality—fit to lead a nation that is still young, still expanding, still going places."

After Dewey was placed in nomination, Norman Judd of Minnesota took the rostrum to argue Stassen's cause, speaking, in Judd's words, "for the millions of Republicans who are tired of winning in June and losing in November." Stassen's demonstration combined enthusiasm and irrelevance, the key ingredients being a successful parade and a curvaceous blonde dressed in a sailor suit rowing a boat over the heads of the delegates ("Man the Oars and Ride the Crest./Harold Stassen, He's the Best").

An overnight recess gave Dewey's opponents a final opportunity to perfect a coalition, but it was hopeless, resting as it did on the far-fetched prospect of Taft helping to nominate someone even further ideologically removed from his thinking than Dewey. On Thursday morning, the balloting at last began, and Russ Sprague's estimate of 429 votes proved to be just five short of Dewey's actual total. Taft had 224 and Stassen 157. On the second ballot, Dewey pulled to within hailing distance of the magic 548, and Jim Duff jumped to his feet to demand a recess. In sheer desperation, the anti-Dewey forces were clutching at straws; Stassen was even trying to reach Eisenhower at Columbia to ask him to rethink his earlier declaration of non-candidacy. (Even that wouldn't have caused undue alarm in Dewey's circle, for Ike and Sprague had met privately before the convention to discuss the General's fear that someone might stampede the hall, à la Willkie, and override his prohibition on personal political activity. Sprague told him not to worry; Dewey would have the delegates when the time came. There wasn't "a Chinaman's chance," in Sprague's words, that Ike would be beneficiary—or victim—of a draft.)[41]

But Duff's motion did present a tactical crisis to the Dewey managers. If they were to contest the move and lose, it would risk a halt in the precious momentum so painstakingly built up all week. The inevitability of victory would be challenged, perhaps beyond repair. On the other hand, to acquiesce in the adjournment was to afford the anti-Dewey forces one final chance to mend their fences and pull a rabbit out of the hat. What made the decision easier was the knowledge that delegates from Connecticut, Arizona, and Michigan, all were chomping at the bit to put Dewey over the top. Without consulting his candidate, Brownell gave the signal: Go along with Duff. Back at his hotel, fearing the worst, Dewey padded down a hallway to another room to find a functioning television set and contact his managers at Convention Hall for an explanation of their tactics. Only after Brownell laid out the justifications in detail did Dewey relax. Giving in on the recess would only postpone victory by a few hours. More important still, it might soothe ruffled feathers and set the scene for a unified party once Taft, Stassen, and the rest recognized the futility of further resistance.[42]

Back to Hamilton's apartment went the opposition, but without Taft, who had tried and failed to get Stassen to agree to accept the vice presidency. A few minutes before the evening session was to start at seven-thirty, Taft phoned the caucus to reveal his plans. "Simple arithmetic," he said, made it impossible to go on. Earl Warren had already reached a similar conclusion, calling Dewey with the news of his withdrawal at seven. When the delegates were back in place inside the hall, they heard John Bricker read a gracious concession from Taft. At the Bellevue-Stratford, a few doors down the hall from Suite 816, Frances Dewey listened to Bricker, closed her eyes, and put her head in her hands. After a few moments, she sighed deeply, rose, and said to no one in particular, "I guess I'd better be putting my hat on."

A few minutes later, she and Tom arrived at the hall, where unity was the new password, marred only by Colonel McCormick, who walked out of the place rather than acquiesce in Dewey's nomination by acclamation. Afterward, slightly calmed, the Colonel allowed as how the choice could have been worse. "It could have been Vandenberg." Some 13,000 victory-starved Republicans awaited delivery from their sixteen years in the wilderness.

Nine times in his acceptance speech, Dewey mentioned the need for political and national unity. Not once did he refer to Truman, domestic Communists, bungled foreign policies, or inflationary domestic ones. The speech was to be a mood setter, an uplifting alternative to the squabbling and shrill partisanship of those in power.

"Mere victory in an election is not our task or our purpose," Dewey said. "Our task is to fill our victory with such meaning that mankind everywhere, yearning for freedom, will take heart and move forward out of this desperate darkness into the light of freedom's paradise." The next presidential term, he said, would see the midway point in "a century of amazing progress and terrible tragedy," of technological triumphs darkened by defeats in "the ancient struggle of men to live together in peace, security, and understanding." To be a Republican in 1948, Dewey went on, "is to dedicate one's life to the freedom of men. As long as this world is half free and half slave, we must peacefully labor to help men everywhere to achieve liberty." It was short—less than fifteen minutes—and dignified, a return to the high road abandoned in 1944, the speech of a man already elected. When it was over, the hall responded warmly if without passion. It was a sobering speech, in a bleak time, suggestive of the campaign to follow.

After returning to his suite, Dewey convened a group of party leaders and sought their advice on a running mate. Leonard Hall, for one, thought that a firm commitment had been made to Halleck, but that was anathema to Dulles, Vandenberg, and the New York *Times,* which chose Wednesday to banner an editorial entitled "Surely Not Mr. Halleck," summarizing, a bit unfairly, Halleck's past isolationism. Both Warren and Halleck waited nearby until the meeting broke up inconclusively at 4:30 A.M. A few minutes later, Dewey called Earl Warren, promised to make the second job more important than in the past, and to elevate it to cabinet status. Would Warren agree to be his running mate? Warren asked for time to think it over, and promised a reply by eleven-thirty. At nine-thirty, a second meeting of the leaders got under way, and it was suggested that Stassen might be asked if he too would run, as insurance against Warren's indecision. Halleck was informed of his elimination in a stormy scene climaxed by his angry declaration that Dewey was "running out" on the Eightieth Congress, and would live to regret it before November.

At eleven-thirty, Warren called to accept Dewey's offer. Sprague broke the news to reporters camped outside his door, and an incipient boom for Stassen was nipped in the bud. "You're sticking your necks into a buzz saw," Halleck told Arizona delegates who wanted to go ahead and nominate Stassen anyway. By twelve-thirty, the Californian was duly nominated. Impartial observers of the Republican ticket agreed that it was the strongest in memory. After all, it combined New York and California, which between them accounted for more than a fourth of the electoral votes needed to win in November. Both men were former prosecutors, with established records of appealing to voters outside the narrow realm of their own party. Both were youthful and vigorous, equipped to take the battle to Truman. Hugh Scott, newly named national chairman, was undoubtedly voicing the opinion of millions when he said, "We have a dreamboat of a ticket."

Scott had already had a taste of how the Dewey operation ran when he was waylaid by Sprague and Jaeckle prior to his formal investiture as chairman and told that the campaign itself would be run by Brownell. "What am I going to do?" Scott asked. "You're to run the Republican party and keep it happy and carry the story of the campaign to it. But the actual strategy and planning is to be done by Brownell himself." If that was what the Governor wanted, Scott concluded, that was what he would do.[43]

The candidate himself now faced the reporters. He said it would be "a frightful imposition" on the Eightieth Congress to call it back into special session to act on a civil rights program, but assured them that such legislation would be enacted as a top priority of a Republican administration. He praised the Congress for enacting European assistance and a tax cut, and said he had "the highest admiration" of its efforts. He faulted Truman's Far East policies, which he called "niggardly . . . and bungling to the point of tragedy." Turning to lighter matters, he said he couldn't give out much by way of an itinerary, but did express the hope, "if we go through Castle Rock again," that the train might go slowly. Calling reporters by their first names, taking pains to insure that everyone got a chance to ask whatever was on his mind, Dewey seemed to the press more relaxed, more self-confident, and more informative than ever before.

He had reason to be optimistic. In the wake of his nomination, omens were universally favorable. Despairing Democratic liberals, fearful of a rout in November, were trying to force Truman off the ticket in favor of Eisenhower or even Justice William O. Douglas. Hubert Humphrey of Minnesota, Mayor William O'Dwyer of New York, Franklin, Jr., and Elliott Roosevelt, and Americans for Democratic Action—all wanted to dump Truman. Columnist Ed Sullivan posted odds on Dewey's election of 1 to 3. Kingsland Macy sent word from Suffolk County that the Governor could count on carrying his home state by a million votes. Henry Luce praised his "noble" acceptance speech, and Ernest Lindley, in *Newsweek*, predicted "only a miracle or a series of political blunders not to be expected of a man of Dewey's astuteness can save Truman . . . from overwhelming defeat." Lindley also expressed relief that the Republicans in Philadelphia had opted for what he called "enlightened conservatism over stand-pattism . . . American leadership in world affairs over isolationism." All Americans could be grateful, he concluded, that 1948 was not to be 1920, a savage backlash against international involvement and domestic liberalism.[44]

Amidst the general euphoria, columnist Dorothy Thompson struck a cautionary note. Readily acknowledging Dewey's gifts for administration, she noted the "bridled enthusiasm" that greeted the New Yorker's second shot at the White House, and wondered aloud if he was the man to rouse something more from the electorate. "In politics, beyond organization," she wrote, "it is understanding that makes for memorable careers, and there is more to understanding than the ability to pick up the best experts to give the best advice. There are imponderables by which greater leadership weathers storms, compounded of sympathy with human feelings, humor, compassion, friendship, loyalty—qualities which evoke affection and faith, which is different from confidence"

In short, Miss Thompson seemed to be saying, only Dewey could defeat Dewey.

15

The Man Who Might Have Been

Sixteen years in the wilderness transforms a party . . . great things happen to its soul as well as to its membership and its ideals. There remain, of course, those who would like to restore the dim, departed, almost forgotten and surely never to be recovered past. The Republican Party of today does not look backward. It looks forward.

—Thomas E. Dewey

If you want to run for Sunday school superintendent, go ahead— but don't you think it will take some time to establish that fact?

—Edwin Jaeckle[1]

In Pawling, Dewey accepted the congratulations of those who reinforced his belief that victory in November was all but assured. Winston Churchill, "the English friend who stopped with you on March 12, 1946," wired discreet best wishes. The *New Republic* conceded the obvious, and sought out silver linings. The most it could come up with was Dewey's opportunity to conduct an unusual campaign, eschewing the commitments ordinarily scattered across the autumnal landscape every four years in an unseemly attempt to nail down the last fluttering banner held aloft by special interests. Raymond Moley, whose Albany pipeline was often clogged with information, wrote that Americans in 1948 had "a real national interest" in the shortest possible campaign. That way, Moley argued, the new president could preserve the "utmost freedom" to pursue new policies.[2]

Others pondered the events at Philadelphia and rejoiced. The editor of the *Country Gentleman,* the magazine hawked by an adolescent Tom Dewey in Owosso, took delight in the Governor's triumph over "the moss-grown old bosses" of the GOP. The editor of *Who's Who* sent Albany an advance copy of the 1949 edition, listing Dewey's address as 1600 Pennsylvania Avenue, Washington, D.C. A Colorado congressman predicted a 75,000-vote win in his state. Don Van Boskirk, moderator of the Dewey-Stassen debate the previous May, now wrote urging the nominee to pursue "an affirmative, progressive campaign" stressing the positive prospects of Republican rule rather than the failures of Roosevelt and Truman. "Possibly," Van Boskirk went on, the actions of the Eightieth Congress "could be explained and justified more clearly in the minds of the people"; but the chairman of Oregon's Multnomah County GOP wanted no repeat of the slam-bang tactics of 1944. Ignore Truman and his henchmen, he wrote, and downplay domestic Communism, about which there had been "entirely too much" discussion already. The American people, in Van Boskirk's words, "are hungry for moral and spiritual guidance . . . it was this tone in your acceptance speech that appealed so greatly to the listening public."[3]

Dewey promised to try and follow Van Boskirk's suggestions. "If I succeed, it will surely make the campaign a better one." He had already given a similar response to others advising him to travel the high road. He was worried, Dewey wrote, by the "precise nature" of the issues confronting voters in 1948, most of which were entirely negative in tone or "too complex for campaign oratory."[4]

No such doubts plagued Harry Truman's advisers. "We've got our backs on our own one-yard line with a minute to play," explained presidential counselor Clark Clifford. "It has to be razzle-dazzle." On the night of July 15, a beleaguered Truman appeared before the national convention of a party coming apart at the seams over civil rights and foreign policy, and he called home the warring elements of FDR's old coalition. "I need your help," he blurted out, before denouncing the opposition as under the control of "special privilege." Truman vowed that he and his running mate, Alben Barkley, would "win this election and make the Republicans like it."

For a moment, the odds were forgotten. So were the jokes, cracked all week in Philadelphia's searing heat, that the delegates deserved embalming fluid rather than bourbon. History had been made amid the gloom; Democrats had heeded the voice of Minneapolis' youthful mayor, Hubert Humphrey, and endorsed the party's first unequivocal civil rights plank. Such bold disengagement from the past exacted its price when delegates from half a dozen Southern states walked out of the hall, promising to bleed further a party already drained by Henry Wallace's defection. The platform, when finally adopted, was militantly liberal, castigating the Eightieth Congress and setting the stage for Truman himself to challenge the Republicans of Capitol Hill.

No less an authority than Samuel Rosenman had taken one look at Dewey's platform and pronounced it fit for any New Dealer to run on. Truman knew better. Having dealt for eighteen frustrating months with the conservative-dominated Eightieth Congress, the President justifiably questioned how much of the GOP platform would prove palatable to the likes of Robert Taft and Joe Martin. So he dropped a bombshell, stuffed with Clifford's razzle-dazzle. He would call Congress back into special session on July 29, "which out in Missouri they call Turnip Day." He would extend to the opposition a chance to make good on all its generous promises in housing and health, civil rights and a minimum wage, education and the economy. The congressmen could keep all their vows in just fifteen days, Truman told a cheering hall, and still find time to go out on the hustings and campaign. Calling the Congress's bluff, the President skillfully exploited the chronic split within GOP ranks, between those favoring a frontal assault on everything that had transpired in America since 1932, and others who hoped to dilute the party's negative image by accepting and transforming New Dealish programs.

Dewey failed to grasp the immediate danger and the obstinacy of his own party's congressional leadership. "The Special Session is a nuisance but no more," he volunteered to his mother on July 12. But he did step up the pace of his criticism. He called the Democratic platform provocative and shrill in claiming for Truman's party credit for "everything from the beginning of time." On July 24, he lobbed some rhetorical shells at American diplomacy as practiced at Yalta, Potsdam, and London: in relying upon "assumptions rather than specific intergovernmental agreements," it had opened the door to the Russians' attempt to isolate Berlin, the city that was considered in millions of minds freedom's outpost. He entertained General Eisenhower at Dapplemere that same week, telling reporters that their conversations had included Berlin, the Communist threat in France, Alcide de Gasperi's achievements in Italy, and the problems of a unified armed services command at home.[5]

A Roper poll confirmed, by a margin of 49 percent to 30 percent, that Americans regarded the foreign threat with greater urgency than domestic problems. Dewey, hemmed in by his own association with bipartisan foreign policy, and cautioned steadily by Dulles and others against saying anything that might undermine the confidence of America's allies in the forthcoming new administration, held back from attacking policies which he, in any case, largely supported. He argued with Frank Gannett, the conservative publisher who wanted him to take a stand against the Marshall Plan. "The European Recovery program costs a few billion," he told Gannett. "War would cost us hundreds of billions, and if we did not have so many friends and allies, would cost our liberty and our country itself."[6]

On another issue, Dewey's hands were tied by personal sentiment. Early in September, Eisenhower reported that his own six-week tour of the country had convinced him that the public's concerns could be boiled down to two words: "Russia" and "inflation." Though perceptive, the General was hardly alone in his estimate. Late that July, a Senate committee had touched off a national uproar with the testimony of Elizabeth Bentley, for five years a courier for a Soviet spy ring with links to the White House itself. Miss Bentley, dubbed "the nutmeg Mata Hari" by *The New Yorker,* pointed an accusing finger at Harry Dexter White, father of the International Monetary Fund and more recently Truman's assistant secretary of the treasury. She also implicated a thirty-two-year-old government economist named William Remington, who all but confirmed her story when he took the stand himself. Remington admitted meeting Bentley in "unusual" places and paying dues to the Communist party. He characterized as "fantastic" his ability to continue working on the Marshall Plan and in the atomic energy field four years after Miss Bentley first identified him as a Communist sympathizer.[7]

Even more sensational disclosures were to come before the House Un-American Activities Committee, when chairman J. Parnell Thomas called to the stand Whittaker Chambers, a disheveled editor from *Time* magazine and a self-confessed Communist who had seen the light and quit the party in disgust. Chambers now stepped forward to identify as an unregenerate subversive one Alger Hiss, currently head of the Carnegie Endowment for World Peace but only three years earlier one of Roosevelt's Yalta advisers. From the White House came a furious retort, all but drowning out Hiss's own denial of the charges on August 5. The investigators, said Truman, were causing "irreparable harm to certain people, seriously impairing the morale of federal employees, and undermining public confidence in the government." Moreover the President flatly refused to allow any federal agencies to turn over to Homer Ferguson's Senate staffers files relating to the government's own loyalty program, a demand arising out of the Remington disclosures. Finally, Truman accepted a reporter's characterization of the House committee's work as "a red herring."

Having already stumbled earlier in the year with an impromptu remark about "good old Joe" who sincerely wanted peace but was frustrated by hardliners on the Soviet Politburo, Truman's red herring phrase might have backfired badly had Dewey chosen to exploit it. But for the moment it was Chambers, not Hiss, who was under suspicion of perjury. To satisfy his own doubts in the matter, Representative Richard Nixon had a long private talk with the witness, who was willing to submit to lie detector tests to prove he had told the truth in identifying Hiss as a onetime colleague and friend. Nixon was satisfied, and on August 11 he went to New York to meet privately with John Foster and Allen Dulles. Foster had known Hiss well enough to write an endorsement of his candidacy for the Carnegie Endowment, on whose board he served. After reviewing transcripts of testimony brought along by Nixon, Dulles concluded, "There's no question about it. It's almost impossible to believe, but Chambers knows Hiss."

Both Dulleses agreed to Nixon's plan for a public confrontation between Hiss and Chambers on August 25. Afterwards, the young Congressman from California summed up the damning evidence against Hiss in a four-page letter. A Dewey aide was dispatched to collect still more of Nixon's material for a speech on domestic Communism. Direct access to congressional discoveries could also have been provided by William P. Rogers, the former assistant in Dewey's D.A. office who was now counsel to the Ferguson Committee. Ferguson himself was a friend who had cooperated fully at the time of the Senate probe of Pearl Harbor in 1946. The information was available. The political dividends promised to be substantial. Brownell, for one, scented the possibilities hinted at by Eisenhower, and late in July he publicly described Communist penetration of high government circles as the most important issue of the campaign.[8]

Yet Dewey never seized on Communism, never tried to employ his special flair for public prosecution. Some thought his reluctance stemmed from Dulles' association with Hiss, however peripheral. A more likely restraining influence was the painful memory of 1944 and his ill-considered attempt to link FDR and Earl Browder. Even now, he ruefully told Breitel, erstwhile friends reminded him of his four-year-old attack on Hillman in Boston. Once burned, Dewey of all men was likely to be twice shy. Then, too, he was tired of running for office as a prosecutor. And there was still another reason for his reluctance to pillory Truman as a dupe of foreign subversion.[9]

"Dewey was perfectly willing to accept America's role as the leading enemy and container of Russian expansion," says Hugh Scott. "But he was no McCarthy. He thought it degrading to suspect Truman personally of being soft on Communism. He wasn't going around looking under beds." Neither was he inclined to make use of *Democratic Diplomacy and Appeasement,* a massive White Paper compiled by the Republican National Committee to provide foreign policy ammunition to the party's candidates. His peculiar stance was illustrated by a discussion he had on August 30 with Styles Bridges and New Hampshire newspaper publisher Bill Loeb, the team who had earlier advised an aggressive courtship of Oregon's primary voters. Now they were back in Albany, this time to press for a hard-hitting campaign emphasizing the Communist danger. Dewey listened to their entreaties, savored the pros and cons of their approach, and then, Solomon-like, rendered a verdict. He would take the Communist issue, he informed Bridges and Loeb, and "fleck it lightly."[10]

When the campaign got under way, Dewey did exactly that. He told audiences everywhere that he had a solution to the problem of Communists on the public payroll much cheaper than Truman's call for $25 million to purge Washington and its agencies: "Elect a Republican administration who won't put them there in the first place." In his major speech on the subject, delivered at Los Angeles on September 25, he took an almost libertarian tack. "We will keep informed and we'll keep the American people informed," he promised. Communist activities would be monitored and exposed. If laws against treason were broken, then "traitors' treatment" would be meted out. Jail would await saboteurs. New laws would be written to contain the threat if old ones proved inadequate. "But in this country we'll have no thought police. We will not jail anybody for what he thinks or believes. So long as we keep the Communists among us out in the open, in the light of day, the United States of America has nothing to fear."

It was, considering the mood of the time, a statesmanlike position. It was also a politically perilous one.

"I do not know about accommodations at the White House for the family, if I am elected," Dewey told his mother on August 9. "There is of course no rush about it." Little else seemed hurried about the Republican nominee's summer. Early in July, Brownell had left on a tour of the South, Sprague had gone fishing in Alaska, and Jaeckle retired to a Buffalo golf course. A reporter asked Dewey if, in the event of his election, he planned to make Dapplemere his summer White House. "There are two ifs in that one," the candidate replied, "and one is too many." With the rest of the nation, Dewey paused briefly to take in the spectacle of Henry Wallace's Progressive party conclave, held in Philadelphia just a few days after the Southern rebels gathered in Birmingham to nominate Strom

Thurmond of South Carolina on a platform of states' rights and reverence for the Constitution—as they interpreted it.[11]

The Dixiecrat affair went on with relative decorum; Henry Wallace's convention was another thing altogether. Vito Marcantonio was chairman of the rules committee. Delegates voted down a resolution introduced by Vermonters warning against any interpretation of the Progressive platform as an endorsement of the policies of a foreign power. Then they adopted a party charter opposing the Marshall Plan and the Truman Doctrine, demanding immediate independence for Puerto Rico, and calling for nationalization of all railroads, utilities, banks, and merchant shipping. H. L. Mencken, full of spleen and ecstatic at the prospect of lancing this "paranoiac confection," earned a formal motion of censure from the Maryland delegation after he described Gideon's Army as a motley blend of "grocery store economists, mooney professors in one-building universities, editors of papers with no visible circulation, preachers of lost evangels and customers of a hundred schemes to cure all the sins of the world."

Wallace might yet be pivotal in deciding the election. Yet he insisted on playing into the hands of his critics—including Truman—by calling for U.S. withdrawal from Berlin, and by accepting a formal endorsement from the Communists. Soon afterward, his candidacy was rejected by the executive board of the CIO, itself struggling to undercut Communist influence in member unions. Only a few months earlier, the former vice president had spoken confidently of polling 10 million votes. Now the first post-convention polls showed him fading. They put Dewey far out in front of Truman—by eleven points, according to George Gallup, by twice that margin in Elmo Roper's survey. A Florida poll, described as "too good to be true" by the candidate, had Dewey ahead in that Democratic bastion. Through Ben Duffey of the New York advertising agency Batten, Barton, Durstine and Osborne, daily telephone conversations were arranged with pollster Archibald Crossley. Both Gallup and Roper offered to make known their findings to Duffey in advance of publication. Gallup did have one question. Why, he asked Duffey, did the Republican campaign want to spend money on polling? The results, after all, were a "foregone conclusion." Roper said as much in announcing on September 9 that he would discontinue his own polling. The race was too obviously one-sided, he explained, to generate even artificial suspense. Whatever he maintained afterward, Truman himself seemed resigned to defeat at this stage of the campaign. Meeting his opponent on July 31 at the dedication of New York's new Idlewild Airport, he whispered in Dewey's ear his hope that the Republican would do something about the White House plumbing once he moved in.[12]

Buoyed by such omens, Dewey involved himself even more than usual in the details of planning the campaign. He relished a "knock-out" of a report from the West Coast, describing California, Oregon, and Colorado as excellent prospects, and setting up a fall battle-ground in the Rocky Mountain states and Washington. He gave permission for Roger Straus to establish a special division to court the heavy Jewish population of cities like Philadelphia and Chicago. He overruled Brownell, and refused to make haste in establishing a farm division in Chicago. He visited with Earl Warren in Albany, where his vice presidential candidate was told the dates, locations, and subject matter for all of Dewey's major speeches, many already composed in draft. Warren's own pet project, federal irrigation as-sistance for the West's water-starved growers, was willingly en-trusted to the Californian. Dewey seemed content to refer reporters to favorable comments he'd made about federal aid in an earlier, definitive speech on the subject. This habit continued, even after newspapers in California's Central Valley pressed for a fresh com-mitment and more details. On Election Day, Dewey lost the Valley by 190,000 votes; he lost California by 18,000.[13]

"I am busy as a one-armed paper hanger," the candidate in-formed his mother as the campaign's formal start neared, "trying to write speeches and seeing too many people as always. The speeches suffer and I will have to write considerably on the train, I am afraid." Among his callers were Senator George Aiken of Vermont, Congressman Clifford Hope of Kansas, and Ed Babcock, his own farm adviser, who briefed him for three days on the agricultural outlook and the finer points of the Hope-Aiken flexible farm price supports bill passed by the Eightieth Congress earlier in the year. On July 24, eighty farm editors were invited to tour Dapplemere and dine with the nominee at the local Grange hall. Dewey cocked an attentive ear as the editors talked about farm surpluses and cattle disease. He described his own farm as "a sort of laboratory," neces-sarily self-supporting "because there is no government to take over the deficits." He pointed proudly to New York's pioneer efforts at promoting artificial insemination as a first step toward more pro-ductive dairy herds, and promised to increase federal soil conserva-tion funding. He had kind words for Hope-Aiken. There were, Dewey said, at least 150 non-basic commodities for which it was im-possible to lay down a single unvarying support price. "You can't class a summer squash with a pound of butter," he explained. The editors, impressed with his plain talk and obvious love of the land, went away happy.[14]

Another session was scheduled for early September; by then, a verbal accident had raised doubts in the minds of at least some farmers. On September 2, Harold Stassen appeared outside the Governor's Albany office to criticize the Truman administration for doing all in its power to keep consumer prices artificially high. At a time of housewives' revolts over the cost of sirloin and pork chops, this seemed smart politics. But Truman's secretary of agriculture, Charles F. Brannan, promptly fired back, accusing the Republicans of wanting to scuttle the entire price support system. For good measure, Brannan threw in a charge, soon disproved, that Dewey profited unduly from the sale of Dapplemere's milk output. It was the first of eighty speeches the fiery Brannan would deliver before November 2, in tandem with the President and Alben Barkley. Truman meanwhile began on a strident campaign on September 18, at the National Plowing Contest in Dexter, Iowa, labeling his opponents "cunning men [who] want a return of the Wall Street economic dictatorship" and prisoners of "that notorious do-nothing Eightieth Congress." What the Tafts and Martins had already stolen away from the farmer was "only an appetizer," said Truman, "for the economic tapeworm of big business."

Having pigeonholed an international wheat agreement and cut the Commodity Grain Corporation's authority to acquire additional storage space for what turned out to be a bumper crop, the Congress was highly vulnerable. But so was Truman. Vandenberg pointed out in a letter to Dewey in mid-July that the Senate's failure to ratify the wheat agreement "stems entirely from the fact that the Administration did not give us remotely adequate time in which to explore a subject of this magnitude and far-reaching implication." The treaty had been submitted on April 30, a full month after its signing. Hearings had been held promptly. But late in May, with the full assent of Democrat Walter George of Georgia and the entire Senate Agriculture Committee, of which he was ranking minority member, it was decided not to press for final approval, since there was too little time to enact supplemental legislation without which the agreement would be ineffective. And to demand an immediate up or down vote was to risk overall defeat. The President and his State Department, Vandenberg concluded, "are far more to be criticized" for their thirty-day delay in transmitting the agreement to the Senate than were the senators themselves, of both parties.[15]

Even on price supports, Truman's attacks were ironic, to say the least. He had issued a call of his own for lowered supports, and for immediate adoption of the flexible support concept (which Hope-Aiken would implement gradually, starting in 1950). Yet Stassen's offhand remark came at an opportune time for the Democrats, who were quick to flog the Republicans with it for their alleged insensitivity to agriculture. It might have been wrested from them two days later, when Truman's commerce secretary, Charles Sawyer, ordered a curb on grain exports over Brannan's protests in the hope that such a move would reduce farm prices ("I think it's time the housewife got a break," Sawyer announced). But Republicans let the comment pass without an answering blast. Having passed up Brownell's advice that the farm campaign should be placed in the hands of Midwesterners, Dewey entrusted his message to agricultural America to Eastern farmers, many of them heavily influenced by the "Cornell School," with its emphasis on consumption of corn and grain by dairy cows. Sawyer's opening was not exploited, for the simple reason that no one in the Dewey camp—except perhaps Brownell—thought it exploitable.[16]

It was a season of frustration for Herb Brownell. In mid-September, angered at the increased authority assumed by Paul Lockwood and others in the Albany circle, the mild-mannered campaign manager wrote out a letter of resignation as campaign director, only to tear it up before the day was out. Brownell was being treated as a technician, not a grand strategist. He carried out Dewey's wishes— aided considerably by a cooperative ABC radio network, which took Eleanor Roosevelt's daily program, shared with her daughter Anna over 200 stations each day at noon, off the air until after the election. He went to Chicago to open a headquarters too obviously planned as a sop to the region's conservative Republicans. And he was made Dewey's ambassador on a fruitless mission to Washington to plead with congressional leaders to get behind the platform and adopt at least a semblance of a responsible program during the special session. As "a last-ditch compromise," Brownell asked for amendments to the Displaced Persons Act, which in its original form discriminated against Catholics and Jewish refugees from European concentration camps, raising hackles throughout urban areas that had been carried by the GOP in 1946.[17]

Taft refused to budge. Angrily, he accused Truman of using the Congress for his own partisan objectives, a charge as truthful as it was irrelevant. Truman's own palace guard testified before congressional committees that his anti-inflation program, a complex omnibus of selective controls, standby rationing authority, credit restrictions, and increases in bank reserves, was of dubious value in attacking inflation at its roots. Marriner Eccles of the Federal Reserve said that the program was like "trying to fill up a bathtub with the stopper out," the stopper, presumably, being the price controls prematurely removed by the President with the help of the Seventy-ninth Congress. Leslie Arends, chairman of the House Rules Committee, spoke for his fellow Republicans. "We'll put controls on turnips," he said, "but nothing else."

Taft did promise Brownell that if committee chairmen would, on their own initiative, permit legislation favored by Dewey to reach the floor, then party leaders would go along. But he refused to pressure W. Chapman Revercomb, the West Virginian who chaired the committee overseeing refugee legislation and who was caught up in a tight re-election battle of his own. Even this grudging cooperation, Brownell was informed, represented generosity of spirit on Taft's part. Most of the rank and file wanted to adjourn immediately; all resented Truman's efforts to make them his "stooges." Taft's ultimatum placed Dewey in a quandary. Feeling boxed in, fearful that any public move to enforce his will on Capitol Hill would be rejected, with disastrous effects for the campaign to come, he did nothing beyond sending Brownell to plead for the refugee amendments and a passage of a $65 million loan to help get the United Nations launched in its new home in New York City.[18]

His attitude toward Taft's colleagues was summed up afterward, when a friendly reporter hankering after a House seat came to seek out Dewey's advice. It was all well and good that a man should want to serve his country in politics, the Governor said, just as long as he didn't win and become "one of those congressional bums."[19]

On August 7, the Congress packed its bags and went home to campaign. In eleven days it had given Truman only two of the eight points in his anti-inflation program. Dewey got even less: the UN loan, which survived a House-Senate conference committee only because Taft agreed to defer to the right wing of his party and withdraw his housing assistance bill. Congress left town without taking any action at all on Truman's request for a $4.3 billion excess profits tax, minimum wage legislation, higher pay for federal workers, broadened Social Security, public power expansion, health insurance—or on the Displaced Persons Act.

Furious with Revercomb, Dewey decided to make the West Virginian an example to others inclined to rebel against his leadership.

He would withhold any support for the hard-pressed senator, informing West Virginia party leaders that he doubted very much whether his schedule would permit a visit to the state before November. If he did come, moreover, Dewey didn't see how he could possibly refrain from denouncing Revercomb's misguided stand on the Displaced Persons Act. Nor would he soften this position after Walter Hallanan, whose strategically timed endorsement at Philadelphia had proved important in nailing down the nomination, made a personal appeal for reconsideration. After all, Hallanan argued, Republicans were worried about control of the new Senate, and whatever else Revercomb might be, he represented a vote to organize the upper body. Having dug in his heels, Dewey refused to change his mind. In the end, Revercomb was defeated, and West Virginia voted for Truman in a Democratic sweep.[20]

The contretemps over Revercomb served to remind voters that all the Republican talk of unity might be at least partly for internal consumption. Behind the smiling facade of a unified GOP, sharp divisions still lurked. None of this surprised party professionals. On the very night of Dewey's nomination in Philadelphia, Hugh Scott had left the hall with a friend to enjoy his first breath of fresh air all week when he ran into Joe Pew, whose money and influence, though both considerable, had not been sufficient to secure Pennsylvania for Taft.

"Well, young man," Pew snapped, "you got your wish. If you can be for the damned little dictator in November, I guess I can. But I'll tell you this: You've shot your career in this state to hell."[21]

Harold Stassen has claimed ever since to have advised Dewey at Pawling that July to move more forcefully in commanding a Congress that wasn't yet his. According to Stassen, he had already spoken with Speaker Martin, and secured a pledge of congressional cooperation. He also took the opportunity to urge passage of a higher minimum wage law, regarded as overdue by businessmen as well as union officials. Stassen recalls vividly seeing Dewey pull out of his pocket an advance copy of the Roper poll, as a prelude to his rejection of any such risky operations. Voters would see through the special session for the political gimmick that it was, Dewey went on. His job was to protect his present lead, and not "rock the boat."[22]

On August 12, Stassen wrote Dewey. "I believe that you came through the special session in good shape. The definite items which were accomplished were sufficient to prevent impartial observers from labeling it a 'do-nothing' session." Others also glanced at the polls and competed in sycophancy. On August 11, Hugh Scott lunched with the Governor at Albany, and he reported on the results of a twenty-eight-state tour among party professionals and precinct captains, whose field marshal he purported to be. Everywhere he had gone, recounted Scott, he had promised a vigorous campaign. As former prosecuting attorneys, Dewey and Warren could be counted on to "read an indictment a mile long" against Truman's failures at home and abroad. Dewey asked how the message had been received, and Scott replied that such a hard-hitting campaign was precisely what the party workers wanted.[23]

"Well," the candidate said, "this will come as news to you, then. That's not what we're going to do." He outlined the feelings of his closest advisers, men like Jaeckle, Sprague, Brownell, Elliott Bell, and speechwriter Stanley High, that a high-level campaign was called for, in keeping with the gravity of world events. Dewey singled out Midwestern coordinator Everett Dirksen, who was telling him to wage a cautious campaign in agricultural America, relying on traditional Republican loyalties among farmers to refute Truman's wild accusations against the Eightieth Congress. To this, Scott replied that the party faithful were hoping to hear speeches between now and November like the blistering attack on FDR delivered at Oklahoma City four years earlier.

"That's the worst speech I ever made," Dewey moaned. For four years he had tried to forget that speech, only to have it thrown up to him now as his best product. His bias was shared with Frances, who believed it undignified and counterproductive to personally attack any incumbent president. "I will not get down into the gutter with that fellow," Dewey told his national chairman. Scott continued to offer resistance, until Dewey asked him to return that evening to the Executive Mansion, "so we can pursue this thing a little more." In awe of the Governor, whom he barely knew, and partially reassured by the solid phalanx of those closer to Dewey who were cautioning against any repeat of 1944, Scott didn't take up the invitation. Dewey was, after all, a busy man, he told himself later; he had said what he came to say.[24]

Out in St. Joseph, Missouri, an elderly GOP worker had conducted a poll of her own among people in hotel lobbies, gas stations, bus depots, and hamburger stands. Then she sat down and wrote Dewey a wary letter. "You are not going to walk away with this election," Irene K. Nims reported. "I have been through a good many presidential campaigns. This one is different. It's peculiar. People don't want to vote for Harry Truman or Henry Wallace, and

they don't know whether they want to vote for you or not. . . . Your
job is to help them make up their minds."[25]

By then, the campaign strategy was set. It was based upon Farley's Law, which held that few souls were saved after August, and
even fewer voters changed their minds after October 1. The respected political reporter Richard Rovere echoed the feelings of
those who looked upon modern-day campaigning as a cynical indulgence. "There are, no doubt, some people in every community
who will vote for the man who says the pleasantest things about the
local crops and the local rainfall," Rovere wrote in *The New Yorker*,
"but their number is probably balanced by the number of intelligent citizens who will decide, the next morning, to vote against the
man who disturbed their children's rest by roaring through the
night, surrounded by a hundred motorcycle cops with a hundred
sirens, so that he could deliver an address pointing out that the Republicans invented the Depression or that the Democrats invented
Communism."

Unity was selected, in the words of one Dewey speechwriter, "as
the clothesline on which speeches would be hung," a tailor-made
prescription for statesmanship at a time of international crisis and
domestic confusion. Berlin was blockaded, China rent by civil war,
the Middle East ravaged by an Arab-Israeli conflict. World War III
could erupt from any one of these flashpoints. Moreover, Dewey and
his men had polling data showing that Truman only benefitted from
sharp attacks leveled against him by Taft or other congressional
leaders. Unlike the magisterial Roosevelt, Truman might easily convert himself into the well-meaning underdog kicked while down.
Dewey had no intention of abetting such a Democratic strategy. Finally, his own overtures to labor and other components of the New
Deal coalition were bearing fruit handsomely. Why abandon a conciliatory posture when it hauled in endorsements from teamster
locals and the 175,000-member Building Service Employees Union,
the Pittsburgh *Courier*, one of the nations' most eminent black newspapers, and Dean Alfange, founder of New York's Liberal party?[26]

Despite his own "high regard" for Truman, Alfange revealed on
September 16, he had concluded that the Democratic party's "feu-
dal dictatorships in the South and corrupt patronage machines in
the North are not the kind of pillars that will support an edifice of
liberalism." To be sure, he went on, the GOP had its own reactionary and isolationist elements. But there was a difference, Alfange
said. Truman had shown no ability to control his own party. Dewey,
by contrast, might influence even the worst malefactors in Republi-

can ranks, in the process restoring the GOP "to its early tradition as the champion of civil liberty and equal opportunity."

The intellectual arguments for an above-the-fray stance were equally compelling: Truman's record of failure predated the Eightieth Congress. His own description of that body as "the worst" in American history—a charge earlier leveled against its immediate predecessor—overlooked the fact that it had been Democrats whose votes had provided the margins to override the President's vetoes of Taft-Hartley and a tax cut bill. It was enlightened Republicans, of the Dewey-Vandenberg stamp, who gave loyal support to the Marshall Plan, aid to Greece and Turkey, a unified defense establishment, and the Vandenberg Resolution, which paved the way for regional alliances with America's allies. It was Southern Democrats, led by Mississippi's Senator John Stennis, who had filibustered to death any civil rights program and placed a roadblock athwart other legislation in the special session.

So there it was: a neat combination of personal preference, bad memories, political necessity, and genuine statesmanship, wrapped up in the unanimous support of trusted advisers and state party leaders. Whatever characterizations would later be made of Dewey's campaign strategy, it was immensely popular at the time among those hoping to persuade a disenchanted, uncertain public.

On Labor Day, Truman went to Detroit and delivered a scathing attack before 150,000 workingmen in Cadillac Square. "These are critical times for labor ... there is great danger ahead," the President warned. Dewey's election would surely usher in a return of the vicious cycle of boom and bust, helping only those who sought to "totally enslave the workingman." Taft-Hartley, Truman continued, was but a preview of the economic hell awaiting labor in a Republican administration, when not only wages and living standards of working people would be imperiled; "our democratic institutions of free labor and free enterprise" themselves might come under attack.

Trailing badly, the President had decided he could afford anything but decorum, and he was determined to bind Dewey "hand and foot" to the Eightieth Congress and its exploitable failures. In Denver on September 21, Truman likened himself to Paul Revere, warning the West against Republican plans to turn the region into an economic colony of Wall Street. Two days later, in Reno, he assailed congressional Republicans as "silent and cunning men, who have developed a dangerous lust for power and privilege." The theme was embellished in El Paso on the twenty-fifth. Republicans opposed public power, in the President's words, "because it means that the big power monopolies cannot get their rake-off at the expense of the public." He attacked Taft, "the Republican wheelhorse of the Senate," for opposing more money for flood control, two weeks before the Columbia River roared over its banks "and washed a whole town away." He quoted a conservative congressman from Pennsylvania who personally believed that "sooner or later you'll have to discontinue the price support program," and asserted that the entire GOP agreed.

The same day, Truman managed jabs at "this Republican gang," at Stassen's remarks about the need to lower farm prices for the benefit of consumers, and at the "economic royalists" who published and read the *Wall Street Journal,* and who were "terribly anxious to take over the country again." In one speech, he invoked the name of Herbert Hoover no fewer than fourteen times. Walter Lippmann expressed disapproval of such tactics. "He is not running against Dewey and Warren at all," wrote the author of *Today and Tomorrow,* "but against the Hoover Administration and against the 80th Congress." Lippmann found it "a palpable absurdity" that Truman and his circle were somehow more liberal than Dewey, Warren, Vandenberg, Stassen, and their closest advisers. "For the slogans and battle cries which Mr. Truman is using in this campaign have almost no connection with the actual prejudices, practices, and habits of thought of his own cronies." The *Oregonian Journal,* a paper of impeccable progressive credentials, agreed, endorsing Dewey with a slap at a "pathetically brave" incumbent "descending to the level of his Missouri training in campaign vilification."

Early in October, the New York *Times* followed suit. So did the Chicago *Tribune.* Dewey, declared the Colonel's editors, was "the least worse" of those in the race. Additional endorsements came from ordinarily Democratic journals—the Newark *Evening News,* the Houston *Chronicle,* the St. Petersburg *Evening Independent,* and the Charlotte *Observer.* Democrats for Dewey signed up Joe Louis, W. C. Handy, Dan Tobin of the teamsters, and former Democratic cabinet member, Jesse Jones. Al Smith's daughter and son-in-law agreed with Jones, a conservative Texan who argued that "patriotism should tell you to forget party labels this year."

"I feel sure," Caroline Gannett wrote Dewey early in September, "that you are the streamlined transition man who will toss off some of the hypocrisies of the old political parties and lead us into a decent, honorable, straightforward way of political life." Polls showed that a majority of Americans inclined to agree. Asked to select adjectives that best described the Republican candidate for president, voters told Elmo Roper that Dewey was "able, aggressive, and intelligent." He might not kindle Rooseveltian affection in many hearts, but he ministered powerfully to the thirst for direction and purposeful application of America's still overwhelming power. Perhaps best of all, he was not Truman.[27]

On September 19, Dewey climbed aboard the last of seventeen rail cars, his portable campaign headquarters carrying forty-one staffers and ninety-two journalists, six speechwriters, Allen Dulles with a cipher machine to provide instantaneous contact with Foster at the UN conference in Paris, Ben Duffey to read and interpret polling data, Ed Jaeckle to leap off at each stop and renew old acquaintances while surveying the lay of the political land, Paul Lockwood and his vast collection of elephants, and Elliott Bell, who was de facto chief of staff and housemother to the speechwriting team. Together, this impressive collection of talent was embarked on a campaign to give meaning to platitudes like "able, aggressive, and intelligent," and incentive to voters to break with Democratic traditions.

Myths form a bridge between implausibility and inevitability. They embroider truth with legend and give irrational history a sleek look of order. The year 1948 has come down to us as a series of myths, appealing images, and contemporary explanations of the pollsters' grievous misjudgment. On the one hand is a courageous bantamweight pursuing vindication on a lonely hell-raising transcontinental tour; on the other, a rival caught up in the certainty of his triumph, dispensing bromides, stingy with specifics. One man fought his way toward Election Day determined to make his party once and for all the majority's spokesman. The other coasted, too embarrassed to mention the record compiled by his party colleagues who were the majority on Capitol Hill. It was the tortoise and the hare, a program versus platitudes, popular hero versus—what? No one could be precisely sure.

But all that was glimpsed only in hindsight. No one riding the *Victory Special* as it chugged through Illinois and Iowa on September 20 could possibly foresee the verdict. It was a jovial, confident Dewey who greeted 10,000 people at Rock Island, giving the state GOP ticket a pat on the back and even finding good omens in the steady rain falling on the crowd. After all, he said, it rained nineteen out of the twenty days he campaigned in Oregon—and everyone knew the results there. Then he turned serious, setting the tone for what was to follow. "We will not tell one part of the American people one program . . . and another part an absolutely contradictory program. We will say the same thing everywhere to all the people of this country and, moreover, we will endeavor during the months ahead to let every nation on earth know that out of this campaign there is no profit for aggressors." In Davenport, he promised to retain price supports, "so essential for the confidence of the farmer"; and he won cheers from an overflow audience at the Drake University fieldhouse in Des Moines with his call for unity in the face of international challenge, and his refusal to indulge in "loose talk, factional quarreling, or appeals to group prejudice." He was as reasonable as Truman was shrill: "I will not contend that all our difficulties today have been brought about by the present national administration . . . only part are deliberately caused for political purposes. It is not too important how these conditions came about. The important thing is that as Americans we turn our faces forward and set about curing them with stout purpose and a full heart."

The truth of America, Dewey said in words addressed to oppressed peoples beyond the sound of his voice, "seeps through every obstacle of iron and steel. . . . Neither barbed wire nor bayonet have been able to suppress the will of men and women to cross from tyranny to freedom." Few specifics of future policies were provided; those, he vowed, would come later. "I have no trick answers and no easy solutions," he told a national radio audience. "The American people have a right to expect honest answers and I propose to give them." The Alsops, like most observers, were impressed. Amid the customary guarantees of instant utopia, the Governor had told the unvarnished truth—"that the road to the happy future is likely to be pretty rocky." Harold Stassen thought the Des Moines address "splendid and beautifully presented." The Des Moines *Register* weighed in with its own brand of approval, greeting Dewey's arrival in the state with a freshly taken poll showing Dewey leading Truman, 51 percent to 30 percent, with native son Henry Wallace trailing in the dust. In a state where Senator J. P. Dollivar once predicted that "Iowa will go Democratic the year hell goes Methodist," Dewey's lead was not surprising. But the same poll indicated a dead heat between Republican Senator George Wilson and his Democratic challenger, Guy Gillette. In Illinois, Dewey found isolationist Republican Curley Brooks in trouble against Paul Douglas. And the GOP weakness was by no means limited to agricultural America. Roy Howard, after a swing around part of the Scripps-Howard circuit in August, expressed his own concern about the party's chances to retain its 51 to 45 margin in the Senate, and Dewey ordered his schedule revised to stress support of such ideologically distant Republicans as Henry Dworshak of Idaho, Curley Brooks, and Oklahoma's Ross Rizely. To help Rizely stave off Robert Kerr, Dewey made thirteen speeches in the state. Vote for John Sherman Cooper, he implored Kentuckians, "even if you don't vote for me."[28]

Throughout his first Western swing, Dewey cited numbers to prove that the Eightieth Congress had appropriated more money than ever before for programs of special interest to the region. And he defended its leading Republican members most of all. He made strenuous efforts to integrate Stassen's loyalists into his campaign. But for Taft there were no national radio hookups, no frequent consultations. Dewey refused to meet Taft supporters lined up by the local organization in Cleveland, where the nominee did nothing to ingratiate himself with county chairman George Bender, a personal friend of Taft's and a man of enormous popularity among the rank and file. The two men rode down Euclid Avenue in an open car, as custom dictated, while groups lining the route shouted, "Hey, George," and waved to attract his attention. Finally, Dewey, genuinely perplexed, turned to his companion and asked, "Who the hell is this guy George?"[29]

His attitude toward the Congress itself was friendlier. Contrasting Republicans and Democrats, Dewey talked early one morning at a Colorado crossroads about "those who go about shouting from the housetops, 'I am for reclamation and flood control. I am for irrigation,' but they don't do anything about it. Then there is the kind of people who don't talk as well sometimes but when you look at the record, they do it." He reminded the crowd that the Eightieth Congress had funded the nearby Big Thompson reclamation project at three times its previous peak levels. "Sometimes we don't talk so good," he concluded, "but we perform. It is my hope that within the next four years in your national government we will have a lot less talking and a lot more performance." He sent Brownell a critical wire as the *Victory Special* neared Cheyenne, Wyoming, labeling a proposed speech draft "fulsome" in distributing praise on administration foreign policy, and "decidedly defensive" in total impression. Dismissing out of hand any reference to "me-too . . . that unworthy accusation" so casually tossed his way by Democratic campaigners, Dewey suggested instead "a spirited defense" of the Eightieth Congress, especially its role in designing and implementing the European Recovery Program.

When the speech was finally delivered, at Salt Lake City on September 30, it was entitled "A Positive American Foreign Policy," and contained pledges of "unstinting support" for the UN and "the great adventure" of the ERP. At the same time, Dewey insisted that European aid must not be considered just another relief program. "We shall use it as a means of pushing, prodding, and encouraging the nations of Western Europe toward the goal of European union." He proposed to put an end to "the tragic neglect of our ancient friend and ally, China," pledged closer ties to Latin America and a stronger outreach to the world to communicate the message of America, which sought "to make all nations our friends; we seek to make none our satellites."

Twenty-four times Dewey was interrupted by applause from the huge crowd filling the Mormon Tabernacle. When he was through, a pleased candidate brought Frances to the front of the stage and asked the throng to join them in singing "America the Beautiful" to inaugurate the Tabernacle's awesome organ, back in service after months of repairs. In that moment, all the talk of unity and national greatness seemed to have meaning. So did the strategy of avoiding Truman's rabbit punches.

At other times on the *Victory Special*'s shakedown tour, Dewey's public utterances had a flabby, listless tone. "Government must help industry and industry must co-operate with government," he told a Denver audience in the campaign's major speech on natural resources. "The mines of our country are vital to our welfare and we must encourage the development of superior technical skills as well as new investment so as to increase our reserves and our national security." Turning to water, Dewey informed his audience that "the ancient civilization of Babylon . . . is now a dead thing" and vowed that "this tragedy . . . must never happen to America." It was at moments like this that Dewey seemed merely to be going through the motions of running for president.

His advisers thought differently. They called him admirably restrained on September 27, when Soviet delegates in Paris threatened to boycott any UN Security Council debate over Berlin, and armed conflict suddenly loomed as a real danger. "Nothing will be said or done on my part or on the part of the Republican party during this campaign," he responded, "which will do anything but strengthen our power, our prestige, our unity to deal with a world situation which is fraught with the gravest of difficulties." Two nights earlier, he had struck a similar tone in addressing the Communist danger before a mass rally in the Hollywood Bowl. Calling for a "war of truth" on Communist propaganda, Dewey checked off a list of consumer goods that took the average Russian worker from four to twenty-eight times as long as his American counterpart to earn. He would go no further in attacking Truman than to bemoan "the tragic fact" that the American government itself "seems to have so far lost faith in our system as to encourage this Communist advance, not hinder it."

The times were too sober, he said in San Francisco, "for threats or recriminations." He did describe Truman's foreign policy as "weak" and "lily-livered," and he zeroed in on domestic problems, particularly inflation, as fit targets for complaint. But even his complaints tended to be softened with analysis and historical allusion, rather than headline-grabbing simplifications. He assessed blame for the price spiral on $80 billion "shot away" in the recent war, aid to postwar Europe, and discouragement of domestic production, coupled with premature lifting of price controls. No "painless, patented panacea" for inflation existed, the candidate said. Referring to Truman's as "an administration which goes on innocently dropping monkey wrenches into the machinery" of the domestic economy, Dewey himself promised nothing more definite than to appoint men and women who understood the workings of the free enterprise system, and who shared his commitment to begin retiring the national debt.

A Roper poll taken early in October found most voters attached words like "dignified," "efficient," "sincere," and "clean," to the Dewey campaign. Only 6 percent found it cold, only 5 percent complained that it was dull (25 percent, by contrast, faulted Truman for mudslinging, 16 percent accused the President of doubletalking, and only 4 percent called his whistle-stopping inspiring). The problem was, Dewey's message was not getting through to the electorate. For instance, 47 percent told Roper they supported price controls as the only mechanism able to corral inflation. When Dewey supporters were asked what they expected their man would do as President, 30 percent replied that he would rely wholly on supply and demand forces, 34 percent expected him to invoke federal powers short of actual controls, and 19 percent predicted he'd impose such controls. Some 69 percent of the voters regarded Truman as a supporter of price controls—clearly the popular position to take, but moreover, strong evidence that the President's pungent campaign style was at least conveying a clear-cut stand on those issues bothering the average American.

Civil rights was another field all but abandoned to Truman.

Dewey might have talked about his own strong record, about New York's pioneering anti-discrimination laws, about the State University and a host of blacks appointed to state jobs. He might have gone after Democratic obstructionists in the Senate, hammer and tongs. Instead, perhaps blinded by the hope of picking up Southern electors, he ignored the issue. The voters groped accordingly. Some 20 percent of Dewey's supporters told Roper they believed their candidate would support federal civil rights legislation—a correct interpretation of the few words he devoted to the subject—but 24 percent were just as convinced that he would leave the issue entirely to the states to handle, and another 20 percent said he would oppose any law, in any jurisdiction.

None of this was perceived by the press. While still in California, Dewey's train passed within four miles of Truman's, and reporters on board the *Victory Special* speculated over what job Harry might possibly hope for after being evicted from the White House. A consensus emerged that, if he was lucky, he might land employment as vice president of an insurance company. The same journalists estimated 376 electoral votes as solid for Dewey, and forecast GOP gains in both houses of Congress. Dewey himself was privy to less encouraging forecasts. On September 23, he looked at a Gallup poll of Earl Warren's state showing his huge post-convention lead cut in half by Truman. In Illinois, where party officials predicted a net loss of 75,000 votes if Henry Wallace was ruled off the ballot, the State Supreme Court did just that. Its action bolstered Truman's slim chance to ride the coattails of Paul Douglas and Adlai Stevenson to an upset win.[30]

About this time, Elmo Roper scanned his national numbers and concluded that, for Dewey at least, nothing much had changed since 1944. He was still polling roughly the 44 percent credited to him at a similar stage in his contest with Roosevelt. What had changed, and dramatically, was the Democratic candidate's standing with traditionally Democratic voters in the South and large cities. Among Democrats, he was down 22 points from 1944. Among independents, too, Truman lagged far behind FDR's showing. Yet nearly all of the deserters had gone over to Wallace, Thurmond, or the don't-know category. So far, Dewey had made no inroads into Democratic strength.[31]

John Burton was disturbed by the campaign's tone. Having participated in all but one of the Governor's earlier races, Burton was an authority on the proper combination of crisp fact and persuasive imagery that gave Dewey on the stump his most potent appeal. For months, the budget director and his research team had been combing the Truman record for ammunition, emptying their pastepots many times over in compiling a damning catalogue of administration promises and blunders. It was only natural for Burton, who shared his boss's normal combativeness, to want the quotes and numbers put to maximum use, shooting holes in Truman's exaggerated claims and straightening out the hangman's noose the President hoped to throw over both Dewey and the Eightieth Congress. Above all, Burton favored a more down-to-earth campaign style, full of bite and vigorous substance.

On the morning of September 24, as the *Victory Special* was pulling into Albuquerque, Burton put through a call from Albany to Elliott Bell, who agreed to consider Burton's suggestions. Just then, Bell spotted Clarence Buddington Kelland, Arizona's Republican national committeeman, who was about to board the train for the ride to Phoenix. Bell said he would take up the matter with Kelland and get back to Burton later in the day. A few hours later, Bell phoned from Phoenix to say that Kelland was in complete agreement with the Dewey high command over the chosen strategy. Avoid controversy, the committeeman had warned. Don't let Truman succeed in his attempts to get under Dewey's skin. Keep the campaign, its pace and its tone, under control. Temporarily mollified, Burton went back to his digging.[32]

Reporters talked of a "new Dewey." In Colorado sugar beet country, the candidate spoke feelingly of his childhood memories, of picking up the beets that fell from wagons lumbering down Owosso's unpaved streets. An Arizona ranch hand interrupted his rear platform talk at seven-thirty one morning to demand to see Frances. "You will, you will!" Dewey said, then he called his wife forward. When a baby started to wail in a Cheyenne high school, Dewey told its father not to remove him from the hall. "I've talked against a lot louder noises than crying babies." When the citizens of Kelso, Washington, presented him with three silver salmon, the candidate expressed his delight that they weren't red herring. He heaped praise on Crater Lake, Arizona's sunshine, Utah's peaches, Oklahoma's Will Rogers, and "the most gorgeous mountains in the world" in Washington. At the end of his little talks, no longer than five minutes at most whistle-stops, Frances came forth to accept flowers or shake hands with a local personage before a final wave of her handkerchief and retreat back into the shadows. "Louise," she remarked to one campaign worker who leapt into the crowds at every desolate prairie town, "you are really enjoying yourself." Phrased as a declaration, it was spoken as a question.[33]

Reporters found themselves coddled and caressed by the Dewey team's famous efficiency. Richard Rovere wrote that riding the *Victory Special* after a stint on Truman's campaign train was like going from district headquarters to the Greenwich Country Club. Speeches were available twenty-four hours in advance, along with plenty of hot coffee, roast beef sandwiches, and eighty-five hotel rooms (and bathtubs) set aside wherever the train pulled in overnight. Reporters covering Truman did their laundry in a Pullman basin; those on the *Victory Special* sent it out and found it waiting for them 500 miles down the line. Truman's circle drank bourbon and played poker; Dewey's preferred martinis and bridge. Before any speech, an advance man left the train, drove to the hall at motorcade pace, inspected the wings where the candidate would await his introduction, and then retraced his steps, stopwatch in hand. The result was perfect radio timing. Each morning, Dewey's throat was sprayed by an Albany specialist brought along for the purpose. Each evening, his personal osteopath gave the candidate a vigorous rubdown. Before the train left any depot, Paul Lockwood stood before the locomotive like Horatius at the bridge, with a whistle and stopwatch, casting a trained eye on reporters who liked to straggle.

In the evening came Dewey's rallies, giant set pieces that never varied in format. The candidate didn't seem to walk onto the stage at these affairs, wrote the observant Rovere, "he comes out like a man who has been mounted on casters and given a tremendous shove from behind." Whatever his propulsion, as he swung into the nation's agricultural heartland, Dewey's speeches took on a feistier, more sardonic tone. "You know that Eightieth Congress that you have been hearing about?" he asked Clifford Hope's Kansas constituents on October 2. "Well, just for the record, let's get it straight that that Eightieth Congress passed the first long-range price support in the history of this country. They did a swell job, and I believe in it wholeheartedly from top to bottom." At St. Louis, in Truman's home state, the largest crowds of the tour mobbed the Republican candidate in a train station at eleven o'clock on a Saturday night, forcing Dewey to leave his car and greet 10,000 well-wishers from the top of a waiting-room bench. Over and over, he lashed out at those in power who "tell the people that the country will go to the dogs if they themselves do not hold office," and who "go around the country blackguarding the Congress." His aunt wrote to congratulate him on "the high, high level of all your addresses," and added, "Mr. Truman is a disgrace to the nation."[34]

Meanwhile, Truman's campaign went boisterously on. Perceiving his weakness among traditional Democratic voting blocs, the President ruthlessly identified himself however he could with Us versus Them, lumping liberals, the poor, blacks, farmers, and the West into a vast, ungainly coalition of the dissatisfied or intimidated. When *Newsweek* headlined its September 27 issue "Who Is Challenger, Champ?" it summed up the increasingly odd character of this campaign, in which the incumbent behaved like an outsider, attacking the institutions of alleged economic domination, while his rival, speaking for a party out of office for sixteen years, was engaged in a continental lecture tour, a series of inaugural addresses aimed less at persuading the undecided than filling time between Labor Day and Election Day. It was turning into a contest of blue smoke and mirrors, of irrelevancies and political vaudeville. At Bonham, Texas, late in September, Truman lambasted Dewey's unity theme. He warned voters about "a unity of the Martins and the Tabers, the Wherrys and the Tafts. It would be unity in giving tax relief to the rich at the expense of the poor—unity in refusing to give aid to our schools—unity in letting prices go sky high in order to protect excessive profits—unity in whittling away all the benefits of the New Deal." At Salt Lake City, Truman said the Republicans were lying in wait to do "a real hatchet job" on New Deal innovations like rural electrification, reciprocal trade, and the Commodity Credit Corporation.

Truman labeled Dewey the New Deal's "chief prosecutor" and a man set on destroying the social gains of the previous decade and a half. Dewey was asked by a Republican worker in Indiana to respond to Truman's barrage of accusation. "Will, nobody believes that stuff anyway," he replied. But Dewey was wrong. There was enough truth in what Truman was saying, especially about the Eightieth Congress and its treatment of farmers, to kindle a heated conflict between farmers' ingrained conservatism and their pocketbooks. Slowly, like a sluggish river that still flows beneath thick ice, rural America was stirring to doubt. Everywhere he went, Dewey was promising a "great housecleaning." What might be swept out in the process? farmers began asking themselves.

Memories of the Depression were still painfully fresh, when a sudden precipitous drop in prices reactivated alarm on the prairies.

Corn in Illinois sold for $2.29 a bushel in June. By October, the price was down to ninety-six cents, even lower than the federal support price, and farmers who had long feared a postwar price collapse akin to that of the 1920s were understandably turning skittish about voting out of office the party that had come to represent agricultural prosperity. One farmer from Van Meter, Iowa, walked into a Des Moines radio station, plunked down eighty-five dollars for air time, and recounted the years when he couldn't possibly have owned his present 540 acres and 500 hogs, his restaurant, and twelve filling stations. Democratic aid to farmers was responsible for the quantum leap in his economic station. Why should others run the risk now of cutting it off for themselves? In Wisconsin dairy country, a farmer sold his herd and retired one month before the election. Later he said he wouldn't have done it if he thought Truman could win.

Americans listened for Dewey's response to their fears, and they heard his invitation to open their hearts to his brand of orderly progress. In Santa Fe on September 22, he had said he had never heard of a single public dispute between two of his Albany teammates in six years. If he ever did, he continued, one of the disputatious advisers "wouldn't be there the next morning." He recycled his four-year-old pledge to bring to bear the finest minds on the nation's problems, and promised to involve the private sector in developing at least some aspects of peaceful atomic energy. He would also set the scientists loose to turn coal into oil (1948 was the first year in which the U.S. was importing more oil than it exported) and to study the feasibility of building atomic plants in the Arctic. None of this reassured the farmers.

Others were having old doubts awakened. Lowell Wadmond took an anguished call from a Montana friend who had recognized a local GOP dignitary wanting to meet the candidate badly enough to leave a trial in progress and race to the station for a chance to pump Dewey's hand. But the admirer was stopped cold in his tracks when he overheard his party's nominee asking a knot of advisers, "When the hell do we get out of this damn town?"[35]

Connecticut's Ray Baldwin had his own grievance. At Bridgeport, he had to personally intervene to prevent that city's mayor from being unceremoniously tossed off the train by campaign aides who didn't recognize the man. Then, with forty-five minutes to kill between stops in New London and New Haven, Dewey had returned to his private car, where he looked up at Baldwin and said, "Ray, you better take your hat and coat and go into one of the other

cars." While Dewey lunched alone, Baldwin and the current governor of the Nutmeg State bought a sandwich from the conductor.
Clearly, the new Dewey had his limits.[36]

Even members of his own inner circle, supposed intimates, were
not immune from sudden blasts of insensitivity. Jim Hagerty incurred the candidate's wrath by including an inaccuracy in a press
release. Summoned to a meeting with Dewey and Bell, Hagerty was
goaded into losing his temper, and he threatened to quit the campaign then and there. Dewey made no effort at all to stop him.
Later, the breach was healed, but Hagerty never pretended to feel
abiding affection for the man who had hired him away from the
Times to build bridges with other working reporters.[37]

Within twenty-four hours of his return to Albany on October 4,
Dewey picked up the first tentative rumors of a bizarre diplomatic
adventure hatched by two White House speechwriters and reluctantly confirmed by the President's men after it leaked out four days
later. Without consulting either Secretary of State George Marshall
or Dulles, Truman had asked Supreme Court Chief Justice Fred
Vinson if he would undertake a personal mission to Moscow in an
effort to achieve in face-to-face talks what had eluded professional
diplomats all summer. When the Secretary of State learned of the
scheme, he blew his stack, forcing Truman to cancel both the plan
and a national broadcast scheduled to make it public. Marshall was
called in for consultations, and Dulles went to Albany in an atmosphere clouded by tension and international puzzlement. Hadn't
Truman been saying for weeks now that the Soviet leaders were men
whose word couldn't be trusted? Then why send Vinson to negotiate
with them? It was the sort of thing one might expect to come out of
Henry Wallace's camp.

Time magazine called the President's action "shocking." The Buffalo *News* accused Truman of "amateurish electioneering" in a harsh
editorial entitled simply "What Next?" Mount Lippmann erupted
with renewed force in an October 12 column charging that Truman
didn't know how to be president, and bemoaning the fact that the
campaign still had three weeks to run. "Although he does not govern," Lippmann said of Truman, "he continues to reign. He still has
the great powers of his office. Unable to use them to form policy, he
is reduced to meddling with policy." Virtually alone among Truman's critics, Dewey chose restraint. Truman's gaffe was so obvious
that it hardly called for a partisan attack. Moreover, Dewey was
chastened by Dulles' constant theme, woven from conversations with

other delegates at the Paris UN conference, that only two votes on the Soviet Politburo stood between war and peace, and that America's allies were badly frightened by Truman's boom-and-bust predictions. It was up to Dewey, said his most trusted foreign policy adviser, to calm the jittery Europeans and treat the Vinson affair with the same self-denial he had exercised at the time of Marshall's Pearl Harbor letters.

Off the record, Dewey considered the mission "a tragic blunder." He told reporters that all Americans would be safer if only Truman would stop interfering with foreign events too large or too delicate for his grasp. Publicly, he refused to make capital of the bungled initiative. The nations of the world, he promised in a statement released in Albany on the eighth, "can rest assured that the American people are in fact united in their foreign policy and will firmly and unshakably uphold the United Nations and our friends of the free world." To a president willing to make a spectacular end-run around the very world organization to which his party and platform pledged fervent allegiance, this was little more than a slap on the wrist. Rumblings of discontent were heard in some Republican circles, along with the feeling that Dewey was passing up a golden opportunity to score points on his rival. Marquis Childs came to his defense.

"In the light of history," Childs wrote, "I believe he will get greater credit for his restraint on the issue of foreign policy than is accorded him today. If peace can somehow be preserved . . . Dewey's contribution will be clear."

On October 9, Dulles returned to Paris, where he told C. L. Sulzberger that he had yet to decide whether to accept State or serve Dewey as an adviser without portfolio. Harry Hopkins and Colonel House, Dulles pointed out, had both enjoyed "much more fun" as unofficial members of the presidential family. Meanwhile, in Washington, Truman sensed the long-term possibilities in his present embarrassment. If nothing else, the failed plan depicted the President as a leader willing to court personal humiliation in the quest for international peace, a stance with powerful appeal to Henry Wallace's dwindling cadre of supporters.

Both Hagerty and Jaeckle, responding to questions from Dewey prior to his departure on the campaign's second major tour, expressed concern about Truman's disquietingly supple performance. There were other grounds for worry: Campaign funds weren't coming in at the expected rate as Wall Street withheld funds from a contest regarded as already won (when the final numbers were tallied, it was discovered that the Democrats had outspent the GOP by over $700,000). In Wisconsin, Republican Senator Alexander Wiley told reporters that overconfidence within his party was reaching disturbing levels. Earl Warren came in from the campaign trail long enough to meet with strategists in Brownell's rented Alexandria home and voice his own unease with the strategy of sweetness and light. "I wish I could call somebody an S.O.B.," Warren muttered.

Dewey decided to try an experiment. He had Hagerty plant a hostile inquiry about Taft-Hartley in the first whistle-stop crowd of the new campaign trip, at Erie, Pennsylvania, on the morning of October 11. Defending the new law so hated by unions, he said it was made necessary by "an administration that liked to play politics with the rights of human beings," to the point where 116 million workdays were lost to strikes in 1946 alone. Not only had Truman come forth with no program of his own to combat labor unrest, but "this miserable administration of ours proposed to the people that men be drafted into the Army because they were on strike. Who stopped it? It was Republicans that stopped it and stood against the totalitarian legislation put forward by an incompetent, pusilanimous administration which wouldn't meet the problem squarely when they had a chance." Truman's justification of his veto of Taft-Hartley was, in Dewey's words, "one of the most wrong, most incompetent, most inaccurate documents ever put out of the White House in 160 years."

Dewey kept up the attack that night in Pittsburgh, reminding a national radio audience that, for all his scorn, Truman had found it convenient to invoke Taft-Hartley seven times in just over a year. The act wasn't perfect, Dewey conceded, but it had reduced time lost to strikes by 50 percent, encouraged collective bargaining, and blunted Communist penetration of the labor movement. As for Truman's assertion that a depression was sure to follow a Republican victory, Dewey called that "an infamous falsehood." The next morning, James Reston saluted Dewey's twelve-point labor program as cogent and well reasoned. According to Reston, the candidate had used "workingman's language" to make his case, effectively refuting opposition charges that he was conducting a campaign of "high-level platitudes." Stassen concurred, saying that the Pittsburgh speech was "greatly strengthened" by its use of specifics. But from the men around Dewey, and from most Republican professionals, there was a groundswell of fear. "Are you trying to lose the election?" he was asked almost as soon as he reboarded the *Victory Special,* according to John Burton.[38]

October 13 was a hectic day for the candidate, who added three stops to an already overlong schedule in Kentucky and Illinois. At his penultimate destination, Beacoup, Illinois, Dewey had just started a fresh defense of the farm price support bill passed by the Eightieth Congress when the *Victory Special* started backing up into the crowd. There were screams from frightened spectators, and Dewey could make out Lillian Rosse amidst the confusion. "That's the first lunatic I've had for an engineer," he barked once the train came to a halt. "He probably ought to be shot at sunrise, but I guess we can let him off because nobody was hurt." Later, he explained his anger: "Lillian would have been the first to go."[39]

Whatever his motive, Dewey's outburst roused lethargic reporters, handing them a colorful tidbit to at last break the tedious perfection of his campaign. "The campaign special train stopped with a jerk," one scribe jokingly proposed as his lead, "who got off and spoke." Truman seized on the incident to ingratiate himself with engineers and, through them, all of organized labor. And the "lunatic" himself? Lee Tindle was a thirty-year veteran of the Louisville and Nashville who didn't allow the affair to change his attitude in the least. "I think as much of Dewey as I did before," Tindle told reporters, "and that's not very much."

On October 15, Dewey drew only 8,000 to a St. Paul Auditorium designed to hold twice as many. Republican strategists blamed the poor turnout on a combination of bad weather and faulty planning. The next day, as if to inject some substance into his campaign, the candidate proposed creation of a department of social progress (an idea embodied in the Department of Health, Education and Welfare in 1953). He was also debating a fresh appeal to farmers. For several days, Republican senators George Aiken and William Langer, both recognized agricultural experts, had been urging a more forceful commitment to price supports and federally guaranteed crop storage facilities. Aiken got no closer to Dewey than John Burton and a Cornell professor who explained that Dewey's closest advisers had "packaged" him, and the package didn't include any effort to outpromise Truman on the farm issue. Langer didn't get that far.[40]

Before speaking in St. Paul, Dewey had canvassed his own advisers. The most important voice was that of H. E. Babcock. Dewey had reason to heed Babcock's judgment, for the man had served brilliantly as his state food commissioner during the war and at Cornell's School of Nutrition. It had been Babcock's "beneficent guidance," in Dewey's words, that put Dapplemere in the black at a time when its owner was forced to cover annual deficits by selling off newborn cattle. When asked for suggestions, Babcock had wired back on October 10, "Thinking over farm speech have arrived at conclusion that unity plea has more appeal to farmers even than the items of farm program. Think you might use school of nutrition as example of the kind of teamwork you propose . . . to solve food and agricultural problems and build stronger America."[41]

To his smallish audience in St. Paul, Dewey reiterated his "wholehearted and unequivocal" support for Hope-Aiken, promised more technical assistance and less politics in soil conservation, and praised congressional action in funding at record levels the rural electrification program. But if Dewey believed he could quell farmers' doubts with an endorsement of flexible price supports, he was underestimating the emotions sweeping the prairies. Truman had sowed fears throughout the region, fears coinciding with a drastic drop in prices, that a Republican administration would take the earliest opportunity to slash supports from 90 percent of parity—the complex federal formula used to gauge farm prosperity, and based on pre-World War I prices—to just 60 percent. Local Democratic organizations ran ads claiming the Republicans would do away with price supports altogether. Government workers fanned out across the region to back up Truman's assertion that the GOP was out to destroy farm co-operatives.

On October 18, a new Gallup poll showed Dewey's lead reduced to six points. John Burton, sitting in an empty compartment on the *Victory Special* as it pulled into the rail yard at Buffalo, looked up to see another pair of feet plunked down on the seat opposite his own.

"Johnny, we are slipping, aren't we?"

Burton told Dewey that the campaign wasn't in the best of shape. He described the President's tumultuous reception in Albany a few days earlier, when 10,000 people braved a soaking rain at seven in the morning to shout, "Give 'em hell, Harry!" Dewey said he wished things were going better, but that it was too late to change the campaign strategy. Besides, Franklin Roosevelt had returned to Albany through Buffalo at the end of his 1932 contest with Herbert Hoover, and all the polls then were showing slippage. "But he won, didn't he?"[42]

The rest of the day provided little reassurance. Dewey forgot himself in Rochester, expressing delight to be in Syracuse ("Oh, I am asleep!") and hurried back to the Executive Mansion, where he ordered a showing of all campaign newsreels. What he saw aroused doubt, genuine doubt, for the first time. It only confirmed the misgivings Lillian Rosse had been entertaining for weeks. Unlike her boss, whose major preoccupation lay in his speeches, she had been opening and reading his mail, including letters like the one from an Indiana woman who had written back in September after the kickoff speech in Des Moines, "We were wondering if you really wanted to be elected or did you just take the nomination to keep someone else from obtaining it. . . . Don't carry this unity business too far."[43]

Thereafter, the mail had taken on "frantic" overtones, prompting her to begin each day with a warning. Elliott Bell urged Dewey to ignore the panic creeping into the letters on Miss Rosse's desk. So did Lockwood. But they could not entirely shut out the qualms of others. "I'm glad the campaign is ending in two weeks," Breitel told Dewey. "You're constantly losing ground." Ed Walsh recalls having been asked by the Governor, "Can I really keep this thing up for another ten days?" Both Walsh and Breitel agreed, albeit with some reluctance, that he could.[44]

A new and noisy controversy arose late in October. Several weeks earlier, following announcement of his plan to sever the infant state of Israel from the Negev and the important port at Haifa, Swedish Count Folke Bernadotte had been assassinated by Zionist extremists. Bernadotte's death did not prevent Secretary Marshall from endorsing his proposed map of the Middle East, or from attempting to enlist Dewey's support through his representative in Paris, John Foster Dulles. Sensitive to the huge Jewish vote in New York, Dewey had no intention of giving such a boost to the Bernadotte Plan. But he and Dulles muted their disapproval, keeping it out of sight lest the Israel question lead to rancor within the U.S. delegation.

All this went by the boards on October 21, when Brownell returned to New York City for discussions with New York State chairman Alger Chapman and others who were worried about Dewey's slippage in his home state. The upshot was a public statement opposing Bernadotte's boundary lines, and calling instead for an Israeli state within the borders originally defined by the United Nations in November 1947.[45]

Truman responded with his own pro-Israel statement two days later, bemoaning the fact that bipartisanship had broken down "ten days before the election" and publicly breaking with his own Secretary of State over the Bernadotte Plan. Not content to undercut his personal spokesman in Paris, the President went Dewey one better by directing all executive agencies to expedite any Israeli loan requests. Then he took off on another campaign swing, and the harshest rhetoric yet in his escalating war of words with the opponent he derided as "the candidate in sneakers." Truman's most vitriolic speech of the campaign was delivered before a vast crowd in Chicago on October 25, in which he dismissed Strom Thurmond's Dixiecrats as "crackpots" and Wallace's followers as part of "the contemptible Communist minority." Then he took dead aim at his Republican rival.

Earlier that day, in a speech at Gary, Indiana, Truman had charged that the GOP were "special privilege boys" who wanted to move the capital to Wall Street, and that "if anybody in this country is friendly to the Communists, it is the Republicans." Now he went further, charging that Dewey's party paid only "lip service" to democracy itself. "In our time we have seen the tragedy of the Italian and German peoples, who lost their freedom to men who made promises of unity and efficiency and sincerity . . . and it could happen here." Pointing a finger at "powerful reactionary forces which are silently undermining our democratic institutions," Truman accused Dewey of being a "front man" for the same cliques that had backed Hitler in Germany, Mussolini in Italy, and Tojo in Japan. He also asked voters to keep the Congress "from turning the country upside down and shaking out its profits."

Dewey heard a broadcast of the speech on board the *Victory Special,* about to depart Albany for its final swing through the Midwest and New England. Realizing that Truman had afforded him one final chance to abandon the pursuit of sweetness and light, Dewey wanted to make the most of it. Holding up a speech draft in his hand, he told his closest advisers he wanted to "tear it to shreds." He meant to take the gloves off, he continued; should have taken them off long before then. He recapped the newsreels he had seen, and the chilling impression of all those faces at all those whistle-stops. Then, having stated his impatience forcefully, he called for a poll of the room. In that moment, his organizational instincts betrayed him. First Hagerty, then Lockwood, then Jaeckle—all insisted he was making a mistake. Frances, going further, reminded him of the horror of Oklahoma City. "If I have to stay up all night to see that you don't tear up that speech, I will," she told her husband.

But Dewey wanted more feedback. Trusting neither his own instincts nor those of his closest advisers, he directed Hagerty to poll reporters on the train, and he sent word to have Brownell in Washington conduct a survey of his own among the entire national committee. The little group waited.[46]

A speechwriter barged into Bell's compartment and found Dewey closeted inside with Lockwood and Bell. Not until 1 A.M. was the writer summoned back and asked to solicit opinions from other campaign staffers about the best way to respond to Truman's broadside. By then, an overwhelming tide of caution was rolling in. Johny Crews of Brooklyn typified the attitude of the GOP professionals polled by Brownell. "You're going to knock hell out of the bastard," he predicted. Another state chairman urged that Dewey be physically restrained, if necessary, to prevent him from throwing away a victory within grasp. Only Kansas's Harry Darby counseled a change in tactics. Chastened by a solid front of certainty (shared by journalists on board his train) Dewey wavered, then gave way. "I can't go against the entire Republican party," he said before turning in. But if he was worried, it wasn't reflected in his schedule. Despite expressions of "grave concern" from state party leaders over the prospects of massive ticket splitting, Dewey scheduled no stops in either Indiana or Ohio en route to Cleveland and a major address on the twenty-seventh.[47]

In his first speech after Truman's blast, also delivered at Chicago, Dewey adopted a tone more of sorrow than of anger. He criticized those who, having failed in office, "are openly sneering at the ancient American ideal of a free and united people. They have attempted to promote antagonism and prejudice. They have scattered reckless abuse along the entire right of way from coast to coast and now, I am sorry to say, reached a new low of mud-slinging. . . . That is the kind of campaign I refuse to wage." Someone in his audience shouted out, "You're an American, that's why," and Dewey answered, "That's right, sir." As for Truman's charges of entrenched monopolies threatening free government, Dewey was indignant. "Who has been in charge of the country all these years?" he demanded. "It was not the Republican party." He issued a warning to workingmen, who would never be safe so long as "an unstable, slippery government" capable of proposing their draft into military service held office.

The next morning, several thousand Ohioans came out to see Dewey's train as it sat shuttered on a track a few miles northeast of Cleveland. The candidate himself stayed inside, refusing even to raise a window shade or bestow a wave upon the curious or committed. Disappointed, the crowd dispersed, leaving John Bricker shaking his head. If Harry Truman had been on that train, thought

Dewey's 1944 running mate, he would have appeared on the rear platform in pajamas and slippers if necessary. That night, Dewey dined alone with Paul Lockwood before going to the Cleveland hall where he was to deliver a speech on foreign policy, while Robert Taft was left to cool his heels in a hotel lobby. When Taft thereafter graciously introduced the man who had beaten him at Philadelphia, Dewey entered the hall all but oblivious; throughout his speech, which attacked "tragic concessions" permitting half a billion people in three years to slip behind the Iron Curtain, he seemed purposely to keep his eyes averted from Taft.[48]

"It is very late and all China is in great peril," Dewey said that night in Cleveland. Again, he refused to engage in sloganeering. The road of easy answers "is the road to disaster. But of one thing we can be sure: we shall not achieve peace by conducting these desperately important matters on a happy-thought basis or by jovially remarking that we like good old Joe." Dewey embellished his theme with ritualistic criticism of Truman's wobbling course, a vow to coordinate American foreign policy more closely with her allies, and a rebuke to the Kremlin's strategy "to divide, then to weaken, then to conquer." But there was nothing as specific, as visceral, as a Vinson mission.

On October 28, the *Victory Special* turned east. At several stops in Massachusetts, Henry Cabot Lodge sampled opinion among party leaders and found a disturbing pattern. At Pittsfield and Springfield, Worcester and Framingham, Lodge was told that the Republican campaign was running behind expectations locally, but everywhere else Dewey was in good shape. Katherine Howard, the Bay State's GOP national committeewoman and secretary of the national committee, sat down to lunch with Rebecca McNabb, an aide to Frances, and asked to know why Dewey was letting Truman "get away with murder." Mrs. McNabb replied that Dewey wanted to light into Truman "desperately. You should hear them, night after night, arguing with the policy group. Everything in his nature longs to attack, and every night, the policy group tells him the same thing: 'Don't get nasty, keep cool, don't make any mistakes and you've got it won.' " Paul Lockwood lost his temper when another old Dewey associate, approached by several worried supporters wishing to express their doubts personally to the candidate, tried to set up an appointment for them. "God damnit," Lockwood exploded, "you've got nothing to do with making appointments for Dewey." To the end, the lines of authority remained inviolable.[49]

Dewey's speech at the Boston Arena was an impassioned call for

Republican support of Social Security, a higher minimum wage, and improved public health benefits, in effect, a public plea that the next Congress change its ways. Only men "of little faith and little vision," Dewey said as Joe Martin sat fifteen feet away, would dare suggest that capitalism was unwilling to provide for the jobless, the sick, the aged or the returning soldier. On October 29, large crowds in Rhode Island and Connecticut cheered Dewey's invigorated attacks on Truman's foreign policy. "You can't buy peace," he shouted before a New Haven assemblage, "by giving away other people's freedom." Thousands more jammed Grand Central Station to greet the *Victory Special* as it pulled in for the last time. And on Saturday night, October 30, Madison Square Garden was packed when Dewey at last took the wraps off and indulged in a flight of sarcasm.

The next night, he told his audience, would be Halloween. "I mention the date because since this campaign began, some people have been trying to give the impression that every night is Halloween. Grown men have been going around the country threatening, 'Vote our way, or the goblins will get you!' We have been hearing blood-curdling stories about 'mossbacks,' 'bloodsuckers,' 'men with calculating machines where their hearts ought to be,' and one shadowy ogre after another. Members of Congress, elected by the people, have had special Halloween treatment by these tellers of tall tales. They are described as 'predatory animals.' . . . They do their dreadful work with 'meat axes, butcher knives and sabers,' and what do these monsters eat? Why, 'red herring' of course."

Halloween would be over within twenty-four hours, Dewey continued, "but next Tuesday the people of America are really going to bring the nightmare to an end." In so grave an hour in world history, a party as splintered and demoralized as Truman's could hardly be entrusted with uniting the country or maintaining a fragile peace. "It has been divided against itself for so long," he went on, "that it has forgotten the meaning of unity, and it never did know the meaning of teamwork or competence." The time had arrived for "a competent, warm-hearted, stable government. . . . Our nation has moved permanently away from the era of dog-eat-dog . . . we are going forward to a greater security for all our people, which will make all America more secure."

At the end, he returned to Olympus.

"In this momentous time our country is called to renew its faith so that the world can begin to have hope again; to renew its strength so that the world can be of good courage again; to renew its vision so that the world can begin to move forward again out of this present darkness toward the bright light of lasting peace. This is the eve of victory. Let us use our victory, not for ourselves—but for an America that is greater than ourselves. Let us humbly pray that our children and their children will look back on this election of 1948 and say, with thankful hearts: 'That was good for the country.' "

On Sunday, Dewey went to church in Pawling, then returned to New York City to await the vote. He confessed to reporters that he was "awfully tired" and in need of both relaxation and exercise after being "walled up in trains for four weeks." Out in St. Louis, en route to Independence and the conclusion of his own fight for re-election, Truman issued a final blast at the press and said of the Tuesday to come, "It can't be anything but a victory."

On Monday, the Hotel Roosevelt braced itself for the history to be made in Suite 1527. One floor below, the A-Pawling Set collected itself, Marge Hogan and Elly Robbins sitting up half the night making imaginary cabinet appointments. A final array of opinion polls showed Dewey well out in front, although his popular vote would likely be of less than landslide proportions. Most observers saw Congress—especially the Senate—as the chief battleground.[50]

Elmo Roper had halted regular polling on the candidates, as he promised he would early in September. But he did take a final sample of voter expectations. In July, just after the conventions, Roper had found that by a margin of 64 to 27 percent the American electorate, regardless of individual choice, believed that Thomas E. Dewey would be the next president. Now, at the end of October, Roper returned to the field. After all the speeches, all the whistle-stops, all the charges and rebuttals, all the editorials and all the polls, the expectation of a Dewey victory had solidified. Three times as many voters believed that Dewey would win as held out hope of a Truman victory. To be sure, the polling data contained in the national surveys was as much as two weeks old. But it was still overwhelming and persuasive. With such favorable portents for their future, Tom and Frances Dewey retired to their room on the night of November 1.

IV

A POSTSCRIPT
TO POWER
1949–1971

16

A Call to Arms

It's a funny thing with this guy. Every time he runs for President,
he gets re-elected Governor.

—JOHNY CREWS

It was a wise man who said, "From the altar of the past take not
the ashes but the fire."

—THOMAS E. DEWEY

America awoke on November 3, 1948, to find its expectations over-
turned and its politics realigned. Dewey had swept the industrial
Northeast, pared Democratic margins in the big cities by a third,
run better than any Republican since Hoover in the South—and
still lost decisively. Truman's popular margin was 2 million, his
Electoral College victory 303 to 189. "We were just caught in a buzz
saw," lamented Jim Hagerty. "The bear got us," Elliott Bell said in
a reference to Moscow and the war threat recreating a fear of
changing horses in midstream. John Foster Dulles wrung his hands
and felt vindicated in his belief that "foreign policy is too complicated a thing to feature in a national election." Francisco Franco,
whose regime had hoped for a Republican victory, struck a mystical
note. "An election," the Spanish caudillo suggested, "is like a jump
into an abyss. Its destiny can never be foreseen." In Munich, Germany, the editor of that city's leading newspaper fretted over a full
page interpreting Dewey's victory and wondered if he should resign.
"What do you suppose Dr. Gallup is going to do?" he asked, plaintively. Closer to home, Nassau County Republican Women replaced
a planned talk, "Our New Republican President" with "It Pays to
Be Ignorant."[1]

Truman wired his defeated rival from Independence, congratu-
lating Dewey on his "fine sportsmanship." Others sent messages of
their own, designed to ease the pain or cushion the shock. Cardinal
Spellman said he was praying for the Deweys. Winston Churchill
had praise for "the dignity and poise with which you received the
heavy political reverse. . . . Such experiences are not agreeable, as I
know only too well myself." Don Van Boskirk told Dewey he was
resigning as GOP chairman in Portland, after blaming defeat on "the
general apathy" with which Republican leaders had had to contend. "I know how long and hard you have worked and how much

543

you have sacrificed to gain the office of President," Van Boskirk added. "I would not blame you for being just a trifle bitter over the whole situation."[2]

George Sokolsky, the columnist, chose to look ahead. "You are 46 years [old]. You have been through an exciting and stimulating life. If you believe that you can retire to writing contracts and looking after reorganizations, you hardly understand your own personality. If you were that kind of person, you could never have fought the battles of the past 16 years. Something has driven you. Whether it was personal ambition, sense of service, or even egotism, it does not matter. The fact is that you have achieved more in a shorter time without accidental factors than any man in the country your age." Beware of a "humdrum existence," Sokolsky cautioned, in which one might become "embittered and narrow." Spend the next few years rebuilding the party in New York and nationally, he urged, and Dewey would be spared "the psychological poison" of becoming a mere scholar of defeat.[3]

To those who asked for explanations, Dewey was crisply matter-of-fact. "You can analyze figures from now to kingdom come," he told Henry Luce, "and all they will show is that we lost the farm vote which we had in 1944 and that lost the election." He gave his uncle the same message, with an added proclamation: "That's that, and I am going to go ahead and enjoy life and live longer." Scientific investigations of the result would begin almost immediately, but none ever seriously contradicted Dewey's own conclusion. Samuel Lubell, citing data from a University of Michigan survey, demolished the myth of Farley's Law. Dewey was ahead until the last two weeks of the campaign, Lubell concluded, when millions of voters switched their allegiance. Some 14 percent of Dewey's own supporters changed their minds; another 13 percent didn't bother to vote. Nowhere did more votes change hands than in the farm belt. Wisconsin, Ohio, Illinois, and Iowa—even Iowa—all washed away in the Truman flood.[4]

Other factors contributed to the upset. Organized labor did a masterful job of pulling out voters for the rest of the Democratic ticket, devastating Republican congressional majorities and incidentally carrying Truman to victory in several states. The very scope of the Democrats' sweep seemed to support Irving Ives's theory that it was "the inability of the Eightieth Congress to get together on a forward-looking, liberal program" that had led to seventy-five new Democratic House members, eleven new Democratic senators and eight additional Democratic governors, including freshmen like

Adlai Stevenson, Chester Bowles, Paul Dever, and G. Mennen Williams. Old Guard Republicans Curly Brooks, Carroll Reece, and Chapman Revercomb all fell from electoral grace. Ed Jaeckle publicly condemned the GOP right wing as "excess baggage," too heavy for his candidate alone to drag across the finish line.

Three days after the disaster, Dewey met with reporters in Albany. Holding a sheaf of messages from college and high school students, he called their interest the most encouraging sign for Republicans who hoped to rebuild their party. "No sir!" he exclaimed when asked if he intended to surrender his position as titular leader. As a matter of fact, Dewey said, he had some "definite ideas" about how the party's comeback might proceed, and he cautioned against interpreting his refusal to seek a third presidential nomination as meaning "I don't intend to be useful to my country."

Then he was off to the El Conquistador Hotel, near Tucson, Arizona, where his sons asked to be excused from dinner to go outside and pitch pennies. Dewey gave his assent. A few minutes later he got a hankering to join the boys himself. Once outside, he removed his coat, rolled up his sleeves, and squatted down in the dust as an Owosso youngster might have done half a century earlier. Frances worried that a photographer might capture her husband in such a pose. She conveyed her misgivings, and Dewey straightened himself, stared off blankly into space for a moment, then said in an even voice, "Maybe if I had done this during the campaign, I would have won."[5]

The upper lip was no less stiff a month later, when Dewey resorted to humor to describe his plight. It reminded him of "a very successful wake" at which a mourner drowned his sorrows and passed out cold, only to be placed in a coffin by solicitous friends. Just as thoughtfully, Dewey explained, they folded his hands across his chest, around the stem of a fragrant lily. And there he remained, until the cold light of dawn—"about the time I got the bad news from Ohio and Illinois." Then the mourner had come to. "He smelled the lily. He observed the tufted white satin of the coffin. Rallying his faculties, he coldly analyzed his predicament: 'If I am alive . . . what I am doing in this coffin? If I am dead, why do I have to go the bathroom?'"

Having made his audience laugh, Dewey turned philosophical. The people had spoken, "and the people of our country are always right." Even had they chosen him president, they would also have saddled him with a Democratic Congress. "So I bid you take heart. It is well that the presidency went with the Congress. Under our political system, the American people . . . are entitled to have a united and responsible government." He assumed "full responsibility" for any mistakes of strategy, "but we will never be embarrassed by the things we said. We have nothing to take back, and we charted a course for a free nation of which I shall always be proud."

Dewey rarely mentioned 1948 in the years thereafter. It was like a locked room in a musty mansion whose master never entered to undrape the chairs or allow sunlight to filter in. From time to time, outsiders could coax an expression of anger against Dirksen, who Dewey said never alerted him to the brewing farm revolt. He seemed a bit bewildered at the unanimous front put up by his Albany advisers, regretted not having taken a final poll when his own senses detected slippage, and couldn't resist a potshot at "that bastard Truman" for having successfully exploited farmers' fears of a new depression. "I have learned from bitter experience," he wrote President Eisenhower in the heat of the 1954 congressional elections, "that Americans somehow regard a political campaign as a sporting event." He flashed a look of genuine disbelief when someone asked if 1948 had gotten the White House out of his system. A man would have "to be touched with madness," Dewey replied, to go through another presidential campaign, enduring the grueling primary schedule, the handshaking, the money-raising, "being dragged from pillar to post, with no time to think," followed by the long ordeal leading up to November, and the distinct possibility that the winner would find himself blocked by a Congress dominated by the opposition.[6]

Dewey kept up a facade of relief. He labeled himself an elder statesman, "which someone has aptly defined as a politician who is no longer a candidate for any office." But the pain was still there, made immeasurably worse by his perfectionism. Clarence Kelland, in league with other conservatives, publicly berated Dewey's campaign as a monumental disgrace (at a tumultuous GOP national committee meeting in Omaha that January, Kelland went after "the Albany Gang" and flatly ruled out any future race for any office by the defeated standard bearer, "and that goes for everything from poundkeeper up"); and a perplexed Clifton White (then a junior member of the Dewey organization, later the field marshal of GOP conservatives who captured their party for Barry Goldwater in 1964) wondered why his boss didn't simply play the tapes of Kelland and all those other committeemen telling Brownell how vital it was to prevent the candidate from going off on a last-minute combative binge.

"I was the boss," Dewey told White. "I could have taken the gloves off."[7]

The public bloodletting in Omaha also included an attack by Harrison Spangler, who charged Dewey with having "thrown away" the election with "weasel words" and "passive and apologetic" support of the Eightieth Congress. Hugh Scott survived in his post on a 54 to 50 vote, but only after loudly proclaiming that Dewey "should not, could not, and will not" be a candidate in 1952. Reporters who looked around the committee's meeting rooms and saw only two black faces, who found on the roster of GOP decision makers no names of Polish, Italian, Irish, or Slavic origin, listened to the Spanglers and Schroders, the Kellands and Owletts, and asked themselves if the same people who drummed Wendell Willkie out of the party weren't now trying to ostracize Dewey.

"How to bring the party back to life in the precincts is the mystery," Dewey himself told a friend on January 22, 1949. "I cannot do it myself. . . . I can try to do it in New York State and I am going to as soon as we get a new chairman. . . . Meanwhile, I think I will start doing a little talking in two Lincoln Day speeches . . . they may stir the animals up a little bit."[8]

On February 8, Dewey did more than rouse his critics to anger. In a Washington speech boycotted by some congressional Republicans, he said the time had come to confront a truth. "The Republican party is split wide open. It has been split wide open for years, but we have tried to gloss it over. . . . We have in our party some fine, high-minded patriotic people who honestly oppose farm price supports, unemployment insurance, old age benefits, slum clearance, and other social programs. These people consider these programs horrendous departures into paternalism. . . . These people believe in a laissez-faire society and look back wistfully to the miscalled 'good old days' of the nineteenth century." But if such efforts to turn back the clock were actually pursued, Dewey said, "you can bury the Republican party as the deadest pigeon in the country." He did not propose to outdo the opposition. "You couldn't outpromise the Democrats if you tried, because they will promise anything to anybody to get a vote." He did insist that the GOP "stop bellyaching about the past" and go on from there to provide progressive alternatives in line with the overwhelming majority who believed that government had to be more than "a cold and impartial umpire."

Go back and read the 1948 platform, he urged his audience. "It must mean something. Unless it was designed to deceive, its various sections say and mean that we are a liberal and progressive party."

As for those who found fault with the platform's guarantees of old age assistance, public housing, water power, and price supports, they "ought to go out and try to get elected in a typical American community and see what happens to them. But they ought not to do it as Republicans." There were differences between the two major parties, "as wide as the ocean." (For one thing, it was Republicans who wanted a foreign policy not limited to Europe.) "Everybody claims to be going to the same place," Dewey said. "But some are going as slaves with chains around their minds and dangling on their heels. Others are going as free men with their heads high and their minds and souls unfettered by the state. The whole difference between freedom and slavery lies in how you advance toward your goals." The GOP, he went on, believed in social progress, "under a flourishing, competitive system of private enterprise where every human right is expanded. . . . We are opposed to delivering the nation into the hands of any group who will have the power to tell American people whether they may have food or fuel, shelter or jobs." Stripping fat from government's frame, replacing political spoils with competent rule, preserving individual freedom and economic incentive, saving Americans from what Dewey called "the tyranny of the few"—these were great and fundamental issues over which there could be no compromising. The speech was warmly received; in the ensuing commotion, Dewey was heard to say it was the kind of address he should have made in the campaign.

Dewey reported "a first class revolt" in his legislature at the end of February, "the inevitable aftermath of running a state with a very firm hand and perhaps of the presidential election." Conservatives were up in arms over his $948 million budget. Liberals wanted to set aside even more than the $100 million already earmarked for increased aid to education. The State Board of Regents, led by George Hinman, hoped to gut legal provisions turning over authority for thirty-one colleges to the State University trustees. The thruway was bogged down, with only forty-three miles under construction that spring and funds for its completion held hostage to inflation. Finally, Democrats in Albany were demanding a full accounting of the Postwar Reconstruction Fund, to which Dewey responded with a forty-five-page document, buttressed by hour after hour of detailed explanations of hundreds of projects on the floor of the Assembly.

The Governor seemed to treat his 1949 legislative agenda as a compensation for the shock of the previous November. He had thrown himself into its preparation and sale to reluctant Republicans with an intensity unusual even for him. His was a long list of requests: a new statewide building code to replace the patchwork quilt of local ordinances, $300 million more for housing and slum clearance, subject to voters' approval, $12 million to begin actual construction of the State University, and, most controversial of all, a new sickness and disability program to be grafted onto existing unemployment insurance. Assemblyman Orlo Brees was one of many GOP legislators who found unpalatable the idea of paying for injuries or sickness not directly the result of work-related factors. Dewey's plan, Brees wrote, "is not consonant with the American system of government, nor with a capitalist economy." Republicans, in Brees's words, should take "a determined stand against further experimentation in the field of socialism and Communist philosophy. . . . The existence of an equality of opportunity is not to be questioned because some of our citizens refuse to put forth the necessary energy to realize that opportunity."[9]

Dewey responded by reminding his colleagues of their earlier opposition to unemployment insurance itself during the Smith and Lehman administrations—followed by enactment of programs placing the burden for its financing entirely upon the employer. His own plan, by contrast, would be funded by equal contributions from worker and boss. It would cost a mere thirty cents a week, and it would do much to ward off "the evils of socialized medicine." Don't squander this opportunity, Dewey blurted out, to win the workingman's support and protect the private sector from something far worse just a few years down the road. In the end, Oswald Heck invoked party caucus rules, and Dewey's sickness disability plan passed the Assembly, 85 to 59. He also repulsed the Regents, and was handed a considerably watered-down version of his building code.[10]

But the biggest fight of the session, one that overshadowed all the other battles between the Governor and his own party's right wing, was a clear-cut setback for Dewey, the worst in his six years in Albany. Walter J. Mahoney, a state senator from Buffalo, led five colleagues from Erie and Westchester counties in rejecting Dewey's budget, as well as the gasoline, business, and income tax increases required to sustain his pay-as-you-go policies. In a statewide radio address on February 27, Dewey detailed the severity of cuts already made: 85 percent in the Health Department's request for new hospitals, 90 percent in the Conservation Department, 100 percent in canals and Military and Naval Affairs. Construction dollars had been slashed from the $315 million requested to $89 million. "My own criticism of this budget," said Dewey, "is that we are not doing enough." Libraries were falling behind the times. Cerebral palsy research could not be expanded as it should. Mental hospitals could not be built to meet demands, nor could scholarships be awarded to young New Yorkers with legitimate need for them. As for state taxes, the Governor said that his requests would merely restore tax rates to where they stood prior to his election in 1942; as a percentage of state incomes, they would actually remain 25 percent below their 1942 levels.

The next night, Mahoney, speaking for the rebels, accused Dewey of "half-truths," and reiterated their demand for sharper cuts in state spending as a price for support of the budget. Mahoney's was a bizarre coalition of orthodox Republicans and free-spending Democrats, united only in its opposition to the Governor. But it would not yield. In one eight-hour session with his leaders, reputed to be the stormiest of his career, Dewey was warned that compromise was unavoidable. Senate Majority Leader Ben Feinberg sent out a feeler to Mahoney, offering to cut $20 million from the budget. The olive branch was rejected, along with a second offer of a $28 million reduction. "The battle goes on and on," Dewey wrote Annie on March 10, just two days before his administration gave way and accepted the conservatives' demands for $48 million less in state spending, elimination of a one-cent gas tax increase, and a 10 percent rollback in income tax raises. Heady with the scent of independence, legislators went on to defeat Dewey's plan to consolidate Civil Service, gutted the compulsory aspects of his building code, and passed a law banning Communists from the classrooms. In a final slap, Republican senators chose Walter Mahoney to be their whip, replacing Kingston's Arthur Wicks, who had moved up to the leadership.[11]

Dewey seemed almost distracted in his response. He accepted docilely the need to finance $48 million of his budget out of an old 1926 bond issue. But he also vetoed a feasibility study of off-track betting, thus alienating Russ Sprague and other political heavyweights who held stock in racetracks. And the old vigor could still overwhelm men with less iron in their constitutions. When a two-year-old dispute between the New York Port Authority and the airlines using Idlewild Airport threatened New York's primacy as a center of air travel, Dewey called the squabbling parties to Suite 1527, locked the doors, and wouldn't let anyone out until a memorandum of agreement (which he wrote out himself) was reached, twenty-three hours later.

Before departing for a European inspection tour, Dewey navigated one more round of political heavy weather. His new state chairman, Bill Pfeiffer, was installed at the start of April, as Kingsland Macy declared an open breach with the man he blamed for his own failure to reach the U.S. Senate in 1944 and 1946. "You have appointed your own advisers and ignored the elected leaders of our Party," Macy complained on April 19. "You have substituted yourself for our Party to an extent where it has almost lost its identity." Refusing to discuss the election of a "rubberstamp" chairman, Macy instead aimed an arrow straight at Dewey's Achilles' heel. "Things might have been so different," he wrote. "No doubt you have tasted deep of the cup of disappointment, but so have others, including myself. I am sure that if you had cultivated consideration for the feelings of others it would have stood you in better stead today."[12]

When Dewey returned from Europe on June 10, he found a nation embroiled in controversy over the world and America's rightful obligation to it. Of all the disillusioning years that followed World War II, 1949 saw the most icons crumble. That January, Chiang Kai-shek fled to the island of Formosa, and within five months Communist forces under Mao Tse-tung were occupying Shanghai. Cardinal Spellman mounted the pulpit at St. Patrick's Cathedral in February to denounce "ostrichlike actions" by those who might unwittingly play into the hands of foreign powers bent on "conquest and annihilation." In March, the U.S., Canada, and ten European nations formed the North Atlantic Treaty Organization to coordinate military preparedness and declare that Soviet aggression against any member would be regarded as an attack on all.

Robert Taft opposed NATO. Dreading a new and expensive arms race, he asked on the Senate floor for what purpose did the U.S. intend to arm her European allies. The Soviets, he said, were already checked by the atomic bomb. "A few more obsolete arms in Europe will not concern them in the least." Besides, Taft argued, ringing Russia with hostile countries, as NATO intended, might actually provide a goad to combat. He feared that the U.S. was slipping toward imperialism, and an attitude in which "war becomes an instrument of public policy rather than its last resort."

Dewey took an opposite view. "A close race is being run," he said in a speech at Williams College on June 19, "between the forces of economic recovery and freedom on the one hand and of economic stagnation and slavery on the other. . . . The race will not be run and ended in a few weeks or in a few months or even in a few years. It is an epochal struggle—perhaps the greatest of all history—in which every human being on earth is involved for the first time in history.... It is a struggle for table stakes representing the whole world." A month later, he returned to the theme. "We cannot keep the peace," he warned, "by denying that there are those who would destroy it." To ratify NATO with anything less than "real enthusiasm" would be abandonment of freedom's cause at a critical juncture, a retreading of the dreary road that led to World War II.

Early in July, Dewey appointed Foster Dulles to the U.S. Senate seat vacated by Robert Wagner. Dulles hurried to Washington, where he engaged Taft in a bitter public debate over America's obligation to arm her NATO partners. Taft feared that American taxpayers would wind up arming "half the world" against the Russians. But Dulles and his allies prevailed, 82 to 13. They won again when Taft tried to cut NATO's military budget.[13]

On July 28, Dewey turned his attention to the Far East, warning against a Truman administration seemingly determined to "throw China into the bottom of the Pacific Ocean." A week later, the White House responded. In a 1,054-page White Paper on American policy toward Chiang's regime, Truman and his new secretary of state, Dean Acheson, virtually cut the line on which the Generalissimo dangled, and accused the former Chinese government of losing the support of its own people through corruption and incompetence.

Whatever the official reasoning behind China's collapse, most Americans chose only to see that Communism now controlled over a quarter of the globe. Acheson himself, tweedy and urbane, educated at Groton, Yale, and Harvard Law School, the sartorial and intellectual apotheosis of the Eastern Establishment, became a lightning rod for criticism of policies that revisionists would assail two decades later as the genesis of the Cold War. One Republican Old Guarder, Hugh Butler, tore into Acheson's "smart-aleck manner and his British clothes," and said that Acheson's very bearing made him want to shout at the Secretary of State, "Get out, get out. You stand for everything that has been wrong with the United States for years."

Dewey and Acheson were, not improbably, friends who shared common temperaments and similar views of the world. Yet later, Dewey never forgave Acheson for what he regarded as a terrible blunder before the National Press Club on Jan. 12, 1950, when Acheson defined the U.S. defense perimeter as running from the Aleutians to Japan, thence to the Ryukyus and the Philippines. Formosa and South Korea, pointedly, were left out of this protective embrace. "No person can guarantee these areas against military attack," Acheson told the Press Club. The best they could expect would be an appeal to the UN—if first they managed to provide "united resistance" sufficient to hold out that long.

Domestic politics meanwhile did not halt for international debate. On July 28, Taft forces on the Republican National Committee avenged their loss at Omaha, choosing New Jersey's Guy Gabrielson to replace Scott as chairman. On Capitol Hill, congressional Republicans more than ever embittered by the 1948 debacle stood staunchly against administration proposals, prompting Dewey's complaint that "what direction they have seems to be straight back to McKinley." He too opposed "socialism, the Brannan Plan, and compulsory medical insurance," he wrote a friend late in the year, and his support for a balanced budget was unwavering. "But if they believe they are going to stop farm price supports, pensions, unemployment insurance, and social advances," he said of his Republican brethren in Washington, "they are crazy and they are likely to lose our freedom for us . . . by leading the country into a one-party system."[14]

Through his state chairmen and local leaders, he was doing his best to strengthen the party at the precinct level, as he promised he would. He was also looking ahead to the not-so-distant future, when he would no longer be governor. It had been rumored after his defeat at Truman's hands that Dewey might resign his office; as the months passed, the story gradually faded. But Dewey was anxious to leave Albany after 1950. Frances wished it. So did Dewey the lawyer, who hadn't forgotten his old ambition to head a great firm and earn the income that went with such an exalted position. But he would not abandon center stage without an impressive understudy in the wings, ready to assume power nationally as well as in the Empire State.

Shortly after his loss to Truman, Dewey had approached Milton Eisenhower, brother of the war hero now ensconced in the president's house at Columbia. He had told Ike's brother that the General must allow Republicans to make him their nominee in 1952. No one else could restore the party to power. Then, on April 11, 1949, Dewey wrote Dwight Eisenhower himself. He had "one or two things of some importance," he said, that he would like to discuss at the General's convenience. Three months later, he was ushered into Eisenhower's study for a two-hour meeting vividly preserved in the General's diary.[15]

"He says he is worried about the country's future—and that *I* am the only one who can do anything about it." Eisenhower noted.

"The Gov. says that I am a public possession—that such standing as I have in the affections or respect of our citizenry is likewise public property. All of this, therefore, must be carefully guarded to use in the service of all the people. (Although I'm merely repeating some-one else's expression," Ike interjected, "the mere writing of such things almost makes me dive under the table). He feels that N.Y. State is vital to any Republican aspirant to Presidency. He assumes I am a Republican and would like to be President (when this last came out I was flabbergasted. I must have had a funny look on my face, because he said, 'I know you disclaimed political ambition in a verbose, wordy document—but that was when you were just a sol-dier'). . . . The Governor then gave me the reasons he believed that only I (if I should carefully preserve my assets) can save this country from going to Hades in the handbasket of paternalism—socialism—dictatorship. He knows that I consider our greatest danger the un-awareness of our majorities while aggregated minorities work their hands into our pockets and their seats to the places of the mighty!"

Dewey outlined a political timetable for the General, "starting very soon." First, he must declare himself a Republican. Then, he should run for and be elected to the governorship of New York. Fi-nally, he could accept a presidential nomination, "but always keep still as to my specific views." (Dewey had his reasons for the last pre-caution.) "All middle class citizens of education have a common be-lief that the tendencies toward centralization and paternalism must be halted and reversed," Eisenhower summed up his visitor's philos-ophy. "No one who voices these views can be elected. He quotes ef-forts of Hoover, Landon, Willkie, Himself. Consequently, we must look around for someone of great popularity and who has not frit-tered away his political assets by taking positive stands against na-tional planning, etc. etc. Elect such a man to Presidency, *after which*, he must lead us back to safe channels and paths."

According to his diary, Eisenhower was tempted to "say what Sherman said," but felt "I'm not sophisticated enough to give any kind of an irrevocable, arbitrary answer at this moment." Ike pleaded lack of interest instead. "I shall never willingly seek a vote. I shall always try to do my duty to U.S. but I *do not* believe that any-thing can ever convince me that I have a *duty* to seek political office." Yet, even as he was saying this, Eisenhower could see in Dewey's eyes an entirely different, and far more cynical interpretation form-ing itself: "Why, surely," he imagined his guest's conclusion, "pro-vided I ever become convinced I can win."

Before leaving, Dewey asked Eisenhower to run for governor of

New York in 1950. Far better than any seat in the Senate, the governorship allowed one to exercise national power without taking "unequivocal stands on national issues." Ike said he didn't want to run for governor, and Dewey replied that he should think it over. He told the General that he must do something of political significance by 1950 or risk political oblivion, to which Eisenhower answered, with a grin, "You've given me the best of reasons for doing nothing."

"Not if you want to preserve democracy," Dewey shot back. Then he injected a final element into the scenario leading up to an Eisenhower administration in 1953. If and when he should be elected to the presidency, Dewey said, "there would never be anything in his gift that I would accept. . . . I wanted no suspicion of self-interest." The partnership was strictly pragmatic.[16]

To Dewey, Ike was a "logical nominee," a hero rather than a politician, a diplomat-soldier whose rather vague ideas on domestic issues were all the more salable for their mystery. In fact, Eisenhower already had displayed signs of innate conservatism. In one 1947 speech, he had complained of the omnipotence of Washington's bureaucratic planners and said that if the only thing of interest to the American people was security, then they could go to jail.[17]

For now, the war hero agreed only not to rule out anything. "His sincerity cannot be questioned," Ike wrote of his visitor that hot July morning, "(he certainly has nothing to gain by my running for state office)." Because of this, and of Dewey's evident importance on the national scene, Eisenhower concluded "the whole matter cannot be lightly dismissed."[18]

In October, Dewey was back at Morningside Heights, invited by Eisenhower to visit before a luncheon on campus, "so that we can have a quarter-hour or so chat together, free from the pressures of the business before us." The General agreed to see "a couple of his trusted advisers," and, late that December, the Governor introduced him to Brownell and Sprague. The four men spent an entire evening in "delightful discussion," which Eisenhower said he had "thoroughly enjoyed." "I do not desire to burden you on the subject we discussed," Dewey wrote on December 23, "but would like to have you feel that I am available, as are my friends . . . when you find it desirable and convenient." Eisenhower replied that he expected the future "will bring many additional opportunities of the same kind."[19]

As if further evidence were needed to prove that Dewey's own presidential fires were banked, he said goodbye at the end of 1949 to two of the most influential members of the Albany Team. Elliott

Bell departed to join McGraw-Hill, and a month later, in a parting that Dewey said "took a piece out of my heart," Charles Breitel was appointed by the Governor to fill a vacancy on the State Supreme Court.

Meanwhile, the pressure on Eisenhower to run mounted steadily. Arthur Vandenberg urged such a course before his death in the spring of 1950. So did James Byrnes, Clare Boothe Luce, and old personal friends like Lucius Clay, Walter Robinson of the New York *Herald Tribune,* and Walter Bedell Smith. Dewey maintained his correspondence with the General after Ike left Columbia to assume command of NATO early in 1951. Ironically, Ike's new post was, from Dewey's standpoint, even better than the governorship, polishing Eisenhower's image as a man above partisan politics and enhancing his silhouette against the greatest events of the age.[20]

Yet circumstances called for discretion. "While I have a very pleasant personal relationship with the General," Dewey told Barak Mattingly in April 1950, in response to Mattingly's question about inviting Ike out to Missouri for an early buildup, "I have refrained from passing invitations on to him because we both agreed that might appear to imply a political relationship which does not exist."[21]

This was in keeping with Dewey's self-imposed restriction, which he called "vitally necessary" to Eisenhower's election. Fearful that Ike might appear a Dewey puppet, keenly aware of the host of enemies accrued over three national campaigns of his own, Dewey vowed, in Eisenhower's words, "to abstain from offering me any direct political advice or counsel." As late as May 1951, when Gardner Cowles invited him to write an article for *Look* on why he was supporting the General for 1952, Dewey turned down the offer—and the $5,000 which might have supported a son through college. He had already rejected similar overtures from *Collier's,* he explained, "while the General is in the early stages of his formidable task." For now, Dewey was reduced to a discreet cross-Atlantic courtship, in phone calls disguised as coming from a "Mr. Lockwood," and in teasing hints of availability brought back from others who could afford to be seen with Eisenhower at his new headquarters just outside Paris.[22]

Eisenhower's precise attitude toward the man who was so persistently urging him to run for president was a combination of bemusement and wariness. At one time he had listened to Dewey lay out all the arguments against his running. Moreover, he looked upon Dewey as a politician to his fingertips and Ike was not a man who felt instinctive rapport with intrigue or ethical calculation. "When Ike learned to say precinct," is the way Cliff White put it, "he thought he knew all about politics." Eisenhower only chuckled when his top civilian aide, Kevin McCann, referred to Dewey as "his pop-eyed excellency," and when the Governor went public with his support near the end of a heated gubernatorial re-election campaign in 1950, Ike questioned the timing of the move to at least one of his Columbia callers. The two men were poles apart in many ways, and would never achieve personal intimacy. Yet Eisenhower felt something akin to awe for the New Yorker's political sagacity. He let himself be surrounded by Dewey men in his first administration. He also perceived early the dichotomy of Dewey's gifts and liabilities.[23]

"He is as likable as he has always been in private conversation," Eisenhower wrote after their July 6, 1949, conference. "It seems that in public he has no appeal, but he is a rather persuasive talker on a tête-à-tête basis." It was a suitably ambiguous assessment, at the start of a largely formal friendship.[24]

Nineteen fifty was a year of bitter headlines, vivid with premonitions of doom. On January 25, Alger Hiss was convicted of perjury. Four days later, Acheson rebuffed those who wanted him to repudiate his old friend. "I do not intend to turn my back on Alger Hiss," the Secretary of State told reporters, foolishly and nobly. Two days after that, Truman revealed his orders to proceed with construction of a hydrogen bomb, prompting Einstein's warning that "general annihilation beckons." On February 3, Britain let it be known that Dr. Klaus Fuchs had confessed to having sold British-U.S. secrets to the Soviets. On the sixth, Taft kicked off the 1950 congressional campaign at a GOP rally in Washington with a scornful reference to "traitors in our ranks." That same week, an obscure first-term Senator from Wisconsin, elected as "Tail-Gunner Joe" in the 1946 wave of returning veterans who were sent on to Washington ("He and millions of other guys kept you from talking Japanese"), rose before a Republican audience in Wheeling, West Virginia, to denounce "the bright young men who are born with silver spoons in their mouths," as personified by Dean Acheson, "that pompous diplomat in striped pants, with phony British accent."

Joe McCarthy's attack was hardly the stuff to frighten Acheson; the imperious, worldly Secretary of State had long since grown accustomed to being pilloried by the congressional Republicans he called "primitives." But McCarthy didn't stop with a ritual barb or two at the architect of Truman's foreign policy. He held up papers which contained what he said were the names of 57—or 205—it was never determined exactly which—"card-carrying members of the Communist party" in the employ of the State Department. Thus was born McCarthyism, the logical bombastic by-product of pent-up national frustrations, whipped to a frenzy by frightened or ambitious men. For the GOP, the long exile from authority had become a retreat from responsibility. Yet Republicans were by no means alone in fanning the flames of suspicion and paranoia. In New York City, Mayor O'Dwyer had, in 1948, removed 150 members of the American Labor party from municipal jobs. Later, firemen, policemen, transit workers, gas inspectors, and even washroom attendants were dismissed as potential security threats.

Dewey himself had signed into law in April 1949 the Feinberg Law, empowering the State Board of Regents to list subversive organizations in which membership might warrant dismissal from teaching posts. The law proved cumbersome and difficult to enforce. So did its streamlined successor, the Security Risk Act of 1951, under whose terms two dozen state workers were fired or forced to resign over an eight-year period. Yet the same month Dewey approved the Feinberg Law, he vetoed another bill, unanimously passed by the Senate, banning all parties advocating the violent overthrow of the government. He refused to halt the left-wing Cultural and Scientific Conference for World Peace in March 1949. To do so, he wrote, "would be abdicating our vital principle of free speech for everyone, even for those with whom our disagreements are fundamental and unbridgeable."

Six months later, when disturbances broke out at a Peekskill, New York, concert appearance by Paul Robeson, Communist sympathizers announced plans for a second concert at the same spot one week later. Three thousand furriers and longshoremen armed with baseball bats and tire irons would keep order. Dewey dispatched state police to the area and issued a plea on behalf of free speech and assembly, "however hateful the views of some who abuse them." On September 4, 15,000 gathered to hear Robeson sing and participate in a wild rampage of stone throwing and club wielding that extended for twenty miles. State troopers did what they could to stem the violence; county police stood by, silent allies of the anti-Robeson crowd. Enraged, Dewey called in the Sheriff and District Attorney of Westchester. Afterwards, he said the facts in the Peekskill riot were "simple and ugly."

"These followers of red totalitarianism," he declared, "which teaches violence and the suppression of individual liberty were themselves made the victims of lawlessness and the suppression of individual rights." He grieved for the foes of Communism, who had fallen into a "bear trap" and he closed with a strong reassertion that "free speech and the right of assembly are as precious to us as life itself." Any violation of such rights, no matter the justification, "can be and will be investigated to the last limit of the powers of the State."

"Remember, fellows," Dewey told a visiting contingent of Boy Scouts in the spring of 1950, "any boy can become President—unless he's got a mustache."

More seriously, the titular head of the Republican party attempted to set forth a positive alternative to both the Democrats and his own conservative critics in a series of lectures delivered at Princeton University that March and April. Published in edited form sixteen years later, after the Goldwater disaster had again opened a way for moderate Republicans, Dewey's Princeton lectures represented the zenith of his mature philosophy, and a search for practical alternatives to the egalitarian left and libertarian right. He railed against the "vociferous few" who demanded neatly divided parties, "impractical theorists" who wished to drive all moderates and liberals into Democratic arms, in return for a purely conservative GOP. Everything would be neatly arranged, said Dewey. "The results would be neatly arranged, too. The Republicans would lose every election and the Democrats would win."

No, his colleagues in Lincoln's party could never expect to win power on "a platform of back-to-Methuselah." Dewey then turned his attention to liberalism, which in its original form meant restriction upon government's power in the death throes of royal absolutism. Yet, a strange alchemy had occurred. Liberalism in the modern era was all but orphaned. The Industrial Revolution had bred in men new kinds of insecurity, as well as a higher standard of living. That insecurity had led straight to controls, many imposed by the state, in the hope of preserving the individual from hazards "entirely beyond his control." A perversion of such liberalism was exemplified by the "modern collectivists" who promised security without risk and the lotus without toil.

In other lands, Dewey claimed, millions had been led astray by utopian promises, "only to find bitter gall at the end of the rainbow." Even at home, government was becoming more centralized, and the national income increasingly the property of a dominant executive department. The future looked bleak if the trend continued.

Such government, in Dewey's words, "can never retreat without admitting failure." Such government fed on the gradual obliteration of state and local authority. Such government offered, in lieu of grassroots taxation, "the counterfeit currency of federal subsidy."

Unless replaced by new theories, the neo-liberalism that Dewey saw as a threat would inevitably destroy the economic mainsprings of society, deadening individual incentive to produce, throttling personal aspiration for what Americans had always liked to consider a dream uniquely theirs. Once accumulated capital dried up, a combination of "high taxes, oppressive regulation, delays, and frustrations due to massive bureaucracies, inflation of prices, and the ominous threat to adequate production" would doom the system to ultimate collapse.

Dewey concluded with a series of questions, his personal test of genuine liberalism. Did welfare measures build up individual independence and responsibility—or foster subservience? Did federal intervention widen or narrow the bounds of personal liberty? Did government try to do itself "what people can and should do for themselves by voluntary action?" Did it remove from productive work large numbers needed to administer its own programs? Did it promote sound finances? Thirty years before the American electorate would install Ronald Reagan in the White House, before a generation of federal intervention and a drooping economy radicalized the voters to Reaganomics, Dewey was doing what he did best: laying out the middle road to a rational prosperity. Perhaps few even in his politically sophisticated Princeton audience could perceive what a sharp break with the past he was proposing.

On March 8, 1950, Dewey entered Columbia Presbyterian Medical Center in New York for removal of three calcium deposits responsible for months of mounting pain in his left shoulder. The patient said afterwards he had "a cute little incision which looks like the seam of a baseball." He expressed happiness with doctors who told him he might be able to swing a golf club within two weeks, and delighted in a cheerful warning from Pat Hogan. "With your mineral deposits and my gas," wrote Dewey's best friend, "you and I are lucky we aren't taxed on our natural resources." The operation also strengthened Dewey's ambition to retire from public life after his present term expired in December. "I've never made any money from public service, all I've got is my salary," he told his Quaker Hill pastor. "I don't have any estate for my family."[25]

By mid-March, rumors were circulating in Albany that Lieutenant Governor Joe Hanley would run in Dewey's place. On the twenty-first, Dewey announced creation of the New York Thruway Authority, an autonomous arm of state government that would market bonds backed by tolls and complete his landmark thruway within five years and without tapping current state revenues. One day later, in a move confirming his own intention to leave office, Dewey appointed Paul Lockwood to the Public Service Commission, Hickman Powell to the St. Lawrence Power Authority, and Burdell Bixby to the Thruway Authority. On June 17, in a one-line statement issued from his office, the Governor made his retirement plans official. Out in Owosso, Annie's reaction was typical: her son, she told friends, "is finally going to make an honest living. "[26]

Within ten days of Dewey's declaration, the U.S. found itself again at war: Harry Truman had committed American troops to repel an invasion of South Korea from the Communist North. "I wholeheartedly agree with and support the difficult decision you have made," Dewey wired the White House on June 28. He was more critical in a letter to his mother. Truman's action in supporting the government of Syngman Rhee "was the only thing to do in the light of the circumstances in which we found ourselves. . . . I think that a more skillful diplomacy and stronger action would have prevented this situation from developing. . . . But here we are and if we did not take this action . . . neither Asia nor Europe would feel that they could any longer rely on us as a bulwark of freedom. Men would not have risked their necks in the cause of free government. The Communists would very quickly take the world."[27]

Apocalyptic as he could sound at such times, Dewey never joined the China Lobby, that mostly Republican, furiously anti-European band who blamed Acheson for having failed Chiang Kai-shek in the hour of his greatest need. For one thing, he was too committed to bipartisanship in foreign policy—even then being expressed by Dulles, back in harness as a consultant at State and working on a peace treaty with Japan. Then too, Dewey was too pragmatic to waste time fighting lost causes; his reaction to 1948 demonstrated that. Steeped in the internationalism of the Eastern Seaboard, suspicious of the Tafts and MacArthurs who proclaimed the primacy of Asia over Europe, he could hardly associate with the China Lobby's leadership, or sympathize with its obsessions. Even while blaming Acheson for the Press Club gaffe that presaged the Korean War, Dewey half excused Mr. Truman, who he said, "wasn't smart enough" to know that Korea was part of the Asian mainland.[28]

The war went badly in its initial weeks. American troops were pushed back into a defensive beachhead around the southern port of Pusan, and at home Taft, cheered on by Senators McCarthy and Jenner, "invited" Acheson to resign. Mr. Republican also questioned, "in the absence of some previous actions by Congress dealing with the subject," the authority of the UN and the need for the U.S. to abide by its strategic decisions. In New York, Dewey warmly endorsed Truman's latest moves to combat international Communism as "a strong step in the right direction." He revealed on July 10 that Lucius Clay, hero of the Berlin airlift (and one of Eisenhower's closest friends) would become the state's civil defense director. The Commerce Department cranked up to work again on war contracts for New York industries. Dewey came under renewed pressure to change his mind about a third term.

In July, he and Frances were apartment hunting in New York City. ("They are expensive as the devil," he told Annie.) By the first week in August, just before MacArthur's master-stroke landing at Inchon, Dewey called the military situation "dreadful" and noted "it is very upsetting to my personal plans." A "lot of people," he wrote on August 16, were making his life "miserable. I hope to succeed in fighting them off." A week later, he was still trying. Other friends were urging him to run, not for governor, but the Senate seat that Lehman would have to defend that fall. "The day you stepped into the Senate," one wrote, "Taft would fold up." Then Truman banished Mayor O'Dwyer to Mexico City, and another wrinkle appeared on the political horizon. With a mayoralty race scheduled in New York City, it became obvious that the GOP would have to go with its strongest statewide contenders or risk being overwhelmed by a heavy Democratic turnout downstate.[29]

Dewey had already been offered a job outside of Albany. He had taken a call from Acheson that August, who said he had "a most confidential matter" to discuss, and wondered where they might meet in absolute privacy. Dewey suggested Roger Straus's home, empty for the summer, and a reluctant Acheson finally went along. It seemed that Lewis Douglas wanted to leave the Court of St. James's, and Truman's secretary of state regarded Dewey as a perfect replacement. The President, insisted Acheson, had been "very pleased" when the idea was broached to him, at the same time remarking that it would be impossible for him to personally discuss anything with his 1948 opponent lest it slip out to the press. "Well," Dewey replied to this, "he's used to the kind of people that don't keep their word."[30]

For five hours, the two men circled the offer warily, Acheson telling Dewey it was his duty to accept in a time of international crisis, Dewey countering that diplomacy had never been his forte. Besides, he said, he couldn't afford St. James's. Acheson reassured him that "special funds and allowances" under his control could take care of the problem nicely. Dewey didn't want to abandon the party of which he was titular leader, or give the impression he was fleeing to London to avoid another term in Albany. The meeting broke up on an inconclusive note, with Dewey saying he'd have to talk it over with Frances, Straus, Dulles, and possibly Brownell. "Oh, Lord," Acheson gasped, "it will leak that way, and the fat will be in the fire." Again, Dewey promised that his people knew the art of discretion; even after he turned down the job, it stayed under wraps for a year.[31]

As August simmered away toward its close, Dewey remained firm in his resolve to return to private practice. But other men wished to take the decision out of his hands. On August 28, a meeting was held in the boardroom of the Chase National Bank in New York City. Frank Gannett was summoned there from Rochester by Roy Howard and informed that his continued support for the Hanley candidacy might imperil his own financial position. Furthermore, it was made clear that Hanley could expect no help from Wall Street. An angry Gannett passed the story on to Kingsland Macy, his partner in lending Hanley $30,000 to help pay campaign costs (who expected to receive in return a U.S. Senate nomination). Later, it was said that Brownell attended the Chase meeting, arranged by Winthrop Aldrich, and that his presence meant a change of heart in Albany. The evidence argues strongly against this.[32]

For one thing, those who knew both men knew that Brownell was less personally close to the Governor than guessed by the public. If he was at the Chase that day, it was almost certainly as a representative to, rather than an emissary from, Dewey. In addition, Dewey had turned over his summer speaking schedule to Hanley, and assigned Jim Hagerty to pave the way for peaceful relations between the heir apparent and the fourth estate. Irving Ives had publicly thrown in the towel on August 8, saying that Dewey could not be persuaded to run. Even after O'Dwyer's diminutive successor in City Hall, Vincent Impellitteri, refused to make way for Ferdinand Pecora, thus insuring a heated three-way contest and a huge fall vote in New York City, Bill Pfeiffer was unable to talk Dewey back into the race. Tom Curran expressed hope for a draft on August 25, only to be slapped down by a gubernatorial statement that the two men had not spoken in over two months. Curran refused to give up, however. He attended the Chase Bank meeting on the twenty-eighth.

Like other experienced politicians, the Manhattan County Chairman knew instinctively that Hanley, seventy-four years old, with a glass eye and fears of total blindness, a man so generous with inside information that his presence was no longer welcomed at the Sunday night skull sessions between the Governor and his legislative team, was just not good enough.[33]

But he had yet to convince Dewey. On August 31, Dewey and Hanley met at Albany before conspicuously attending a civil defense meeting together. Later that day, the Governor left for Forest Hills, where the national tennis championships were scheduled for the weekend. Hanley went into conference with Pfeiffer and his own campaign manager, Representative Dean Taylor. (Later it was said, only half in jest, that Taylor and Pfeiffer had threatened to push Hanley out of a plane if he did not voluntarily step aside.) A call went out to Russ Sprague: Hanley wanted to pull out. Sprague then reached Alger Chapman at the Roosevelt Hotel, where Dewey had yet to return from Forest Hills. When the Governor did appear, he found a cache of political advisers strenuously urging him to take advantage of the changed situation. A statewide poll had been taken, showing Hanley losing in a landslide to any prospective Democratic nominee. Hanley, it was said, couldn't raise adequate funds. There was a presidential election coming up in two years—and what impact could New York expect to have with a Democrat in Albany? Finally, there was the Governor's vanity to be appealed to. This was a chance to win vindication, Dewey was told "for the screwing you took in '48."[34]

To all this and more, Dewey turned a deaf ear. Chapman asked if his friend really wished to leave public office this way, when he could win a November election with one hand tied behind his back? Dewey only stared at the man he called Alger B. Then he hollered for Frances. Earlier in the year, the two had made what Chapman calls "a blood pact" to leave Albany in 1950. Now, to his utter astonishment, Frances said she had been listening to the radio, and hearing the latest weekly casualty reports from Korea—the worst numbers yet. So long as Americans were dying in Asian fields, she continued, her husband could hardly justify retreat to a private law office. "I'm afraid you have a New England conscience," Dewey quoted her later. "If you don't run, you'll never forgive yourself."[35]

The next day, September 1, the New York *Times* published an editorial appeal to the Governor to reverse his stand. That night, Suite

1527 was filled with heated argument, as Pfeiffer, Taylor, and Hanley himself joined the fray. At three in the morning, with Hanley sound asleep in an adjoining room, Dewey told his visitors, "The hell with you. I'm going to bed." When he awoke, the pleadings resumed, until finally Dewey gave in—with one important stipulation. Fearing that upstate Republicans would hold him responsible for Hanley's replacement, Dewey insisted that his lieutenant governor agree to run for the Senate against Lehman. Reluctantly, Hanley gave his assent. On September 5, Democrats chose Walter J. Lynch, a fifty-six-year-old Bronx congressman, who was both obscure and vulnerable by way of his close ties to Boss Flynn, to run against Dewey. The same day, GOP delegates gathered in Saratoga in an atmosphere of surface harmony. "It is pretty tough to ask everybody to serve," Dewey wrote Annie, after a unanimous renomination, "if you are unwilling to do so yourself." Only a short while before, he had been negotiating an apartment lease on the East Side of New York. Then came "two tumultuous weeks . . . and so here I am running again, much against my will."[36]

For those who liked their politics bare-knuckled, the 1950 race for governor of New York had everything. It featured party splits and charges of bribery, assertions of dictatorship and name-calling on a grand scale, police scandals and, for good measure, some waving of the Communist bloody shirt. Dewey started the ball rolling, claiming at Saratoga that the Democratic ticket was pulled from Boss Flynn's phone book, and taking aim at Truman. The American people were "sick of midnight reversals, sick of policies which invite war, sick of weakness," he said, "sick of an administration which in five years reduced America from the greatest power on earth and put its . . . brains in mothballs." He called Flynn's slate "a crew of wreckers" and "boss-ridden puppets." On September 21, he caused an uproar in a welcoming speech to the UN General Assembly, referring to Soviet slave labor camps and Russian "barbarism."

"These are not times to cover up ugly issues with polite words. Imperialist slavery has conquered one-third of the world and is obviously determined to conquer the rest." With that, chief Soviet delegate Andrei Vishinsky led a walkout of Moscow's diplomats from the Waldorf-Astoria ballroom; Dewey said that he was "complimented by the withdrawal of those who plot the destruction of the world." The 1,500 remaining diners rose to their feet and cheered. So did most New Yorkers. Mayor Impellitteri refused to apologize to the Russians for the Governor's "splendid remarks," and Dewey himself told his mother that Vishinsky had done him a favor. Before making his comments, he had read his text over the phone to Acheson, who oddly failed to perceive the likely impact. When Dewey kept the call a secret, a grateful Acheson told Truman that if any of "our people" went after the Governor, he, the Secretary of State, would be forced to come to his assistance.[37]

Outside of diplomatic circles, Dewey heaped scorn on those accusing him of squandering the Postwar Reconstruction Fund. It was a "delightful fantasy" presented to the voters of New York, he said on September 25, "Democrats running on an economy platform. Now I've seen everything—except sunrise at seven o'clock at night." Then he went out to dedicate new colleges and hospitals made possible through the surplus funds. He accused Truman of "political obstruction" over the St. Lawrence power project, and reaped favorable headlines when a bookmaking scandal in Brooklyn was followed by revelations that millions of dollars of New York City school funds had been mishandled or unappropriated. The city, he wrote on October 1, was "a complete mess, but that may help us."[38]

Lynch fought back, calling Dewey "little Stalin" and his political machine "a politburo." To offset the gambling scandal downstate, Lynch alleged Republican inactivity in the face of bookmaking in Saratoga and other upstate counties. "Order your county bosses to take the fetters off the district attorneys" he wired the Governor on October 3, "and make them do their duty." Dewey dredged up Lynch's vote to draft striking rail workers into the Army, "something you would expect to find only in Soviet Russia." Lynch called his opponent "Chase Bank Dewey," a pliant tool of Winthrop Aldrich. Dewey regained center stage with an experimental question and answer program on statewide television. Sitting on a desk, his jacket sloughed off under the hot lights, chuckling when asked about his mustache and cigarette holder, reeling off facts and figures to support his case for the thruway, the State University, and educational assistance to local communities, Dewey came across as mellow and conversational. He took an instant shine to the new medium, booking several more appearances before Election Day, including a final eighteen-hour marathon on November 4.

Beyond the studio, too, he warmed to the fight. He made extemporaneous speeches for the first time since the 1937 district attorney's contest, saying they would prolong his life by twenty years. He stopped a rural motorcade in defiance of schedulers to greet two dozen Girl Scouts drawn up to wish him well. He stood outside in a biting wind to shake hands with 150 prison guards at Dannemora, referred to the thruway colloquially as "the bloomin' thing," and spent forty-five minutes posing for pictures wearing a fireman's hat while standing on the running board of the town of Malone's newest engine. On October 10, the New York *Times* endorsed him, saying his two administrations ranked with the best in state history. Some national observers even speculated that a big win in November might propel Dewey yet again into the thick of presidential contention. As if to head this off, he telephoned Eisenhower at Columbia on October 13, prior to an appearance on *Meet the Press,* and informed the General of his intention to make a public declaration of support for an Eisenhower candidacy.

Ike noted in his diary that there seemed to be no "double-talking" about the matter. His own response, he told Dewey, would be a chaste "no comment." Dewey's motives were not purely altruistic. Russ Sprague, for one, was insisting that he renounce the 1952 nomination or face potential revolution in Nassau. Brownell disagreed, thinking it best to keep all options open and gubernatorial influence at a maximum. Dewey came down on Sprague's side, and on October 15, told the television audience that he was "definitely and finally removed" from the race. He intended to work for Eisenhower, he continued, "if I should be re-elected Governor and have influence with the New York delegation." Next morning's headlines were full of his announcement. Reading them, Dewey prepared himself for an even bigger story about to break.[39]

For weeks, rumors had floated about of a mysterious, potentially lethal letter from Joe Hanley to Kingsland Macy. On October 16, it became evident that the Democratic state committee possessed such correspondence and would soon make it public. At the Roosevelt Hotel, near-panic ensued. No one knew better than Dewey the validity of the rumors. Five weeks earlier, in a midnight conference with Macy, Dewey had urged the disaffected Suffolk leader to burn the letter. But Macy refused, and before long copies reached Frank Gannett and Helen Reid, among others. The Governor's counsel, Ed Walsh, learned from a Gannett reporter that the source of the leak was Jim Leary, Saratoga County GOP chairman and a man who stood to lose a great deal should Dewey make good on his threats to crack down on gambling and racetrack abuses in Saratoga. Others speculated that disgruntled Taft Republicans had supplied the Democrats with Hanley's letter, while the New York *World-Telegram* fingered Macy himself as its source.[40]

However it reached the opposition, the letter was bound to explode with tremendous force. At the urging of Alger Chapman, Dewey's campaign manager, Hanley held a press conference late on the afternoon of the sixteenth. Hoping to defuse some of the fallout, seeking sympathy as well as understanding, Hanley denounced a "whispering campaign" and said that he had been in debt practically all his life, stemming from a failed Iowa bank in which he and his widowed mother held stock. But he could not overshadow the inflammatory text in which he told Macy of a September 4 conference with Dewey. Hanley said he had received "certain unalterable and unquestionably definite propositions." If he consented to run for the Senate, a very dicey proposition, "I am definitely assured of being able to clean up my financial obligations within ninety days. . . . Also I have an ironclad arrangement whereby I will be given a job with the state which I would like and enjoy (I have been told what it is). . . . I cannot afford to gamble with my future." Win or lose, the Lieutenant Governor would thus be taken care of—a powerful incentive to one with thousands of dollars in debts over his head. Hanley also apologized to Macy for having "let you down" and promised to pay back whatever he owed. He described himself as "humiliated, disappointed and heartsick."

Taken in context, Hanley's letter could be the feeble attempt of an old man to placate a ruthless one to whom he had given his word. Dewey himself regarded his lieutenant governor's behavior as "pathetic." His anger was reserved for Macy and Leary. But he could not fail to see how for the first time in his own political career, there was mud splattering his white charger. Lynch, scenting the vulnerability, accused Dewey of "the blackest page in New York State's political history" and "a nefarious crime" against "a broken-hearted old man." The Democratic nominee also relished the prospect of "the great prosecutor" reduced to "a craven, evasive defendant." In common with everything else about this campaign, Lynch's response to Hanley's indiscretion was an exaggeration. Dewey himself blustered his way through a press conference on the seventeenth, acknowledging that a job for Hanley with the Thruway Authority had been discussed. "There is nothing to investigate," he said with a straight face. "It is all as clear as day." His offer to Hanley was "a simple act of friendship," and Lynch's charge that the Lieutenant Governor had been bludgeoned into running for the Senate "the most violent fixed fraud in all fiction."[41]

That night, he struck back, quoting from Flynn's own book, *You're the Boss,* to recount a deal whereby Franklin Roosevelt was enabled to run for governor in 1928 by transferring debts run up by his

Warm Springs Foundation to Democratic angel John J. Rascob, "God rest his soul." It was also well known that Flynn had tried to buy Impellitteri off with a fourteen-year term on the bench, in order to give Ferdinand Pecora a clear field in the mayoral race; this made Democratic outrage over the Dewey-Hanley deal hard to swallow. When the likes of Flynn could pin a crime on any Republican, Dewey told a shrieking New Rochelle crowd, "then hell will move over and heaven will takes its place." The New York *Times* published a tolerant editorial, saying Hanley's letter proved only that "politicians should telephone, not write." On October 19, Roy Howard's *World-Telegram* unearthed a letter of its own, this one from Herbert Lehman to Alger Hiss, dated August 1948 and containing assurances of Lehman's "complete confidence in your loyalty."

Dewey even tried to turn the furor to advantage. "If it is wrong for a man to have debts," he said at Newburgh on October 20, "then millions of people in the State of New York are wrong. . . . Here you have a politician who has been in office for twenty-four years and he hasn't got a dime. He owes money. The people of New York know they have a chance to elect an honest man to the U.S. Senate and I am for him." It was brazen but effective, especially since Lehman was a multimillionaire. Encouraged by the popular response, Dewey began calling his own rival "Flynch." He claimed that the Democrat was backed by "thieves, bums, fakers, and crooks." Lynch was forced to backpedal to earlier themes, including the hard-to-credit charge that Dewey's was a spendthrift administration. Dewey reveled in the allegation. He reeled off some of his achievements in office—the sickness-disability insurance, the free X rays and tuberculosis care, ("They took better care of cows with t.b.," he said of his Democratic predecessors, "than they did of human beings"), the twenty-one cancer clinics newly opened, the swimming pools and picnic groves, the grade crossings and state parks. "If that is squandering money, ladies and gentlemen, I propose to continue it."

When Lynch took him to task for the condition of New York's highways, Dewey reminded the voters that it had been Democratic legislators who unanimously opposed the thruway. "The roads aren't all that good," he said to one rural audience, "believe you me, I know. I have to ride them. I am the first governor in history that has ridden the whole length of Route 17. . . . Somebody put a sign, 'Dewey's Washboard' on it. He made a mistake. That highway was left to me by twenty years of Democrats, along with 13,000 miles of highways, half of which are crooked Indian trails . . . and lo and behold, now that we have come to election time, they get religion; they

are for highways, ladies and gentlemen, believe it or not: they say
we'll fix up the rotten highways which the Democrats left you. They
say just trust them. . . . Oh, how these people can pretend at election
time."

He hammered away at Flynn and the New York City scandals,
beseeched the voters not to let Tammany "get their hands on the
State of New York," and belittled the Democratic ticket as "nice,
patient, time-serving fellows who . . . couldn't find the State Capitol
without a guide." He pointed to stories of Frank Costello's powerful
grip over Tammany, quoting Costello's own remark, "I've never
been a junior partner in anything I ever went into." If Lynch was
elected, Dewey predicted, Costello would be governor of New York.
Lynch fired back, assailing Dewey as "a traitor to honest politics."
On October 22, he demanded "full details" of the four-year-old pardon and deportation of Lucky Luciano. It was an old and seamy
story, given birth almost immediately upon Luciano's departure for
Sicily in February 1946, and it varied with the teller. Some said that
Lucky had purchased his freedom by donating $90,000 to Dewey's
1944 presidential campaign. Others made it $40,000 and the 1946
race for re-election. Now, the whispers were out in the open. They
brought an immediate denial by Frederick Moran, the Democratic
chairman of the State Parole Board, who described Dewey's "unbroken practice" of referring all applications for executive action to
the board for independent investigation. Moran pointed out that
the board had granted a unanimous recommendation in favor of
Luciano's pardon and deportation, a practice followed in fifty-one
such cases since Herbert Lehman took office in 1933. "I am the guy
who spent a year and a half of his life in convicting Luciano,"
Dewey told New Yorkers. Ed Walsh went further, calling Lynch "an
oratorical thug."

The story was filed away with other last-minute allegations. But it
refused to die. It has stuck stubbornly to Dewey's memory ever since,
even though the man who pardoned Luciano held in his possesson
plenty of evidence to dispel the doubts over his conduct. Once again,
Dewey had heeded the pleas of military men to keep what he knew
secret.

Herbert Lehman was still governor in March 1942, when Captain
Roscoe C. McFall of the Navy's New York District Intelligence Office hatched a plan to utilize underworld help in securing the water-
fronts of the East Coast for Allied shipping. Pearl Harbor was then a
painfully fresh memory. Nazi submarines were sinking American

vessels off Long Island and the ship *Normandie,* being converted to a troopship, was considered a victim of enemy sabotage after it burned one February night at a North River pier. Fishing fleets were suspected of providing enemy subs with fuel and supplies. Rum runners were thought to be selling assistance with the same loose morality employed in their normal line of business. On March 7, 1942, McFall went to the office of District Attorney Frank Hogan, Dewey's successor, and met with Hogan and chief rackets investigator Murray Gurfein in hopes of obtaining their help in his scheme.

Another meeting took place two weeks later. This time, McFall's place was taken by C. Radcliffe Heffernden, head of the B-3 section of Naval Intelligence, charged with investigating sabotage and frustrating espionage. Out of these meetings, Gurfein arranged a conference with Socks Lanza, then under indictment for conspiracy and extortion, and well known as a powerful force in waterfront circles. Gurfein met Lanza and his attorney on a park bench at Riverside Drive and 131st Street on the night of March 26, at which time the criminal boss agreed to do what he could to get information on subversive activities in his bailiwick.

Lanza, aided by Meyer Lansky, helped Naval Intelligence men land jobs as ship loaders, dock workers, waiters, and hotel clerks. Union cards were provided for agents who eavesdropped on fishing boats and grilled drunks in bars for information about possible enemy activity along the waterfront. But Lanza's influence was geographically limited. Soon he was urging that overtures be made to Luciano, still in jail on his thirty- to fifty-year prison sentence from the prostitution racket case. Moses Polakoff, who hadn't seen his former client in three years, was persuaded to visit him at Dannemora; and on April 29, Gurfein asked State Corrections Commissioner John A. Lyons to approve Luciano's transfer to Great Meadow Prison, closer to New York and thus more convenient for the series of important visitors who now began a steady progress to the cell of the onetime monarch of the underworld. At first reluctant to do anything for New York, Lucky finally relented and sent word to Lansky to clear things all along the waterfront south of Manhattan.

Luciano wished the details of his assistance kept as secret as possible; that way, if the Nazis did finally win the war, he could go home to Italy safe from assassination. Through him, other mobsters were brought into the sensitive activities of Naval Intelligence, among them Johnny Dunn, Frank Costello, and Willie Moretti. Lookouts were posted throughout the waterfront, the International Longshoremen's Association was cultivated, subversives were pursued in a Harlem printing plant and cabaret. In 1943, when Heffernden moved up to a new division, this one gathering information for an invasion of Sicily, Luciano's contacts were again tapped. Sicilians expelled by Mussolini proved willing to help devise maps of possible landing sites. The island coastline and the contour of land off the coast were assessed with the help of underworld informants. Later, Heffernden estimated that 40 percent of the tips provided him turned out to be accurate.[42]

In February of that year, Luciano petitioned Judge McCook to reduce his sentence. McCook met with both Heffernden and Gurfein, but advised the prisoner to think instead of executive clemency. That way, as McCook later explained, the Navy could get the "fullest possible benefit" of Luciano's cooperation. Two years later, on V-E Day, Luciano filed a request with the Govenor's office, now occupied by Dewey. The State Parole Board undertook a lengthy investigation. Heffernden recounted Lucky's aid to the war effort. Gurfein did likewise in an affidavit from Paris, where he was employed by the OSS. After seven months, the board recommended that Dewey grant the petition, then deport Luciano as other governors had done in the past. Early in 1946, Dewey agreed, saying that Luciano had rendered wartime service, although its exact dimension was cloudy. One month later, on February 9, Lucky found himself on a boat bound for Sicily, with the provision that should he ever re-enter the country, he would be treated as an escaped convict, and be forced to serve out his maximum sentence.

Stories alleging a payoff began to circulate. They reached the surface in Dewey's campaign against Lynch, and reappeared in February 1953, when an author asserted on Kate Smith's NBC television program that Dewey had sold Luciano his pardon. On that occasion, Charles Breitel called network officials, provided them with background on the case, and won an on-air retraction and apology. Dewey himself asked William Herlands, his new director of investigations, to conduct an exhaustive probe of Luciano's wartime role, and the circumstances leading up to the pardon. What emerged, in more than 2,600 pages of testimony and interpretation, was a portrait of naval paranoia in 1942, followed by the approach to District Attorney Hogan, the Lanza involvement, and Lucky's own contribution. The final report was ready by the spring of 1954. It was shown to Navy officials in Washington for clearance, and on July 26 the Chief of Naval Operations, Carl F. Espe, confirmed to Herlands Luciano's role in the wartime linkup between the Navy and the underworld. Later, after his own review of Herlands' findings, he told

Dewey's investigator that its release at that time might "jeopardize operations of a similar nature" in the future and cause "a rash of thriller stories" that could severely embarrass the Navy "public-relations wise."[43]

"Unless there are compelling reasons for making the report public," Espe concluded, "I hope that Mr. Dewey may find it consistent with his personal interests to hold it against the future. . . . It's publication can do the Navy no good; it might do it harm."[44]

The report was locked up among Dewey's most private papers; it was not made public until after his death. But those hearing the rumors of Dewey's willingness to trade in pardons did not require the sensitive facts contained in the Herlands report to cause second thoughts. There was the Parole Board's own independence, and the tradition of deportation for criminals New York no longer wished to support at public expense. There was Dewey's ironclad rule against politicizing the pardoning process. "Parole," he informed Barak Mattingly in the fall of 1952, "is one matter in which I quite properly never intervene" after Mattingly put in a good word for Joey Fay. There was Dewey's hypersensitive attitude about unknown contributors to consider, and his own innate caution. Goody Goodrich read the accusations and was puzzled. "If he got $75,000, where was it?" he asked at one point. "I went over every contribution." Finally, those willing to believe Luciano's deportation the result of a bribe did not take into account Dewey's attitude, as expressed to intimates, that Lucky's original sentence was punitive. Ten years in jail, whatever the extent of his wartime aid, seemed to Dewey long enough for a man whose conviction had come on a charge of aiding and abetting prostitution.[45]

In the Hanley affair, Dewey may be fairly criticized. His conduct verged on the illegal or unethical. In pardoning Luciano, he followed tradition and instinct, and paid a price by refusing to make public information the Navy itself acknowledged as accurate and likely to bring exoneration.

Not even Joe Hanley's sudden hospitalization for exhaustion during the last weekend of the campaign—the Democrats said he was hiding from Senate investigators up from Washington to probe the now-famous letter, Dewey claimed he was the persecuted victim of uncaring politicians—could reverse enough votes to give Lynch a shot at the executive mansion. Dewey won by 572,000, which, considering the tone of the campaign and the political obituaries written only days before, was a more than respectable margin. George

Hinman, reconciled to the Governor after their bitter fight over the State University, wrote to congratulate him on his "never say die, hit 'em where they live campaign." Dewey's own mood, tinged with bitterness and colored by the awareness that he would be governing for four more years without his favorite Team, was less exuberant. "I don't know what I'm still doing here," he muttered to a friend a few weeks after the election. The war precluded major innovations. Such ventures, he wrote in January 1951, would have to be postponed, "until we can see a little more clearly that we are going to survive to enjoy them." He worried more than ever about Republicans committed to what he called "the isolationist line," and his worst doubts seemed confirmed just before Christmas, when Herbert Hoover won headlines with a speech declaring that air and sea support alone should replace American ground forces in Europe, and proposing that the northern and southern hemispheres unite as a "Western Gibraltar . . . a sure dam against the Red flood."[46]

America was about to embark on what would later be called her Great Debate and Dewey suddenly was to discover a reason for running once again—for an office he did not particularly want.

17

The President Maker

I am still not quite sure why I ran again, but . . . having no ambitions or expectations of having any other office, I am free to proselyte to the limit of my capacity . . . and intend to do so.
—THOMAS E. DEWEY TO WINSTON CHURCHILL[1]

Your performance was a masterpiece of effectiveness.
—DWIGHT D. EISENHOWER TO DEWEY[2]

The "Great Debate" into which Dewey and the nation plunged early in 1951 was initiated by Senator Kenneth Wherry's proposal that Congress check Truman's plan—supported by Generals Marshall and Bradley—to shift up to 70,000 American soldiers to Europe without congressional sanction. Taft sided with his Old Guard colleague from Nebraska. Such military commitment, he argued, would seriously strain the national economy. In fact, Taft let it be known, he was considering a formal ceiling of 20 percent of the nation's ground forces that could be assigned overseas. Dewey disagreed. It was the "utmost folly," he said on *Meet the Press* early in February, to believe that air and sea power alone could win a modern contest. "I thought everyone had learned that in Korea." That Americans could negotiate as equals with Stalin so long as Russian troops outnumbered our own 10 to 1 in Europe was "a stupid jackass idea."

In somewhat more lofty language, he made the same point in a Lincoln Day address on February 12. "Operation withdrawal," he said, "is operation suicide. . . . The day of decision is upon us. . . . Freedom was never bought in a bargain basement. Freedom was never saved by timidity, selfishness, half-measures or appeasement." He wrote an article for *Collier's* urging that NATO be expanded to include Greece, Turkey, and Spain. "Take courage," he advised the non-Communist world, "America is coming. Be strong; you can remain free." He proposed additional American aid to friendly regimes in Iran, Iraq, Israel, and Saudi Arabia. On February 24, he went to Washington to deliver a stinging, 4,000-word rebuke to Wherry and others out to undermine "the present virile effort developing in Europe for its own defense." He could remember the time—"and it seems only yesterday—when many were saying that the Marshall Plan . . . was Operation Rat-Hole," yet the physical and economic rehabilitation of Europe was progressing a year and a half ahead of schedule. Britain, for example, had already signed off on further assistance from its wartime ally.

In singling out Western Europe for military neglect, Dewey said that the Wherry Resolution was in fact "the last gasp of effort" of those who really hoped that America might "withdraw from all the world to our own shores." He decried Wherry's logic. There were already 117,000 American troops on the continent and in nearby North Africa. Passage of the resolution would be, in Dewey's words, "a simple, direct notice to Stalin that we do not intend to back up our men in Europe and that they and Europe are his for the asking." He held up a list of "seventy-one critical materials," like bauxite from Surinam, cobalt from Equatorial Africa, columbite from Nigeria, and manganese from India, all vital to American survival. "No," he concluded. "Fortress America is an illusion . . . the free world is indivisible. The loss of any part of it is the loss of a vital living organism of human freedom. . . . The defense of America is . . . in Europe and Japan."

Wherry's resolution was rejected, and Dewey found himself confiding to Churchill his hope "that a Grand Alliance will emerge." His own efforts at combating the isolationist impulse drew praise from an unlikely quarter. "All of us who have worked so long in the cause of internationalism," wrote Russell Davenport on February 8, "owe you a debt of gratitude." Dewey was less vocal in April, when Truman fired General Douglas MacArthur for pursuing military victory in Korea in defiance of the President's own attempts at a negotiated settlement. A one-paragraph statement issued in Albany that afternoon hailed MacArthur, soon to become a martyr for the right, as "a towering figure of strength." In private, Dewey regarded the Olympian general as a posturer, whose dismissal had been bungled by Washington. "Things never should have been allowed to get to the point of insubordination and crisis," he wrote Ben Duffey on April 12. Now little more remained than to "try and pick up the pieces, which are getting smaller and smaller."[3]

Unwilling to absolve "terrible management in Washington," neither did he intend to lend a hand in canonizing the military man he distrusted and politically feared. When MacArthur came home to a hero's welcome—including the largest crowd ever assembled in New York City—Dewey was not among his cheering admirers. He had fled the state in order to avoid the fervent tributes, telling the press he was feeling unwell, and on doctor's orders was retiring to Bermuda.[4]

Dewey could not escape other problems so easily. Joe McCarthy sent him a lengthy study of General Marshall's career, entitled *America's Retreat from Victory*. Dewey dutifully replied that he would read it "with interest." He begged off on an immediate critique of a McCarthy speech because of legislative business. But when Queens GOP boss Frank Kenna asked him to act on reports that Charles and Mary Beard of the Columbia faculty were Communist sympathizers, Dewey reacted angrily. The Beards were among America's most distinguished historians, he replied, and in reviewing the other names on Kenna's list, he found one man who had been dead for twenty years, and three "exceedingly fine authors who have never been associated in any way with Communist work." He recalled a time in the 1930s when his own name had found its way onto such a roster, "so having been falsely accused myself, I am suspicious of lists that are so palpably false."[5]

The struggle for the soul of the Republican party had begun and Dewey behaved accordingly. Early in 1951 he asked a friend hoping to draft him for a third presidential nomination to cease and desist. "Wholly aside from my personal choice . . . there are too many old sores that would be reopened to make it a reasonable proposal." Indeed, what was required was circumspection on his part; that, and a willingness to publicly yield the spotlight to others who were trying to persuade the reluctant Eisenhower to come home from Europe. Bertrand Shanley, a national committeeman from New Jersey, was asked by several GOP governors to undertake a holding operation, the upshot of which was Harold Stassen's agreement in writing to serve as a stalking horse for Ike. Dewey had no illusions about Stassen's strength or reliability. "Right now he will be useful as a counterirritant during the present difficult period," he wrote early in December, "and later in winning Minnesota . . . and perhaps the Wisconsin primary." As for his own course, "I intend to continue acceding to his every request for conference . . . even though nobody else in our group trusts him or is willing to talk with him."[6]

In May, Dewey met with another old rival, Jim Duff of Pennsylvania, and the two men agreed to pool their resources in the movement to draft Eisenhower.

A few weeks later, Dewey sent his state party chairman, Bill Pfeiffer, out before reporters to endorse Eisenhower and pledge all ninety-six of New York's convention delegates to the cause. Russ Sprague boarded the bandwagon the same day. But nationally, the Eisenhower campaign was bogged down in petty rivalries, uncertainty over the General's true intentions, and a lack of organized authority at the top. Harry Darby and Frank Carlson of Kansas, Henry Cabot Lodge, Duff, and a smattering of liberal GOP governors all seemed to be working at cross-purposes. In September, Dewey met in Washington with several of the friendly senators. They discussed, among other priorities, Duff's wish that a Washington office be established to coordinate campaign activities. "I think I made some progress," Dewey reported to Annie on September 11, 1951. Soon, Tom Stephens was brought down from New York to oversee the new headquarters, under the nominal supervision of Darby and others.[7]

That same month, Eisenhower told Roy Roberts, who was visiting NATO headquarters to add his own brand of political inducement, that he was "a good Kansas Republican." Roberts wrote home to the would-be drafters, "I think you can get him." But tensions within the Eisenhower camp remained high. In October, Duff flew to Paris to secure assurances from the General that he would at least accept a nomination, and warn him that if he failed to run, the party would find itself rent by another Taft-Dewey showdown, with Taft the likely winner. Taft himself was making halfhearted efforts to cultivate his old foe. "How in the world can I placate Mr. Dewey?" he asked Tom Curran and Lowell Wadmond at a University Club lunch that fall. "Can I promise to make him Attorney General or something? Would that do it?" Wadmond said he doubted very much whether Dewey could be bought off with any appointment.[8]

Taft tried the direct approach. He denied a recent report that he had been secretly pleased by the 1948 results, telling Dewey late in October, two weeks after announcing his own candidacy, that no election had ever been more of a disappointment of him. He could afford to be gracious. An NBC poll of the 1948 delegates put him far out in front of Warren, Eisenhower, and Stassen. The Democratic National Committee forecast his nomination on an early ballot. On December 8, Guy Gabrielson, acting in concert with the pro-Taft Republican National Committee, revealed that all the key posts at the Chicago convention, including rules, credentials and platform assignments, would go to Taft supporters. Best of all from the Ohioan's viewpoint, the Eisenhower movement remained fractious and disorganized.[9]

Dewey moved forcefully to put an end to the drift. Early that fall, he invited General Lucius Clay to visit the Roosevelt Hotel. When Clay arrived, he found Brownell and Sprague already in Suite 1527. Discarding preliminaries, Dewey said he wanted to know what Clay thought of the possibility of an Eisenhower candidacy. For his own part, the Governor was convinced that Ike was the only Republican who could regain the White House in 1952, "if we could get him to run." Clay was dubious. If no strong organization existed, and if no genuine popular demand could be shown to the General, he thought his old friend's answer "would be a very positive no." Clay did agree to meet with Dewey's cohorts Duff, Lodge, Darby, and Barak Mattingly, as well as Brownell and Sprague, on November 10.[10]

That session, again held at the Roosevelt, produced a campaign manager in the form of Henry Cabot Lodge, a New England patrician whose previous allegiance to Willkie and Vandenberg freed him of any onus as a Dewey man. Dewey himself preferred Mattingly, but gave in to Duff's insistence on a better-known candidate. "You're the manager," Dewey now told Lodge. "You tell me what you'd like me to do." Before the meeting broke up, plans were made to open a headquarters at the Commodore Hotel in New York. "And don't forget," Darby recalls Dewey saying, "let's get a hell of a lot of money." Harold Talbott promised to do just that. So did John Hay Whitney. Sig Larmon of the Young and Rubicam ad agency joined the campaign to handle publicity. Elliott Bell lent Gabe Hauge to do research and compile a dossier of Eisenhower's previous statements. Hauge also established an economic intelligence unit along with a statistical group. Dewey seized on an encouraging Gallup poll and urged Lodge "to rub this in by mailing it to all the Republican workers" in thirteen states, a suggestion Lodge thought "a ten-strike."[11]

On November 13, after the Roosevelt meeting but before the formal announcement of Lodge's appointment, Dewey rejoiced in news from Paris passed along by Bill Robinson, and he wrote Helen Reid, owner of the paper Robinson edited, "Two months of grief have finally culminated with what I hope will be success before the week is out." It may well have been a reference to Eisenhower's attitude in the wake of his meeting with Taft ten days earlier, at which the two men failed to reach agreement on the principle of mutual security and NATO's unique significance to international cooperation. According to Milton Eisenhower, this was the turning point in the road that led his brother away from military life and toward a political career. Brownell agrees: "Taft could take the insolationist route. That was the whole thing. Nothing else had any appeal to Eisenhower at all." On New Year's Eve 1951, Eisenhower in Paris called to his side a military aide. He wanted to know what it would take "to get Mamie and me back home." Of course, if the aide wished to come along too, they would be delighted. If he wished to complete his tour of duty, then that, too, would be understood.[12]

At the end of September 1951, Dewey had attended the annual governors' conference at Gatlinburg, Tennessee. When it concluded, he filed a report on the presidential preferences of each Republican there. He was worried, he said, about what he called "this 'but' business," the reluctance of many governors to commit themselves to a man who hadn't even given permission to his own supporters to enter his name in the upcoming primaries. He hoped that Lodge, about to embark on another diplomatic mission to Paris, might be able to correct this. Meanwhile, Dewey considered himself a bridge between the governors and the draft-Eisenhower amateurs. He continued to shun center stage. "So far as I am concerned," he noted when Duff pressed him for his own man at Washington headquarters, "I will take Mickey Mouse if only he's undeviatingly loyal, has unlimited enthusiasm, and will work all day and all night with the people who know how to do the job." In later years, while acknowledging that "there were more self-appointed ambassadors in this particular operation than any other I ever saw," he credited Clay with doing most to bring Eisenhower around.[13]

Still, the draft movement lagged. Late in December, Dewey wrote another secret memorandum. "The time has finally come when I must regretfully impose myself upon our Friend," he noted, almost certainly to Clay for transmission to Paris. He was not worried by Taft's current lead; December promises tend to "evaporate in June heat." At least half of his own supporters in forty states "are still with us." Many more were sitting on the fence, awaiting developments. The early polls out of New Hampshire were almost too good, "and I have proposed that some opposition be artificially stimulated," to raise the stakes and generate headlines. "After many nerve-racking experiences" with the Wisconsin primary, he continued, "I want no part of it." Wisconsin should be left to Stassen. He was "shocked" at the assumption that Ike would enter Oregon, since "Once people talk you into entering these primaries they then start crying bloody murder for you to come out and save the bacon when the going gets rough."

Dewey dismissed as "hysterical" the demands made in weekly conferences for an immediate public announcement from Paris. Instead, he proposed, "solely on my own" that in New Hampshire "a brother should . . . by January 15 answer a letter of inquiry from the Governor . . . concerning party affiliation. A very gracious but clear and flat reply can be given, with assurances of ultimate knowledge of our Friend's views that, of course, he adheres to the principles of the Party and always has. The next day I propose that our Friend answer a newspaper query about the letter by saying: 'My brother has never misrepresented my views' or something of that kind—but no more." Such a statement would "galvanize the movement and . . . stop dead in its tracks any opposing bandwagon. The politicians will stop to look and listen." As to those pressing for an immediate declaration of candidacy, Dewey pugnaciously wrote, "I insist with equal vigor that the one thing the American people want most is the one thing they cannot get."[14]

On January 6, 1952, Lodge released a letter being sent to Governor Sherman Adams of New Hampshire in reply to Adams' own inquiry of prospective candidates. Assuring Adams that Eisenhower was a Republican in sympathy with "enlightened Republican doctrine" and that the General would indeed "consider a call to political service by the will of the party and the people to be the highest form of duty," Lodge threw Ike's hat in the ring precisely as Dewey wished. Reporters pressed for the General's personal feelings about all this. "Ask him and see," Lodge replied. The next day, a statement issued in Paris said that Lodge had given "an accurate account of the general tenor of my political convictions and of my Republican voting record." Eisenhower also stipulated that only "a clear-cut call to political duty" would persuade him to forsake "the vital task to which I am assigned."

"The announcement was a smashing success," Dewey concluded five days later. Taft's "sniping and smears" would undoubtedly be accelerated, but to little effect. As for his own stance, "I plan to continue to stay completely in the background." His people did not. Brownell and Sprague went to work for Eisenhower at a January national committee meeting. Dewey himself encouraged an Oklahoma publisher to keep up the pressure on Ross Rizely, the publisher's counsel, and member of his board of directors as well as of the credentials committee in Chicago. He persuaded a delegation from Hawaii that the General was interested in the Pacific as well as Europe. He kept up negotiations with Stassen, even after the ambitious Minnesotan entered the New Hampshire primary on his own. He sent Mattingly out to California to soothe Earl Warren's bruised feelings after one of what he scornfully called "the bandwagon boys" threatened the proud Californian with political oblivion unless he went along with Ike's crusade. He denounced Taft's withdrawal from New Jersey's primary as "pretty shameful" and thanked his Alabama friend Frank M. Johnson (later the judicial architect of integration in George Wallace's state) for news that two delegates from that state's Seventh District might be counted upon. He listened to faked reports of gloom from Tom Stephens in New Hampshire, and fretted with Clay and others over the precise timing of Eisenhower's return. "God damn it," Clay exploded at one lugubrious meeting, "we've been telling this man we can do this and we can do that—the time has come when we have to call on him to do it."[15]

On February 16, Clay secretly met with Eisenhower in London (the General was in town for the funeral of King George VI). Before leaving, he extracted a promise that Ike would in fact come home at the right moment and take personal charge of the preconvention campaign. But as the weeks went by, and Taft seemed as strong as ever despite losing in New Hampshire and a towering Eisenhower write-in in Minnesota ("I am doing everything within my power," Dewey wrote on March 29. "Certainly, it was not gremlins who wrote his name on all those ballots in Minnesota"), Dewey himself changed his mind about the necessity for prompt action. Frustrated and uncertain about his candidate's stomach for the battle, he hit on a unique incentive. He wrote out in longhand—no copy was ever made—for transmission to Paris a warning that, unless Eisenhower gave an immediate signal to his supporters back home, Douglas MacArthur might well sweep the convention. A week later, on April 12, noting that "circumstances of my personal life have markedly changed," Eisenhower asked to be relieved of his military command.[16]

Ed Jaeckle dropped in on Dewey late in March. "I don't think your candidate's doing very well," he needled the Governor. He would know better himself in a few days, Dewey replied. Brownell was in Paris talking with the General. "Cabot Lodge had no experience in this area," Dewey said afterward of the original campaign manager. "He had great charm and great intelligence, but this wasn't a field in which he had much experience." Brownell, the obvious choice to assume command of the delegate hunt, was reluctant to do so. For one thing, he had promised his law firm not to engage in further politicking. He had also witnessed firsthand the rifts between Eisenhower's early supporters and shied away from deeper involvement unless given a free hand. But Dewey continued pressing him to see Eisenhower, and on the heels of the victory in New Hampshire, Brownell finally consented.[17]

Ike was already being briefed by Lucius Clay. "I keenly realize," he wrote Dewey on March 18, "that I am of no particular help in all the matters of policy and decision with which you people are continuously faced. But I feel . . . that as long as I am performing a military duty and doing it with all my might, I am possibly providing as much ammunition for your guns as I could in any other way." When Ike and Brownell met for the first time, they enjoyed a wide-ranging talk. They discussed the mechanics of a presidential campaign, scheduling, speeches, platforms, and organizational needs. Social Security came up, along with race relations and budget cuts. Eisenhower got out correspondence from others who had urged him to run, and he asked for background information from the well-connected Brownell. He wanted a better fix on Dewey's own position. The talks went well; anticipating such results, Dewey advised Eisenhower to get in "some last few games of golf and . . . some rest, which will stand you in good stead later."[18]

When a friend wrote in mid-April to complain that the draft campaign was going poorly and to urge Dewey to take a more active role in it, the Governor was able to report that Brownell was finally in charge of the delegate search. (He told Annie that his old friend was performing "superlatively well.") Contrary to the public impression, "I have been working like a Trojan, but quietly. It is always better, when there are so many involved, to avoid arousing jealousies, and this I have succeeded in doing, meanwhile giving what I believe has been effective organizing work."[19]

On April 22, New York Republican voters went to the polls and elected an overwhelming pro-Eisenhower slate of delegates to the Chicago convention. Dewey had personally selected most of the delegation, which was heavily populated with county chairmen and state committeemen. He had called upon the 135 Federation of Women's Republican Clubs and 140 Young Republican chapters for help in subduing Taft forces in Erie, Westchester, Orange, Rockland, and New York counties. Low turnouts were a tradition of New York primaries, but wherever his forces were on the defensive, Dewey made certain they flocked to the polls. "The organization must have voted the cows," commented Hamilton Fish, himself defeated in his bid for a seat on the delegation. In Buffalo, Harry J. Forhead saw his carefully chosen slate of organization men go down in a 3-to-1 rout at the hands of gubernatorial allies. When Forhead a few weeks later attended the state party's annual $100-a-plate fund-raising dinner in New York City, he found himself seated behind a pillar.[20]

The main speaker that night was Richard M. Nixon, the fresh-man California senator best known for his role in exposing Alger Hiss. Nixon spoke forcefully, without notes, arguing the need for a Republican candidate in 1952 to attract millions of Democratic and independent voters. When he was finished, Dewey stamped out a cigarette and took Nixon's hand. "That was a terrific speech," he said. "Make me a promise; don't get fat, don't lose your zeal, and you can can be President someday." Later that evening, Dewey in-vited Nixon up to his suite. There, the Senator learned of Dewey's interest in him as a possible vice president. According to Dewey, Nixon implied in response that he would be "greatly honored." The Governor then made certain he was introduced to both Sprague and Brownell. "I thought he was a fine speaker," he explained later of his choice. "He had a very fine voting record in both the House and the Senate, good, intelligent, middle of the road, and at this time it was important to get a Senator who knew the world was round. . . . His age was a useful factor. He had a fine record in the war. Most of all, however, he was an extraordinarily intelligent man, fine balance and character."[21]

While laying plans for the Republican convention, Dewey con-tinued to spread the alarm about Communism. In the spring of 1952, he was putting finishing touches on *Journey to the Far Pacific*, which, following its publication in June, became a bestselling ac-count of the Governor's sixty-day Asian trip of the previous summer. The book was deceptively genial, a series of thumbnail sketches of foreign lands and colorful leaders. Dewey noted how the President of Vietnam liked to be accompanied to state dinners by his pet ele-phant, how American troops in Korea enjoyed talking about dairy farming over a glass of beer, and how shrewdly poor Taiwanese housewives bought pigs as a hedge against inflation. "There are no blacks and whites in the incredible complexities of Asia," he wrote, "as in the best Chinese paintings, there are only various shades of gray."

Yet Dewey seemed to regard Indochina as a black and white case of Communist aggression. He believed a wave of terrorist attacks in-spired by a northern Vietnamese Marxist named Ho Chi Minh in December 1946 to be the genesis of France's resolve to commit over 100,000 soldiers and a sixth of her national budget to the defense of the chunky, sharkskin-clad emperor Bao Dai. Dewey noted how even Saigon's zoo, once teeming with life, was reduced to a single sad-looking elephant. "Perhaps," he concluded, "when human beings fall out, honest animals keep their freedom."

In long private talks with the electrifying French commander in Vietnam, Jean Marie de Lattre de Tassigny, Dewey heard the Viet Minh described as natural-born guerrillas. De Lattre taught his distinguished visitor how the followers of Ho lived off the land, relying on propaganda, subversion, and corruption of local officials as preludes to military action. "This is the critical fight of the world," the General told Dewey. If Indo-China were to fall to the Communists, then all Southeast Asia would follow. India would be threatened; Japan might starve for lack of food and raw materials. Dewey echoed the message in his own book. "The crisis today is in Southeast Asia. . . . Wherever we have undertaken treaties assuring collective action in advance, there is no war. Peace has thus far been preserved by strength. In the Pacific we have done only patchwork jobs, and that area is racked by five wars."

Dewey's prescription was a mutual defense treaty, similar to NATO. It entailed risks, he acknowledged. But in times like those, "the only question is where lies the greater risk: in building united defense now or in waiting until catastrophe strikes? . . . The torch fell from our hands after the First World War; it must not fall again." He never ceased to believe in the rightness of America's mission in Southeast Asia. Even when Secretary of Defense Melvin Laird persuaded him to try to pressure the Nixon White House in 1969 into moving forward with Laird's Vietnamization program, under which American ground forces were extricated as responsibility for the actual fighting was transferred to South Vietnamese soldiers, Dewey was only exercising the good lawyer's prerogative, choosing the larger good over personal preference. The larger good, then as always, lay with the Republican party.[22]

Eisenhower returned to Abilene, his Kansas boyhood home, on June 4. In a stilted homecoming speech delivered before television cameras, he sounded a bland call to national faith and cooperation "in an atmosphere of goodwill and confidence." He told reporters that he was opposed to a national Fair Employment Practice Commission—FEPC ("I do not believe we can cure all of the evils in men's hearts by law"), and struck a hesitant note in remarks dealing with labor relations, farm price supports, and Korea. Taft cracked that after a few more such performances the General, if nominated, would prove "as weak a candidate as Dewey turned out to be." The immediate problem was simple: Eisenhower's folksy charisma was inhibited by a formal text. Ten days after his dismal Abilene performance, he roused a Denver audience with a high-voltage display of impromptu speechmaking—much as he had impressed Dewey at Columbia in 1947.

"Hosannah," his most prominent backer wired that night. "The speech was magnificent and rung every bell. I repeat—I hope you never use a text again."[23]

But the momentary success of Denver could not obscure Taft's rapidly accumulating delegate strength, nor the disadvantages faced by Eisenhower in his long-shot campaign. Absent from the country and its political debates for much of the previous decade, his ignorance of domestic matters was embarrassingly plain. He was hamstrung from attacking the State Department by his own leading role in Truman's European policies. A Gallup poll published on May 2 showed his greatest appeal lay with independents—who preferred him over Taft nearly 4-to-1—but independents would have little voice among the party regulars who gathered in Chicago the second week of July. Clearly, something dramatic was needed to shift the focus of the contest. On May 27, something happened, in Texas.

Three weeks earlier, 75,000 people, the largest GOP turnout in the state's history, had clogged living rooms and precinct caucuses. Many were Democrats or independent voters, who endangered regular control of the party even as they boosted Ike's chances in his native state. "I'd rather lose with Bob Taft than win with Eisenhower," grumped Party Chairman Henry Zweifel, who ran the Taft steamroller over Eisenhower forces at the state convention in Mineral Wells on the twenty-seventh. Zweifel chose to overlook the fact that almost all the newcomers had agreed to sign a loyalty oath, promising to support whomever the party nominee might be. He chose instead to decry the Eisenhower backers as captives of the New and Fair deals, labor, internationalists, the CIO, "and left-wingers so far left that the Texas Democrats don't want them." The executive committee agreed, carefully tossing out all but nine of 519 pro-Eisenhower delegates before going on to award the delegation to a so-called "uninstructed" slate. The GOP, boasted Zweifel, had been rescued from "mob rule."

A bolt was inevitable. By the end of the day, two opposing delegations claimed to represent Texas Republicans. Each clamored for recognition from the national party. David Ingalls and Carroll Reece fought the Taft fight in Mineral Wells that day; Herb Brownell was there for the Eisenhower forces. Brownell never forgot the tactics used by regulars to disenfranchise pro-Eisenhower voters. "They just didn't count the vote," he said nearly thirty years later. "They changed caucuses to houses across the street. . . . It was a crude, rough deal. They'd been doing it since the Civil War. Taft's father did it before him. . . . The idea that the public should be allowed in a Republican caucus was unheard of in places like Texas, Mississippi, Alabama."[24]

Recognizing the threat posed by Texas, Taft called upon the national committee "in a judicial atmosphere and with the calm judgment required to reach a legal and equitable determination," to examine the merits of both sides in the dispute. Eisenhower himself found the offer attractive. But the olive branch was followed within twenty-four hours by a lunch at which Dewey, Lodge, and others stiffened Ike's resistance. A moral outrage was required if Taft's lead was to be reversed, and Texas was the best shot going. Lodge, for one, loftily rejected any settlement. "It is never right to compromise with dishonesty," he said. Soon afterward, Eisenhower left for a Southern tour, where he talked of "rustlers" in Texas who had flouted majority rule, "the very basis of free government." Cries of "steamroller" and "theft" filled the air. Herbert Hoover found himself rebuffed after proposing that the matter be settled by a panel of three "eminent citizens," himself included.

Meanwhile, Brownell was reviewing the record and rules of the 1912 convention, and devising a plan to prevent any contested delegate from voting on any business until the entire convention affirmed his right to sit on the floor. Dewey told a group of his old racket busters that Brownell's plan, by shifting delegates away from Taft to Eisenhower, would tip the scales in favor of the General. Taft fought back; he called on Eisenhower to condemn George Marshall for the loss of China, and verbally pummeled what he called "the New Deal wing of the Republican Party." As if anyone needed to be told the specific target of his criticisms, Taft publicly identified Dewey as the real mastermind behind the Eisenhower campaign. Dewey pronounced himself "highly complimented."[25]

"Things look steadily better for Eisenhower," he wrote Annie on June 26, just prior to departing for Houston and the annual governors' conference, "and I think we have a slight edge. The Taft people will not control the voting. They just control the mechanics of the convention, and I think we can beat them even on that score." The governors convened at the Shamrock Hotel in counterpoint to the national committee's debate over contested delegations from

Texas, Louisiana, and Georgia. On June 30, Dewey met with other state executives in the hotel room of his New Hampshire colleague Sherman Adams. Some of those present wanted an outright endorsement of Eisenhower. Others held out for a more cautious approach, convinced that if fewer than the thirteen Republicans who earlier had protested the Texas "steal" now went public for Ike it would reverse momentum. Dewey outlined the parliamentary strategy devised by Brownell, and the rules change that would deprive Taft of crucial early support at Chicago.[26]

In the background, Wisconsin's Walter Kohler and Nebraska's Val Peterson sought the proper high moral level on which to pitch at least a protest against the alleged Southern thievery. Once the meeting broke up, Dewey and Governor John Davis Lodge retired to Kohler's room to hammer out just such a statement. Others contributed their own phrases, until Adams and Peterson felt confident of obtaining near-unanimous support. Even Taft's supporter J. Bracken Lee of Utah signed the document (without bothering to read beyond its pious, uncontroversial first page). His price: a share of the public glory dished out at a joint press conference with Dan Thornton of Washington that was called to announce—erroneously at the time—that all twenty-three Republican governors approved the "Manifesto of Houston." The governors' declaration argued that their party would enter an already difficult campaign under a black cloud of suspicion unless popularly elected delegates reflected the actual preferences of those who sent them to Chicago.[27]

Dewey went further still, holding that if illegally chosen delegates were permitted a hand in selecting the candidate, then the nomination would be no more valid than William Howard Taft's in 1912, "which was achieved by similar tactics." The manifesto was released to the public on July 2, one day after the national committee, yielding to the demands of Taft's manager, Clarence Brown, forbade television cameras from covering the debate over Texas and other contested delegations. Foolishly, one Taft supporter blamed the ban on Dewey, who immediately fired off an angry telegram insisting that cameras be let in "so the American people can see and judge the scandalous way Taft delegates were chosen here in Texas and elsewhere. . . . Let the people see and hear the evidence. Any other course would do irreparable injury to public confidence in the integrity of the party." Taft dismissed the telegram, and bristled at Dewey's allegations that he was condoning a "Russian dictatorship" in the national committee. "No one has been a more ruthless political dictator than Governor Dewey when he had the chance," the

Senator sputtered. Simultaneously, fresh rumors were circulated by Taft supporter John Hamilton that Dewey would place Eisenhower's name in nomination. Lodge stepped in to slap down the reports.

Tom Coleman, another Taft manager ("If Taft had had one good manager instead of four lousy ones," said Lodge, "he might have won"), accused General Motors and Ford of pressuring Michigan's Arthur Summerfield, (one of the state's largest auto dealers) who held the key to that state's uncommitted delegation. He said that Pennsylvania's Governor John Fine, also neutral in the Taft-Eisenhower fight, was being dictated to by the Mellons. In New York, a rump anti-Dewey faction calling itself the "Committee for the Preservation of the Integrity of the Republican Party" sent out letters to all the Empire State's delegates censuring the Governor as a me-too Republican. Two Harlem delegates, miffed over Eisenhower's failure to support FEPC, staged a brief rebellion. It was put down when Dewey reminded one that his livelihood depended on a $4,000-a-year job with the Board of Elections, and the other was called home by the sudden death of his daughter—his place to be taken by a pro-Eisenhower alternate.[28]

"I have come to carry water," Dewey modestly informed reporters who met him at the Chicago airport on July 3, "run errands and help in any way I can." He dismissed reports of dissension within the New York delegation; the New Yorkers, avowed their governor, would "do the right thing" when the time came. At his hotel, Dewey found more evidence of the bitterness generated by the battle. Draped over the door of his suite was a bedsheet and a sign identifying it as a "Dewey-Lodge Crying Towel." Outside, brochures were being handed out in the streets of Chicago urging delegates to reject "Ike the Kike, financed by Phooey Dewey's international bankers." On the fortieth floor of the nearby Hilton, Brownell, Bill Rogers, and a battery of lawyers were collecting testimony for presentation to the credentials committee, and plotting strategy for the floor fight sure to follow rejection of their case in the Taft-dominated committee. Brownell, like Sprague, had been in the city for ten days already, choosing Sherman Adams as Ike's floor manager, cultivating ostensibly uncommitted power brokers and giving more than a stray thought to a running mate for the General. His agenda for victory included a series of procedural votes leading up to adoption of the critical rules change.[29]

On Sunday night, the sixth (with an AP poll showing Taft leading Eisenhower in delegate strength, 533 to 427), Lodge convened a meeting to debate a name for the amendment, now rewritten slightly to preclude voting by any delegates objected to by one-third of the national committee. Lodge and Brownell favored TR's old slogan, "Square Deal." Then Hugh Scott piped up. What about "Fair Play"? he asked. "After all, who could be against fair play?" On a vote of 28 to 2, the motion was adopted, and while a fruit-less meeting aimed at compromise went on until two-thirty in the morning in William Knowland's suite, the Eisenhower forces sharp-ened their weapons for the key test to come Monday morning.[30]

It was a night of high drama and blunt orders. John Fine told the big Pennsylvania delegation, "This is the way I want it," in in-structing a vote for Fair Play. Dewey was more direct still at a caucus of the New York delegation, which had shown signs of restiveness all weekend. Earlier in the day, a reporter had asked the Governor how things were going. "There are a couple sons of bitches in this delegation," Dewey replied, "I'd like to give mickey finns to." Now, for two hours, the New Yorkers were told that honor was at stake as well as loyalty. Oswald Heck called the upcoming vote a clear-cut choice between a "clean convention" and "fraud." Dewey himself denounced "the rape of the Republican party that went on in the national committee." Where moral suasion failed to persuade, hardball tactics were employed.[31]

He would be governor for two and a half more years, Dewey re-minded the delegates, "and remember that." Bill Pfeiffer reinforced the argument, telling those assembled that he and the Governor had "good memories." Dewey called the roll, inviting each delegate to identify himself and the number of state patronage jobs at his dis-posal. Once all seventy-five completed their reports, he coolly in-formed the group that a vote against Fair Play would result in a dis-appearance of such jobs. "There's not going to be a split in this delegation. . . . If you think that Taft has a steamroller," Dewey chortled, "wait until you see our steamroller operate." The head of Monroe County's delegates, Fred Parrish, told Dewey later that he was uncommitted. "I've already committed you," the Governor in-formed him. Lowell Wadmond, a Manhattan delegate friendly to Taft, listened for most of one afternoon to the Governor's blandish-ments, until Wadmond in exasperation asked his old friend if he wasn't taking himself "a little too seriously." A Brooklyn court em-ployee told Wadmond he wished he could be equally indepen-dent—but he had to eat. From Dutchess County and Harlem came words that state jobholders, fearing for their paychecks, were calling wavering delegates in droves.[32]

The tensions gripping Chicago were pervasive. Dewey tried for hours to find Tom Curran, his secretary of state, who had deliberately stayed away to avoid such pressures. "My God," he finally gasped, "you better figure out how to get a hold of him or he's going to be an ex." John Wayne jumped out of a cab to shout at an old mess sergeant in an Eisenhower sound track, "Why don't you get a red flag?" Taft supporters marched in the streets singing "Onward, Christian Soldiers." On Monday morning, after hours of haggling failed to produce a settlement of the disputed delegates, Guy Gabrielson brought down his gavel, and a complex circling of each camp finally led to the showdown vote on a move by Clarence Brown to exempt seven Louisiana delegates from Fair Play. Taft lost, 658 to 548; Dewey announced the New York vote as 94 to 2. Backtracking, the Credentials Committee opened the doors to TV before voting to seat Taft supporters from Georgia, Florida, and Mississippi. It was a temporary victory for the Ohioan, susceptible to the will of his combined opposition on the convention floor. The Fair Play amendment had been adopted, and Taft almost certainly deprived of nearly seventy delegates from the reliable Southern boroughs.[33]

There was a gory majesty to the proceedings, a fearful courage and a sense of history being made as Dewey and his allies finally broke Taft's twelve-year-long siege of the Republican citadel. The strategy was working. On Monday night, New York delegates boycotted Douglas MacArthur's leaden keynote address. Sprague said it was "unfortunate" that the pro-Taft general had been scheduled to speak just as an important Eisenhower strategy session was convening. Told that MacArthur's eloquence had failed to stir the crowd, Dewey replied, "That's good!" and said his own advice to Taft would be to surrender. At the Hilton's Suite 1102, registered in Lodge's name but host to the strategy team dominated by Brownell and Sprague, Jim Hagerty monitored reports from former Dewey staffers in the D.A.'s office sent out to infiltrate the enemy camp. Dewey himself, to make certain that his forces would be heard should convention microphones suddenly go dead, sent out to a Pennsylvania firm for fourteen bullhorns. On Tuesday afternoon, he got into a verbal fight with John Conway, twice his campaign manager in Louisiana and now one of the Taft supporters threatened with expulsion under Fair Play.

"Damn it, Tom," Conway pleaded, "you can't vote to throw me out."

"Are you with us or against us?" Dewey demanded. Conway failed to persuade his erstwhile hero.

On Tuesday, the fighting moved to the trenches. Sprague discovered Frank Kenna of Queens under a bleacher stand with Dave Ingalls, and denounced Kenna as an ingrate. In fact, Kenna may have been calling Ingalls' bluff, telling Taft's cousin that his eight-member bloc was willing to support the Ohioan only if Taft forces could guarantee seventeen votes within the entire delegation. Armed with this knowledge, Sprague made a deal of his own. If he could disprove the Taft claims, then Kenna would join Dewey in supporting Ike on the important vote over Georgia's delegation on Wednesday night. One New Yorker later recalled seeing Dewey and Kenna engaged in heated discussion as the Governor demanded a list of all seventy-one jobs in Queens allocated by his own patronage men. "That's it, Frank," Dewey told the county leader after being handed the list, "Think it over and give me your answer very shortly." Finally, Kenna capitulated, receiving a warm handshake from Dewey in return. Taft's hopes for a split in New York were fading.[34]

Overkill by his supporters accounted for much of Taft's loss. Attacks on the Governor that spread through the convention hall infuriated many of the New Yorkers, including Fred Bontecou, who until Wednesday was honestly undecided. "He's a son of a bitch," said Bontecou of his 1938 running mate, "but he's my son of a bitch. Put me down." Outside, loudspeakers sang a tune called "Poor Blind Ike." Inside, Dewey apologized to his fellow delegates for the tiny caucus room assigned them prior to the Georgia vote. "This is the way we're being treated at this convention," he muttered, before asserting that the vote on Georgia was now a test of personal standing. He had been called "a thief" by the other side, Dewey raged; those who voted Taft's way on Georgia would be voting to approve such tactics. Lowell Wadmond disagreed, saying that he had always supported Dewey. To prove it, Wadmond now offered a resolution that passed unanimously, reiterating support for the embattled Governor. But Dewey refused to be put off with kind words. He wanted the votes, committed and irrevocable. Before the caucus broke up, he had them. By a margin of 91 to 0, with 5 abstentions, Dewey's control was reaffirmed. Russ Sprague had won his bet with Kenna. Westbrook Pegler was beside himself with anger. "This Dewey," he wrote, "who was such a mincing, falsetto campaigner . . . is manipulating Taft right out of his nomination . . . with Ike just standing

around and doing as he is told and wondering what it is all about."
George Sokolsky called Dewey "a new Mark Hanna."[35]

Within the Taft organization, a new debate broke out. How
should Everett Dirksen, assigned to argue Taft's position on Georgia, treat the issue? It was decided to try to, in the words of partici-
pant Ray Bliss, "soften up Dewey," who was looked upon by Eisenhower's foes as the General's chief shield and defender. Break
Dewey, engulf the floor in a controversy over his alleged dictation,
and not only wavering New Yorkers but other delegates raised to a
fever pitch of resentment might bolt Eisenhower's ranks. Dirksen
took the advice. That night, he reached out to his "good friends
from the Eastern Seaboard" and asked them to "re-examine your
hearts." Staring down at Dewey, who sat well below and to the right
of the podium, Dirksen shook his finger at the Governor. "We followed you before and you took us down the path to defeat."[36]

Before the sentence was out of his mouth, Dirksen was bathed in
waves of protest and approval. In the Ohio delegation, Taft supporters were booing their hated foe lustily. A fist fight broke out in
the Michigan delegation, most of whose members booed Dirksen for
his slur upon a favorite son. A New York alternate fainted and had
to be carried off the floor. Turmoil swept the galleries, where guests
of the convention stood on chairs and shook their fists, screaming at
the little man who sat imperturbably, with the faintest trace of a
smile pursing his lips. "Sit down, sit down," people yelled at Dirksen, while the aisles were jammed with indignant Republicans and
photographers swarming around the New York standard in hopes of
an emotional display by the offended party. Wayne Morse was already there, having rushed over from his place with Oregon's contingent to vent his outrage. "He's not hurting me," Dewey murmured in reply. "He's hurting himself." With a cold stare fixed on
Dirksen, and the din around him reverberating in millions of homes,
Dewey called to mind the words of H. L. Mencken about another
controversial broker at an earlier convention. "He did not sweat. . . .
He did not puff," Mencken wrote of the senior Henry Cabot Lodge
at Chicago in 1920. "He did not fume. It was delightful to observe
the sardonic glitter in his eye, the occasional ill-concealed snort, his
general air of detachment . . . and behind the voice . . . the sneer."

A friend later interpreted Dewey's "happy look of assurance" as a
fearful rebuke to his opponents. Happy or not, his confidence was
well placed. Before the night ended, Eisenhower's position on Georgia prevailed, 607 to 531, and Jack Porter's friendly slate from Texas
was formally seated. At 2:35 A.M. on Thursday, a weary, embittered

convention went home for a few hours' sleep and a final dosage of vitriol before closing the door on Robert Taft's presidential aspirations.[37]

Overnight, the tempest winds surrounding Dewey reached hurricane force. On Thursday morning, a broadside signed by David Ingalls and issued by the Taft Committee singled him out for stinging attack. "SINK DEWEY!!" the poster-sized flyer proclaimed. "End Dewey's Control of Our Party. Eight Years of *Deweyism and Defeat.*" In a shower of abuse, the Taft command called Dewey "the most cold-blooded, ruthless, selfish political boss in the United States today. He stops at nothing to enforce his will. He is the greatest menace that the Republican party has. Twice he led us down the road to defeat, and now he is trying the same trick again, hidden behind the front of another man." Old resentments surfaced, of "the same old gang of Eastern internationalists and Republican New Dealers who ganged up to sell the Republican party down the river in 1940, in 1944, and in 1948." Fair play, according to Ingalls, "is only a two-word phrase to the Dewey boys," who practiced slander and vilification behind a screen of sweetness and light. The Governor of New York had meant "only sorrow and defeat" for the GOP; not until Dewey and Deweyism were crushed once and for all would the party be safe from New Dealers "whatever their party label."

That night, in another calculated affront, Taft's name was placed in nomination by Dirksen, and seconded by a rebel from Manhattan. Richard Neville decried Dewey as "the Pied Piper who has led us to defeat time after time." Two husky Taft supporters loomed menacingly close to Dewey as Maryland's Theodore McKelden nominated Eisenhower. They were turned aside by Johny Crews, just as someone asked the New Yorker how it felt to be a whipping boy.

"I don't mind it at all," he replied, a smile creasing his face. "It's been going on for fifteen months. We're going to win, and that's all that counts." Boos welled up from the galleries when Dewey rose to announce New York's vote on the first and only ballot—for Taft 4, for Eisenhower 92. This time, however, the General's supporters were primed to respond, and Dewey answered the cacophony with a smile and a mocking little wave to the crowd. "Here we go," he muttered when Minnesota's Warren Burger sought recognition to switch 19 votes to Eisenhower, sending him over the top. Now Dewey was surrounded by admirers, pumping his hand, slapping his back. He hugged Sprague, Pfeiffer, and Ives, pronounced the result "wonderful," and ignored jeering Taftites as he hurried out of the hall to the Blackstone Hotel, where Eisenhower's running mate would be selected. Herb Brownell had no such option; standing in an elevator with some Ohio delegates whose verbal contempt for Dewey was rich and inventive, Brownell correctly sensed that the bitterness felt throughout convention week would not soon fade.[38]

Ben Tate, one of Taft's close advisers, had to restrain an impulse to strike Dewey when he caught sight of the New Yorker later in the day. Taft himself was being gracious. Someone urged him to try again in 1956; the Senator said he would be too old by then. He received his victorious rival, who crossed the street in an unprecedented gesture to pay respect to "a very great American."

Taft began the tortuous process of reuniting a badly splintered party; but he did not forgive Dewey. Neither would his spiritual heirs. Twelve years later, Republicans would engage in another violent debate between instinct and pragmatism. In 1964, the rival spokesmen for the party's warring liberals and conservatives would be named Rockefeller and Goldwater. By then, the Republican center of gravity had shifted so far to the right that Dewey, having unsuccessfully attempted to line up delegates for Rockefeller's stand-in, William Scranton, skipped the San Francisco convention that turned into a Goldwater coronation. Eisenhower's victory represented Dewey's zenith. He would never again exercise the degree of power that now led him to the Blackstone to act out a carefully scripted drama leading to Richard Nixon's nomination for vice president.[39]

Nixon may have been chosen as early as May 8, the night of his stellar performance before the New York Republicans. Lodge, attributing it to Nixon's role in the Fair Play fight, says he knew of the selection two weeks before Chicago. "I couldn't think of anybody else who could keep the California delegation in line," explains the pre-convention campaign manager. Bill Pfeiffer, who as Dewey's state party chairman was privy to much of the strategy devised at the Roosevelt Hotel, said flatly that the California senator was "a fifth column" assigned to undermine Warren's position within his own delegation. There is evidence to support Pfeiffer. Nixon had already sent out a poll to 23,000 constituents soliciting their opinion of "the strongest candidate that Republicans could nominate for President." Coming on the heels of California's June 3 primary, this was interpreted as a virtual break with Warren and the Governor's friend and intensely loyal supporter Senator William Knowland. The youthful Senator Nixon had denounced the "Texas grab" as the corrupt handiwork of a small clique of Lone Star politicians, cynically freezing out the public. On the train carrying California's delegates to Chicago from Denver, he could be seen making a strong pitch for Fair Play—an argument successfully renewed at a heated caucus which overrode Warren's wish to split the delegation precisely in half on the controversial rules vote.[40]

With Eisenhower poised only a few votes short of a first-ballot victory, a reporter spying Jim Hagerty on the floor wanted to know why Ike's supporters didn't turn to California, a delegation known to harbor dozens of potential converts. "We don't want them from California," Hagerty replied. The reason why became apparent after the Blackstone meeting settled on Nixon. Eisenhower himself had dined with Brownell the previous evening. "I thought the convention had to do that," the General answered when approached for suggestions on a running mate. Finally, he submitted a list of seven names, including Nixon's. Brownell had already discussed the matter with Dewey and Clay, who agreed that Nixon, as a Westerner of relative youth, with expertise in domestic issues and considerable debating skill, would complement Eisenhower's nonpartisan appeal. By Thursday, the Californian's only real obstacle was his fellow senator, Bill Knowland. Brownell went to Murray Chotiner, a longtime Nixon associate, who nonetheless was managing Knowland's reelection campaign, and secured the none-too-surprising estimate that Nixon would prove a better campaigner.[41]

Ike's nomination was nailed down a few minutes before two o'clock on the afternoon of the eleventh. Before the convention could reconvene at four, two dozen preselected party leaders went into conclave at the Blackstone. Brownell left the room and his place as chairman was taken by Dewey. Senator Alexander Smith of New Jersey proposed Taft. (As Sprague told it later, there was considerable evidence to suggest that Eisenhower himself preferred his defeated rival as a major step toward party harmony.) Taft called to recommend Dirksen, prompting a sour expression from the chairman, and a contemptuous declaration from another governor that "after what he said . . . I wouldn't wipe my feet on that fellow." More names were raised and discarded, including Dan Thornton of Colorado, Earl Warren, and Bill Knowland. Finally, during a lull in the debate, Dewey looked around the room and said, "What about Nixon?" He proceeded to a lucid outline of the Senator's advantages, stressing age and campaigning gifts. Quickly, the rest of the group fell in. Brownell returned and placed a call to Nixon, while Tom Stephens emerged to send word to Pat Nixon to keep a smile on her face for convention hall TV cameras.[42]

In the words of William Rogers, Brownell's call reached a man who was "surprised as hell." If so, then Nixon was as good an actor as he was a politician. The nomination was ratified by acclamation (Dewey had hoped to nominate Nixon himself, according to Pfeiffer, but relinquished the job in light of the intense controversy swirling about his convention-week activities). He could, however, savor a purge of Taftites on the national committee. Chicago had been "pretty rugged," he told a friend who wrote with congratulations, but then everything had turned out "gloriously" in the end. Another convert, scenting the Governor's newfound proximity to national power, urged retaliation against his foes, particularly Richard Neville, whose offensive seconding speech qualified him for "a good shellacking" by the local organization.[43]

Eisenhower wired that he and Mamie were on their way west for some relaxation, and that Dewey likewise should get some rest. "I am still lost in wonder at your performance," the nominee concluded. A few days later, a fuller expression of gratitude arrived in Albany. Eisenhower said it was "amazing" how closely Dewey had kept to his original restriction on public leadership or private guidance. He was similarly impressed with the Governor's effectiveness in New York, where strenuous efforts had been made to challenge his control. "All this is reinforced," Eisenhower went on, "by the fact that you were willing to devote many days and weeks counseling with others and planning—always completely in the background— to bring about the result that was finally attained in Chicago." Another friend expressed pleasure in the outcome, and a happy rationalization. "Thank heaven . . . that the shadow of the presidency has been lifted so that the nation could see the real Dewey again, forceful, smiling, astute and in complete and intelligent charge of the situation."[44]

Other voices were raised in anger. "Mr. Dewey is at best a contemptible person," grumped the Chicago *Tribune*, "animated chiefly by the desire to spoil things for Senator Taft, out of the evident fear that if Taft had his chance before the people, he would make Dewey look as sick as Truman." In Colonel McCormick's opinion, the shame of Dewey's methods was not something to be washed off "with a quick shower." The Colonel began making noises, soon echoed by fellow conservatives Hamilton Fish, Kingsland Macy, and Frank Gannett, about forming a new American party, perhaps headed by McCormick's favorite general, Albert C. Wedemeyer. Such discontent on the fringe might be overlooked. What troubled many Republicans that July was that Taft himself seemed strangely aloof from the developing campaign.

In an account of his defeat privately circulated among friends, Mr. Republican blamed his loss on "the New York financial interests," businessmen "subject to New York influence," newspapers which "turned themselves into propaganda sheets for my opponent," the Republican governors, and men like John Fine, Arthur Summerfield, and, of course, Tom Dewey. "The continuation of the New Deal for four years may not be as tragic," Taft told John Hamilton on August 27, "as putting certain of [Eisenhower's] principal associates in command of the Republican Party for the next two decades." It appeared that Ike's election, Taft noted in an unrelated memorandum, "will . . . put into power a New Deal Republican Administration, perhaps dominated by Dewey. . . . Consequently, a Republican success would probably bring an end to any power that I might have in Congress . . . and I would be forced into a position more or less antagonistic to the Administration."[45]

What rescued Taft from such a bleak prospect was Ike's own failure to arouse the country in the weeks immediately following his nomination. It was like Abilene all over again. "Ike, When Do We Start?" asked the Scripps-Howard papers late in August. The New York *World-Telegram* said Eisenhower's campaign was "running like a dry creek." For the Democrats had nominated Illinois' eloquent and moderately liberal governor, Adlai E. Stevenson, and millions of Americans were soon captivated by Stevenson's charm, his wit, and his proclamation that "we must look forward to great tomorrows." One of Dewey's most trusted informants warned that the General was due for "a pasting" unless there was a drastic change in the tone and tempo of his campaign.[46]

Dewey was more concerned with patching together a winning organization for Eisenhower. He talked with the General by phone, and it was agreed that the national headquarters would be returned to New York from Chicago. Harold Keller was dispatched to put some bite into the candidate's speeches. Stanley High and Merlyn Pitzele, both veterans of the 1948 campaign, joined Keller. So did Jim Hagerty and Tom Stephens, who would later serve in the Eisenhower White House. Bernie Katzen went to Washington to see Ives and Nixon, and then into battle to counter charges of anti-Semitism left over from the savage Nixon-Douglas senatorial fight of

1950. Dewey asked Frank Stanton at CBS to provide data on ad agencies, and Stanton volunteered to round up trade press editors who might confidentially recommend two or three of the best agencies. When Eisenhower's speechwriters came up with the electrifying proposal that he announce his intention to go to Korea following his election, *Time* publisher C. D. Jackson and columnist Emmet Hughes hoped that the speech draft would not fall into Dewey's hands; they feared he might tear it apart. They needn't have worried. Dewey and Ike met that same evening, and the Governor, who had already listened to similar suggestions at Pawling from Ben Duffey, thought the Korean proposal excellent.[47]

On September 12, Taft and Eisenhower had breakfast at Columbia University. In a memo composed beforehand, Taft indicated that his support for the ticket might rest on assurances that Dewey would be kept out of the cabinet, that Taft supporters would receive fair treatment in the scramble for federal positions, and that the federal tax collections would be held below the $60 billion level by the second year of the Eisenhower presidency. When the General seemed to accept most of Taft's agenda, critics in the press labeled their meeting "the surrender of Morningside Heights." Adlai Stevenson said it meant that "Ike would be in the White House, Taft in Blair House, and Dewey in the doghouse." Dewey seemed to pay little attention to the controversy. His advice to Eisenhower to stay out of McCarthy's Wisconsin went unheeded, to be sure, and the General found himself in the distasteful position of endorsing a man he privately detested. But good news outweighed bad. The campaign was finally jelling. Ike's speeches picked up noticeably, and a pent-up desire for change after twenty years of Democratic rule boded well to overwhelm Stevenson's graceful appeals and sometimes inept attempts at putting distance between himself and those he acknowledged in a verbal slip to bear responsibility for "the mess in Washington." He was "still hopeful," Dewey told his mother on September 16, of a Republican victory in November. Within forty-eight hours, events would shake that confidence, pushing him again to center stage just when rivals thought him confined permanently to the wings.[48]

"Secret Rich Men's Trust Funds Keeps Nixon in Style Far Beyond His Salary."

With that sensational blast, the New York *Post* kicked off on September 18 the Fund Crisis, a warmed-over sensation already rejected by Drew Pearson but seized upon by hungry Democrats as manna from heaven. According to Nixon's own explanation, backed by a detailed accounting, some $18,000 had been collected from seventy-six contributors, mostly Southern California businessmen, to help pay for office expenses, Christmas cards, travel, and other items not covered by Nixon's senatorial salary. Coming from the *Post*, the allegations of wrongdoing might have been dismissed as a partisan jab. But then Democratic National Chairman Stephen Mitchell called for Nixon's repudiation, and the vice presidential candidate himself overreacted in a California whistle-stop, calling the story a Communist smear and reminding voters that his Democratic counterpart, John Sparkman, employed his wife on the public payroll.

On Friday the nineteenth, Nixon learned that the New York *Herald Tribune* and the Washington *Post* were about to print editorials seconding Mitchell's motion. He assigned Bill Rogers to determine Dewey's attitude. Eisenhower campaign headquarters had already received two telegrams from the Governor. The first, fired off the day the *Post* story broke, pleaded the necessity of Nixon's visiting New York to overcome what Dewey called a "smear campaign." On Friday, Dewey contacted Ike's advisers again. "Keep your respective chins up," he advised, "and do not let smears or sniping bother you." Twenty-four hours later, Eisenhower himself said that his running mate would have to prove himself "clean as a hound's tooth," and Nixon phoned Albany to deny the charges and tell his patron of plans for a major speech rebutting the story. Dewey's response was characteristic: He took a poll. On his own, he invited Jerry Lambert to interview a cross-section of Republican voters, and was shortly able to report that fewer than 20 percent of them were disturbed by the allegations against Nixon.[49]

On Sunday morning, Ike left his train at Jefferson City, Missouri, to take a call from Lucius Clay. Despite his own antipathy to Nixon, Clay urged that no action be taken until the candidate could talk face to face with Brownell the next day in Cincinnati. That same day, according to Nixon, he was called by Dewey, who said that he had been in touch with the men around Eisenhower. Except for a couple of friends, Dewey said, Ike's inner circle was "a hanging jury." Yet he also believed that Eisenhower himself had yet to make a decision, and he had a scheme to force his hand. "I think you ought to go on television," Dewey told Nixon. "I don't think Eisenhower should make this decision. Make the American people do it. At the conclusion of the program, ask people to wire their verdict in to you. You will probably get over a million replies, and that will give you three or four days to think it over. At the end of that time, if

it is 60 percent for you and 40 percent against you, say you are get-
ting out. . . . If it is 90 to 10, stay on. If you stay on, it isn't blamed on
Ike, and if you get off, it isn't blamed on Ike. All the fellows here in
New York," Dewey concluded, "agree with me."[50]

Nixon responded that something along those lines was already
being considered. Dewey argued that timing was of the essence.
That night, for the first time since the Fund story appeared, Nixon
talked with Eisenhower. The General agreed to the television speech
but offered nothing else by way of encouragement to his embattled
running mate. The Republican National Committee purchased a
half-hour of TV time for Tuesday night for $75,000, and Dewey told
his mother that the address would settle the issue, once and for all.
As for his own feelings in the matter, he found the Nixon exposures
"disturbing, but I have heard nothing to indicate that he is not an
absolutely honest man who has behaved extremely well."[51]

Here events grow fuzzy, and individual accounts divergent. Nixon
himself wrote with evident testiness of a call from Dewey less than
an hour before he was to go on the air. According to Nixon's account
of the call, Dewey said that a meeting had just taken place of Eisenhower's "top advisers," from which a consensus had emerged that
he, Nixon, ought to use his television time to submit his resignation.
"As you know," Nixon quoted Dewey, "I have not shared this point
of view, but it is my responsibility to pass this recommendation on to
you." Dewey was evasive when pressed for Ike's personal opinion. In
an almost surreal afterthought, he suggested that Nixon also quit his
Senate seat as well. That way, he could win vindication in a special
election. "What shall I tell them you are going to do?" he asked.
Nixon paused. He didn't have "the slightest idea," he finally answered; they could watch the broadcast and discover for themselves.
"And tell them I know something about politics too," Nixon heatedly concluded. Then he hung up.

Dewey did call Nixon, and he had spoken with Eisenhower's advisers. According to George Shapiro, his counsel at the time, the
Governor had taken a call from the campaign train—most likely
from Leonard Hall—asking him to contact Nixon at Ike's request
and persuade him to drop off the ticket at the conclusion of his
speech. Dewey said as much in later years to his friend Dwayne Andreas, and implied that the request to dissuade Nixon from remaining on the ticket came from Eisenhower himself. One who was present when the call was placed to Los Angeles' Ambassador Hotel
says it was made by Alger Chapman, who talked with Bill Rogers
and discovered that Nixon was in an adjoining room "crying his

eyes out." Hearing this, Dewey gruffly took the phone and demanded to talk with the candidate. To believe that he was acting as more than a messenger for Eisenhower's own fainthearted advisers is to overlook the pivotal role he had played in nominating Nixon in the first place, the Lambert poll, his assessment of Nixon's behavior given to Annie, Nixon's own recollections, and the testimony of close associates that, after what one calls "twenty-four hours of indecision," Dewey had rallied to Nixon's side, albeit with undeniable misgivings.[52]

When Nixon finally did go on the air, he delivered a memorable defense. Citing a complete audit of the fund, he called on Stevenson and, by implication, Eisenhower to bare their own finances, and in a maudlin aside, vowed not to return a cocker spaniel named Checkers given to his daughters by an admirer. Off to one side, tense and sympathetic, sat Pat Nixon, owner of "a respectable Republican cloth coat" in place of the minks symbolic of influence peddling in Truman's Washington. Nixon challenged Stevenson to provide details of his own fund collected from Illinois businessmen to supplement state workers' salaries. He went on the offensive against "the Truman-Acheson administration," praised Ike extravagantly—and irrelevantly—as a man who owed nothing "to the big city bosses," and closed by asking viewers to wire their opinions on his status to the Republican National Committee. "Let them decide whether my position on the ticket will help or hurt. . . . Whatever their decision is, I will abide by it."

Cut off before he could give the committee's address, Nixon nevertheless had succeeded in removing the decision from Eisenhower's hands. Hundreds of thousands of wires deluged county and state GOP headquarters. Some 107 committee members replied unanimously that the Senator should remain on the ticket. In Cleveland, Mamie Eisenhower watched the broadcast in tears; even Bill Robinson, hitherto Nixon's severest critic, was converted. Dewey hailed the program as "a superb statement by a man of shining integrity." Russ Sprague chimed in. To oust Nixon now, said the boss of Nassau, would rank as "the crime of the century." Eisenhower recognized the inevitable. He invited Nixon to meet him at Wheeling, West Virginia, the next day, and raced up the plane steps to embrace the young Californian, whom he now hailed as "my boy."

Nixon had done a "fine job," Dewey concluded, privately, before taking a poke at "this business of putting out income tax returns." Such ideas were "a lot of silly nonsense," he argued, which might well prevent the ablest men in the country from ever joining public service. As for the fund itself, Dewey thought it perfectly justified. How else could someone from a large state possibly get his message across to his constituents, or visit them often enough to stay in the Senate? Besides, he confided to a friend, Vice President Barkley charged a thousand dollars a speech whenever he toured.[53]

Nixon could thank Dewey for more than the means by which public opinion salvaged his place on the ticket. "He thought Dewey was about the toughest guy who ever came down the pike," said Bryce Harlow, a fixture of both the Eisenhower and the Nixon White House. For evidence, he needed to look no further than the way Dewey ran the party in New York. Billy Hill, Dewey's veteran ally in the Southern Tier counties, once threatened to castrate Murray Chotiner if he set foot in the state. "To a guy like Nixon," said Cliff White, "this was impressive stuff." So were Dewey's campaign tactics, light-years removed from the tea-and-crumpets gentility of 1948. During a statewide broadcast on October 9, the Governor pointed to a huge blowup of the Alabama state ballot, complete with a Democratic rooster labeled "white supremacy" and demanded to know why Senator John Sparkman did not reject the "Jim Crow banner" of a party turning into "a two-headed monster." Three weeks later, Dewey invited viewers to join him on a tour of "Harry's Haunted House." The elaborate set included closets full of mink coats and deep freezers, skeletons wearing barrels, a foundation laid by big-city machines, and the State Department's own nook housing the ghost of Alger Hiss. Dewey looked into a dusty file cabinet marked "File and Forget," and retrieved a Truman promise of peace in the Far East. He said he didn't blame the President for wanting to forget most of his administration, but Harry's Haunted House, Dewey insisted, was "rotten from top to bottom."[54]

Eisenhower was among those impressed by Dewey's television personality. On October 22, the candidate made himself late for a Brooklyn radio broadcast so that he might finish watching Dewey's televised appeal on behalf of the GOP ticket. When it was over, Ike called what he had just witnessed "the most masterful performance I've ever seen." This was all the more remarkable in light of an incident earlier in the day. Halfway through an exhausting motorcade through metropolitan New York, in which Dewey had peeved Eisenhower with his constant instructions on how to greet upcoming parishes, or where to bestow a smile and wave, the car carrying the Governor, the General, and Bertrand Shanley halted. Dewey turned to a county chairman and asked what arrangements had been made for lunch. It had been canceled, the man replied. Dewey asked if the decision had been made at the Commodore Hotel campaign head-quarters. Actually, the local party leader explained, a slip-up had occurred, and field organizers had made the decision on their own. Dewey exploded, demanding to know on whose authority such an order had been given and why the original schedule had not been adhered to strictly. After five minutes of this, an embarrassed Eisen-hower turned and whispered into Shanley's ear, "Jesus Christ, no wonder he was never elected President."[55]

On November 4, Eisenhower easily defeated Stevenson. Swept into office on his coattails was the first Republican Congress since the ill-fated Eightieth. Dewey waited at the Roosevelt Hotel that night until victory was assured; then he walked over to the Commo-dore, where jubilant Republicans camped out in a ballroom chanted his name during lulls in the returns. "It really does feel as though we have been let out of jail, doesn't it," he told a friend. "At least that awful crowd is going to be out of Washington." He was still glowing six weeks later, remarking, "The air seems a lot cleaner in this country already." From London, Winston Churchill relayed discreet congratulations. "I watched with great interest the impor-tant part you played," wrote the PM, "but I could not say a word until the race was won."[56]

There wasn't much time in which to savor the triumph. Barely had the votes been counted than Eisenhower asked Dewey to join him at Augusta, Georgia, where the President-elect had gone for some rest following the hectic campaign. Eisenhower's call stirred fresh debate among gubernatorial counselors. As Burdell Bixby, then the Governor's secretary, put it, "Ike wasn't asking him to go down there to play nine holes." Bixby listened as Dewey grappled with the prospect of joining the new administration. After a while, he pointed to the lights and buzzers employed to call individual staff members to the Governor's office. If he went to Washington, Bixby reminded his chief, he would find a buzzer on his own desk—with Sherman Adams on the other end.[57]

"That does it," Dewey said decisively. He would wish Ike well. He would hold himself available for occasional responsibilities or advi-sory capacities. But he would not abrogate his three-year-old ban on full-time service in an Eisenhower administration. "Next to you," he told his old friend Jerry Lambert, "I am the most goddamned arro-gant person in the country." Neither of them, Dewey explained, ever worked for someone else; neither would ever be happy trying. On

November 11, three days before he publicly reiterated his refusal to Eisenhower at Augusta, Dewey informed Churchill that he would not be entering the national government, "because I have obligations here in the State."[58]

Did Ike want Dewey in his cabinet? Herb Brownell, remembering Ike's coolness after the day-long campaign swing through upstate New York, says the General was "not anxious" for such a teammate. Yet Dewey told Lillian Rosse after Augusta that the new President raised the chief justiceship, if and when Fred Vinson vacated the position. Dewey asked his family what they would think of such a promotion; and when Vinson died in September 1953, Richard Nixon's presence at a prearranged Dapplemere weekend fueled rumors that he had been authorized to offer the job to Dewey. It may well have been offered; in notes dictated for his autobiography, Dewey scribbled a fragmentary recollection indicating that he had been asked, for a second time, to succeed Vinson. He replied, as he would fifteen years later when Nixon offered him the chief justiceship upon the retirement of Earl Warren, that his was not a judicial temperament. He had no desire to be buried in the kind of monastic scholarship pursued by the justices. "I'm a warrior," he said when Kitty Carlisle Hart asked why he turned Nixon down. "I don't want to be up there judging. I want to be down there in the arena, fighting."[59]

If not Chief Justice, then why not Secretary of State? Lucius Clay was by no means alone in believing that Dewey was Dulles' only possible rival for the job. Early in 1958, with Dulles dying of cancer, Eisenhower invited Dewey, by then happily ensconced in private practice, for an off-the-record chat. It was an almost verbatim repeat of a similar private conversation between Eisenhower and Dewey two weeks after the 1956 election, at which Ike was "edging up" to asking the former governor to take over for Charles Wilson, his departing Secretary of Defense. Dewey then headed the President off before any formal offer could be made. He would be glad to run "a few errands," he assured his host. That would be both "privilege and . . . pleasure." But there was no public office he would possibly consider filling. Left unmentioned was Dewey's own need to earn a living, and the extreme distaste Frances felt for the idea of living in Washington. By the time Nixon offered Dewey his choice of federal positions, Mrs. Dewey was, in the words of a close friend, "so fed up with official life she could vomit." By then, too, Frances was suffering from a fatal cancer.[60]

Dewey didn't merely refuse to take a job in the new administration. He established—and adhered to—a firm policy of never picking up the phone to give the new President advice. "I have no desire," he said more than once, "to be known as the pain in the ass who's telling Ike how to be President." He did meet with Eisenhower on sixteen occasions during the eight-year tenure of the thirty-fourth President, who came to value highly his political insights. Eisenhower was especially pleased in June of 1954, when Dewey dropped by with a plan to lance Joe McCarthy before the Wisconsin senator did irreparable harm to the nation's defense and intelligence community. As soon as the Army-McCarthy hearings were over, Dewey suggested, the President should move "in a dramatic way," proposing establishment of an independent office of investigation, similar to New York's Moreland Act Commission. Seventeen states already had such offices; Ike looked upon the idea with favor. In effect, he said, it would allow him to have an Inspector General for every executive department. "If there is any wrongdoing, I could appoint a commission or commissioner to investigate and clean up the matter fast."[61]

Eisenhower anticipated congressional opposition to the plan, but said he was more than willing to face down those who might resent it on McCarthy's behalf. Eisenhower's reaction to the idea was suggestive of a warming trend between Dewey and the President. When Dewey composed a lengthy memo urging the President to do more in helping Republican congressional candidates in 1954, Ike took pains in a two-and-a-half-page response to explain his own reluctance to add still more to an already "appallingly heavy" schedule. He said that nothing about Truman had so "shocked my sense of the fitting and appropriate" as his predecessor's "barnstorming" while still in the Oval Office. He questioned the historical effectiveness of those chief executives who attempted to transfer their own popularity to others running on the party label. And there was another factor to take into consideration. "After all," Ike wrote, "I am 64 years old." He would do his best to aid the GOP cause, he told Dewey. He would consider "very carefully and prayerfully" everything the Governor had urged. "But I do get impatient with some of these candidates who see no way of getting elected except by getting someone else to do the work for them."[62]

Dewey was "embarrassed," he said in reply. "When I have a point of view to drop into the pot for discussion, I beg of you, please don't bother to answer it, or I will never again express one," he told Eisenhower. "You just have too much to do to answer any letters of mine and I do hope you won't take the trouble." Later that month, Ike

did go to New York to campaign for Dewey's chosen successor, Irving Ives, and to tour the nearly completed thruway. (At one point,
Eisenhower commented wistfully that he thought he'd gone into the
wrong profession; seeing a revolutionary bridge taking shape at
Tappan Zee as part of the thruway system, the chief executive remarked that he should have been an engineer.) When Dewey completed a round-the-world tour in 1955, he was promptly invited to
the White House for a report. He became an infrequent guest at Eisenhower's stag dinners, jovial evenings when the ordinarily reserved
President unloosened with favorite anecdotes and pungent observa-
tions of those in the political world, where he still regarded himself
as a novice.[63]

Dewey was present as Ike's guest for his second inaugural in January 1957. He enjoyed the inauguration parade in the company of
young David Eisenhower, the President's grandson, who insisted on
"shooting" most of the marchers as rebels, until Dewey stepped in
and managed to save the lives of a few. Later that year, Dewey si-
lenced a protesting Republican who was upset at the administration's fiscal policies by advising a look over the shoulder. "I can
prove in five minutes that if Truman was still President," he wrote,
"the budget would be at least $10,000,000,000 higher." He gladly
represented Ike at the 1959 inauguration of the new president of
Venezuela. He thought Eisenhower's handling of the Geneva Conference in July of 1955, where he delivered his famous "open skies"
speech and vowed that the U.S. would never take part in an aggressive war, the crowning achievement of "a master world statesman."
With his own people in so many key positions (Dulles at State,
Brownell at Justice, Tom Stephens the presidential appointments
secretary, Gabe Hauge an economic adviser, among others), Dewey
could hardly take issue with an administration he had done much to
install and staff. He did take pains to disclaim personal influence
with the White House. "I assure you solemnly that I had nothing to
do with it," he insisted to Barak Mattingly when John Harlan was
appointed to the Supreme Court in the fall of 1954.[64]

He shaded the truth. For if he didn't recommend candidates for
the federal bench, then Dewey most certainly had a hand in weed-
ing out ideological undesirables. Ray Bliss asked him in 1966 what
had gone wrong with William J. Brennan, a New Jersey appeals
judge recommended for the Supreme Court by Dewey's staunch political supporter in the state, Arthur T. Vanderbilt. Dewey shook his
head. Looking puzzled, he replied to Bliss, "I don't know. We investigated that guy from hell to breakfast—he just changed on us."

Another justice who "just changed on us" was Earl Warren, who gave Brownell what Bryce Harlow calls "an absolute assurance" that he would be a conservative chief justice. He proved anything but, and Dewey was appalled. He came to regard Warren as Eisenhower's single greatest error, a judicial wrecker who pulled out the very underpinning of what was designed to be a conservative-to-moderate administration. Before he died, Dewey took to calling his onetime running mate "the big dumb Swede."[65]

His own disappointment with Eisenhower's presidency stemmed from the feeling that a great political opportunity had been missed. Republicans were no closer to being America's majority party in 1960 than in 1952, and Dewey and Nixon alike blamed much of the drift upon a president for whom politics was always a distasteful adjunct to national leadership. Eisenhower himself struggled for years to find a word or phrase to accurately describe his own political outlook. He finally settled on "responsible progressive," an awkward compromise that nonetheless encapsuled Dewey's own brand of pay-as-you-go liberalism. In policy terms, Dewey was careful to proclaim his admiration for a president both "brave and bright," for eight years of peace, and six of prosperity. But the sense of continuity with Roosevelt and Truman before him, the reluctance to break sharply with established economic or foreign traditions, and the willingness by the White House to yield the political initiative to others—all this created a dangerous vacuum once Eisenhower left the scene and Nixon failed to attain the presidency in his close contest with John F. Kennedy.[66]

Dewey lived the last decade of his life with the avenging ghost of Republican conservatism triumphant. He had to wonder if he or anyone else would have governed in a way that might have institutionalized more moderate attitudes in the party and the nation. He had learned the recurring lesson of American political history: that generals are far better at giving commands than they are at fashioning majorities.

18

A Graceful Retreat

> They tell me that politics is a disease, and I know that old fire-horses never lose their interest in fires.
>
> —THOMAS E. DEWEY[1]

> It is time to be old, to take in sail . . . leave the many and hold the few.
>
> —EMERSON

"For some reason or other," Dewey mused in early 1953, halfway through his final term in Albany, "I seem to have more trouble and be working harder than I did my first year." Even if he wasn't personally part of the Eisenhower administration, enough job hopefuls assumed that he was a power within its highest echelons and flooded his office with resumés and self-appraisals. Felix Frankfurter was put out when Dewey refused to join his campaign to make Whitney North Seymour solicitor general. He had already recommended Seymour for a judgeship, Dewey replied, and Brownell was warning about an overabundance of New Yorkers at the Justice Department. "I don't share that view," the governor said, "but I am not making the appointments and do not have to live with the complainers."[2]

At home, New York City was indulging in its latest flirtation with bankruptcy, and appealing to Albany for permission to do what came naturally, raise taxes. Dewey's anger was undisguised. After years of "improvidence and incompetence," the stock in trade of bartering politicians seeking "an easy path to popularity," Dewey declared on March 9, the most beautiful city in America was on the verge of becoming a ghost town. Six times since 1945, new taxes had been levied; eight times, existing ones had been increased—all hurrying the judgment day of permanent insolvency. Young Bob Wagner, challenging the inept Impellitteri for mayor, didn't hesitate to join in City Hall's criticism of the state. Dewey retaliated with his favorite weapon, numbers. New York City received two-thirds of all state welfare assistance, he claimed, and 80 percent of all housing subsidies. Aid to education under his administration had doubled—even as the New York school system taught 200,000 fewer students. New York residents in 1940 hadn't received a nickel for public health care; now they were getting $19 million a year.

The city was home to 53 percent of New York's population. It received 53 percent of all state aid. Those suggesting anything else were playing hard and loose with fact. Those who continued to demand more services and simultaneously vote for less taxation were guilty of "the oldest trick of the lowest level of American politics." Dewey refused to call a special session of the legislature to meet the city's cash crisis. Instead, he would await the findings of his own commission studying the structure of municipal government. (When the panel reported in June, the Governor made no secret of his preference for a city manager instead of a mayor.) He was equally scornful of New York's woeful subway and bus system, a political football grown "dirty, rundown and overcrowded." The subways, in particular, were a commuter's horror, a Stygian underworld of screeching, unreliable trains and filthy, often dangerous stations. In March, acknowledging that his efforts were unlikely to be appreciated, Dewey went public with his proposal to create a New York Transit Authority. The city itself, he said, "ought to get out of the bus business."[3]

An even darker corner of New York was soon illumined with gubernatorial indignation. For months now, Dewey's Crime Commission had been probing into a seamy duet involving organized crime and Tammany ward heelers. The old and familiar song played on: judgeships for sale, no-show jobs, salary kickbacks, friendly ties between political bosses and underworld characters like Frank Costello, Tommy Luchese, and Joe Adonis. In June 1953, the commission took dead aim at the New York waterfront, where 40,000 longshoremen serviced 900 piers and docks, and a corrupt International Longshoremens Association sanctioned a heyday of extortion, robbery, and shakedowns. Seven hundred witnesses filled five thick volumes with the sad tale of the decline of America's greatest port. In a business where a single day's delay in turnover cost shipowners $5,000, a lot of owners were willing to pay vast sums to greedy union officers. One fur importer was assessed an extra $70,000 to unload his cargo; perishables like fruit or tulip bulbs were even more vulnerable. Stevedoring companies disguised payoff money as an investment in opposing Communists on the docks. One shipper handed over $11,000 to pay for the wedding of a business agent's daughter. Another union boss was blithely unconcerned about the source of his engorged vacation fund. "You can't go to Florida without spending a lot of money," he informed the Crime Commission.

In three years, cargo theft alone along the New York piers had exceeded $13 million. Combined with antiquated facilities, the inflated cost of doing business in the Port of New York was threatening both its standing and the long-range security of its employees. On June 8 and 9, Dewey presided at public hearings designed to find an equitable solution to the problem. He was reluctant to encourage new regulations. The state already kept a watchful eye over everything "from hairdressers to private detectives," he cautioned. But in the end, a new regulatory board was created, shared by two states (New Jersey as well as New York) in an unprecedented "compact" requiring the approval of Congress. The Port Authority was given additional investigating powers, while the states on their own required all dockworkers to submit to questions about possible criminal records. Three weeks after the Waterfront Labor Act took effect on December 1, dockworkers in a bitterly contested election narrowly retained the ILA over the rival AFL.

There was plenty of evidence to support Dewey's angry contention that the vote was fraudulent, and that the ILA leadership was what he called it, "a ruthless mob attempting to preserve by force . . . power which it gained by force." Six months later, he hailed as "a great victory for decency" the decision handed down by the National Labor Relations Board in Washington overturning the election. Some conditions along the waterfront improved. Others festered in ingrained illegality long after Dewey died. But most of the Crime Commission's recommendations took effect. Minimum standards were established for police departments, along with simpler procedures to force removal of corrupt mayors or police chiefs. A third measure strengthened witnesses' immunity before all courts, grand juries, and legislative or administrative agencies.

This was timely protection. In Washington, Joe McCarthy was riding a crest of national alarm over Communists and Communism. Frances Dewey, her husband reported, was among the tens of millions of Americans following McCarthy's televised investigation of the Army in the spring of 1954. ("Disgusting but, of course, fascinating.") Personally, he felt "terribly sorry" for the parents of G. David Schine, who with McCarthy's chief counsel, Roy Cohn, had undertaken a book-burning expedition to overseas libraries maintained by federal information agencies and was now serving Cohn as "chief consultant" in the hunt for Communist sympathizers in the Pentagon. (To the end of his life, Dewey looked upon Cohn as "the most unscrupulous man I ever met.")[4]

On April 1, 1954, as the Wisconsin Senator dueled with Army lawyers for the mind and soul of the nation, Dewey signed into law a first-of-its-kind fair procedure code. The conduct of investigations, he argued, must be reconciled with the rights of individuals. In "an atmosphere of smears, countersmears, headlines, and fragmentary information," truth was usually the first victim. Henceforth in New York, those subpoenaed were entitled to know the subject being investigated, to obtain a copy of testimony, to be accompanied by counsel at public or private hearings, and to file a sworn statement for inclusion in the record. Anyone whose reputation was adversely affected by testimony had the right to rebut the allegations, either in person or in a sworn statement. Evidence could not be disclosed without the consent of a majority of any investigatory panel. Dissenters were encouraged to file minority reports to prevent "distortion or one-sided presentations."

Most of all, Dewey worried about the effects of McCarthyism on America's standing abroad. In a June 1954 speech in which he asserted that the world had shrunk to the size of an orange, he cautioned against hasty judgments about foreign political practices alien to democracy. After all, he said, if other lands were to judge Americans "by our preoccupation with the stupidities or ... the cruelties of single individuals," the result might be harsh indeed.

The leitmotif of New York City's politics in 1953 was the highly publicized hostility between Dewey and every candidate not enrolled in Republican ranks. When Liberal mayoral nominee Rudolph Halley, distrusted in Albany since his role in the Kefauver hearings, challenged Dewey on the amount of welfare assistance going to the city, the Governor said Halley was as "stupid and ignorant as he is shallow and venomous." Mayor Impellitteri, buried by Robert Wagner in the Democratic primary, was "a pleasant man with a weakness for blaming the State for his failure as mayor." But it was Wagner who most roused Dewey's ire. The Democratic nominee took advantage of a 15 percent increase in rent control ceilings, as well as transit fares that were certain to go up under the Governor's subway plan. Late in the campaign, Wagner asserted in lurid language that one of the most important men in the country had intervened with Dewey on behalf of Joey Fay, the convicted labor racketeer serving a lengthy sentence at Sing Sing. "I always thought the boy was stupid," Dewey cracked, "but I never before thought he was crazy."

Wagner said no more about the charge, but his relations with the Dewey administration were never more than cool. Later, after he took office in 1954, the new mayor came to see the state's chief executive. He brought with him a proposed municipal budget and funding plan for the Governor's perusal. Dewey scanned the documents for a few minutes. Then he stretched out one arm to dangle them over a wastebasket while with the other hand he took hold of his nose, as if an odor of impossible foulness had suddenly filled the room. Wordlessly, he dropped the city's financial package into the basket. Wagner and his budget were dismissed.[5]

Even as Dewey fought vainly to elect his own mayor in the 1953 election, two embarrassing disclosures touched off a storm of accusation. On August 28, a labor leader was found murdered at a racetrack in Yonkers. In the aftermath, investigators discovered that at least thirty-five employees of the track had criminal pasts. The management acknowledged paying $165,000 over the previous three and a half years to what it chose to call "labor troubleshooters," and Dewey shut the place down pending a complete examination of all eight of the state's harness tracks. Pitifully inadequate for such purposes was the state's Harness Racing Commission, a three-member part-time board appointed in the days before the sport became a quarter-billion-dollar-a-year industry. In their place, a special investigative group went to work. It uncovered a pastime grown corrupt and corpulent since pari-mutuel betting first was authorized in 1939.

Then a rural pastime, favored by county fair goers, harness racing had mushroomed fortyfold in twelve years. Worse yet, a third of all racetrack stock was in the hands of public officeholders or party officials. The Democratic Senate Minority Leader held a one-half interest in a track. Four GOP county leaders and numerous members of the Assembly owned substantial shares on their own. By far the most embarrassing investor in a business now badly tainted in the public view was J. Russel Sprague. Sprague's holdings in Roosevelt Raceway, although managed by other men, amounted to half a million dollars. His connection with racing, he told Dewey in a public letter dated November 13, was tenuous. Yet it would be "foolish and unrealistic" to overlook public reaction, and so Sprague was tendering his resignation as a Republican national committeeman and terminating a career in GOP politics that neatly bracketed that of Thomas E. Dewey. Only a few days earlier, in an unrelated move, Dewey's state party chairman, Bill Pfeiffer, had decided to call it quits after four years in the job.

Dewey issued a halfhearted appeal to Sprague to reconsider (it's hard to imagine he meant what he said), and then went about the task of reforming the state's racing code. He proposed a single full-time commissioner with the power to impose "sweeping and drastic" controls over the sport. He secured a significantly higher share of racing revenues for Albany; this, Dewey reasoned, would cut down "excessive profits," which led to abuses. Finally, he fought for and won passage of "a draconian measure" that would require the fingerprinting of all track employees, outlaw the closed shop, and absolutely forbid ownership of racetrack stock, by state or local officers, including party functionaries.[6]

"I just got one darn thing finished," he wrote at the height of the racetrack scandals, "and then another comes along. I can never complain that my life is dull." That was precious little consolation for what Arthur Wicks was about to do. Wicks, a dapper sixty-five-year-old state senator distinguished mostly for the cut of his clothes, had once been a Tammany Democrat. Perceiving brighter possibilities as an upstate Republican, Wicks outlasted enough of his colleagues to become majority leader when Ben Feinberg was appointed to the Public Service Commission. Then, when Frank Moore resigned to go into private business, the GOP convert suddenly found himself acting lieutenant governor under terms of the state constitution. On the day he was sworn in, October 1, he chose to pay a visit to Joey Fay at Sing Sing, where Fay was serving a sentence of seven and a half to fifteen years for extorting over $400,000 while an officer of the operating engineers' and hod carriers' union. Dewey learned of the visit, and demanded a public explanation. Wicks replied that his visits to Fay—there had been others earlier, it was revealed—were necessary to prevent labor troubles in his home district (otherwise known as the Kremlin).[7]

Fay was summarily transferred to another prison. On October 8, Dewey and Wicks met privately for four hours ("I always knew he was no good" was the Governor's verdict), following which the Majority Leader let it be known that he would not under any circumstances tender his resignation. "Mr. Dewey didn't elect me Majority Leader," Wicks said. "The Senate did." Dewey announced a special session of the legislature for November 17 for the purpose of electing a successor to Wicks. The Senator fired back, comparing his visits to Fay with those that set the stage for Luciano's deportation. With Wagner's election and Sprague's departure, it began to look as if the Dewey machine was creaking badly. Actually, his fight against Wicks helped reinstate him as the state's leading opponent of graft. "We think the Governor is ruthless in his actions," reported the Oneonta *Star* on October 13, "but we also think he will countenance nothing that smacks of trickery and dishonesty in public administration."[8]

As the date of the special session neared, colleagues tried to persuade Wicks to quit voluntarily. That way, he was told, his appointees might expect to stay in office, a gubernatorial concession to senatorial prerogative. On the morning of the seventeenth, the GOP caucus was postponed. Wicks, it was hoped, might yet be persuaded to fold his tent. When he refused, the lawmakers were ordered to remain in session by the Governor until he had Wicks's scalp and a new majority leader was chosen. On November 19, Dewey got his wish. Wicks was out as majority leader and acting lieutenant governor. But he would be permitted to remain in the Senate, uncensured, and seek vindication from the voters of his district. In his place, Republican caucus selected Dewey's old foe Walter J. Mahoney, twice before defeated by candidates more to the executive office's liking. The battle had been bloody, its outcome mixed. "When something bad turns up, it has to be cleaned out," Dewey explained to a friend, "most particularly in a political party," no matter how difficult or painful the operation. Wicks's own behavior inspired only bewilderment. "I honestly think he enjoyed the publicity of being kicked out," Dewey sputtered.[9]

The next year, the voters of Ulster and Sullivan counties dutifully returned Arthur Wicks to the Senate, where he stayed until his thirtieth anniversary in the upper body. Vice President Nixon sent a congratulatory telegram to the testimonial dinner held in Wicks's honor in 1956, a salute organized by a racetrack promoter. Similarly effusive messages were read from other colleagues from both sides of the aisle. Among the state's leading politicians, only Tom Dewey refused to give Wicks a verbal pat on the back.

For all the frustrations of his third term, Dewey could count an array of solid achievements. Besides the New York–New Jersey compact, he won approval at last from Washington to proceed with state development of the Niagara Power Project. One legislator wondered if the Governor's plan didn't represent creeping socialism, and Dewey, harkening back to TR and Hughes, said any creeping had been done forty years ago. Simple justice, he argued, demanded for New York residents the same access to cheap electricity as provided those in the Tennessee or Columbia River valleys. Even the New York *Post* concluded that his presentation before a hostile congressional committee in July 1953 had been "most persuasive." Later on that year, he won over Eisenhower with the contention that turning over the Niagara to private power companies would be a major political blunder. This paved the way to divide the Niagara project from the St. Lawrence Seaway, and for New York State to achieve the first important step in what would become the Northeast Power Pool.[10]

Dewey won in the courts his fight to establish the New York Transit Authority and, across a bargaining table, the right to keep the bankrupt Long Island Railroad out of permanent state ownership. His Long Island Transit Authority persuaded the Pennsylvania Railroad to invest $58 million in a twelve-year overhaul of the decrepit line's cars and tracks. In exchange for exemption from state taxes and reductions in local levies, the Penn agreed to forgo any return on its first $100 million. Fare increases would result, but at Dewey's insistence they would be 20 percent lower than the figure originally called for by the Interstate Commerce Commission. Upstate, the thruway was leaping ahead through marshlands and hillsides of solid granite. Eighty million cubic yards of earth were moved to build the road, and enough steel installed in 507 bridges along the way to construct a railroad track between New York City and Omaha. Still, at $1,350,000 per mile, the thruway was coming in at a lower cost than major highways in neighboring states. Even before Dewey ceremoniously opened 366 miles of the road in October 1954, property values around the Syracuse section were multiplying tenfold.

Forty-three million passengers traveled the thruway in each of its first three years of operation. By 1964, when Dewey's name was given the highway (Averell Harriman had vetoed a similar bill four months after his predecessor left office), there were a quarter billion trips being made on the 562-mile-long main street of New York. By then, the thruway was flanked by other concrete arteries planned in the final years of the Dewey regime: the Albany–Canada Northway, the Long Island Expressway, and superhighways in the Southern Tier and the Thousand Islands regions. Eisenhower made Bert Tallamy, chief architect of the thruway, his national highway administrator, charged with constructing the Interstate Highway System.

Even the Wicks affair led to something positive as Dewey won enactment of the state's first code of ethics for public officials. New Yorkers, he had said on January 6, 1954, were entitled to expect from their public servants "a set of standards far above the morals of the marketplace." The Governor wanted the legislature to regulate both the business and professional activities of its members, forbid their practicing law before state agencies, and hold an ethical umbrella over party officers as well as public officeholders. In only one major area of interest did Dewey fail to win legislative support. He left office with no plan for compulsory auto insurance in effect. But he did not despair. "That too," he informed Annie confidently, "will pass someday not too long from now."[11]

Poignant evidence of time's passage came early that summer, when Dewey learned that Robert Taft was dying of cancer. The news "appalled" him, he told a friend. Alone and without advance warning, he slipped into Memorial Hospital, where Taft had registered under an assumed name on June 7. For half an hour, the two old antagonists chatted; no controversy was permitted to intrude on this final burying of the hatchet. Afterward, hardly recovered from his surprise, Taft managed a joke. "Tom came around," he told a nurse, "to see whether I am really out of the running." Six weeks later, he was dead. Dewey was among the admirers who donated money to build him a memorial belltower on Capitol Hill, not far from the chamber he dominated and the presidential mansion he coveted in vain. Now it calls him back every hour, a soft chime on the wind in memory of one who pursued principles better than power.[12]

Dewey did not lose his partisan bite. "It seems a sardonic twist of fate," he wrote after Attorney General Brownell raised the specter of Harry Dexter White's White House connections, "that an expression of fact concerning Harry Truman is believed to have done damage to the Administration, whereas for twenty years, every Democrat has been denouncing and lying about Herbert Hoover. The distinction eludes me." When Mayor Wagner pressed for $50 million in new real estate taxes in 1954, Dewey threw the request back in his face. The city's own management survey, he said, had concluded that the New York tax rate should be lowered. Now Wagner was superseding the management experts with a "rump committee" of his own choosing, "the crudest kind of Tammany Hall politics and a clumsy attempt," in Dewey's words, "to isolate New York City from the rest of the state."[13]

On June 3, he told Hagerty at the White House that he would not seek a fourth term. Irving Ives would run instead, Dewey informed his old press secretary, and he would beat young Franklin Roosevelt (at the time the most likely Democratic nominee, and one of whom it was claimed by Johny Crews, "He's as light as a Panama hat") by 400,000 votes. "Sheer nonsense," he said to rumors of his replacing Dulles at State. "After twenty-four years," Dewey went on, "I should like a little private life for a change." The time had come "for me to pass from the scene," he confessed to Clare Boothe Luce. It had been "a pretty rugged summer," Dewey told a statewide televi-

sion audience on September 13. In the broader sense, they had
shared twelve years "of monumental problems and heartbreaks, of
crisis and triumph." Now that it was over, he hoped New Yorkers
might understand and sympathize with his desire to retire from office. His own interest in the cause of good government would never
falter, he reassured them, and he looked forward to participating
vigorously in the campaign to elect a successor.[14]

Two weeks later, Dewey was established in a Saratoga hotel command post, where Jacob Javits discovered him on a daybed, arms
folded, feet up. "Jack," he asked point-blank, "why should we nominate you for attorney general?" Javits replied that he was the only
Republican capable of defeating Franklin Roosevelt, Jr. He chose
his argument well; Dewey detested young FDR almost as much as
did Carmine de Sapio, the state Democratic Committee chairman,
who had, out of bitter personal enmity, refused the late President's
son a gubernatorial nomination. Some thought it a mistake to slot
Javits for the state's top legal post. He should be paired with Irving
Ives, Ed Jaeckle told Dewey, where he might attract Jewish support
away from the Democratic ticket headed by W. Averell Harriman.

With his patrician features and political naiveté (he gave money,
secretly so he thought, to both FDR and Willkie in 1940, only to
have the beneficiaries compare amounts after the election), Harriman struck many observers as the sort of virtuous stiff New York
Republicans usually rallied to. Eisenhower regarded him as a nin-
compoop, "a Park Avenue Truman."[15]

Yet Harriman's very probity made him a safe interruption in Republican government, and an appealing alternative to the Tammany wheelhorses led out in previous statewide contests. Irving Ives
found himself stymied by such a rival. Ives was also bucking a national trend toward the Democrats, and a powerful shadow cast by
the outgoing governor. "A marble block is very good, smooth, and
hard," one Dewey supporter wrote, "but not so hard as a granite
block. That is the difference between Ives and you." Ives was urged
to open fire on Harriman as anti-union and a payer of bribes to secure a twenty-year-old pier lease in New York City. Dewey could use
such language convincingly. Coming from the mild-mannered Ives,
it all sounded merely desperate. The GOP itself was disorganized,
three different state chairmen having come and gone during the previous year, and Dewey's own operatives were scattered into private
niches of government or industry.[16]

By mid-October, Dewey was pessimistic. "We have changed over
from a Republican to a Democratic country now," he lamented to

Annie, "and we might as well get used to it." Anticipating a sharp break in the market, he was soon selling stocks. On election night, he went to Javits, who was trailing Roosevelt, and all but ordered him to concede. Javits refused, contending that upstate precincts were yet to be counted; and an angry Dewey stalked over to Ives's head-quarters nearby. A few minutes later, Javits looked out in the hall and saw Ives on his way to make a concession. "Are you crazy?" Javits demanded. "It's only ten o'clock." Ives said that he was be-hind Harriman by 230,000 votes, and might as well be a good sport about it. Then, miraculously, the trend began to reverse. By two in the morning, Javits was sitting with the other candidates in Suite 1527 when Dewey turned his way, a look of amazement on his face. "Jack, you're ahead."[17]

In hopes of repeating Javits' come-from-behind victory for his candidate, Dewey now impounded every ballot box in the state. It didn't work; Ives lost by 11,000 votes, the smallest margin in the state's history. The legislature was still in Republican hands, and Nelson Rockefeller's election in four years would prove Harriman only a pause in Dewey's electoral revolution. But for now, change was in order. For the outgoing governor, politics seemed remote al-ready. He bought a ten-room apartment on East Seventy-second Street, and enthusiastically wrote Annie of the "hard hitting, able group" of law partners who would make up his professional circle once he left Albany. He busied himself with official housekeeping, deeding more than a million pieces of paper to the University of Rochester, hundreds of boxes filled with the fragments of history to which he had been privy. On November 15, he announced formally his coming affiliation with a New York law firm. Meanwhile, news-papers competed in paying tribute to the man who had filled the governor's office longer than any other New Yorker save George Clinton.[18]

Dewey confronted a far more wrenching farewell on November 23, when his mother died in Owosso. "Mater went the way she wanted to," he wrote, "suddenly and in her sleep in the night. . . . She hoped that if she ever had a serious attack, it would be a com-plete one." Two months later, he told his uncle it was hard to imag-ine she was really gone, "but she was such a wonderful spirit that she will be with all of us who knew and loved her all of our lives." Not long after, he sold the house on West Oliver Street for $11,000. But he could not so easily obliterate memories of the strong-willed woman whom he had loved uncritically.

Years later, Dewey suddenly stopped dictating to Miss Rosse.

"Why didn't you take a picture of my mother?" he demanded, in a non sequitur that Lillian immediately understood. One night in Albany, with both Frances' and the Governor's mothers visiting the executive mansion, Lillian had asked the women to her house. Audie Lee Hutt had accepted the invitation, and stayed long enough to have a striking photograph taken. But Annie Dewey did not go to Lillian's that night; Frances had objected to her mother-in-law becoming close to her husband's professional colleagues. Miss Rosse explained this to Dewey, whose anger cooled. Long after, she thought back to the incident and was reminded of how much mother and son resembled one another. "She was the person he would have been," Lillian mused in 1980, "if it wasn't for Mrs. Dewey and his own vulnerability in public."[19]

Dewey had never ceased to be a lawyer. Now he was back in home port, at the firm headquartered at 31 Nassau Street and known in the vernacular of New York's legal establishment as Root-Clark. Founded by Elihu Root in 1909, raised to the heights of prestige and prosperity by the likes of Emory Buckner and Arthur Ballantine, recommended to ambitious young men by unofficial recruiters like Felix Frankfurter, Root-Clark had more lately entered a period of genteel but unmistakable decline. Grenville Clark retired in 1945. A split within the firm peeled off some of its best talent soon thereafter. John Harlan, its best litigator, was elevated to the federal bench in March 1954. And the Bank of Manhattan, soon to merge with Chase, seemed certain to follow the Chase to its lawyers at Milbank, Tweed.

So when Dewey let it be known in the summer of 1954 that he was interested in returning to private practice, the men at Root-Clark were especially ardent. Not everyone appreciated the new senior partner. Elihu Root, Jr., resigned, and his sumptuous office was assigned to the newcomer. Dewey's name went to the head of a shingle that, after January 1, 1955, read Dewey Ballantine Bushby Palmer & Wood. But whatever offense his high-powered methods might have caused among traditionalists, Dewey soon demonstrated his value to the firm. At the outset, he said he had no intention of emulating other defeated presidential candidates, who were content to lend their names to firms which provided in return a comfortable base for political or literary operations. "I'm going to be a full-time lawyer," he announced. "When people come to see Thomas E. Dewey, he's going to be here."[20]

The promise was kept, and the firm prospered. Around Wall Street, it was rumored that Dewey brought an extra $10 million in business to Dewey, Ballantine. The government of Turkey paid $150,000 for Dewey's services. The Japanese Trade Council signed on, and a lucrative deal divided neatly the legal business of Chase Manhattan between Dewey's firm and Milbank, Tweed. Some of the senior partner's time was devoted to the bank. In other hours, he limbered up his skills as a trial lawyer on behalf of Schenley Industries, Eli Lilly and Company, and the State of New York.[21]

The senior partner of Dewey, Ballantine was a working lawyer and administrator. Nature had not equipped him to be a sage. Most mornings, he was behind his desk by nine-forty-five, ready to review important cases or welcome new associates until lunch, which usually was at the Recess or some other suitably fashionable downtown address. In the afternoon, he took a twenty-minute nap. Dewey kept his promise about devoting himself exclusively to the work at hand. He refused to join outside boards or serve as an at-large delegate to a 1966 state constitutional convention. Those seeking a political entree to Washington were politely ushered from his office. He was usually out of the office by six, sometimes carrying an old Parisian cane that could turn into a sword as protection against a would-be assailant.[22]

For the first time in his life—aided immeasurably by his generous share of the firm's profits—Dewey did not have to worry about money. He died worth more than $3 million. When a fire destroyed several outbuildings at Dapplemere in July 1955, Dewey was determined to rebuild, whatever the cost. The farm had been their home for too many years, he told his eldest son, "to go through the wrench of a change now." When he and Frances attended the opera these days, it was as Rudolph Bing's personal guests. They became friendly with the Duke and Duchess of Windsor, dining out with the royal exiles in New York and getting lost en route to the Windsors' well-concealed mansion in Paris' Bois de Boulogne. Travel was one of the most pleasant indulgences they allowed themselves.[23]

In October 1955, they visited young Tom in Rome, where he was on leave from the Army, and they spent five weeks in Europe. "Nothing will ever convince Frances that I am a gay boulevardier," Dewey informed Lowell Thomas after a visit to Paris. Scotland's shimmering lochs, he concluded, were "more famous than their beauty warrants." France seemed "just a little dirtier, the people a little more grasping," than before. "Something has certainly died in

France," he declared in the fall of 1957. "The people like an unstable government, so they can pull it down any day it does something they don't like."[24]

On the other hand, Dewey was enchanted by the Taj Mahal. He took advantage of a lunch with Prime Minister Jawaharlal Nehru to invite Gandhi's disciple to visit the United States. He had praise for Nehru's "charming daughter," and felt a warmth for the PM that later years eroded when he decided that India's crusading advocate of nonviolence was less than entirely faithful to his tenets. "The world's biggest racketeer" was the way he put it. His overseas journeys contributed much to Dewey's satisfaction with his lot. "Bix," he said to his former Albany secretary, "aren't we glad I didn't make it?" The allusion to 1948 was all but unspoken. "This way, I'm the head of a great law firm. That couldn't have happened if I'd been President." Bixby saw his boss's contentment. "Now he had everything he'd been denied," he recalled. "He was making a very handsome living. He didn't have to respond to the press. He didn't have to run all over hell's half-acre. He had great personal joy without great stress."[25]

For Frances, great personal joy was infrequent in the post-Albany years. She would be happy soon, a friend prophesied near the end of Tom's term as governor. Her husband would belong to her, her sons, and her mother-in-law once more. And Frances' own "patient, long-suffering contributions" would someday be noted. "Without you," her friend wrote, "what would Tom ever have done in the gray and difficult hours?" But her sons were now adults ("How I wish we, too, had a daughter to announce her engagement," she told a prospective bride's mother), and New York City was an aimless sequel to the hectic official schedule of the Executive Mansion. Her family caused worry as well as pride. Young Tom married Ann Reynolds Lawler, a daughter of Westchester who shared his passion for the golf links and proved an admirable mother to his children. ("That girl's a gem" was the verdict from Ann's ordinarily astringent father-in-law.) Prior to their marriage in September 1959, Tom settled into a promising financial career at Kuhn, Loeb Company. His brother was less decided about a vocation. John Dewey impressed those who knew him as bright, curious, and argumentative. He allowed his father to steer him toward a legal career for which he had little taste, only to rebel and spend the last years of the elder Dewey's life as a kind of buttoned-down edition of the 1960s' alienated young.[26]

The Governor stood over John, tearing each page of the boy's

Princeton thesis from a typewriter as his son raced to meet an extension deadline. Frances worried about John, sided with him in family disputes, appreciated his passion for music over law, and silently cringed in restaurants when John and his father got into heated arguments. "It has really been a really wretched summer for me," she told her brother in August 1959, a few weeks before Tom, Jr., was wed and his brother enrolled in Harvard Law School. Her ailments persisted, and unable to take several medicines, frustrated no doubt by the empty hours and cruel disillusionment of her newest life, Frances began drinking more than in the past. Maids from Miss Patterson's Agency returned with disturbing tales of life at 141 East Seventy-second Street. To please her husband, she formally changed her religious affiliation, from Southern Methodist to Episcopal, completing a process of conversion begun in a Chicago music studio thirty-five years before. There were good times; there were also mornings at Dapplemere, increasingly frequent, when a maid found the guest room used by the man of the house.[27]

Dewey and Nixon had struck up a close relationship, and the former governor went out of his way to defend the Vice President against Harold Stassen and others who were after his scalp in 1956. At the convention in San Francisco that summer, Dewey delivered a speech of scathing sarcasm against Democrats worried about American alliances in the world, quoting one of the opposition's own "former favorite authors," Harry Truman, to the effect that the West had never been better positioned to meet the Soviet threat. He also seized the opportunity to settle an old score. When Everett Dirksen rose to address the convention on its second night, a small, dapper-looking man left his seat in the New York delegation and proceeded to stride the long central aisle that divided the Cow Palace, pursued all the way by television cameras.

Later that same night, Dewey appeared in the Fairmont Hotel office of the convention's arrangements chairman, Meade Alcorn. "Tom," Alcorn said, "that was a long walk you took tonight." Dewey smiled grimly. "I've been waiting to take that walk for four long years," he said.[28]

In November, voters bore out Dewey's prediction of a 10-million-vote margin for Eisenhower over Adlai Stevenson. At the same time, New York Republicans faced a continuing political vacuum. From time to time, rumors circulated that Dewey might be willing to return to Albany. He topped other prospective gubernatorial contenders in a January 1958 poll of GOP voters. His name turned up frequently in the headlines, as in June 1957, when he delivered a strong pitch for a permanent program of foreign aid. Only with such an American investment, he told a University of Rochester audience, could mankind avoid "the planetary shambles of a nuclear war." A few weeks later, Dewey was in the news again, lunching with a minister of the government of Ghana who had been denied service in a Dover, Delaware, restaurant because of his color. He became chairman of an American Bar Association commission on international law, and his known influence in Washington and on Wall Street made him a continuing power in Republican politics[29]

But he had no intention of leaving the good life at 31 Nassau. Another man, with formidable resources of his own, was more interested in taking the helm of New York Republicanism. Dewey and Nelson Rockefeller had known each other casually for twenty years. The Rockefeller family had been a mainstay of GOP finances long before that. But Dewey harbored disturbing memories as well as gratitude. Three times during the 1952 campaign, he had been called upon to deflect Nelson's attempts to carve out an important role for himself in Eisenhower's campaign apparatus. Two years later, top Republicans laughed off the idea of Rockefeller succeeding Dewey in Albany, and Dewey himself advised Rocky to forget the whole thing in 1957. As Rockefeller later recalled before a group of New Hampshire Republicans, "When I decided to run, I went to see Tom Dewey, and I told him of my plans. He slapped my knee and laughed out loud and said, 'Nelson, you're a great guy, but you couldn't get elected dogcatcher in New York.' "[30]

Following his victory, Rockefeller unfurled an administration that bore financially only the faintest resemblance to Dewey's. The state budget quintupled, to more than $8 billion by 1972. "I like you Nelson," Dewey once remarked, "but I don't think I can afford you." Dewey was aghast at Rockefeller's methods of funding grandiose building projects like the Albany Mall, brilliant subterfuges in which independent agencies (or, in this case, Albany County itself) acted as surrogate spenders for the state. The inveterate foe of bond-floating looked on in horror as his expansive successor created autonomous extensions of state government like the Urban Development Corporation, endowed with authority to bond for hundreds of millions of dollars until it nearly collapsed in a pool of red ink after Rockefeller left office.[31]

Governor Rockefeller himself was capable of resentment when reminded of the way things had been done under the last Republican administration. "I don't want to hear what Tom Dewey did," he finally told one persistent reminiscer. For his part, Dewey tried to give Rocky a free rein. "It's Nelson's show now," he said, turning down invitations to attend the legislative correspondents' dinner. He lent Burdell Bixby to run Rockefeller's 1962 re-election campaign, and kept to himself his disapproval of the Governor's decision to remarry in 1963 following his divorce from his first wife. It was Rockefeller's private life, he told a friend, and one never knew the motives behind private actions. Four years before, when Rockefeller was sounding out national opinion before deciding whether to challenge Nixon for the 1960 presidential nomination, Dewey was among those he consulted with at length. (Rockefeller had made the right decision in leaving the field to Nixon, Dewey said afterward.)[32]

His support for Rockefeller in 1964, when Nixon was out of contention, was open and strong. He was especially pleased with the Governor's excellent civil rights record. He personally enjoyed Rocky more than Nixon, whom he regarded as a more commanding figure in the field of foreign affairs. In 1968, when both men contended for the prize, Dewey managed to stay publicly noncommittal. Privately, say close friends, he favored Nixon—which didn't prevent him from funneling outside contributions to the late-starting Rockefeller campaign. When the former vice president defeated both Rockefeller and Ronald Reagan on the first ballot at the Miami convention, Dewey found a way out of the dilemma posed by having two presidential candidates from his own backyard. He suggested Rockefeller for Nixon's running mate, an idea that was brushed aside in favor of Maryland's Spiro T. Agnew.[33]

Dewey looked upon John Kennedy as a young man of considerable charm and little qualification to be president. A friend passed on the news that JFK had been seen in an exclusive New York restaurant with actress Angie Dickinson; Dewey wasn't surprised. Everyone knew, he said, that Jack Kennedy ran around with dozens of young girls. Doing anything about such knowledge was quite another thing. "That's the one thing you can't discuss in a campaign," he remarked to Miss Rosse. "It will boomerang on anyone who tries."[34]

In between speeches for the Nixon-Lodge ticket in which he termed Kennedy's foreign politics naive and accused the candidate's brother Robert of injecting religion as a campaign issue, Dewey stumped for other Republicans as well. Sitting alone at the back of a room in which an Oregon Senate candidate and his advisers were discussing the latest poll results, he suddenly piped up, "You may recall that I don't have much confidence in polls." When Kennedy won, Dewey offered Nixon a job with his law firm. In the first week of the new administration, he caused a stir at the Kennedy Justice Department by proposing creation of a federal agency outside Justice to ease anti-trust laws governing foreign investments by American firms. Kennedy had a different idea of American assistance to developing lands; the Peace Corps was born two days later.

For all his partisanship, Dewey sympathized with the young President's attempts to limit nuclear testing. No matter what the frustrations, he told a friend at the time of his sixtieth birthday in March 1962, negotiations toward such a ban would have to continue with the Soviets, "in the hope that their own increasing internal problems will lead them . . . to respect the peaceful aims of the West and gradually quiet their belligerency. Among other things, some day the Chinese are going to give them enough to worry about so that they can stop worrying us, perhaps." His own attitude toward the Russians was less broadminded; he refused permission for a visiting Soviet delegation to tour Dapplemere.[35]

On November 21, 1963, the Governor of Nebraska publicly urged Dewey to seek the White House in 1964. "If anybody is going to tie William Jennings Bryan's record," Dewey cracked, "it will have to be Adlai, not me." The next day, he was due to meet Nixon for lunch, followed by a weekend on the golf course. John Kennedy's murder put a halt to the plans.

The new President, Lyndon B. Johnson, took a liking to the diminutive New Yorker, in so many ways his polar opposite. Dewey reciprocated, regarding Johnson as a man he could deal with as an equal, two country boys who had never surrendered rural wiles to big-city sophistication. Dwayne Andreas, Dewey's close friend and a self-made agribusiness millionaire, introduced him to Hubert Humphrey, and the two men hit it off instantly. Dewey insisted on buying Humphrey some new golf shoes, so he'd look presentable on Andreas' course at the Seaview, a resort hotel in Bal Harbour, Florida, where Tom and Frances became familiar faces in the 1960s, and Dewey paid $57,000 for a two-room co-op there in 1968. HHH might be a Democrat, Dewey told his friends, "but he's about the best liberal around." He advised Andreas to get their friend a divorce from Norman Cousins and "the ban-the-bomb, surrender-quickly crowd," and did Humphrey a favor in 1964 that sealed a friendship still largely hidden from public view.[36]

Dewey considered Bobby Kennedy a dangerous man, a vicious upstart who was unqualified to be Attorney General and was determined to force his way onto Lyndon Johnson's ticket as vice-president. Complaining of this to Andreas one day in the summer of 1964 ("I see something that terrifies me"), he was urged to take up his complaint with Johnson personally. Reluctant to risk exposure, Dewey finally agreed to see LBJ in private late one afternoon a few weeks before the Democratic convention opened in Atlantic City. "If there's one thing I know something about," he told the President, "it's conventions, and I tell you, Bobby can stampede this one." Look at the convention schedule, he went on. The first day was "Kennedy day," what with Jackie there and Bobby there, and a movie on the life of the late President to be shown. "It'll be a real tearjerker," Dewey counseled Johnson. "And then they'll go out and stampede the convention." The President was not blind to the danger posed. Picking up the phone, he told Marvin Watson, then his top political operative, "You move Kennedy day from the first day to the last day." When Humphrey won the vice presidential nomination, he wanted to know how to repay the favor. Dewey replied that he'd appreciate a chance to comment on federal judgeships before they were filled—not select them, he hastened to add, just be asked for his views. That, he added to Andreas, was something he thought he could do "for the country."[37]

In 1965, a few months after his inauguration for a full term, Johnson was pursuing Dewey with an urgent request of his own. The President had in mind a national crime commission, with Dewey to serve as its chairman. First, however, he solicited advice on crime in the District of Columbia. Dewey talked with Attorney General Nicholas Katzenbach, who did little to allay his fears of the time commitment such a job would entail. Johnson turned on the charm, saying in a letter dated May 19, 1965, that he was "hoping and praying" for a positive response, and adding in a handwritten postscript, "I know I can work with you for our country and our children and I want to do so—don't let your partners say no." On June 17, Dewey was at the White House to discuss the matter with the President himself. Johnson employed every trick in his legendary book of persuasion to change Dewey's mind about chairing the commission. Flight after flight back to New York was missed, cocktails and discussion took the place of an evening at home, and it was insisted that Dewey must spend the night. Dinner wasn't served until eleven o'clock. After a hurriedly prepared meal, the First Lady escorted her unexpected guest to the Lincoln Bedroom, a toothbrush in one hand and a pair of her husband's oversized pajamas in the other.[38]

In the morning, the barrage of entreaties began anew. When Johnson finally requested his opinion of capital punishment, Dewey saw an escape hatch. "I'm for it foursquare and 100 percent," he proclaimed. Soon after, he managed to slip out of the Oval Office. But he continued to correspond with the towering Texan, writing scornfully in November 1965 of "confused" Americans who pressed for a withdrawl of U.S. ground forces from Vietnam. The President, wrote Dewey, was "everlastingly right" in pursuing his course of military action against North Vietnam's guerrillas. "Every President before you has had to resist . . . the confused and the treacherous in doing the right but sometimes unpopular thing. You are doing it well and bravely and history will record it." Johnson replied warmly, and a month later Dewey was again his guest at the White House, this time at a state dinner honoring visiting German Chancellor Ludwig Erhard.[39]

In 1964, following the Goldwater disaster of that year, the new GOP chairman, Ray Bliss, had come up with the Republican Co-Ordinating Committee, a round table of past and future party leaders (including Eisenhower and Dewey, Romney and Ford) who would draw up a GOP manifesto and keep up a steady drumfire of criticism at Johnson administration policies. Dewey agreed to serve on the committee, where he rapidly impressed Bliss and others with his grasp of the issues. Dean Burch said he didn't know why Nixon showed up for the group's meetings. Dewey made him look ridiculous.[40]

Some in his circle thought Dewey resented the ingratitude of those for whom his brand of modern Republicanism had built housing and highways and health clinics. More accurately, he was questioning the limits of effective government in a welfare state. Around him there seemed to be only ever-greater grasping for benefits, and more social license. At firm gatherings, he looked more bewildered than critical of long hair and casual dress. He feared for educational standards at the nation's colleges. What saved him from more resentment was his own curiosity; that and a charming permutation. Dewey aged into a man whose hard qualities assumed the aura of eccentricity. He told friends to meet him at the park at 5:03—and sure enough, there they found him, dark glasses and a homburg, his slightly comical protection against recognition. He readily complied with a request for some bifocals from something called the Famous People's Eye Glass Museum. He made a production out of presenting his original dollar-a-year men with silver dollars withheld for thirty years. Earnest as ever about his golf, he didn't blink an eye when British Open champion Archie Campson consented to give him lessons, then informed him he held a club "like a fucking piccolo player." His driving grew worse than ever. "Funny, I never noticed that bump before," he muttered after running over a curb instead of turning right, then left at the light at a Miami intersection. He asked friends to play golf on the Lake Placid course following his address to a judicial conference, and finding congestion at the first hole, drove "like a bat out of hell" in the words of a companion, to the tenth tee. In his wake, a trail of clubs scattered across the entire course marked his path. The cart halted, and one of the men climbed down.

"Governor," he asked, "do you know where our clubs are?"

For the first time, Dewey looked behind him. "I'll be goddamned."[41]

Dewey didn't look back much in the twilight. His autobiography languished, its author unable to summon the same enthusiasm for describing his own life as he had for sounding the alarm on Asia. "I don't know why I'm writing this book," he groaned one day. "No one's going to read it." In the end, it never did get finished. There had been too many honors, too many controversies, too many campaigns, to etch themselves on a memory reserved for contemporary battles. When Kitty Carlisle Hart asked for some pointers in her new job with the State Arts Council, Dewey told her he didn't remember a single thing about state government; it had all washed away. But he was not immune to reminiscence, and he looked forward to reunions of his gangbusting partners, young men no longer young, whose names he was apt to forget without Paul Lockwood at his side to prompt. He dreaded what he called the indignities of getting old, the gray hair and eyeglasses and slowed step. His own health was robust, marred only by an occasional attack of gout or a tendency to develop minor skin malignancies in the sun. As ever cautious, he asked his doctor if it was all right to take a medicinal nightcap of whiskey to help him sleep. By all means, Wilbur Duryee replied.[42]

He reached the age of funeral-going, even as Tom and Ann presented him, in October 1963 with his first grandson, Thomas III. Old faces were disappearing: political allies like Tom Curran and Russ Sprague, elder statesmen like Herbert Hoover, and cherished personal friends from Pawling. Lyn Sumner died in 1953. Charlie

Murphy followed him to the grave six years later. In a shattering double loss, Pat and Marge Hogan died within a few months of each other in 1968. The Hill seemed a community of ghosts now. "I get so lonesome for your father," Dewey wrote Patsy Hogan, "that once in a while I just call Jack up to talk. . . . To me it is almost the same as talking to your father, who was God's leading nobleman to me." One of the younger men from the D.A.'s office moved out of New York City and forgot to send a Christmas card to his old employer. He received one from Dewey anyway, along with a postcard several weeks later wondering why he hadn't heard from him. This, too, he neglected, until a phone call came through one day from Dewey, Ballantine, and the Chief was asking in a concerned voice about his health and status. He was worried, the younger man concluded, and probably lonely.[43]

In April 1964, Frances discovered she was suffering from breast cancer. An immediate operation was followed by months stretching into years of cobalt treatments and gradually diminishing strength. She pledged Tom to absolute secrecy about her illness. Miss Rosse, who paid the hospital bills, was one of the few who guessed it wasn't the polyp removal described by Dewey. Frances herself broke down one night when her husband was out of the living room and told Herb and Doris Brownell the nature of her illness. When he returned, she gathered herself together and went on with a pleasant evening. For the first time in years, she had no complaints of hay fever or allergies, schedules or neglect. It was as if, finally entrusted with a major fight all her own, Frances was calling upon hidden reserves of fortitude. Most days, she stayed in bed, playing cards or Scrabble, husbanding strength before going out with Tom as he entertained business clients or attended the theater. More and more of her time was spent in the sun of Andreas' Seaview, followed by new drugs and doctors' reports. Her husband was solicitous, perhaps a little guilty. He would stay on the phone with her for an hour as she debated whom to invite to their box at the opera. He interrupted his dictation to Miss Rosse to check in with Frances every half hour or so, returning from her bedroom with a grim look. He didn't have to say anything about the TV that was kept going all day, or the open bottle next to her bed; his bewilderment at what seemed like helplessness was expressed eloquently on his face.[44]

"Between the two of us," Nixon wrote Dewey on the eve of announcing his 1968 candidacy, "we should at least be able to come up with pretty relevant conclusions as to how to conduct a presidential campaign."

"Or how *not* to," Dewey replied a few days later. "It might be said that I have a double qualification in that specialty."[45]

Dewey spoke at the convention that endorsed Nixon in July 1968, raised money for the campaign, and supplied counsel on a regular basis to Nixon aides and counselors like Melvin Laird and Bryce Harlow. He confessed to doubts about John Mitchell, the nominal campaign manager. "He may be the best bond lawyer in New York," he said, "but he's no politician." Dewey tried one day to get a message through to Nixon on a campaign train, only to be informed by William Rogers that he couldn't see the candidate himself. He hoped for victory, but acknowledged Nixon was slipping weeks before Election Day. "The candidate has to conduct his campaign at his own pace," he told those who worried out loud about a possible repeat of 1960—or was it 1948? "No one else can make that decision for him." His fondness for Hubert Humphrey may have eased the prospect of defeat. He remarked to Andreas that there weren't five degrees separating Nixon and Humphrey on the political spectrum, and said it was a good thing, too, that in America, "all the votes are still to be found in the middle of the road."[46]

Nixon called Dewey with concern in his voice in the early hours of November 6, when his election hung on late returns from Illinois and Ohio. But Nixon's fears of vote theft proved groundless, and Dewey spent much of the day trying to get through to the defeated Democratic nominee to express his condolences. He might have been thinking ahead to the new administration when he described his own career in public life as that of "a political engineer . . . a conservative facing up to the political facts of life."[47]

"I'm not especially fond of reading about myself in the papers."

Thus Dewey explained the reticence surrounding his role in Nixon's administration. Frances' health and his own distaste for office insured he would never sit on the Supreme Court or at the State Department. Instead, he became an unofficial adviser to the President, joining Dean Acheson on the Foreign Intelligence Advisory Board. He gave his approval to Warren Burger's nomination as Chief Justice in the summer of 1969, after first telling Nixon, "Now Dick, this is the most important thing you'll do in four years." Dewey slipped into the White House often. He was on the phone to Nixon in the early months of the new administration even more frequently. In league with Defense Secretary Melvin Laird, he pressed for the Vietnamization program and a freer hand for Laird himself at the Pentagon. Personally, Dewey told Laird that his cabinet appointment was a mistake—he ought to have been in the White House. As events unfolded, the comment would assume ironic proportions. Another source close to the President says Nixon leaned on Dewey heavily in his first year in office as a counterweight to Henry Kissinger, his national security adviser, who was still regarded with some suspicion in the Nixon White House as a Rockefeller man.[48]

Shrewdly, Kissinger himself cultivated Dewey, sending him unclassified descriptions of Soviet weapons and attending the opera in New York City in his company. Soon, Dewey was calling Nixon's secretary-of-state-in-all-but-name "a genius" and himself nothing more than "a fascinated spectator" to the workings of Kissinger's mind. In April 1970, he was asked to meet with aides to Laird and William Rogers as a prelude to assuming command of an undercover diplomatic mission aimed at retrieving American prisoners of war from the clutches of the North Vietnamese. The idea died aborning once American ground forces moved into the Parrot's Beak section of Cambodia that May. In the wave of protest that swept American campuses in the aftermath of Nixon's "incursion" and which lapped at the White House itself, the President again turned for solace and support to his friend from earlier days. One of a barrage of phone calls Nixon placed in a night-long outreach, before his famous dawn visit to the Lincoln Memorial and protesters camped out there, went to Dewey.[49]

There had been other calls, a great many others, since January 20, 1969, at all hours of the day and night, according to Dewey intimates. But they began to tail off in 1970, when Dewey urged the White House to make inflation, rather than domestic disturbances and Vice President Agnew's strident attacks upon "radiclibs," the major theme of that year's congressional elections. Dewey himself entertained growing doubts about the Nixon White House. After a lengthy call from the President late one night, on the eve of a major policy initiative yet to be decided, Dewey emerged from his study on East Seventy-second Street shaking his head and saying, "That is the single most indecisive man I have ever come across." On visits to Washington, he listened as Rose Mary Woods complained of her isolation at the hands of presidential aides H. R. Haldeman and John Ehrlichman. Dewey told Arnulf Mueller it was "a very bad setup" in the White House, and the more he saw of the men around Nixon, the less confidence he felt in their judgment. The President, too, seemed different. "I don't know what's happened to Dick," Dewey said late in 1970. "He just doesn't listen anymore." Nixon tried to keep the old relationship on an even keel. He invited Dewey to the family's private Christmas party that December, where the older man sang carols and the President played the piano. He sent to New York a volume of collected speeches with a warm expression of thanks for the help Dewey had given him over the years.[50]

In the wake of the 1970 elections, little more than a holding action for Republicans, a movement was launched to purge both Haldeman and Ehrlichman. Five members of the cabinet individually paid visits to Bryce Harlow, who had recently left the White House staff and was known to share the cabinet officers' disdain for what he called "the great macho spirit in the White House, biceps and all that stuff." The message from all five differed only in emphasis: Something was poisoning the atmosphere around the President. George Bush gave a dinner for the cabinet, which was recalled as "a very spleeny affair" by one who was present. Again, criticism of Nixon's chief of staff and domestic policy adviser filled the air. The upshot of all this was a plan to replace, or at least to circumvent, both Haldeman and Ehrlichman with a new chief of staff, Mel Laird. Laird wanted nothing to do with it. He said he wouldn't even consider the idea unless given a free hand in cleaning out the White House staff. This didn't prevent the plotters from proceeding to the next logical step: Who could be persuaded to sell the plan to the President himself? Harlow couldn't, for he was soon back on the White House staff. None of the cabinet members had sufficient clout. Neither did Bush (although the extent of his participation in the whole scheme is cloudy at best).

Someone was needed who was not only genuinely disinterested but who *appeared* disinterested, and tough enough to tell Nixon that he was risking his presidency out of misguided loyalty. A consensus emerged that there was only one man capable of pulling off such a hazardous mission, if he could be persuaded to undertake it. It was agreed that Tom Dewey would be contacted, just as soon as he returned from a golfing vacation in Florida in March 1971. Dewey did not return, alive, and the plan fizzled out. Three years later, Nixon's White House was embroiled in Watergate. Hugh Scott echoes others who knew Dewey well in speculating about his own reaction to such a cancer in his presidency. "Everybody would have been out on their hindquarters within a week," says Scott. "And it would be a week because that's how long it would have taken to make sure he was being fair to everyone."[51]

. . .

In 1969, after a series of radiation treatments briefly raised Dewey's hopes, Frances underwent a second mastectomy. She spent most of that winter at the Seaview, still able on occasion to dance with her husband—a hobby he pursued with relish once out of public office—or join him and friends in singing favorite songs around a piano at Dapplemere long after midnight. Her breath grew shorter as the weeks passed, and her mobility decreased, until it was a chore to climb a flight of steps. In June of 1970, she managed to attend an anniversary dinner at New York's 21 Club. A few days later, she had Arnulf Mueller and his wife to dinner at the farm, before leaving for New York and a hospital bed she knew she would never leave. When the meal was finished, she called her friends to her side. "God bless you, my children," she said. Then she entered Memorial Hospital, where she died on July 17.[52]

"Something very sweet went out of all our lives with Frances," a family friend wrote. Dewey himself, who had had six years to brace for this moment, had told his older son that he was descended from the sturdy stock of Michigan, where farmers sometimes outlived two or three wives. But he could not persuade himself. On July 20, a thousand mourners gathered at St. James Episcopal Church on Madison Avenue for a brief farewell marked by the Apostles Creed and three hymns. It was a simple way to end a marriage of forty-two years, but no less emotional for being unornamental. The Governor sat between his sons in a front-row pew. He made no attempt to brush away the tears streaming down his face.[53]

Pawling residents who happened along Dewey Lane in the months after Frances' death encountered a solitary man, with little to say as he walked over the hill to his fields. Only a handful had ever known how close the couple had been, or how few decisions Dewey made without consulting his wife. Closer friends took calls from him now, as he worked on his autobiography and ostensibly sought confirmation of dates. "That was the last time Frances went to a restaurant," he would say, or "That was the last time Frances had company." He didn't have to be alone, but he seemed to will it. He often let a Chinese couple in his employ go home before he was fully dressed for dinner or the opera. Friends asked him out, only to be refused—he didn't want to impose. A couple of times he organized golfing weekends, but when that sport lost its allure he was prone to sit alone and ask what he could possibly do with himself in the city. Pawling he visited less often; there were too many memories.[54]

So when Kitty Carlisle Hart entered his life that September, Dewey seemed like a new man. They had first met three years earlier, at a fund-raising dinner where Mrs. Hart, widow of the playwright Moss Hart, expressed alarm over her son, who was in Washington for a march on the Pentagon. A year later, they renewed their acquaintance at the same dinner, where Dewey impressed the fashionable television star by asking if Chris Hart had gotten home all right from his protest. Still later, he became her lawyer; and when Frances died, it shouldn't have been too surprising that the lonely widower turned to the dashing widow, who shared his love of music and who introduced him to a side of New York—its opening nights, social glitter, and literati—that he had always been too busy to sample. They went to the movies, something he hadn't done in twenty years, and he sputtered about the unreality of the black comedy *Catch-22*. The army wasn't like that at all, he told Kitty. "Relax," she admonished him, "it's supposed to be funny." They sat on hard wooden benches, the oldest people in the theater, and watched the absurdist Off-Broadway drama *Waiting for Godot*. As usual, Dewey had done his homework; he arrived at the theater knowing more about the play than his sophisticated lady friend.[55]

They talked about John. Mrs. Hart told Dewey to spend more time with his younger son. "Be a father to him." They disputed political issues, she jokingly describing herself as "an old-line socialist" and railing against banks; he replying that without banks none of the housing she thought so necessary to the poor could ever be constructed. She berated some of his actions in support of the Nixon administration, and he cut her off with the abrupt declaration "I'm a party man." In December, he brought her to the Seaview, where her glamorous lifestyle clashed with the athletic tastes of Dewey's friends. She liked nightclubs, they liked golf clubs. But despite frictions within his own family, Dewey continued to see Mrs. Hart. She made him feel alive to New York's esthetic vitality. She made him laugh. Most of all, she encouraged his self-confidence. Returning from Pawling late one Sunday evening, he missed the Triborough Bridge and FDR Drive. Soon Dewey found himself fast approaching the George Washington Bridge and New Jersey on the other side. In the middle of a crowded access lane, he calmly announced his intention to turn around. He couldn't possibly do that, Kitty told him, before sinking down in the car and covering her face in her hands.[56]

Suddenly, she heard people calling out, "Hi, Governor," She looked out the window, and the other cars were halting for them, their drivers waving and wishing well to the familiar-looking man at the wheel. "See," Dewey said after they were headed back in the right direction, "I told you I could turn around."[57]

By February 1971, their relationship had become serious. One day in March, they sang for hours around the piano at Mary Sumner's house on the Hill. "Just one more!" Dewey insisted after each tune. He seemed younger than his years that afternoon. About this time, he proposed marriage to Kitty (among the incentives, he asked if she'd like to become the first "ambassadress" to China), who turned him down. She wasn't willing to give up her career, according to one Dewey intimate. A mutual friend of the couple puts it another way: "She thought his friends were the most boring people in the world, and her friends the most fascinating." Possibly she had never gotten over Moss Hart. Whatever the reason for her reluctance to wed him, Dewey left New York for his golfing vacation at the Seaview determined to change her mind. He went away, Kitty Hart recalls, not a happy man, but an optimistic one."[58]

A few weeks earlier, Dewey had experienced a heart incident, something his New York doctor diagnosed as short of a full-scale attack. At Dwayne Andreas' urging now, he visited the Miami Heart Institute for some tests, which confirmed his basically good health but detected possible warning signs of occlusive vascular disease. Dr. Richard Elias of the institute staff found enough in a thrombosing test to warrant a warning that Dewey should cut out his smoking (something the former governor was reluctant to do, claiming it made him lose his voice); and he wrote a prescription for heparin. This may have prompted a series of impulsive actions, from his proposal to Mrs. Hart, to a request that Bill Rogers consider coming back to New York from Washington to join Dewey, Ballantine.[59]

Frank Hogan reported after a chat with his old friend that the Chief was in one of his sentimental moods, hopeful of convening soon another reunion of the Dewey Associates. On March 13, 1971, Dewey flew north to Washington, to attend the Gridiron Dinner. Earlier, he had secured a promise from Andreas to extract him from the crowded hall no later than eleven o'clock. But he found himself so enjoying the familiar faces and stories that he stayed past midnight, a drink in one hand, exuberant and teasing. Only once did his happy mood dissipate; to Hugh Scott he confessed that the Republican party in this third spring of the Nixon presidency was in "a hell of a mess." Just that week, Robert Finch of the White House staff had asked Dewey to review some of the President's ideas on reorganizing the nation's intelligence system, and serve as co-chairman of a citizen's committee to promote the plan. Nixon himself told a group of women reporters at the White House how Dewey had been the first person to discuss the vice presidency with him, back in 1952.[60]

On the flight back to Miami, Andreas' friend surprised him with a sudden monologue on funeral arrangements. What among his personal possessions, Dewey wanted to know, would he like to have set aside for him in Dewey's will? On Monday, the fifteenth, the two men played golf with Andreas' son-in-law and the younger man's former college roommate, Boston Red Sox slugger Carl Yastrzemski, whom Dewey plied with questions about the game and his own career on the field. The next morning, he called Kitty Carlisle Hart, who was still in bed, and they had a long talk, ended when she announced her intention of going to the television studio where she taped her weekly quota of *To Tell the Truth*. He made sure their Thursday night dinner plans were still set. Then Dewey went out on the golf course. He played good golf that day, managing a rare victory in the dollar-a-match games with Andreas.[61]

After eighteen holes, Dewey suggested nine more, interrupted for a horse's neck and Andreas' cautioning him to put on his hat—he looked a little red in the sun. In the locker room afterward, he turned to his friend and said, "By God, Dwayne, you and I are a couple of damned fools. There's no reason in the world why I have to sit up there in New York in my office." He insisted on blocking out three golfing trips with his friend. Back at the Seaview, Dewey hurriedly prepared to return to Washington, where he was expected at the White House that evening for the announcement of Tricia Nixon's engagement to New York lawyer Edward Finch Cox. Thoughtfully, the First Family wanted him there to celebrate the occasion. It was 2:30 P.M. when Dewey walked into Suite 711-12 to dress and pack for the flight north. He took a call from Miss Rosse, instructed her on how to answer a message, exulted over his golf game and asked to be reminded to have one of the tests done at the Miami Heart Institute repeated in New York.[62]

At three-ten, he called down to Andreas' chauffeur, Tony Finn, who would drive him to the airport. A bellboy was sent up. He returned without the Governor. Finn, knowing of Dewey's punctuality, expressed concern to Andreas, who called the suite and got no answer. Both men hurried to the seventh floor. Inside suite 711-12, the found Dewey fully dressed, lying on his back on the bed, the victim of a heart attack as swift and massive as the one that carried his mother off in the middle of the night. The phone was in its place, the room undisturbed. His bags were packed. Neatly placed on top of the luggage, sitting on the bed beside the dead man, was Dewey's hat. Even death had not disturbed his passion for order.[63]

Epilogue
"There Goes the Warrior"

> Dreamer, sleep deep,
> Toiler, sleep long,
> Fighter, be rested now,
> Commander, sweet good night.
> —CARL SANDBURG

When Dewey's life ended, so did the dignity he prized. He became autopsy subject #A-30-71 at the Miami Heart Institute, where doctors exacerbated an old and sore spot: Thomas E. Dewey, they reported, was "a well-developed, well-preserved, well-nourished white male" of five feet, six inches in height. A casket could not be admitted through the narrow doorway of Dwayne Andreas' private plane, so the body was wrapped in a sheet and disguised as cargo, the only way to get around Florida's law about transporting the dead and an ironic climax to the career of America's most renowned law enforcer.[1]

In New York, where the news was flashed to the Dewey, Ballantine law firm within minutes, messages of sympathy began to pour in. Herb Brownell called. So did Abba Eban, Nelson Rockefeller, Kitty Carlisle Hart, and the government of Taiwan. A butler who had served on the Executive Mansion staff during Dewey's years in residence left a white mass card. Richard Nixon interrupted the festivities surrounding his daughter's engagement to announce the sad news; in a formal statement, the President said that all Americans were poorer that evening for the loss of "a great patriot" whose "wise counsel" he had found personally invaluable over many years. John Bricker, more distant from office and thus more conversant with honest emotion, said his 1944 running mate was "a great citizen and a fine lawyer, and I'm mighty sorry to see him go." Harry Truman said nothing.[2]

In Owosso, Martha Woodward recalled a classmate who had never missed football practice, and whose perfectionism had a way of interfering with popularity. "He knew all the answers and made us look like ninnies," she said of Annie Dewey's boy. "Some of us didn't like him for that." In Paris, *Le Monde* had a different reaction. It assessed the dead man as "the first important victim of public opinion polls." That night, when Lowell Thomas went on the air, he

639

said it was difficult to do his regular newscast. He had just learned of
the death of a special friend, who in addition to being someone who
could always be counted upon, "especially when the going was
rough," was also the father of modern Republicanism, a lawyer's
lawyer, and "just about the most impressive man I ever knew."
Frank Hogan stressed Dewey's "insatiable curiosity" and quoted
Emerson: "He knew the depth, the draught of water of every one of
his men."

By Wednesday morning, when the body went on view at Frank
Campbell's funeral home, the nation's newspapers were filled with
recollections. Most stressed 1948. Many brushed over the gangbusting, Eisenhower's nomination, and the dead man's historical importance in soldering together a bitterly divided party in the shadow of
Roosevelt's New Deal. All day long, mourners, mostly of Dewey's
generation, filed past his open casket. At one point, a class of schoolchildren were led in to gaze upon the face of a man whose public life
was largely over before they were born. In Albany, the state legislature adjourned in memory of the governor it once resented as a
bully, and black leaders planned a memorial service emphasizing
Dewey's contributions to civil rights in New York. Across the state,
flags flew at half-mast, per order of Governor Rockefeller. Resolutions of sympathy were passed by the legislatures of Texas and
Maine, Washington and New Mexico.

On Friday afternoon, the nineteenth, the polished African ma-
hogany casket, draped with a blanket of red carnations, was carried
to the altar of St. James Church, where Frances had been mourned
nine months earlier. Outside, several hundred New Yorkers stood
under umbrellas as distinguished guests filed into the old brownstone church, with its somber redwood carving and rose window.
Richard Nixon was there, along with Pat and Tricia. So were members of the cabinet like William P. Rogers. Hubert Humphrey
slipped in alone, ashen with grief. In a special section of the church
sat the Dewey men, veterans of the war on crime in the 1930s. Cardinal Cooke sat near John Lindsay. Justice John Harlan could see
Haldeman and Ehrlichman.

The service was short, thirty minutes in all, more musical than
eulogistic. When it was over, the congregation stood and sang
"America" and Kitty Carlisle Hart looked at the flower-covered
casket and thought to herself, "There he goes. There goes the warrior." The President rose, and without pausing to speak to the family in the pew across the aisle, walked down the nave and out of the
church. The rest went to young Tom's apartment nearby.[3]

The next morning, rain still flirted with the city, as a long gray hearse left Campbell's and headed north, toward Pawling. There, a knot of perhaps a dozen local residents stood on a windswept hill just outside of town. No presidential aides scoured the area, no Secret Service men cleared the way or kept back crowds, no senators hunched against the chill. There were just seven pallbearers, all workers on the Dewey farm, the Reverend Ralph Lankler and a couple members of the local press. At eleven o'clock, they caught sight of the hearse pulling in from Coulter Street, slowly making its way back around the steep hill forming the rear of the cemetery, past the grave of John L. Worden, commander of the *Monitor* in her historic clash with the *Merrimac,* up and around the hilltop where a Dewey mausoleum was in progress, then back down again to the public receiving vault where Frances had lain since the previous July.

The pallbearers looked a little uncomfortable in their Sunday suits. Their work-hardened hands showed red as they strained to lift the casket and place it in the vault. The calm was broken by Mr. Lankler. "Eternal God, we are grateful for all good men who have sought public office—not for the power it represents, nor for the prestige it gives—but for the opportunity it presents to serve the people and the public good. . . . We believe, O God, that Thomas Dewey tried to be faithful to the words of your Prophet Micah, who said, 'He hath showed you, O man, what is good and what the Lord requires of you but to do justly, to love mercy and to walk humbly with you, O God.' " Lankler asked that the dead man might hear the words desired by all: "Well done, good and faithful servant, you have been faithful over a few things, now I will set you as master over many; enter now into the joy of your Lord."[4]

A breeze stirred, knocking a carnation from the casket to the muddy ground, where it was picked up by one of the farmhands, who wrapped it carefully in a handkerchief and put it in his coat pocket. " . . . ashes to ashes and dust to dust," the minister concluded his prayer, and the pallbearers stepped forward. Ten minutes after it began, the ceremony was over. The men climbed back into their cars, the hearse set off to return to the big city, and the clouds resumed their leaden watch over the hillside where Pawling laid its dead.

Three months would elapse before Tom and Frances Dewey were moved to a permanent resting place, a granite house of death prepared to Dewey's specifications but never built during his lifetime.

After the interment service, a group of friends and family retreated up Purgatory Hill to Dapplemere, which Lowell Thomas hoped to preserve for ownership by the state. Nelson Rockefeller wouldn't agree to the plan, and so it was that Thomas called a local realtor and told her to show the big white house. It didn't sell for a long time—the farm outbuildings, it was explained, were too close to the residence—and when it was purchased, by a family who planned to raise horses for sale to Jersey racetracks, people in the village enjoyed a few weeks of speculative gossip. It wasn't called Dapplemere anymore. It became Dewey Lane Farm, a prosaic title only accidentally reminiscent of its famous owner.[5]

Little remained to mark the history made in Pawling during the period when it was a major source of the day's news, a prospective summer White House, and a popular attraction for tourists eager to get a glimpse of the Gangbuster's country hideout. To find Thomas Dewey, one has to go back down Reservoir Road to the rather lonely little burial ground, where he lies in his sleek cool box of granite, in death as in life a little apart from the rest of his neighbors. The casual visitor might not notice the personal trimmings that relieve the blank face of the tomb, the carved lyre and rose, symbols of music and love. Otherwise, the mausoleum reflects the symmetry of a life unbalanced only by ambition.

It isn't easy, gazing off at the Berkshires and thinking thoughts as spectacular as the scenery, to restrain a gnawing sense of what might have been. But then one remembers other pastoral places, a sluggish river in Owosso, a grocery store's cellar for a playpen, a provincial school, and Earl Putnam's farm. One ponders the significance of chance: the timely scholarship in a Chicago music school, the first encounter with a future bride, the greed of Annie Kaufman, and the confidence of George Medalie. One exclaims at precocity: the headlines ringing in the ears at age thirty-three, the polls showing a lead over an immensely popular president at thirty-seven, the acclaim for precisely those qualities of exhaustiveness and precision that would later curdle into criticism of artificiality and reserve. How does one assess a man who came so far, so fast—too fast for his own good, as he readily admitted—in spite of a personality that never had a chance to grow up to his dazzling potential? One recalls a political party wrapped in frock-coated conservatism, and the same party a dozen years later, less in love with slogans, more willing to accept America's central role in defending globally a way of life.

His talents were limited by serious flaws, by a temperament too rational for politics, a daunting competence, and an unwillingness to accept the changed rules of a game reinvented by Franklin Roosevelt. Dewey's times demanded broadly sympathetic leaders. He sought only to set fire to logic. Neither a crusader nor a hero in the conventional sense, he had instincts for thoroughness, order, and expertise, that were the precise opposite of what modern politicians mistake for leadership. He would undoubtedly have made an abler president than candidate, and the history of his country might have been profoundly different had he succeeded in articulating a compelling vision contrary to that of FDR or Truman. Instead, he chose to prosecute a popular revolution.

"Everything came too early for me," he said near the end of his life. He had been spoiled by the calendar, raised up by a capricious destiny before he could grasp its implications. He had become a prisoner of his own perfectionism, a victim of emotions alien to the "scientific humanism" of his youth. When he was most anxious to govern her, America was not ready to yield the impulses of her heart to any mere efficiency expert, no matter how many atrocities he avenged or administrative inventions he fathered. Only later, when both the country and the office seeker achieved perspective, would a time come when regrets might be in season. By then, the youthful candidate was too old to attain anything but wisdom and wealth. Power would lie just beyond his grasp. Perhaps that is why a scent of tragedy will always hover around Dewey's hilltop. It is hard to imagine for such a man a restful eternity.[6]

Notes

Prologue: *The Man in Suite 1527*

1. James Fleming–Hickman Powell, Sept. 12, 1937; *Twenty Against the Under-world,* Thomas E. Dewey, edited by Rodney Campbell, Doubleday, New York, 1975, p. 440 (hereafter referred to as TAU).
2. Interview with Dr. George Gallup, April 26, 1980; interview with Lowell Thomas, Feb. 4, 1980.
3. Interview with Harry O'Donnell, May 15, 1980.
4. Interview with T. Norman Hurd, May 19, 1980; interview with Herbert Brownell, Jan. 17, 1980.
5. Letter from George Aiken to author, Dec. 10, 1979.
6. Interview with Frank Hnida, March 8, 1980; interview with Harry Darby, Jan. 29, 1980.
7. Interview with Esther Tufty, May 5, 1980.
8. Minutes of Feb. 14, 1948, political meeting, Hotel Roosevelt; interview with Thomas E. Stephens, May 9, 1980.
9. Interview with Abe Poeretz, Feb. 17, 1980.
10. TED–David Hinshaw, Sept. 30, 1931; interview with Robert Thayer, Feb. 18, 1980.
11. Interview with George Shapiro, March 13, 1980.
12. Interview with Kitty Carlisle Hart, Jan. 18, 1980; interview with Mrs. Joseph Stone, March 14, 1980; interview with Arnulf Mueller, Jan. 20, 1980; interview with the Rev. Ralph Lankler, Jan. 8, 1980; David Dressler interview, Columbia Oral History Project (hereafter referred to as COHP).
13. Interview with David Rockefeller, Feb. 13, 1980.
14. Interviews with Thomas E. Dewey, Jr., Oct. 6, 1980, March 14, 1980; interview with Elly Robbins, Feb. 19, 1980.
15. Interview with John Dewey, Feb. 15, 1980; Mueller interview, Dressler, COHP; Hart interview.
16. Interview with F. Clifton White, Feb. 12, 1980; interview with the Rev. Laman Bruner, April 26, 1980; interview with Arthur Barnett, March 5, 1980.
17. Dewey interview, John Foster Dulles Oral History Project, Princeton University, Jan. 23, 1965.
18. Interview with William Pfeiffer, May 13, 1980.
19. O'Donnell interview; Shapiro interview; interview with June Martin, March 18, 1980.
20. Interview with Stanley Fuld, Feb. 15, 1980; Barnett interview; Dewey interview, Dulles OHP; interview with Lou Golden, May 19, 1980.
21. Hurd interview.
22. Shapiro interview; Mueller interview.
23. Confidential source.
24. Interview with Leo O'Brien, May 10, 1980.
25. Interview with John Dewey, May 16, 1980; interview with Alger Chapman, April 15, 1981.

26. Interview with Louise Gore, May 14, 1980.
27. Gallup interview.
28. Interview with Lillian Rosse, Jan. 28, 1980.
29. Gore interview; Brownell interview. With characteristic good humor, Brownell told me how, over thirty years after that long, increasingly gloomy election night, people still wanted to know one thing: Had Dewey hit him with a lamp, as alleged in Cholly Knickerbocker's column? In this case, the retraction printed by the columnist has never quite caught up with the original story.
30. Interview with Lillian Rosse, Feb. 1, 1980; Frances Dewey–Harold Hutt, Sept. 30, 1944.
31. Interview with Jack Hogan, Feb. 1, 1980; Gore interview.
32. Martin interview.
33. Thayer interview.
34. Poeretz interview.
35. Interview with McGeorge Bundy, Feb. 14, 1980.
36. Interview with Jack Cotten, March 3, 1980.
37. Hogan interview; interview with Joseph Gasarch, Jan. 24, 1980. Dewey's judgment of midnight notwithstanding, the election stayed close throughout the night. At a 3 A.M. strategy conference on the Roosevelt's mezzanine, Brownell refused to brook talk of conceding. Dewey's assistant counsel in Albany was dispatched to investigate the ground rules of an election thrown into the House of Representatives. The Chicago *Tribune*'s confident headline reinforced Brownell's opinion; and in fact, not until Tom and Frances rose after ninety minutes of sleep on Wednesday morning, and first Illinois, then Ohio and California slipped through their grasp, was defeat confirmed.
38. Interview with Hugh Scott, Jan. 23, 1980.
39. Interview with Bert Sarafan, April 23, 1980.
40. Interview with Lillian Rosse, Feb. 9, 1980; interview with Robert Ray, May 20, 1980.
41. Interview with Frank Kirsie, Jan. 18, 1980.

1. The Right Side of the Tracks

1. TAU, p. 23–24. Much of the material on Dewey's ancestors and his own boyhood in Owosso was collected by Harlan Phillips, who spent two weeks in the town in 1957 combing old editions of the *Times* and *Argus-Press,* and talking with residents who remembered Dewey's parents, grandparents, or the boy himself.
2. Dewey–Phillips, Oct. 14, 1957; E. Grace Dewey–TED, March 23, 1949.
3. Interview with John Welch, March 27, 1980; TAU, p. 25.
4. Lemoyne Jones–Rupert Hughes, July 20, 1939. Among the most useful sources on Dewey's early years are the rough drafts of Hughes's campaign biography, prepared in exhaustive collaboration with the candidate. The original draft contains considerable anecdotal information later edited out as superfluous—or too revealing.
5. Interview with Mrs. W. B. Davis, March 17, 1980; interview with Harold Hutt, March 26, 1980; interview with Harlow Ross, April 19, 1980.

6. Interview with George Campbell, June 2, 1980; Davis interview; Hutt interview; Thomas E. Dewey, Jr., interview, March 14, 1980; interview with John Dewey, March 7, 1980.

7. Thomas E. Dewey, Jr., interview, Oct. 6, 1980; interview with Anna Hynes, May 19, 1980; interview with Mrs. Phillip Welch, March 17, 1980.

8. Tufty interview.

9. TAU, p. 43.

10. TAU, pp. 36–37; interview with Mrs. Leon Vosburgh, March 17, 1980.

11. Interview with Lillian Rosse, Feb. 14, 1980; interview with George Champion, April 21, 1980; Dewey–Phillips, Oct. 14, 1957.

12. Interview with A. Wilbur Duryee, July 10, 1980.

13. Hutt interview. Dr. Hutt recalled how, following Annie's death in 1955, Dewey decided to sell the old house on West Oliver Street. Going through its contents one day, he came across the cuckoo clock. Feeling even less sentimental than usual, he was about to throw the clock out, until Hutt stopped him. "Who the hell wants that old thing?" Dewey asked. Hutt assured him that, if no one else did, then he would.

14. TAU, pp. 33–34.

15. TED–Annie T. Dewey, June 25, 1944 (later entries in this correspondence are listed TED–ATD).

16. George Valentine–TED, April 23, 1931.

17. Hart interview.

18. Interview with Earl Putnam, March 17, 1980.

19. Scott interview.

20. Teapot Dome was a Wyoming oil reserve leased by Harding's interior secretary, Albert B. Fall, to the Sinclair oil interests. In return, Fall and friends received hundreds of thousands of dollars. Actually, Teapot Dome was only one of numerous scandals tainting Harding's administration. Others included theft in the Veterans Bureau and the sale of pardons and liquor permits by Attorney General Harry Daugherty. But Teapot Dome caught the public fancy—as Watergate, fifty years later, became a generic term, a corrupt umbrella held over presidential abuse of power.

2. *Foundations and Cathedrals*

1. TED–Gretchen Dick, Aug. 17, 1927.

2. TAU, p. 56; interview with John Dewey, Aug. 20, 1980.

3. TED–Barry Byers, Sept. 11, 1959; TAU, p. 57.

4. Hutt interview; Thomas E. Dewey, Jr., interview, March 14, 1980.

5. Hutt interview.

6. Hutt interview; interview with Elly Robbins, March 11, 1980.

7. TAU, pp. 59–60; letter to the author from Ken McCormick, Sept. 11, 1980.

8. Lillian Rosse–Charles Garside, March 5, 1948.

9. Phillips interview with Joseph Panuch, April 29, 1959.

10. Phillips–Panuch; Phillips interview with Marland Gale, April 28, 1959.

11. Phillips interview with James Dealey, April 28, 1959; Fuld interview.

12. Interview with Arthur Schwartz, April 23, 1980.

13. Phillips–Gale.

14. Dewey–Phillips, Dec. 11, 1957.

15. Dewey–Phillips, March 24, 1958; TAU, pp. 64–65.
16. Phillips–Panuch.
17. Interview with Lowell Wadmond, June 19, 1980; Party Policy Report, January 1929, New York Young Republican Club file.
18. NYYRC File, 1931.
19. Ibid.
20. Sam Koenig–TED, May 11, 1927; Clarence Fay–TED, Oct. 24, 1927; TED–Junior Republican Committee of One Hundred, Nov. 27, 1927.
21. Wadmond interview; TED–Sam Koenig, April 18 and 19, 1929.
22. Dewey circular to NYYRC Speakers' Bureau, October 1930.
23. Phillips–Dealey; Arthur Schwartz, then as later a close friend, confirms that young Dewey was "not well liked" at Larkin, Rathbone and Perry.
24. Phillips interview with Raymond Seymour, May 19, 1959.
25. Ibid.
26. TED–George L. Storer, July 18, 1927; Dewey's silence regarding his father is testified to by numerous intimates as well as members of his own family.
27. Regis Sternberg–TED, April 25, 1940; John Dewey interview, Feb. 15, 1980; TED–Joseph Baldwin, June 8, 1928.
28. Phillips–Gale; Schwartz interview.
29. TED–E. P. Lovejoy, Feb. 16, 1929.
30. TED–E. P. Lovejoy correspondence, Jan. 28 and Feb. 16, 1929.
31. Phelps Phelps–TED, Aug. 28 and Sept. 17, 1929.
32. TED–Grace Dewey, Aug. 22, 1929; TED–Charles Bullard, Aug. 24, 1929.
33. Phillips–Gale.

3. *The Ruby Nose of Uncle Sam*

1. TED–Grace Dewey, Dec. 29, 1929.
2. TED–Emory Thomas, Dec. 15, 1930.
3. Phillips–Seymour; TAU, pp. 73–75; Dewey–Phillips, March 27, 1958.
4. Phillips interview with William Herlands, Nov. 19, 1958.
5. Phillips–Herlands, ibid.
6. Wadmond interview; Phillips–Panuch. That Wadmond was Medalie's first choice to be his chief assistant, a view held by both Wadmond and Panuch based on their own conversations with the new U.S. Attorney, is confirmed by Arthur Schwartz, himself head of the prohibition division at the time of Tuttle's departure. Ira Wolfert's article on Dewey's selection, written for the North American News Alliance on July 21, 1935, provides additional details of the casual invitation extended by the older man to his young protégé.
7. Wadmond interview.
8. TED–George Medalie, Feb. 18 and March 6, 1931.
9. Phillips–Seymour; ATD–TED, undated.
10. Allen Brownhall–TED, April 1, 1931.
11. Letter to author from Joseph Stone, Sept. 9, 1980.
12. Interview with Jacob Grumet, Jan. 17, 1980.
13. Interview with Joseph Stone, March 14, 1980; Dewey memos, April 8 and 17, 1931; TAU, p. 79.
14. TAU, p. 81; Phillips interview with William Herlands, Dec. 1, 1958.

15. TAU, p. 79; Phillips–Herlands, ibid.
16. Interview with Jacob Grumet, Oct. 5, 1980.
17. Confidential source.
18. Minutes of District Attorney staff meeting, May 21, 1938; TED–Joseph Finnegan, April 9, 1931.
19. Schwartz interview; Arthur Schwartz–TED, May 20, 1969.
20. 1931 Charter of the New York Young Republican Club.
21. TED–J. D. Lodge, Oct. 31, 1931.
22. Phillips interview with Herbert Brownell, undated.
23. Francis E. Rivers–TED, Nov. 16, 1931.
24. Phillips–Panuch.
25. Schwartz interview.
26. TED–Ken McCormick, June 25, 1969.
27. Dewey memo to Justice Department, Aug. 2, 1933.

4. *The Baby Prosecutor*

1. TED–Edward Bernays, Oct. 24, 1932; Phillips–Panuch.
2. Interview with Irene Grumet, Oct. 5, 1980. Dewey's sensitivity to discrimination against New York's minorities was the chief reason he agreed to creation of a state university in 1948. But it had its limits. "Why do all the Jewish boys want to be judges?" he asked the wife of a friend who harbored such ambitions. "I don't want to be a judge." "You don't have to be," the woman replied. "You can be President of the United States. A judge is all they can ever be."
3. TED–R. Emerson Swout, Aug. 15, 1932.
4. TED–Melvin C. Eaton, Nov. 13, 1932.
5. TAU, p. 119.
6. Interview with Thurston Green, April 23, 1930; TED–Leonard Reid, Jan. 22, 1934.
7. TED–William O. Douglas, Nov. 26, 1934; Dewey account books.
8. Thomas E. Dewey, Jr., interview, March 14, 1980; interview with Herbert Fabricant, March 1, 1980; interview with Wilbur Duryee, Jan. 20, 1980.
9. Interviews with Lillian Rosse, Feb. 1 and 9, 1980.
10. TED–William Herlands, June 18, 1934.

5. *The Chief*

1. Judge John Woolsey–TED, July 11, 1935.
2. TED–E. J. Davis, May 21, 1935.
3. Interview with Thomas G. Corcoran, May 27, 1980.
4. Rosse interview, Feb. 9, 1980; TED–Leonard Reid, June 25, 1935.
5. Bob School–TED, undated, July 1935; Green interview; J. M. Stratton–TED, July 5, 1935.
6. TED–Harry G. Herman, July 25, 1935.
7. Diary of Henry J. Morgenthau, vol. 8, p. 48, FDR Library.
8. Phillips interview with Manny Robbins, June 17, 1958.
9. Green interview; Phillips–Gelb.
10. TED–Abbot Southall, July 8, 1935; Phillips–Fuld.

11. Dewey–Phillips, May 8, 1958; Phillips–Paul Lockwood, Dec. 16, 1958.
12. Phillips–Gelb.
13. Interview with Victor Herwitz, Feb. 14, 1980.
14. Interview with Lillian Rosse, Aug. 20, 1980.
15. Green interview.
16. Phillips–Robbins; Rosse interview, Feb. 1, 1980.
17. Minutes of District Attorney's staff meeting, May 13, 1938.
18. Confidential source.
19. TAU, pp. 175–78; Phillips–Robbins.
20. TED–Judge John Woolsey, July 13, 1935.
21. D.A. staff meeting minutes.
22. Interview with John L. Mowry, Feb. 24, 1980; Herwitz interview.
23. Interview with David Worgen, March 14, 1980; interview with Whitman Knapp, Feb. 14, 1980.
24. Knapp interview; Grumet interview.
25. Interview with James O'Malley, March 13, 1980.
26. TED–Harold Hutt, Oct. 16, 1935; Rosse interview, Sept. 12, 1980.
27. Herwitz interview.

6. *"An NRA of Prostitution"*

1. Phillips interview with Harris Steinberg, May 29, 1958; Phillips interview with Charles Breitel, December, 1958.
2. William A. Allen interview, COHP.
3. Dewey–Phillips, May 8, 1958.
4. Frank Hogan–TED, March 19, 1970.
5. Rosse interview, Aug. 20, 1980; Phillips–Breitel.
6. Phillips–Gelb; TAU, pp. 162–166; Hogan memorandum.
7. Green interview; Phillips–Breitel.
8. Minutes of D.A. staff meeting, May 13, 1938.
9. Interview with Eva Gurfein, April 28, 1980.
10. Rosse interview, Aug. 28, 1980; Fuld interview.
11. Interview with Ray Bliss, Jan. 15, 1980; interview with William P. Rogers, June 5, 1980; Rosse interview, Aug. 20, 1980.
12. Interview with Livingston Goddard, Feb. 28, 1980.
13. TAU, pp. 193–194.
14. Rosse interview, Aug. 28, 1980. Dewey's own notes for his memoirs, and rough drafts of the manuscript itself, support Miss Rosse's recollection of how he first came to learn of Luciano's personal involvement in the prostitution racket.
15. Memo, Lillian Rosse to R. Burdell Bixby, undated; Rosse interview, Aug. 28, 1980.
16. Gurfein interview.
17. Phillips–Breitel.
18. Ibid; TAU, p. 195.
19. Interview with Oscar J. Cohen, March 1, 1980; Herwitz interview.
20. TED–ATD, Feb. 4, 1936.
21. TED–ATD, March 10, 1936; Goddard interview; interview with Irving Hest, May 5, 1980.

22. Gasarch interview.
23. TAU, pp. 212–13.
24. TAU, pp. 227–252.
25. Frank Hogan–TED, March 19, 1970.
26. Interview with Richard Korn, March 8, 1980.

7. *"Tonight, I Am Going to Talk About Murder"*

1. Sarafan interview.
2. Phillips–Steinberg; Dewey–Phillips, May 8, 1958.
3. Murray Gurfein–TED, July 10, 1969. Duces tecum had historically meant the voluntary turning over of evidence. In the rackets cases, suspects usually destroyed the evidence before the customary waiting period required for the mails to return what a prosecutor sought. So Dewey reworded the subpoenas, duces tecum forthwith—which meant that one of his men could walk into a shop or office and legally expect to walk out with company records or financial books in his hands.
4. Gurfein memo to TED, September 1969 (one of a series of written recollections used by Dewey in composing his memoirs).
5. Phillips–Breitel; TAU, pp. 282–285.
6. TED remarks to New York printers' union, Oct. 22, 1937.
7. TED remarks at Benny Gottesman tribute, Oct. 26, 1937.
8. TAU, pp. 278–282; Hest interview; Phillips–Steinberg.
9. TAU, pp. 288–290.
10. TED–ATD, March 24, 1937.
11. Interview with Henry Root Stern, May 1, 1980.
12. Confidential source.
13. Stern interview.
14. E. F. Thomas–TED, March 7, 1939; David W. Peck to author, July 21, 1980; interview with Alfred M. Landon, July 20, 1972.
15. Alfred M. Landon–Roger Dunn, May 5, 1945.
16. TED–Chase Osborne, June 7, 1939; Dewey–Phillips, Nov. 26, 1958.
17. TAU, pp. 298–303; Murray Gurfein–TED, Nov. 17, 1969.
18. Murray Gurfein–TED, Aug. 26, 1968: Grumet interview, Oct. 5, 1980.
19. Murray Gurfein–Victor Herwitz, March 24, 1969; TAU, pp. 312–313.
20. TED–ATD, April 19, 1938; interview with John Dewey, Oct. 7, 1980.
21. Interview with John Dewey, Sept. 5, 1980.
22. Rosse interview, Sept. 12, 1980; interview with Henry Elkind, March 10, 1980; TED–ATD, March 7, 1938.
23. Interview with Arnold Bauman, Feb. 22, 1980.
24. TED–ATD, Feb. 15, Feb. 25, 1938; interview with the Rev. Ralph Lankler, Jan. 8, 1980.
25. Dewey interview, Dulles OHP; Dewey–Phillips, May 8, 1958.
26. William A. Allen, COHP.
27. Dewey–Phillips, May 8, 1958.
28. Diary of Adolf Berle, July 24, Dec. 17, 1937, FDR Library.
29. Berle diary, Aug. 12, 1937.
30. Ibid.
31. Berle diary, Aug. 13 and 17, 1937; interview with Warren Moscow, March 13, 1980.

32. Berle diary, Aug. 17, 1937.
33. Dewey interview, Dulles OHP.
34. TED–ATD, Aug. 25, 1937.
35. Interview with Bernie Katzen, Feb. 14, 1980; interview with Florence Shientag, March 18, 1980; the elaborate phone banks were described in "Dewey-Up-to-Date," a trio of background articles published in the *Wall Street Journal* in June 1944.
36. TED–ATD, Sept. 9, 1980.
37. Dewey interview, Dulles OHP; interview with Herbert Brownell, Jan. 17, 1980.
38. Dewey–Phillips, May 8, 1958.
39. Frances H. Dewey–ATD, undated letter, November 1938.
40. TED–Leonard Reid, Dec. 9, 1937; TED–Leo J. Casey, Dec. 15, 1937.

8. *Mr. District Attorney*

1. TED–ATD, April 19, 1938.
2. Sarafan interview.
3. In April 1937, a policeman was killed in a stick-up on the Lower East Side. Among those implicated in the shooting was one Isidore Zimmerman. The killing took place before Dewey became district attorney. It became one of the first cases to be prosecuted by Jacob Rosenblum as head of the new D.A.'s Homicide Bureau. According to those who knew him, Rosenblum was a tough prosecutor, proud of his near-unblemished string of courtroom victories. Moreover, since this was a cop killing, and since guarantees of defendant's rights in 1938 were not what they are in our time, it is entirely possible, according to one of Rosenblum's colleagues, that the New York police "overdid" their zeal in seeing the accused brought to justice.

In the event, Zimmerman, along with the others, was convicted in the spring of 1938. Another accused accomplice, turning state's evidence, testified against Zimmerman. The defendant's court-appointed lawyer, James D. C. Murray, knew that such testimony had been given Rosenblum, but shied away in the courtroom from doing anything that might call the statements into question. Rosenblum went so far as to toy publicly with his rival, taunting him in the hope that the witness's prior statements would be produced. Still, Murray refused to take the bait. In so refusing, he virtually conceded that the statement was damning evidence. In fact, the witness had produced contradictory testimony. In a modern courtroom, the district attorney would be required to come forward with such dubious evidence; in 1938, no such clear-cut responsibility existed.

Zimmerman went to jail, stayed there for twenty-five years. When the case was appealed, no allegation of improper conduct was made against anyone in Dewey's operation. Neither was this claimed twenty years later, when attorneys for Zimmerman based their appeal on violation of due process—specifically police conduct during the investigation. The court of appeals sent the case down for reargument, tossing out the original grounds and turning instead to a position successfully argued in an earlier decision by Judge Stanley Fuld, once head of Dewey's Indictments Bureau. It was

Fuld who argued that failure to turn over to the court or opposing attorneys evidence that is suspect constitutes suppression of due process.

So it was that the court of appeals granted Zimmerman's plea, but for reasons of its own. By 1962, it was far too late to restage the original trial, and Isidore Zimmerman launched a campaign to prove his innocence and win financial retribution from the State of New York. His case attracted press interest; at one point in the summer of 1981, Zimmerman claimed to have fifty offers from movie producers interested in filming his story. Three times Nelson Rockefeller vetoed claim bills passed by the legislature on Zimmerman's behalf—for the same reason that Dewey, as governor, vetoed such bills routinely, for fear of establishing dangerous precedents. But in 1981, Governor Hugh Carey signed a bill paving the way for Zimmerman to sue the state for $10 million.

Ironically, the whole question of Zimmerman's guilt or innocence became obscured; even more ironic was the fact that Zimmerman was released from prison because an appeals court found errors by his own lawyer, and based its ruling upon an opinion by Stanley Fuld. Dewey's own role in the Zimmerman case is cloudy; cynics argued that his office was eager to procure as many convictions as possible at a time when the boss's presidential hopes were gaining force. This overlooks the fact that conviction rates can easily be doctored, and that in other cases where Dewey found extenuating evidence, he did not hesitate to thrust himself personally into appeals for leniency. Moreover, it simplifies Dewey's role in a largely delegated authority assumed by each bureau head. The cops and Rosenblum, not to mention Murray's bungling in court, had far more to do with the guilty verdict than any vendetta pressed by the D.A.

4. Interview with Henry Clay, May 10, 1938. Leonard Reid, Dewey's Chicago cousin, an established lawyer in the Windy City, wrote to praise the new D.A.'s administrative instincts. On the other hand, said Reid, many of the innovations planned for 137 Centre Street, were "entirely too idealistic to suit me."

5. Interview with Richard Denzer, March 8, 1980.

6. Interview with Thomas Gilchrest, Feb. 12, 1980.

7. Katzen interview.

8. Knapp interview; interview with Lawrence Walsh, April 23, 1980.

9. Interview with Louis Pagnucco, March 12, 1980.

10. Rogers interview. Rogers recalls Dewey's bluntness—how he convened a dinner for New York's judges only to muddy the hospitality by welcoming the magistrates as follows: "It's nice to get to know you all. It's not easy to know you during the afternoons because so many of you go to the racetracks."

11. Interview with Augustus Marchetti, Feb. 9, 1980.

12. Confidential source.

13. Interview with Charles Tillinghurst, May 19, 1980, Pagnucco interview; interview with Joseph Czechlewski, April 23, 1980.

14. Knapp interview; Grumet interview, Oct. 5, 1980.

15. Knapp interview; Gilchrest interview.

16. Leonard Reid–TED, Jan. 22, 1938.

17. TED–Alfred M. Landon, April 24, 1938; Landon–TED, July 15, 1941. At their first meeting, in May 1938, Landon urged the White House on Dewey,

etching a cataclysmic image of the country's future should FDR win again in 1940. Such an event, in Landon's words, would mean "we had seen the last free election in America."

18. Rosse interview, Feb. 9, 1980; Harold Keller–Dale Carnegie, Feb. 15, 1938.
19. Letter to author from Lester Arrow, Feb. 26, 1980; TED–ATD, Jan. 21, 1938.
20. TED–ATD, May 21, 1938.
21. Ibid.
22. Phillips–Gelb.
23. The blue ribbon jury was a favorite tool of many prosecutors, who reasoned that those who had previously served as jurors would better grasp the complex details of cases involving racketeering or tax evasion. Technically, the juries were that and nothing more. In practice, they tended to include a high proportion of the affluent or professional, and critics attacked them as little more than hanging juries.
24. TED–ATD, Aug. 10, 1938.
25. Interview with A. Wilbur Duryee, Jan. 20, 1980.
26. TED–E. F. Thomas, May 8, 1938; James Farley–Claude Bowers, July 1, 1938, Farley papers, Library of Congress; TED–ATD, June 17, 1938.
27. Herbert Lehman interview, COHP.
28. Leonard Reid–TED, July 30, 1980; interview with John Burton, March 1, 1980; Dewey–Phillips, May 27, 1938.
29. Goddard interview; interview with Thomas G. Corcoran, May 22, 1980. Corcoran did not deny a visit to Judge Pecora at the time of the Hines trial (he spent a month in New York City at Roosevelt's behest organizing a primary challenge to Representative John J. O'Connor, an insufficiently New Dealish Democrat who was one of the President's few actual victims in his purge campaign). He could not remember talking with the judge about the 1938 gubernatorial race, but readily acknowledged a close friendship with Pecora, as well as the crucial importance of that year's elections to Roosevelt, at a time when the New Deal was coming under spreading attack.
30. Phillips–Gelb; Dewey–Phillips, May 27, 1958.
31. Herwitz interview; Rosse interview, Feb. 4, 1980; Phillips–Gelb.
32. Alfred M. Landon–TED, Sept. 3, and 24, 1938.
33. Gallup interview; TED–ATD, Sept. 28, 1938.
34. Lehman's brother-in-law, indicated that the Governor changed his mind about running again after hearing Dewey's attempt to label him "a front man" for corrupt politicians in the state. Dewey himself told Harlan Phillips that he found this hard to credit.
35. Interview with Edwin F. Jaeckle, May 11, 1981.
36. Dewey–Phillips, Jan. 14, 1959.
37. TED–Alfred M. Landon, Oct. 11, 1938; James Farley–James Roosevelt, Oct. 19, Farley papers, LOC.
38. Jaeckle interview. I have also been permitted to read and profit from lengthy interviews of Jaeckle conducted by Professor William Dietz of the University of Rochester. I am grateful to both men for their kindnesses.
39. Ibid.
40. Breitel interview.
41. Jaeckle interview.

42. Arthur Sulzberger–TED, Sept. 30, 1938; FDR–John G. Saxon, Oct. 11, 1938, P.P.F. 1763 FDR Library.

43. Another incident, which might have had even wider repercussions than Bontecou's blunder, took place at a Dewey rally for Syrian and Armenian voters in New York City. Barent Ten Eyck, with heavy humor, preceded the candidate by addressing the rally goers as "mongrel Americans" and reminded his audience that the mongrel was "the most faithful of dogs." Dewey was livid. "The son of a bitch will cost me the election," he muttered to a friend on the platform. Only later did he learn that Paul Lockwood, equally sensitive to the ramifications of Ten Eyck's gaucherie, had saved the day by spilling drinks all over reporters at his table, drowning out the speaker with some artificial commotion.

44. Dewey–Phillips, May 27, 1958.

45. Hickman Powell–TED, Dec. 7, 1939.

9. *The Charge of the Electric Light Brigade*

1. William Allen White–Chase Osborne, Sept. 5, 1939.

2. Rupert Hughes–TED, Jan. 31, 1940.

3. TED–ATD, April 26, 1939.

4. Kingsland Macy–TED, Nov. 11, 1938; Ward Jenks–TED, Nov. 18, 1938; Phillips–Lockwood.

5. Notes of conversation between Herbert Hoover and Burton Heath, Oct. 5, 1939; Heath sought and Hoover readily granted permission to pass the substance of their talks on to Dewey.

6. Interview with Oren Root, Jan. 17, 1980.

7. TED–Barry Byers, Sept. 11, 1959; Herwitz–Gurfein memo, March 24, 1969.

8. Herwitz–Gurfein memo, ibid.

9. TED–ATD, Jan. 29, 1939.

10. Herwitz interview; Rosse interview, Feb. 1, 1980.

11. Phillips–Gelb; Sarafan interview; interview with Amos Wylie, Feb. 28, 1980.

12. TAU, pp. 467–73 for Dewey's own account of the second Hines trial; I have supplemented this with reference to a half-dozen New York dailies and interviews with several participants in the prosecution.

13. Millard Ellison–Harold Keller, May 19, 1939.

14. Dewey–Phillips, Dec. 3, 1958; TED–Wheeler Sammons, Jan. 22, 1939; TED–ATD, April 4, 1939; TED–Leonard Reid, April 14 and 18, 1939.

15. Elliott V. Bell–TED, April 10, 1939; interview with Gabriel Hauge, March 27, 1981; Rosse interview, March 8, 1980.

16. Gallup interview; Gerard Lambert–TED, April 26, 1939; John Burton memo to TED, June 20, 1939.

17. TED–Hickman Powell, Dec. 5, 1939.

18. Berle Diary, Dec. 7, 1939; Hickman Powell–TED, Dec. 7, 1939.

19. Interview with Irene Kuhn, April 15, 1981; TED–Joseph Patterson, Dec. 17, 1943.

20. Phillips–Brownell; Dewey–Phillips, May 27, 1958; Stanley Isaacs interview, COHP.

21. Robert H. Thayer–TED, Dec. 6, 1938.

22. Ken Simpson–Millard Ellison, Dec. 30, 1937; Harold Keller–J. Russel Sprague, April 25, 1940; Phillips interview with J. Russel Sprague, Jan. 13, 1959.

23. Dewey interview, Herbert Hoover Oral History Project, Nov. 25, 1969.

24. The text of Dewey's remarks, off the record under the rules of the legislative correspondents, is to be found in his papers at Rochester. Warren Moscow, who was present at the dinner, vividly recalls Simpson practically being led out of the room in a state of shock. At the same time, Moscow attributed to Dewey the remark that, so far as he was concerned, Simpson had "a permanent case of laryngitis," a deviation from the actual text that is subtle but significant. On balance, it seems safe to say that Dewey caused a stir with what he had to say about Simpson, but still less than an outright public break.

25. TED–Herbert Hoover, April 3, 1939; Wadmond interview.

26. Hart interview.

27. Phillips–Sprague; Chase Osborne–TED, March 13, 1939; Corcoran interview; TED–John H. Perry, Sept. 5, 1939.

28. Barak Mattingly–TED, May 31, 1939; TED reply, June 9, 1939; Hoover–Heath conversation.

29. TED–ATD, Feb. 21, 1940; TED–Ruth Simms, Feb. 9, 1940.

30. James Farley–Franklin D. Roosevelt, Feb. 2, 1940, FDR Library. (Farley was enclosing a copy of the Portland *Oregonian*, dated Jan. 28, 1940, and dealing with Dewey's metronomic scheduling, for presidential perusal.)

31. Kuhn interview.

32. Dewey–Phillips, Dec. 3, 1958; Dewey interview Dulles OHP.

33. Jaeckle interview.

34. Carl T. Hogan–TED, May 17, 1940.

35. Interview with John Burton, July 5, 1980.

36. J. J. Kavenaugh–TED, May 16 and 18, 1940.

37. Wadmond interview.

38. Raymond Baldwin interview, COHP.

39. Dewey–Phillips, Dec. 3, 1958.

40. Dewey interview, Hoover OHP; Dewey–Phillips, Dec. 3, 1958.

41. Dewey interview, Hoover OHP; Dewey–Phillips, Dec. 3, 1958.

42. Eleanor B. Roosevelt–TED, July 27, 1944; Dewey–Phillips, Dec. 3, 1958.

43. Jaeckle interview.

44. Moscow interview; Dewey–Phillips, Dec. 3, 1958.

45. Baldwin interview, COHP; Dewey–Phillips, Dec. 3, 1958.

46. TED–Alfred M. Landon, July 19, 1940.

47. Herbert Hoover–TED, July 17, 1940.

48. TED–James T. Patterson, Oct. 20, 1969. Dewey told Professor Patterson, then preparing a biography of Robert Taft, that he had "no recollection at all" of any agreement forestalling pressure upon him to take the vice presidency on a ticket headed by Taft. At the same time, there is plenty of evidence of cooperation between the two men in Philadelphia. There was a Taft observer at the Walton all week; the candidates themselves talked more than once; Sprague and Mrs. Simms visited David Ingalls on Tuesday night; Jaeckle arranged additional negotiations in an attempt to stop Willkie; and Dewey released his delegates with a request they support Taft against Willkie. In the end, Taft's drive fell just short.

10. *The View from Purgatory Hill*

1. Mueller interview.
2. Interview with Florence Akin, May 10, 1980; Thomas E. Dewey, Jr., interview, March 14, 1980; interview with Anna Hynes, May 21, 1980.
3. Letter from Lowell Thomas to author, March 11, 1980; Jack Hogan interview, Feb. 1, 1980; TED–ATD, May 13, 1938; TED–Harold Hutt, Feb. 24, 1944; Thomas E. Dewey, Jr., interview, April 15, 1981.
4. TED–Regis Sternburgh, Oct. 9, 1939.
5. Rosse interview, Feb. 9, 1980; Gallup interview.
6. TED–Dudley Swain, June 19, 1945; Rosse interview, Feb. 9, 1980; Gallup interview.
7. TED–Lowell Thomas, Nov. 8, 1939; Thomas reply, Nov. 9, 1939; Lowell Thomas–TED, March 13, April 12, Sept. 13, Oct. 7, 1939.
8. Lowell Thomas–TED, Dec. 6, 1939; Thomas E. Dewey, Jr., interview, March 14, 1980; Rosse interview, May 28, 1980.
9. John Dewey interview, May 16, 1980; TED–ATD, Aug. 1, 1938.
10. TED–Ward Jenks, Feb. 10, 1938; TED–ATD, July 15, 1941; Thomas E. Dewey, Jr., interview, July 10, 1980.
11. TED–Carl T. Hogan, Nov. 8, 1941; interview with Mary Pickens Sumner, Jan. 20, 1980; Charles Murphy–Carl T. Hogan, Nov. 14, 1952.
12. Charles Murphy–TED, March 26, 1959; Dec. 18, 1958; interview with Charles Murphy, Jr., May 7, 1980.
13. Interview with Charles Stewart, March 13, 1980; Sumner interview.
14. Mueller interview.
15. Interview with Howard Smith, March 25, 1980; Thomas E. Dewey, Jr., interview, March 14, 1980.
16. Hynes interview; John Dewey interview, May 9, 1980; Mueller interview.
17. John Dewey interview, May 9, 1980; Sumner interview; Mueller interview.
18. TED–ATD, Oct. 7, 1941; Duryee interview; letter from Norman Vincent Peale to author, May 28, 1980.
19. TED–Ruth Simms, July 9, 1940; confidential source, told the story by Willkie himself. Dewey told Rupert Hughes on July 24 that Willkie would make "a fine candidate" with an excellent chance of winning. As for himself, he sounded relieved. "The presidency is a sentence to hard labor with abuse and punishment," he wrote Hughes.
20. TED–Ruth Simms, July 9, 1940; Wendell Willkie–TED, July 8, 1940.
21. Ruth Simms–TED, July 16, 1940.
22. Robert A. Taft–TED, Sept. 17, 1940; TED reply, Sept. 19, 1940.
23. Gallup interview.
24. Undated memo dictated by Allen W. Dulles, John Foster Dulles file, Dewey papers.
25. TED–Alfred M. Landon, Oct. 21, 1940; Landon–TED, Sept. 17, 1940; TED–Landon, Oct. 2, 1940.
26. TED–Chase Osborne, Nov. 29, 1940; Dewey–Phillips interview, Dec. 3, 1958.
27. TED–Charles Garside, Dec. 21, 1940; TED–Gerard Lambert, Dec. 20, 1940.

28. Simpson death certificate, Jan. 26, 1941; W. Kingsland Macy–TED, April 19, 1949.
29. TED–Ruth Simms, Nov. 30, 1940.
30. TED–ATD, Feb. 24, 1941; Oswald Heck–TED, Dec. 30, 1940; TED reply, Jan. 2, 1941.
31. Robert A. Taft–George F. Stanley, Sept. 8, 1944, Taft papers, Library of Congress.
32. TED–Edward A. Bacon, Jan. 25, 1941, Eisenhower Library; TED–Alfred M. Landon, March 4, April 27, 1941.
33. Alfred M. Landon–TED, Jan. 21, 1941: Landon–Harold Johnson, Aug. 15, 1941.
34. Harrison Spangler–TED, Sept. 10, 1941.
35. Dewey–Phillips, Jan. 14, 1959.
36. TED–ATD, May 22, 1941. Much of the background on Dewey's USO travels is to be found in private reports compiled by Cal Tinney, a publicist who accompanied the D.A.
37. TED–Harrison Spangler, Sept. 18, 1941.
38. Dewey–Phillips, Jan. 14, 1959; TED–Harrison Spangler, Sept. 18, 1941; undated Dewey memo to Henry Stimson, Sept. 1941.
39. TED–Ward Jenks, Sept. 19, 1941.
40. Herwitz interview.
41. TED–Alfred M. Landon, April 27, Sept. 19, 1941: TED–ATD, Sept. 18, 1941.
42. TED–Businessmen's Committee for O'Dwyer, Oct. 23, 1941.
43. TED–Alfred M. Landon, Nov. 17, 1941; Dewey–Phillips, Jan. 14, 1959; TED–ATD, Aug. 1, 1941.
44. TED–ATD, Oct. 30, Dec. 11, 1941; TED–Leonard Reid, Dec. 11, 1941.
45. Marchetti interview.
46. Interview with Joseph Sarafite, March 14, 1980.
47. Robbins interview, March 11, 1980.
48. Moscow interview.
49. TED–ATD, April 6, 1942.
50. Transcript of Hamilton Fish telephone call to Dewey, May 22, 1942; Warren Moscow, for one, believes that Dewey had his political headquarters tapped in 1942, something Lillian Rosse firmly denies. The few phone conversations transcribed in the Rochester collection could easily have been recorded by a secretary listening in on an extension.
51. Otto Schuler–TED, June 16, 1942. Schuler had asked Dewey for a response should Fish's name surface in Mahopac, and supplied afterward an eyewitness account of an uncompromising stand against the Congressman. At the same time, Hagerty's reputation among his peers was impeccable, something Dewey himself testified to by making him his Albany press secretary.
52. TED–Leonard Reid, June 19, 1942; TED–ATD, July 29, 1942.
53. Jaeckle interview.
54. Interview with Dean Alfange, May 19, 1980; TED–ATD, July 29, 1942.
55. Brownell–Phillips; Jaeckle interview.
56. Interview with Herbert Brownell, Jan. 17, 1980; Brownell–Phillips.
57. TED–ATD, Sept. 9, 1942; TED–George Z. Medalie, undated.
58. Roger Straus–TED, Nov. 9, 1942; on the same date, Dewey wrote Ruth

Simms, pronouncing disinterest in 1944, while claiming that Willkie "wants the presidential nomination more than life itself."
59. Jaeckle interview.

11. *The Governor*

1. Bruner interview.
2. TED–Ruth Simms, Jan. 17, 1943.
3. TED–Alfred E. Smith, Dec. 17, 1943.
4. O'Donnell interview.
5. TED–Ward Jenks, Dec. 7, 1942; confidential source.
6. John Dewey interview, May 9, 1980; TED–ATD, Jan. 26, 1943. Additional details of Frances' transformation of the mansion were provided in a radio conversation in 1948 between Marge Hogan and NBC interviewer Mary Margaret McBride.
7. Rosse interview, May 9, 1980; Hogan interview; Thomas E. Dewey, Jr., interview, March 14, 1980.
8. John Dewey interview, March 26, 1980; Hutt interview; Robbins interview, March 11, 1980.
9. John Dewey interview, ibid; Rosse interview, Feb. 4, 1980; Hynes interview.
10. Interview with Ken McCormick, March 11, 1980.
11. Interview with Alger W. Chapman, March 27, 1981; Jaeckle interview; TED–A. H. Kirchofer, April 18, 1943.
12. Breitel interview.
13. Jaeckle interview.
14. Breitel interview.
15. TED–M. C. Haber, July 7, 1943; TED–Mrs. W. F. Davenport, July 23, 1943.
16. David Dressler interview, COHP.
17. John Dewey interview; Grumet interview; Yeargin interview.
18. Czechlewski interview.
19. TED–Elliott V. Bell, May 5, 1944.
20. Interview with Murray Kempton, May 4, 1980.
21. TED–ATD, March 25, 1943.
22. TED–Ruth Simms, April 22, 1943.
23. Hurd interview.
24. TED–Westbrook Pegler, May 15, 1946; Oct. 29, 1945.
25. Moscow interview.
26. TED–ATD, Feb. 18, 1943: TED–John Foster Dulles, July 17, 1943.
27. Barak Mattingly–TED, Nov. 3, 1943; TED reply, Nov. 5, 1943; Alfred M. Landon–TED, Nov. 5, 1943.
28. TED–A. H. Kirchofer, Aug. 8, 1943; TED–Alfred M. Landon, June 15, 1943.
29. Herbert Hoover–TED, Aug. 30, 1943.
30. William Bleakley memo of 1940 convention delegate preferences, undated; Rupert Hughes–TED, May 24, 1948.
31. TED–Arthur Vandenberg, March 23, 1946.
32. TED–ATD, Sept. 14, 1943.
33. Alfred M. Landon–TED, Oct. 5, 1943; Dewey reply, Oct. 19, 1943.

34. Report on Mackinac Conference, Sept. 7, 1943, PSF: Dewey Box 143; John Franklin Carter-Steve Early, Feb. 1, 1944, FDR Library.

35. TED–Ruth Simms, July 13, 1943; Karl Mundt–TED, Sept. 3, 1943; TED reply, Sept. 16, 1943.

36. Ruth Simms–TED, Oct 25, 1943; TED reply, Nov. 19, 1943.

37. Barak Mattingly–TED, Sept. 3, 1943; TED–Ruth Simms, Dec. 23, 1943; Simms reply, Jan. 6, 1944; TED–Alfred M. Landon, Dec. 30, 1943; Jaeckle interview.

38. Carl Rix–Arthur T. Vanderbilt, Jan. 13, 1944; Dec. 20, 1943.

39. Herbert Hoover–TED, April 5, 1944; Carl Rix–TED, April 7, 1944; TED–ATD, April 12, 1944; TED–Ruth Simms, April 12, 1944.

12. *Taking on the Champ*

1. John Hamilton–A. L. Schultz, April 26, 1944, Hamilton Papers, Library of Congress; Herbert Hoover–TED, April 12, 1944; Ruth Simms–TED, April 21, 1944; Alfred M. Landon–TED, April 5, 1944.

2. John Cowles–Elliott Bell, May 1, 1944; Walter Lippmann–John Foster Dulles, April 30, 1944.

3. TED–ATD, May 21, 1944.

4. Gallup interview; TED–Ruth Simms, May 18, 1944.

5. Phillips–Brownell; TED–Elliott Bell, May 25, 1944; TED–ATD, May 14. Dewey's attitude toward the governors' conferences was expressed to Earl Warren in October 1943. In reality, they weren't conferences at all, he wrote his California colleague. "It is a convention at which the Governors sit and listen to speeches . . . go on sightseeing tours and go to banquets. Every discussion is public and is under the restraint involved in talking for home consumption. Can't we have a Governors' Conference," he asked plaintively, "where we really have a conference?" and suggested a three-day affair with no speeches and an agenda limited to discussion of state government.

6. Wadmond interview; TED–Alfred M. Landon, June 6, 1944.

7. Brady interview; Corcoran interview.

8. As evidence of Dewey's sometimes regal bearing, a friend recalls seeing the Governor at a reception beside Francis Cardinal Spellman, formally clad and radiating authority. One awed New Yorker knelt to kiss his Cardinal's ring, rose, approached Dewey, and started to repeat the process instinctively. Hnida interview.

9. Ruth Simms–TED, June 5, 1944.

10. Interview with John Bricker, Nov. 26, 1979; Jaeckle interview.

11. Breitel interview.

12. Scott interview.

13. TED–Clarence Kelland, Aug. 21, 1944; A. H. Kirchofer–TED, Aug. 18, 1944.

14. Herbert Hoover–TED, July 7, 1944; Dewey reply, July 20, 1944.

15. Phillips–Brownell.

16. Phillips–Brownell; Robert McCormick–TED, July 24, 1944.

17. TED–Herbert Brownell, Aug. 17, 1944; TED–Harrison Spangler, Aug. 12, 1944.

18. Jaeckle interview.
19. Bricker interview.
20. TED–Robert McCormick, July 20, 1944.
21. Franklin D. Roosevelt–Fred Adams, Aug. 18, 1944, FDR Library.
22. Raymond Baldwin interview, COHP; Harry Hopkins memo, Aug. 11, 1944, Sherwood–Hopkins files, FDR Library.
23. Memo of Dewey-Willkie conversations, dictated July 20, 1944.
24. Moscow interview.
25. TED–Cordell Hull, Aug. 25, 1944; Hull reply, Sept. 4, 1944.
26. TED–Stanley High, Sept. 5, 1944; Dewey interview, Dulles OHP.
27. Brownell interview, Feb. 1, 1974; Phillips–Brownell; interview with Edith Willkie, June 9, 1974.
28. John Foster Dulles–TED, Oct. 7, 1944.
29. Tom Reynolds-Steve Early, from Dewey campaign train, Sept. 24, 1944, FDR Library.
30. TED–Stanley High, Sept. 5, 1944; Alfred M. Landon–TED, Sept. 7, 1944.
31. A. H. Kirchofer–TED, Sept. 11, 1944; TED–Alfred M. Landon, Oct. 4, 1944; Reynolds memo to Early, ibid.
32. Rupert Hughes–TED, March 29, 1948; Phillips–Brownell.
33. Tufty interview.
34. A. H. Kirchofer–TED, Oct. 19, 1944; Phillips–Brownell.
35. Rosse interview, Jan. 28, 1980; Walter Trohan–Carl T. Hogan, Sept. 21, 1944.
36. Reynolds memo to Early, ibid.; Barnett interview.
37. Rupert Hughes–TED, Sept. 25, 1944; Brownell interview.
38. Walter Trohan–Carl T. Hogan, Sept. 21, 1944; James Farley–John Nance Garner, Sept. 27, 1944. Farley Papers, Library of Congress.
39. Brownell interview, Feb. 1, 1974. Dewey used the same phrase in describing the Oklahoma City speech to Hugh Scott four years later. Obviously, the memory rankled.
40. Unpublished article, "Inside Dewey's Incredible '48 Defeat," John Burton.
41. Report on Marshall–Dewey exchange, Colonel Carter C. Clarke, September 1944. This report, compiled for Clarke's superiors in the wake of his visits to Dewey, was declassified by the National Security Agency early in 1981. It can be found at the National Archives in Washington.
42. Ibid.
43. Ibid.; the letter itself appeared in public for the first time late in 1945, at the conclusion of a congressional inquiry into Pearl Harbor.
44. Ibid.
45. Ibid; Lillian Rosse interview, Jan. 28, 1980.
46. Rosse interview, Jan. 28, 1980; Phillips–Brownell; Burton interview.
47. Hopkins memo, updated, October 1944, FDR Library. After the election, Marshall sent another associate to Albany to thank Dewey for his cooperation and display recent evidence obtained from the disputed Japanese codes. Dewey, aware that a congressional investigation of the affair was likely, volunteered to do what he could to dampen Republican enthusiasm for such a probe. Marshall, equally gracious, said that he had already embarrassed the Governor once; he had no intention of doing so again.
48. Arthur Goldberg–TED, March 30, 1946; updated memo, John Chamberlain to Dewey. After Dewey's death, Chamberlain revealed for the first time

how he was contacted by the Governor, who wanted him to publish the facts surrounding the Marshall letters, without in any way identifying the source of his information. One can guess at the reporter's excitement, listening to Dewey's story unfold as the two men drove along the shores of Saranac Lake.

49. Rupert Hughes–TED, Oct. 2, 1944; Republican National Committee newsletter, September–October 1944.

50. TED–Stanley High, Sept. 5, 1944.

51. TED–Ward Jenks, Oct. 4, 1944; Herbert Brownell–TED, Oct. 3, 1944; Moscow interview.

52. Herbert Brownell–TED, Sept. 11, 1944. Brownell's informant passed along a letter promoting the Thousand Club signed by Estes Kefauver, then a Tennessee congressman. Membership in the exclusive organization carried with it a special copperplated identification plate, "which is all the pass they need here in Washington to go anywhere." Presumably, anywhere included the corridors of power where lucrative war contracts were decided upon. Among its other distinguished members, the Thousand Club included Jesse Jones, Josephus Daniels, Marshall Field, and most of the Roosevelt cabinet. TED–Henry J. Taylor, April 8, 1970; Phillips–Brownell.

53. Breitel interview.

54. Harry Hopkins memo, Nov. 10, 1944, FDR Library; Robert Wood–John Hamilton, Oct. 12, 1944, Hamilton papers, Library of Congress.

55. Hopkins memo, ibid.

56. Gore interview.

57. TED–Franklin D. Roosevelt, Nov. 10, 1944; FDR reply, Nov. 13, 1944, PSF: Dewey; Franklin D. Roosevelt–Hamilton Holt, Nov. 20, 1944, P.P.F. 345, FDR Library.

13. *The Science of Politics*

1. TED–Lowell Thomas, Nov. 8, 1944; TED–Ward Jenks, Jan. 8, 1945.

2. John Hamilton–C. C. Ketchum, Nov. 16, 1944, Hamilton papers, Library of Congress.

3. The Political Action Committee of which Brownell spoke was the unwitting grandfather of more recent PAC's, which by the 1980 campaign were exercising more influence than ever on the electoral process. Most ironic was the best-known PAC of all—the National Conservative Political Action Committee, widely held responsible for defeating a dozen liberal Democrats in the Senate, and contributing to Ronald Reagan's presidential sweep.

4. Robert A. Taft–TED, Dec. 13, 1944; Dewey memo, undated.

5. O'Malley interview; Vandenberg's account of the Roosevelt session is contained in his diary, published as edited by his son in 1955.

6. Phillips–Brownell.

7. TED–Henry Luce, Feb. 10, 1945.

8. Robert A. Taft–TED, Feb. 26, 1945.

9. Interview with Eleanor Lansing Dulles, Jan. 12, 1980.

10. Interview with Charles Breitel, May 16, 1980; Walsh interview; Alvin Johnson–Helen Reid, July 29, 1952.

11. Alvin Johnson–TED, Sept. 19, 1946.

12. Shapiro interview. Another version of events leading up to the bill's passage is given by Warren Moscow, who recalls a conversation in which Ives recounted his visit to the second floor to appeal for the legislation. Dewey didn't seem to share his own fervor about the bill, at one point turning to the Assembly leader and exclaiming, "For God's sake, Irv, you really care about this thing. Why?" Ives, according to Moscow, replied simply, "For God's sake."

13. TED–Harry S. Truman, April 12, 1945; Truman reply, April 30, 1945; Edward D. McKim–TED, May 5, 1945; Truman–TED, May 24, 1945; Dewey reply, May 30, 1945.

14. James Farley–Cordell Hull, April 17, 1945, Farley papers, Library of Congress; Leonard Reid–TED, April 21, 1945; Dewey reply, April 25, 1945.

15. TED–John Perry, May 17, 1946.

16. Interview with John Burton, March 1, 1980.

17. TED–ATD, Feb. 26, 1946.

18. O'Brien interview; minutes of second annual reunion of Castle Rock Survivors Association, Dec. 12, 1946.

19. O'Donnell interview.

20. TED–ATD, Aug. 20, 1947.

21. TED–ATD, Oct. 14, 1947, July 2, 1946; Frances H. Dewey–Helen Stohl, Oct. 9, 1950; Hutt interview.

22. Rosse interview, Jan. 28, 1980; Hutt interview; TED–ATD, Oct. 25, 1948, Sept. 3, 1947, Oct. 1, 1946; TED–George H. Sibley, Dec. 16, 1946; Frances H. Dewey–Peggy Talbott, Feb. 5, 1943.

23. Rosse interview, Sept. 20, 1980.

24. TED–Emory Thomas, March 14, 1946.

25. TED–Winston Churchill, Nov. 6, 1946.

26. TED–Arthur H. Vandenberg, May 22, 1946; TED–J. Edgar Hoover, Sept. 21, 1945.

27. TED–ATD, Sept. 18, 1946.

28. Psychological Corporation Poll, Dewey poll files.

29. TED–John Perry, June 9, 1946; TED–Frank Gannett, Oct. 10, 1946. Among other things, Marcantonio was a co-founder of the Civil Rights Congress, listed in 1947 by Truman's Attorney General, Tom Clark, as a subversive organization. The CRC regularly bailed out Communist leaders (the Bail Fund was supported by Dashiell Hammett, among others, who went to jail for six months for refusing to identify other contributors). In the House, Marcantonio opposed the Marshall Plan as nothing more than a windfall for Wall Street. In 1950, Richard Nixon won election to the Senate partly by comparing the voting records of his Democratic opponent, Representative Helen Gahagan Douglas, with Marcantonio, who lost his own seat that same year.

30. Dulles interview.

31. Chapman interview.

32. TED–Wheeler Sammons, Nov. 7, 1946; TED–ATD, Nov. 10, 1946.

14. *A Second Chance*

1. TED–ATD, Sept. 3, 1947.
2. Kingsland Macy–TED, Jan. 13, 1947; TED–Macy, Nov. 14, 1948.
3. Ben Duffey–TED, Sept. 30, 1948; TED–John Perry, April 5, 1947.
4. Shapiro interview; Schwartz interview.
5. Alvin Johnson–TED, Jan. 30, 1953.
6. Clellan S. Forsyth–Herbert Brownell, April 1, 1947.
7. TED–Frank Gannett, Jan. 3, 1946.
8. TED–H. E. Babcock, March 18, 1947.
9. Herbert Brownell–TED, April 15, 1947.
10. Walter S. Mack–TED, Dec. 9 and 18, 1947; Mack memo to Tom Curran, Jan. 22, 1949; TED–Mack, Jan. 6, 1948.
11. TED–Herbert Brownell, April 7, 1947.
12. TED–Henry Luce, April 23, 1947; Jaeckle interview.
13. TED–Werner Schroder, Jan. 15, 1947; John Perry–TED, Feb. 13, 1948; Dewey reply, Feb. 18, 1948.
14. Thomas E. Stephens–Herbert Brownell, May 16, 1947; Robert H. Thayer–Paul Lockwood, April 10, 1947; Stephens memo to TED, April 8, 1947; Brownell–TED, March 6, 1947.
15. Chapman interview; Scott interview; John Callen O'Loughlin–Roger W. Straus, Nov. 17, 1947.
16. Brownell interview.
17. David Hinshaw–Bradley Nash memo, Dec. 29, 1947.
18. TED–Barak Mattingly, Dec. 15, 1947.
19. Jaeckle interview; Stephens interview; TED–ATD, Jan. 20, 1948.
20. Moscow interview; Harold Stassen–TED, May 16, 1944; Stassen interview, May 29, 1980.
21. Oswald Heck–TED, Feb. 24, 1948; TED–ATD, Feb. 17, 1948.
22. Minutes of political meeting at Hotel Roosevelt, Feb. 14–15, 1948; Pfeiffer interview, New Hampshire primary budget, Harold Keller, Feb. 11, 1948; Robert Blood–Herbert Brownell, April 1, 1948.
23. TED–Leonard Reid, Nov. 13, 1947.
24. TED–ATD, April 14, 1948; TED–Rupert Hughes, April 5, 1948.
25. Phillips–Brownell; Brownell interview with author; interview with Herbert E. Moore, Feb. 28, 1980.
26. Ralph Moores–William Pfeiffer, March 26, 1948; Oregon organizational file, Dewey papers.
27. Herbert Brownell–Paul Lockwood, undated; Thomas E. Stephens–TED, April 17, 1948; Ralph Moores–Brownell, Jan. 22, 1948; Brownell interview; William Pfeiffer–Gerber Advertising Agency, April 20, 1948.
28. Paul Lockwood–Herbert Brownell, undated telegram; Harold Keller–Lockwood, May 5, 1948; Keller–Thomas E. Stephens, undated; O'Brien interview; Brownell memo, April 15, 1948.
29. Lockwood organizational chart of Oregon; TED–Lockwood, April 27, 1948; TED–ATD, April 27, 1948; Thomas E. Stephens–TED, April 17, 1948.
30. Phillips–Brownell.
31. Ibid.
32. J. Parnell Thomas, as chairman of the House Un-American Affairs Com-

mittee, after 1946, oversaw congressional investigations into alleged Communist infiltration of Hollywood, the atomic energy program, and the State Department. Thomas saw much of his thunder stolen by young Republican Richard M. Nixon in the case of Alger Hiss—only weeks before Thomas was indicted on a charge of pocketing funds supposedly paid to staff members. He spent eighteen months in a federal jail at Danbury, Connecticut—the same prison housing Hollywood writers held in contempt of his committee.

33. Ralph Moores–Herbert Brownell, July 9, 1948; Brownell himself was in Missouri the night of the debate, where he could feel a sea change in sentiment among grassroots Republicans who listened in to the Portland confrontation. After that night, he felt good about the Show Me state for the first time. His confidence was justified in Philadelphia. Missouri went for Dewey.

34. Alfred M. Landon interview, Robert Taft project, COHP.

35. Herbert Brownell–Thomas E. Stephens, May 1, 1948.

36. Interview with Ray Bliss, Jan. 15, 1980; Phillips–Brownell; Brownell interview with author.

37. Marge Hogan–Mrs. Charles Weis, Jr., May 22, 1948; Weis–Thomas E. Stephens, May 20, 1948.

38. Jaeckle interview; Edward Martin–TED, Sept. 25, 1947; Scott interview.

39. Phillips–Brownell. Much of the jockeying for delegates centered on the second spot on the ticket. Brownell was candid to say that his own candidate for vice president, Dwight Green, left him "flatfooted" following his declaration for Taft. He believed he had persuaded Green to come out for Dewey, until Colonel McCormick got wind of the plan and ordered his governor to do nothing of the kind. With Green out of the running, Dewey felt increasing pressure to choose someone less clearly associated with the Old Guard. The result: Earl Warren, soon regarded as a major mistake by those in the campaign's upper echelons. Raymond Baldwin interview, COHP.

40. Brownell interview; Jaeckle interview; Stephens interview; Maris McLean–Dwight D. Eisenhower, Dec. 6, 1951. McLean, an Indiana delegate, claimed afterward that Halleck had an assurance "straight from Dewey." The preponderance of evidence suggests, as Tom Stephens argues, that a reasonable man could and probably should have interpreted Halleck's conversations with Sprague and Brownell as a promise.

41. Stern interview; interview with General Robert L. Schultz, May 9, 1980; interview with Kevin McCann, May 8, 1980. The idea of Eisenhower's meeting secretly with a Dewey operative and expressing an interest in the nomination himself is completely at odds with everything known about Ike's attitude toward politics at the time. Yet that is the story told by Russ Sprague to friends after the convention. By then embittered at his own exclusion from the Eisenhower White House, Sprague may also have misinterpreted the General's expressions of alarm over a possible draft with a positive interest in one. The Eisenhower Library has no record of any such meeting. However, both McCann and Schultz confirm that it took place, with Schultz, then Eisenhower's closest military aide, saying there was nothing secret about it, and that it did not take place, as Sprague hinted, during convention week in a secluded hotel room. On the contrary, both men agree that Ike wished to make absolutely clear his own disinterest in political office—a feeling reiterated only a few days later in a public decla-

ration of non-candidacy released to quell efforts by dissident Democrats to dump Truman in favor of the charismatic war hero.

42. Phillip–Brownell; Jaeckle interview; Dewey memo on 1948 convention, undated, Autobiography File.
43. Scott interview.
44. Kingsland Macy–TED, June 26, 1948; Henry Luce–TED, June 25, 1948.

15. *The Man Who Might Have Been*

1. Jaeckle interview.
2. Winston Churchill–TED, June 29, 1948.
3. Robert H. Reed–H. E. Babcock, June 25, 1948; TED–Wheeler Sammons, July 1, 1948; J. Edgar Cherworth–Herbert Brownell, July 5, 1948; Donald R. Van Boskirk–TED, July 1, 1948.
4. TED–Donald R. Van Boskirk, July 6, 1948; TED–George Sokolsky, Jan. 30, 1948.
5. TED–ATD, July 12, 1948.
6. TED–Frank Gannett, Oct. 18, 1948.
7. Dwight D. Eisenhower–TED, Sept. 10, 1948.
8. O'Malley interview; Rogers interview.
9. Breitel interview.
10. Scott interview. The interview with Loeb and Bridges, along with several other revealing incidents, is described in Loeb's article "Thomas E. Dewey—Almost President," written at the time of Dewey's death and appearing in the *Vermont Sunday News* on July 11, 1971.
11. TED–ATD, Aug. 9, 1948.
12. TED–Herbert Brownell, Aug. 20, 1948; TED–John Perry, Sept. 9, 1948; Brownell–TED, Aug. 27, 1948; Ben Duffey–Brownell, Sept. 1, 1948.
13. TED–Herbert Brownell, Aug. 19, 1948; Roger W. Straus–TED, Sept. 2, 1948.
14. TED–ATD, Sept. 14, 1948; Aiken letter to author, Dec. 11, 1979; transcript of July 24, 1948, meeting of Dewey and farm editors at Dapplemere.
15. Arthur H. Vandenberg–TED, July 14, 1948.
16. Phillips–Brownell.
17. Tom Stephens interview, May 9, 1980; Ben Duffey–Herbert Brownell, Aug. 24, 1948; Phillips–Brownell.
18. Phillips–Brownell.
19. O'Brien interview.
20. Interview with Joe Bartlett, March 4, 1980.
21. Scott interview.
22. Stassen interview.
23. Harold Stassen–TED, Aug. 12, 1948; Scott interview.
24. Scott interview; Rosse interview, April 5, 1980.
25. Irene K. Nims–TED, Aug. 18,1948.
26. Barnett interview; interview with R. Burdell Bixby, Jan. 17, 1980; Burton article.
27. Caroline Gannett–TED, Sept. 2, 1948.
28. Harold Stassen–TED, Sept. 21, 1948; Roy Howard–TED, Aug. 18, 1948.
29. Bartlett interview.

30. O'Brien interview; Ben C. Odell–William Pfeiffer, Sept. 2, 1948.
31. Ben Duffey–Elliott V. Bell, Sept. 19, 1948; Duffey–TED, Sept. 30, 1948.
32. Burton article.
33. Gore interview. Ed Jaeckle says that he advised the candidate to have his wife precede him to the platform. This was after Frances received especially warm applause at several stops. As Jaeckle bluntly put it, "People who won't vote for you may vote for your wife." After that, Frances never appeared until the end of her husband's speech.
34. Grace Dewey–TED, Oct. 2, 1948.
35. Wadmond interview.
36. Raymond Baldwin interview, COHP.
37. Jaeckle interview.
38. Harold Stassen–TED, Oct. 12, 1948; Burton article. Leo O'Brien, who was on board the *Victory Special,* confirms the unanimous and almost ferocious rebuke given the candidate when he came back in from his brief, vigorous partisan jabs at the Erie stop.
39. Rosse interview, Sept. 20, 1980.
40. Aiken letter to author, Dec. 11, 1979. According to the Vermonter, Langer cited a threat to the campaign in nine agricultural states.
41. TED–H. E. Babcock, March 2, 1948; Babcock–TED, Oct. 10, 1948. As early as February 1947, Babcock did tell Dewey his opinion that farm surpluses were likely to be a major issue in the next year's elections.
42. Burton article.
43. Burton article; Rosse interview, Jan. 28, 1980; Anna Strong–TED, Sept. 27, 1948.
44. Rosse interview, Jan. 28, 1980; Breitel interview; Walsh interview.
45. Letter from Bernard Katzen to author, March 25, 1980; Katzen interview, March 7, 1980; Chapman interview.
46. Rosse interview, Jan. 28, 1980.
47. Barnett interview; Schwartz interview; Scott interview; Rosse interview, ibid. William Pfeiffer–Herbert Brownell, Oct. 22, 1948.
48. Bricker interview.
49. Interview with Henry Cabot Lodge, Dec. 14, 1979; interview with Katherine Howard, Dec. 21, 1979; Thayer interview.
50. Robbins interview, March 11, 1980.

16. *A Call to Arms*

1. Ray interview.
2. Harry S. Truman–TED, Nov. 3, 1948; Francis Cardinal Spellman–TED, Nov. 3, 1948; Winston Churchill–TED, Feb. 28, 1949; Donald R. Van Boskirk–TED, Dec. 6, 1948.
3. George Sokolsky–TED, Nov. 5, 1948.
4. TED–Henry Luce, Dec. 15, 1948; TED–Emory Thomas, Dec. 15, 1948.
5. Robbins interview, Feb. 19, 1948.
6. Interview with Gabriel Hauge, March 27, 1981; McCormick interview; interview with Tim Seldes, March 11, 1980; Pfeiffer interview; TED–Dwight D. Eisenhower, Oct. 5, 1954; Shapiro interview.
7. Interview with F. Clifton White, Feb. 15, 1980.

8. TED–Jack Mack, Jan. 22, 1949.

9. TED–ATD, Feb. 28, 1949; Orlo M. Brees–TED, Dec. 20, 1948.

10. Shapiro interview; TED–ATD, March 25, 1949.

11. TED–ATD, March 10, 1949.

12. Kingsland Macy–TED, April 19, 1949. Macy was not alone in his resentment. When Bill Pfeiffer asked Jaeckle for advice about taking the vacant job of party chairman, the former chairman was less than encouraging. "They clipped me," he said, in an obvious reference to Dewey. "They'll clip you."

13. Herbert Hoover–TED, July 26, 1949. "You were right not to announce that matter," Hoover wrote of Dewey's offer of the Senate seat to him—also offered to Eisenhower before it finally went to Dulles. "We want Mr. Dulles to have all the prestige possible in these times." Dewey himself maintained afterward publicly that no such offer had been made to Hoover; Dewey interview, Hoover OHP; Dwight D. Eisenhower diary, July 7, 1949, Eisenhower Library.

14. TED–Jack Mack, Dec. 29, 1949.

15. Letter from Milton S. Eisenhower to author, Feb. 11, 1981; TED–Dwight D. Eisenhower, April 11, 1949.

16. Eisenhower diary, July 7, 1949; Eisenhower Library.

17. Dewey interview, Hoover OHP; Dewey interview, Eisenhower Project, COHP.

18. Eisenhower diary, ibid.

19. Dwight D. Eisenhower–TED, Oct. 13, 1949; Eisenhower–TED, Dec. 27, 1949; TED–Eisenhower, Dec. 23, 1949.

20. Eisenhower diary, Sept. 27, 1949, Nov. 25, 1949, Eisenhower Library.

21. TED–Barak Mattingly, April 10, 1950.

22. Dwight D. Eisenhower–TED, Aug. 1, 1952; TED–Gardner Cowles, May 24, 1951; Schultz interview.

23. Eisenhower letter to author, Feb. 11, 1981; Scott interview; White interview; McCann interview.

24. Eisenhower diary, July 7, 1949, Eisenhower Library.

25. TED–ATD, March 13, 1950; Carl T. Hogan–TED, March 10, 1950; Lankler interview. The Reverend Lankler recalls his slightly impertinent efforts to persuade Dewey to seek a third term, brushing aside the Governor's insistence on earning a living for his family with the comment that public service was more important. Dewey stared at his friend for a moment, expressionless, and then said, "You know Ralph, I wouldn't let many people say that to me."

26. Campbell interview.

27. TED–Harry S. Truman, June 28, 1950; TED–ATD, June 28, 1950.

28. Gallup interview.

29. TED–ATD, July 13, Aug. 3, Aug. 16, Aug. 24, 1950; John Franklin Carter–TED, July 28, 1950; Thomas E. Dewey, Jr., recalls hearing his father express concern about hewing to his original decision of not running again, almost as soon as the Korean hostilities broke out at the end of June 1950.

30. Dewey–Phillips interview, Oct. 10, 1957; Jaeckle once heard Dewey express an interest in being Secretary of Defense, while Tommy Corcoran was advising him to strike out for just such a post early in 1951, and a Washington

friend was reporting that Defense might well be preferable to a seat in the Senate. After all, as the friend quoted Corcoran, the Ohioan would be out to "crucify" Dewey the moment he appeared on Capitol Hill. John Carter Franklin–TED, Jan. 12, 1951.

31. Dewey–Phillips, ibid.
32. Moscow interview. Both Frank Moore and Kingsland Macy told the *Times* reporter about the meeting at the Chase. Additional details surfaced in January 1955, when Dewey, by then out of office, testified in Macy's libel suit against the *World-Telegram.*
33. Jaeckle interview. Jaeckle earlier had been called by Hanley, who was seeking his support for the governorship. Jaeckle refused, telling the Lieutenant Governor that he didn't believe Dewey's assertions of friendship. This being the case, Jaeckle had no intention of climbing out on a limb. "I don't want to embarrass myself," he told Hanley. As events unfolded, his caution was justified.
34. Chapman interview; Jaeckle interview; Pfeiffer interview.
35. Chapman interview.
36. Pfeiffer interview; TED–ATD, Sept. 8, 1950.
37. TED–ATD, Sept. 24, 1950.
38. TED–ATD, Oct. 1, 1950.
39. Eisenhower diary, Oct. 13, 1950, Eisenhower Library; Chapman interview; Golden interview.
40. Chapman interview; undated memo from Lawrence Walsh; Moscow interview.
41. Chapman interview.
42. Report of Herlands investigation, May 5, 1954; Rosse interview, March 8, 1980.
43. Rosse interview, March 8, 1980; Walsh interview; Carl F. Espe–William Herlands, July 26, 1954.
44. Carl F. Espe–William Herlands, Nov. 22, 1954.
45. Rosse interview, Feb. 4, 1980; TED–Barak Mattingly, Sept. 24, 1952; Chapman interview. Heffernden himself died in December 1952. His F section files were destroyed at the time of V-J Day.
46. George Hinman–TED, Nov. 8, 1950; Herwitz interview; TED–A. H. Kirchofer; TED–Jack Mack, Dec. 26, 1950.

17. *The President Maker*

1. TED–Winston Churchill, Dec. 22, 1950.
2. Dwight D. Eisenhower–TED, Aug. 1,1952.
3. TED–Winston Churchill, March 13, 1951; Russell Davenport–TED, Feb. 8, 1951; Shapiro interview; TED–Ben Duffey, April 12, 1951.
4. TED–ATD, April 11, 1951; Chapman interview.
5. Joseph McCarthy–TED, June 25, 1951; TED reply, June 28, 1951; TED–McCarthy, March 12, 1951; TED–Frank Kenna, Jan. 10, 1951.
6. TED–Alvin Johnson, Feb. 21, 1951; interview with Bernard Shanley, June 5, 1980; Dewey memo, undated; Harold Stassen–TED, May 21, 1951.
7. Letter from Hugh Scott to author, June 9, 1980; Scott interview; TED–ATD, Sept. 11, 1951.

8. Gene Pulliam–Harry Darby, Oct. 11, 1951; Wadmond interview.
9. Robert A. Taft–TED, Oct. 29, 1951.
10. Lucius Clay interview, COHP.
11. Interview with Henry Cabot Lodge, Dec. 14, 1979; Darby interview; TED–Henry Cabot Lodge, Nov. 17, 1951; Lodge reply, Nov. 26, 1951.
12. TED–Helen Reid, Nov. 13, 1951; Milton Eisenhower to author, Feb. 11, 1981; Brownell interview; interview with Gen. Robert L. Schultz, May 9, 1980.
13. Dewey memo, undated; Dewey interview, COHP.
14. Dewey memo, undated.
15. Dewey memo, Jan. 12, 1952; TED–Herb Brownell, May 15, 1952; TED–Ben Duffey, Feb. 15, 1952; Stephens interview, May 9, 1980; Harold Stassen–TED, March 25, 1952; Frank M. Johnson–TED, March 21, 1952.
16. Clay interview, COHP; TED–Wheeler Sammons, March 29, 1952; Rosse interview, April 5, 1980.
17. Jaeckle interview, May 11, 1980; Dewey interview, COHP; Herbert Brownell interview, COHP.
18. Dwight D. Eisenhower–TED, March 18, 1952; Brownell interview, COHP; TED–Dwight D. Eisenhower, March 20, 1952.
19. TED–Gardner Cowles, April 19, 1952; TED–ATD, April 19, 1952.
20. White interview; New York Confidential Political Report, March 16, 1953, Eisenhower Library. Interestingly, a Gallup poll of presidential preferences among New York Republicans about the time Dewey's forces were sweeping the state showed Taft actually favored over Eisenhower, 36 percent to 26 percent. Rank and file opinion counted little in a state whose primary law historically gave an enormous advantage to the organization.
21. Dewey interview, COHP; Nixon's recollection of the dinner is to be found in his *RN: The Memoirs of Richard M. Nixon,* published by Grosset and Dunlap in 1977.
22. Interview with Melvin Laird, June 3, 1980.
23. TED–Dwight D. Eisenhower, June 14, 1952.
24. Brownell interview.
25. Brownell interview; Herwitz interview.
26. TED–ATD, June 26, 1952; interview with Sherman Adams, July 14, 1980.
27. Walter Kohler–TED, Nov. 21, 1958; Sherman Adams interview, COHP.
28. Interview with Henry Cabot Lodge, May 28, 1980.
29. Interview with R. Burdell Bixby, May 28, 1980; Rogers interview.
30. Hugh Scott to author, June 9, 1980.
31. O'Brien interview.
32. Pfeiffer interview; Wadmond interview. It should be noted that Pfeiffer does not recollect so bald a threat from Dewey, yet others in Chicago do, and newspaper accounts then and later reinforce those memories.
33. White interview.
34. Bixby interview, May 28, 1980; Moscow interview; letter from Warren Moscow to author, April 22, 1980.
35. Bixby interview, May 28, 1980; White interview; Wadmond interview.
36. Interview with Ray Bliss, Jan. 15, 1980.
37. Mrs. Gardner Cowles–TED, July 14, 1952.
38. Brownell interview.

39. Interview with David W. Peck, Jan. 14, 1980; letter from David W. Peck to author, July 21, 1980.

40. Lodge interview, May 28, 1980; Pfeiffer interview; interview with Ab Herman, May 8, 1980; interview with Tom Bewley, May 29, 1980. Herman, then and later an important cog in the Republican National Committee, watched Nixon from a good vantage point in Chicago "obviously working California for Ike." Bewley, Nixon's first law partner, rode on the same train with the Senator from Denver to Chicago. While his friend remained up front with what Bewley called "the big shots" for most of the trip, he says it was no secret among the Californians that Nixon and Earl Warren were engaged in "a hullabaloo . . . over who would run the delegation."

41. Moscow interview; Bixby interview, May 28, 1980; Brownell interview, COHP.

42. Lucius Clay–TED, March 30, 1970; Sherman Adams interview, COHP; Stern interview; Darby interview; Robbins interview.

43. Rogers interview; Pfeiffer interview; Stephens interview; TED–Mrs. Gardner Cowles, July 15, 1952; Livingston Platt–TED, July 25, 1952.

44. Dwight D. Eisenhower–TED, undated telegram; Eisenhower–TED, Aug. 1, 1952; Elizabeth T. Fraser–TED, Sept. 24, 1952.

45. Robert A. Taft–John D. M. Hamilton, Aug. 27, 1952, Hamilton papers, Library of Congress; Taft memo, undated, Taft papers, Library of Congress.

46. John Franklin Carter–TED, Aug. 18, 1952.

47. Golden interview; Pfeiffer interview; Bernie Katzen memo to TED, Sept. 10, 1952; Frank Stanton–TED, Aug. 25, 1952; Sherman Adams interview; COHP; Hogan interview.

48. Taft memo, undated, Taft papers, Library of Congress; Sherman Adams interview, COHP; TED–ATD, Sept. 16, 1952.

49. TED–Sherman Adams, Sept. 18 and 19, 1952; confidential source; Sherman Adams interview, COHP.

50. Brownell interview, COHP; Nixon's most thorough account of the Fund Crisis is to be found in Six Crises, published in 1962 by Doubleday.

51. TED–ATD, Sept. 23, 1954.

52. Shapiro interview; confidential source; interview with Dwayne Andreas, Dec. 24, 1979.

53. TED–ATD, Sept. 30, 1952; TED–Elizabeth T. Fraser, Sept. 29, 1952.

54. Interview with Bryce Harlow, Jan. 26, 1980; White interview.

55. Stephens interview; Shanley interview.

56. Ben Duffey–TED, Nov. 11, 1952; TED–Mrs. Gardner Cowles, Dec. 6, 1952; TED–Elizabeth T. Fraser, Dec. 22, 1952; Oliver Franks–TED, Nov. 8, 1952.

57. Interview with R. Burdell Bixby, Feb. 19, 1981. Bixby's own phrase for what happened at Augusta, and it is probably the best description extant, is that Eisenhower invited Dewey down to "explore his availability."

58. Bixby interview, Jan. 17, 1980; TED–Winston Churchill, Nov. 11, 1952. The line from Dewey to Lambert is contained in Lambert's book All Out of Step, published by Macmillan in 1955.

59. Brownell interview; interview with Lillian Rosse, July 17, 1980; interview with Thomas E. Dewey, Jr., April 15, 1981. Ed Walsh recalls a discussion of the chief justiceship by Dewey early in the Eisenhower administration.

60. Lucius Clay interview, COHP; Rosse interview, Feb. 9, 1980; Dewey interview, COHP; Hart interview; Champion interview; Andreas interview.

61. TED–Dwight D. Eisenhower, Oct. 5, 1954; interview with Burdell Bixby, April 23, 1980; Eisenhower diary, Oct. 10, 1956; James Hagerty diary, June 3, and 8, 1954, Eisenhower Library. According to Thomas E. Dewey, Jr., his father played a leading role in hiring Joseph Welch, the Boston attorney who began McCarthy's downfall at the 1954 hearings.
62. TED–Dwight D. Eisenhower, Oct. 5, 1954; Eisenhower reply, Oct. 8, 1954.
63. TED–Dwight D. Eisenhower, Oct. 11, 1954; Tallamy interview; Eisenhower–TED, Nov. 29, 1955; Eisenhower–John Foster Dulles, Feb. 2, 1956, Eisenhower Library; interview with Meade Alcorn, April 28, 1980.
64. TED–Dwight D. Eisenhower, Jan. 22, 1957; TED–George Leib, June 10, 1957; TED–Thomas E. Dewey, Jr., July 28, 1955; TED–Barak Mattingly, Nov. 12, 1954.
65. Shanley interview; Bliss interview; interview with Bryce Harlow, Jan. 25, 1980; Alcorn interview; Andreas interview; confidential source.
66. Interview with Thomas E. Dewey, Jr., Nov. 16, 1973; Brownell interview; Harlow interview, Jan. 26, 1980; Dewey interview, COHP.

18. *A Graceful Retreat*

1. TED–James Hagerty, May 26, 1954.
2. TED–Felix Frankfurter, May 2, 1953; Frankfurter–TED, Aug. 5, 1953; TED reply, Aug. 18, 1953.
3. TED–ATD, March 20, 1953.
4. TED–ATD, May 4, 1954; Rosse interview, Feb. 9, 1980.
5. Moscow interview.
6. TED–ATD, March 15, 1954.
7. TED–ATD, Oct. 17, 1953; O'Donnell interview, May 15, 1980.
8. TED–ATD, Nov. 13, 1953.
9. White interview; TED–Alfred Kirchofer, Nov. 6, 1953; TED–ATD, Nov. 20, 1953.
10. Eisenhower diary, Dec. 11, 1953, Eisenhower Library.
11. TED–ATD, March 22, 1954.
12. John Franklin Carter–TED, June 25, 1953; TED reply, June 26, 1953.
13. TED–John Franklin Carter, Nov. 27, 1953.
14. Jim Hagerty diary, June 3 and July 12, 1954, Eisenhower Library; TED–Joseph Robinson, June 28, 1954; TED–Clare Boothe Luce, Oct. 16, 1954.
15. TED–ATD, Sept. 29, 1954; Jaeckle interview; confidential source; Javits' own account of his encounter with Dewey is contained in *Javits: The Autobiography of a Public Man* published in 1981 by Houghton Mifflin.
16. Alvin Johnson–TED, Sept. 9, 1954; John Franklin Carter–TED, Nov. 4, 1953.
17. TED–ATD, Oct. 16 and Nov. 4, 1954.
18. TED–ATD, Nov. 12, 1954.
19. TED–Emory Thomas, Dec. 13, 1954, Feb. 9, 1955; Rosse interview, Feb. 9, 1980.
20. Interview with R. Burdell Bixby, Feb. 14, 1980.
21. Bauman interview; Rosse interview, May 27, 1980; John Dewey interview, May 16, 1980.

22. Stewart interview; Rosse interview, May 27, 1980; John Dewey interview, May 16, 1980.

23. Thomas E. Dewey, Jr., interview, March 14, 1980; TED–Thomas E. Dewey, Jr., July 28, 1955, Jan. 3, 1955.

24. TED–Emory Thomas, Nov. 7, 1955; TED–Lowell Thomas, June 11, 1961; private notes of 1957 trip; TED–Emily Warren, Aug. 20, 1957.

25. Notes on 1957 trip; Thomas E. Dewey, Jr., interview, March 14, 1980; Bixby interview, Jan. 17, 1980.

26. Mrs. Joseph Robinson–Frances H. Dewey, Nov. 28, 1954; Frances H. Dewey–Amelia Bell, Dec. 8, 1952; Rosse interview, May 27, 1980.

27. Rosse interview, May 27, 1980; Frances H. Dewey–Harold Hutt, Aug. 13, 1957; Thomas E. Dewey, Jr., interview, March 14, 1980; John Dewey interview, Feb. 15, 1980; confidential source. There is no evidence of any drinking problem until the last years of Frances' life, and then, believe intimates, it was aggravated by her medical condition and inability to take medicines as prescribed.

28. Richard M. Nixon–TED, Jan. 13, 1960; Alcorn interview.

29. Charles Murphy–Carl T. Hogan, Nov. 12, 1956. Perhaps made permanently cautious by 1948, Elliott Bell forecast an Eisenhower plurality of only 4.5 million votes, and nearly 80 fewer electoral votes than the President actually received.

30. Burton interview, July 5, 1980; Shapiro interview; interview with Robert Bass, May 9, 1980.

31. Pfeiffer interview; John Dewey interview, May 16, 1980; Harry O'Donnell–TED, April 3, 1962.

32. Martin interview; O'Donnell interview, April 26, 1980; Mueller interview.

33. TED–Harry O'Donnell, Nov. 4, 1962; Thomas E. Dewey, Jr., interview, March 14, 1972; Brownell interview; Dwayne Andreas–TED, May 7, 1968; Laird interview.

34. Rosse interview, Feb. 4, 1980.

35. TED letter, March 26, 1962 (recipient unknown); Mueller interview.

36. Thomas E. Dewey, Jr., interview, Oct. 6, 1980; Andreas interview; Hurd interview; TED–Walter Kohler, Dec. 27, 1968; TED–Dwayne Andreas, Dec. 15, 1964.

37. Rosse interview, Feb. 4, 1980; Mueller interview; Andreas interview.

38. Lyndon B. Johnson–TED, March 8, May 19, May 27, 1965; TED–Johnson, May 20, 1965.

39. O'Donnell interview, May 15, 1980; TED–Lyndon B. Johnson, Nov. 18, 1965.

40. Bliss interview; interview with Jo Goode, Nov. 28, 1979. Bryce Harlow recalls how Dewey, joined by Eisenhower, raised "pluperfect hell" over a draft statement within the ROC that strongly tilted toward the Israeli position in the crisis over the Middle East. Both men voiced alarm over American-Arab relations, and in the end succeeded in watering down the text.

41. Rosse interview, May 27, 1980; Hart interview; TED–Dr. M.J. Bagley, July 10, 1963; Hogan interview; Kohler interview; TED–William H. Timbers, April 28, 1956; interview with William H. Timbers, April 23, 1965.

42. Rosse interview, Jan. 28, 1980; Hart interview; Marchetti interview; John Dewey interview, Feb. 15, 1980.

43. TED–Patsy Hogan Welles, Oct. 5, 1970; interview with Carroll Boynton, Feb. 28, 1980.

44. Champion interview; Rosse interview, Jan. 28, 1980; Brownell interview; Thomas E. Dewey, Jr., interview, March 14, 1980.

45. Richard M. Nixon–TED, Nov. 17, 1967; TED reply, Nov. 21, 1967. According to Dwayne Andreas, Nixon also invited Dewey to join him on a planned visit to the People's Republic of China, a journey called off in the spring of 1967 following sharp condemnation of the Peking regime by Secretary of State Dean Rusk for its support of North Vietnamese forces.

46. Laird interview; Rosse interview, Feb. 9, 1980; Charles S. Rhyne–TED, Oct. 7, 1968; Bauman interview; Andreas interview.

47. TED–David W. Peck, Nov. 6, 1968; Mueller interview; Andreas interview.

48. Alexander Haig–TED, March 9, 1971; Andreas interview; Laird interview; confidential source.

49. Henry Kissinger–TED, March 2, 1970; TED–Kissinger, Feb. 16, 1970; Rosse interview, Feb. 9, 1980; TED–Kissinger, July 15, 1970; Melvin Laird–TED, April 20, 1970.

50. Interview with John Dewey, Feb. 23, 1980; Hutt interview; Rosse interview, Feb. 9, 1980; Mueller interview; Richard M. Nixon–TED, Dec. 5, 1970.

51. Confidential source; Scott interview.

52. Andreas interview; Mueller interview.

53. Charlotte Kohler–TED, July 30, 1970; Thomas E. Dewey, Jr., interview, March 14, 1980; Rosse interview, Sept. 20, 1980.

54. Interview with Tela Cook, March 8, 1980; Kohler interview; Rosse interview, Jan. 28, 1980.

55. Hart interview.

56. Hart interview; Kohler interview.

57. Hart interview.

58. Sumner interview; Hart interview; Mueller interview; confidential source.

59. Thomas E. Dewey, Jr., interview, March 14, 1980; Rosse interview, Sept. 20, 1980; Dr. Richard Elias–Dr. A. Wilbur Duryee, Feb. 15, 1971; confidential source.

60. Interview with Edward Rose, March 1, 1980; Andreas interview; Scott interview; Robert Finch–TED, March 4, 1971.

61. Andreas interview; interview with Bill McMurtrie, Jan. 28, 1980; Hart interview; Rosse interview, Jan. 28, 1980.

62. Andreas interview; McMurtrie interview; Rosse interview, Jan. 28, 1980.

63. Kohler interview; Andreas interview. Additional details of the events surrounding Dewey's death are to be found in the Miami *Herald* of March 17, 1971.

Epilogue: *"There Goes the Warrior"*

1. Dewey autopsy report, March 16, 1971; Andreas interview.

2. Message file from the time of Dewey's death.

3. Hart interview; Thomas E. Dewey, Jr., interview, March 14, 1980.

4. Ralph Lankler–Thomas E. Dewey, Jr., April 12, 1971.

5. Mueller interview; Cook interview.

6. Rosse interview, Feb. 1, 1980.

Sources

INTERVIEWS

Sherman Adams, Meade Alcorn, Dean Alfange, Florence Akin, Dwayne Andreas, Lester Arrow, Arthur Barnett, Joseph Bartlett, Robert Bass, Arnold Bauman, Thomas Bewley, R. Burdell Bixby, Raymond Bliss, Carroll Boynton, Dorothy Brady, Charles Breitel, John Bricker, Herbert Brownell, Laman Bruner, McGeorge Bundy, Valerie Busby, John Burton, George W. Campbell, George Champion, Alger Chapman, Henry J. Clay, Oscar J. Cohen, Tela Cook, Thomas Cook, Thomas G. Corcoran, Jack Cotten, Paul Curran, Joseph Czechlewski.

Harry Darby, Mrs. W. B. Davis, Richard Denzer, Vincent Dermody, John Dewey, Thomas E. Dewey, Jr., Eleanor Lansing Dulles, A. Wilbur Duryee, Norman Diamond, Henry Elkind, Winthrop S. Emmet, Herbert Fabricant, Thomas Fay, Jr., Stanley Fuld, George Gallup, Robert Gamarche, Joseph Gasarch, Thomas Gilchrest, Livingston Goddard, Jo Goode, Lou Golden, Louise Gore, Thurston Green, Irene Grumet, Jacob Grumet, Mrs. Murray Gurfein, Katie Haas, Bryce Harlow, Helen Harrelson, Kitty Carlisle Hart, Charles Hattauer, Gabriel Hauge, Ab Herman, Victor Herwitz, Irving Hest, Frank Hnida, Mrs. Frank Hogan, Jack Hogan, Katherine Howard, T. Norman Hurd, Harold Hutt, Anna D. Hynes.

Edwin Jaeckle, Bernard Katzen, Florence Kelly, Page Benson Kelly, Murray Kempton, Frank Kirsie, Whitman Knapp, Charlotte Kohler, Richard Korn, Irene Kuhn, Melvin Laird, Alexander Lankler, Ralph Lankler, Eugene Leibman, Henry Cabot Lodge, J. Edward Lubard, Augustus Marchetti, Ben Margolin, Janet Martin, Kevin McCann, Ralph McAfee, Kenneth McCormick, Harold McGowan, William Mertens, Gae Mitchell, Robert Moore, Warren Moscow, John L. Mowry, Arnulf Mueller, Charles Murphy, Jr., Thomas Murphy, William McMurtrie, Leo O'Brien, Harry O'Donnell, James O'Malley, Jack Pace, Louis Pagnucco, David Peck, William Pfeiffer, Abraham Poeretz, Earl Putnam, Robert Ray, David Rockefeller, Elly Robbins, William P. Rogers, Oren Root, Edward Rose, Harlow Ross, Lillian Rosse.

Bert Sarafan, Joseph Sarafite, Robert L. Schultz, Arthur Schwartz, Hugh Scott, Gavin Scotti, Tim Seldes, Betty Seeley, Bernard Shapiro, George Shapiro, Florence Shientag, John Simmons, Bertrand Shanley, William Sirignano, Howard Smith, Harold Stassen, Thomas E. Stephens, Henry Root Stern, Jr., Charles Stewart, Joseph Stone, Mary Pickens Sumner, Lois Sutton, Bert Tallamy, Robert Thayer, Lowell Thomas, Charles Tillinghurst, William H. Timbers, Esther Tufty, Julia Umsheid, Rudi Umsheid, William Umsheid, Vincent Viciano, Mrs. Leon Vosburgh, Lowell Wadmond, Isabel Walsh, Lawrence Walsh, Robert Warren, Mr. and Mrs. John Welch, Mr. and Mrs. Phillip Welch, Patsy Hogan Welles, F. Clifton White, David Worgen, John E. F. Wood, Stephine C. Wooden, James Yeargin.

UNPUBLISHED MATERIAL

Columbia Oral History Project: Though not all are quoted in the text, all of the following interviews in some way shed light on Dewey and his times: Sherman

Adams, William A. Allen, Raymond Baldwin, Herbert Brownell, Lucius Clay, Thomas E. Dewey (on the Eisenhower administration), David Dressler, Milton S. Eisenhower, Stanley Fuld, Jonah J. Goldstein, Gabriel Hauge, Stanley Isaacs, Alfred M. Landon, Herbert Lehman, J. Edward Lumbard, Newbold Morris, David W. Peck, Ferdinand Pecora, Warren Moscow. The following interviews are copyrighted © by the Trustees of Colombia University in the City of New York and are used by permission. David Dressler (1972), William A. Allen (1972), Herbert Lehman (1972), Stanley Isaacs (1972), Warren Moscow (1972), and Lucius Clay (1976).

Harlan Phillips Interviews, all of which are contained in the Dewey Collection at Rochester, include the following: Charles Breitel, Herbert Brownell, James Dealey, Thomas E. Dewey, Stanley Fuld, William Herlands, Marland Gale, Sol Gelb, Paul Lockwood, Joseph Panuch, Manny Robbins, Raymond Seymour, J. Russel Sprague, Harris Steinberg.

At the Library of Congress, I benefited from use of the papers of Joseph Barnes, a close friend of Willkie's, whose biography of the 1940 nominee was published eight years after Willkie's death; James Farley; Hamilton Fish; John D. M. Hamilton; and Robert A. Taft. Two other Oral History transcripts, involving Dewey's relations with John Foster Dulles and Herbert Hoover, are cited in the chapter notes.

NEWSPAPERS

The daily press was generous to Dewey, at least when it came to space. His exploits won headlines in virtually every American journal in the 1930s, and, of course, his presidential campaigns filled news pages for another decade after that. In New York City, I have made extensive use of the New York *Times, Herald Tribune, Star, Mirror, Daily News, World-Telegram, Journal-American, Sun,* and *P.M.* Elsewhere in New York State, the Albany *Times-Union* and *Knickerbocker News* are both helpful for coverage of the Dewey years in the capital. The Buffalo *News,* edited by the governor's friend A. H. Kirchofer, provides another inside perspective.

Other journals yielded considerable background, and more than a little hard fact: The Brooklyn *Eagle,* White Plains *News,* Yonkers *Record,* Amsterdam *Recorder,* Jamaica *Press,* and *Newsday.* Upstate, there were the Schenectady *Union-Star,* Niagara Falls *Gazette,* Newburgh *News,* Massena *Observer,* Kingston *News,* Ithaca *Journal,* Troy *Observer,* Rome *Sentinel,* Binghamton *Sun,* Syracuse *Herald,* Syracuse *Post-Standard,* Utica *Press,* Watertown *News,* Elmira *Advertiser,* Rochester *Democrat and Chronicle,* and Rochester *Times-Union.*

Outside of New York, no look at the Republican party during the period of Dewey's leadership would be complete without Colonel McCormick's acid-tongued clarion of Midwestern conservatism, the Chicago *Tribune.* The Washington *Post,* Washington *Evening Star,* Philadelphia *Bulletin,* and Boston *Herald* also furnished helpful information. Much of my account of Dewey's final days, and of the story surrounding his death, comes from three thick cartons of newspaper clippings compiled in March 1971 and now housed at Rochester.

PERIODICALS

The nation's magazines and news journals were equally attracted to Dewey as a subject. His gangbusting exploits made a natural subject for popular reporting. His campaign activities engendered controversy. His personality excited debate. *Time, Newsweek,* the *Literary Digest, Life,* and *U.S. News & World Report* provided a steady stream of weekly reports. More probing coverage, often critical, can be found in the brittle assessments of *The New Yorker, Harper's, American Mercury,* the *Nation,* and the *New Republic. Collier's, Fortune,* and the *Saturday Evening Post* generally treated Dewey with admiration. *Liberty* and *American* magazine were downright friendly, *Real Detective* wide-eyed, and *Reader's Digest* a willing platform for Dewey, Willkie, Hoover, and other anti–New Deal spokesmen.

It would be virtually impossible to list all the articles that shaped this book; suffice it to say that my interpretation of Dewey is heavily indebted to his journalistic contemporaries. Some of the most useful included profiles of the youthful crime fighter in the March 1934 issue of *American* magazine, the October 1936 *Real Detective,* and J. T. Flynn's look at "New York's War on Rackets" in *Collier's* for October 5, 1935. Dewey's own article in the November 1937 *Reader's Digest,* "What Every Citizen Should Know About Crime," is worth looking at. Raymond Moley covered Dewey in several *Newsweek* columns; his "Dewey the Prosecutor" dated August 8, 1938, is revealing. A far less flattering examination of the man and his methods can be found in "St. George and the Dragnet," by Woollcott Gibbs and John Bainbridge in *The New Yorker,* May 24, 1940, and in Benjamin Stolberg's savage profile "Thomas E. Dewey, Self-made Myth," published in *American Mercury,* June 1940.

Forrest Davis contributed a comprehensive review of the Gangbuster in "Smashing the Rackets," a five-part series that ran in the *Saturday Evening Post* from mid-October 1937 until January 15, 1938. A similar story is Henry F. Pringle's "Putting Down Crime: Dewey's Amazing War on the Racketeers," *Woman's Home Companion,* September 1937. Jack Alexander's profile of Dewey in the September 27, 1938, issue of *Life* is balanced and credible. Hickman Powell, although a close friend of the candidate, contributed a surprisingly candid look at Dewey in *Cosmopolitan*'s September 1938 edition; and for a fascinating look behind the headlines being generated out of the District Attorney's office, there is a series of articles published in the July and August 1939 issues of *Collier's,* written by Dixie Davis under the umbrella title "Things I Couldn't Tell Until Now."

The *Nation* could always be counted upon for critical coverage of New York's latest phenomenon. Oswald G. Villard weighed in with "Facts about Mr. Dewey" in February 24, 1940, issue; and, not to be outdone, John Richmond contributed a scathing profile of Dewey, one of the "Men Who Would Be President," less than a month later, on March 16. Barent Ten Eyck answered Richmond's piece with an interesting rejoinder in the April 27 issue. No such rebuttal appeared in the *New Republic* after its critical essay "Young Mr. Dewey" appeared on February 12, 1940.

"Tom Dewey," by Noel Busch, in the April 22, 1940, issue of *Life,* is typical of the slightly bewildered, slightly cynical attitude toward the Gangbuster held by many in the press of the period. Henry Pringle contributed "Mr. and Mrs. Dewey" to the *Ladies' Home Journal* for August 1939; "Meet the Deweys," by Lowell Thomas, appeared in the same publication in November 1944. E. B.

White's funny imaginary conversation "Breakfast on Quaker Hill" ran in the October 28, 1944, issue of *The New Yorker*.

Politics of the late 1930s revolved around no issue so heated as isolationism, and no personality as charismatic as Wendell Willkie. The first is argued by Herbert Hoover in "Shall We Send Our Youth to War?" in *Reader's Digest*, September 1937. Willkie's name turned up often during this period—sometimes on the by-line of articles preaching his vaguely liberal, vaguely nostalgic, definitely anti-Roosevelt gospel. "The Faith That Is America" appeared in the July 1939 *Reader's Digest*. "We the People," *Fortune's* special pro-Willkie edition of April 1940, is invaluable, as is Janet Flanner's lively profile of "Rushville's Renowned Son-in-Law" that ran in the October 12, 1940, *New Yorker*. "The Man Who Talked Back," in the *Saturday Evening Post* for February 25, 1939, is a less equivocal tribute to the utilities tycoon who suddenly found himself the voice of enlightened Republicanism.

Two scholarly articles on the Republican opposition to Roosevelt are Ronald Bridges' "The Republican Program Committee" in *Public Opinion Quarterly*, April 1939, and "Republican Opposition during Wartime, 1941–45," by Donald R. McCoy, in *Mid-America*, July 1967. The period leading up to Dewey's 1944 nomination brought forth a spate of profiles, few of them neutral. Critical articles include Richard Rovere's highly negative "Dewey: The Man in the Blue Serge Suit," which appeared in the May 1944 issue of *Harper's;* I. F. Stone's "Thomas E. Dewey," the *Nation*, May 20, 1944, and Elliot Janeway's "Birth of the Tickets," in the August 1944 *Fortune*. More favorable pieces include Hickman Powell's "My Friend, Tom Dewey," *Collier's*, June 24, 1944; "The Great Albany Enigma," Forrest Davis' two-part look at a reluctant candidate that ran in the *Saturday Evening Post* on January 22 and January 29, 1944; and Stanley Walker's "Snapshots of Tom Dewey," *Reader's Digest*, August 1944.

The 1944 campaign saw some of the best coverage of Dewey. Little, if any, surpassed Roger Butterfield's superb review of the candidate's early years published in the October 9 issue of *Life*. The men around Dewey were examined as well: Forrest Davis wrote about Elliott Bell and others in "Dewey's April Decision," *Saturday Evening Post*, August 12, 1944. *Life* ran a profile of "Dewey's Man Jaeckle" in its June 12 edition; *Collier's* profiled Herbert Brownell on September 2. Additional articles of interest include I. F. Stone's "Thomas E. Dewey: Close-up of a Candidate," the *Nation*, May 20, 1944; "The Dewey Personality," by Marquis Childs, *Liberty*, October 7, 1944; Russell Davenport's "Why I Cannot Vote for Dewey," *American Mercury*, October 1944; the *New Republic's* special edition on Dewey and his career dated September 25, 1944; and *Look's* advice to the Republicans contained in its September 19 issue. An article of special interest in Louise Overader's "Presidential Campaign Funds in 1944," appearing in *American Political Science Review* for October 1945.

John Chamberlain's article on what Dewey knew and didn't know about Pearl Harbor created a sensation when it appeared in *Life* on September 24, 1945. Less sensational but equally revealing about the GOP at a time of rancorous dispute is a long look at the party's leading personalities in the April 1947 issue of *Fortune*. Henry C. Turner authored "Tolerance in Industry: The Record," for the New York *Times Magazine* of August 24, 1947, an excellent overview of Dewey's civil rights laws and their impact upon black employment in New York. The same magazine carried an article on Dewey and Mead at the tail-end of their bitter 1946 gubernatorial fight, on October 27, 1946. Edward Rigby's "Thomas

Dewey's First Eleven" in the August 2, 1947, issue of the *Saturday Evening Post* is another reminder of how important team government was in Dewey's Albany. "Mr. Dewey's Methods," *U.S. News & World Report,* July 19, 1948, and Stanley High's "The Case for Tom Dewey," *Saturday Evening Post,* March 22, 1948, are self-explanatory. So is Robert G. Spivack's "Tactics of a Scared Candidate," published in the *Nation* on May 8, 1948, in the crucial weeks before Oregonians went to the polls and reversed Stassen's lead. The *Collier's* profile "Governor Dewey," May 1, 1948, is especially useful on Dewey's foreign policy attitudes and work habits. Robert Bendiner wrote a *Nation* profile dated July 3, 1948, entitled, "The Nominee Nobody Loves." A less partisan look at the candidate came in *Life's* September 13, 1948, preview of a Dewey administration based upon his Albany record.

Kiplinger's magazine for November 1948 is a treasure trove of Dewey predictions, with a fat preview of the new administration put together with considerable help from inside sources. Ernest K. Lindley's reporting of the 1948 campaign in *Newsweek* is eye-opening; the same can be said of Richard Rovere's work for *The New Yorker,* especially his delightful "Letter from a Campaign Train," October 16, 1948. Alden Hatch's "Men Around Dewey," *Harper's,* October 1948, is useful, as is "What Kind of President Will Dewey Make?" by Joseph and Stewart Alsop, *Saturday Evening Post,* October 16, 1948. *Business Week* in its October 9, 1948, issue looked at Dewey's Pawling farm, while *American* magazine for the month of October 1948 contains a charming, if wistful, look at Quaker Hill and the people of Pawling. One biting newspaper article deserves mention: the New York *Star's* "Barefoot Boys with Screws On," written by Hurd S. Corners (a pseudonym), a profile of Dewey's boyhood that appeared on October 11, 1948.

Post-1948 articles of value include *"Thomas E. Dewey,"* in the *Nation,* February 19, 1949; Dewey's own series of articles on foreign policy for *Collier's* on February 10 and May 12, 1951; the reports of his Pacific journey that ran in the magazine on December 1, 8, and 15, 1952; "Why I'm for Eisenhower," another Dewey piece that ran in the May 17, 1952, *Collier's;* and Andrew J. Vigliotta's firsthand account of the riotous maneuvering on the convention floor that led to Eisenhower's nomination, "Our Delegation Helped Dewey Put Ike Over," *Long Island Press,* March 21, 1971. Harold Ickes contributed a predictably partisan commentary on "The Great Hanley Scandal" to the *New Republic,* October 30, 1950. Nine months later, Ickes was back in the same journal with "What's Dewey Doing?" July 16, 1951. Another old Dewey foe, Warren Moscow, speculated about a turning point in New York politics in the *Nation* for July 31, 1954, "End of a GOP Era: Has Dewey Had Enough?"

Among the many articles that appeared in the press at the time of Dewey's death, the most authoritative include recollections by Leo O'Brien in the Albany *Times-Union* for March 17, 1971; Kurtland King, Windsor, Ontario, *Star,* March 17, 1971, and Dan Winegar, the Batavia *News,* March 24, 1971. *Time* and *Newsweek* for March 29, 1971, are worth a look; William A. Rusher's touching obituary in the April 6, 1971, issue of *National Review* is far more evocative. "The Tom Dewey I Knew," by Edward Bernays, the Boston *Herald,* March 21, 1971, is revealing. The New York *Times* coverage of Dewey's funeral is surprisingly thin. The best reportage of that event was by Joan Douglas in the Pawling-Patterson *News Chronicle* for March 25, 1971. Her account is a lovely tapestry of atmosphere and understatement. A final article, of somewhat specialized interest, is a tribute to Dewey's work at his law firm by his partner John E. F. Wood. It appeared in the firm's *Bulletin* for March 29, 1971.

Additional background on Owosso was provided by a local promotional booklet published in the boom year of 1908 and lent me by Thomas E. Dewey, Jr. Pherbia Thornburg's *Historical Footnotes of Quaker Hill and Vicinity,* published in 1964, sheds anecdotal light on the area, as does *Quaker Hill,* a booklet Lowell Thomas wrote in 1940 as part of his promotional campaign to populate his dream community.

SPEECHES AND PUBLIC MESSAGES

The most valuable source by far are *The Public Papers of Governor Thomas E. Dewey,* published in twelve volumes covering the years 1943–1954. Nearly all my quotations from speeches, legislative messages, vetoes, etc., for this period come from this collection. Earlier quotes were culled from a master speech file kept at Rochester; a handful of these, as well as several of Dewey's later statements, derive from the daily or weekly press.

BOOKS

Abbott, Berenice. *New York in the Thirties* (photographs). New York, 1939.

Abels, Jules, *Out of the Jaws of Victory.* New York, 1969.

Acheson, Dean. *Present at the Creation.* New York, 1969.

———. *Sketches from Life of Men I Have Known.* New York, 1959.

Adams, Sherman. *First Hand Report: The Story of the Eisenhower Administration.* New York, 1961.

Alexander, Herbert E. *Financing Politics: Money, Elections and Political Reform.* Washington, D.C., 1976.

Alexander, Holmes. *The Famous Five.* New York, 1958.

Allen, Frederick Lewis. *Only Yesterday.* New York, 1957.

———. *Since Yesterday.* New York, 1972.

Allen, Robert S., and Shannon, William V. *The Truman Merry-Go-Round.* New York, 1950.

Andrews, Bert. *Washington Witch Hunt.* New York, 1948.

Asbury, Herbert. *The Gangs of New York.* New York, 1928.

Barber, James David. *Presidential Character.* Englewood Cliffs, N.J., 1972.

Barnes, Joseph. *Willkie.* New York, 1954.

Bean, Louis H. *Ballot Behavior: A Study of Presidential Elections.* Washington, D.C., 1940.

Bell, Daniel. *The End of Ideology.* Glencoe, Illinois, 1960.

Bell, Jack. *The Splendid Misery.* New York, 1960.

Berger, Meyer. *The Eight Million.* New York, 1942.

Bernstein, Barton J., and Matusow, Allen J. *The Truman Administration: A Documentary History.* New York, 1966.

Binkley, Wilfred E. *American Political Parties: Their Natural History.* New York, 1958.

Bishop, Jim. *F.D.R.'s Last Year.* New York, 1974.

Blum, John Morton. *The Price of Vision: The Diary of Henry A. Wallace, 1942–1946.* Boston, 1973.

————. *V Was for Victory*. New York, 1976.

Boorstin, Daniel. *The Americans: The Democratic Experience*. New York, 1974.

Botkin, B. A. *New York City Folklore*. New York, 1956.

Bowles, Chester. *Promises to Keep: My Years in Public Life, 1941–1969*. New York, 1971.

Brayman, Harold. *The President Speaks Off the Record*. Princeton, N.J., 1976.

Browning, Frank, and Gerassi, John. *The American Way of Crime: From Salem to Watergate*. New York, 1980.

Burns, James MacGregor. *Roosevelt: The Lion and the Fox*. New York, 1956.

————. *Roosevelt: Soldier of Freedom*. New York, 1970.

Butler, Nicholas Murray. *The Rise of a University*. New York, 1937.

Byers, Barry. *Thomas E. Dewey: A Study in Political Leadership*. New York, 1978.

Caro, Robert. *The Power Broker: Robert Moses and the Fall of New York*. New York, 1974.

Casdorph, Paul D. *A History of the Republican Party in Texas, 1865–1965*. Austin, 1965.

Catledge, Turner. *My Life and the Times*. New York, 1971.

Caute, David. *The Great Fear: The Anti-Communist Purge under Truman and Eisenhower*. New York, 1978.

Childs, Marquis. *I Write from Washington*. New York, 1942.

Ciridi, Ronald J. *The Korean War and American Politics: The Republican Party as a Case Study*. Philadelphia, 1969.

Clapper, Raymond. *Watching the World, 1934–1944*. New York, 1944.

Conkin, Paul K. *FDR and the Origins of the Welfare State*. New York, 1967.

Coon, Horace. *Columbia: Colossus on the Hudson*. New York, 1947.

Cuneo, Ernest. *Life with Fiorello*. New York, 1955.

Dahl, Robert. *Congress and Foreign Policy*. New York, 1950.

Danforth, Harold and Horan, James D., *The D.A.'s Man*, New York, 1957.

Darilek, Richard E. *A Loyal Opposition in Time of War: The Republican Party and the Politics of Foreign Policy from Pearl Harbor to Yalta*. Westport, Connecticut, 1976.

Davenport, Marcia. *Too Strong for Fantasy*. New York, 1967.

David, Paul M. *Presidential Nominating Politics in 1952*. Baltimore, 1954.

De Toledano, Ralph. *One Man Alone: Richard Nixon*. New York, 1969.

————. *The Winning Side*. New York, 1963.

Dewey, George M. *Autobiography*. New York, 1916.

Dewey, Thomas E. *The Case Against the New Deal*. New York, 1940.

————. *Journey to the Far Pacific*. New York, 1952.

————. *On the Two-Party System*. New York, 1966.

————. *Twenty Against the Underworld*. New York, 1975.

Dewey, Walter E. *Family Genealogy*. 1912.

Dillon, Mary E. *Wendell Willkie*. New York, 1952.

Divine, Robert A. *Foreign Policy and U.S. Presidential Elections: 1940–1948*. New York, 1974.

Donahoe, Bernard F. *Private Plans and Public Dangers: The Story of FDR's Third Nomination*. South Bend, Indiana, 1965.

Donovan, Robert J. *Conflict and Crisis: The Presidency of Harry S. Truman*. New York, 1977.

————. *Eisenhower, The Inside Story*. New York, 1956.

Douglas, William O. *Go East, Young Man*. New York, 1974.

————. *The Court Years.* New York, 1980.

Einaudi, Mario. *The Roosevelt Revolution.* New York, 1959.

Eisenhower, Dwight D. *The White House Years* (volume I): *Mandate for Change, 1953–1956.* New York, 1963.

Eldridge, Paul. *Crown of Empire: The Story of New York State.* New York, 1957.

Ellis, David M., Frost, James A., Syrett, Harold C., Carman, Harry F. *A History of New York State.* Ithaca, 1967.

Ellis, Edward Robb. *The Epic of New York.* New York, 1966.

Ellis, Franklin. *History of Shiawassee and Clinton Counties.* Detroit, 1880.

Ernst, Morris, and Loth, David. *The People Know Best: The Ballots Versus the Polls.* Washington, D.C., 1949.

Ewald, William B. *Eisenhower the President.* New York, 1981.

Fairlie, Henry. *The Parties.* New York, 1978.

Farley, James. *Behind the Ballots.* New York, 1938.

Feder, Sid, and Joesten, Joachim. *The Luciano Story.* New York, 1954.

Ferrill, Robert H. *The Eisenhower Diaries.* New York, 1981.

————. *Off the Record: The Private Papers of Harry S. Truman.* New York, 1980.

Fink, William B. *Getting to Know New York State.* New York, 1971.

Finnegan, James E. *Tammany at Bay.* New York, 1933.

Fitch, Charles Eliott. *Official New York: From Cleveland to Hughes.* New York, 1911.

Flynn, Edward J. *You're the Boss.* New York, 1947.

Frank, Glenn. *America's Hour of Decision.* New York, 1934.

————. *A Program for a Dynamic America.* Washington, D.C., 1940.

Franklin, Jay. *Republicans on the Potomac.* New York, 1953.

Freidel, Frank. *FDR—The Apprenticeship.* Boston, 1952.

————. *FDR—Launching the New Deal.* Boston, 1973.

Gardner, Joseph L. *Departing Glory: Theodore Roosevelt As Ex-President.* New York, 1973.

Goldman, Eric F. *The Crucial Decade and After: America 1945–1960.* New York, 1956.

Gornick, Vivian. *The Romance of American Communism.* New York, 1973.

Gosch, Martin A., and Hammer, Richard. *The Last Testament of Lucky Luciano.* Boston, 1975.

Gouldon, Joseph C. *The Best Years: 1945–1950.* New York, 1976.

Gunther, John. *Roosevelt in Retrospect.* New York, 1950.

Hamby, Alonzo. *The New Deal.* New York, 1969.

Harris, Louis. *Is There a Republican Majority?* New York, 1954.

Hartman, Susan M. *Truman and the 80th Congress.* Columbia, Missouri, 1971.

Healey, Laurin Hall, and Kutner, Luis. *The Admiral.* New York, 1944.

Heath, Burton. *Yankee Reporter.* New York, 1947.

Hershkowitz, Leo. *Tweed's New York.* New York, 1978.

Hoffman, Paul. *Lions in the Street.* New York, 1973.

Hofstadter, Richard. *The Age of Reform.* New York, 1955.

Hoopes, Townsend. *The Devil and John Foster Dulles.* Boston, 1973.

Hoover, Herbert. *Challenge to Liberty.* New York, 1934.

————, and Gibson, Hugh. *The Problems of Lasting Peace.* New York, 1942.

Howard, Katherine G. *With My Shoes Off.* New York, 1977.

Hughes, Rupert. *Thomas E. Dewey: Attorney for the People.* New York, 1940.

Hull, Cordell. *Memoirs.* New York, 1948.

Ickes, Harold. *The Secret Diary of Harold Ickes.* New York, 1953–54.

Irey, Elmer L. *The Tax Dodgers*. Garden City, New York, 1949.

Jacob, Herbert, and Vines, Kenneth. *Politics in the American States*. Boston, 1965.

Javits, Jacob, and Sternberg, Rafael. *Javits: The Autobiography of a Public Man*. Boston, 1981.

Johnson, Claudia Alta (Lady Bird). *A White House Diary*. New York, 1969.

Johnson, Donald B. *The Republican Party and Wendell Willkie*. Urbana, Illinois, 1960.

Jones, Charles O. *The Minority Party in Congress*. Boston, 1970.

———. *The Republican Party in American Politics*. New York, 1965.

Josephson, Hannah and Matthew. *Al Smith: Hero of the Cities*. Boston, 1969.

Joyner, Conrad. *The Republican Dilemma: Conservatism or Progressivism*. Tucson, 1963.

Kimball, Francis P. *The Capital Region of New York State, Crossroads of Empire*. New York, 1942.

Kirk, Russell. *The Political Principles of Robert A. Taft*. New York, 1967.

Krock, Arthur. *Memoirs*. New York, 1968.

Lamb, Karl. *John Hamilton and the Revitalization of the Republican Party, 1936–1940*. Ph.D. thesis, Hamilton Papers, Library of Congress.

Lambert, Gerard. *All Out of Step: A Personal Chronicle*. New York, 1956.

Larson, Arthur. *A Republican Looks at His Party*. New York, 1956.

Lash, Joseph P. *Roosevelt and Churchill: The Partnership That Saved the West*. New York, 1976.

Laurie, Leonard. *The King Makers*. New York, 1971.

———. *The Running of Richard Nixon*. New York, 1972.

Lodge, Henry Cabot. *The Storm Has Many Eyes: A Personal Narrative*. New York, 1973.

MacKaye, Milton. *The Tin Box Parade*. New York, 1934.

Manchester, William. *The Glory and the Dream*. New York, 1975.

Mann, Arthur. *La Guardia: A Fighter Against His Times, 1882–1933*. Philadelphia.

———. *La Guardia Comes to Power, 1933*. Philadelphia, 1965.

Martin, Joseph. *My First Fifty Years in Politics*. New York, 1960.

Mayer, George H. *The Republican Party, 1854–1964*. New York, 1964.

Mazo, Earl. *Nixon: A Political Portrait*. New York, 1969.

Melosi, Martin V. *The Shadow of Pearl Harbor: Political Controversy over the Surprise Attack*. College Station, Texas, 1977.

Mitgang, Herbert. *The Man Who Rode the Tiger*. Philadelphia, 1963.

Moley, Raymond. *The Republican Opportunity*. New York, 1962.

Moos, Malcolm. *Politics, Presidents and Coattails*. Baltimore, 1952.

———. *The Republicans*. New York, 1956.

Moquin, Wayne and Van Doren, Charles, eds. *The American Way of Crime*. New York, 1976.

Morris, Newbold. *Let the Chips Fall*. New York, 1955.

Moscow, Warren, *Politics in the Empire State,* New York, 1948.

———. *Roosevelt and Wilkie*. Englewood Cliffs, 1968.

———. *What Have You Done For Me Lately?* Englewood Cliffs, 1967.

Mosley, Leonard. *Dulles: A Biography of Eleanor, Allen, and John Foster Dulles and Their Family Network*. New York, 1978.

Mosteller, Frederick. *The Pre-Election Polls of 1948*. New York, 1949.

Nevins, Allan. *Herbert H. Lehman and His Era*. New York, 1963.

New York State Department of Commerce. *The New York State Capital.* Albany, 1951.

New York State Thruway Authority. *Forging Ahead on the New York State Thruway.* Albany, 1951.

New York State University. *Futures: State University of New York and Your Children.* Albany, 1962.

Nixon, Richard M. *Memoirs.* New York, 1977.

————. *Six Crises.* New York, 1962.

Northrup, W. B. and John B. *The Insolence of Office.* New York, 1932.

Papp, John P. *Albany's Historic Street.* Albany, 1918.

Parmet, Herbert. *Eisenhower and the American Crusades.* New York, 1972.

————, and Hecht, Marie B. *Never Again.* New York, 1967.

Patterson, Robert T. *Mr. Republican: A Biography of Robert A. Taft.* Boston, 1975.

Pearce, Neal. *The Megastates of America.* New York, 1972.

Pearson, Drew. *Diaries, 1949–1959.* Edited by Tyler Abell, New York, 1974.

Peckham, Howard. *The Making of the University of Michigan.* Ann Arbor, 1967.

Peel, Roy V. *The Political Clubs of New York City.* New York, 1935.

Perrett, Geoffrey. *Days of Sadness, Years of Triumph: The American People, 1939–1945.* New York, 1973.

Phillips, Kevin P. *The Emerging Republican Majority.* Garden City, 1978.

Pogue, Forrest C. *George C. Marshall, Organizer of Victory, 1943–1945.* New York, 1973.

Powell, Hickman. *Ninety Times Guilty.* New York, 1939.

Ray, Robert. *A Comparison of the Speaking Styles of Franklin D. Roosevelt and Thomas E. Dewey in the 1944 Presidential Campaign.* Ph.D. Thesis, University of Iowa, Iowa City, 1947.

Reid, Edward. *The Shame of New York.* New York, 1953.

Republican National Committee. *Choices for America.* Washington, D.C., 1968.

————.*Official Proceedings of the 22nd Republican National Convention.* Washington, D.C., 1940.

————.*Official Proceedings of the 23rd Republican National Convention.* Washington, D.C., 1944.

————.*Official Proceedings of the 24th Republican National Convention.* Washington, D.C., 1948.

————. *Official Proceedings of the 25th Republican National Convention.* Washington, D.C., 1952.

————. *The Republican News,* September 1945–October 1948. Washington, D.C.

————. *The Truman Chronology.* Washington, D.C., 1948.

Robbins, Jhan and June. *Eight Weeks to Live: The Last Chapter in the Life of Senator Robert A. Taft.* Garden City, 1954.

Roosevelt, Elliott, and Brough, James. *The Roosevelts of Hyde Park: An Untold Story.* New York, 1973.

————. *The Roosevelts of the White House: A Rendezvous With Destiny.* New York, 1975.

Root, Oren. *Persons and Persuasions.* New York, 1974.

Roper, Elmo. *You and Your Leaders.* New York, 1956.

Rosenman, Samuel and Dorothy. *Presidential Style: Some Giants and a Pygmy in the White House.* New York, 1976.

Ross, Irwin. *The Loneliest Campaign.* New York, 1968.

Rossiter, Clinton. *Conservatism in America.* New York, 1955.

Rovere, Richard H. *Affairs of State: The Eisenhower Years.* New York, 1956.

————. *Senator Joe McCarthy.* New York, 1959.

Russell, Francis. *The Shadow of Blooming Grove: Warren G. Harding and His Times.* New York, 1968.

Sagandorph, Kent. *Michigan: The Story of the University.* New York, 1948.

Sann, Paul. *Kill the Dutchman: The Story of Dutch Schultz.* New York, 1971.

————. *The Lawless Decade: A Pictorial History of a Great American Transition.* New York, 1957.

Sarasohn, Stephen and Vera. *Political Party Patterns in Michigan.* Detroit, 1957.

Schapsmeier, Edward L. and Frederick H. *Henry A. Wallace and the War Years, 1940–1965.* Ames, Iowa, 1970.

Schlesinger, Arthur. *The Coming to Power: Critical Presidential Elections in American History* (contains "The Election of 1940," by Robert E. Burke). New York, 1972.

Schnapper, Morris B. *Grand Old Party: The First Hundred Years of the Republican Party, A Pictorial History.* Washington, D.C., 1955.

Scott, Hugh. *Come to the Party.* Garden City, 1966.

Sherman, Richard B. *The Republican Party and Black America from McKinley to Hoover, 1896–1933.* Charlottesville, Virginia, 1973.

Sherwood, Robert E. *Roosevelt and Hopkins.* New York, 1948.

Smith, Charles. *Highway to Republican Victories.* Boston, 1942.

Smith, Gene. *The Shattered Dream.* New York, 1970.

Simon, James. *Independent Journey: A Life of William O. Douglas.* New York, 1980.

Simon, Kate. *Fifth Avenue: A Social History.* New York, 1978.

Sinclair, Andrew. *The Available Man.* New York, 1965.

————. *Prohibition: The Era of Excess.* Boston, 1962.

Sparks, C. Nelson. *One Man—Wendell Willkie.* New York, 1942.

Stassen, Harold. *Where I Stand.* Garden City, 1947.

Steel, Ronald. *Walter Lippmann and the American Century.* Boston, 1980.

Still, Bayrd. *Mirror for Gotham.* New York, 1956.

Stone, Irving. *They Also Ran.* Garden City, 1966.

Streeter, Floyd Benjamin. *Political Parties in Michigan, 1837–1860.* Lansing, 1918.

Strelton, A. P. *Republican Reveille.* New York, 1939.

Stromberg, Roland. *Collective Security and American Foreign Policy: From the League of Nations to NATO.* New York, 1963.

————. *Republicanism Reappraised.* College Park, 1969.

Sulzberger, C. L. *A Long Row of Candles: Memoirs and Diaries, 1934–1954.* New York, 1969.

Taft, Robert A. *A Foreign Policy for Americans.* New York, 1951.

Thomas, Lowell. *Good Evening, Everybody.* New York, 1976.

————. *The New York Thruway Story.* Buffalo, 1955.

————. *So Long Until Tomorrow.* New York, 1977.

Thompson, Craig, and Raymond, Allen. *New York under Gang Rule.* New York, 1940.

Tompkins, C. David. *Arthur H. Vandenberg: The Evolution of a Modern Republican, 1884–1945.* Ann Arbor, 1970.

Trohan, Walter. *Political Animals.* New York, 1975.

Truman, Harry S. *Memoirs: Years of Trial and Hope* (vol. II). New York, 1956.

Truman, Margaret. *Harry S. Truman.* New York, 1973.

————. *Souvenirs.* New York, 1956.

Tugwell, Rexford G. *In Search of Roosevelt.* Cambridge, Massachusetts, 1972.

Tully, Andrew. *Treasury Agent.* New York, 1958.

Turkus, Burton B., and Feder, Sid. *Murder, Inc.* New York, 1951.

Tyler, Gus. *Organized Crime in America.* Ann Arbor, 1962.

Vandenberg, Arthur H., Jr. *The Private Papers of Senator Vandenberg.* Boston, 1952.

Viorst, Milton. *Fall from Grace: The Republican Party and the Puritan Ethic.* New York, 1968.

Waldrop, Frank C. *McCormick of Chicago.* New York, 1966.

Walker, Stanley. *Thomas E. Dewey: An American of this Century.* New York, 1944.

Walsh, George. *Gentleman Jimmy Walker.* New York, 1974.

Ware, Caroline F. *Greenwich Village, 1920-1930.* Boston, 1935.

Warren, Earl. *The Memoirs of Earl Warren.* New York, 1977.

Wecter, Dixon. *The Hero in America.* New York, 1941.

Werner, M. P. *Tammany Hall.* Garden City, New York, 1932.

White, Theodore H. *The Making of the President, 1964.* New York, 1965.

White, William Allen. *A Puritan in Babylon: The Story of Calvin Coolidge.* New York, 1938.

White, William S. *The Taft Story.* New York, 1954.

Willkie, Wendell. *An American Program.* New York, 1944.

———. *One World.* New York, 1943.

Wilson, Willis H. *Quaker Hill in the 18th Century.* Pawling, New York, 1905.

Wiltz, John. *From Isolation to War, 1931-1941.* New York, 1968.

WPA Writers Program. *A Guide to the Empire State.* New York, 1940.

Zdrinczyk, David. *One Hundred Years of the New York State Legislature.* Albany, 1978.

INDEX